JavaScript by Example

Second Edition

JavaScript by Example

Second Edition

Ellie Quigley

PRENTICE
HALL

Upper Saddle River, NJ • Boston • Indianapolis • San Francisco
New York • Toronto • Montreal • London • Munich • Paris • Madrid
Capetown • Sydney • Tokyo • Singapore • Mexico City

Many of the designations used by manufacturers and sellers to distinguish their products are claimed as trademarks. Where those designations appear in this book, and the publisher was aware of a trademark claim, the designations have been printed with initial capital letters or in all capitals.

The author and publisher have taken care in the preparation of this book, but make no expressed or implied warranty of any kind and assume no responsibility for errors or omissions. No liability is assumed for incidental or consequential damages in connection with or arising out of the use of the information or programs contained herein.

The publisher offers excellent discounts on this book when ordered in quantity for bulk purchases or special sales, which may include electronic versions and/or custom covers and content particular to your business, training goals, marketing focus, and branding interests. For more information, please contact:

> U.S. Corporate and Government Sales
> (800) 382-3419
> corpsales@pearsontechgroup.com

For sales outside the United States, please contact:

> International Sales
> international@pearson.com

Visit us on the Web: informit.com/ph

Library of Congress Cataloging-in-Publication Data

Quigley, Ellie.
JavaScript by example / Ellie Quigley.—2nd ed.
    p.   cm.
Includes index.
ISBN 978-0-13-705489-3 (pbk. : alk. paper)
1. JavaScript (Computer program language) I. Title.
QA76.73.J39Q54 2010
005.13'3—dc22

                           2010020402

ISBN-13: 978-0-13-705489-3
ISBN-10:   0-13-705489-0
Text printed in the United States on recycled paper at Edwards Brothers Malloy in Ann Arbor, Michigan.
Third printing, August 2012

Editor-in-Chief
Mark L. Taub

Managing Editor
John Fuller

Full-Service Production Manager
Julie B. Nahil

Production Editor
Dmitri Korzh
Techne Group

Copy Editor
Teresa Horton

Indexer
Potomac Indexing, LLC

Proofreader
Beth Roberts

Editorial Assistant
Kim Boedigheimer

Cover Designer
Anne Jones

Composition
Techne Group

Contents

10 It's the BOM! Browser Objects   271

11 Working with Forms and Input Devices   327

12 Working with Images (and Links)   413

Preface

This second edition of *JavaScript by Example* is really more than a new edition; it is a new book! So much has changed since the first edition in 2002, and now with the newfound popularity of Ajax, JavaScript is on a roll! Almost every personal computer has JavaScript installed and running and it is the most popular Web scripting language around, although it comes under different aliases, including Mocha, LiveScript, JScript, and ECMAScript. There are a lot of books out there dedicated to some aspect of the JavaScript language and if you are new to JavaScript, it would be difficult to know where to start. This book is a "one size fits all" edition, dedicated to those of you who need a balance between the technical side of the language and the fun elements, a book that addresses cross-platform issues, and a book that doesn't expect that you are already a guru before you start. This edition explains how the language works from the most basic examples to the more complex, in a progression that seemlessly leads you from example to example until you have mastered the basics all the way to the more advanced topics such as CSS, the DOM, and Ajax.

Because I am a teacher first, I found that using my first edition worked well in the classroom, but I needed more and better examples to get the results I was looking for. Many of my students have been designers but not programmers, or programmers who don't understand design. I needed a text that would accommodate both without leaving either group bored or overwhelmed. This huge effort to modernize the first edition went way beyond where I had expected or imagined. I have learned much and hope that you will enjoy sharing my efforts to make this a fun and thorough coverage of a universally popular and important Web programming language.

Acknowledgments

Many thanks go to the folks at Prentice Hall: Mark L. Taub, editor-in-chief, and the most supportive person I know; Julie Nahil, Full-Service Production Manager; John Fuller, Managing Editor; and Ann Jones, Cover Designer. Thanks also to Dmitri Korzh, Production Editor at Techne Group. Finally, a special thank you to Thomas Bishop who spent hours reviewing and sending constructive criticism that greatly improved the quality of the book; to Brendon Crawford for reviewing the manuscript; and to Elizabeth Triplett for her artwork to give the chapters a cheerful beginning.

Ellie Quigley
September, 2010

chapter
1

Introduction to JavaScript

1.1 What JavaScript Is

JavaScript is a popular general-purpose scripting language used to put energy and pizzaz into otherwise dead Web pages by allowing a page to interact with users and respond to events that occur on the page. JavaScript has been described as the glue that holds Web pages together.[1] It would be a hard task to find a commercial Web page, or almost any Web page, that does not contain some JavaScript code (see Figure 1.1).

JavaScript, originally called LiveScript, was developed by Brendan Eich at Netscape in 1995 and was shipped with Netscape Navigator 2.0 beta releases. JavaScript is a scripting language that gives life, hence LiveScript, to otherwise static HTML pages. It runs on most platforms and is hardware independent. JavaScript is a client-side language designed to work in the browser on your computer, not the server. It is built directly into the browser (although not restricted to browsers), Microsoft Internet Explorer and Mozilla Firefox being the most common browsers. In syntax, JavaScript is similar to C, Perl, and Java; for example, *if* statements and *while* and *for* loops are almost identical. Like Perl, it is an interpreted language, not a compiled language.

Because JavaScript is associated with a browser, it is tightly integrated with HTML. Whereas HTML is handled in the browser by its own networking library and graphics renderer, JavaScript programs are executed by a JavaScript interpreter built into the browser. When the browser requests such a page, the server sends the full content of the document, including HTML and JavaScript statements, over the network to the client. When the page loads, HTML content is read and rendered line by line until a JavaScript opening tag is read, at which time the JavaScript interpreter takes over. When the closing JavaScript tag is reached, the HTML processing continues.

---

1. But the creator of JavaScript, Brendan Eich, says it's even more! In his article, "Innovators of the Net: Brendan Eich and JavaScript," he says, "Calling JavaScript 'the glue that holds web pages together' is short and easy to use, but doesn't do justice to what's going on. Glue sets and hardens, but JavaScript is more dynamic than glue. It can create a reaction and make things keep going, like a catalyst."

JavaScript handled by a browser is called client-side JavaScript. Although JavaScript is used mainly as a client-side scripting language, it can also be used in contexts other than a Web browser. Netscape created server-side JavaScript to be programmed as a CGI language, such as Python or Perl, but this book will address JavaScript as it is most commonly used—running on the client side, your browser.

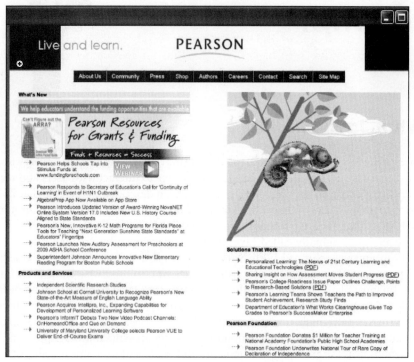

Figure 1.1   A dynamic Web page using JavaScript to give it life. For example, if the user rolls the mouse over any of the text after the arrows, the text will become underscored links for navigation.

1.2   What JavaScript Is Not

JavaScript is not Java. "Java is to JavaScript what Car is to Carpet"[2] Well, that quote might be a little extreme, but suggests that these are two very different languages. Java was developed at Sun Microsystems. JavaScript was developed at Netscape. Java applications can be independent of a Web page, whereas JavaScript programs are embedded in a Web page and must be run in a browser window.[3] Java is a strongly typed language with strict guidelines, whereas JavaScript is loosely typed and flexible. Java data

---

2. From a discussion group on Usenet, also p. 4 *Beginning JavaScript with DOM Scripting and Ajax* by Christian Heilmann, APRESS, 2006.

types must be declared. JavaScript types such as variables, parameters, and function return types do not have to be declared. Java programs are compiled. JavaScript programs are interpreted by a JavaScript engine that lives in the browser.

JavaScript is not HTML, but JavaScript code can be embedded in an HTML document and is contained within HTML tags. JavaScript has its own syntax rules and expects statements to be written in a certain way. JavaScript doesn't understand HTML, but it can contain HTML content within its statements. All of this will become clear as we proceed.

JavaScript is not used to read or write the files on client machines with the exception of writing to cookies (see Chapter 16, "Cookies"). It does not let you write to or store files on the server. It does not open or close windows already opened by other applications and it cannot read from an opened Web page that came from another server.

JavaScript is object based but not strictly object oriented because it does not support the traditional mechanism for inheritance and classes found in object-oriented programming languages, such as Java and C++. The terms private, protected, and public do not apply to JavaScript methods as with Java and C++.

JavaScript is not the only language that can be embedded in an application. VBScript, for example, developed by Microsoft, is similar to JavaScript, but is embedded in Microsoft's Internet Explorer.

1.3 **What JavaScript Is Used For**

JavaScript programs are used to detect and react to user-initiated events, such as a mouse going over a link or graphic. They can improve a Web site with navigational aids, scrolling messages and rollovers, dialog boxes, dynamic images, and so forth. JavaScript lets you control the appearance of the page as the document is being parsed. Without any network transmission, it lets you validate what the user has entered into a form before submitting the form to the server. It can test to see if the user has plug-ins and send the user to another site to get the plug-ins if needed. It has string functions and supports regular expressions to check for valid e-mail addresses, Social Security numbers, credit card data, and the like. JavaScript serves as a programming language. Its core language describes such basic constructs as variables and data types, control loops, *if/else* statements, *switch* statements, functions, and objects.[4] It is used for arithmetic calculations, manipulates the date and time, and works with arrays, strings, and objects. It handles user-initiated events, sets timers, and changes content and style on the fly. JavaScript also reads and writes cookie values, and dynamically creates HTML based on the cookie value.

---

3. The JavaScript interpreter is normally embedded in a Web browser, but is not restricted to the browser. Servers and other applications can also use the JavaScript interpreter.

4. The latest version of the core JavaScript language is JavaScript 1.8.1, supported by Mozilla and Microsoft Internet Explorer.

1.4   JavaScript and Its Place in a Web Page

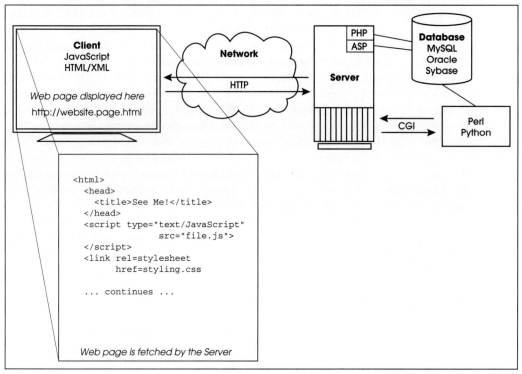

Figure 1.2   The life cycle of a typical Web page.

1.4.1   Analysis of the Diagram

The Players.   The players in Figure 1.2 are the applications involved in the life cycle of a Web page:

1. A browser (Firefox, Internet Explorer, Safari, Opera). This is where JavaScript lives!
2. A network (HTTP).
3. A server (Apache, Windows IIS, Zeus).
4. A server module (PHP, ASP.NET, ColdFusion, Java servlet).
5. External files and/or a database (MySQL, Oracle, Sybase).

The Steps.   Figure 1.2 illustrates the life cycle of a Web page from when the client makes a request until it gets a response.

1. On the left hand side of the diagram, we see the client, or browser where the request is made. The user makes a request for a Web site by typing the address

of the Web site in the browser's URL location box. The "request" is transmitted to the server via Hypertext Transfer Protocol (HTTP). The Web server on the other side accepts that request. If the request is for an HTML file, the Web server responds by simply returning the file to the client's browser. The browser will then render the HTML tags, format the page for display, and wait for another request. If the page contains JavaScript tags, the JavaScript interpreter will handle that code based on a user-initiated event such as clicking a button, rolling a mouse over a link or image, or submitting a form. It is with JavaScript that the page becomes interactive. JavaScript detects whatever is happening on the page and responds. It handles fillout forms, feedback, animation, slide-shows, and multimedia. It responds to a key press, a mouse moving over an image, or a user submitting a form. It can read cookies and validate data. It can dynamically change a cell in an HTML table, change the text in a paragraph, or add a new bullet item to a list. But it doesn't do everything. It cannot close a window it didn't open, query a database, update the value in a file upload field, or write to files on a server. After the JavaScript interpreter has completed its tasks, and the page has been fully rendered, another request can be made to the server. Going back and forth between the browser and the server is known as the Request/Response loop, the basis of how the Web works.

2. The cloud between the client side and the server side represents the network. This can be a very large network such as the Internet consisting of millions upon millions of computers, an intranet within an organization, or a wireless network on a personal desktop computer or handheld device. The user doesn't care how big or small the network is—it is totally transparent. The protocol used to transfer documents to and from the server is called HTTP.

3. The server side includes an HTTP Web server such as Apache, Microsoft's IIS, or lighttpd. Web servers are generic programs capable of accepting Web-based requests and providing the response to them. In most cases, this response is simply retrieving the file from server's local file system. With dynamic Web sites, which require processing beyond the capabilities of JavaScript, such as processing form information, sending e-mail, starting a session, or connecting to a database, Web servers turn over the request for a specific file to an appropriate helper application. Web servers, such as Apache and Internet Information Service (IIS) have a list of helper applications that process any specific language. The helper application could be an external program, such as a CGI/Perl script, or one built right into the server, such as ColdFusion, ASP.NET, or a PHP script. For example, if the Web server sees a request for a PHP file, it looks up what helper application is assigned to process PHP requests, turns over the request to the PHP module, and waits until it gets the result back.

1.5   What Is Ajax?

Ajax stands for Asnychronous JavasScript and XML, a term that was coined by Jesse James Garrett in 2005. Ajax is not new. It's been around since 1996, and is a technique used to create fast interactivity without having to wait for a response from the server. As shown in our Web cycle example in Figure 1.2, the browser sends a request to the server and waits for a response, often with a little wheel-shaped icon circling around in the location bar reminding you that the page is loading. As you wait, the browser sits with you and waits, and after each subsequent request, you must wait for the entire page to reload to get the contents of the new page. Ajax lets you send data back and forth between the browser and server without waiting for the whole page to reload. Only parts of the page that change are replaced. Several requests can go out while you are scrolling, zooming in and out, filling out a form, and so on, as those other parts are loaded in the background. Because this interactivity is asynchronous, feedback is immediate with no long waiting times between requests. Some examples of Ajax applications are Ajax Stock Qutos Ticker (SentoSoft LTD), Flickr for photo storage and display, Gmail, Google Suggest, and perhaps the best example, Google Maps at *maps.google.com* (see Figure 1.3).

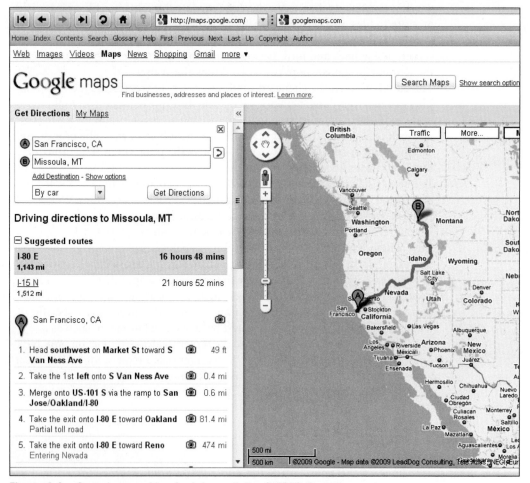

Figure 1.3 Google uses Ajax for interactivity. © 2010 Google.

When you use this Web page, you have complete and fast interactivity. You can zoom in, zoom out, move around the map, get directions from one point to another, view the location's terrain, see traffic, view a satellite picture, and so on. In Chapter 18 we discuss how this technique works, but for now think of it as JavaScript on steroids.

1.6   What JavaScript Looks Like

Example 1.1 demonstrates a small JavaScript program. The Web page contains a simple HTML table cell with a scrolling message (see Figure 1.4). Without JavaScript the message would be static, but with JavaScript, the message will continue to scroll across the screen, giving life to an otherwise dead page. This example will be explained in detail later, but for now it is here to show you what a JavaScript program looks like. Notice that the *<script></script>* tags have been highlighted. Between those tags you will see JavaScript code that produces the scrolling effect in the table cell. Within a short time, you will be able to read and write this type of script.

EXAMPLE   1.1

```html
<html>
   <head><title>Dynamic Page</title>
      <script type="text/javascript">
         // This is JavaScript. Be patient. You will be writing
         // better programs than this in no time.
         var message="Learning JavaScript will give your Web
                      page life!";
         message += " Are you ready to learn? ";
         var space="...";
         var position=0;
         function scroller(){
            var newtext = message.substring(position,message.length)+
            space + message.substring(0,position);
            var td = document.getElementById("tabledata");
            td.firstChild.nodeValue = newtext;
            position++;
            if (position > message.length){position=0;}
            window.setTimeout(scroller,200);
         }
      </script>
   </head>
   <body bgColor="darkgreen" onload="scroller();">
      <table border="1">
         <tr>
            <td id="tabledata" bgcolor="white">message goes here</td>
         </tr>
      </table>
   </body>
</html>
```

Figure 1.4 Scrolling text with JavaScript (output of Example 1.1).

1.7 JavaScript and Its Role in Web Development

When you start learning JavaScript, JavaScript code will be embedded directly in the content of an HTML page. Once we have covered the core programming constructs, you will see how a document is structured by using the document object model (DOM), and how JavaScript can get access to every element of your page. Finally you will be introduced to cascading style sheets (CSS), a technology that allows you to design your page with a stylized presentation. The combination of HTML, CSS, and JavaScript will allow you to produce a structured, stylized, interactive Web page. As your knowledge grows, so will your Web page, until it becomes necessary to create more pages and link them together. And then you still have to be sure your visitors are having a pleasant experience, no matter what browser they are using, at the same time trying to manage the site behind the scenes. To keep all of this in perspective, Web designers have determined that there are really three fundamental parts to a Web page: the content, the way the content is presented, and the behavior of that content.

1.7.1 The Three Layers

When a Web page is designed on the client (browser) side, it might start out as a simple HTML static page. Later the designer might want to add style to the content to give the viewer a more visually attractive layout. Last, to liven things up, JavaScript code is added to give the viewer the ability to interact with the page, make the page do something. A complete Web page, then, can be visualized as three separate layers: the content or structural layer, the style or presentation layer, and the behavior layer (see Figure 1.5). Each of these layers requires careful planning and skill. Designers are not necessarily programmers and vice versa. Separating the layers allows the designer to concentrate on the part he or she is good at, while the programmer can tweak the code in the JavaScript application without messing up the design. Of course, there is often a blurred line between these layers but the idea of separating content structure and style from behavior lends to easier maintenance, less repetition, and hopefully less debugging.

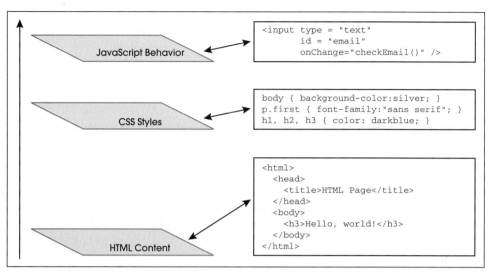

Figure 1.5 Three layers that make up a Web page.

Content or Structure. In Web development, HTML/XML markup makes up the content layer, and it also structures the Web document. The content layer is what a viewer sees when he or she comes to your Web page. Content can consist of text or images and include the links and anchors a viewer uses to navigate around your Web site. Because HTML/XML elements are used to create the structural content of your page, misusing those elements might not seem relevant for a quick visual fix, but might be very relevant when applying CSS and JavaScript. For example, using headings out of order to force a change in font size, such H1, H3, and then H2 tags, in that order is invalid HTML. These tags are intended to define the structure of the document on the display. The browser views the Web page as a tree-like structure, a model consisting of objects, where each HTML element (e.g., HEAD, BODY, H1) is an object in the model. This document tree, the DOM, defines the hierarchical logic of your document, which becomes an important tool for creating dynamic content. Because the structure is so important, valid markup should be a priority before going to the next layer: the CSS presentation layer. See Section 1.12 for markup validation tools.

Style or Presentation. The style or presentation layer is how the document will appear and on what media types. This layer is defined by CSS. Prior to CSS, nearly all of the presentation was contained within the HTML markup; all font colors, background styles, element positions and alignments, borders, and so on, had to be explicitly, often repeatedly, included in the HTML markup for the page. If, for example, you decided you wanted your page to have a blue font for all headings, then you would have to change each heading in the document. CSS changed all that. It gave designers the ability to move the presentational content into separate style sheets, resulting in much simpler HTML markup. Now you could change the font color in one place to affect all of the pages in your site. Although styles can be embedded within a document and give you control over selected elements, it is more likely they will be found in separate *.css* files to let you produce sweeping changes over an entire document. With one CSS file you can control the style of one or thousands of documents. External style sheets are cached, reduce the amount of code, and let you modify an entire site without mangling the HTML content pages. And CSS works with JavaScript and the DOM to create a dynamic presentation, often known as DHTML.

Behavior.   The behavior layer is the layer of a Web page that makes the page perform some action. For most Web pages, the first level of behavior is JavaScript. JavaScript allows you to dynamically control the elements of the Web page based on user interaction such as an individual keystroke, moving a mouse, submitting form input, and so on. JavaScript also makes it easy to perform style changes on the fly. Although traditionally CSS and JavaScript are separate layers, now with the DOM, they work so closely together that the lines are somewhat blurred. JavaScript programs are often stored in external files, which are then put in libraries where other programmers can share them. See *http://JavaScriptlibraries.com/*.

Unobtrusive JavaScript.   When you hear this phrase, "Make sure you use unobtrusive JavaScript," and you will hear or read about it once you have started really using JavaScript, it refers to the three layers we just discussed. It is a technique to completely separate JavaScript from the other two layers of Web development by putting JavaScript code in its own file and leaving the HTML/XHTML/XML and CSS in their own respective files. In the following chapters we have included most of the JavaScript examples in the same the HTML document because the files are small and serve to teach a particular aspect of the language. So for the time being, we will be obtrusive.

Once you have learned the JavaScript basics and start working on larger applications, you might want to understand this more fully. For the seven rules of unobtrusive Java-Script, go to *http://icant.co.uk/articles/seven-rules-of-unobtrusive-JavaScript/*.

1.8   **JavaScript and Events**

HTML is static. It structures and defines how the elements of a Web page will appear in the browser; for example, it is used to create buttons, tables, text boxes, and fillout forms, but it cannot by itself react to user input. JavaScript is not static; it is dynamic. It reacts asynchronously to events triggered by a user. For example, when a user fills out a form; presses a button, link, or image; or moves his or her mouse over a link, JavaScript can respond to the event and interact dynamically with the user. JavaScript can examine user input and validate it before sending it off to a server, or cause a new image to appear if a mouse moves over a link or the user presses a button, reposition objects on the page, even add, delete, or modify the HTML elements on the fly. Events are discussed in detail in Chapter 13, "Handling Events," but you should be made aware of them right at the beginning because they are inherently part of what JavaScript does, and there will be many examples throughout this text that make use of them.

The events, in their simplest form, are tied to HTML. In the following example, an HTML form is created with the *<form>* tag and its attributes. Along with the *type* and *value* attributes, the JavaScript *onClick* event handler is just another attribute of the HTML *<form>* tag. The type of input device is called a *button* and the value assigned to the button is *"Pinch me"*. When the user clicks the button in the browser window, a Java-Script event, called *click*, will be triggered. The *onClick* event handler is assigned a value that is the command that will be executed after the button has been clicked. In our example, it will result in an alert box popping up in its own little window, displaying *"OUCH!!"*. See the output of Example 1.2 in Figures 1.6 and 1.7.

EXAMPLE 1.2

```
         <html>
           <head><title>Event</title></head>
           <body>
1            <form>
2              <input type ="button"
3                    value = "Pinch me"
4                    onClick="alert('OUCH!!')" />
5            </form>
           </body>
         </html>
```

Figure 1.6   User initiates a click event when he or she clicks the mouse on the button.

Figure 1.7   The *onClick* event handler is triggered when the button labeled "Pinch me" is pressed.

Some of the events that JavaScript can handle are listed in Table 1.1.

Table 1.1   JavaScript Event Handlers

Event Handler	*What Caused It*
onAbort	Image loading was interrupted.
onBlur	The user moved away from a form element.
onChange	The user changed a value in a form element.
onClick	The user clicked a button-like form element.
onError	The program had an error when loading an image.
onFocus	The user activated a form element.
onLoad	The document finished loading.
onMouseOut	The mouse moved away from an object.
onMouseOver	The mouse moved over an object.
onSubmit	The user submitted a form.
onUnLoad	The user left the window or frame.

1.9 Standardizing JavaScript and the W3C

ECMAScript, which is more commonly known by the name JavaScript™, is an essential component of every Web browser and the ECMAScript standard is one of the core standards that enable the existence of interoperable Web applications on the World Wide Web.

—Ema International

During the 1990s Microsoft Internet Explorer and Netscape were competing for industry dominance in the browser market. They rapidly added new enhancements and proprietary features to their browsers, creating incompatibilities that made it difficult to view a Web site the same way in the two browsers. These times were popularly called the Browser Wars, ending with Microsoft's Internet Explorer browser winning. For now there seems to be peace among modern browsers, due to the fact that the World Wide Web Consortium (W3C) set some standards. To be a respectable browser, compliance with the standards is expected.

   To guarantee that there is one standard version of JavaScript available to companies producing Web pages, European Computer Manufacturers Association (ECMA) worked with Netscape to provide an international standardization of JavaScript called ECMAScript. ECMAScript is based on core JavaScript and behaves the same way in all applications that support the standard. The first version of the ECMA standard is documented in the ECMA-262 specification. Both JavaScript (Mozilla) and JScript (Microsoft IE) are really just a superset of ECMAScript and strive to be compatible with ECMAScript even though they have some of their own additions.[5] After ECMAScript was released, W3C began work on a standardized DOM, known as DOM Level 1, and recommended in late 1998. DOM Level 2 was published in late 2000. The current release of the DOM specification was published in April 2004. By 2005, large parts of W3C DOM were well supported by common ECMAScript-enabled browsers, including Microsoft Internet Explorer version 6 (2001), Gecko-based browsers (like Mozilla Firefox, and Camino), Konqueror, Opera, and Safari. In fact 95% of all modern browsers support the DOM specifications.

For the latest information on the latest ECMA-252 edition 5, see *http://www.ecmascript.org/*.

1.9.1 JavaScript Objects

Everything you do in JavaScript involves objects, just as everything you do in real life involves objects. JavaScript sees a Web page as many different objects, such as the browser object, the document object, and each element of the document as an object; for example, forms, images, and links are also objects. In fact every HTML element in the page can be viewed as an object. HTML H1, P, TD, FORM, and HREF elements are all examples of objects. JavaScript has a set of its own core objects that allow you to manipulate strings, numbers, functions, dates, and so on, and JavaScript allows you to create your own objects. When you see a line such as:

```
document.write("Hello, world");
```

the current page is the document object. After the object, there is a dot that separates the object from the *write* method. A method is a function that lets the object do something. The method is always followed by a set of parentheses that might or might not contain data. In this example the parentheses contain the string "Hello, world" telling JavaScript to write this string in the document window, your browser. In Chapter 8, "Objects," we discuss objects in detail. Because everything in JavaScript is viewed as an object, it is important to understand the concept from the start.

1.9.2 The Document Object Model

What is the DOM? A basic Web document consists of HTML/XML markup. The browser's job is to turn that markup into a Web page so that you can see text, input devices, pictures, tables, and so on in your browser window. It is also the browser's job to store its interpretation of the HTML page as a model, called the Document Object Model. The model is similar to the structure of a family tree, consisting of parents, children, siblings, and so on. Each element of the tree is related to another element in the

---

5. ECMAScript 5th edition adds some new features and is now available for review and testing (2009).

tree. These elements are referred to as nodes, with the root parent node of the tree at the top. With this upside down tree model every element of the document becomes an object accessible by JavaScript (and other applications), thus giving the JavaScript programmer control over an entire Web page; that is, the ability to navigate, create, add, modify, or delete the elements and their content dynamically.

As mentioned earlier, the DOM, Level 1[6] (see *http://www.w3.org/DOM*), a standard application programming interface (API) developed by the W3C is implemented by all modern browsers, including Microsoft Internet Explorer version 6 (2001), Gecko-based browsers (like Mozilla Firefox and Camino), Konqueror, Opera, and Safari.

After you learn the fundamentals of JavaScript, you will see how to create and manipulate objects, how to use the core objects, and then how to use JavaScript to control every part of your Web page with the DOM. With CSS, the DOM, and JavaScript you can reposition elements on a page dynamically, create animation, create scrolling marquees, and change the style of the page with fancy fonts and colors based on user input or user-initiated events, such as rolling the mouse over an image or link, clicking an icon, submitting a fillout form, or just opening up or closing a new window. Figure 1.8 demonstrates

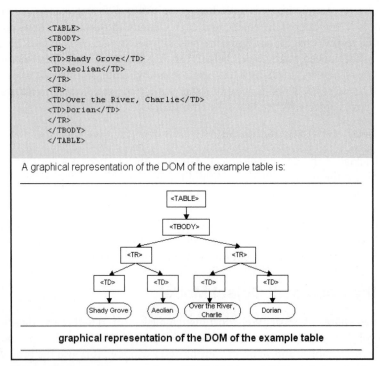

Figure 1.8   http://www.w3.org/TR/DOM-Level-2-Core/introduction.html.

---

6. DOM Levels 2 and 3 have also been developed by W3C, but DOM Level 1 is supported by most browsers.

an HTML table and how it is represented as a tree where each element is related to its parent and siblings as described by the W3C shown at *http://www.w3.org/DOM*.

1.10 What Browser?

When a user receives a page that includes JavaScript, the script is sent to the JavaScript interpreter, which executes the script. Because each browser has its own interpreter, there are often differences in how the code will be executed. And as the competing companies improve and modify their browsers, new inconsistencies may occur. There are not only different types of browsers to cause the incompatibilities but also different versions of the same browser. Because modern browsers conform to the W3C standards, these inconsistencies tend to be less of a distraction than they were in the past. Popular browsers today are shown in Table 1.2.

Table 1.2   Modern Browsers

Browser	Web Site
Internet Explorer	*microsoft.com/windows/ie*
Firefox	*mozilla.org/products/firefox*
Safari	*apple.com/safari*
Opera	*opera.com*
Google Chrome	*google.com/chrome*
Konqueror	*konqueror.org/*

The little script in Example 1.3 should tell you what browser you are using. Even though the application name might display Netscape for Firefox and Microsoft Internet Explorer for Opera, if you examine the user agent, you will be able find Firefox or Opera as part of the output string (see Figure 1.9). Programs that determine the browser type are called browser sniffers. We have a complete example in Chapter 10, "It's the BOM! Browser Objects."

EXAMPLE 1.3

```
<script type="text/javascript">
   alert("User appName is "+ navigator.appName +
         "\nUser agent is "+ navigator.userAgent);
</script>
```

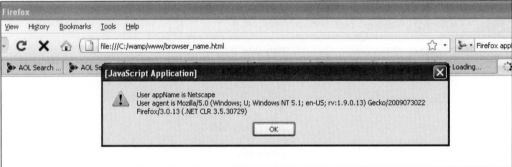

Figure 1.9 Output from Example 1.3.

1.10.1 Versions of JavaScript

JavaScript has a history. Invented by Netscape, the first version was JavaScript 1.0. It was new and buggy and has long since been replaced by much cleaner versions. Microsoft has a scripting language comparable to JavaScript called JScript. Table 1.3 lists versions of both JavaScript and JScript. For a discussion of JavaScript versions and development see *http://ejohn.org/blog/versions-of-JavaScript/*.

Table 1.3 JavaScript Versions

JavaScript or JScript Version	Browsers Supported
JavaScript 1.0 1996	Netscape Navigator 2.0, Internet Explorer 3.0
JavaScript 1.1 1996	Netscape Navigator 3.0, Internet Explorer 4.0
JavaScript 1.2 1997	Netscape Navigator 4.0–4.05, Internet Explorer 4.0

Table 1.3   JavaScript Versions (continued)

JavaScript or JScript Version	*Browsers Supported*
JavaScript 1.3 1998	ECMA-232, Netscape Navigator 4.06–4.7x, Internet Explorer 5.0
JavaScript 1.5 2000	ECMA-232, Netscape Navigator 6.0+, Mozilla Firefox, Internet Explorer 5.5+, JScript 5.5, 5.6, 5.7, 6
JavaScript 1.6 2006	Mozilla Firefox, Safari
JavaScript 1.7 2006	Mozilla Firefox, Safari, Google Chrome
JavaScript 1.8 2008	Mozilla Firefox

JavaScript is supported by Firefox, Explorer, Opera, and all newer versions of these browsers. In addition, HotJava 3 supports JavaScript, as do iCab for the Mac, WebTV, OmniWeb for OS X, QNX Voyager and Konqueror for the Linux KDE environment. NetBox for TV, AWeb and Voyager 3 for Amiga, and SEGA Dreamcast and ANT Fresco on RISC OS also support JavaScript.

Figure 1.10   JavaScript2 and the Web, an informative paper by Brendan Eich.

So where is JavaScript now? As of December 2009, the ECMA-262 Standard is in its 5th edition. JavaScript is a dialect of ECMAScript, but JavaScript 1.8 is comparable to ECMAScript, edition 3 and is currently the most widely used version (JavaScript 1.9 is available for download). To understand some of the proposals for a JavaScript2 version (ECMAScript Edition 4), Brian Eich, the creator of JavaScript, wrote an interesting article a few years ago that he published on the Web. If nothing else, it tells you some of the pros and cons of the current state of the JavaScript language and the obstacles faced in trying to change it. See Figure 1.10.

1.10.2   Does Your Browser Follow the Standard?

Modern browsers are using versions of JavaScript 1.5 or above, which generally follow the standards set by the W3C. The snippet of code in Example 1.4 tests to see if you are using a modern version of JavaScript that follows the standard DOM (see Figure 1.11). Both the *getElementById* and *createTextNode* are part of the W3C standard, which supports the DOM.

EXAMPLE 1.4

```
<script type="text/javascript">
   if (document.getElementById && document.createTextNode){
      alert("DOM supported by " + navigator.appName);
   }
</script>
```

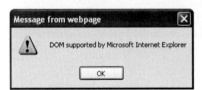

Figure 1.11   Internet Explorer supports the standard.

1.10.3   Is JavaScript Enabled on Your Browser?

To see if JavaScript is enabled on your browser, you can check the options menu of Firefox by going to the Tools menu/Options/Content. If using Apple's Safari browser, go to Safari menu/Preferences/Security and with Internet Explorer, go to the Tools menu/Internet Options/Security/Custom Level and enable Active scripting (see Figure 1.12). If using Opera go to the Opera menu/Preferences/Advanced/Content and click Enable JavaScript. An easy way to test if your browser has JavaScript enabled is to go to the Web site http://www.mistered.us/test/alert.shtml and follow directions (see Figure 1.13).

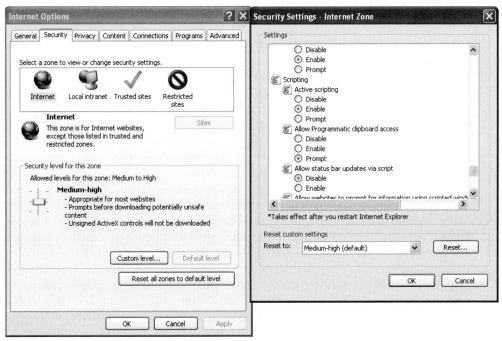

Figure 1.12   Enabling JavaScript on Microsoft Internet Explorer.

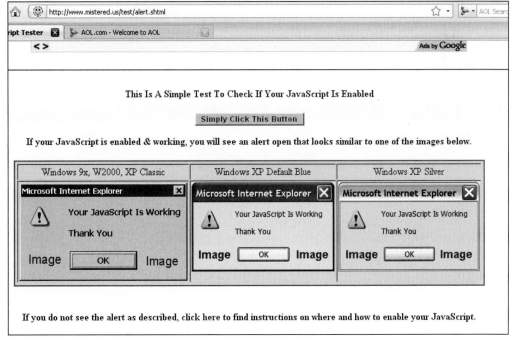

Figure 1.13   Is your browser JavaScript enabled?

1.11 Where to Put JavaScript

Before learning JavaScript, you should be familiar with HTML and how to create an HTML document. This doesn't mean that you have to be an expert, but you should be familiar with the structure of HTML documents and how the tags are used to display various kinds of content on your browser. Once you have a static HTML document, then adding basic JavaScript statements is quite easy. (Go to *http://www.w3schools.com* for an excellent HTML tutorial.) In this text we have devoted a separate chapter to CSS. CSS allows you to control the style and layout of your Web page by changing fonts, colors, backgrounds, margins, and so on in a single file. With HTML, CSS, and JavaScript you can create a Web site with structure, style, and action.

Client-side JavaScript programs are embedded in an HTML document between HTML head tags *<head>* and *</head>* or between the body tags *<body>* and *</body>*. Many developers prefer to put JavaScript code within the *<head>* tags, and at times, as you will see later, it is the best place to store function definitions and objects. If you want text displayed at a specific spot in the document, you might want to place the JavaScript code within the *<body>* tags (as shown in Example 1.5). Or you might have multiple scripts within a page, and place the JavaScript code within both the *<head>* and *<body>* tags. In either case, a JavaScript program starts with a *<script>* tag, and ends with a *</script>* tag. And if the JavaScript code is going to be long and involved, or may be shared by multiple pages, it should be placed in an external file (text file ending in *.js*) and loaded into the page. In fact, once you start developing Web pages with JavasScript, it is customary to separate the HTML/CSS content from the programming logic (Java-Script) by creating separate files for each entity.

When a document is sent to the browser, it reads each line of HTML code from top to bottom, and processes and displays it. As JavaScript code is encountered, it is read and exe-cuted by the JavaScript interpreter until it is finished, and then the parsing and rendering of the HTML continues until the end of the document is reached.

EXAMPLE 1.5

```
1  <!DOCTYPE HTML PUBLIC "-//W3C//DTD HTML 4.01//EN"
          "http://www.w3.org/TR/html4/strict.dtd">
2  <html>
3    <head><title>First JavaScript Sample</title></head>
4    <body bgcolor="yellow" text="blue">
5      <script type="text/javascript">
         document.write("<h2>Welcome to the JavaScript World!</h2>");
6      </script>
7      <big>This is just plain old HTML stuff.</big>
8    </body>
9  </html>
```

EXPLANATION

1   The doctype declaration tells the Web browser what version of the markup language will be used for this page and should be the very first thing in an HTML document, and must be included in an XHTML document. The doctype declaration refers to a Document Type Definition (DTD). The DTD specifies the rules for the markup language, so that the browsers can render the content correctly. This document is declared to be HTML 4.01 Strict. HTML 4.01 Strict is a version of HTML 4.01 that emphasizes structure over presentation. Deprecated elements and attributes, frames, and link targets are not allowed in HTML 4 Strict. In most of the examples in this book, this declaration will be omitted just to save space, but when you create your own documents, you should include the doctype declaration.

2   This is the starting tag for an HTML document.

3   This is the HTML *<head>* tag. The *<head>* tags contain all the elements that don't belong in the body of the document, such as the *<title>* tags, as well as JavaScript tags.

4   The *<body>* tag defines the background color and text color for the document.

5   This *<script>* tag is the starting HTML tag for the JavaScript script, which consists of a mix of textual content and JavaScript instructions. JavaScript instructions are placed between this tag and the closing *</script>* tag. JavaScript understands JavaScript instructions, not HTML.

   The JavaScript *writeln* method is called for the document. The string enclosed in parentheses is passed to the JavaScript interpreter. If the JavaScript interpreter encounters HTML content, it sends that content to the HTML renderer and it is printed into the document on the browser. The normal HTML parsing and rendering resumes after the closing JavaScript tag is reached.

6   This is the ending JavaScript tag. The output is shown in Figure 1.14.

7   HTML tags and text continue in the body of the document.

8   The body of the document ends here.

9   This is the ending tag for the HTML document.

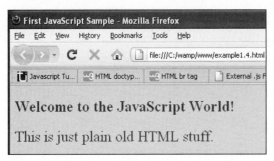

Figure 1.14 Example 1.5 output: JavaScript has been inserted in a document.

1.11.1   JavaScript from External Files

When scripts are long or need to be shared by other pages, they are usually placed in external files, separate from the HTML page. Keeping the JavaScript separate (unobtrusive JavaScript) from the HTML or CSS files is important when developing a Web site. It enables you to apply one set of functions to every page of the site, so that when you need to make a change, you can do it in one document rather than going through each individual page to apply the change. A JavaScript external file contains just plain JavaScript code and is saved as a .js file. The .js file is linked to the Web page by including it between the *<head>* tags of the HTML document and within its own *<script>* tags. The external JavaScript file is assigned to the *src* attribute of the *<script>* tag in the HTML file. The external file name includes the full URL if the script is on another server, directory path or just the script name if in the local directory. You can include more than one .js script in a file.

```
<script type="text/javascript"
        src="http://servername/JavaScriptfile.js">
</script>
```

The following examples, although very small, give you the idea of how external files are used. The welcome.js script contains a JavaScript function (see Chapter 7, "Functions").

EXAMPLE 1.6

```
// The external file called "welcome.js"
function welcome(){
   alert("Welcome to JavaScript!");
}
```

EXAMPLE 1.7

```
      <!DOCTYPE HTML PUBLIC "-//W3C//DTD HTML 4.01//EN"
          "http://www.w3.org/TR/html4/strict.dtd">
      <html>
        <head>
          <title>External .js File</title>
1         <script type="text/javascript" src="welcome.js">
2         </script>
        </head>
        <body bgColor="lavender">
          We are working with an external file.<br />
3         <input type="button" onClick="welcome()" value="Welcome Me!" />
        </body>
      </html>
```

EXPLANATION

1   The JavaScript *<script>* tag's *src* attribute is assigned the name of a file (name must end in *.js*) that contains JavaScript code. The file's name is *welcome.js* and it contains a JavaScript program of its own containing a simple JavaScript function that will be called when the user clicks the "Welcome Me!" button. See Figure 1.15.

2   The JavaScript program ends here.

3   This is an HTML button input device. When the user clicks the button, a JavaScript function called *welcome()* will be called. It is defined in the external file, *welcome.js*.

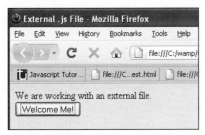

Figure 1.15   After clicking the "Welcome Me!" button, a function from the external .js file is called.

As you can see in Figure 1.16, Pearson Education uses many external JavaScript files (.js) files to produce their Web site.

```
Source of: http://www.pearsoned.com/ - Mozilla Firefox
File   Edit   View   Help
<!DOCTYPE html PUBLIC "-//W3C//DTD XHTML 1.0 Transitional//EN" "http://www.w3.org/TR/xhtml1/DTD/xhtml.
<html>
<head>
<title>Pearson Education - Live and Learn</title>
<meta name="description" content="Educating 100 million people worldwide, Pearson Education is the gl
<meta name="keywords" content="pearson education, publishing, textbooks, student management, testing,
<script language="JavaScript" type="text/JavaScript"></script>
<script LANGUAGE="JavaScript" SRC="js/browser-detect.js" TYPE='text/javascript'></script>
<script language="JavaScript1.2" src="js/mm menu.js"></script>
<link rel="stylesheet" href="css/ie.css" type="text/css"/>
</head>

<body bgcolor="#086BBD" leftmargin="0" topmargin="0" marginwidth="0" marginheight="0" >
<!-- ClickTale Top part -->
<script type="text/javascript">
var WRInitTime=(new Date()).getTime();
</script>
<!-- ClickTale end of Top part -->
```

Figure 1.16   Viewing the source code for a Web site using external JavaScript files.

1.12 Validating Your Markup

Because your JavaScript code does not stand alone but is integrated with HTML/XHTML and CSS, it is important to find validation tools to verify that your markup is correct, especially when conforming to the DOM and W3C standards. There are a number of free tools on the Web to help you make sure your markup is valid.

1.12.1   The W3C Validation Tool

The W3C validation tool is shown in Figure 1.17. This tool allows you to validate by URI, file upload, or by direct input. This validator checks the markup validity of Web documents in HTML, XHTML, SMIL, MathML, and so on, but to evaluate specific content such as RSS/Atom feeds or CSS stylesheets, MobileOK content, or to find broken links, there are other validators and tools available.

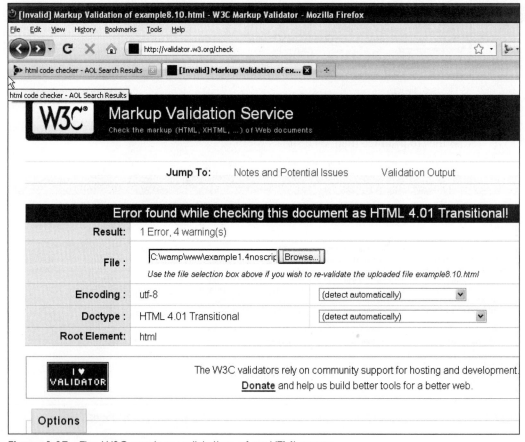

Figure 1.17   The W3C markup validation of an HTML page.

1.12.2   The Validome Validation Tool

The validator at *www.validome.org* is another excellent tool for validating an online page or an XHTML document. Just go to the Validome Web page and select the URL or Upload option to get a file from your hard drive. Once you have selected a file, just click Validate (see Figure 1.18).

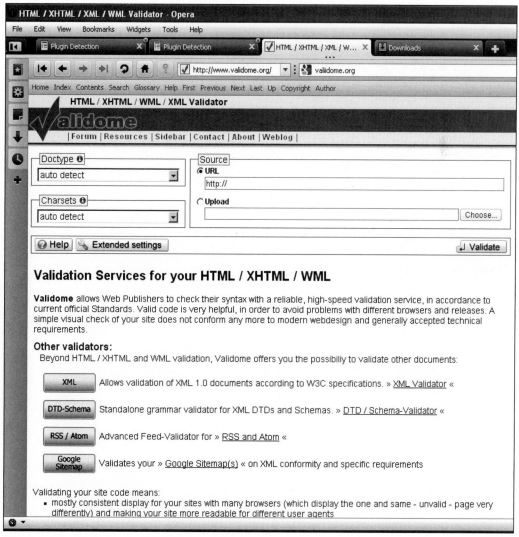

Figure 1.18   The Validome validation tool.

1.13 What You Should Know

This first chapter introduces you to the JavaScript programming language, its history, why it is important in Web development, and how it fits into a Web page. Before going further, you should know:

1. The difference between a compiled and scripting language.
2. Where JavaScript is defined, the client or server?
3. What JavaScript is used for.
4. How JavaScript makes a page interactive.
5. Where JavaScript programs are stored.
6. What a JavaScript program looks like.
7. What Ajax stands for and an example of how it is used.
8. What W3C stands for.
9. Why the DOM was standardized.
10. What is meant by unobtrusive JavaScript.
11. Where on the Web to find a good HTML tutorial.

Exercises

1. Describe the life cycle of a Web page.

2. What browser are you using? What version? How do you know?

3. What is an example of a JavaScript event handler? Copy Example 1.2 into your editor and run the program in your browser.

4. What is the difference between JavaScript and JScript?

5. Where do JavaScript tags go in an HTML page? Does JavaScript understand HTML?

6. What is the DOM?

7. Define the three layers of a Web page.

8. How do you set up JavaScript in an external file?

9. Write a JavaScript program that prints a welcome message in a large blue font. Check to see if JavaScript is enabled. Use comments to explain what you are doing.

chapter

2

Script Setup

2.1 The HTML Document and JavaScript

Unlike Perl and Python scripts, JavaScript scripts are not stand-alone programs. They are run in the context of an HTML document. When programming on the client side, the first step will be to create an HTML document in your favorite text editor, such as UNIX vi or emacs, or Windows Notepad,[1] WordPad, or TextPad (see Figure 2.1). There are a number of popular integrated development environments (IDEs) such as NetBeans, Komodo Edit, and Eclipse, with highlighting, validation, debugging features, and so on you might prefer to use. A list of recommended IDEs can be found at *http://JavaScript-ide.software.informer.com/downloads/*. Because the file you create is an HTML document, its name must include either an *.html* or *.htm* extension. JavaScript programs can be embedded within the HTML document between the *<script>* and *</script>* tags. Figures 2.1 and 2.2 show an HTML file containing JavaScript code.

```
TextPad - [C:\wamp\www\example2.1.html]

File  Edit  Search  View  Tools  Macros  Configure  Window  Help
1    <!DOCTYPE HTML PUBLIC "-//W3C//DTD HTML 4.01//EN"
2    "http://www.w3.org/TR/html4/strict.dtd">
3    <html lang=en>
4       <head><title>Hello</title></head>
5       <body>
6       <h3>
7          <script type="text/javascript">
8             <!-- Hide script from old browsers.
9             document.write("Hello, world!");
10            // End the hiding here. -->
11         </script>
12         <p>So long, world.</p>
13      </h3>
14      </body>
15   </html
```

Figure 2.1 JavaScript in TextPad editor.

---

1. If you are using Windows Notepad, be sure to turn off word wrap (under the Format menu) to avoid errors in your program.

29

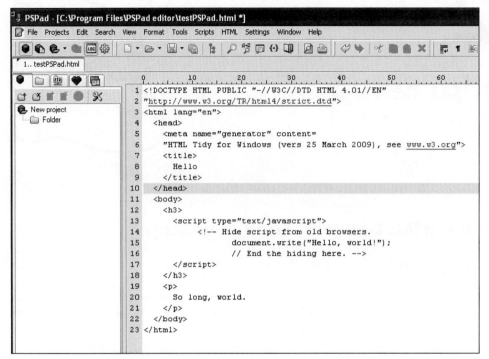

Figure 2.2   JavaScript in PSPad Editor, a popular free IDE with many features.

2.1.1   Script Execution

Because a JavaScript program is embedded in an HTML document, you will execute it in your browser window. If you are using an IDE, the browser is part of the integrated environment, but either way, you can execute a JavaScript program directly in the browser. If using Mozilla Firefox, Opera, or Internet Explorer, follow these instructions:

1. Go to the File menu and open the HTML file by browsing for the correct one.

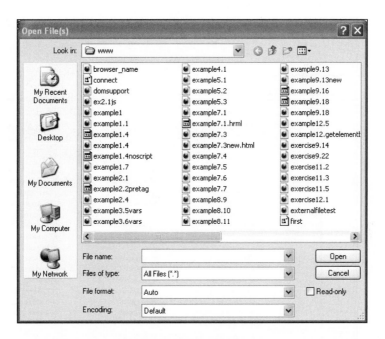

2. All files in the www folder are displayed. (The .html extension on the files will appear in the browser's URL.)

3. The file example 2.1.html is highlighted. (The .html extension is not visible.)

4. Or you can type the URL (complete address) in the navigation bar of your browser as shown here. (Note the .html extension appears in the URL.)

2.2 **Syntactical Details**

Rules, rules, rules. Just like English, French, or Chinese, all programming languages have their rules. Many of the rules are similar and many have individual quirks, but to do anything at all, you have to obey the rules, or your program simply won't work. If you have experience programming in other languages, you will find the JavaScript rules and syntax quite familiar. When you write JavaScript programs, you have to deal with HTML rules (and CSS rules), as well as JavaScript rules, because JavaScript does not stand alone.

2.2.1 Case Sensitivity

The HTML tags in a document are not case sensitive. If you type the *title* tag as *<title>*, *<Title>*, *<TItle>*, or any combination of upper or lowercase characters, the HTML renderer will not care. But JavaScript names, such as variables, keywords, objects, functions, and so on, are case sensitive. If, for example, you spell the Boolean value *true* with any uppercase letters (e.g., TrUE), JavaScript will not recognize it and will produce an error or simply ignore the JavaScript code. Although most names favor lowercase, some JavaScript names use a combination of upper and lowercase (e.g., *onClick*, *Math.floor*, *Date.getFullYear*).

2.2.2 Free Form and Reserved Words

JavaScript ignores whitespace (i.e., spaces, tabs, and newlines) if the whitespace appears between words. For example, a function name, such as *onMouseOver()*, *toLowerCase()*, or *onClick()*, cannot contain whitespace even though it consists of more than one word.

```
1. var name="Tom";          1 and 2 are equivalent statements
2. var     name    =
          "Tom";

3. onMouseOver()            3 and 4 are not the same
4. on  Mouse Over()
```

Whitespace is preserved when it is embedded within a string or regular expression. For example, the whitespace in the string, *"Hello   there"* will be preserved because it is enclosed within double quotes. Of course, you can't break up a word such as *switch*, *if*, *else*, *window*, *document*, and so on, because it would no longer be the same word. Because extra whitespace is ignored by the JavaScript interpreter, you are free to indent, break lines, and organize your program so that it is easier to read and debug.

There are a number of reserved words (also called keywords) in JavaScript. Being reserved means that keywords are special vocabulary for the JavaScript language and cannot be used by programmers as identifiers for variables, functions and labels, and the like. Words such as *if*, *for*, *while*, *return*, *null*, and *typeof* are examples of reserved words. Table 2.1 gives a list of reserved words.

Table 2.1   Reserved Keywords

abstract	boolean	break	byte	case	catch
char	class	const	continue	default	delete
do	double	else	extends	false	final
finally	float	for	function	goto	if
implements	import	in	instanceof	int	interface
long	native	new	null	package	private
protected	public	return	short	static	super
switch	synchronized	this	throw	throws	transient
true	try	typeof	var	void	volatile
while	with				

2.2.3   Statements and Semicolons

Just like sentences (which represent complete thoughts) in the English language, Java-Script statements are made up of expressions. The statements are executed top down, one statement at a time. If there are multiple statements on a line, the statements must be separated by semicolons. Although not a rule, it is good practice to terminate all statements with a semicolon to make it clear where the statement ends. Because JavaScript is free form, as long as statements are terminated with a semicolon, the lines can be broken, contain whitespace, and so on. A statement results in some action unless the statement is a null statement, in which case it does nothing.

The following two lines are both technically correct:

```
var name = "Ellie"     <- no semicolon, valid
var name = "Ellie";    <- better
```

The following line is incorrect:

```
var name = "Ellie"  document.write("Hi "+name);  <- wrong, two statements
```

It should be:

```
var name = "Ellie";  document.write("Hi " + name);  <- semicolon needed
                                                        to separate two
                                                        statements on the
                                                        same line
```

If the statements are grouped in a block of curly braces, they act as a single statement.

```
if ( x > y) { statement;  statement; } <- Statements enclosed in curly
                                          braces act as a single
                                          statement
```

2.2.4 Comments

A comment is text that describes what the program or a particular part of the program is trying to do and is ignored by the JavaScript interpreter. Comments are used to help you and other programmers understand, maintain, and debug scripts. JavaScript uses two types of comments: single-line comments and block comments.

Single-line comments start with a double slash:

```
// This is a comment
```

For a block of comments, use the /* */ symbols:

```
/* This is a block of comments
   that continues for a number of lines
*/
```

2.2.5 The *<script>* Tag

JavaScript programs must start and end with the HTML *<script>* and *</script>* tags, respectively. Everything within these tags is considered JavaScript code, nothing else. The script tag can be placed anywhere within an HTML document. If you want the Java-Script code to be executed before the page is displayed, it is placed between the *<head>* and *</head>* tags. This, for example, is where function definitions are placed (see Chapter 7, "Functions"). If the script performs some action pertaining to the body of the document, then it is placed within the *<body>* and *</body>* tags. A document can have multiple *<script>* tags, each enclosing any number of JavaScript statements.

FORMAT

```
<script>
  JavaScript statements...
</script>
```

EXAMPLE 2.1

```
<script>
  document.write("Hello, world!<br />");
</script>
```

Attributes.   The *<script>* tag also has **attributes** to modify the behavior of the tag. The attributes are

- *language*
- *type*
- *src*

Any JavaScript-enabled browser can identify that the scripting language is JavaScript, if the *language* attribute is set to *JavaScript*[2] rather than, for example, *VBScript* or *JScript*. You normally set the language attribute as follows:

```
<script language="JavaScript">
```

According to the W3C recommendation, the value assigned to this attribute is an identifier for the scripting language, but because these identifiers are not standard, this attribute has been deprecated in favor of the *type* attribute.

The *language* attribute can be assigned a version number to specify what version of JavaScript is supported to view the page. If the browser doesn't recognize the version, the script will be totally ignored. You shouldn't have to worry about this if you are using the latest version of a particular browser, but just in case, here's how you specify a version number.

```
<script language="JavaScript1.5">
</script>
```

The *type* attribute is used to specify both the scripting language and the Internet content type. It is used mainly to validate JavaScript as part of a well-formed document and is the preferred way to start JavaScript in all modern browsers.

```
<script language="JavaScript"
  type="text/javascript">
</script>
```

---

2. Although common to most scripts, the *language* attribute has been deprecated as of HTML 4.0 in favor of the *type* attribute.

The *src* attribute is used when the JavaScript code is in an external file, the file name ending with a *.js* extension. The *src* attribute is assigned the name of the file, which can be prefixed with its location (e.g., a directory tree or URL).

```
<script type="text/javascript"
   src="sample.js">
</script>

<script type="text/javascript"
   src="directory/sample.js">
</script>

<script type="text/javascript"
   src="http://hostname/sample.js">
</script>
```

2.3   Generating HTML and Printing Output

When you create a program in any language, the first thing you want to see is the output of the program displayed on a screen. In the case of JavaScript, you'll see your output in the browser window. Of course, browsers use HTML to format output. Although Java-Script doesn't understand HTML per se, it can generate HTML output with its built-in methods, *write()* and *writeln()*.

2.3.1   Strings and String Concatenation

A string is a character or set of characters enclosed in matching quotes. Because the methods used to display text take strings as their arguments, this is a good time to talk a little about strings. See Chapter 9, "JavaScript Core Objects," for a more complete discussion. All strings must be placed within a matched set of either single or double quotes; for example:

```
"this is a string"   or   'this is a string'
```

Double quotes can hide single quotes; for example:

```
"I don't care"
```

And single quotes can hide double quotes; for example:

```
'He cried, "Ahoy!"'
```

Either way, the entire string is enclosed in a set of matching quotes.

Concatenation is caused when two strings are joined together. The plus (+) sign is used to concatenate strings; for example:

```
"hot" + "dog"  or  "San Francisco" + "<br />"
```

For more information on strings, see Chapter 3, "The Building Blocks: Data Types, Literals, and Variables."

2.3.2   The *write()* and *writeln()* Methods

One of the most important features of client-side JavaScript is its ability to generate pages dynamically. Data, text, and HTML itself can be written to the browser on the fly. The *write()* method is a special kind of built-in JavaScript function used to output HTML to the document as it is being parsed. When generating output with *write()* and *writeln()*, put the text in the body of the document (rather than in the header) at the place where you want the text to appear when the page is loaded.

Method names are followed by a set of parentheses. They are used to hold the arguments. These are messages that will be sent to the methods, such as a string of text, the output of a function, or the results of a calculation. Without arguments, the *write()* and *writeln()* methods would have nothing to write.

JavaScript defines the current document (i.e., the HTML file that contains the script) as a document object. (You will learn more about objects later.) For now, whenever you refer to the document object, the object name is appended with a dot and the name of the method that will manipulate the document object. In the following example the *write()* method must be prepended with the name of the document object and a period. The browser will display this text in the document's window. The syntax is

```
document.write("Hello to you");
```

The *writeln()* method is essentially just like the *write()* method, except when the text is inserted within HTML *<pre>* or *<xmp>* tags, in which case *writeln()* will insert a newline at the end of the string. The HTML *<pre>* tag is used to enclose preformatted text. It results in "what you see is what you get." All spaces and line breaks are rendered literally, in a monopitch typeface. The *<xmp>* tag is an obsolete HTML tag that functions much like the *<pre>* tag.

EXAMPLE 2.2

```
<html>
   <head><title>Printing Output</title></head>
   <body bgcolor="yellow" text="blue">
      <big>
      <b>Comparing the <em>document.write</em> and
                    <em>document.writeln</em> methods</b><br />
      <script type="text/javascript">
1        document.write("One, ");  // No newline
2        document.writeln("Two, ");
```

EXAMPLE 2.2 (CONTINUED)

```
          document.writeln("Three, ");
3         document.write("Blast off....<br />");  // break tag
4         //document.write("The browser you are using is " +
          //                navigator.userAgent + "<br />");
5     </script>
6     <pre>
7     <script type="text/javaScript">
          /*Lines are broken due to size of this page. If you cut
            and paste these programs into an editor, make sure
            strings start and end with qutoes!!!*/
8         document.writeln("With the <em>HTML &lt;pre&gt;
                           </em> tags, ");
          document.writeln("the <em>writeln</em> method produces a
                           newline.");
          document.writeln("Slam");
          document.writeln("Bang");
          document.writeln("Dunk!");
9     </script>
10    </pre>
      </big>
    </body>
  </html>
```

EXPLANATION

1 The *document.write()* method does not produce a newline at the end of the string it displays. HTML tags are sent to the HTML renderer as the lines are parsed.

2 The *document.writeln()* method doesn't produce a newline either, unless it is in an HTML *<pre>* tag.

3 Again, the *document.write()* method does not produce a newline at the end of the string. The *
* tag is added to produce the line break.

4 The *document.write()* method does not produce a newline. The *
* tag takes care of that. *userAgent* is a special *navigator* property that tells you about your browser.

5 The first JavaScript program ends here.

6 The HTML *<pre>* tag starts a block of preformatted text; that is, text that ignores formatting instructions and fonts.

7 This tag starts the JavaScript code.

8 When enclosed in a *<pre>* tag, the *writeln()* method will break each line it prints with a newline; otherwise, it behaves like the *write()* method (i.e., you will have to add a *
* tag to get a newline).

9 This tag marks the end of the JavaScript code.

10 This tag marks the end of preformatted text. The output is shown in Figure 2.3.

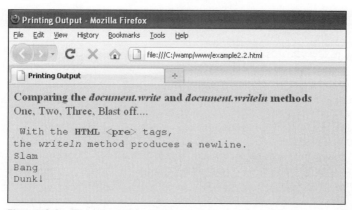

Figure 2.3 The output from Example 2.2 demonstrates the difference between the *document.write()* and *document.writeln()* methods.

2.4 About Debugging

Have you ever tried to draw a picture or do your resume for the first time without a mistake either in the layout, order, type, style, or whatever? In any programming language, it's the same story, and JavaScript is no exception. It's especially tricky with JavaScript because you have to consider the HTML as well as the JavaScript code when your page doesn't turn out right. You might get errors on the console or get a totally blank page. Finding errors in a script can get quite frustrating without proper debugging tools. Before we go any further, this is a good time to get acquainted with some of the types of errors you might encounter.

2.4.1 Types of Errors

Load or Compile Time.   Load-time errors are the most common errors and are caught by JavaScript as the script is being loaded. These errors will prevent the script from running at all. Load-time errors are generally caused by mistakes in syntax, such as missing parentheses in a function or misspelling a keyword. You might have typed a string of text and forgotten to enclose the string in quotes, or you might have mismatched the quotes, starting with single quotes but ending with double quotes.

Runtime.   Runtime errors, as the name suggests, are those errors that occur when the JavaScript program actually starts running. An example of a runtime error would be if your program references an object or variable that doesn't exist, or you put some code between the *<head></head>* tags and it should have been placed within the *<body></body>* tags, or you referenced a page that doesn't exist.

Logical.   Logical errors are harder to find because they imply that you didn't anticipate an event or that you inadvertently misused an operator, but your syntax was okay.

For example, if you are checking to see if two expressions are equal, you should use the == equality operator, not the = assignment operator.

2.5 Debugging Tools

To see your where errors have occurred in your JavaScript programs, modern browsers provide an error console window.

Table 2.2   Browser Error Console

Browser	How to Invoke Error Console
Internet Explorer	Double-click the little yellow triangle in the left corner
Firefox	Tools/Error Console
Safari	Develop/Show Error Console
Opera9	Tools/Advanced/Error Console script Options/

2.5.1 Firefox

Error Console.   You can bring up the error console for Firefox by going to "Tools/Error Console" The Console displays the lines containing the errors. Leave the console open and watch your errors build up. There is a "Clear" option to refresh the error console window. The following JavaScript program contains an error that will be displayed in the Error Console window as shown in Figure 2.4.

EXAMPLE 2.3

```
     <html>
       <head>
         <title>First JavaScript Sample</title>
       </head>
       <body bgcolor="lavender">
         <font size="+2">

1        <script type = "text/javascript">
2           document.writeln("<h2>Welcome to the JavaScript World!</h2>);
                              // Bug in line2:  Missing double quote!!
         </script>

            This is just plain old HTML stuff.
         </font>
       </body>
     </html>
```

EXPLANATION

1   JavaScript code starts here.

2   In this line, the string starts with a double quote, but doesn't terminate with one. Because the quotes are not matched, JavaScript produces an error. Each browser has a way of handling error messages. Figure 2.4 uses the Firefox error console to detect the error.

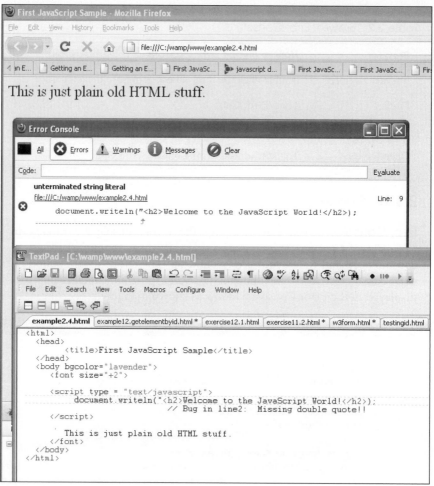

Figure 2.4   Firefox Error Console (go to Firefox Tools/Error Console).

Firebug.   Firebug is a Firefox extension that has become very popular with Web developers for editing, debugging, and monitoring CSS, HTML, and JavaScript live in any Web page (see Figures 2.5 and 2.6). It is easy to download and can be found in the Firefox Tools menu.

Figure 2.5   The Firebug Web site.

You can also use a version of Firebug in Internet Explorer, Opera, and Safari called Firebug Lite. See *http://getfirebug.com/lite.html*.

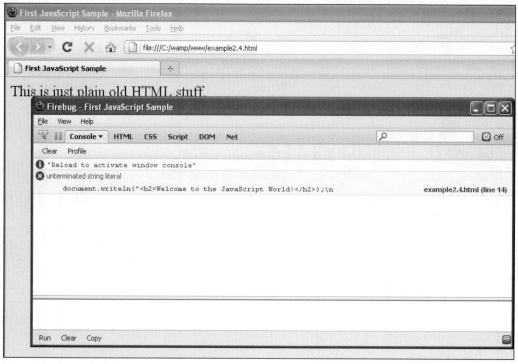

Figure 2.6   The Firebug Debugging window.

2.5.2   Debugging in Internet Explorer 8

When an error occurs in your JavaScript program, a little yellow triangle appears in the bottom left corner of the browser window. If you double-click the triangle, a debugging window opens explaining the error and the line number where it occurred (see Figure 2.7).

Internet Explorer Developer Tools.   Every installation of Internet Explorer 8 comes with the Developer Tools for debugging JavaScript (Microsoft JScript), HTML, and CSS on the fly. It comes with a plethora of features including the ability to control script execution, set break points, inspect variables, profile performance, edit and prototype new designs, and so on. See *http://msdn.microsoft.com/en-us/library/dd565628(VS.85).aspx*.

To start debugging your JavaScript programs, open the Developer Tools and switch to the Script tab, then click Start Debugging. When starting the debugging process, the Developer Tools will refresh the page and you will have all the functionality you expect from a debugger (see Figure 2.8). Once you are done, click Stop Debugging. Go to Internet Explorer Tools/Developer Tools and the debugger window will appear. Click Script, and then restart your program in the browser.

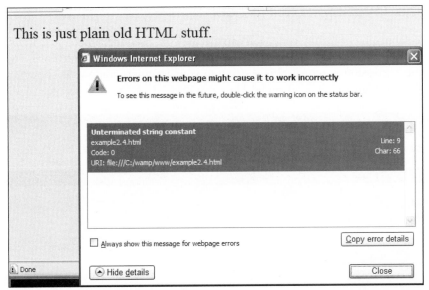

Figure 2.7 Internet Explorer 8 after clicking the little yellow triangle in the bottom left corner.

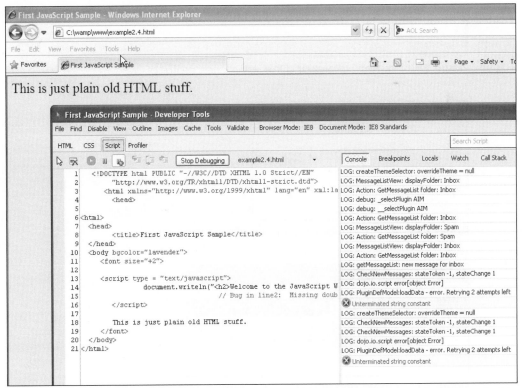

Figure 2.8 Internet Explorer 8 Developer Tools (go to the Tools menu and then Developer Tools).

2.5.3 The *JavaScript:* URL Protocol

For simple debugging or testing code, you can use the URL pseudoprotocol, *JavaScript:* followed by any valid JavaScript expression or expressions separated by semicolons. The result of the expression is returned as a string to your browser window, as shown in Example 2.4 and Figures 2.9, 2.10, and 2.11.

FORMAT

```
JavaScript: expression
```

EXAMPLE 2.4

```
JavaScript: 5 + 4
```

Figure 2.9 Internet Explorer and the *JavaScript:* protocol.

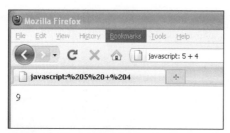

Figure 2.10 Mozilla Firefox and the *JavaScript:* protocol.

Figure 2.11 Opera and the *JavaScript:* protocol.

2.6   JavaScript and Old or Disabled Browsers

2.6.1   Hiding JavaScript from Old Browsers

Is JavaScript Enabled?   The answer is most probably "yes." There are many versions of browsers available to the public and the vast majority of the public uses Firefox, Opera or Internet Explorer. So why worry? Well, just because a browser supports JavaScript does not mean that everyone has JavaScript enabled. There are also some older text browsers that don't support JavaScript, but today it's more likely that JavaScript has been disabled for security reasons or to avoid cookies than because the browser is old. Cell phones, Palm handhelds, and speech browsers for the visibly disabled provide browser support, but do not necessarily have JavaScript. There has to be some alternative way to address those Web browsers (see *http://www.internet.com*).

Hiding JavaScript.   If you put a script in a Web page, and the browser is old and doesn't know what a *<script>* tag is, the JavaScript code will be treated as regular HTML. But if you enclose JavaScript code within HTML comment tags, it will be invisible to the HTML renderer and, therefore, ignored by browsers not supporting JavaScript. If the browser has JavaScript enabled, then any HTML tags (including HTML comments) inserted between the *<script> </script>* tags will be ignored. Hiding JavaScript in comment tags is a common practice used in JavaScript programs. It is introduced here so that when you notice these embedded comments in other's programs, you will understand why. See Example 2.5.

EXAMPLE 2.5

```
   <html>
      <head><title>Old Browsers</title></head>
      <body><font color="0000F">
         <div align=center>
1           <script type="text/javascript">
2              <!-- Hiding JavaScript from Older Browsers
3              document.write("<h2>Welcome to Maine!</h2>");
4              // Stop Hiding JavaScript from Older Browsers -->
5           </script>
            <img src="BaileyIsland.jpg" width="400" height="300" border=1>
            <br />Bailey's Island
         </div></font>
      </body>
   </html>
```

EXPLANATION

1   The JavaScript program starts here. Browsers that don't support JavaScript will skip over this opening *<script>* tag.

2   The *<!--* symbol is the start of an HTML comment and will continue until *-->* is reached. Any browser not supporting JavaScript will treat this whole block as a comment. JavaScript itself uses two slashes or C-style syntax, */* */*, and will ignore the HTML comment tags.

Continues

EXPLANATION(CONTINUED)

3   The *document.write* method displays this line in the page. Any HTML tags inserted in the quoted strings will be handled by the HTML renderer. JavaScript does not know how to interpret HTML by itself. If the browser supports JavaScript, the line *Welcome to Maine!* will appear just above the image. If the browser does not support JavaScript, or has it disabled, this section of code is ignored. See the two examples of output shown in Figures 2.12 and 2.13.

4   This line starts with two slashes, the start of a JavaScript comment. This is done so that if JavaScript is interpreting this section, it won't see the HTML closing comment tag, -->. Why don't we want JavaScript to see the closing tag if it could see the opening tag? Because JavaScript would see the double dash as one of its special operators, and produce an error. Firefox's error:

5   The JavaScript program ends here with its closing *</script>* tag.

Bailey's Island

Figure 2.12   Example 2.5 output in a JavaScript-disabled browser.

Figure 2.13   Example 2.5 output in a JavaScript-enabled browser.

The *<noscript>* Tag.   Modern browsers provide a set of tags called *<noscript></noscript>* that enable you to provide alternative information to browsers that are either unable to read JavaScript or have it turned off. All JavaScript-enabled browsers recognize the *<noscript>* tag. They will just ignore whatever is between *<noscript>* and*</noscript>*. Browsers that do not support JavaScript do not recognize the *<noscript>* tags. They will ignore the tags but will display whatever is in between them. See Example 2.6.

EXAMPLE 2.6

```
         <html>
           <head>
             <title>Has JavaScript been turned off?</title>
           </head>
           <body bgColor="blue">
             <font color="white">
             <h3>
1            <script type="text/javascript" >
2              document.write("Your browser supports JavaScript!");
             </script>
3            <noscript>
               Please turn JavaScript on if you want to see this page!<br>
               <em>
4                 Firefox &gt; Tools &gt; Options &gt; Content &gt;
                    Enable JavaScript<br />
                  IE &gt; Tools &gt; Internet Options &gt; Security &gt;
                    Custom Level &gt;Security Setting &gt; Scripting &gt;
                    Enable<br />
               </em>
5            </noscript>
```

Continues

EXAMPLE 2.6 (CONTINUED)

```
        </h3>
        </font>
    </body>
</html>
```

EXPLANATION

1   The JavaScript program starts here with the opening *<script>* tag.
2   This line is displayed on the Web page only if JavaScript is enabled.
3   The *<noscript>* tag is read by browsers that support JavaScript. They will ignore everything between the *<noscript>* and *</noscript>* tags. Disabled browsers will not recognize the *<noscript>* tag and thus ignore them, displaying all enclosed text.
4   JavaScript-disabled browsers will display the message shown in Figure 2.14.
5   The *</noscript>* tag ends here.

Figure 2.14   Output from Example 2.6.

2.7   What You Should Know

This chapter introduced you the JavaScript, the language. You should now be able to create a simple script and execute it in the browser window. Here are some things you should know:

1. How HTML and JavaScript coexist.
2. Understand the syntax, or how to write correct JavaScript statements.
3. How to execute a JavaScript program.
4. About case sensitivity, special words called reserved words or keywords, and how JavaScript handles whitespace, that it is free form.
5. Three ways to comment text that is used to explain what is going on in your program and ignored by the interpreter.
6. How to use *<script> </script>* tags, its attributes, and where to put them.

7. How and why you would create a .js file.
8. How to create and quote a string, and how to use the *writeln()* method.
9. Identify three types of errors and use your browser's debugging tools.
10. How to hide JavaScript from old browsers.

Exercises

1. What is a reserved word? Give an example.

2. Is JavaScript case sensitive?

3. What is the purpose of enclosing statements within curly braces?

4. What is the latest version of JavaScript? Where can you find this information?

5. What is the difference between the JavaScript *src* and *type* attributes?

6. How would you concatenate the following three strings with JavaScript?

   ```
   "trans"    "por"    "tation"
   ```

7. Write a script that demonstrates how concatenation works.

8. Create a JavaScript program that will print "Hello, world! Isn't life great?" in an Arial bold font, size 14, and make the background color of the screen light green.

9. Add two strings to the first JavaScript program—your first name and last name—concatenated and printed in a blue sans serif font, size 12.

10. In the Location field of your browser, test the value of an expression using the *JavaScript:* protocol.

11. Find the errors in the following script:

    ```html
    <html>
    <head>
       <title>Finding Errors</title>
    </head>
    <body bgcolor="yellow" text="blue">
       <script type="text/javascript"
          document.writeln("Two, ")
          document.writeln ("Three, ")
          document.write('Blast off....<br />");
       </script>
    </body>
    </html>
    ```

chapter

3

The Building Blocks: Data Types, Literals, and Variables

3.1 Data Types

A program can do many things, including calculations, sorting names, preparing phone lists, displaying images, validating forms, ad infinitum. But to do anything, the program works with the data that is given to it. Data types specify what kind of data, such as numbers and characters, can be stored and manipulated within a program. JavaScript supports a number of fundamental data types. These types can be broken down into two categories, primitive data types and composite data types.

3.1.1 Primitive Data Types

Primitive data types are the simplest building blocks of a program. They are types that can be assigned a single literal value such as the number 5.7, or a string of characters such as *"hello"*. JavaScript supports three core or basic data types:

- numeric
- string
- Boolean

In addition to the three core data types, there are two other special types that consist of a single value:

- null
- undefined

Numeric Literals. JavaScript supports both integers and floating-point numbers. Integers are whole numbers and do not contain a decimal point, such as 123 and –6. Integers can be expressed in decimal (base 10), octal (base 8), and hexadecimal (base 16), and are either positive or negative values. See Example 3.1.

Floating-point numbers are fractional numbers such as 123.56 or –2.5. They must contain a decimal point or an exponent specifier, such as 1.3e–2. The letter "*e*" for exponent notation can be either uppercase or lowercase.

JavaScript numbers can be very large (e.g., 10^{308} or 10^{-308}).

EXAMPLE 3.1

```
12345          integer
23.45          float
.234E-2        scientific notation
.234e+3        scientific notation
0x456fff       hexadecimal
0x456FFF       hexadecimal
0777           octal
```

String Literals and Quoting.   String literals are rows of characters enclosed in either double or single quotes.[1] The quotes must be matched. If the string starts with a single quote, it must end with a matching single quote, and likewise if it starts with a double quote, it must end with a double quote. Single quotes can hide double quotes, and double quotes can hide single quotes:

```
"This is a string"
'This is another string'
"This is also 'a string' "
'This is "a string"'
```

An empty set of quotes is called the null string. If a number is enclosed in quotes, it is considered a string; for example, "5" is a string, whereas 5 is a number.

Strings are called constants or literals. The string value "*hello*" is called a string constant or literal. To change a string requires replacing it with another string.

Strings can contain escape sequences (a single character preceded with a backslash), as shown in Table 3.1. Escape sequences are a mechanism for quoting a single character.

Table 3.1 Escape Sequences

Escape Sequence	What It Represents
\'	Single quotation mark
\"	Double quotation mark
\t	Tab

---

1. Any string without quotation marks surrounding it is considered the name of a variable.

Table 3.1 Escape Sequences (continued)

Escape Sequence	What It Represents
\n	Newline
\r	Return
\f	Form feed
\b	Backspace
\e	Escape
\\	Backslash
Special Escape Sequences	
\XXX	The character with the Latin-1 encoding specified by up to three octal digits XXX between 0 and 377. \251 is the octal sequence for the copyright symbol.
\xXX	The character with the Latin-1 encoding specified by the two hexadecimal digits XX between 00 and FF. \xA9 is the hexadecimal sequence for the copyright symbol.
\uXXXX	The Unicode character specified by the four hexadecimal digits XXXX. \u00A9 is the Unicode sequence for the copyright symbol.

EXAMPLE 3.2

```
    <html>
      <head><title>Escape Sequences</title></head>
      <body>
1       <pre>
        <big>
2         <script type="text/javascript">
            <!-- Hide script from old browsers.
3           document.write("\t\tHello\nworld!\n");
4           document.writeln("\"Nice day, Mate.\"\n");
5           document.writeln('Smiley face:<font size="+3"> \u263a\n');
            //End hiding here. -->
          </script>
        </big>
        </pre>
      </body>
    </html>
```

EXPLANATION

1   The escape sequences will work only if in a *<pre>* tag or an alert dialog box.

2   The JavaScript program starts here.

3   The *write()* method sends to the browser a string containing two tabs (\t\t), *Hello*, a newline (\n), *world!,* and another newline (\n).

4   The *writeln()* method sends to the browser a string containing a double quote (\"), *Nice day, Mate.,* another double quote (\"), and a newline (\n). Because the *writeln()* method automatically creates a newline, the output will display two newlines: the default value and the \n in the string.

5   This string contains a backslash sequence that will be translated into Unicode. The Unicode hexadecimal character 263a is preceded by a \u. The output is a smiley face. See Figure 3.1.

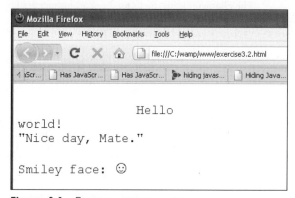

Figure 3.1 Escape sequences.

Putting Strings Together.   The process of joining strings together is called concatenation. The string concatenation operator is a plus sign (+). Its operands are two strings. If one string is a number and the other is a string, JavaScript will still concatenate them as strings. If both operands are numbers, the + will be the addition operator. The following examples output *"popcorn"* and *"Route 66"*, respectively.

```
document.write("pop" + "corn");
document.write("Route " + 66);
```

The expression *5 + 100* results in *105*, whereas *"5" + 100* results in *"5100"*.

Boolean Literals.   Boolean literals are logical values that have only one of two values, *true* or *false*. You can think of the values as yes or no, on or off, or 1 or 0. They are used to test whether a condition is true or false. When using numeric comparison and equality operators, the value *true* evaluates to 1 and *false* evaluates to 0. (Read about comparison operators in Chapter 5, "Operators.")

```
answer1 = true;
```

or

```
if (answer2 == false) { do something; }
```

The *typeof* Operator.   The *typeof* operator returns a string to identify the type of its operand (i.e., a variable, string, keyword, or object). The values returned can be "number", "string", "boolean", "object", "null", and "undefined". You can use the *typeof* operator to check whether a variable has been defined because if there is no value associated with the variable, the *typeof* operator returns *undefined.*

FORMAT

```
typeof operand
typeof (operand)
```

EXAMPLE

```
typeof(54.6)
typeof("yes")
```

EXAMPLE 3.3

```
<html>
   <head>
      <title>The typeof Operator</title>
   </head>
   <body bgcolor="gold">
      <big>
      <script type="text/javascript">
1       document.write(typeof(55),"<br />");   // Number
2       document.write(typeof("hello there"),"<br />");   // String
3       document.write(typeof(true),"<br />");  // Boolean
      </script>
      </big>
   </body>
</html>
```

EXPLANATION

1   The integer, *55*, is a *number* type.

2   The text *"hello there"* is a *string* type.

3   The *true* or *false* keyword represent a *boolean* type. See Figure 3.2.

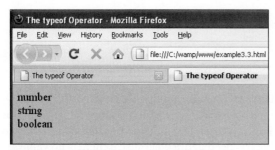

Figure 3.2   Output from Example 3.3.

***Null* and *Undefined*.**   The difference between null and undefined is a little subtle. The *null* keyword represents "no value," meaning "nothing," not even an empty string or zero. It is a type of JavaScript object (see Chapter 8, "Objects"). It can be used to initialize a variable so that it does not produce errors or to clear the value of a variable, so that there is no longer any data associated with that variable, and the memory used by it is freed. When a variable is assigned *null*, it does not contain any valid data type.

A variable that has been declared, but given no initial value, contains the value *undefined* and will produce a runtime error if you try to use it. (If you declare the variable and assign *null* to it, *null* will act as a placeholder and you will not get an error.) The word *undefined* is not a keyword in JavaScript. If compared with the == equality operators, *null* and *undefined* are equal, but if compared with the identity operator, they are not identical (see Chapter 5, "Operators").

EXAMPLE 3.4

```
<html>
   <head>
      <title>The typeof Operator with Null and Undefined</title>
   </head>
   <body bgColor="gold">
      <big>
         <script type="text/javascript">
            document.write("<em>null</em> is type "+
1                        typeof(null),"<br />");
            document.write("<em>undefined</em> is type "+
2                        typeof(undefined),"<br />");
         </script>
      </big>
   </body>
</html>
```

EXPLANATION

1   The *null* keyword is a type of object. It is a built-in JavaScript object that contains no value.

2   Undefined is returned when a variable has been given no initial value or when the *void* operator is used (see Table 5.19 on page 120). See output in Figure 3.3.

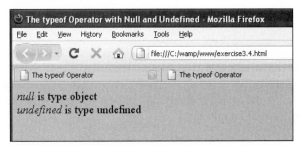

Figure 3.3 Output from Example 3.4.

3.1.2 Composite Data Types

We mentioned that there are two types of data: primitive and composite. This chapter focuses on the primitive types: numbers, strings, and Booleans—each storing a single value. Composite data types, also called complex types, consist of more than one component. Objects, arrays, and functions, covered later in this book, all contain a collection of components. Objects contain properties and methods, arrays contain a sequential list of elements, and functions contain a collection of statements. The composite types are discussed in later chapters.

3.2 Variables

Variables are fundamental to all programming languages. They are data items that represent a memory storage location in the computer. Variables are containers that hold data such as numbers and strings. Variables have a **name**, a **type**, and a **value**.

```
num = 5;              // name is "num", value is 5, type is numeric
friend = "Peter";     // name is "friend", value is "Peter",
                      // type is string
```

The values assigned to variables can change throughout the run of a program whereas constants, also called literals, remain fixed. JavaScript variables can be assigned three types of data:

- numeric
- string
- Boolean

Computer programming languages like C++ and Java require that you specify the type of data you are going to store in a variable when you declare it. For example, if you are going to assign an integer to a variable, you would have to say something like:

```
int n = 5;
```

And if you were assigning a floating-point number:

```
float x = 44.5;
```

Languages that require that you specify a data type are called "strongly typed" languages. JavaScript, conversely, is a dynamically or loosely typed language, meaning that you do not have to specify the data type of a variable. In fact, doing so will produce an error. With JavaScript, you would simply say:

```
n = 5;
x = 44.5;
```

and JavaScript will figure out what type of data is being stored in *n* and *x*.

3.2.1   Valid Names

Variable names consist of any number of letters (an underscore counts as a letter) and digits. The first character must be a letter or an underscore. Because JavaScript keywords do **not** contain underscores, using an underscore in a variable name can ensure that you are not inadvertently using a reserved keyword. Variable names are case sensitive; for example, *Name, name*, and *NAme* are all different variable names. Refer to Table 3.2.

Table 3.2   Valid and Invalid Variable Names

Valid Variable Names	*Invalid Variable Names*
name1	*10names*
price_tag	*box.front*
_abc	*name#last*
Abc_22	*A-23*
A23	*5*

3.2.2   Declaring and Initializing Variables

Variables must be declared before they can be used. To make sure that variables are declared first, you can declare them in the head of the HTML document. There are two ways to declare a variable: with or without the keyword *var*. Although laziness might get the best of you, it is a better practice to always use the *var* keyword.

You can assign a value to the variable (or initialize a variable) when you declare it, but it is not mandatory, unless you omit the *var* keyword. If a variable is declared but not initialized, it is "undefined."

FORMAT

```
var variable_name = value;    // initialized
var variable_name;            // uninitialized
variable_name;                // wrong
```

To declare a variable called *firstname*, you could say

var first_name="Ellie"

or

first_name ="Ellie";

or

var first_name;

You can declare multiple variables on the same line by separating each declaration with a comma. For example, you could say

var first_name, middle_name, last_name;

EXAMPLE 3.5

```
   <html>
     <head><title>Using the var Keyword</title>
       <script type="text/javascript">
1        var language="English";   // Variable is initialized
2        var name;                 // OK, undefined variable
3        age;                      //  Not OK! var keyword missing ERROR!
       </script>
     </head>
     <body bgcolor="silver">
       <big>
         <script type="text/javascript">
           document.write("Language is " + language + "<br />");
           document.write("Name is "+ name + "<br />");
4          document.write("Age is "+ age + "<br />");
         </script>
       </big>
     </body>
   </html>
```

EXPLANATION

1 The variable called *language* is defined and initialized. The *var* keyword is not required here, but is recommended.

2 Because the variable called *name* is not initialized, the *var* keyword is required here.

Continues

3   The variable called *age* is not assigned an initial value. The *var* keyword is required. Without it, the program produces errors, shown in the output for Firefox
and Explorer, in Figure 3.4 and Figure 3.5 (on page 63), respectively.
4   This line will not be printed until the variable called *age* is defined properly. Just
use the *var* keyword as good practice, even if it isn't always required!

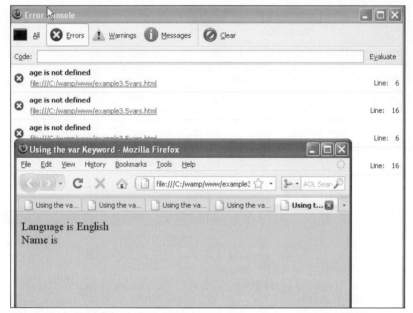

Figure 3.4   Firefox error (JavaScript Error Console). The variable *age* was
referenced twice on lines 6 and 16 in the actual program (lines numbered 3 and 4
in Example 3.5). Program was tested twice.

3.2.3   Dynamically or Loosely Typed Language

Remember, strongly typed languages like C++ and Java require that you specify the type
of data you are going to store in a variable when you declare it, but JavaScript is loosely
typed. It doesn't expect or allow you to specify the data type when declaring a variable.
You can assign a string to a variable and later assign a numeric value. JavaScript doesn't
care and at runtime, the JavaScript interpreter will convert the data to the correct type.
Consider the following variable, initialized to the floating-point value of 5.5. In each successive statement, JavaScript will convert the type to the proper data type (see Table 3.3).

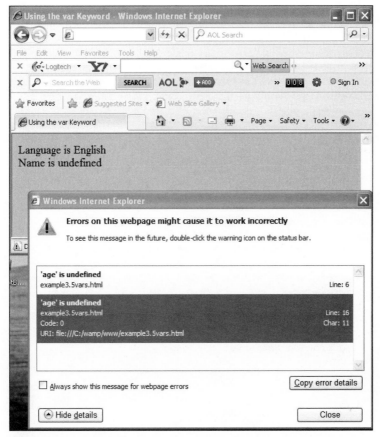

Figure 3.5 Internet Explorer error (Example 3.5).

Table 3.3 How JavaScript Converts Data Types

Variable Assignment	Conversion
`var item = 5.5;`	Assigned a float
`item = 44;`	Converted to integer
`item = "Today was bummer";`	Converted to string
`item = true;`	Converted to Boolean
`item = null;`	Converted to the null value

EXAMPLE 3.6

```
     <html>
       <head><title>JavaScript Variables</title>
1        <script type="text/javascript">
2          var first_name="Christian"; // first_name is assigned a value
3          var last_name="Dobbins";    // last_name is assigned a value
4          var age = 8;
5          var ssn;      // Unassigned variable
6          var job_title=null;
       </script>
7      </head>
8      <body bgcolor="lightgreen">
         <big>
9          <script type="text/javascript">
10           document.write("<b>Name:</b> " + first_name + " "
                            + last_name + "<br />");
11           document.write("<b>Age:</b> " + age + "<br />");
12           document.write("<b>SSN:</b> " + ssn + "<br />");
13           document.write("<b>Job Title:</b> " + job_title+"<br />");
14           ssn="xxx-xx-xxxx";
15           document.write("<b>Now SSN is:</b> " + ssn , "<br />");
         </script>
         <p>
           <img src="Christian.gif" /></body>
         </p>
       </big>
     </body>
   </html>

Output:

10   Name: Christian Dobbins
11   Age: 8
12   SSN: undefined
13   Job Title: null
15   Now Ssn is: xxx-xx-xxx
```

EXPLANATION

1   This JavaScript program is placed within the document head. Because the head of the document is processed before the body, this assures you that the variable definitions will be defined first.

2   The string *"Christian"* is assigned to the variable called *first_name*.

3   The string *"Dobbins"* is assigned to the variable called *last_name*.

4   The number *8* is assigned to the variable called *age*.

5   The variable called *ssn* is not assigned any value at all. It is an uninitialized variable. The return value is *undefined*.

EXPLANATION

6   The value *null* is assigned to the variable called *job_title*. *Null* is used to set a variable to an initial value different from other valid types, but if used in an expression the value of *null* will be converted to the appropriate type.

7   The document head ends here.

8   The body of the document starts here.

9   A new JavaScript program starts here. All the variables declared in the head of the document are available here. Variables that are available throughout the entire document are called global variables.

10 The *document.write()* method concatenates the values of the strings with the + sign and sends them to the browser to display on the screen.

11 The value of the variable called *age* is displayed.

12 The variable called *ssn* was declared, but not initialized. It has no value, which JavaScript calls *undefined*.

13 The variable *job_title* was assigned *null*, a placeholder value. The *null* string is returned.

14 The variable *ssn* is assigned a string value. It is no longer *undefined*. Even though the variable was declared in the head of the document, as long as it was declared, it can be assigned a value anywhere else in the document.

15 The value of the variable *ssn* is displayed. Figure 3.6 shows the output in Internet Explorer.

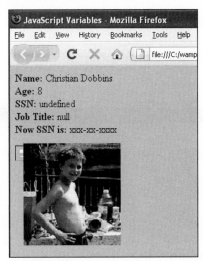

Figure 3.6   Declaring and displaying variables.

3.2.4 Scope of Variables

Scope describes where a variable is visible, or where it can be used, within the program. JavaScript variables are either of global or local scope. A global variable can be accessed from any JavaScript script on a page, as shown in Example 3.6. The variables we have created so far are global in scope.

It is often desirable to create variables that are private to a certain section of the program, thus avoiding naming conflicts and accidentally changing a value in some other part of the program. Private variables are called local variables. Local variables are created when a variable is declared within a function. Local variables must be declared with the keyword, *var*. They are accessible only from within the function from the time of declaration to the end of the enclosing block, and they take precedence over any global variable with the same name. (See Chapter 7, "Functions.")

3.2.5 Concatenation and Variables

To concatenate variables and strings together on the same line, the + sign is used. The + sign is an operator because it operates on the expression on either side of it (each called an operand). Sometimes the + sign is a string operator and sometimes it is a numeric operator when used for addition. Addition is performed when both of the operands are numbers. In expressions involving numeric and string values with the + operator, JavaScript converts numeric values to strings. For example, consider these statements:

```
var temp = "The temperature is " + 87;
 // returns "The temperature is 87"
var message = 25 + " days till Christmas";
// returns "25 days till Christmas"
```

But, if both operands are numbers, then addition is performed:

```
var sum = 10 + 5; // sum is 15
```

EXAMPLE 3.7

```
<html>
  <head><title>Concatenation</title></head>
  <body>
    <script type="text/javascript">
1      var x = 25;
2      var y = 5 + "10 years";
3      document.write( x + " cats" , "<br />");
4      document.write( "almost " + 25 , "<br />");
5      document.write( x + 4, "<br />");
6      document.write( y, "<br />");
7      document.write(x  +  5 + " dogs" , "<br />");
8      document.write(" dogs"  + x + 5 , "<br />");
    </script>
```

EXAMPLE 3.7 (CONTINUED)

```
    </body>
  </html>
```

Output:

```
3   25 cats
4   almost 25
5   29
6   510 years
7   30 dogs
8   dogs255
```

EXPLANATION

1. Variable *x* is assigned a number.
2. Variable *y* is assigned the string *510 years*. If the + operator is used, it could mean the concatenation of two strings or addition of two numbers. JavaScript looks at both of the operands. If one is a string and one is a number, **the number is converted to a string** and the two strings are joined together as one string, so in this example, the resulting string is *510 years*. If one operand were *5* and the other *10*, addition would be performed, resulting in *15*.
3. A number is concatenated with a string. The number *25* is converted to a string and concatenated to " *cats*", resulting in *25 cats*. (Note that the *write()* method can also use commas to separate its arguments. In these examples the **
** tag is not concatenated to the string. It is sent to the *write()* method and appended.)
4. This time, a string is concatenated with a number, resulting in the string *almost 25*.
5. When the operands on either side of the + sign are numbers, addition is performed.
6. The value of *y*, a string, is displayed.
7. The + operators works from left to right. Because *x* and *y* are both numbers, addition is performed, *25 + 5*. *30* is concatenated with the string " *dogs*".
8. Because the + works from left to right, this time the first operand is a string being concatenated to a number, the number is converted to string *dogs25* and concatenated with string *5*.

3.3 Constants

The weather and moods are variable; time is constant, and so are the speed of light, midnight, *PI*, and *e*. In programming, a constant is a special kind of placeholder with a value that cannot be changed during program execution. Many programming languages use a special syntax to define a constant to distinguish it from a variable. JavaScript declares constants with the *const* type (which replaces *var*) and the name of the constant is in uppercase letters, by convention only. Constants are assigned values at the time of the declaration, and it is impossible to modify them during the run of the program. Caveat: Firefox, Opera, Safari, Netscape, and many browsers support the JavaScript reserved keyword *const* to declare constants (see Figure 3.7). It is important to note that Internet Explorer 7 and 8 do not support it, as shown in Figure 3.8.

EXAMPLE 3.8

```
      <html>
        <head><title>Using the const Keyword</title>
          <script type="text/javascript">
1           const NOON = 12;
2           const FREEZING = 32;      // Can't change
          </script>
        </head>
        <body bgcolor="silver">
          <big>
            <script type="text/javascript">
              document.write("Farenheit temp is " + FREEZING + ".<br />");
3             FREEZING = 32 + 10;
4             NOON = NOON + " noon";
5             document.write("Make it warmer " + FREEZING + ".<br />");
              document.write("See you at ", NOON, ".<br />");
            </script>
          </big>
        </body>
      </html>
```

EXPLANATION

1   The constant NOON is assigned 12, a value that will not change throughout the execution of this program.

2   The constant FREEZING is assigned 32, a value that will not change throughout the execution of this program.

3   Now if we try to add 10 to the constant, the value of the constant doesn't change. It's still 32.

4   This time, we try to concatenate a string to the constant NOON. It will not be changed.

5   The constants FREEZING and NOON are displayed. They were not changed.

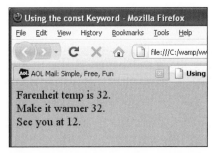

Figure 3.7   Firefox 3.5.7 supports the *const* keyword.

Figure 3.8   Internet Explorer 8 does not support the *const* keyword.

3.4 Bugs to Watch For

Try to declare all your variables at the beginning of the program, even if you don't have values for them yet. This will help you find misspelled names faster. Watch that you use proper variable names. Don't used reserved words and words that are too long to remember or type easily. Remember that variable names are case sensitive. *MyName* is not the same as *myName*. Avoid giving two variables similar names, such as *MyName* and *myNames*. Avoid one-character differences in variable names, such as *Name1* and *Names1*. Even though you aren't always required to use the *var* keyword, do it anyway. It's safer. And, of course, be sure that the variables you use are spelled properly throughout the script.

When you use strings don't forget to enclose the strings in either double or single quotes. Quoting will get the best of programmers every time!

3.5   **What You Should Know**

This chapter introduced you to the fundamental building blocks of the JavaScript language; that is, the kinds of data that can be stored and manipulated within a program, such as strings and numbers. To proceed to the next chapters, you should know:

1. What is meant by primitive data types.
2. What numeric literals are.
3. How to concatenate strings.
4. The two values for a Boolean.
5. What the *typeof* operator returns.
6. What is meant by *null, undefined*.
7. The difference between a variable and a constant.
8. The difference between loosely typed and strongly typed languages.
9. What scope is.
10. What types can be assigned to a variable.
11. How to name a variable.
12. When *var* is used.

Exercises

1. Create a script that uses the three primitive data types and prints output for each type. In the same script, print the following:

   ```
   She cried, "Aren't you going to help me?"
   ```

2. Go to *http://www.unicode.org/charts/PDF/U2600.pdf* and find a symbol. Use Java-Script to display one of the symbols in a larger font (+5).

3. Write a script that displays the number 234 as an integer, a floating-point number, an octal number, a hexadecimal number, and the number in scientific notation.

4. When is it necessary to use the *var* keyword?

5. Write a script that contains four variables in the head of the document: The first one contains your name, the second contains the value 0, the third one is declared but has no value, and the last contains an empty string. In the body of the document, write another script to display the type of each (use the *typeof* operator).

chapter

4

Dialog Boxes

4.1 Interacting with the User

Programs like to talk, ask questions, get answers, and respond. In the previous chapter, we saw how the *write()* and *writeln()* methods are used to send the document's output to the browser. The document is defined in an object and *write()* and *writeln()* are methods that manipulate the document, make it do something. The document object is defined within a window. The window is also an object and has its own methods.

The window object uses dialog boxes to interact with the user. The dialog boxes are created with three methods:

- *alert()*
- *prompt()*
- *confirm()*

4.1.1 The *alert()* Method

The window's *alert()* method is used to send a warning to the user or alert him or her to do something. For example, you might let the user know he or she has not entered his or her e-mail address correctly when filling out a form, or that his or her browser doesn't support a certain plug-in, and so on. The alert box is also commonly used for debugging to find out the results of a calculation, if the program is executing in an expected order, and so on.

The *alert()* method creates a little independent window—called a dialog box—that contains a a user-customized message placed after a small triangle, and beneath it, an OK button. See Figure 4.1. When the dialog box pops up, all execution is stopped until the user clicks the OK button in the pop-up box. The exact appearance of this dialog box might differ slightly on different browsers, but its functionality is the same.

Unlike the *write()* method, the *alert()* method doesn't require the window object name in front of it as *window.alert()*. Because the window is the top-level browser object, it doesn't have to be specified. This is true with any window object methods you use.

The message for the alert dialog box is any valid expression, variable, or a string of text enclosed in matching quotes, and sent as a single argument to the *alert()* method. HTML tags **are not rendered** within the message string but you can use the escape sequences, \n and \t. A word of caution: Don't overuse the alert box on your Web site. It can be seriously annoying for visitors. Use the alert box for its intended purpose: to alert visitors about input or processing problems and briefly explain how to correct them.

FORMAT

```
alert("String of plain text");
alert(expression);
```

EXAMPLE

```
alert("Phone number is incorrect");
alert(a + b);
```

EXAMPLE 4.1

```
    <html>
      <head><title>Dialog Box</title></head>
      <body bgcolor="yellow" text="blue">
        <b>Testing the alert method</b><br />
        <h2>
1         <script type="text/javascript">
2           document.write("It's a bird, ");
            document.write("It's a plane,<br />");
3           alert("It's Superman!");
          </script>
        </h2>
      </body>
    </html>
```

EXPLANATION

1   The *<script>* tag starts the JavaScript program. The JavaScript engine starts executing code from here until the closing *</script>* tag. JavaScript does not understand HTML tags unless they are embedded in a string.

2   The *document.write()* method sends its output to the browser.

3   The *alert()* method will produce a little dialog box, independent of the current document, and all processing will be stopped until the user clicks the OK button. This little box can be moved around the screen with your mouse.

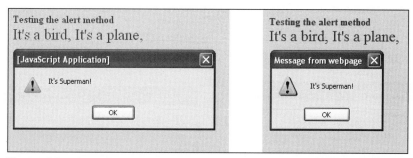

Figure 4.1 Using the *alert()* method with Firefox (left) and Internet Explorer (right).

EXAMPLE 4.2

```
    <html>
      <head>
        <title>Using JavaScript alert box</title>
1       <script type="text/javascript">
2         var message1="Match your Quotes and ";
          var message2="Beware of Little Bugs ";
3         alert("Welcome to\nJavaScript Programming!");
4         alert(message1 + message2);
        </script
      </head>
    </html>
```

EXPLANATION

1   The JavaScript program starts here with the *<script>* tag.

2   Two variables, message1 and message2 are assigned text strings.

3   The *alert()* method contains a string of text. Buried in the string is a backslash sequence, *\n*. There are a number of these sequences available in JavaScript (see Table 3.1 on page 54). The *\n* causes a line break between the two strings. The reason for using the *\n* escape sequence is because HTML tags such as *
* are not allowed in this dialog box. After the alert dialog box appears on the screen, the program will stop until the user clicks the OK button.

4   The *alert()* method not only accepts literal strings of text, but also variables as arguments. The + sign is used to concatenate the values of the two strings together and create one string. That string will appear in the alert dialog box as shown in the output in Figure 4.2.

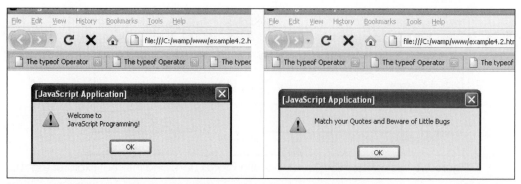

Figure 4.2   After the first alert box appears and the user clicks OK, the second box appears.

4.1.2   The *prompt()* Method

A *prompt()* method asks the user for some small amount of information such as a password, completion of a form input, or personal information, such as nickname or title. Because JavaScript does not provide a simple method for accepting user input, the prompt dialog box and HTML forms are used (forms are discussed in Chapter 11, "Working with Forms and Input Devices"). The prompt dialog box pops up with a simple textfield box. After the user enters text into the prompt dialog box, its value is returned. This method takes two arguments: a string of text that is normally displayed as a question to the user, prompting the user to do something, and another string of text that is the initial default setting for the box. If this argument is an empty string, nothing is displayed in the box. The *prompt()* method always returns a value. If the user clicks the OK button, all the text in the box is returned; otherwise *null* is returned.

FORMAT

```
prompt(message);
prompt(message, defaultText);
```

EXAMPLE

```
prompt("What is your name? ", "");
prompt("Where is your name? ", name);
```

EXAMPLE 4.3

```
<html>
  <head>
    <title>Using the JavaScript prompt box</title>
  </head>
  <body>
    <script type = "text/javascript">
1       var name=prompt("What is your name?", "");
        alert("Welcome to my world! " + name);
2       var age=prompt("Tell me your age.", "Your age: ");
3       if ( age == null){     // If user clicks the Cancel button
           alert("Not sharing your age with me");
        }
        else{
4          alert(age + " is young");
        }
5       alert(prompt("Where do you live? ", ""));
    </script>
  </body>
</html>
```

EXPLANATION

1   The *prompt()* method takes two arguments, one is the text that will prompt the user to respond. This text will appear above the prompt dialog box. The second argument provides default text that will appear at the far left, inside the box. If the second argument is an empty string, the prompt box will be empty. After the user types his or her response in the prompt textbox, the response is returned and assigned to the variable *name*. The *alert()* method displays that value on the screen.

2   The variable called *age* will be assigned whatever the user types into the prompt box. This time a second argument, *"Your age: "*, is sent to the *prompt()* method. When the prompt box appears on the screen, *Your Age:* will appear inside the box where the user will type his or her response.

3   If the user clicks the Cancel button, the value returned by the *prompt()* method is *null*. This *if* statement tests to see if the value of *age* is *null*.

4   If the return value was *null*, this line is printed in the alert dialog box.

5   The *prompt()* method is sent as an argument to the *alert()* method. After the user has clicked OK in the prompt box, the return value is sent to the *alert()* method, and then displayed on the screen. See Figures 4.3 through 4.7.

Figure 4.3   Prompt without a second default argument.

Figure 4.4   Prompt with a second default argument.

4.1.3   The *confirm()* Method

The confirm dialog box is used to confirm a user's answer to a question. The user must agree before the action is completed. You'll often see this when placing an online order or deleting a file where a yes or no confirmation determines what will happen next. A question mark will appear in the box with an OK button and a Cancel button. If the user clicks the OK button, *true* is returned; if he or she clicks the Cancel button, *false* is returned. This method takes only one argument, the question you will ask the user.

EXAMPLE 4.4

```
<html>
  <head>
    <title>Using the JavaScript confirm box</title>
  </head>
```

EXAMPLE 4.4 (CONTINUED)

```
    <body>
      <script type="text/javascript">
1       if(confirm("Are you really OK?") == true){
2          alert("Then we can proceed!");
        }
        else{
3          alert("We'll try when you feel better? ");
        }
      </script>
    </body>
  </html>
```

EXPLANATION

1   The confirm dialog box takes only one argument, the question that you want to ask the user. It returns *true* if the user clicks the OK button and *false* if the user clicks the Cancel button. He or she has to click either one to continue. If the return value is equal to *true*, then the *alert()* method on line 2 will be executed. The *if/else* constructs are not discussed until Chapter 6, "Under Certain Conditions," but the way they are used here is to test a true or false alternative to make the example a little more meaningful.

2   The user clicked OK. The alert dialog box will display its message (see Figure 4.7).

3   If the user clicked Cancel, this alert dialog box will display its message (see Figure 4.7).

Figure 4.5   The confirm dialog box (Firefox).

Figure 4.6   The confirm dialog box (Internet Explorer).

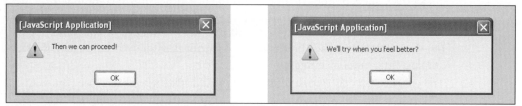

Figure 4.7   After the user clicks OK (left) or Cancel (right).

4.2 **What You Should Know**

This is a short chapter, but important for interacting with users. You will find yourself using the *alert()* method more than the *prompt()* and *confirm()* methods because it offers a quick way to help debug your programs, such as finding out what is being stored in variables, what is returned from functions, the flow of execution, and so on. Before going on, you should know:

1. To what object the *alert()*, *prompt()*, and *confirm()* methods belong.
2. Why you don't specify the name of the object with these methods.
3. The purpose of the alert dialog box.
4. How the prompt box works and how many arguments it takes.
5. When you would use the *confirm()* dialog box.

1. What is wrong with the following alert box?

   ```
   alert("Hello<br />", "world!<br />");
   ```

   Create a JavaScript program that produces the previous alert box. When the alert dialog box appears, what does the program do?

2. What is the return value of the prompt method if the user doesn't enter anything? Where is the return value stored?

3. Create a JavaScript program that prompts the user for a phone number and then asks the user for confirmation.

chapter

5

Operators

5.1 About JavaScript Operators and Expressions

Data objects can be manipulated in a number of ways by the large number of operators provided by JavaScript. Operators are symbols, such as +, −, =, >, and <, that produce a result based on some rules. An operator manipulates data objects called operands; for example, 5 and 4 are operands in the expression 5 + 4. Operators and operands are found in expressions. An expression combines a group of values to make a new value, $n = 5 + 4$. And when you terminate an expression with a semicolon or a newline, you have a complete statement (e.g., $n = 5 + 4;$).

```
var sum          =          5          +          4
```
new variable operator operand operator operand

In the numeric **expression**, $5 + 4 - 2$, three numbers are combined. The **operators** are the + and − signs. The **operands** for the + sign are 5 and 4. After that part of the expression is evaluated to 9, the expression becomes 9 − 2. After evaluating the complete expression, the result is 7. Because the plus and minus operators each manipulate two operands, they are called binary operators. If there is only one operand, the operator is called a unary operator. If there are three operands, it is called a ternary operator. We'll see examples of these operators later in the chapter.

The operands can be either strings, numbers, Booleans, or a combination of these. We have already used some of the operators: the concatenation operator to join two strings together, the *typeof* operator to determine what data type is being used, and the assignment operator used to assign a value to a variable. Now let's look at a plethora of additional JavaScript operators and see how they manipulate their operands.

5.1.1 Assignment

An assignment statement evaluates the expression on the right side of the equal sign and assigns the result to the variable on the left side of the equal sign. The equal sign is the assignment operator.

```
var total = 5 + 4;
var friend = "Tony";
```

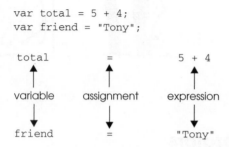

5.1.2 Precedence and Associativity

When an expression contains a number of operators and operands, such as $5 * 4 + 3 / -2.2$, and the order of evaluation is ambiguous, then JavaScript must determine what to do. This is where the precedence and associative rules come in. They tell JavaScript how to evaluate such an expression. Precedence refers to the way in which the operator binds to its operand, such as, should addition be done before division or should assignment come before multiplication? The precedence of one operator over another determines what operation is done first. As shown in Table 5.1, the operators are organized as a hierarchy, the operators of highest precedence at the top, similar to a social system where those with the most power (or money) are at the top. In the rules of precedence, the multiplication operator is of higher precedence than the addition operator, technically meaning the operator of higher precedence binds more tightly to its operands. The assignment operators are low in precedence and thus bind loosely to their operand. In the expression *sum = 5 + 4* the equal sign is of low precedence, so the expression *5 + 4* is evaluated first and then the result is assigned to *sum*. Parentheses are of the highest precedence. An expression placed within parentheses is evaluated first; thus, in the expression *2 * (10 – 4)*, the expression within the parentheses is evaluated first and that result is multiplied by 2. When parentheses are nested, the expression contained within the innermost set of parentheses is evaluated first.

Associativity refers to the order in which an operator evaluates its operands: left to right in no specified order, or right to left. When all of the operators in an expression are of equal precedence, normally the association is left to right; in the expression *5 + 4 + 3*, the evaluation is from left to right. In Example 5.1, how is the expression evaluated? Is addition, multiplication, or division done first? And in what order, right to left or left to right?

In Table 5.1 the operators on the same line are of equal precedence. The rows are in order of highest to lowest precedence.

Table 5.1   Precedence and Associativity

Operator	*Description*	*Associativity*
()	Parentheses	Left to right
++ --	Auto increment, decrement	Right to left
!	Logical NOT	Right to left
* / %	Multiply, divide, modulus	Left to right
+ -	Add, subtract	Left to right
+	Concatenation	Left to right
< <=	Less than, less than or equal to	Left to right
> >=	Greater than, greater than or equal to	Left to right
== !=	Equal to, not equal to	Left to right
=== !==	Identical to (same type), not identical to	Left to right
&	Bitwise AND	Left to right
|	Bitwise OR	
^	Bitwise XOR	
~	Bitwise NOT	
<<	Bitwise left shift	
>>	Bitwise right shift	
>>>	Bitwise zero-filled, right shift	
&&	Logical AND	Left to right
||	Logical OR	Left to right
? :	Ternary, conditional	Right to left
= += -= *= /= %= <<= >>=	Assignment	Right to left
,	(comma)	

EXAMPLE 5.1

```
<html>
   <head><title>First JavaScript Sample</title>
      <script type = "text/javascript">
1        var result = 5 + 4 * 12 / 4;
      </script>
   </head>
   <body bgcolor="yellow" text="blue">
      <big>
         <script type="text/javascript">
2           document.write("result = " + result,"<br />");
         </script>
      </big>
   </body>
</html>
```

EXPLANATION

1   The order of associativity is from left to right. Multiplication and division are of a higher precedence than addition and subtraction, and addition and subtraction are of higher precedence than assignment. To illustrate this, we'll use parentheses to group the operands as they are grouped by JavaScript. In fact, if you want to force precedence, use the parentheses around the expression to group the operands in the way you want them evaluated. The following two examples produce the same result:

```
var result = 5 + 4 * 12 / 4;
```

could be written

```
result = (5 + ( ( 4 * 12 ) / 4));
```

2   The expression is evaluated and the result is assigned to variable, *result*. The value of *result* is displayed on the browser (see Figure 5.1).

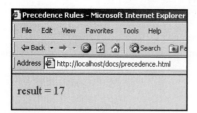

Figure 5.1　Output from Example 5.1: Precedence and associativity.

EXAMPLE 5.2

```
        <html>
          <head>
            <title>Precedence and Associativity</title>
          </head>
          <body>
            <h3>
            <script type = "text/javascript">
1             var x = 5 + 4  * 12 / 4;
2             document.writeln( "The result is " + x + "<br />");
3             var x = ( 5 + 4 )  * ( 12 / 4 );
4             document.writeln("The result is " + x);
            </script>
            </h3>
          </body>
        </html>
```

EXPLANATION

1   The variable, called *x*, is assigned the result of the expression.

```
var x = 5 + 4 * 12 / 4;
```

results in

```
x = 5 + 48 / 4
```

results in

```
x = 5 + 12
```

results in

```
17
```

Because multiplication and division are higher on the precedence table than addition, those expressions will be evaluated first, associating from left to right.

2   The result of the previous evaluation, the value of *x*, is sent to the browser.

3   The expressions enclosed in parentheses are evaluated first and then multiplied.

```
var x = ( 5 + 4 )  * ( 12 / 4 );
```

results in

```
x = 9 * 3
```

results in

```
27
```

4   The result of the previous evaluation, the value of *x*, is sent to the browser. The output of the script is shown in Figure 5.2.

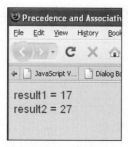

Figure 5.2   Output from Example 5.2: Precedence and associativity.

5.2   Types of Operators

5.2.1   Arithmetic Operators

Arithmetic operators take numerical values (either literals or variables) as their operands and return a single numerical value. The standard arithmetic operators are addition
(+), subtraction (–), multiplication (*), and division (/). See Table 5.2.

Table 5.2   Arithmetic Operators

Operator/Operands	Function
$x + y$	Addition
$x - y$	Subtraction
$x * y$	Multiplication
x / y	Division[a]
$x \% y$	Modulus

a.   The / operator returns a floating-point division in JavaScript, not a truncated division as it does in languages
such as C or Java. For example, 1/2 returns 0.5 in JavaScript and 1/2 returns 0 in Java.

EXAMPLE 5.3

```
<html>
   <head><title>Arithmetic Operators</title></head>
   <body>
      <h2>Arithmetic operators</h2>
      <h3>
```

EXAMPLE   5.3 (CONTINUED)

```
1              <script type="text/javascript">
2                var num1 = 5;
                 var num2 = 7;
3                var result = num1 + num2;
4                document.write("num1 + num2 = "+ result);
5                result = result + (10 / 2 + 5);
6                document.write("<br />12 + (10 / 2 + 5) = " + result);
7              </script>
            </h3>
          </body>
        </html>
```

EXPLANATION

1   This is the start of a JavaScript program.

2   Variables *num1* and *num2* are declared and assigned values 5 and 7, respectively.

3   The variable *result* is assigned the sum of *num1* and *num2*.

4   The results are displayed by the browser. Note that the + sign in this expression is used to concatenate two strings. When a string is concatenated to a number, Java-Script converts the number to a string. The value stored in the variable *result* is converted to a string and joined to the string on the left side of the + sign.

5   The expression on the right side of the = sign is evaluated and assigned to the variable, *result*, on the left side of the = sign. (The parentheses are not needed, but used for clarity.) The browser output is shown in Figure 5.3.

6   The variable result is concatenated to a string and displayed.

7   Script ends here.

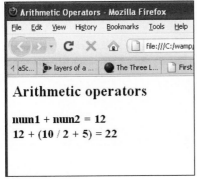

Figure 5.3   Output from Example 5.3.

5.2.2   Shortcut Assignment Operators

The shortcut assignment operators allow you to perform an arithmetic or string operation by combining an assignment operator with an arithmetic or string operator. For example, *x = x + 1* can be written *x+=1*. See Table 5.3.

Table 5.3   Assignment Operators

Operator	Example	Meaning
=	var x = 5;	Assign 5 to variable x.
+=	x += 3;	Add 3 to x and assign result to x.
−=	x −= 2;	Subtract 2 from x and assign result to x.
*=	x *= 4;	Multiply x by 4 and assign result to x.
/=	x /= 2;	Divide x by 2 and assign result to x.
**=	x **= 2;	Square x and assign result to x.
%=	x %= 2;	Divide x by 2 and assign remainder to x.

EXAMPLE 5.4

```
    <html>
      <head>
        <title>Assignment and Shortcut Operators</title>
      </head>
      <body bgcolor="gold">
        <big>
1         <script type= "text/javascript">
2           var num=10;
3           document.write("num is assigned " + 10);
4           num += 2;
            document.write("<br />num += 2; num is " + num );
5           num -= 1;
            document.write("<br />num -= 1; num is " + num);
6           num *= 3;
            document.write("<br />num *= 3; num is " + num);
7           num %= 5;
            document.write("<br />num %= 5; num is " + num);
8         </script>
        </big>
      </body>
    <html>
```

EXPLANATION

1   JavaScript program starts here.

2   The variable *num* is assigned *10*.

3   Output is sent to the browser.

4   The shortcut assignment operator, +=, adds 2 to the variable *num*. This is equivalent to *num = num + 1;*.

5   The shortcut assignment operator, −=, subtracts 1 from the variable *num*. This is equivalent to *num = num - 1;*.

6   The shortcut assignment operator, *, multiplies the variable *num* by 3. This is equivalent to *num = num * 3;*.

7   The shortcut assignment modulus operator, %, yields the integer amount that remains after the scalar *num* is divided by 5. The operator is called the modulus operator or remainder operator. The expression *var %= 5* is equivalent to *num = num % 5;*.

8   JavaScript ends here. The output is shown in Figure 5.4.

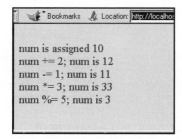

Figure 5.4   Output from Example 5.4: Shortcut operators.

5.2.3   Autoincrement and Autodecrement Operators

To make programs easier to read, to simplify typing, and, at the machine level, to produce more efficient code, the autoincrement (++) and autodecrement (−−) operators are provided.

The autoincrement operator performs the simple task of incrementing the value of its operand by 1, and the autodecrement operator decrements the value of its operand by 1. The operator has two forms: the first form **prefixes** the variable with either ++ or −− (e.g., ++x or −−x); the second form **postfixes** (places the operator after) the variable name with either ++ or −− (e.g., x++ or x−−). For simple operations, such as x++ or x−−, ++x or −−x, the effect is the same; both ++x and x++ add one to the value of x, and both −−x and x−− subtract one from the value of x.

Now you have four ways to add 1 to the value of a variable:

- x += 1;
- x += ;
- x++;
- ++x;

and four ways to subtract 1 from the value of a variable:

- x = x – 1;
- x –= 1;
- x––;
- ––x;

Refer to Table 5.4. In section "Loops" on page 131, you'll see these operators are commonly used to increment or decrement loop counters.

Table 5.4 Autoincrement and Autodecrement Operators

Operator	Function	What It Does	Example	
++x	Pre-increment	Adds 1 to x	x = 3; x++;	x is now 4
x++	Post-increment	Adds 1 to x	x = 3; ++x;	x is now 4
––x	Pre-decrement	Subtracts 1 from x	x = 3; x––;	x is now 2
x––	Post-decrement	Subtracts 1 from x	x = 3; ––x;	x is now 2

Autoincrement and Autodecrement Operators and Assignment.   The placement of the operators does make a difference in more complex expressions, especially when part of an assignment; for example, y = x++ is not the same as y = ++x.

Start with: y = 0 ; x = 5;

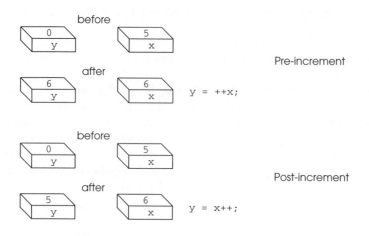

EXAMPLE 5.5

```
  <html>
    <head><title>Auto-increment and Auto-decrement</title></head>
    <body>
      <h3>
        <script type="text/javascript">
1         var x=5;
          var y=0;
2         y = ++x;        // add one to x first; then assign to y
          document.write("Pre-increment:<br />");
3         document.write("y is " +  y + "<br />");
          document.write("x is " + x + "<br />");
          document.write("----------------------<br />");
4
          var x=5;
          var y=0;
5         y=x++;      // assign value in x to y; then add one to x

          document.write("Post-increment:<br />");
6         document.write("y is " + y + "<br />");
          document.write("x is " + x + "<br />");
        </script>
      </h3>
    </body>
  </html>
```

EXPLANATION

1 The variables, *x* and *y*, are initialized to *5* and *0*, respectively.

2 The pre-increment operator is applied to *x*. This means that *x* will be incremented **before** the assignment is made. The value of *x* was *5*, now it is *6*. The variable *y* is assigned *6*. *x* is *6*, *y* is *6*.

3 The new values of *y* and *x* are displayed in the browser window.

4 The variables *x* and *y* are assigned values of *5* and *0*, respectively.

5 This time the post-increment operator is applied to *x*. This means that *x* will be incremented **after** the assignment is made. The number *5* is assigned to the variable *y*, and then *x* is incremented by *1*. So *x* is *5* and *y* is *6*.

6 The new values of *y* and *x* are displayed in the browser window. See Figure 5.5.

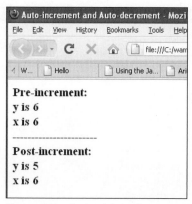

Figure 5.5   Output from Example 5.5. Auto-increment and auto-decrement operators.

5.2.4   Concatenation Operator

As shown in previous examples, the + sign is used for concatenation and addition. The concatenation operator, the + sign, is a string operator used to join together one or more strings. In fact, the concatenation operator is the only operator JavaScript provides to manipulate strings.

In the example, *"correct"* + *"tion"* + *"al"* , the result is *"correctional"*. If the operands are a mix of strings and numbers, JavaScript will convert the **numbers to strings**. For example, *"22"* + *8* results in *"228"*, not *30*. If the operands are numbers, then the + sign is the addition operator as in *5 + 4*. But suppose we say, *"22" * 1 + 4*. In this case, JavaScript sees the multiplication operator (*) and converts the string *"22"* to a number, resulting in *22 + 4* or *26*. Firefox provides the JavaScript console for testing these expressions or you can type *JavaScript:* in the URL, followed by the expression you want to test, as shown in Figures 5.6 and 5.7.

The concatenation operator is summarized in Table 5.5. To explicitly convert strings to numbers, JavaScript provides built-in functions called *parseInt()* and *parseFloat()*, discussed in Sections 5.3.1 and 5.3.2, respectively.

Figure 5.6   Evaluating expressions in the *JavaScript:* URL. The result of the test, *26*, is displayed in the browser window.

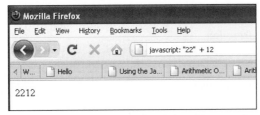

Figure 5.7   Concatenation of a string and a number.

Table 5.5   The Concatenation Operator

Operator	Example	Meaning
+	*"hot"* + *"dog"*	Concatenates (joins) two strings; creates *"hotdog"*.
	"22" + *8*	Converts number *8* to string *"8"*, then concatenates resulting in *"228"*. In statements involving other operators, JavaScript does not convert numeric values to strings.
+=	*x =*"cow"; *x +=* "boy";	Concatenates two strings and assigns the result to *x*; *x* becomes *"cowboy"*.

5.2.5   Comparison Operators

When operands are compared, relational and equality operators are used. The operands can be numbers or strings. The result of the comparison is either *true* or *false*—a Boolean value. Strings are compared letter by letter (lexographically) using Unicode[1] values to represent the numeric value of each letter; thus, *"A"* is less than *"B"*, and when comparing *"Daniel"* with *"Dan"*, *"Daniel"* is greater than *"Dan"*. When comparing strings, JavaScript pads *"Dan"* with three spaces to make it the same length as *"Daniel"*. Refer to Table 5.6.

Table 5.6   Comparison Operators

Operator/Operands	Function
$x == y$	x is equal to y
$x \mathrel{!=} y$	x is not equal to y
$x > y$	x is greater than y

Continues

---

1. Unicode is not supported in versions of JavaScript prior to 1.3. Unicode is compatible with ASCII characters. The first 128 Unicode characters correspond to the ASCII character set and have the same byte value.

Table 5.6 Comparison Operators (continued)

Operator/Operands	Function
$x >= y$	x is greater than or equal to y
$x < y$	x is less than y
$x <= y$	x is less than or equal to y
$x === y$	x is identical to y in value and type
$x !== y$	x is not identical to y

What Is Equal?   In an ideal world, there would be equality between the sexes and among the races and religions, but in the real world equality is a debatable topic, often determined by governments. In JavaScript, operators determine the equality or inequality of their operands, based on more specific rules. When using the == or != equality operators, the operands may be of any given data type—numbers, strings, Booleans, objects, arrays, or a combination of these—and there are rules that govern whether they are equal. For example, two strings are equal when they have the same sequence of characters, same length, and same characters in corresponding positions. Two numbers are equal when they have the same numeric value. If a string is compared with a number, they are equal if the number has the same characters as the string; for example, *"500"* is equal to *500*. *NaN* (Not a Number) is not equal to anything, including *NaN*. Positive and negative zeros are equal. Two objects are equal if they refer to the same object. Two Boolean operands are equal if they are both *true* or both *false*. *Null* and *undefined* types are equal. To test any of the expressions shown in Table 5.7, use the JavaScript Console. Figure 5.8 shows an example using Firefox.

Table 5.7 Equality Test with Strings and Numbers

Test	Are They Equal?
"William" == "William"	*true*
"william" == "William"	*false*
5 == 5.0	*true*
"54" == 54	*true*
"5.4" == 5.4	*true*
NaN == NaN	*false*
null == null	*true*
−0 == +0	*true*

Table 5.7 Equality Test with Strings and Numbers (continued)

Test	Are They Equal?
false == false	*true*
true == 1	*true*
null == undefined	*true*

Figure 5.8 Testing the equality of two strings. Is *"William"* equal to *"william"*? Nope.

What Is Identical?   Men are equal; clones are identical. The **===** and **!==** equality operators test that its operands are not only of the same value, but also of the same data type. String "54" is equal to number 54, but **not identical** because one is a string and the other is a number, even though their values are equal. See Table 5.8.

Table 5.8 Identity Test with Strings and Numbers

Test	Are They Identical?
"William" === "William"	*true*
"william" === "William"	*false*
5 === 5.0	*true*
"54" === 54	*false*
NaN === NaN	*false*
null === null	*true*
-0 === +0	*true*
false === false	*true*
true === 1	*false*
null === undefined	*false*

Comparing Numbers.   When the comparison operators are used to compare numbers, numeric values are compared; as in, is *50 > 45?* A Boolean value of either *true* or *false* is returned.

Table 5.9   Comparison Operators

Example	How Operator Compares Numbers
x > y	*x* is greater than *y*
x >= y	*x* is greater than or equal to *y*
x < y	*x* is less than *y*
x <= y	*x* is less than or equal to *y*

EXAMPLE 5.6

```
        <html>
         <head>
          <title>Comparing Numbers</title>
         </head>
         <body>
          <h3>
1          <script type = "text/javascript">
2            var x = 5;
             var y = 4;
3            var result = x > y;
4            document.writeln("The result is "+ result + ".<br />");
5            result = x < y;
6            document.writeln( "The result is " + result + ".<br />");
7          </script>
          </h3>
         </body>
        </html>
```

EXPLANATION

1   The JavaScript program starts here.

2   The variables x and y are assigned values to be compared later in the program.

3   If the value of *x* is greater than the value of *y*, a Boolean value of either *true* or *false* is returned and assigned to the variable *result*.

4   The Boolean result of the comparison is displayed by the browser. It is *true*; x is greater than y.

5   If *x* is less than *y*, *true* is assigned to the variable, *result*; otherwise it is assigned *false*.

6   The Boolean result of the comparison is displayed by the browser. It is *false*; *x* is not greater than *y*.

7   This tag marks the end of the JavaScript program. The output is shown in Figure 5.9.

Figure 5.9   Output from Example 5.6: Numeric comparison.

Comparing Strings.   The difference between comparing strings and numbers is that numbers are compared numerically and strings are compared alphabetically, based on the ASCII character set. The strings are compared letter by letter, from left to right, and if they are exactly the same all the way to end, they are equal (see Table 5.10). Once a letter in one string differs from the corresponding letter in the second string, the comparison stops and each of the differing letters is evaluated. For example, if the string *"Dan"* is compared with *"dan"*, the comparison stops at the first letters *D* and *d*. *"Dan"* is smaller than *"dan"*, because the letter *D* has a lower ASCII value than the letter *d*. *D* has an ASCII decimal value of 68, and *d* has an ASCII value of 100.

To avoid the case-sensitivity issue when comparing strings, JavaScript provides the built-in string functions, *toUpperCase()* and *toLowerCase()*, discussed in section "Free Form and Reserved Words" on page 33 and Table 9.10 on page 253.

Table 5.10   Comparison Operators

Example	*How Operator Compares Strings*
"string1" > *"string2"*	*"string1"* is greater than *"string2"*
"string1" >= *"string2"*	*"string1"* is greater than or equal to *"string2"*
"string1" < *"string2"*	*"string1"* is less than *"string2"*
"string1" <= *"string2"*	*"string1"* is less than or equal to *"string2"*

EXAMPLE 5.7

```
<html>
  <head>
    <title>Comparing Strings</title>
  </head>
  <body>
1     <script type="text/javascript">
2        var fruit1 = "pear";
         var fruit2 = "peaR";

3        var result = fruit1 > fruit2;
4        document.write( "<h3>The result is "+ result + ".<br />");

5        result = fruit1 < fruit2;
6        document.write( "The result is " + result + ".<br />");

7        result = fruit1 === fruit2;
         // Are they identical; i.e., value and type are the same?
8        document.write( "The result is " + result + ".<br />");
    </script>
  </body>
</html>
```

EXPLANATION

1   This is the start of the JavaScript program.

2   The variables, *fruit1* and *fruit2*, are assigned to string values, differing by only one letter.

3   The string values are compared and a Boolean value of *true* or *false* will be returned and assigned to the variable, *result*. *"pear"* is greater than *"peaR"* because the *r* has an ASCII value of 114 and the *R* has an ASCII value of 82.

4   The result of the comparison in line 3 is *true* and the result is sent to the browser.

5   This time *"pear"* is compared to *"peaR"* with the less than operator. The result is *false*.

6   The result of the comparison in line 5 is *false* and the result is sent to the browser.

7   The identical equality operator is used. Because the strings are not identical, the result is *false*.

8   The result of the comparison in line 7 is *false* and the result is sent to the browser. The output of the script is shown in Figure 5.10.

```
The result is true.
The result is false.
The result is false.
```

Figure 5.10   Output from Example 5.7: String comparison.

5.2.6 Logical Operators

The logical operators allow you combine the relational operators into more powerful expressions for testing conditions and are most often used in *if* statements. They evaluate their operands from left to right, testing the Boolean value of each operand in turn: Does the operand evaluate to true or false? In the expression *if (x > 5 && x < 10)*, the *&&* is a logical operator. The expression simplified means, "if *x* is greater than 5 and *x* is also less than 10, then do something"; in the case of the logical AND (*&&*), if the first expression returns *true* and the second expression also returns *true*, then the whole expression is true. If instead of *&&* we used ||, the operator means OR and only one of the expressions must be true.

Sometimes the result of a test is not Boolean. When logical operators have numeric operands, such as *5 && 6*, the result of the entire expression is evaluated from left to right, and the value returned is that of the last expression. A numeric operand is true if it evaluates to any number that is not zero. *5, –2,* and *74* are all true. *0* is false. For example, when using the *&&* (AND) operator, both operands must be true for the whole expression to be true. The value returned from an expression such as *5 && 6* is *6*, the last value evaluated by the operator. *5* is not zero (true) and *6* is not zero (true), therefore, the expression is true. If the expression contained a 0 as in *5 && 0, 0 && 0* and *0 && 5* all yield *0*, which is false. Because the && operator wants all of its operands to be nonzero values, as soon as the value 0 is encountered in the expression, 0 is the result of the whole expression. See Table 5.11.

The three logical operators are the logical AND, logical OR, and logical NOT. The symbol for AND is *&&*, the symbol for OR is ||, and the symbol for NOT is *!*.

Table 5.11 Logical Operators and Their Functions

Operator/Operands	*Function*
num1 && num2	True, if *num1* **and** *num2* are both true. Returns *num1* if *num1* is false; otherwise returns *num2*. If operands are Boolean values, returns *true* if **both** operands are true; otherwise returns *false*.
num1 || num2	True, if *num1* is true **or** if *num2* is true.
! num1	**Not** num1; true if *num1* is false; false if *num1* is true.

The && Operator (Logical AND). We all know the meaning of the English statement, "If you have the money **and** I have the time...." Whatever is supposed to happen is based on two conditions, and both conditions must be met. You must have the money **and** I must have the time. JavaScript uses the symbol *&&* to represent the word AND. This operator is called the logical AND operator. If the expression on the left side of the *&&* evaluates to zero, null, or the empty string "", the expression is false. If the expression on the left side of the operator evaluates to true (nonzero), then the right side is evaluated, and if that expression is also true, then the whole expression is true. If the left side evaluates to true, and the right side is false, the expression is false. If evaluated as Booleans, the same rules apply, except the returned value will be either Boolean *true* or *false*. See Table 5.12.

Table 5.12 Logical AND Examples

Expression	What It Evaluates To
true && false	*false*
true && true	*true*
"honest" && true	*true*
true && ""	(empty string)
true && "honest"	*honest*
5 && 0	*0*
5 && –6	*–6*
5 && false	*false*
null && 0	*null*
null && ""	*null*
null && false	*null*
"hello" && true && 50	*50*
"this" && "that"	*that*

EXAMPLE 5.8

```
        <html>
          <head>
            <title>Logical AND Operator</title>
          </head>
          <body bgcolor="lightblue">
            <big>
            <script type="text/javascript">
1           var answer = prompt("How old are you? ", "");
2           if (answer > 12 && answer < 20) {
               alert("Teenagers rock!");
            }
            </script>
            </big>
          </body>
        </html>
```

EXPLANATION

1   The user is prompted for his or her age. The variable called *answer* is assigned the value the user enters. (See Figure 5.11.)

2   If the value of *answer* is greater than 12 and also less than 20, the statement enclosed within the curly braces is executed: an alert box appears displaying *Teenagers rock!* (See Figure 5.12.) If the user enters any other value, nothing happens.

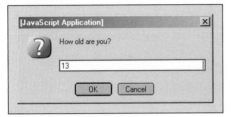

Figure 5.11   The user enters his or her age.

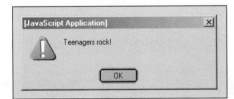

Figure 5.12   If the user enters his or her age and it is greater than 12 and less than 20, this alert box appears.

The | | Operator (Logical OR).   In the English statement "If you have some cash **or** I have a credit card..." the word *or* is used in the condition. With the *or*, only one of the conditions must be met (hopefully that you have the cash!). JavaScript uses the || symbol to represent the logical OR. If the expression on the left side of the || operator is evaluated as true (nonzero), the value of the expression is true, and no further checking is done. If the value on the left side of the || operator is false, the value of the expression on the right side of the operator is evaluated, and if true, the expression is true; that is, only one expression must be true. Once an expression returns true, the remaining expressions can be either true or false. It doesn't matter, as long as **one expression is true**. Refer to Table 5.13.

Table 5.13   Logical OR Examples

Expression	What It Evaluates To
true || false	*true*
true || true	*true*

Continues

Table 5.13 Logical OR Examples (continued)

Expression	What It Evaluates To
"honest" || true	honest
true || ""	true
true || "honest"	true
5 || 0	5
5 || –6	5
5 || false	5
null || 0	0
null || ""	(empty string)
null || false	false
"hello" || true || 50	hello
"this" || "that"	this

EXAMPLE 5.9

```
    <html>
      <head>
        <title>Logical OR Operator</title>
      </head>
      <body bgcolor="lightblue">
        <big>
        <script type="text/javascript">
1         var answer = prompt("Where should we eat? ", "");
2         if ( answer == "McDonald's" || answer == "Taco Bell" ||
              answer == "Wendy's"){
3           alert("No fast food today, thanks.");
          }
        </script>
        </big>
      </body>
    </html>
```

EXPLANATION

1 The user is prompted to choose a place to eat. The variable called *answer* is assigned the value he or she enters. (See Figure 5.13.)

2 If the value of *answer* is any one of *McDonald's* or *Taco Bell* or *Wendy's*, the statement enclosed within the curly braces is executed: An alert box appears displaying *No fast food today, thanks*. (See Figure 5.14.) If the user enters any other value, nothing happens.

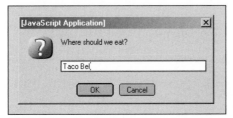

Figure 5.13 The user enters a value.

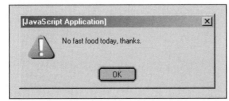

Figure 5.14 If the user enters any one of the values in line 2, this alert box appears.

The ! Operator (Logical NOT). In the English statement "That's **not** true!" the word *not* is used for negation: Not true is false, and not false is true. JavaScript provides the NOT (!) operator for negation. The ! operator is called a unary operator because it has only one operand; for example, ! *true* or ! 5. It returns *true* if the expression evaluates to false and returns *false* if the expression evaluates to true. See Table 5.14.

Table 5.14 Logical NOT Examples

Expression	What It Evaluates To
! "this"	false
! 0	true
! 2	false
! false	true
! null	true
! undefined	true

EXAMPLE 5.10

```
       <html>
       <head>
          <title>Logical NOT Operator</title>
       </head>
          <body bgcolor="lightblue">
          <big>
            <script type="text/javascript">
1             var answer = true;
2             alert("Was true. Now it is " + ! answer);
            </script>
          </big>
          </body>
       </html>
```

EXPLANATION

1   The Boolean value *true* is assigned to the variable *answer*.
2   The expression sent to the alert dialog box, *! answer*, negates the value *true* (not true), making it *false*. (See Figure 5.15.)

Figure 5.15   The logical "not" operator changes true to false or false to true. The *!* operator caused *true* to become *false*.

In summary, Example 5.11 illustrates the logical operators and the values they return.

EXAMPLE 5.11

```
       <html>
         <head>
           <title>Logical (Boolean) Operators</title>
         </head>
         <body>
           <h3>
           <script type = "text/javascript">
1            var num1=50;
             var num2=100;
             var num3=0;
```

EXAMPLE 5.11 (CONTINUED)

```
2        document.write("num1 && num2 is "+(num1 && num2)+".<br />");
3        document.write("num1 || $num2 is "+(num1 || num2)+".<br />");
4        document.write("! num1 is " + !num1+".<br />");
5        document.write("!(num1 && num2) is "+!(num1 && num2)+".<br />");
6        document.write("!(num1 && num3) is "+!(num1 && num3)+".<br />");
    </script>
    </h3>
  </body>
</html>
```

EXPLANATION

1   Three variables, *num1*, *num2*, and *num3*, are initialized.

2   The *&&* operator expects both of its operands to be true, if the expression is to be true. A true value is any number that is not zero. In the expression, *50 && 100*, both operands are true. The value of the last true operand, *100*, is returned.

3   The || operator expects only one of its operands to be true if the whole expression is to be true. *50 || 100* is true because the first operand evaluates to a nonzero value. Because *50* is true and only one operand must be true, the evaluation stops here and *50* is returned.

4   The *!* (NOT) operator negates its operand. *! 50* means *! true*; that is, *false*.

5   Because the expression *num1 && num2* is enclosed in parentheses, it is evaluated first, resulting in *50 && 100*, *true*. Then the *!* (NOT) operator evaluates *!* (true), resulting in Boolean *false*.

6   The expression, *num1 && num3*, enclosed in parentheses, is evaluated first. Because *num3* is *0*, the expression evaluates to false. *!* (false) is *true*. See Figure 5.16.

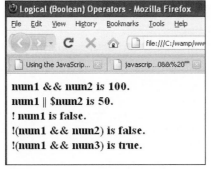

Figure 5.16 Output from Example 5.11.

5.2.7 The Conditional Operator

The conditional operator is called a ternary operator because it requires three operands. It is often used as a shorthand method for *if/else* conditional statements. (See Chapter 6, "Under Certain Conditions.") Although we cover *if/else* in Chapter 6, the following format shows both the conditional operator and how it translates to an *if/else* statement.

FORMAT

```
conditional expression ? expression : expression
```

EXAMPLE

```
x ? y : z     If x evaluates to true, the value of the expression
              becomes y, else the value of the expression becomes z

big = (x > y) ? x : y     If x is greater than y, x is assigned to
                          variable big, else y is assigned to
                          variable big

 An if/else statement instead of the conditional statement:

if (x > y) {
   big = x;
}
else{
   big = y;
}
```

EXAMPLE 5.12

```
   <html>
     <head>
        <title>Conditional Operator</title>
     </head>
     <body bgcolor="lightblue">
       <big>
       <script type ="text/javascript">
1         var age = prompt("How old are you? ", "");
2         var price = (age > 55 ) ? 0 : 7.50;
3         alert("You pay $" + price + 0);
       </script>
       </big>
     </body>
   </html>
```

EXPLANATION

1   The user is prompted for input. The value he or she enters in the prompt box is assigned to the variable *age*. (See Figure 5.17.)

2   If the value of *age* is greater than 55, the value to the right of the *?* is assigned to the variable *price*; if not, the value after the : is assigned to the variable *price*.

3   The alert dialog box displays the value of the variable *price*. (See Figure 5.18.)

Figure 5.17   The user enters *12*. This value is assigned to the variable *age* in the program.

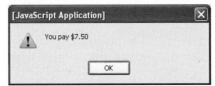

Figure 5.18   Because the age is not greater than *55*, the price is assigned *7.50*.

5.2.8   Bitwise Operators

Most of us represent numbers in decimal base 10, a number system based on 10 values starting from 0 to 9; such as $50.00 or 2011. The HTML color codes are represented in hexadecimal, base 16, which uses 16 distinct symbols: 0–9 and A–F. The color cyan is #00FFFF and fuschia is #FF00FF. Computers store data in binary, base 2, two values either 0 or 1, called bits. A byte is made up of 8 bits, a word is two bytes, or 16 bits, and two words together are called a double word or dword, which is a 32-bit value. Today, 64-bit processors have become the standard for most modern systems. Because the processor uses binary numbers, when performing low-level programming, such as writing device drivers, graphics, and data compression, bitwise operations are necessary, tasks that are more suitable to languages like C or Java.

"Bitwise operators treat their operands as a set of 32 bits (zeros and ones), rather than as decimal, hexadecimal, or octal numbers. For example, the decimal number nine has a binary representation of 1001. Bitwise operators perform their operations on such binary representations, but they return standard JavaScript numeric values."

https://developer.mozilla.org/En/Core_JavaScript_1.5_Reference/Operators/Bitwise_Operator (refer to Table 5.15).

Table 5.15 Bitwise Operators

Operator	Function	Example	What It Does
&	Bitwise AND	*x & y*	Returns a *1* in each bit position if both corresponding bits are *1*.
|	Bitwise OR	*x | y*	Returns a *1* in each bit position if one or both corresponding bits are *1*.
^	Bitwise XOR	*x ^ y*	Returns a *1* in each bit position if one, but not both, of the corresponding bits are *1*.
~	Bitwise NOT	*~x*	Inverts the bits of its operands. *1* becomes *0*; *0* becomes *1*.
<<	Left shift	*x << y*	Shifts *x* in binary representation *y* bits to left, shifting in zeros from the right.
>>	Right shift	*x >> y*	Shifts *x* in binary representation *y* bits to right, discarding bits shifted off.
>>>	Zero-fill right shift	*x >>> b*	Shifts *x* in binary representation *y* bits to the right, discarding bits shifted off, and shifting in zeros from the left.

When using the bitwise operations &, |, ^, and ~, each bit in the first operand is paired with the corresponding bit in the second operand: first bit to first bit, second bit to second bit, and so on. For example, the binary representation for *5 & 4* is *101 & 100.*

```
    101        101        101
  & 100      | 100      ^ 100
  -----      -----      -----
    100        101        001
```

Bitwise Shift Operators.   The bitwise shift operators take two operands: The first is a quantity to be shifted, and the second specifies the number of bit positions by which the first operand is to be shifted. The direction of the shift operation is controlled by the operator used.

- << (left shift)
  This operator shifts the first operand the specified number of bits to the left. Excess bits shifted off to the left are discarded. Zero bits are shifted in from the right.

- >> (sign-propagating right shift)
  This operator shifts the first operand the specified number of bits to the right. Excess bits shifted off to the right are discarded. Copies of the leftmost bit are shifted in from the left.
- >>> (zero-fill right shift)
  This operator shifts the first operand the specified number of bits to the right. Excess bits shifted off to the right are discarded. Zero bits are shifted in from the left. For example, *19>>>2* yields 4, because 10011 shifted two bits to the right becomes 100, which is 4. For nonnegative numbers, zero-fill right shift and sign-propagating right shift yield the same result.

Shift operators convert their operands to 32-bit integers and return a result of the same type as the left operator.

EXAMPLE 5.13

```
<html>
  <head>
    <title>Bitwise Operators</title>
  </head>
  <body bgcolor="lightblue">
    <font size="+1" face="arial">
    <h3> Testing Bitwise Operators</h3>
      <script type="text/javascript">
1       var result = 15 & 9;
        document.write("15 & 9 yields: " + result);
2       result = 15 | 9;
        document.write("<br /> 15 | 9  yields: " + result);
3       result = 15 ^ 9;
        document.write("<br /> 15 ^ 9  yields: " + result);
4       result = 9 << 2;
        document.write("<br /> 9 << 2 yields: " + result);
5       result = 9 >> 2;
        document.write( "<br /> 9 >> 2 yields: " + result);
6       result = -9 >> 2;
        document.write( "<br /> -9 >> 2 yields: " + result);
7       result = 15 >>> 2;
        document.write( "<br /> 15 >>> 2 yields: " + result);
      </script>
    </font>
  </body>
</html>
```

EXPLANATION

1 The binary representation of 9 is 1001, and the binary representation of 15 is 1111. When the bitwise *&* (AND) operator is applied to *1111 & 1001*, the result is binary 1001 or decimal 9.

Continues

EXPLANATION(CONTINUED)

2   When the bitwise | (OR) operator is applied to *1111 | 1001*, the result is binary 1111 or decimal 15.

3   When the bitwise ^ (Exclusive OR) is applied to *1111 ^ 1001*, the result is binary 0110 or decimal 6.

4   9<<2 yields 36, because 1001 shifted two bits to the left becomes 100100, which is decimal 36.

5   9>>2 yields 2, because 1001 shifted two bits to the right becomes 10, which is decimal 2.

6   –9 >> 2 yields –3, because the sign is preserved.

7   15 >>> 2 yields 3, because 1111 shifted two bits to the right becomes 0011, which is decimal 3. For nonnegative numbers, zero-fill right shift and sign-propagating right shift yield the same result. (See Figure 5.19.)

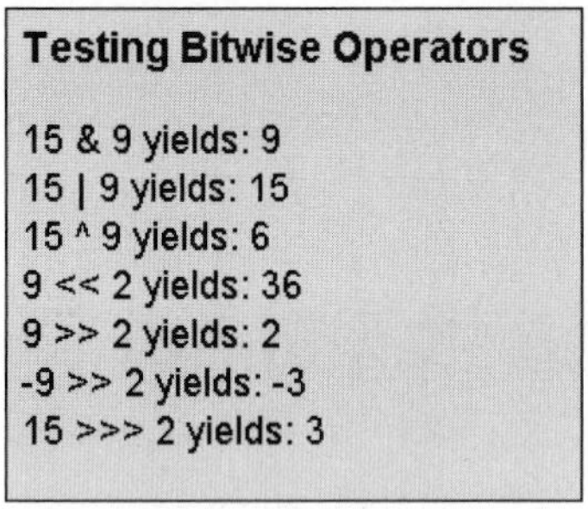

Testing Bitwise Operators

15 & 9 yields: 9
15 | 9 yields: 15
15 ^ 9 yields: 6
9 << 2 yields: 36
9 >> 2 yields: 2
-9 >> 2 yields: -3
15 >>> 2 yields: 3

Figure 5.19   Output from Example 5.13.

5.3   Number, String, or Boolean? Data Type Conversion

As defined earlier, JavaScript is a loosely typed language, which really means that you don't have to be concerned about what kind of data is stored in a variable. You can assign a number to *x* on one line and on the next line assign a string to *x*, you can compare numbers and strings, strings and Booleans, and so on. JavaScript automatically converts values when it assigns values to a variable or evaluates an expression. If data types are mixed (i.e., a number is compared with a string, a Boolean is compared with a number, a string is compared with a Boolean), JavaScript must decide how to handle the expression. Most of the time, letting JavaScript handle the data works fine, but there are times when you want to force a conversion of one type to another. For example, if you prompt a user for input, the input is set as a string. But, suppose you want to perform calculations on the incoming data, making it necessary to convert the strings to numbers. When using the + operator you want to add two numbers that have been entered as strings, not concatenate them, so you will then need to convert the data from string to number.

JavaScript provides three functions to convert the primitive data types. They are:

- *String()*
- *Number()*
- *Boolean()*

EXAMPLE 5.14

```
        <html>
          <head><title>The Conversion Functions</title></head>
          <body>
            <p>
            <h3>Data Conversion</h3>
            <script type="text/javascript">
1             var num1 = prompt("Enter a number: ","");
              var num2 = prompt("Enter another number: ","");
2             var result = Number(num1) + Number(num2);
              // Convert strings to numbers
3             alert("Result is "+ result);
4             var myString=String(num1);
5             result=myString + 200;          // String + Number is String
6             alert("Result is "+ result);    // Concatenates 200 to the
                                              // result; displays 20200
7             alert("Boolean result is "+ Boolean(num2));  // Prints true
            </script>
          </body>
        </html>
```

EXPLANATION

1   The user is prompted to enter a number (see Figure 5.20). Even though the user typed a number, JavaScript treats user input as string data and assigns it to the variable *num1* as a string. On the next line, *num2* is assigned another string (see Figure 5.21).

2   The JavaScript *Number()* function converts strings to numbers. After the variables *num1* and *num2* have been converted to numbers, the + sign will be used as an addition operator (rather than a concatenation operator), resulting in the sum of *num1* and *num2*. Unless converted to numbers, the string values "30" + "20" would be concatenated, resulting in *3020*.

3   The *alert* box displays the sum of the two numbers entered by the user (see Figure 5.22).

4   The variable *num1* is converted to a string; its value is assigned to the variable, *result*.

5   The value of *myString, 20,* is concatenated to *200* and assigned to *result*. The result is *20200*.

6   The *alert()* box displays the result from line 5.

7   The value of *num2* is converted to Boolean, either *true* or *false*. Because the value of *num2* is not 0, *true* is displayed in the *alert()* dialog box.

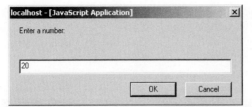

Figure 5.20   The user is prompted to enter a number.

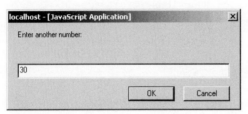

Figure 5.21   The user is prompted to enter another number.

Figure 5.22   The result is displayed.

5.3.1   The *parseInt()* Function

This function converts a string to a number. It starts parsing at the beginning of the string and returns all integers until it reaches a noninteger and then stops parsing. If the string doesn't begin with an integer, *NaN* (not a number) is returned. For example, *parseInt("150cats")* becomes *150*, whereas *parseInt("cats")* becomes *NaN*. However, if the string begins with a leading 0x or 0X or a leading 0, then JavaScript assumes you want the 0x to represent the beginning of a hex value and a single 0 to represent the start of an octal value. You can also use octal and hexadecimal numbers. In the two-argument format, the first argument to *parseInt()* is a string containing a number base (radix) ranging from 2 to 36. The default is base 10. In the statement, *parseInt("17", 8)*, the result is *15*. The first argument is the string to be parsed and the second argument, 8, is the number base of the number (here, octal 17). The value returned is decimal *15*. Refer to Tables 5.16 and 5.17.

FORMAT

```
parseInt(String, NumberBase);      Default base is 10
parseInt(String);
```

EXAMPLE

```
parseInt("111", 2);     7   (111 in base 2 is 7)
parseInt("45days");    45
```

Table 5.16   parseInt(String)

String	Result
"hello"	NaN
"Route 66"	NaN
"6 dogs"	6
"6"	6
"-6"	–6
"6.56"	6
"0Xa"	10
"011"	9

Table 5.17   parseInt(String, NumberBase)

String	Base	Result (Decimal)
"111"	2 (binary)	7
"12"	8 (octal)	10
"b"	16 (hex)	11

EXAMPLE   5.15

```
<html>
  <head><title>Using the parseInt() Function</title></head>
  <body><font face="arial size="+1">
    <b>
    <script type= "text/javascript">
1     var grade = prompt("What is your grade? ", "");
        // Grade entered as a string
2     grade=parseInt(grade);    // Grade converted to an integer
3     document.write("grade type is<em> " + typeof(grade));
4     grade+=10;
```

Continues

EXAMPLE 5.15

```
5       document.write("</em><br />After a 10 point bonus, your grade "
                        + is grade + "!<br />");
     </script>
     </font>
   </body>
</html>
```

EXPLANATION

1   The user is prompted to enter a grade. The string value entered in the prompt box is assigned to the variable *grade* (see Figure 5.23).

2   The *parseInt()* function will convert the grade to an integer value.

3   The *typeof()* operator returns the data type of the variable *grade*.

4   The value of *grade* is incremented by 10.

5   The new value of *grade* is sent to the browser (see Figure 5.24).

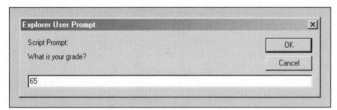

Figure 5.23   The user enters a grade.

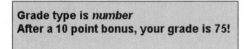

Figure 5.24   The new value of *grade* is displayed in the browser.

5.3.2   The *parseFloat()* Function

The *parseFloat()* function is just like the *parseInt()* function except that it returns a floating-point[2] number. A floating-point number is a number that contains a fractional part, such as 3.0, –22.5, or .15. The decimal point is allowed in the string being parsed. If the string being parsed does not start with a number, *NaN* (not a number) is returned (see Table 5.18).

---

2. The term "floating point" means that there are not a fixed number of digits before or after the decimal point; the decimal point floats.

FORMAT

```
parseFloat(String);
```

EXAMPLE

```
parseFloat("45.3 degrees");
```

Table 5.18 *parseFloat(String)*

String	Result
"hello"	NaN
"Route 66.6"	NaN
"6.5 dogs"	6.5
"6"	6
"6.56"	6.56

EXAMPLE 5.16

```
    <html>
      <head>
        <title>Using the parseFloat() Function</title>
        <script type = "text/javascript">
1         var temp = prompt("What is your temperature? ", "");
2         temp=parseFloat(temp);
3         if(temp == 98.6){
4           alert("Your temp is normal");
          }
5         else{
            alert("You are sick!");
          }
        </script>
      </head>
      <body></body>
    </html>
```

EXPLANATION

1   The user is prompted for input and the result is assigned as a string to the variable *temp* (see Figure 5.25).

2   The *parseFloat()* function converts the string into a floating-point number and assigns it to *temp*.

Continues

EXPLANATION

3   Although we haven't formally covered *if* statements, we have used them in several examples, and they should be easy to follow. (See Chapter 6, "Under Certain Conditions," for a formal introduction). If the value of *temp* is equal to *98.6*, then the following block of statements will be executed.

4   If is the user entered 98.6, the alert box sends the message "*Your temp is normal*" to the browser.

5   If line 3 is not true, the block of statements following *else* is executed. An alert box will appear in the browser window saying, "*You are sick!*" (see Figure 5.26).

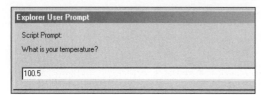

Figure 5.25   User enters a string. The *parseFloat()* function will convert it to a floating-point number.

Figure 5.26   Output from Example 5.16.

5.3.3 The *eval()* Function

The *eval()* function evaluates a string as a JavaScript expression, returning the result of the execution.[3] If there is no result, *undefined* is returned.

FORMAT

```
eval(String);
```

EXAMPLE

```
eval("(5+4) / 3");
```

---

3. The *eval()* function takes a primitive string as its argument, not a *String* object. If a *String* object is used, it will be returned as is.

```
    <html>
      <head>
        <title>The eval() Function</title>
      </head>
      <body bgcolor="lightblue">
        <big>
        <script type="text/javascript">
1         var str="5 + 4";
2         var num1 = eval(str); // results in 9
3         var num2 = eval(prompt("Give me a number ", ""));
4         alert(num1 + num2);
        </script>
        </big>
      </body>
    </html>
```

EXPLANATION

1   The string "5 + 4" is assigned to the variable *str*.

2   The *eval()* function evaluates the string expression "5 + 4" as a JavaScript instruction. The variable *num1* is assigned 9, the sum of 5 + 4.

3   The *eval()* function evaluates the string value that is entered into the prompt dialog box (see Figure 5.27). The *prompt()* method always returns a string value. If the value in the string is a number, *eval()* will convert the string to a number, return the number, and assign it to *num2*.

4   The *alert()* method displays the sum of *num1* and *num2* in the browser window.

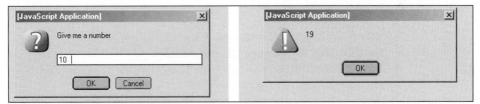

Figure 5.27   The *eval()* function converts the user input, a string, to a number (left) to allow calculation (right).

5.4   Special Operators

In this chapter, we have covered the most commonly used JavaScript functions. Table 5.19 lists some of the other operators available to be discussed in later chapters when they are applicable.

Table 5.19   Other Useful JavaScript Operators

Operator	What It Does
, (comma)	Evaluates two expressions and returns the result of the second expression.
delete	Deletes an object, an object's property, or an element at a specified index in an array.
function	Defines an anonymous function.
in	Returns true if the property is a property of a specified object.
instanceof	Returns true if the object is of a given object type.
new	Creates an instance of a user-defined object type or of one of the built-in object types.
this	Keyword that you can use to refer to the current object.
void	Specifies an expression to be evaluated without returning a value.

5.5   **What You Should Know**

An operator runs a forklift, finds a phone number, or performs an appendectomy. Java-Script operators manipulate operands, any combination of numbers, strings, and Bool-eans. This chapter covered the many JavaScript operators and the rules that govern them, called precedence and associativity. Some of the important points you should have derived from this chapter are:

1. What is precedence?
2. What is associativity?
3. How to evaluate the expression: 5 + 4 - 3 * (12 % 5) / 2
4. The difference between equal and identical.
5. Another way to write x++
6. The rules for the "+" operator.
7. How comparison operators work with numbers and strings.
8. How to use the logical && and || in expressions such as: true && false, 5 || 0, and so on.
9. How to use the conditional operator.
10. What the parseInt() and parseFloat() functions are used for.

Exercises

1. In the expression *6 + 4 / 2 % 2* what are the operands and in what order are they evaluated? Show operator preference by using parentheses.

2. How can JavaScript tell if the + is used for concatenation or addition? Write a short program to demonstrate.

3. a. If *x* is assigned the value of 5, what is *y* in the following two statements:
   ```
   y = --x;
   y = x--;
   ```
   b. Explain the output of the preceding two statements.

4. a. Are the following true or false?
   ```
   22 == "22"
   22 === "22"
   "2" > "100"
   ```
   b. Write a script to prove your answers to the preceding. In the same script, use the following two statements:
   ```
   document.write("3" + "4");
   document.write(3 + 4);
   ```
   c. Explain the output of the two preceding statements.

5. Example 5.8 prompts the user for his or her age. The user's response is assigned to the variable *answer* as a string value. Rewrite the program to assure that the age entered is a number before testing it. How do you do this?

6. Ask the user for a Fahrenheit temperature, and then convert it to Celsius. Use *parseFloat()*. To specify the precision of the number, see "The Number Object" on page 259 in Chapter 9. Formula for conversion: C = 5/9(F – 32).

7. The user is visiting Thailand. He or she has 65 U.S. dollars. Tell the user how many Thai baht that amounts to. Display an image of the Thai flag on the same page.

chapter

6

Under Certain Conditions

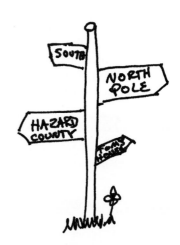

6.1 Control Structures, Blocks, and Compound Statements

If you were confronted with the above signpost, you'd have to decide which direction to take. People control their lives by making decisions, and so do programs. In fact, according to computer science books, a good language allows you to control the flow of your program in three ways. It lets you

- Execute a sequence of statements.
- Branch to an alternative sequence of statements, based on a test.
- Repeat a sequence of statements until some condition is met.

Well, then JavaScript must be a good language. We've already used programs that execute a sequence of statements, one after another.

Now we will examine the branching and looping control structures that allow the flow of the program's control to change depending on some conditional expression.

The decision-making constructs (*if, if/else, if/else if, switch*) contain a control expression that determines whether a block of statements will be executed. The looping constructs (*while, for*) allow the program to execute a statement block repetitively until some condition is satisfied.

A compound statement or block consists of a group of statements surrounded by curly braces. The block is syntactically equivalent to a single statement and usually follows an *if, else, while,* or *for* construct.

6.2 Conditionals

Conditional constructs control the flow of a program. If a condition is true, the program will execute a block of statements and if the condition is false, flow will go to an alternate block of statements. Decision-making constructs (*if, else, switch*) contain a control expression that determines whether a block of expressions will be executed. If the condition after the *if* is met, the result is true, and the following block of statements is executed; otherwise the result is false and the block is not executed.

FORMAT

```
if (condition){
   statements;
}
```

EXAMPLE

```
if ( age > 21 ){
   alert("Let's Party!");
}
```

The block of statements (or single statement) is enclosed in curly braces. Normally, statements are executed sequentially. If there is only one statement after the conditional expression, the curly braces are optional.

6.2.1 *if/else*

"You better pay attention now, or else . . . " Ever heard that kind of statement before? JavaScript statements can be handled the same way with the *if/else* branching construct. This construct allows for a two-way decision. The *if* evaluates the expression in parentheses, and if the expression evaluates to true, the block after the opening curly braces is executed; otherwise the block after the *else* is executed.

FORMAT

```
if (condition){
   statements1;
}
else{
   statements2;
}
```

EXAMPLE

```
if ( x > y ){
   alert( "x is larger");
}
else{
    alert( "y is larger");
}
```

EXAMPLE 6.1

```
      <html>
        <head>
          <title>Conditional Flow Control</title>
        </head>
        <body>
          <h3>
1           <script type="text/javascript">
            <!--  Hiding JavaScript from old browsers
2           var age=prompt("How old are you? ","");
3           if( age >= 55 ){
4              document.write("You pay the senior fare! ");
5           }
6           else{
7              document.write("You pay the regular adult fare. ");
            }
            //-->
8           </script>
          </h3>
        </body>
      </html>
```

EXPLANATION

1   JavaScript program starts here.

2   The prompt dialog box will display the message *"How old are you?"*. Whatever the user types into the box will be stored in the variable *age* (see Figure 6.1).

3, 4   If the value of the variable *age* is greater than or equal to 55, line 4 is executed (see Figure 6.2).

5   This closing curly brace closes the block of statements following the *if* expression. When there is only one statement in the block, the curly braces are not required.

6, 7   The *else* statement, line number 7, is executed if the expression in line 3 is false.

8   This tag marks the end of the JavaScript program.

Figure 6.1   The user is prompted for input.

Figure 6.2   If the age entered was greater than 55, this message is displayed.

The Conditional Operator.   The conditional operator, called a ternary operator, was discussed in Chapter 5, "Operators." Because it is often used as a shortcut for the *if/else* conditional statement, it is reviewed again here.

FORMAT

```
conditional expression ? expression : expression
```

EXAMPLE

```
x ? y : z      If x evaluates to true, the value of the expression
               becomes y, else the value of the expression becomes z

big = (x > y) ? x : y      If x is greater than y, x is assigned to
                           variable big, else y is assigned to
                           variable big
```

An *if/else* statement instead of the conditional statement:

```
if (x > y) {
   big = x;
}
else{
   big = y;
}
```

EXAMPLE 6.2

```
    <html>
      <head>
        <title>Conditional Operator</title>
      </head>
      <body bgcolor="lightblue">
        <big>
        <script type ="text/javascript">
1         var age = prompt("How old are you? ", "");
2         var price = (age > 55 ) ? 0 : 7.50;
```

EXAMPLE 6.2 (CONTINUED)

```
3          alert("You pay $" + price + 0);
        </script>
        </big>
      </body>
    </html>
```

EXPLANATION

1   The user is prompted for input. The value he or she enters in the prompt box is assigned to the variable *age*.

2   If the value of *age* is greater than 55, the value to the right of the *?* is assigned to the variable *price*; if not, the value after the *:* is assigned to the variable *price*.

3   The alert dialog box displays the value of the variable *price*.

6.2.2   *if/else if*

"If you've got $1, we can go to the Dollar Store; else if you've got $10, we could get a couple of movies; else if you've got $20 we could buy a CD . . . else forget it!" JavaScript provides yet another form of branching, the *if/else if* construct. This construct provides a multiway decision structure.

FORMAT

```
if (condition) {
   statement(s);
}
else if (condition)  {
   statement(s);
}
else if (condition)  {
   statement(s);
}
else{
   statement(s);
}
```

If the first conditional expression following the *if* keyword is true, the statement or block of statements following the expression is executed and control starts after the final *else* block. Otherwise, if the conditional expression following the *if* keyword is false, control branches to the first *else if* and the expression following it is evaluated. If that expression is true, the statement or block of statements following it are executed, and if false, the next *else if* is tested. All *else if*s are tested and if none of their expressions are true, control goes to the *else* statement. Although the *else* is not required, it normally serves as a default action if all previous conditions were false.

EXAMPLE 6.3

```
        <html>
          <head>
            <title>Conditional Flow Control</title>
          </head>
          <body>
            <h2>
1             <script type="text/javascript">
              <!--
2             var age=eval( prompt("How old are you? ",""));
3             if( age > 0 && age <= 12 ){
4                 alert("You pay the child's fare. ");
              }
5             else if( age > 12 && age < 60 ){
6                 alert("You pay the regular adult fare. ");
              }
              else {
7                 alert("You pay the senior fare! ");
              }
              //-->
8             </script>
            </h3>
          </body>
        </html>
```

EXPLANATION

1   JavaScript program starts here.

2   The prompt dialog box will display the message *"How old are you?"*. Whatever the user types into the box will be converted to a number by the *eval()* method and then stored in the variable *age*.

3, 4 If the value of the variable *age* is greater than *0* and *age* is also less than or equal to *12*, then line 4 is executed and the program continues at line 8.

5, 6 If the expression on line 3 is false, the JavaScript interpreter will test this line, and if the age is greater than 12 and also less than 60, the block of statements that follow will be executed and control goes to line 8. You can have as many *else ifs* as you like.

7   The *else* statement, line number 7, is executed if all of the previous expressions test false. This statement is called the default and is not required.

8   This tag marks the end of the JavaScript program.

6.2.3 *switch*

The *switch* statement is an alternative to *if/else if* conditional construct (commonly called a "case statement") and may make the program more readable when handling multiple options.

FORMAT

```
switch (expression){
case label :
   statement(s);
   break;
case label :
   statement(s);
   break;
   ...
default : statement;
}
```

EXAMPLE

```
switch (color){
case "red":
   alert("Hot!");
   break;
case "blue":
   alert("Cold.");
   break;
default:
   alert("Not a good choice.");
   break;
}
```

The value of the *switch* expression is matched against the expressions, called labels, following the *case* keyword. The *case* labels are constants, either string or numeric. Each label is terminated with a colon. The default label is optional, but its action is taken if none of the other cases match the *switch* expression. After a match is found, the statements after the matched label are executed for that case. If none of the cases are matched, the control drops to the *default* case. The default is optional. If a *break* statement is omitted, all statements below the matched label are executed until either a *break* is reached or the entire *switch* block exits.

EXAMPLE 6.4

```
<html>
  <head>
    <title>The Switch Statement</title>
  </head>
  <body>
```

Continues

EXAMPLE 6.4 (CONTINUED)

```
        <script type="text/javascript">
        <!--
1       var day_of_week=Math.floor((Math.random()* 7)+1);
        // Get a random number between 1 and 7
        // Monday is 1, Tuesday is 2, etc.
2       switch(day_of_week){
3         case 1:
          case 2:
          case 3:
          case 4:
4           alert("Business hours Monday through Thursday are from
                    9am to 10pm");
5           break;
          case 5:
            alert("Business hours on Friday are from 9am to 6pm");
            break;
          case 6:
            alert("Business hours on Saturday are from
                    11am to 3pm");
            break;
6         default:
            alert("We are closed on Sundays and holidays");
7           break;
8       }
        //-->
        </script>
      </body>
    </html>
```

EXPLANATION

1   The random number function generates a random number between 1 and 7 inclusive when the script is executed. The random number is stored in a variable called *day_of_week*.

2   The *day_of_week* value of the *switch* expression is matched against the values of each of the *case* labels below.

3   The first *case* that is tested is *1*. If the random number is 1, the message "*Business hours Monday through Thursday are from 9am to 10pm*" will be displayed in the alert dialog box. The same is true for case 2, 3, and 4.

4   This statement is executed if case 1, 2, 3, or 4 are matched. Note there are no *break* statements associated with any of these 4 case statements. Program control just drops from one case to the next, and if cases 1, 2, 3, or 4 are not matched, execution control goes to the next case (case 5) for testing.

5   The *break* statement causes program control to continue after line 8. Without it, the program would continue executing statements into the next *case*, "*yellow*", and continue doing so until a *break* is reached or the *switch* ends—and we don't want that. The *break* statement sends control of the program to line 8.

EXPLANATION (CONTINUED)

6   The default statements are executed if none of the cases are matched.

7   This final *break* statement is not necessary, but is good practice in case you should decide to replace the *default* with an additional *case* label.

8   The final curly brace ends the *switch* statement. Figure 6.3 displays examples of the output.

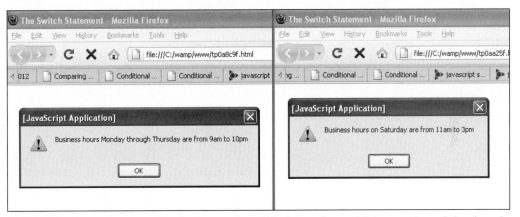

Figure 6.3   A random number between 1 and 7 determines which *case* is matched and executed.

6.3 Loops

Loops are used to execute a segment of code repeatedly until some condition is met. JavaScript's basic looping constructs are

- *while*
- *for*
- *do/while*

6.3.1 The *while* Loop

The *while* statement executes its statement block as long as the expression after the while evaluates to true; that is, nonnull, nonzero, nonfalse. If the condition never changes and is true, the loop will iterate forever (infinite loop). If the condition is false, control goes to the statement right after the closing curly brace of the loop's statement block.

The *break* and *continue* functions are used for loop control.

FORMAT

```
while (condition) {
   statements;
   increment/decrement counter;
}
```

EXAMPLE 6.5

```
       <html>
         <head>
           <title>Looping Constructs</title>
         </head>
         <body>
           <h2>While Loop</h2>
           <font size="+2">
1          <script type="text/javascript">
2             var i=0;     // Initialize loop counter
3             while ( i < 10 ){       // Test
4                document.writeln(i);
5                i++;     // Increment the counter
6             }      // End of loop block
7          </script>
           </font>
         </body>
       </html>
```

EXPLANATION

1   The JavaScript program starts here.

2   The variable *i* is initialized to *0*.

3   The expression after the *while* is tested. If *i* is less than *10*, the block in curly braces is entered and its statements are executed. If the expression evaluates to false, (i.e., *i* is not less than *10*), the loop block exits and control goes to line 6.

4   The value of *i* is displayed in the browser window (see Figure 6.4).

5   The value of *i* is incremented by 1. If this value never changes, the loop will never end.

6   This curly brace marks the end of the *while* loop's block of statements.

7   The JavaScript program ends here.

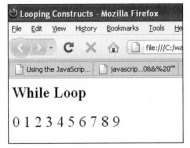

Figure 6.4 Output from Example 6.5.

6.3.2 The *do/while* Loop

The *do/while* statement executes a block of statements repeatedly until a condition becomes false. Owing to its structure, this loop necessarily executes the statements in the body of the loop at least once before testing its expression, which is found at the bottom of the block. The *do/while* loop is supported in Mozilla/Firefox and Internet Explorer 4.0, JavaScript 1.2, and ECMAScript v3.

FORMAT

```
do
   { statements;}
while (condition);
```

EXAMPLE 6.6

```
      <html>
        <head>
          <title>Looping Constructs</title>
        </head>
        <body>
          <h2>Do While Loop</h2>
          <font size="+2">
          <script type="text/javascript">
1            var i=0;
2            do{
3               document.writeln(i);
4               i++;
5            } while ( i < 10 )
          </script>
          </font>
        </body>
      </html>
```

EXPLANATION

1   The variable *i* is initialized to *0*.

2   The *do* block is entered. This block of statements will be executed before the *while* expression is tested. Even if the *while* expression proves to be false, this block will be executed the first time around.

3   The value of *i* is displayed in the browser window (see Figure 6.5).

4   The value of *i* is incremented by 1.

5   Now, the *while* expression is tested to see if it evaluates to true (i.e., is *i* less than *10*?). If so, control goes back to line 2 and the block is re-entered.

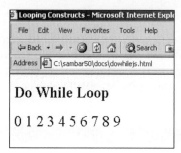

Figure 6.5   Output from Example 6.6, the *do/while* loop.

6.3.3 The *for* Loop

The *for* loop consists of the *for* keyword followed by three expressions separated by semicolons and enclosed within parentheses. Any or all of the expressions can be omitted, but the two semicolons cannot. The first expression is used to set the initial value of variables and is executed just once, the second expression is used to test whether the loop should continue or stop, and the third expression updates the loop variables; that is, it increments or decrements a counter, which will usually determine how many times the loop is repeated.

FORMAT

```
for(Expression1;Expression2;Expression3)
   {statement(s);}
for (initialize; test; increment/decrement)
   {statement(s);}
```

The preceding format is equivalent to the following *while* statement:

```
Expression1;
while( Expression2 )
   { Block; Expression3};
```

```
<html>
    <head>
        <title>Looping Constructs</title>
    </head>
    <body>
        <h2>For Loop</h2>
        <font size="+2">
        <script type="text/javascript">
1           for( var i = 0; i < 10; i++ ){
2               document.write(i);
3           }
        </script>
        </font>
    </body>
</html>
```

EXPLANATION

1   The *for* loop is entered. The expression starts with step 1, the initialization of the variable *i* to *0*. This is the only time this step is executed. The second expression, step 2, tests to see if *i* is less than *10*, and if it is, the statements after the opening curly brace are executed. When all statements in the block have been executed and the closing curly brace is reached, control goes back into the *for* expression to the last expression of the three. *i* is now incremented by one and the expression in step 2 is retested. If true, the block of statements is entered and executed.

2   The value of *i* displayed in the browser window (see Figure 6.6).

3   The closing curly brace marks the end of the *for* loop.

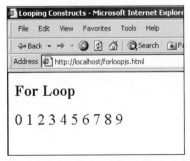

Figure 6.6 Output from Example 6.7.

6.3.4 The *for/in* Loop

The *for/in* loop is like the *for* loop, except it is used with JavaScript objects. Instead of iterating the statements based on a looping condition, it operates on the properties of an object. This loop is discussed in Chapter 9, "JavaScript Core Objects," and is only mentioned here in passing, because it falls into the category of looping constructs.

6.3.5   Loop Control with *break* and *continue*

The control statements, *break* and *continue*, are used to either break out of a loop early or return to the testing condition early; that is, before reaching the closing curly brace of the block following the looping construct.

Table 6.1   Control Statements

Statement	What It Does
break	Exits the loop to the next statement after the closing curly brace of the loop's statement block.
continue	Sends loop control directly to the top of the loop and re-evaluates the loop condition. If the condition is true, enters the loop block.

EXAMPLE 6.8

```
    <html>
      <head>
        <title>Looping Constructs</title>
      </head>
      <body>
1       <script type="text/javascript">
2         while(true) {
3            var grade=eval(prompt("What was your grade? ",""));
4            if (grade < 0 || grade > 100) {
               alert("Illegal choice!");
5               continue;    // Go back to the top of the loop
             }
             if(grade > 89 && grade < 101)
6               {alert("Wow! You got an A!");}
7            else if (grade > 79 && grade < 90)
                {alert("You got a B");}
             else if (grade > 69 && grade < 80)
                {alert("You got a C");}
             else if (grade > 59 && grade < 70)
                {alert("You got a D");}
8            else {alert("Study harder. You Failed.");}
9            answer=prompt("Do you want to enter another grade?","");
10           if(answer != "yes"){
11              break;    // Break out of the loop to line 12
             }
12        }
        </script>
      </body>
    </html>
```

1   The JavaScript program starts here.

2   The *while* loop is entered. The loop expression will always evaluate to true, causing the body of the loop to be entered.

3   The user is prompted for a grade, which is assigned to the variable *grade*.

4   If the variable *grade* is less than 0 or more than 100, "*Illegal choice*" is printed.

5   The *continue* statement sends control back to line 2 and the loop is re-entered, prompting the user again for a grade.

6   If a valid grade was entered, and it is greater than 89 and less than 101, the grade "A" is displayed (see Figure 6.7).

7   Each *else/if* branch will be evaluated until one of them is true.

8   If none of the expressions are true, the *else* condition is reached and "*You Failed*" is displayed.

9   The user is prompted to see if he or she wants to enter another grade.

10, 11   If the answer is not *yes*, the *break* statement takes the user out of the loop, to line 12.

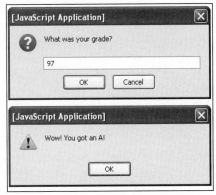

Figure 6.7 The user enters a grade, clicks OK, and gets another alert box.

6.3.6   Nested Loops and Labels

Nested Loops.   A loop within a loop is a nested loop. A common use for nested loops is to display data in rows and columns. One loop handles the rows and the other handles the columns. The outside loop is initialized and tested, the inside loop then iterates completely through all of its cycles, and the outside loop starts again where it left off. The inside loop moves faster than the outside loop. Loops can be nested as deeply as you wish, but there are times when it is necessary to terminate the loop owing to some condition.

EXAMPLE 6.9

```
     <html>
       <head>
         <title>Nested loops</title>
       </head>
       <body>
         <script type="text/javascript">
           <!--  Hiding JavaScript from old browsers
1          var str = "@";
2          for ( var row = 0; row < 6; row++){
3            for ( var col=0; col < row; col++){
               document.write(str);
             }
4            document.write("<br />");
           }
           //-->
         </script>
       </body>
     </html>
```

EXPLANATION

1   The variable *str* is assigned a string "@".

2   The outer *for* loop is entered. The variable *row* is initialized to *0*. If the value of *row* is less than 6, the loop block (in curly braces) is entered (i.e., go to line 3).

3   The inner *for* loop is entered. The variable *col* is initialized to *0*. If the value of *col* is less than the value of *row*, the loop block is entered and an @ is displayed in the browser. Next, the value of *col* will be incremented by 1, tested, and if still less than the value of *row*, the loop block is entered, and another @ displayed. When this loop has completed, a row of @ symbols will be displayed, and the statements in the outer loop will start up again.

4   When the inner loop has completed looping, this line is executed, producing a break in the rows (see Figure 6.8).

```
@
@@
@@@
@@@@
@@@@@
```

Figure 6.8   Nested loops: rows and columns. Output from Example 6.9.

Labels. Labels allow you to name control statements (*while, do/while, for, for/in,* and *switch*) so that you can refer to them by that name elsewhere in your program. They can be named the same as any other legal identifier that is not a reserved word. By themselves, labels do nothing. Labels are optional, but are often used to control the flow of a loop. A label looks like this, for example:

```
topOfLoop:
```

Normally, if you use loop-control statements such as *break* and *continue*, the control is directed to the innermost loop. There are times when it might be necessary to switch control to some outer loop. This is where labels most often come into play. By prefixing a loop with a label, you can control the flow of the program with *break* and *continue* statements as shown in Example 6.10. Labeling a loop is like giving the loop its own name.

EXAMPLE 6.10

```
     <script type="text/javascript">
1    outerLoop: for ( var row = 0; row < 10; row++){
2        for ( var col=0; col <= row; col++){
             document.write("row "+ row +"|column " + col, "<br />");
3            if(col==3){
                 document.write("Breaking out of outer loop at column
4                    " + col +"<br />");
5                break outerLoop;
             }
         }
6        document.write("************<br />");
7    }    // end outer loop block
     </script>
```

EXPLANATION

1   The label *outerLoop* labels the *for* loop that follows it. It's like giving the for loop its own name so that it can be referenced by that name later.

2   This is a nested *for* loop. As the program executes the row and column numbers are displayed.

3   If the expression is true, the *break* statement, with the label, causes control to go to line 8; it breaks out of the *outer:* loop. A *break* statement without a label would cause the program to exit just the loop to which it belongs.

4   The value of *row* and *col* are displayed as the inner loop iterates.

5   The *break* statement with the label causes control to go to line 8.

6   Each time the inner loop exits, this row of stars will be printed (see Figure 6.9). Notice that the row of stars is not printed when the loop is exited on line 5.

7   The closing curly brace closes the outer *for* loop block on line 1.

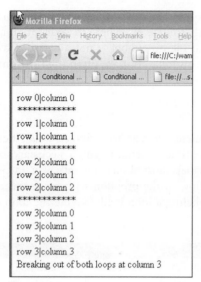

Figure 6.9   Using a label with a loop.

6.4   **What You Should Know**

"Two roads diverged in a wood, and I—" wrote Robert Frost. This chapter was about making decisions about the flow of your program, what road to take, how to repeat a sequence of statements, and how to stop the repetition. At this point, you should understand:

1. How to use conditional constructs to control the flow of your program; *if/else*, *switch*, and so on.
2. What a block is and when to use curly braces.
3. How and why you would use a *switch* statement.
4. How the *while* and the *do/while* loops differ.
5. How to use a *for* loop.
6. How to use *break* and *continue* with loops.
7. The purpose of nested loops.
8. How to make an infinite loop and how to get out of it.
9. The purpose of labels in loops.
10. How *else/ifs* work.

Exercises

1. Create a *while* loop that displays numbers as: 10 9 8 7 6 5 4 3 2 1. Put the numbers in HTML table cells.

2. Ask the user what the current hour is. If the hour is between 6 and 9 a.m., tell the user, "Breakfast is served." If the hour is between 11 a.m. and 1 p.m., tell the user, "Time for lunch." If the hour is between 5 and 8 p.m., tell the user, "It's dinner time." For any other hours, tell the user, "Sorry, you'll have to wait, or go get a snack."

3. Create a conversion table using the following formula:

   ```
   C = (F - 32) / 1.8;
   ```

   Start with a Fahrenheit temperature of 20 degrees and end with a temperature of 120 degrees; use an increment value of 5. The table will have two columns, one for Fahrenheit temperature values and one for those same temperatures converted to Celsius.

4. Ask the user for the name of the company that developed the JavaScript language. Alert the user when he or she is wrong, and then keep asking the user until he or she gets the correct answer. When the user gets it right, confirm it.

5. Use a *switch* statement to rewrite the following JavaScript code. Prompt the user for the number of a month rather than setting it to 8.

   ```
   <script type=text/javascript>
       month = 8;

       if (month == 1) {
           alert("January");
       }
        else if (month == 2) {
           alert("February");
       }
        else if (month == 3) {
           alert("March");
       }
        else if (month == 4) {
           alert("April");
       }
        else if (month == 5) {
           alert("May");
       }
   ```

```
        else if (month == 6) {
            alert("June");
        }
         else if (month == 7) {
            alert("July");
        }
        else if (month == 8) {
            alert("August");
        }
        else if (month == 9) {
            alert("September");
        }
        else if (month == 10) {
            alert("October");
        }
        else if (month == 11) {
            alert("November");
        }
        else if (month == 12) {
            alert("December");
        }
        else{
            alert("Invalid month");
        }
    </script>
```

6. Consider the following example:

```
var start_time = (day == weekend) ? 12 : 9;
```

Rewrite the conditional statement using an *if/else* construct.

chapter

7

Functions

7.1 What Is a Function?

A pocket calculator performs certain functions. You push the buttons, send information to the calculator, it performs a calculation, and sends back the results. You don't care about what transpires inside the calculator, you just want the results. That's what a function does. Functions are self-contained units of a program designed to accomplish a specified task such as calculating mortgage payments, displaying random images, or checking for valid input. They can be used over and over again and thus save you from repetitive programming. They are also used to break up a program into smaller modules to keep it better organized and easier to maintain. JavaScript has a large number of its own built-in functions, and now you can create your own.

By definition, a function is a block of statements that not only performs some task, but also returns a value. A function is an independent part of your program and not executed until called. A function is often referred to as a "black box." It's like the pocket calculator: Information goes into the black box (or calculator) as input and the action or value returned from the box is its output. What goes on inside the box is transparent to the user. The programmer who writes the function is the only one who cares about those details. When you use *document.write()*, you send something like a string of text to the function, and it sends some text back to the browser. You don't care how it does its job, you just expect it to work. If you send bad input, you get back bad output or maybe nothing, hence the expression "Garbage in, garbage out."

Functions are like miniscripts. They contain JavaScript statements that behave as a single command and can be called repeatedly throughout a program without rewriting the code.

The terms "function" and "method" are often used interchangeably. A method refers to a function that is used with JavaScript objects (covered in Chapter 8, "Objects"). A function, as used in this chapter, is a stand-alone block of statements, independent of the program until invoked by a caller.

7.1.1 Function Declaration and Invocation

Functions must be declared before they can be used. Normally functions are placed in the *<head>* tag of the HTML document to ensure that they are defined before used. Within the *<script>* tag itself, they can go anywhere. Function definitions are often stored in external JavaScript files or libraries (see "JavaScript from External Files" on page 22 of Chapter 1).

To define a function, the *function* keyword is followed by the name of the function and a set of parentheses. The parentheses are used to hold parameters, values that are received by the function. The function's statements are enclosed in curly braces.

```
function bye() { document.write ("Bye, adios, adieu, au revoir..."); }
```

Once you define a function, you can use it. JavaScript functions are invoked by calling the function; for example, *bye()*. A function can be called directly from within the *<script>* tag, from a link, or when an event is triggered, such as when the user presses a key. When called, the function's name is followed by a set of parentheses that may contain messages that will go to the function. These messages are called arguments.

To check whether the function has been defined or if it is truly a function, use the *typeof* operator; for example, *typeof(function_name)*.

FORMAT

Function definition:

```
function function_name () {statement; statement;}
function function_name (parameter, parameter){statement; statement;}
```

Function call:

```
function_name ();
function_name(argument1, argument2, ...)
```

EXAMPLE 7.1

```
    <html>
      <head><title>A Simple Function</title>
        <script type="text/javascript">
1         function welcome(){  // Function defined within <head> tags
2           var place="San Francisco";
3           alert("Welcome to "+ place + "!");
4         }
        </script>
      </head>
```

```
      <body bgcolor="lightblue">
        <big>
        <div align="center">
          <script type="text/javascript">
5           welcome();
          </script>
          <b>San Francisco</b><br />
6         <img src="sf.jpg" width="400" height="300" border="1">
        </div>
        </big>
      </body>
    </html>
```

EXPLANATION

1. Functions must be defined before they can be used. Therefore, functions are normally placed in a JavaScript program, between the HTML *<head></head>* tags. In this example, the function is defined, but it will not do anything until it is called from somewhere in the file.

   The *function* keyword is followed by the user-defined name of the function called *welcome* and a set of parentheses. The parentheses are used to hold parameters, information being received by the function. What the function actually does is defined in a set of statements enclosed within curly braces. The function statements are enclosed in a set of curly braces.

2, 3. This is the code that is run whenever the function is called. It is called the function definition. When this function is called, the string *San Francisco* will be assigned to the variable called *place* and the alert dialog box will display *"Welcome to San Francisco!"* in the browser window (see Figure 7.1).

4. This is the final closing curly brace that ends the function definition.

5. This is where the function is invoked or called. When the function *welcome()* is called, the statements within its definition will be executed.

6. The function is defined in the head of the document and called from the body of the document before the *<img>* tag is reached. This image will not appear until the user clicks the OK button in the alert dialog box (see Figure 7.2).

Figure 7.1 After the function *welcome()* is called, output is sent to the browser.

Figure 7.2 After the user clicks the OK button in the alert box, this image loads.

Passing Arguments.   If a user wants to send values to a function, the values are enclosed in the parentheses right after the function name and sent as a comma-separated list of arguments when the function is called. The arguments are received by the function in a list of corresponding values called parameters (see Figure 7.3). The names of the arguments are not necessarily the same names in the parameter list, but they correspond to the same values. These values can be assigned to local variables within the function. Local variables disappear when the function exits. JavaScript doesn't keep track of the number of arguments sent to the function to make sure they match up with the number of parameters specified in the function definition at the other end. If you send three arguments, and there are only two parameters defined within the function, the third argument is ignored. If you send three arguments, and there are four parameters waiting within the function, then the fourth parameter is *undefined*. It's similar to sending messages to an answering machine. If you send a message and the message machine is full, your message is ignored, and if you send a message and there's room for more messages, the message you sent is stored, and the unused space is still there, but not defined.

```
function_name(argument1, argument2, ...);    // function call (caller)



function_name(parameter1, parameter2...){    // function definition (receiver)
   var result= parameter1 + parameter2;
  ...
}    // curly braces required
```

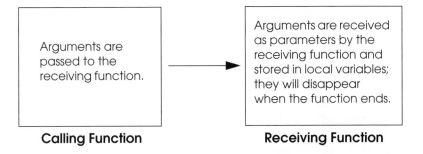

Calling Function   **Receiving Function**

Figure 7.3   In the analogy of the pocket calculator, you are the caller when you press the buttons, and the internal functions inside the calculator are the receiver.

EXAMPLE 7.2

```
      <html>
      <head><title>Passing Arguments</title>
        <script type="text/javascript">
1         function greetings(pal){  // "Birdman!" is stored in pal
2         alert("Greetings to you, " + pal);
        }
        </script>
      </head>
      <body background="birdman.jpg">
3       <script type="text/javascript">
4         greetings("Birdman!");  // Passing an argument
        </script>
      </body>
      </html>
```

EXPLANATION

1   The function, *greetings()*, has one parameter, called *pal*. This parameter holds a value that is sent to the function when it was called. The parameter name is any valid Java-Script variable name. At this point, the function has been defined but not called.

2   The alert method will display the string, *"Greetings to you, "* concatenated to the value stored in *pal*; in this example that value is *"Birdman!"*.

3   The JavaScript program is in the body of the document. It contains a function call that will invoke a function defined in the head of the document.

4   The function *greetings()* is called with one argument, *"Birdman!"*. This argument will be sent to the function, and assigned to the parameter, *pal*. If the function had been called in the head of the document as it was in Example 7.1, the background image would not appear until after the user clicks the OK button in the alert box (see Figure 7.4), but in this example, the image was loaded before the function was called.

Figure 7.4 Output from the *greetings()* function in Example 7.2.

Calling a Function from a Link.   A function can be called directly from a link, by using the JavaScript pseudoprotocol, *JavaScript:*, instead of a normal URL. The *Java-Script:* protocol and the function call are placed within quotes and assigned to the *href* attribute of the *<a>* tag. When the user clicks his or her mouse on the link, instead of the program going to the URL of another page, a JavaScript function will be called.

EXAMPLE **7.3**

```
    <html>
      <head><title>Functions</title>
1       <script type="text/javascript">
2         function greetings(){  // Function defined within <head> tags
              document.bgColor="lightblue";
              alert("Greetings to you!");
3         }
      </script>
    </head>
    <body bgcolor="silver">
      <div align="center">
4       <a href="JavaScript:greetings()"><big>Click here for
          Salutations</big>
        </a><br />
      </div>
    </body>
  </html>
```

EXPLANATION

1   The JavaScript program starts here in the head of the document. The function is defined within the head of the document to guarantee that it will be defined before being called.

2, 3   The function *greetings()* is defined. It is very simple. It causes the background color of the document to be a light blue color and causes an alert box to appear with a greeting message.

4   The *href* attribute of the link tag is assigned a string consisting of the *JavaScript:* pseudoprotocol, followed by the name of the function to be called. When the user clicks this link, JavaScript calls the function, *greetings()*. (See Figure 7.5.)

Figure 7.5   After clicking the link, the function is called, causing the alert dialog box to appear.

Calling a Function from an Event.   An event is triggered when a user performs some action, like clicking a button or moving the mouse over a link. The function assigned to the event is called an event handler. When the event is triggered, the function is called. In the following example, when the user clicks the Welcome button, the function is called.

EXAMPLE 7.4

```
        <html>
          <head><title>Functions and Events</title>
            <script type="text/javascript">
1             function greetings(you){  // Function definition
2               document.bgColor="lavender";
                alert("Greetings and Salutations! " + you);
              }
            </script>
          </head>
```

Continues

EXAMPLE 7.4 (CONTINUED)

```
3      <body>
        <div align="center">
4       <form>
5         <input type="button"
6           value="Welcome button"
7           onClick="greetings('Dan');"
        />
        </form>
        </div>
      </body>
    </html>
```

EXPLANATION

1   The JavaScript program starts here. The function is defined in the head of the document.

2   The function *greetings()* is defined here.

3   The body of the page starts here.

4   An HTML form starts here. It will be used to create a button input device.

5   The type of input device is a button.

6   The value that will be displayed in the button is *"Welcome button"* (see Figure 7.6).

7   When the user presses or clicks the button, the *onClick* event handler will be triggered, causing the *greetings()* function to be called. The value assigned to the *onClick* event handler is a JavaScript function enclosed in quotation marks (see Figure 7.7).

Figure 7.6   When the button is clicked, the event is triggered.

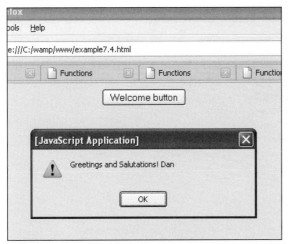

Figure 7.7 A function is called after the event is triggered. The function "handles" the event.

Calling a Function from JavaScript.   In the first examples of this chapter, functions were defined in one JavaScript script and called from another. Although it is valid to define and call the function from the same JavaScript program, it is often desirable to define the function in the head of the document, to be sure it has been defined before it is called. Then you can call the function from a link, an event, or another JavaScript program. Because the document is defined within the *<body></body>* tags, the body is often the place from where you will call functions. The general rule of thumb is: If your script is designed to write data to the page, put the *<script></script>* tags within the *<body></body>* tags. Example 7.2 called a function from one JavaScript program within the body, but defined the function in another JavaScript program within the head. Finally, you might want to store function definitions in an external library (.js file) where they can be reused and shared by other programs.

Scope of Variables in Functions.   The scope of a variable describes where the variable is visible in the program; that is, where it can be used in the program. Variables declared outside of functions are global in scope, meaning they can be used or changed anywhere in the program. A variable is also global if declared within a function unless it is declared within a function with the *var* keyword. The *var* keyword makes the variable local in scope; that is, the variable can be used only within the function where it is defined and is no longer visible once the function ends.

EXAMPLE 7.5

```
        <html>
          <head><title>Function Scope</title>
            <script type="text/javascript">
1             var name="William";    // Global variable
              var hometown="Chico";
2             function greetme(){
3               var name="Daniel";    // Local variable
                var hometown="Husingen";
4               alert("In function the name is " + name +
                " and hometown is "+ hometown);
5             }
            </script>
          </head>
          <body>
            <script type="text/javascript">
6             greetme();  // Function call
7             alert("Out of function, name is "+ name +
8                " and hometown is " + hometown);
            </script>
          </body>
        </html>
```

EXPLANATION

1   The variables called *name* and *hometown* are global in scope. They are visible throughout the JavaScript program.

2   The function called *greetme()* is declared and defined.

3   Any variables declared within a function with the *var* keyword are local to that function. In fact, you must use the *var* keyword when declaring local variables; otherwise, the variables will be global. The variable called *name* has been declared inside the function. This is a local variable and has nothing to do with the global variable of the same name on line 1. The function variable will go out of scope; that is, it will no longer be visible, when the function ends on line 6, at which point the global variable will come back in scope. If the variable, *name*, had been given a different name, within the function, such as *name2* or *myName*, then the global variable would have remained in scope within the function.

4   The variable called *name* and *hometown* were defined inside this function and are local in scope. They will stick around until the function exits.

5   The closing curly brace marks the end of the function definition.

6   The function *greetme()* is called here.

7   The global variable called *name* has come back into scope.

8   The global variable called *hometown* is still in scope (see Figure 7.8).

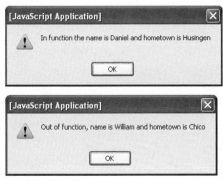

Figure 7.8 Output from Example 7.5.

7.1.2 Return Values

Functions can return values with a *return* statement. The *return* keyword is optional and can only exist within a function. When the *return* keyword is reached in a function, no further processing within the function occurs. A *return* can be used to send back the result of some task, such as a calculation, or to exit a function early if some condition occurs. If a function doesn't have a *return* statement, it returns the *undefined* value.

FORMAT

```
return;
return expression;
```

EXAMPLE

```
function sum (a, b) {
   var result= a + b;
   return result;
}
```

If the call to the function is made part of an expression, the returned value can be assigned to a variable. In Example 7.6 the *sum* function is called with two arguments, 5 and 10. The *sum* function's return value will be assigned to the variable *total*.

```
var total=sum(5, 10);
```

EXAMPLE 7.6

```
      <html>
        <head><title>Return Value</title>
          <script type="text/javascript">
1            function mileage(miles, gas){
2               return miles/gas;    // Return the result of the division
             }
          </script>
        </head>

        <body bgcolor="lightgreen">
          <font face="arial" size="+1">
          <div align="center">
          <img src="car-wave.gif">
          <script type="text/javascript">
3            var distance=eval(prompt("How many miles did you
                 drive? ", ""));
             var amount=eval(prompt("How much gas did you use?", ""));
4            var rate = mileage(distance, amount);
                 // Return value assigned to rate
5            alert("Your mileage "+ rate  +" miles per gallon.\n");
          </script>
          </div>
          </font>
        </body>
      </html>
```

EXPLANATION

1   A function called *mileage()* is defined in this JavaScript program located between the *<head>* tags of the document.

2   The *return* statement sends back to the caller of the function the result of the division. That returned value will be assigned to the variable, *rate*, on line 4.

3   The user is asked for input. The number of miles driven and the amount of gas used are assigned to the variables called *distance* and *amount*, respectively (see Figure 7.9).

4   The *mileage()* function is called, passing two arguments. Because the *mileage()* function is on the right side of the assignment operator (the = sign), whatever is returned from the function will be assigned to the variable, called *rate*, on the left side of the = sign.

5   The alert dialog box displays the value returned from the function: the number of miles used per gallon (see Figure 7.10).

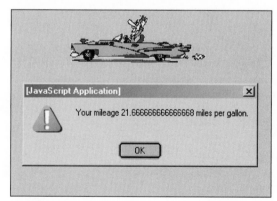

Figure 7.9 The user is asked for input.

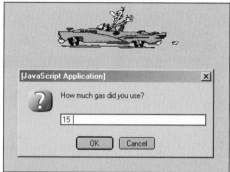

Figure 7.10 The number of miles per gallon is returned by the *mileage()* function.

7.1.3   Anonymous Functions as Variables

A function definition can be assigned directly to a variable. The variable is like any other variable except that its value is a function definition and this variable is used as a reference to the function. The () is a JavaScript operator, indicating that a function is to be called. Pay close attention to the use of the () operator in the next example and how it affects the outcome of the function variable. Later we will use these anonymous functions with event methods as follows:

```
window.onload = function() {
        alert("Welcome");
    }
```

When the Web page has finished loading, the onload event is triggered and JavaScript will execute the anonymous function statements, in this case an alert box.

EXAMPLE 7.7

```
    <html>
      <head><title>Anonymous Function</title>
        <script type="text/javascript">
1         var greetings= function(){  // Anonymous function has no name
2           message="Greetings to you! "; // Function definition
3           return message;
          }
        </script>
      </head>
      <body>
        <big>
        <script type="text/javascript">
4         text=greetings;
          // greetings is a variable;
          // its value is the function definition
          document.write(text +"<br />");

5         text=greetings();   // Call function
          document.write(text +"<br />");
        </script>
        </big>
      </body>
    </html>
```

EXPLANATION

1   A function without a name, called an anonymous function, is given its definition between the curly braces. The definition of the function is assigned to the variable *greetings*. We can say then that *greetings* is the name of a variable whose value is a function definition and that *greetings* is a reference to the function.

EXPLANATION

2 In the function a variable called *message* is assigned a string. Rather than using an alert box to send the message, it will be returned to the caller.

3 The *return* statement sends the message back to the caller of the function.

4 Notice that in this line we are displaying the value of the variable *greetings*. The definition of the function is shown.

5 In this line the variable name is appended with parentheses, the () operator. This operator causes JavaScript to call *greetings* as a function and return the result. In the previous line, without the () operator, the value of the variable, a function definition, is displayed (see Figure 7.11).

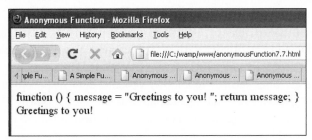

Figure 7.11 A variable with an anonymous function as its value

EXAMPLE 7.8

```
<html>
   <head><title>Functions as Variable</title>
     <script type="text/javascript">
1        var greetings=function (visitor){
            // Function body is assigned to greetings
            message="Greetings to you, " + visitor + "! ";
2           return message;
         }
     </script>
   </head>
   <body>
     <big>
     <script type="text/javascript">
3        var salutation=greetings("Elfie");
         document.write(salutation + "<br />");
4        var hello = greetings;
            // Function variable assigned to another variable
5        var welcome = greetings;
6        document.write(hello("Stranger") +"<br />");
            // Call the function
```

Continues

EXAMPLE 7.8 (CONTINUED)

```
7              document.write(welcome("your Majesty") +
                  " May I take your coat? </br />");
           </script>
           </big>
        </body>
      </html>
```

EXPLANATION

1   A function definition is assigned to the variable named *greetings*. This time the function will take an argument called *visitor*.

2   The *return* statement sends back to the caller the value of the message string assigned on the previous line .

3   Because the value of the variable *greetings* is a function definition, to activate the function, we need to add parentheses to the variable name. Now the variable acts as a function call.

4   We can assign the *greetings* variable to another variable. Now *hello* contains the function definition. To call the function add parentheses to *hello* as *hello()*.

5   Now the variable *welcome* is assigned the name of the function called *greetings*. To call the function, we add parentheses: *welcome()*.

6   The value of the variable, *hello*, is a function definition. To use the variable as a function call, parentheses are added to its name, and any arguments passed within the parentheses just as with any ordinary function call, e.g. *hello("Stranger")*.

7   The value of the variable, *welcome*, is a function definition. The function is called by adding parentheses to the variable name, *welcome* (see Figure 7.12).

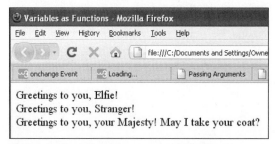

Figure 7.12   Variables used as functions

7.1.4   Closures

A closure is an a anonymous function defined within another function. When the outer function exits, it returns a reference to the inner anonymous function, making it possible to call the inner function via the reference. A closure means that the local variables can remain accessible to the inner function even when it seems they should have gone out of scope. The closure causes the variables to hang around until they are no longer needed.

A common use for a closure is to set up the parameters for a function that will be called at some time in the future. JavaScript's *setTimeout()* function is used to set a timer in your program. The first argument may be a reference to a function that will be called after some time interval has passed. You will see in future chapters that JavaScript also uses closures with event handling and information hiding.

Douglas Crawford writes (*http://www.crockford.com/JavaScript/private.html*), "The pattern of public, private, and privileged members is possible because JavaScript has closures. What this means is that an inner function always has access to the vars and parameters of its outer function, even after the outer function has returned. This is an extremely powerful property of the language. There is no book currently available on JavaScript programming that shows how to exploit it. Most don't even mention it."

On the other hand, accidentally creating closures can have harmful side effects such as Internet Explorer memory leaks and reduced efficiency of code. A very detailed article on both the pros and cons of using closures, written by Richard Cornford, can be found at *http://www.jibbering.com/faq/faq_notes/closures.html.*

In the following example the outer function is called *paint()* and the inner function is anonymous. The *paint()* function receives two parameters. It then creates a local string variable called *str* and assigns the parameter values to it. When *paint()* exits, those variables and their values continue to exist even though they seem like they should have gone out of scope. Why? Because the anonymous function needs access to the variables in *paint()* until it has been called and exits.

EXAMPLE 7.9

```
      <html>
        <head><title>Closures</title>
          <script type="text/javascript">
1           function paint(type, color) {
2             var str = "The " + type + " is " + color; //local variable
3             var tellme = function() {   // Anonymous function
                 document.write("<big>"+str+".</big><br />")
              }
4             return tellme;   // return a reference to the function
            }
          </script>
        </head>
        <body bgColor="lightgreen">
          <h2>Testing a closure</h2>
          <script type="text/javascript">
5           var say1 = paint("rose","red"); /* A reference to the
                                                anonymous is
                                                function is returned */
6           var say2 = paint("sun", "yellow");
7           alert(say1); // See the value in say1 Figure 7.13
8           say1();   // Call the anonymous function
9           say2();
          </script>
        </body>
      </html>
```

EXPLANATION

1   A function called *paint()* is defined. It takes two parameters: a type and a color.

2   The local variable called *str* is assigned a string containing the value of type and color.

3   The variable *tellme* is a reference to an anonymous function. Defining a function within another function is called a closure. This function will print the value of *str* and a newline when it is called. But it is only defined here. It will not be called until after the *paint()* function exits. Even though this function has no local variables of its own, it reuses the *str* variable declared in the outer function.

4   The *paint()* function returns the variable *tellme* whose value happens to be a reference to an anonymous function.

5   The returned value, a reference to the anonymous function defined within the *paint()* function, is assigned to *say1*.

6   The returned value, a reference to the anonymous function defined within the *paint()* function, is assigned to *say2*.

7   Let's look at the value of the variable *say1*. In the alert box (Figure 7.13) you can see that the value of *say1* is the complete definition for the anonymous function declared on line 3.

8   By adding parentheses to the reference *say1*, so that now it is *say1()*, the anonymous function is called and the statement within it is displayed (see Figure 7.14).

9   The variable *say2* is also a reference to an anonymous function; *say2()* calls that anonymous function.

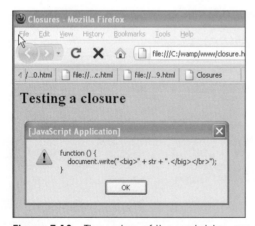

Figure 7.13   The value of the variables, *say1* and *say2*, is a function definition.

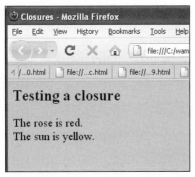

Figure 7.14 The closure remembers the values of local variables.

7.1.5 Recursion

Definition of recursion:

recursion: See recursion.

This definition says it all! JavaScript supports recursion. So what is it? Have you ever taken apart a Russian doll? Open up the outside doll and there's another smaller duplicate doll inside it, take that one out, and you find another, and so on, until you get down to a tiny doll at the end. Then when you put them back, you start with the last doll you opened and keep returning each doll until you get back to the first one you opened. A recursive function is a function that calls itself. It's a chain of function calls to the same function. The first time it calls itself is the first level of recursion, the second time is the second level, and so on. When a function calls itself, execution starts at the beginning of the function, and when the function ends, the program backs up to where it was when it called the function and starts executing from that point. Most important, there must be a way to stop the recursion, or it will be infinite, and probably cause the program to crash.

An example often used to describe recursion can be demonstrated with a function to produce a Fibonacci sequence of numbers: 0, 1, 1, 2, 3, 5, 8, 13, 21, 34, 55, and so on. Here is a little bit of history about how this formula was derived.

In the beginning of the 13th century, an Italian mathematician, Leonardo Fibonacci, was trying to solve the following problem presented at a mathematical competition in Pisa: How many rabbits would be produced in a year if, beginning with a single pair of rabbits, every month each pair reproduces a new pair of rabbits, which become productive when they are one month old, and none of them die, and so on? Fibonacci came up with a formula, named after himself, to answer the rabbit question. The sequence starts with 0 and 1, and then produces the next number by adding the two previous numbers together; so 0 + 1 is 1, 1 + 1 is 2, 1 + 2 is 3, 2 + 3 is 5, and so on.

In Example 7.10, the Fibonacci sequence recurses 20 times and as you can see, if these numbers represent rabbits, we have over 4,000 rabbits in a short period of time!

EXAMPLE 7.10

```
      <html>
        <head><title="Fibonacci Series"</title>
          <script type="text/javascript">
1         var count = 0;
2         function fib(num){
3            count++;
             switch(num){
               case 0 :
4                  return(0);
                   break;
               case 1:
5                  return(1);
                   break;
               default:
6                  return(fib(num - 1) + fib( num - 2 ));
                   break;
             }
          }
        </script>
      </head>
      <body>
        <big>
        <div align = "center">
        <table border="1">
          <tr>
          <script type = "text/javascript">
7           for( n=0; n < 20; n++){
8              value = fib(n);
               document.write("<td>" + value + "</td>");
            }
9           alert("Function called itself "+ count + " times!!");
          </script>
          </tr>
        </table>
        </div>
        </big>
      </body>
      </html>
```

EXPLANATION

1   The variable, *count*, is initialized outside the function, making it global. It will keep track of the number of times the *fib()* function is called.

2   The *fib()* function introduces the concept of recursion, a function that calls itself. This function starts the initial task and in itself is not recursive. When the same task needs to be repeated, that is when *fib()* will call itself.

3   Each time the function is called, the value of *count* is incremented by 1.

4   The first two Fibonacci numbers are 0 and 1, and each remaining number is the sum of the previous two. The *switch* statement is used to check for the incoming values of a number, *num*. If *num* is 0, the value returned will be 0; if it is 1, the value returned is 0 + 1. Because these cases are so simple there is no need for recursion. If the number is greater than 1, then the default case is entered.

5   The first values in the sequence are 0 and 1. The value 1 is returned.

6   This is the heart of the recursive program. If the number is not 0 or 1, the default case is entered, and the remaining number is the sum of the previous two numbers. The function *fib()* is used within its own definition. The result of the first call to the *fib()* function is added to the result of next call to *fib()* , returning the result to line 8.

7   The loop iterates 20 times. For each iteration, the function *fib()* is called, which calls itself.

8   Each time through the for loop, the function *fib()* is called passing the value *n* as its argument (see line 6).

9   The value of the *count* variable increases by one every time the *fib()* function is called. With recursion, the function was called 35,400 times (see Figure 7.15).

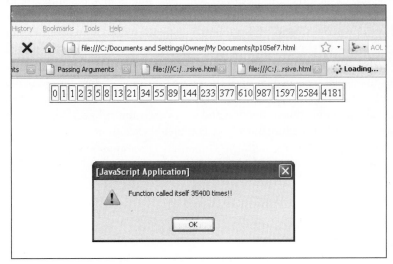

Figure 7.15   Recursion with the Fibonacci series.

EXAMPLE 7.11

```
<html>
  <head>
    <title>Recursion</title>
      <script type="text/javascript">
1         function upDown(num){
2            document.write("<b><font size='+1'>Level "
                           + num + "</b><br />");
3            if(num < 4){
4               upDown(num + 1);    // Function calls itself
5               document.write("<em>Level "+ num + "<em><br />");
            }
         }
      </script>
  </head>
  <body bgcolor="lightblue">
    <h2>Recursion</h2>
    <script type="text/javascript">
6         upDown(1);
      </script>
  </body>
</html>
```

EXPLANATION

1   The first time this function is called it is passed the number 1.

2   The function prints out the level number, Level 1.

3   If the value of *num* is less than 4, the function calls itself.

4   When the function calls itself, it adds 1 to the value of *num* and restarts execution
    at the top of the function, this time with the value of *num* equal to 2. Each time
    the function calls itself, it creates a new copy of *num* for that recursion level. The
    other copy is on hold until this one is finished. The function keeps calling itself
    and printing level numbers in bold text until the *if* statement fails; that is, until
    the value of *num* is not less than 4.

5   This line won't be executed until the recursion stops—when the value of *num* is
    4. When that happens, the current version of *upDown*() is finished, and we back
    off to the previous called function and start execution at line 5. This process con-
    tinues until all of the functions have completed execution.

6   This is the first call to the *upDown*() function. The argument is the number *1*. The
    output is shown in Figure 7.16.

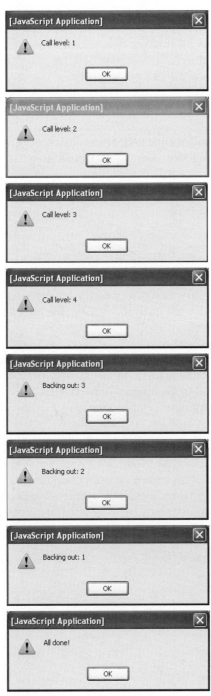

Figure 7.16 Output from Example 7.11. Alert box displays: Call level: 1, Call level: 2, Call level: 3, Call level: 4, Backing out: 3, Backing out: 2, Backing out: 1, All done.

7.1.6   Functions Are Objects

For a discussion on how functions behave as objects. See "Classes and User-Defined Functions" on page 182 in Chapter 8, "Objects."

7.2   Debugging Techniques

Now that we have covered some of the fundamental JavaScript constructs, this is a good time to introduce some debugging techniques. As your programs grow, so do your chances to create errors. Getting to know how to deal with these problems will save you much time and frustration.

7.2.1   Function Syntax

When working with functions there are some simple syntax rules to watch for:

1. Did you use parentheses after the function name?
2. Did you use opening and closing curly braces to hold the function definition?
3. Did you define the function before you called it? Try using the *typeof* operator to see if a function has been defined.
4. Did you give the function a unique name?
5. When you called the function is your argument list separated by commas? If you don't have an argument list, did you forget to include the parentheses?
6. Do the number of arguments equal to the number of parameters?
7. Is the function supposed to return a value? Did you remember to provide a variable or a place in the expression to hold the returned value?
8. Did you define and call the function from within a JavaScript program?

Figure 7.17 shows function errors displayed by the JavaScript Error Console in Firefox. This is a very useful debugging tool for immediate error checking. Just click the Tools menu and go to Error Console. These error messages make troubleshooting your scripts much easier. Figures 7.18 through 7.20 show errors in other browsers.

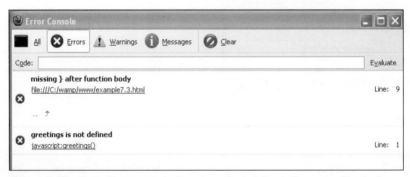

Figure 7.17   Function errors in the JavaScript Error Console (Firefox).

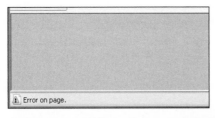

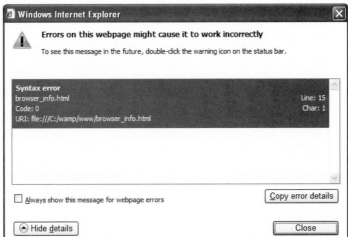

Figure 7.18   Windows Internet Explorer—Look in the bottom left corner of the page. Double-click the yellow icon. A window will appear with the line and character where the error was found.

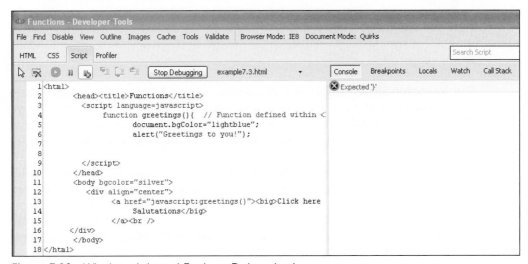

Figure 7.19   Windows Internet Explorer Debug tool.

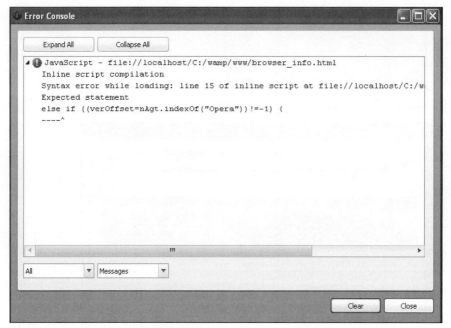

Figure 7.20 Opera's Error Console.

7.2.2 Exception Handling with *try/catch* and *throw*

An exception is a runtime error that the program might encounter during its execution, such as an undefined variable, an index value that is referenced but doesn't exist, a function that receives a bad parameter, and so on. Exception handlers make it possible to catch errors and resolve them gracefully. By catching the exception and controlling the error message, the program will be much nicer for an unwary user who is not used to the kinds of error messages you see all the time. As of JavaScript1.5 exception handling is now supported.

The *try/catch* Statements.   You can enclose and test those parts of a program where you expect potential problems in a *try* statement. If an exception occurs within the *try* block, control will shift to the *catch* block. The *catch* block will contain statements to clarify what went wrong. If there were no errors, the *catch* block will be ignored. See Examples 7.12 and 7.13.

When an exception is thrown in the *try* block, the variable shown as *e* in *catch(e)* holds the value of the type of exception (Table 7.1) that was thrown in the *try* block. You can use this variable to get information about the exception that was thrown. (The variable *e* can have any name and is local to the *catch* block.) You can use the name and message properties with the *catch* variable to get the name of the exception and a message explaining what caused the exception.

Table 7.1 Primary Error Types (JavaScript 1.5+)

Error Name	When It Is Raised
EvalError	If the *eval()* function is used in an incorrect manner
RangeError	If a numeric variable or parameter exceeds its allowed range
ReferenceError	If an invalid reference is used; e.g., the variable is undefined
SyntaxError	If a syntax error occurs while parsing code in an *eval()*
TypeError	If the type of a variable or parameter is a valid type
URIError	Raised when `encodeURI()` or `decodeURI()` are passed invalid parameters

EXAMPLE 7.12

```
    <html>
      <head><title>Try/Catch</title>
        <script type="text/javascript">
1         try
          {
            alert("Current balance is $:" + get_balance());
          }
2         catch(err)
          {
            alert("Something went wrong! \n"+
3           err.name + ": "+ err.message);
          }
        </script>
      </head>
    </html>
```

EXPLANATION

1 The *try* block contains the JavaScript that will be tested for errors.
2 If an error occurred in the *try* block, it would be caught in the *catch* block.
3 The argument, *err*, contains the reason for the error. Without the *try/catch* statements, this example would display a blank page and the error would show up in the browser's error console. If the exception is caught in your program, it will not show up in the browser's console window (see Figure 7.21).

Figure 7.21 An error was caught and its name and the reason for it are displayed.

The _throw_ Statement.   The _throw_ statement allows you to create your own conditions for exceptions. Used within in the _try_ block, a specific error condition can be tested and thrown to the _catch_ block. In the _catch_ block you can create customized error messages to correspond to a particular error. See Example 7.13.

The _finally_ Clause.   You can use the _finally_ clause to execute statements after the _try_ statement finishes, whether or not an exception occurred.

    You can use the _finally_ clause to make your script fail gracefully when an exception occurs; for example, you might need to release a resource that your script has tied up. The following example opens a file and then executes statements that use the file (server-side JavaScript allows you to access files). If an exception is thrown while the file is open, the _finally_ clause closes the file before the script fails.

EXAMPLE 7.13

```
    <html>
      <head><title>Catch me if you Can!</title></head>
      <body>
        <script type="text/javascript">
1         var age=eval(prompt("Enter your age:",""));
2         try{
3           if(age>120 || age < 0){
              throw "Error1";
            }
            else if(age == ""){
4             throw "Error2";
            }
            else if(isNaN(age)){
              throw "Error3";
            }
          }
5         catch(err){
6           if(err=="Error1"){
              alert("Error! The value is out of range");
            }
```

EXAMPLE 7.13 (CONTINUED)

```
            if(err=="Error2"){
               alert("Error! You didn't enter your age");
            }
            if(err=="Error3"){
               alert("Error! The value is not a number");
            }
         }
7        if (age < 13){
            alert("You pay child's fare!");
         }
         else if(age < 55 ){
            alert("You pay adult fare.");
         }
         else { alert("You pay senior fare.");
         }
      </script>
   </body>
</html>
```

EXPLANATION

1   This simple example is here to show you how the *try/catch/throw* statements can be used for handling errors. For something like this, you will probably find it easier to test the program in the *if* conditionals, but we'll use it to demonstrate how to throw exceptions. First, the user is prompted for his or her age.

2   The *try* block is entered to test for the possible error conditions defined by the programmer.

3   If an invalid age is entered (i.e., an age less than 0 or greater than 120). An error string, "Error1" is thrown and picked up in the *catch* block to be tested.

4   If the user didn't enter anything, the string "Error2" is thrown and picked up in the *catch* block.

5   In the *catch* block, the errors will be handled based on the error string that was thrown from the *try* block.

6   The *err* value being passed to the catch block is one of the values that was thrown from the *try* block; for example, "Error1", "Error2", "Error3".

7   Because all the testing and error handling was handled in the *try/catch* blocks, the rest of the program can continue with no further testing of the age variable (see Figure 7.22).

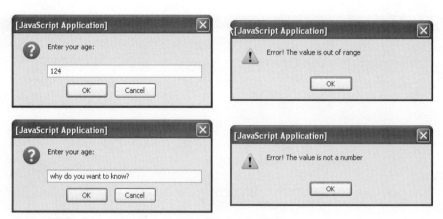

Figure 7.22   Example of output for Example 7.13.

7.3   **What You Should Know**

Functions are fundamental to programming in any programming language. There are JavaScript built-in functions such as *eval*(), *parseInt*(), and *Number*(), among others, and there are user-defined functions. This chapter was all about defining and calling your own functions. We will be creating functions throughout the rest of this text to perform tasks based on user-initiated events such as clicking a link, clicking a button, rolling a mouse over an image, or submitting a form. Functions will be defined within JavaScript code or from another file. They may be used to create objects, respond to HTTP requests, validate data, perform calculations, customize output, and so on. After reading this chapter, you should know:

1. How to declare and define functions.
2. Where to put functions in a JavaScript program.
3. How to call a function with arguments and use parameters.
4. What can be returned from a function.
5. The difference between global and local variables.
6. How to trigger a function call.
7. How to assign a function to a variable.
8. What closure is.
9. What recursion is.
10. How *try* and *catch* work.
11. How to debug programs with browser tools.

Exercises

1. Copy the following file and execute it in your browser. What's wrong with it and why? Can you fix it?

```
<html>
  <head><title>link</title>
    <script type="text/javascript">
      function addem(){
        var n = 2;
        var y = 3;
        document.write( n + y , "<br />");
      }
    </script>
  </head>
  <body bgcolor="red">
    <a href="JavaScript:addem()">Click here</a>
    <h2>Hello</h2>
  </body>
</html>
```

2. Write a function that will calculate and return the amount that should be paid as a tip for a restaurant bill. The tip will be 20 percent of the total bill.

3. Create a function called *changeColor()* that will be called when the user presses one of two buttons. The first button will contain the text "*Press here for a yellow background*". The second button will contain the text "*Press here for a light green background*". The function will take one parameter, a color. Its function is to change the background color of the current document; for example, bgColor="yellow".

4. Write a function called *isLeapYear()* that will return true if this is a leap year and false if it isn't.

5. Write an anonymous function that will calculate and return the distance you have traveled using the formula, *rate * time*. The function definition will be assigned to a variable. The function will be called using the variable.

6. The following example is written in the C language. It is a very common recursive function call *factorial*. Can you explain how this function works and can you write it in JavaScript?

```
unsigned int factorial(unsigned int n){
   if (n <= 1) {
      return 1;
   } else {
```

```
            return n * factorial(n-1);
        }
    }
```

7. Write a function that returns the total cost of any number of buckets of paint.
   Ask the user how many buckets he or she is going to buy and for the cost of one
   bucket. Ask the user the color of the paint. Calculate and return what he or she
   owes. Change the color of the font to the color of the paint. Use the
   catch/try/throw statements to check for invalid input if the user doesn't give you
   a valid value for the number of buckets, such as a number less than 0, or gives
   you no input, or types in a string, and so on, check that the user doesn't give
   you a color of paint that is the same color as the background of your document
   or you will not be able to see the color of the font.

chapter
8

Objects

8.1 What Are Objects?

JavaScript is all about objects. Windows and buttons, forms and images, links and anchors are all objects. Programming languages like Java, C++, and Python that focus on objects are called object-oriented programming (OOP) languages. JavaScript is called an object-based language because it doesn't technically meet the criteria of the more heavy-duty languages, but it certainly behaves as an object-oriented language. Some people are apprehensive at the thought of tackling this kind of programming, although the mystique is somewhat diminished from what it was back in the last century when the top-down procedural approach to programming was more in vogue. In the real world, you may see a book or a cup or a hat as an object. JavaScript can represent data such as a string or a number as an object, and JavaScript lets you create your own objects. When talking about JavaScript data types in Chapter 3, "The Building Blocks: Data Types, Literals, and Variables," we discussed two types: primitive and composite. Objects are composite types. They provide a way to organize a collection of data into a single unit. Object-oriented languages, such as C++ and Java, bundle up data and behavior and call it an object. So does JavaScript.

When you learn about objects, they are usually compared to real-world things, like a cat, a book, or a triangle. Using the English language to describe an object, the object itself would be like a noun.

Nouns are described with adjectives. A cat might be described as fat, furry, smart, or lazy. The book is old, with 400 pages, and contains poems. The triangle has three sides, three angles, and red lines. The adjectives that collectively describe these objects are called **properties** or **attributes**. The object is made up of a collection of these properties or attributes.

In English, verbs are used to describe what the object can do or what can be done to it. The cat eats, sleeps, and meows. The book is read, its pages can be turned forward and backward, and it can be opened or closed by the reader. The triangle's sides and angles can be increased and decreased, it can be moved, and it can be colored. These verbs are called **methods** in object-oriented languages. JavaScript sees your browser window as an object, a window that can be resized, opened, closed, and so on. It sees all the frames, documents, images, and widgets inside the window as objects. And these objects have properties and methods.

JavaScript supports several types of objects, as follows:

1. User-defined objects defined by the programmer.
2. Core or built-in objects, such as Date, String, and Number (see Chapter 9, "JavaScript Core Objects").
3. Browser objects, the BOM (see Chapter 10, "It's the BOM! Browser Objects").
4. The Document objects, the DOM (see Chapter 15, "The W3C DOM and Java-Script").

This chapter focuses on user-defined objects, objects that you will create and manipulate. Once you understand the syntax and how these objects work, JavaScript's core objects will be much easier to understand and use.

8.1.1   Objects and the Dot Syntax

An object model is a hierarchical tree-like structure used to describe all of the components of an object (see Figure 8.1). For example, in Chapter 1, "Introduction to Java-Script," we discussed the DOM (see more in Chapter 15), a tree-like structure that represents an HTML document and all of its elements, and this tree-like model is also used to represent the browser and its components (BOM; see Chapter 10). JavaScript objects and user-defined objects use this same model. When accessing an object in the tree, the object at the top of the tree is the root or parent of all parents. If there is an object below the parent it is called the child, and if the object is on the same level, it is a sibling. A child can also have children. A dot (.) is used to separate the objects when descending the tree; for example, a parent is separated from its child with a dot. In the following example, the *Object* object is the primitive JavaScript object from which all other objects are derived and the *Object* object has its own properties and methods that all objects will have access to. (We list these properties and methods in Tables 8.1 and 8.2.) The *cat* object and the *dog* object are derived from the *Object* object. To get the cat's name, you would say *cat.name,* and to get the dog's breed you would say *dog.breed.* The *Object* object is not named when going down in the hierarchy.

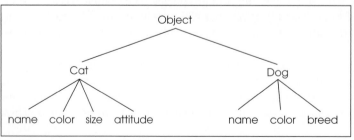

Figure 8.1   A hierarchical tree-like structure used to describe components of an object.

8.1.2 Creating an Object with a Constructor

JavaScript allows you to create an object in a number of ways. One way is with a constructor. A **constructor** is a special kind of function that creates the blueprint for an object. The *new* keyword precedes the name of the constructor that will be used to create the object. By convention, constructor names start with a capital letter to distinguish them from ordinary functions.

```
var myNewObject = new Object(argument, argument, ...)
```

To create the *cat* object, for example, you could say:

```
var cat = new Object();
```

The *new* Operator.   The *new* operator is used to create an instance of an object. To create an object, the *new* operator is followed by the name of a function. The *new* operator treats the function as a constructor. This function may be a JavaScript constructor or one that is user-defined. JavaScript comes with several built-in constructors, such as *Object()*, *Array()*, *Date()*, and *RegExp()*. With them you use the *new* operator followed by the constructor function and any arguments it takes. A reference to the object is returned and assigned to a variable.

```
var car = new Object();
var friends = new Array("Tom", "Dick", "Harry");
var holiday = new Date("July 4, 2011");
var rexp = new RegExp("^[a-zA-Z]");
```

The *Object()* Constructor.   JavaScript provides a special predefined constructor function called *Object()*, used with the *new* keyword, to build a generic object. The return value of the *Object()* constructor is assigned to a variable. The variable contains a reference to an instance of a new object. See Example 8.1. Later we will create a user-defined function that will act as a constructor.

FORMAT

```
var myobj = new Object();
```

EXAMPLE 8.1

```
    <html>
      <head><title>The Object() Constructor</title>
        <script type = "text/javascript">
1           var cat = new Object();
2           alert(cat);
        </script>
      </head>
      <body></body>
    </html>
```

EXPLANATION

1   The *Object()* constructor creates and returns a reference to a *cat* object.

2   The returned value from the *Object()* constructor is a reference to an object, as shown in the Figure 8.2. *[object Object]* means that the cat is a descendant of the *Object* object from which all objects are derived.

Figure 8.2   *cat* is an object.

8.1.3   Properties of the Object

Properties describe the object. The object name is followed by a dot and a property. The properties are accessible only via their object. In Figure 8.3, the top object is the *Object* object. If we create a new *cat* and a *dog* object, as shown in Example 8.2, they are descendants of the *Object* object. Although the *dog* and the *cat* are objects in their own right, they are considered properties of the *Object* object. In fact, any object subordinate to another object is also a property of that object. The *cat* and the *dog* are descendants of the *Object* object. They also have properties that describe them, such as *name*, *color*, *size*, and so forth. The *Object* object is not listed in the hierarchy when using the dot syntax.

To assign properties to the *cat* object, the syntax would be as follows:

```
cat.name = "Sneaky";
cat.color="yellow";
```

In Example 8.2 a new object is created with the *new* keyword and the *Object()* constructor. Properties are assigned to the object and their values retrieved.

EXAMPLE   8.2

```
       <html>
          <head><title>User-defined objects</title>
1            <script type = "text/javascript">
2               var toy = new Object(); // Create an instance of the object
3               toy.name = "Lego";        // Assign properties to the object
                toy.color = "red";
                toy.shape = "rectangle";
4            </script>
          </head>
          <body bgcolor="lightblue">
```

EXAMPLE   8.2 (CONTINUED)

```
5        <script type = "text/javascript">
6           document.write("<b>The toy is  a " + toy.name + ".");
7           document.write("<br />It is a " + toy.color + " "
                           + toy.shape+ ".");
8        </script>
      </body>
   </html>
```

EXPLANATION

1   JavaScript code starts here.

2   The *Object()* constructor is called with the *new* keyword to create an instance of an object called *toy*. A reference to the new object is assigned to the variable, *toy*. (All objects are descendants of the *Object* object.)

3   The *toy* object's *name* property is assigned *"Lego"*. The properties describe the characteristics or attributes of the object. Properties are **not** variables. Do not use the *var* keyword.

4   This is the end of the JavaScript program.

5   A new JavaScript program starts here in the body of the page.

6   The global object called *toy* is available within the script. The value of the *toy* object's *name* property is displayed.

7   The values for the *color* and *shape* properties of the *toy* object are displayed.

8   This is the end of the JavaScript program. The output is shown in Figure 8.3.

```
The toy is a Lego.
It is a red rectangle.
```

Figure 8.3   The *toy* object and its properties.

In JavaScript you might see the syntax:

```
window.document.bgColor = "lightblue";
```

The *window* is the top object in the Browser Object Model. It is the parent of all parents; the *document* is an object but, because it is subordinate to the *window*, it is also a property of the *window* object. Although the background color, *bgColor*, is a property of the document object, by itself it is not an object. (It is like an adjective because it describes the document.)

```
window
   document
      bgColor
```

8.1.4 Methods of the Object

Methods are special functions that object-oriented languages use to describe the object's behavior. Methods are attached to the object with a dot and are only accessible via that object. Methods, like verbs, are action words that perform some operation on the object. The cat purrs and the dog barks. The *cat* object may have a method called *sleep()* or *play()* and the *dog* object may have a method called *sit()* or *stay()*, and both of them could have a method called *eat()*.

The dot syntax is used to call the methods just as it was used to separate objects from their properties. When invoked, a set of parentheses are postfixed to the name of the method. Omitting the parentheses when using a method results in an error.

```
cat.play();
```

Methods, like functions, can take arguments, messages that will be sent to the object:

```
dog.fetch("ball");
```

A JavaScript example:

```
window.close();
document.write("Hello\n");
```

Example 8.3 demonstrates how to create an object and assign properties. But we need to complete the definition of an object by assigning methods to it. Instead of assigning a value such as a string or number to the property of an object, you assign a function to it. Methods let the object do something or let something be done to it. There is little difference between a function (see Chapter 7, "Functions") and a method, except that a function is a stand-alone unit of statements and a method is attached to an object, is accessed only via the object, and can be referenced by the *this* keyword. Like functions, methods also take arguments and can return a value.

EXAMPLE 8.3

```
       <html>
          <head><title>User-defined objects</title>
            <script type= "text/javascript">
1              var toy = new Object();    // Create the object
2              toy.name = "Lego";        // Assign properties to the object
               toy.color = "red";
               toy.shape = "rectangle";
3              toy.display=printObject;  // Function name is assigned as a
                                          // property of the object
4              function printObject(){
                  document.write("<b>The toy is a " + toy.name + ".<br>");
```

EXAMPLE 8.3 (CONTINUED)

```
                document.write("It is a " + toy.color + " " + toy.shape
                                + ".<br />");
           }
        </script>
     </head>
     <body>
        <script type = "text/javascript">
5           toy.display();   //Object method is called
6           toy.color="blue";
7           toy.display();
        </script>
     </body>
   </html>
```

EXPLANATION

1   The *Object()* constructor is called with the *new* keyword to create an instance of a
    new object. A reference to the new object is assigned to the variable, *toy*. We now
    have a *toy* object.

2   The properties describe the characteristics or attributes of the object. Properties
    act as variables for the object, but do not use the *var* keyword. The *toy* object's
    name property is assigned *"Lego"*, its color property is assigned *"red"*, and its
    shape property is assigned *"rectangle"*. The *display* property is assigned the name
    of a function.

3   When the name of a function is assigned to a property, the property will serve as
    a method for the object. The name of a function, *printObject*, is assigned to the
    display property. Lines 5 and 7 demonstrate how to invoke the new method *dis-
    play()*.

4   *printObject()* function is defined. It will be used as a method for the *toy* object,
    allowing the *toy* object to display its properties. Instead of *display*, we could use
    the same name for this property; that is, *toy.printObject = printObject*. By giving the
    property a different name, in this case, *display*, it is clear that the property is being
    assigned a function name and that the object's **method name** is *display*, not *print-
    Object*.

5   The object's *display()* method is called. Its function is to print the *color* and *shape*
    properties of the *toy* object.

6   The global object called *toy* is available within the script. The value of the *toy* ob-
    ject's *color* property is changed.

7   The object's *display()* method is called again showing that the value of the color
    property has been changed to *"blue"*. The result is shown in Figure 8.4.

Figure 8.4 An object and its properties.

8.2 Classes and User-Defined Functions

8.2.1 What Is a Class?

JavaScript ain't got no class! If you are familiar with Java or C++ you may be wondering how to create a class in JavaScript. A class is a template or blueprint that describes the properties and behavior of all objects that belong to that specific class, so you may have a Car class or a House class or a Widget class. A Car class would be defined with the properties and methods for a Car and then you could create as many Car objects as you want using the class as a template. But JavaScript doesn't have classes in the traditional sense. It doesn't have a *class* keyword. We must develop the notion of classes in a different way. A new JavaScript class is defined by creating a simple function. The name of the function will serve as the class name for an object, and the function will define its properties and methods; it serves as a blueprint or prototype of the object. When the function is called with the *new* keyword, it acts as a constructor; that is, it builds the new object and then returns a reference to it. We can say that if you call the *Book()* constructor function, it returns a reference to a new *Book* object, an instance of the Book class.

8.2.2 What Is *this*?

Internally, JavaScript creates an object, and then calls the constructor function. Inside the constructor, the variable *this* is initialized to point to this newly created object. The *this* keyword is a sort of shorthand reference that keeps track of the current object. When a function is used as a constructor, the *this* keyword is used to set the properties for the object that was just created. In this way you can create as many objects as you need and JavaScript *this* will refer to the current object. In Example 8.4, a function is used to create a Book class with two properties, a title and an author. The *this* keyword refers to the current Book object.

   Methods can be assigned to an object in the constructor function so that the method can be applied to multiple instances of an object. In Example 8.5, two methods are created in the Book constructor function called *uppage()* and *backpage()*. Any Book object has access to these methods.

EXAMPLE 8.4

```
<script type="text/javascript">
1    function Book(){   // Create a Book class
2        this.title = "The White Tiger";   // Properties
         this.author = "Aravind Adiga";
     }
3    var bookObj = new Book;  // Create new Book object
     alert(bookObj.title + " by " + bookObj.author);
</script>
```

EXPLANATION

1   The *Book()* function defines a class. When called with the *new* keyword, the function acts as a constructor function.

2   The properties describe the characteristics or attributes of the object. The *this* keyword is a reference to the current object. The title and author are defined for this book object.

3   A new Book object is created and a reference to it assigned to the variable *bookObj*. The *new* keyword, used with the *Book()* function, causes the function to behave as a constructor. You can create as many book objects as you want, but in this example, they would all have the same title and author. See Figure 8.5 for the output.

Figure 8.5   An instance of the Book class.

EXAMPLE 8.5

```
<html>
    <head><title>User-defined objects</title>
        <script type ="text/javascript">
1            function Book(title, author, publisher){   // Receiving
                                                         // parameters
2                this.pagenumber=0;        // Properties
                 this.title = title;
                 this.author = author;
                 this.publisher = publisher;
3                this.uppage = pageForward;    // Create methods
4                this.backpage = pageBackward;
             }
```

Continues

EXAMPLE   8.5 (CONTINUED)

```
5          function pageForward(){      // Functions to be used as methods
               this.pagenumber++;
               return this.pagenumber;
           }
6          function pageBackward(){
               this.pagenumber--;
               return this.pagenumber;
           }
        </script>
     </head>
     <body>
        <script type = "text/javascript">
7          var myBook = new Book("JavaScript by Example",
               "Ellie Quigley", "Prentice Hall" );    // Create new object
8          myBook.pagenumber=5;  //Assign a page number
9          document.write( "<b>"+ myBook.title +
                            "<br>" + myBook.author +
                            "<br>" + myBook.publisher +
                            "<br>Current page is " + myBook.pagenumber );
           document.write("<br>Page forward: " );
10         for(i=0;i<3;i++){
11             document.write("<br />" + myBook.uppage());
               // Move forward a page
           }
           document.write("<br />Page backward: ");
           for(;i>0; i--){
12             document.write("<br />" + myBook.backpage());
               // Move back a page
           }
        </script>
     </body>
   </html>
```

EXPLANATION

1   This is the constructor function that will represent a class called "Book". The function creates the object and assigns it properties and methods. The parameter list contains the values for the properties *title, author*, and *publisher*. Each time this function is called a new Book class is instantiated.

2   The *this* keyword refers to the *Book* object. The *Book* object is given a *pagenumber* property initialized to *0*.

3   A method is defined by assigning the function to a property of the *Book* object. *this.uppage* is assigned the name of the function, *pageForward*, that will serve as the object's method. Note that only the **name of the method** is assigned to a property, i.e., a reference to the function's definition. There are no parentheses following the name. This is important. If you put parentheses here, you will receive an error message. But when the method is called you must use parentheses.

EXPLANATION(CONTINUED)

4   The property *this.backpage* is assigned the name of the function, *pageBackward*, that will serve as the object's method.

5   The function *pageForward()* is defined. Its purpose is to increase the page number of the book by *one*, and return the new page number.

6   The function *pageBackward()* is defined. Its purpose is to decrease the page number by *one* and return the new page number.

7   A new object called *myBook* is created. The *new* operator invokes the *Book()* constructor function with three arguments: the title of the book, the author, and the publisher.

8   The *pagenumber* property is set to *5*.

9   The properties of the object are displayed in the browser window.

10 The *for* loop is entered. It will loop three times.

11 The *uppage()* method is called for the *myBook* object. It will increase the page number by 1 and display the new value, each time through the for loop.

12 The *backpage()* method is called for the *myBook* object. It will decrease the page number by 1 and display the new value each time through the loop. The output is shown in Figure 8.6.

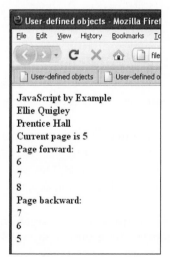

Figure 8.6 An instance of the Book class, its properties, and methods.

8.2.3   Inline Functions as Methods

Rather than naming a function outside the class, an inline or anonymous function can be assigned directly to a property within the constructor function. (Every instance of the class will have a copy of the function code.) In Example 8.6, the *calculate* property is assigned an inline or anonymous function. Because it is part of the definition of the *Distance()* constructor, only objects of the Distance class will have access to the method, thereby encapsulating the method. In previous examples the functions that served as methods were defined outside of the constructor, making available to any class.

EXAMPLE 8.6

```html
<html>
    <head><title>functions</title>
        <script type="text/javascript">
1           function Distance(r, t){ //Constructor function
2               this.rate = r;
                this.time = t;
3               this.calculate=function() { return (this.rate * this.time); }
                // anonymous
            }
        </script>
    </head>
    <body>
        <script type ="text/javascript">
4           var trip1 = new Distance(50, 1.5);
5           var trip2 = new Distance(75, 3.2);
6           alert("trip 1 distance: "+ trip1.calculate());
            alert("trip 2 distance: "+ trip2.calculate());
        </script>
    </body>
</html>
```

EXPLANATION

1 This is the constructor function for the *Distance* class. It takes two parameters, *r* and *t*, and returns a reference to an object.

2 Properties are assigned to the object. The *this* keyword is a reference to the current object.

3 When a function is assigned to a property, it is called a method. This is an inline or anonymous function. It has no name but has been defined and assigned to the object as a method.

4 A new object called *trip1* is created with the *new* constructor. Two arguments are passed, the rate (how fast) and the time (in hours). This is the first instance of the *Distance* class.

5 Another object, *trip2*, is created and sends different argument values.

6 See Figure 8.7. The method called *calculate()* is invoked for each object. The alert box displays the value returned from the *calculate()* method; that is, the distance traveled.

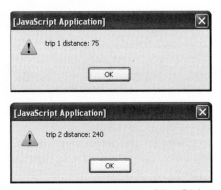

Figure 8.7   Two objects of the Distance class call the *calculate()* method.

8.3   **Object Literals**

Object literals enable you to create objects that support many features without directly invoking a function. When a function acts as constructor you have to keep track of the order of arguments that will be passed, and so on. Not so with object literals. They are similar to hashes in other languages using key/value pairs to represent fields. The fields can be nested. The basic syntax for an object literal is:

1. A colon separates the property name from its value.
2. A comma separates each set of name/value pairs from the next set.
3. The comma should be omitted from the last name/value pair.[1]
   Even with nested key/value pairs, the last key/value pair does not have a comma.
4. The entire object is enclosed in curly braces.

The value assigned to a property can be of any data type, including array literals and object literals (arrays are covered in Chapter 9). Using the *new* operator with the *Object()* constructor or an object literal is both simple and logical, but the biggest shortcoming is that the code is not reusable; that is, you would have to retype the code to use it again within the program, whereas you can use a constructor function to create multiple instances of an object. In Example 8.7, one soldier object is created as an object literal, but we cannot create two soldier objects unless we redefine another entirely new object. (See JSON in Chapter 18, "An Introduction to Ajax (with JSON)," for a good reason to use object literals.)

---

1. Firefox will not complain if the last field is terminated with a comma; Internet Explorer will raise an exception.

FORMAT

```
var object = { property1: value, property2: value };
```

EXAMPLE

```
var area = { length: 15, width: 5 };
```

In the next example, two methods are created for the object literal. Once an object literal has been defined you can later add more properties to it as demonstrated in Example 8.7.

EXAMPLE 8.7

```
      <html>
        <head><title>working with literal objects</title>
          <script type="text/javascript">
1           var soldier = {
2             name: undefined,
3             rank: "captain",
4             picture: "keeweeboy.jpg",
5             fallIn: function() {
                  alert("At attention, arms at the side, head and
                        eyes forward.");
              },
6             fallOut: function() {
                  alert("Drop out of formation, step back, about face!");
              }
            };
          </script>
        </head>
        <body>
          <big>
          <script type="text/javascript">
7           soldier.name="Tina Savage";   // Assign value to object
                                           // property
8           document.write("The soldier's name is ",
                            soldier.name,".<br />");
            document.write(soldier.name+"'s rank is ",
                            soldier.rank+".<br />");
9           document.write("<img src='"+soldier.picture+"'>")
10          soldier.fallIn();   //call object's methods
11          soldier.fallOut();
          </script>
          </big>
        </body>
      </html>
```

EXPLANATION

1 A literal object called *soldier* is defined with properties and methods.

2 The property *name* is separated from its value with a colon. The value is *undefined* at this point.

3 The property is *rank*. Its value is a string, "captain".

4 This property is *picture*; its value is a JPEG file.

5 The property *fallIn* is assigned an anonymous function that will serve as a method for this object.

6 The property *fallOut* is assigned an anonymous function that will server as another method for this object.

7 The object's property *name* is assigned a value, "Tina Savage". It is initially assigned "undefined".

8 In this and the next line the value of the *name* and *rank* properties is printed.

9 A picture of the soldier is assigned to the *img* tag's *src* property and displayed in the document.

10 The method for the object, *fallIn()*, is called. Note that by appending the () operator to the *fallIn* property, the function assigned to it on line 5 is called and executed.

11 The method for the object, *fallOut()*, is called. By appending the () operator to the *fallOut* property, the function assigned to it on line 6 is called and executed. The output is shown in Figure 8.8.

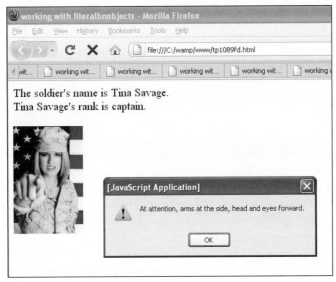

Figure 8.8 A literal object with properties and methods.

EXAMPLE 8.8

```
        <html>
          <head><title>Object Literals</title>
            <script type = "text/javascript">
1             var Car = {  // Create a Car object
2               make:undefined,
                year:2006,
                price:undefined,
3               owner:{
                        name:"Henry Lee",
                        cell_phone: "222-222-2222",
4                       address:{street: "10 Main",
                                  city: "SF",
                                  state: "CA"
                        }
                },
                dealer: "SF Honda",
5               display: function() {details="Make: "+Car.make+"\n";
                                      details += "Year: "+Car.year+"\n";
                                      details += "Price: $"+Car.price+"\n";
                                      details += "Owner: "+
                                                   Car.owner.name+"\n";
                                      alert(details);
                }
            };
          </script>
        </head>
        <body>
          <script type="text/javascript">
6           Car.make="Honda Civic";  // Assign value
7           Car.year=2009;  // Update the year
8           Car.price=30000;
9           Car.display();
          </script>
        </body>
      </html>
```

EXPLANATION

1   An object literal *Car* is created and initialized.

2   The properties for the *Car* object are assigned. Properties are separated from their corresponding values with a colon and each property/value pair is separated by a comma, except the last one. Watch the commas. Internet Explorer is very particular about this rule.

3   The *owner* property contains another set of property/value pairs. The value of the *owner* property is another nested object literal with key/value pairs enclosed in curly braces.

4   The owner has an address field that contains its set of property/value pairs.

5   This property will act as the object's method. It is assigned an inline function defined to display properties of the object.

6   With object literals there is no constructor function. This line assigns a value to an undefined Car property called *make*.

7   This Car's year property is assigned a new value.

8   The Car object's price property, originally undefined, is assigned a value.

9   The Car object's method called *details()* is called to display the properties of the object. Be sure to observe the syntax differences; that is, an equals sign rather than colon between property and value, and an optional semicolon rather than comma at the end of the assignment. The output is shown in Figure 8.9.

Figure 8.9   Nesting property/value pairs in an object literal. Output of Example 8.8 literal objects.

8.4 Manipulating Objects

8.4.1 The *with* Keyword

The *with* keyword is used as a kind of shorthand for referencing an object's properties or methods. The object specified as an argument to *with* becomes the current object for the duration of the block that follows. The properties and methods for the object can be used without naming the object or using the dot syntax. A caveat: This shorthand might save typing, but it will also take a lot longer to run because JavaScript checks each variable within the *with* block to see whether or not it is a property of the object it references.

FORMAT

```
with (object){
   < properties used without the object name and dot>
}
```

EXAMPLE

```
with(employee){
   document.write(name, ssn, address);
}
```

EXAMPLE 8.9

```
      <html>
        <head><title>The with Keyword</title>
          <script type = "text/javascript">
1           function book(title, author, publisher){
2              this.title = title;   // Properties
               this.author = author;
               this.publisher = publisher;
3              this.show = show;   // Define a method
            }
4           function show(){
5              with(this){    // The with keyword with this
6                 var info = "The title is " + title;
                  info += "\nThe author is " + author;
                  info += "\nThe publisher is " + publisher;
7                 alert(info);
               }
            }
          </script>
        </head>
        <body bgcolor="lightblue">
          <script type = "text/javascript">
8           var childbook = new book("A Child's Garden of Verses",
                                      "Robert Lewis Stevenson",
                                      "Little Brown");
9           var adultbook = new book("War and Peace",
                                      "Leo Tolstoy",
                                      "Penguin Books");
10          childbook.show(); // Call method for child's book
11          adultbook.show(); // Call method for adult's book
          </script>
        </body>
      </html>
```

EXPLANATION

1 The *book* constructor function is defined with its properties.

2 The *book* object is described with three properties: *title*, *author*, and *publisher*.

3 The *book* object's property is assigned the name of a function. This property will serve as a method for the object.

4 A function called *show* is defined.

5 The *with* keyword will allow you to reference the properties of the object without using the name of the object and the dot or the *this* keyword. (See "The Math Object" on page 241 in Chapter 9.)

6 A variable called *info* is assigned the property values of a *book* object. The *with* keyword allows you to specify the property name without a reference to the object (and dot) preceding it.

7 The *alert* box displays the properties for a book object.

8 The constructor function is called and returns an instance of a new book object called *childbook*.

9 The constructor function is called and returns an instance of another book object called *adultbook*.

10 The *show()* method is called for the *childbook* object (see Figure 8.10).

11 The *show()* method is called for the *adultbook* object (see Figure 8.11).

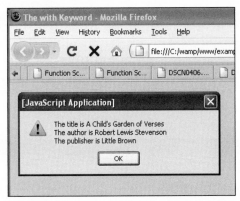

Figure 8.10 The *childbook* object and its properties.

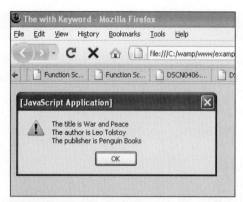

Figure 8.11   The *adultbook* object and its properties.

8.4.2 The *for/in* Loop

JavaScript provides the *for/in* loop, which can be used to iterate through a list of object properties or array elements. The *for/in* loop reads: for each property in an object (or for each element in an array) get the name of each property (element), in turn, and for each of the properties (elements), execute the statements in the block that follows.

The *for/in* loop is a convenient mechanism for looping through the properties of an object.

FORMAT

```
for(var property_name in object){
   statements;
}
```

EXAMPLE 8.10

```
    <html>
      <head><title>User-defined objects</title>
        <script type = "text/javascript">
1           function book(title, author, publisher){
2               this.title = title;
                this.author = author;
                this.publisher = publisher;
3               this.show=show;    // Define a method for the object
            }
```

EXAMPLE 8.10 (CONTINUED)

```
4          function show(obj, name){
           // Function to show the object's properties
           var result = "";
5          for (var prop in obj){
6             result += name + "." + prop + " = " +
                  obj[prop] + "<br />";
           }
7          return result;
        }
     </script>
  </head>
  <body bgcolor="lightblue">
     <script type="text/javascript">
8       myBook = new book("JavaScript by Example", "Ellie",
                          "Prentice Hall");
9       document.write("<br /><b>" + myBook.show(myBook, "myBook"));
     </script>
  </body>
</html>
```

EXPLANATION

1   The function called *book* will define the properties and methods for a *book* object. The function is a template for the new object. An instance of a new *book* object will be created when this constructor is called.

2   This is the first property defined for the *book* object. The *this* keyword refers to the current object.

3   A *show* property of the object is assigned a function name also called *show*, thus creating a method for the object.

4   The function called *show()* is defined, tasked to display all the properties of the object.

5   The special *for/in* loop executes a set of statements for each property of the object.

6   The name and value of each property is concatenated and assigned to a variable called *result*. The value *obj[prop]* is used to key into each of the property values of the *book* object.

7   The value of the variable *result* is sent back to the caller. Each time through the loop, another property and value are displayed.

8   A *new book* object called *myBook* is created (instantiated).

9   The properties for the book object are shown in the browser window; see Figure 8.12. Notice how the method and its definition are displayed.

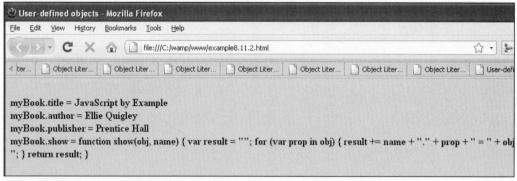

Figure 8.12 The *book* object's properties.

8.5   Extending Objects with Prototypes

In object-oriented languages, like Java and C++, the object, along with its properties (state) and methods (behavior), is bundled up into a container called a class. These programming languages all allow classes to reuse and extend an existing class; that is, inherit commonly used state and behaviors from other classes. A new class, called a subclass, can be derived from an existing class. For example, if you have a Pet class, let's say all pets have an owner, a gender, and some methods for setting and getting the properties. We could create subclasses of the Pet, such as a Dog and Cat, because both the Dog and Cat share the same properties as a Pet. The code for the Pet can be extended to the Dog and the Cat by using inheritance. Then each subclass can be refined further by adding its own specific features.

Let's look at an example of how JavaScript might use inheritance. A constructor function called *divStyle()* has been defined. It will be used to create *div* containers to style a Web page. The constructor defines the properties for a *div*, for example, the borders, padding, background color, and so on, and has a *divGet()* method to display the *div* in the document. Later we want to make *divStyle* objects but change or add properties; perhaps change the width of the border or set a border color. We can reuse or extend the *divStyle* code by using inheritance.

Section 8.2 explained that unlike Java and C++, JavaScript doesn't have a class mechanism per se, but inheritance involves reusing or extending a class. With JavaScript we can simulate a class with a constructor function and the *new* keyword. And to implement inheritance JavaScript extends a the class with a **prototype**. (For those of you who are Java or C++ programmers, JavaScript does not use keywords like *extended, protected, private, public*, etc.). How does prototype inheritance work?

JavaScript functions are automatically given an empty *prototype* object. If the function acts as a constructor function for a class of objects, the prototype object can be used to extend the class. Each object created for the class is also given two properties, a *constructor* property and a *prototype* property. The *constructor* property is a reference to the function that created this object, and the prototype property a reference to its prototype object. This property allows the object to share properties and methods.

Like any other object, you can assign properties and methods to the prototype object. You do this with the prototype property. When values are assigned to an object's prototype property, they are automatically extended to all instances of the class. After an object has been created, new properties and methods can be added to the *prototype* object, and any objects created after that will automatically inherit the new properties and methods. This is how JavaScript implements inheritance. It allows you to reuse code and customize an object.

Let's say we define a constructor function called *Book()* with a set of properties such as *title* and *author*. The *Book()* constructor function is JavaScript's way of creating a class. The constructor function is called with the *new* keyword and creates an instance of the Book class, an object called *book1*, and then the constructor function is called again and creates another Book object called *book2*, and so on. Now, after creating *book1*, we add another property such as *book1.publisher*. This property affects *book1*, and only *book1*. The *publisher* property is not extended to *book2*. The property would have to be added separately to each Book object that needs it or by adding it to the Book's prototype.

Adding a new property without using the prototype property

EXAMPLE 8.11

```
    </html>
       <head><title>Object Properties</title>
1        <script type="text/javascript">
           function Book(title, author){
              this.title =title;
              this.author=author;
           }
         </script>
    </head>
    <body bgColor="#E0FFFF">
       <big>
       <script>
2        var book1 = new Book("Kidnapped","R.L.Stevenson");
         var book2 = new Book("Tale of Two Cities", "Charles Dickens")
3        book1.publisher="Penguin Books";
         document.write(book1.title + " is published by "+
4        book1.publisher + "<br />");
         document.write(book2.title + " is published by " +
5        book2.publisher);   //Doesn't have this property
       </script>
       </big>
    </body>
    </html>
```

EXPLANATION

1   The constructor function called *Book* will define the properties and methods for a *Book* class. The function takes two parameters.

2   Two new Book objects are created, *book1* and *book2*.

Continues

EXPLANATION(CONTINUED)

3   A new property, called *publisher*, is assigned to the *book1* object. It is available for this instance of the object.

4   JavaScript retrieves and displays the value of the publisher for the *book1* object.

5   The second book object does not have access to the *publisher* property. It is *undefined* (see Figure 8.13).

Figure 8.13   Defining a new property for an object.

8.5.1   Adding Properties with the Prototype Property

What if in the previous example *book2* we want to add a *publisher* property so that it is extended to all instances of the Book class? All objects have a prototype property. We can use the Book's *prototype* property to assign new properties to the Book class that will now be available to the Book class and any instances of the class; that is, all Book objects will have the new properties. In Example 8.12, we will add new properties to the Book class.

EXAMPLE 8.12

```
    <html>
      <head><title>Object Properties</title>
        <script type="text/javascript">
1         function Book(title, author){
            this.title =title;
            this.author=author;
          }
        </script>
      </head>
      <body bgColor="#E0FFFF">
        <big>
        <script>
2         var book1 = new Book("Kidnapped","R.L.Stevenson");
          var book2 = new Book("Tale of Two Cities", "Charles Dickens")
3         Book.prototype.publisher = "Penguin Books";
```

```
                document.write(book1.title + " is published by "+
4                   book1.publisher + "<br />");
                document.write(book2.title + " is published by " +
                    book2.publisher);
            </script>
            </big>
        </body>
    </html>
```

EXPLANATION

1   The constructor function called *Book* will define the properties and methods for a *Book* class. The function takes two parameters.

2   Two new Book objects are created, *book1* and *book2*.

3   The Book class has a *prototype* object. It is assigned a property called *publisher*. Now the *publisher* property and its value are available to all Book objects.

4   In the last example only *book1* got the new property. Now both *book1* and *book2* have inherited the *publisher* property found in the Book's prototype (see Figure 8.14). If you don't want all books to be published by "Penguin Books" you could set the value of the publisher to "Unknown" as a default and change it later; for example, *book2.publisher="Viking Press"* and the *book2* object would get the value *"Viking Press."*

Figure 8.14   Using the prototype for inheritance.

8.5.2   The Prototype Lookup Chain

When the program tries to retrieve an object's property, JavaScript first looks to see if the property was defined directly for that object; for example, does the Book object have a *title* property? Does the Book object have a *author* property? If so, JavaScript retrieves the property. If the property has not been defined, then JavaScript looks at the object's **prototype** to see if the property is defined there. If it is not defined there, JavaScript will go up to the parent object. This process of going up the hierarchy, called the prototype lookup chain, can continue until JavaScript reaches the top of the chain. You might recall that the top object is called the *Object* object and it too has a *prototype*.

Example 8.13 uses the prototype for the *Object* object and the prototype for the Book object to create new properties. To retrieve a property for a Book object, JavaScript would look up the property in the following order:

1. The object itself
2. The Book.prototype
3. The Object.prototype

First JavaScript starts with a Book object. If looking for the Book's *title* and *author*, then there is no need to look further; if, on the other hand, we want to get the *publisher* or *category*, then JavaScript will go up the chain and look at the Book's prototype, and finally, if not there, go to the top Object object and look there (see Figure 8.15). If the *Object* object has not defined the property, it is *undefined*. (Much of the information in this paragraph should be credited to a paper on objects written by Mike Koss at *http://mckoss.com/jscript/object.htm.*)

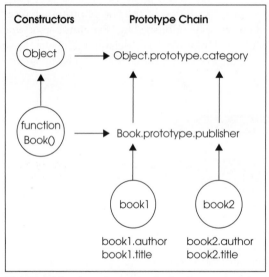

Figure 8.15   JavaScript looks for the property with Example 8.13.

Using The Prototype Property

EXAMPLE 8.13

```
    <html>
      <head><title>Object Properties</title>
      <script type="text/javascript">
1         function Book(title, author){
            this.title =title;
            this.author=author;
          }
      </script>
    </head>
    <body bgColor="#E0FFFF">
      <big>
      <script>
2         var book1 = new Book("Kidnapped","R.L.Stevenson");
          var book2 = new Book("Tale of Two Cities", "Charles Dickens")
3         Object.prototype.category="Fiction";
4         Book.prototype.publisher = "Penguin Books";
          document.write(book1.title + " is published by "+
5            book1.publisher + " and is in the " + book1.category +
             " category <br />");
          document.write(book2.title + " is published by "+
             book2.publisher + " and is in the " + book1.category +
             " category <br />"); </script>
      </script>
      </big>
    </body>
    </html>
```

EXPLANATION

1   The constructor function called *Book* will define the properties and methods for a *Book* class. The function takes two parameters.

2   Two new Book objects are created, *book1* and *book2*.

3   By assigning a property to the *Object* object's prototype, all instances of the Book class (or any class) will have access to the *category* property. Note that on line 5, the book uses the *category* property. (This is just an example to show how the prototype property is used, not meant to be practical.)

4   The Book class has a *prototype* object. It is assigned a property. Now the *publisher* property and its value are available to all Book objects.

5   When JavaScript tries to retrieve the value of the *category* property, the property was not directly assigned in the constructor function. JavaScript checks to see if a Book *prototype* has been defined in the property. It has not. Going up the chain, the next level up is the *Object* object. It does have this *prototype* property. The value is retrieved (see Figure 8.16).

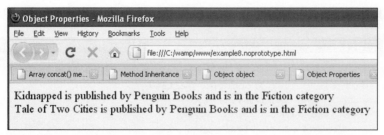

Figure 8.16 Going up the prototype chain.

8.5.3 Adding Methods with Prototype

JavaScript methods are just properties that have been assigned functions for their values. A common use for prototypes is to extend a class by giving it new methods. You can use a prototype to assign methods that are common to all objects in a given class. The benefit of using the prototype is that the method does not have to be created and initialized every time an object is created, and there is no duplication of function code. All objects in the class share the same prototype method.

In Example 8.14, a new method is defined for the Book class to add a tax to the price of each book. All Book objects will have access to this method.

EXAMPLE 8.14

```
        <html>
          <head><title>Method Inheritance</title>
            <script type = "text/javascript">
1             function Book(title, author, price){  // The Book constructor
                  this.title = title;   // Book properties/attributes
                  this.author = author;
                  this.price=price;
2                 this.show=showProps;  // Book method
              }
3             function showProps(){
                  var result = "";
                  for (var i in this){
                      result +=  i + " = " + this[i] + "<br />";
                  }
                  return result;
              }
            </script>
          </head>
          <body>
            <script type="text/javascript">
              // Add a new method with prototype
```

EXAMPLE 8.14

```
4          Book.prototype.addTax=function addTax(){
              this.price *= 1.18;
              return(this.price.toFixed(2));
           }
5          var famousBook=new Book("War and Peace","Leo Tolstoy", 30.00);
           var myBook=new Book("JavaScript by Example", "Ellie
                             Quigley", 25);
6          document.write("<br /><b>" + famousBook.show()+"<br />");
           document.write("<br /><b>" + myBook.show()+"<br />");
7          document.write("With tax \""+ famousBook.title +"\" costs $"+
           famousBook.addTax() +".<br />");
           document.write("With tax \""+ myBook.title + "\" costs $" +
8          myBook.addTax() +".<br />");
        </script>
     </body>
  </html>
```

EXPLANATION

1   The constructor function called *Book* defines the properties and methods for a *Book* class. (*Book* is a JavaScript representation of a class.) The constructor function has a prototype object containing those properties that are inherited by all Book objects.

2   A function called *showProps* is defined on line 3. Its name is assigned to the property called *show*, making it a method for the Book class.

3   The function *showProps* uses the special *for* loop to iterate through all the properties of an object.

4   The Book's *prototype* property is used to add a function called *addTax()*. It calculates and returns the price of the book with an 18 percent sales tax added. This function will be added as a method to the Book class and available to all objects in that class. JavaScript creates only one copy of the function and all book objects will point to that copy.

5   A new *Book* object, called *myBook*, is created. It has inherited all of the original properties of the *Book* class, including the new method defined by the *prototype* property, called *addTax*.

6   The *show()* method is called for the object, *famousBook*. The entire object, properties and methods are displayed. You can see that *addTax* has been included.

7   The new method, *addTax()* is called for the object *famousBook*.

8   Again, *addTax()* is called for the object *myBook*. The result is shown in Figure 8.17.

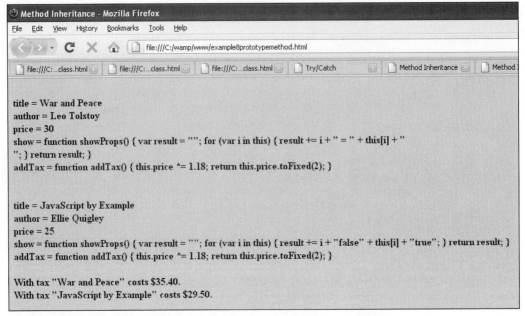

Figure 8.17 Adding a new method with a prototype.

8.5.4 Properties and Methods of All Objects

As we have seen, all user-defined objects and built-in objects are descendants of the object called *Object*. The *Object* object has its own properties and methods that can be accessed by any objects derived from it.

All objects have the properties and methods shown in Tables 8.1 and 8.2.

Table 8.1 Object Properties

Property	What It Provides
constructor	A reference to the function that created the object.
prototype	A reference to the object prototype for the object. This allows the object to share properties and methods.

Table 8.2 Some Object Methods

Method	What It Does
toString()	Returns a string representing a specified object.
valueOf()	Returns a primitive value for a specified object.

Table 8.2   Some Object Methods (continued)

Method	What It Does
hasOwnProperty(property)	Returns true if the specified property belongs to this object, not inherited from its prototype object chain.
isPrototypeOf(object)	Returns true if this object is one of the parent prototype objects of the specified child object.

You can also use the *instanceof* operator to test if the specified object is of the specified object type. If it is, *true* is returned.

FORMAT

```
var isInstance = objectName instanceof objectType;
```

EXAMPLE

```
var str1 = new String("good morning");// Create a new string object
var result = sr1 instanceof String;
if( result == true ){ }
```

EXAMPLE 8.15

```
        <html>
         <head><title>Object object</title>
          <script type="text/javascript">
1         function Book(title, author){
             this.title =title;
             this.author=author;
          }
         </script>
        </head>
        <body bgColor="#E0FFFF">
          <big>
          <script>
2         Book.prototype.publisher="Oxford Press";
3         Object.prototype.category="Fiction";
4         var tale = new Book("Kidnapped","R.L.Stevenson");
5         document.write("The value of Object's category property is "+
                 Object.prototype.category +"<br />");
6         if(tale.constructor == Book){
             document.write("tale is a Book object<br />");
             document.write("The Book's constructor is defined as: "+
7                tale.constructor + "<br />");
          }
```

Continues

EXAMPLE   8.15 (CONTINUED)

```
  8          if(tale.hasOwnProperty("author")){
                document.write("The object has an author property.<br />");
             }
  9          if(Book.prototype.isPrototypeOf(tale)){
                document.write("Book is a prototype of object tale.<br />");
             }
 10          if(tale instanceof Book){
                document.write("tale is an instance of Book.<br />");
             }
 11          if(tale instanceof Object){
                document.write("tale is an instance of Object.<br />");
             }
          </script>
          </big>
        </body>
      </html>
```

EXPLANATION

1   The constructor function called *Book* defines the properties and methods for a *Book* class.

2   The Book class starts with an empty prototype object. Now we assign it a property. The *publisher* property and its value are available to all Book objects.

3   By assigning a property to the *Object* object's prototype, all instances of the Book class (or any class) will have access to the *category* property.

4   A new instance of the Book class is created, a reference to an object called *tale*.

5   The value of the *Object* object's *prototype* property, *category*, is displayed.

6   The *constructor* property is inherited from the *Object* object and can be used with any of its descendants. This line tests if this object has a constructor. It does, so the block is entered.

7   The value assigned to the *constructor* property is the constructor function and the names of all of its arguments and properties.

8   The *hasOwnProperty()* method returns true if the property (its argument) belongs to the object being tested; in this case the object is *tale* and the method is checking to see if the *author* property belongs to it and is not inherited from the prototype chain.

9   Next we test to see if the *tale* object is inheriting from the Book class; that is, Book is a prototype for the *tale* class.

10   The *instanceof* operator returns *true* if the specified object, *tale*, is of the specified object type; that is, *tale* is a Book type.

11   The *instanceof* operator returns *true* if the specified object, *tale*, is of the specified object type; that is, *tale* is also an Object type. The output is shown in Figure 8.18.

The value of Object's category property is Fiction
tale is a Book object
The Book's constructor is defined as: function Book(title, author) { this.title = title; this.author = author; }
The object has an author property.
Book is a prototype of object tale.
tale is an instance of Book.
tale is an instance of Object.

Figure 8.18 Testing objects.

8.5.5 Creating Subclasses and Inheritance

In the previous examples, we used the *prototype* object to extend properties and methods for a given class. In the next chapter you will see how to use prototyping to customize JavaScript's built-in objects such as *Date* and *String*.

Now, to demonstrate how inheritance works, we will define a base class called Pet, which will have its own properties and methods and can create instances via the "new" operator. Then we will use this base class to create two additional subclasses called Cat and Dog. Each of these subclasses (derived classes) will use the prototype property to inherit the properties and methods of the Pet class (see Figure 8.19). Both the Cat and the Dog class will be customized to have their own *speak()* method. Even though the name of the method is the same for both the Cat and Dog class, JavaScript will call the *speak()* method for the object to which it belongs; that is, when the *speak()* method is called for a Cat object, it will return "Meow", and when called for a Dog object, it will say "Woof". See Example 8.15 for the program code.

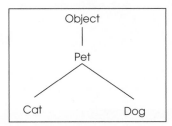

Figure 8.19 A hierarchical tree-like structure used to describe base class and derived classes.

EXAMPLE 8.16

```
      <html>
        <head><title>Creating a subclass</title>
          <script type="text/javascript">
1           function Pet(){    // Base Class
2             var owner = "Mrs. Jones";
              var gender = undefined;
3             this.setOwner = function(who) { owner=who;};
              this.getOwner = function(){ return owner; }
4             this.setGender = function(sex) { gender=sex; }
              this.getGender = function(){ return gender; }
            }
5           function Cat(){}   //subclass constructor
6           Cat.prototype = new Pet();
7           Cat.prototype.constructor=Cat;
8           Cat.prototype.speak=function speak(){
              return("Meow");
            };
9           function Dog(){};   //subclass constructor
10          Dog.prototype= new Pet();
            Dog.prototype.constructor=Dog;
            Dog.prototype.speak = function speak(){
              return("Woof");
            };
          </script>
        </head>
        <body><big>
          <script>
11          var cat = new Cat;
            var dog = new Dog;
12          cat.setOwner("John Doe");
            cat.setGender("Female");
13          dog.setGender("Male");
14          document.write("The cat is a "+ cat.getGender()+ " owned by "
                + cat.getOwner() +" and it says " + cat.speak());
            document.write("<br>The dog is a "+ dog.getGender() + " " +
                " owned by " + dog.getOwner() + " and it says "
                + dog.speak());
          </script>
          </big>
        </body>
      </html>
```

EXPLANATION

1   The constructor function called *Pet* will define the properties and methods for a
    Pet class. The Pet constructor creates a class of Pets and is the base class for the
    Dog and *Cat* classes defined later in the program.

2   Local variables are set for the object. All Pet objects will have an owner and a gen-
    der. The default value for the owner is Mrs. Jones. The gender is *undefined*.

EXPLANATION (CONTINUED)

3   The *setOwner* and *getOwner* methods are defined for the Pet. All Pet objects will have access to these methods.

4   The *setGender* and *getGender* methods are defined for the *Pet*.

5   An empty function called *Cat* is declared. It will be used as the constructor function for a *Cat* class.

6   By creating a new *Pet* object and assigning it to the Cat's *prototype*, all properties and methods of the *Pet* will now be available to the *Cat*. This is how JavaScript implements inheritance.

7   The *constructor* property returns a reference to the function that initialized the object; in this case, the Pet. (The value of this property is a reference to the function itself, not a string containing the function's name). By updating the *constructor* property, it will contain a reference to the new Cat class constructor, not its parent, the Pet. Now the Cat constructor is the constructor for all Cat objects.

8   We are creating a new method for the *Cat*, called *speak*. It will be a property of the Cat's prototype. All cat objects will have access to this method and all cats will speak "Meow".

9   An empty function, called *Dog*, is created.

10   By creating a new *Pet* object and assigning it to the Dog's *prototype*, all properties and methods of the *Pet* will now be available to the *Dog*. The *Dog* inherits from the *Pet*. The *constructor* property is also updated so that it will reference the Dog class. The Dog will also have a *speak()* method. How does JavaScript know which *speak()* method to call? The object that calls this *speak* method has its own copy of it.

11   A new object called *cat* is instantiated. And in the next line, a *dog* object is instantiated. They both inherit from the *Pet* class.

12   The *cat* object calls the *setOwner()* method with a new value. It inherited this method from the *Pet*.

13   The dog calls the *setGender()* method, inherited from the *Pet*.

14   Using the *getOwner()* and *getGender()* and *speak()* methods, we display the properties of the *cat* object and the *dog* object. The output is shown in Figure 8.20.

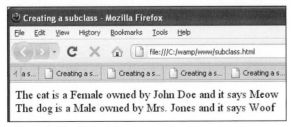

Figure 8.20   Subclasses and their properties.

8.6   What You Should Know

Because JavaScript is based on all kinds of objects such as windows, documents, input devices, buttons, and so on, in this chapter we talked about what objects are and how they are used. The purpose of creating your own objects before talking about JavaScript's core objects and DOM objects is to give you an understanding of the terminology and syntax and how objects relate to each other in an object model. Now you should understand:

1. Why an object is a composite type.
2. Several ways to create an object.
3. How to use an object constructor.
4. The difference between properties and methods.
5. The difference between a method and a function.
6. How a function can act as a constructor.
7. What the *this* keyword is used for.
8. How to create an object literal.
9. How to use the *with* keyword.
10. How to extend an object with its prototype.

Exercises

1. Create a *circle* object with the *Object()* constructor and a method that will calculate its circumference.

2. Write a function that will create a *clock* object.
   a. It will have three properties: *seconds*, *minutes*, and *hours*.
   b. Write two methods: *setTime()* to set the current time and *displayTime()* to display the time.
   c. The user will be prompted to select either a.m./p.m., or military time. The value he or she chooses will be passed as an argument to the *displayTime()* method.

3. The output will be either

   ```
   14:10:26 or 2:10:26 pm
   ```

   depending on what argument was passed to the *display()* method.

4. The following function acts as a constructor to create an Employee object. Use this function to create three new employees. Set the properties and print the employees' names. Add a *phone* property to this function.

   ```
   <script type="text/javascript">
       function Employee(){
           var = name;
           this.getName = function(){
               return this.name;
           }
           this.setName = function(name){
               this.name = name;
           };
       }
   ```

5. Create an object literal called Customer. The Customer will have properties: a name, gender, photo, and occupation. There will be one method called *showCustomer()*. The user will be prompted for each of the property values. Use the *showCustomer()* method to display the data in an HTML table.

6. Using JavaScript prototyping, extend the Employee (Exercise 4). Create two new subclasses from the Employee: a Salesman and a Manager class. Use a prototype to create a salary property for the new employees (*setSalary*, *getSalary*), and a *setRaise()* method to add 15 percent to the salary. Check to see if each of the new Employees is an instance of the Employee class.

chapter

9

JavaScript Core Objects

9.1 What Are Core Objects?

Like an apple, JavaScript has a core, and at its core are objects. Everything you do in JavaScript will be based on objects; you may create your own as we did in Chapter 8, "Objects," or use JavaScript's core objects. Core objects are built right into the language. JavaScript provides built-in objects that deal with the date and time, math, strings, regular expressions, numbers, and other useful entities. The good news is that the core objects are consistent across different implementations and platforms and were standardized by the ECMAScript 1.0 specification, allowing programs to be portable. Although each object has a set of properties and methods that further define it, this book does not detail every one, but highlights those that will be used most often. For a complete list of properties and objects, go to *http://www.echoecho.com/jsquickref.htm*.

9.2 Array Objects

An array is a collection of like values—called **elements**—such as an array of colors, an array of strings, or an array of images. Each element of the array is accessed with an index value enclosed in square brackets (see Figure 9.1). An index is also called a subscript. There are two types of index values: a nonnegative integer and a string. Arrays indexed by numbers are called **numeric arrays** and arrays indexed by strings are called **associative arrays** (see Figure 9.2). In JavaScript, arrays are built-in objects with some added functionality.

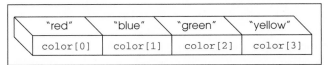

Figure 9.1 A numeric *Array* object called *color*. Index values are numbers.

213

Figure 9.2   An associative *Array* object called *hex*. Index values are strings.

9.2.1   Declaring and Populating Arrays

Like variables, arrays must be declared before they can be used. Let's examine some ways to create an array.

Creating an Array Object with
new. The *new* keyword is used to dynamically create the Array object. It calls the Array object's constructor function, *Array()*, to create a new Array object. The size of the array can be passed as an argument to the constructor, but it is not necessary. Values can also be assigned to the array when it is constructed, called a dense array, but this is not required either. The following array is called *array_name* and its size is not specified.

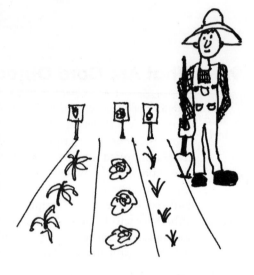

FORMAT

```
var array_name = new Array();
```

Example:
```
var months = new Array();
months[0]="January";
months[1]="February";
months[2]="March"
```

In the next example, the size or length of the array is passed as an argument to the *Array()* constructor. The new array has 100 undefined elements.

```
var array_name = new Array(100);
```

And in the following example, a dense array is given a list of initial values at the same time it is being declared:

```
var weekday = new Array("Sunday", "Monday", "Tuesday");
```

The values can be of any data type or combination of types. Although you can specify the size of the array when declaring it, it is not required. JavaScript allocates memory as needed to allow the array to shrink and grow on demand. To populate the array, each element is assigned a value. Each element is indexed by either a number or string. If the array index is a number, it starts with 0. JavaScript doesn't care what you store in the array. Any combination of types, such as numbers, strings, Booleans, and so forth, are acceptable. Example 9.1 creates a new *Array* object called *book* and assigns strings to each of its elements.

Another popular way to declare an array is with the literal notation. This is a quick and easy way to declare and populate an array in one step:

```
var friends = [ "John", "Jane", "Niveeta", "Su" ];
```

Using the *new* Constructor. To create an *Array* object, call the *Array()* constructor with the *new* keyword and optionally pass information to the constructor if you know the size and/or what elements you want to assign to the array. When a size is supplied but not values, the empty elements will be assigned *undefined*. JavaScript provides a number of methods to manipulate the array (these are listed in the "Array Methods" on page 227).

EXAMPLE 9.1

```
        <html>
          <head><title>The Array Object</title>
            <h2>An Array of Books</h2>
            <script type="text/javascript">
1             var book = new Array(6);    // Create an Array object
2             book[0] = "War and Peace"; // Assign values to its elements
              book[1] = "Huckleberry Finn";
              book[2] = "The Return of the Native";
              book[3] = "A Christmas Carol";
              book[4] = "The Yearling";
              book[5] = "Exodus";
            </script>
          </head>
          <body bgcolor="lavender">
            <big>
            <script type="text/javascript">
3             for(var i in book){
4               document.write("book[" + i + "] "+ book[i]  + "<br />");
              }
            </script>
            </big>
          </body>
        </html>
```

EXPLANATION

1   The variable *book* is assigned a reference to a new *Array* object containing six elements. You can leave out the size 6 and JavaScript will dynamically build the array as you add elements to it.

2   The first element of the *book* array is assigned the string *"War and Peace"*. Array indexes start at zero.

3   The special *for* loop is used to access each of the elements in the *book* array where *i* is a variable used to represent the index value.

4   Each of the elements of the *book* array are displayed in the browser (see Figure 9.3).

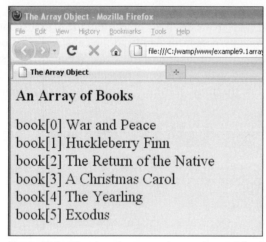

Figure 9.3 The book array elements and their values.

Creating an Array Literal.   The array literal is a quick way to create and populate an array. To use the literal notation (array), the array is given a name and assigned a list of elements. The elements are separated by commas and enclosed between a set of square brackets.

```
var myarray=["Joe", "Bob", "Ken"]
```

Once declared, a literal array behaves like a normal array using index values starting at 0, and so on. Current best-practice tells us that the literal way of creating an array is preferred to using the *new* keyword.

Can you see the difference between the following array declarations?

```
var array1 = new Array(10);
var array2 = [ 10 ];
```

The first array is specified to be a 10-element array. The second array is initialized with the value of the first element being the number 10.

EXAMPLE 9.2

```html
<html>
    <head><title>The Literal Way</title>
        <h2>An Array of Pets</h2>
        <script type="text/javascript">
1            var pet = [ "Fido", "Slinky", "Tweetie","Wanda" ];
        </script>
    </head>
    <body bgcolor="lavender">
        <font size="+2">
        <script type="text/javascript">
2        for(var i in pet){
3            document.write("pet[" + i + "] "+ pet[i]  + "<br />");
            }
        </script>
        </font>
    </body>
</html>
```

EXPLANATION

1   The variable *pet* is assigned a list enclosed in square brackets. This is called an array literal.

2   The special *for* loop is used to access each of the elements in the *pet* array where this example represents the index value, whether a number or a string.

3   Each of the elements of the *pet* array is displayed in the browser (see Figure 9.4).

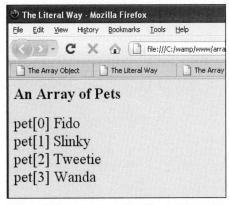

Figure 9.4 An array literal and its output.

Populating an Array with a *for* Loop.   Populating an array is the process of assigning values to it. In Example 9.3, the *for* loop is used to fill an array. The initial value of the index starts at zero; the looping will continue as long as the value of the index is less than the final size of the array.

EXAMPLE   9.3

```
    <html>
      <head><title>The Array Object</title></head>
      <body>
        <h2>An Array of Numbers</h2>
        <script type="text/javascript">
1         var years = new Array(10);
2         for(var i=0; i < years.length; i++ ){
3             years[i]=i + 2000;
4             document.write("years[" + i + "] = "+ years[i]
                           + "<br />");
          }
        </script>
      </body>
    </html>
```

EXPLANATION

1   The *Array()* constructor is called to create a 10-element array called *years*.

2   The *for* loop starts with an initial value of *i* set to 0, which will be the value of the first index in the array. As long as the value of *i* is less than the length of the array, the body of the loop will be executed. Each time through the loop, *i* is incremented by 1.

3   The array is populated here. Each time through the loop, *years[i]* is assigned the value of *i + 2000*.

4   The value of the new array element is displayed for each iteration of the loop (see Figure 9.5).

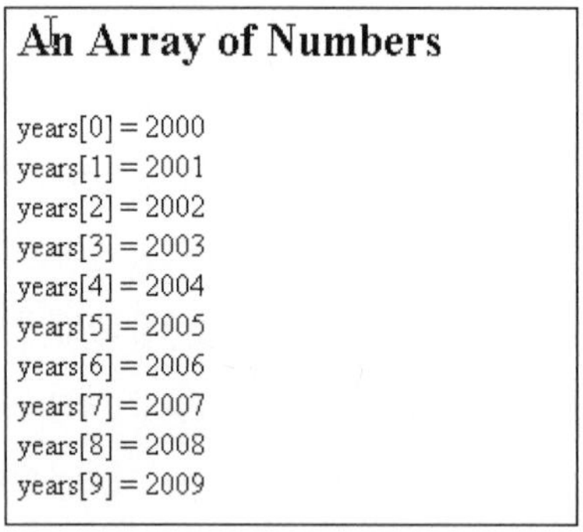

An Array of Numbers

years[0] = 2000
years[1] = 2001
years[2] = 2002
years[3] = 2003
years[4] = 2004
years[5] = 2005
years[6] = 2006
years[7] = 2007
years[8] = 2008
years[9] = 2009

Figure 9.5   A *for* loop is used to populate an array: Output from Example 9.3.

Creating and Populating an Array in One Step.   When creating an array, you can populate (assign elements to) it at the same time by passing the value of the elements as arguments to the *Array()* constructor. Later on, you can add or delete elements as you wish. See Example 9.4.

EXAMPLE 9.4

```
<html>
  <head><title>The Array Object</title></head>
  <body>
    <h2>An Array of Colored Strings</h2>
    <script type="text/javascript">
1      var colors = new Array("red", "green", "blue", "purple");
2      for(var i in colors){
3        document.write("<font color='"+colors[i]+"'>");
4        document.write("colors[" + i + "] = "+ colors[i]
                      + "<br />");
      }
    </script>
  </body>
</html>
```

EXPLANATION

1   A new array called *colors* is created and assigned four colors.

2   The special *for* loop iterates through each element of the colors array, using *i* as the index into the array.

3   The color of the font is assigned the value of the array element.

4   The value of each element of the colors array is displayed. The color of the font matches the value (see Figure 9.6). Make sure the background color is not the same color as the font or you won't be able to see the font.

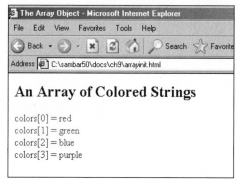

Figure 9.6   Each string is a different font color: Output from Example 9.4.

9.2.2 *Array* Object Properties

The *Array* object only has three properties, *constructor*, *length*, and *prototype* (see Table 9.1). In Chapter 8, we talked about the *constructor* property and the *prototype* property. The value of the *constructor* property is the name of the constructor function that created the object. The *prototype* property allows you to customize objects. All objects have this property, which allows you to add new properties and methods.

The property most used with arrays is the *length* property, which determines the number of elements in the array, that is, the size of the array. You can also use this property to set the size of an array; for example, if you set the length to 0, all elements of the array will be removed.

Table 9.1 Array Properties

Property	What It Does
constructor	References the object's constructor.
length	Returns the number of elements in the array.
prototype	Extends the definition of the array by adding properties and methods.

EXAMPLE 9.5

```
    <html>
       <head><title>Array Properties</title>
          <h2>Array Properties</h2>
          <script type="text/javascript">
1          var book = new Array();   // Create an Array object
           book[0] = "War and Peace"; // Assign values to elements
           book[1] = "Huckleberry Finn";
           book[2] = "The Return of the Native";
           book[3] = "A Christmas Carol";
           book[4] = "The Yearling";
           book[5] = "Exodus";
          </script>
       </head>
       <body bgcolor="lightblue">
          <big>
          <script type="text/javascript">
2          document.write("The book array has "  + book.length +
                           " elements<br />");
           document.write("The book's constructor is: "+
3                          book.constructor + "<br />");
4          book.length=0;
           document.write("The book has been trashed! The first book is"+
5                          book[0] );
6          document.write("<br />The size is now "+ book.length);
          </script>
          </big>
       </body>
    </html>
```

EXPLANATION

1   An *Array* object is declared.

2   The *length* property is used to get the length of the array. The length is 6.

3   The *book* is an *Array* object created by the *Array()* constructor. The *constructor* property shows that this is native (primitive) code and the name of the constructor function is *Array()*.

4   The *book* array object is set to a length of 0, meaning all elements with an index of 0 or more will be removed from the array, leaving an empty array. If you set the length to 2, all values with index value of 2 or more will be removed.

5   The value is *undefined*. It was removed by setting the length of the array to 0.

6   All the elements of the array have been removed; its length is now 0. Figure 9.7 shows the output.

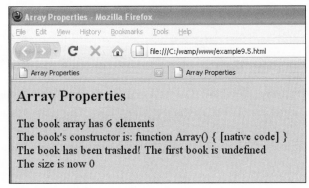

Figure 9.7   Array properties.

9.2.3   Associative Arrays

JavaScript allows use of a string value as an index of an array. An array that uses a string as an index value instead of a number is called an associative array. There is an association between the index and the value stored at that location. The index is often called a **key** and the value assigned to it, the **value**. Key/value pairs are a common way of storing and accessing data. In the following array called *states*, there is an association between the value of the index, the abbreviation for a state (e.g., *"CA"*), and the value stored there—the name of the state (e.g., *"California"*). The special *for* loop can also be used to iterate through the elements of an associative array. We will see many examples throughout the rest of the text where associative arrays are used.[1]

---

1. This type of array has nothing to do with the built-in Array object. Saying object["property"] is just another way of saying object.property. It's another way of representing an object's property. This means that the Array object's *length* property is not used with associative arrays, nor do the *Array* methods apply, which are covered later in this chapter.

EXAMPLE   9.6

```
    <html>
      <head><title>Associative Arrays</title></head>
      <body>
        <h2>An Array Indexed by Strings</h2>
1       <script type="text/javascript">
2         var states = new Array();
3         states["CA"] = "California";
          states["ME"] = "Maine";
          states["MT"] = "Montana";
4         for( var i in states ){
            document.write("The index is:<em> "+ i );
            document.write(".</em> The value is: <em>" + states[i]
                          + ".</em><br />");
          }
        </script>
      </body>
    </html>
```

EXPLANATION

1   The JavaScript program starts here.

2   The *Array()* constructor is called and returns a new *Array* object called *states*.

3   The index into the array element is a string of text, "CA". The value assigned is "*California*". Now there is an association between the index and the value.

4   The special *for* loop is used to iterate through the *Array* object. The variable, *i*, represents the index value of the array, and *states[i]* represents the value found there. It reads: For each index value in the array called *states*, get the value associated with it (see Figure 9.8).

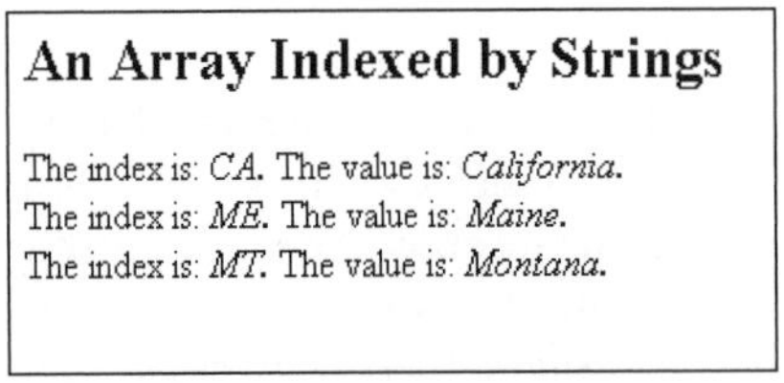

An Array Indexed by Strings

The index is: *CA*. The value is: *California*.
The index is: *ME*. The value is: *Maine*.
The index is: *MT*. The value is: *Montana*.

Figure 9.8   An associative array.

Bracket vs. Dot Notation.   This is an important note: any object, not just the *Array* object, can use the square bracket notation to reference it's properties. The following two expressions are interchangeable:

```
cat.color = "black";
cat["color"] = "black";
```

The bracket notation allows you to use either a string or variable as the index value, whereas the dot notation requires the literal name of the property.

```
      <script type="text/javascript">
1         cat = new Object();
2         c = "color"
3         cat["name"] = "Powder"; // same as cat.name = "Powder"
4         cat[c] = "gray"; // same as cat.color = "gray";
5         document.write(cat.name + " is " + cat.color + "<br />");
          document.write(cat["name"] + " is " + cat[c] + "<br />");
      </script>
```

EXPLANATION

1   A new *cat* object is instantiated.

2   The variable *c* is assigned the string "color".

3   The square brackets contain an index value that also represents a property for the object. We could have written this as cat.name = "Powder".

4   The variable *c* is used as the index value within the square brackets. Using this notation would allow you to easily change the value of the variable, thereby changing the property of the object.

5   A property of the *cat* object can be accessed directly with the dot notation, or represented with a string or variable within the square brackets (see Figure 9.9).

Figure 9.9   Properties of the *cat* object accessed with bracket or dot notation.

9.2.4 Nested Arrays

An array can consist of another set of arrays. Take, for example, a row of seats in a movie theater. One row of seats would represent a one-dimensional array, but the theater has more than one row. To get to your seat you need to not only know what row, but the number of the seat as well.

To create a two-dimensional array, each row is a new array. To find an element in the array we will use two index values, one for the row and one for the column; for example, *array_name[0][0]* represents the first element in the first row. The array in Figure 9.10 consists of three rows and three columns:

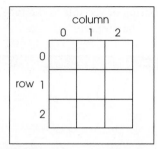

Figure 9.10   An array of three arrays.

Using the *Array* constructor, the following example is an array consisting of three arrays.

```
var array_name=new Array(new Array(77,88,99),
                         new Array(50,60,99),
                         new Array(99,88,78)
                         );
```

or the literal and easier way:

```
var array_name= [ [77,88,99],
                  [50,60,99],
                  [99,88,78]
                ];
```

The first row is *array_name[0]*, the first element in the first row is *array_name[0][0]*, and the last element is *array_name[2][2]*. (JavaScript will not complain if the number of elements in each of the nested arrays varies.)

EXAMPLE 9.8

```
     <html>
        <head><title>Two-dimensional array</title></head>
        <body>
           <table border="2" bordercolor="blue">
              <caption>Grade Sheet</caption>
              <tr>
              <script type="text/javascript">
 1               var grades= [ [77,88,99,75],
                               [50,60,99,89],
                               [99,88,78,92]
                             ];

                 // alert(grades.length);   Output is 3
                 // alert(grades);     Output is 77,88,99,75,50,60,99,89,
                 //                             99,88,78,92
```

EXAMPLE 9.8 (CONTINUED)

```
2            for (var i=0; i < grades.length; i++) {
3            for (var j=0; j < grades[i].length; j++) {
                 document.write(
4                    "<td bgcolor='#fff00'>"+grades[i][j] + "</td>");
                 }
5                document.write("</tr>");
             }
         </script>
     </table>
   </body>
</html>
```

EXPLANATION

1   A two-dimensional array (array of arrays) is created using the literal notation. The outer set of square brackets surrounds the set of rows nested within them. Each nested row is enclosed in its own set of square brackets and each row separates with a comma (see Figure 9.11).

2   This outer *for* loop will cycle through each row. The length property determines the size of the row, which is 3.

3   The nested *for* loop is used to cycle through each of the elements in a row.

4   The two index values represent the rows, *i*, and its element, *j*, respectively.

5   The </tr> tag closes the table row.

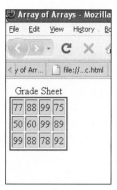

Figure 9.11   Two-dimensional array.

A Key in an Associative Array with More Than One Value.   It is possible that the key of an associative array is associated with more than one value. To accomplish this, rather than a single value, a new array object is assigned as a set of values, as shown in Example 9.9.

EXAMPLE 9.9

```
      <html>
        <head><title>Associative Array</title></head>
        <body>
          <p style="font-size:150%">
          <script type="text/javascript">
1           var student=new Array();
2           student["Name"]="John Doe"; //one key, one value
3           student["Courses"]=new Array("Math","English", "PE");
4           student["Phones"]=new Array("415-333-1234","530-345-5432");

5           document.write("The student's name is " + student["Name"] +
                           ".<br />");
6           document.write("His courses are " + student["Courses"] +
                           ".<br />");
7           document.write("His favorite course is "+
                           student["Courses"][2] + ".<br />");
8           document.write("His cell phone number is " +
                           student["Phones"][0] + ".<br />");

          </script>
          </p>
        </body>
      </html>
```

EXPLANATION

1 A new array object called *student* is instantiated.

2 An index or key in the *student* array is a string of text, *"Name"* assigned a single value, *"John Doe"*. Now there is an association between the index and the value.

3 The index key is *"Courses"*. The student takes more than one course. A new Array is created with the values of the courses assigned to the key, an array with a nested array.

4 The index key is *"Phones"*. The student has two phones. A new Array is created with two phone numbers assigned to the key, an array with a nested array.

5 To get the name of the student, the *"Name"* is used as an index, also called the key.

6 To get a list of all the courses, the key/index in the array is *"Courses"*.

7 To get one of the courses out of the list, two index values are needed, one to key into the courses and one to select a specific course. Because array index values start at 0, student *["Courses"][2]* gets the third course, *"PE"*.

8 Again two index values are need to get one of the phone numbers. *student["Phones"][0]* gets the value of the first phone. The output is shown in Figure 9.12.

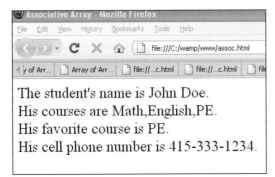

Figure 9.12 An associative array—one key associated with more than one value.

9.3 Array Methods

Because an array is an object in JavaScript, it has properties to describe it and methods to manipulate it. The *length* property of an array was used in previous examples to determine the size of an array. Now we will look at methods that allow you to manipulate arrays such as adding a new element at the beginning or end of an array, removing an element from the end of an array, reversing an array, and so on. JavaScript provides a whole set of methods for doing all of these things and more (see Table 9.2).

Table 9.2 Array Methods

Method	What It Does
concat()	Concatenates elements from one array to another array.
join()	Joins the elements of an array by a separator to form a string.
pop()	Removes and returns the last element of an array.
push()	Adds elements to the end of an array.
reverse()	Reverses the order of the elements in an array.
shift()	Removes and returns the first element of an array.
slice()	Creates a new array from elements of an existing array.
sort()	Sorts an array alphabetically or numerically.
splice()	Removes and/or replaces elements of an array.
toLocaleString()	Returns a string representation of the array in local format.
toString()	Returns a string representation of the array.
unshift()	Adds elements to the beginning of an array.

The *concat()* Method.   The *concat()* method concatenates the elements passed as arguments onto an existing array (JavaScript 1.2), returning a new concatenated list. The method does not change the existing array in place. You must assign results to either an existing array or a new one.

FORMAT

```
newArray=oldArray.concat(new elements);
```

EXAMPLE

```
names = names.concat("green, "blue");
```

EXAMPLE 9.10

```
    <html>
      <head>
        <title>Array concat() methods</title>
      </head>
      <body>
        <script type="text/javascript">
1           var names1=new Array("Dan", "Liz", "Jody" );
2           var names2=new Array("Tom", "Suzanne");
            document.write("<b>First array: "+ names1 + "<br />");
            document.write("<b>Second array: "+ names2 + "<br />");
            document.write("<b>After the concatenation <br />");
3           names1 = names1.concat( names2);
            document.write(names1);
        </script>
      </body>
    </html>
```

EXPLANATION

1   The first *Array* object, called *names1*, is created.

2   The second *Array* object, called *names2*, is created.

3   After concatenating the *names2* array to *names1*, the result is returned written to *names1* (see Figure 9.13). Without assigning the return value to *names1*, *names1* will not be changed. You can return the results to a completely different array. The *concat()* method allows the elements of one array to be added to another.

```
First array: Dan,Liz,Jody
Second array: Tom,Suzanne
After the concatenation
Dan,Liz,Jody,Tom,Suzanne
```

Figure 9.13   The Array *concat()* method before and after.

The *pop()* Method. The *pop()* method deletes the last element of an array and returns the value popped off.

FORMAT

```
var return_value=Arrayname.pop();
```

EXAMPLE

```
var popped = myArray.pop();
```

EXAMPLE 9.11

```
   <html>
      <head><title>Array pop() method</title></head>
      <body>
         <script type="text/javascript">
1           var names=new Array("Tom", "Dan", "Liz", "Jody");
2           document.write("<b>Original array: "+ names +"<br />");
3           var newstring=names.pop();   // Pop off last element of array
4           document.write("Element popped: "+ newstring);
5           document.write("<br />New array: "+ names + "</b>");
         </script>
      </body>
   </html>
```

EXPLANATION

1 The *Array()* constructor creates a new array called *names* and initializes the array with four values: *"Tom"*, *"Dan"*, *"Liz"*, and *"Jody"*.

2 The contents of the array called *names* is displayed.

3 The last element of the array is removed. The value removed is returned and assigned to the variable called *newstring*.

4 The popped value is displayed.

5 The shortened array is displayed (see Figure 9.14).

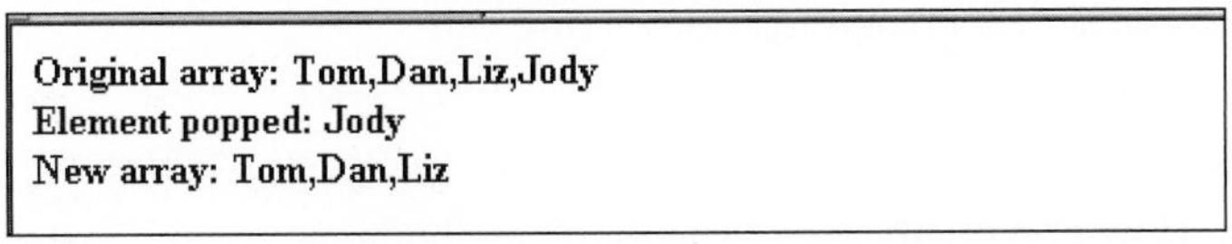

```
Original array: Tom,Dan,Liz,Jody
Element popped: Jody
New array: Tom,Dan,Liz
```

Figure 9.14 The Array *pop()* method.

The *push()* Method. The *push()* method adds new elements onto the end of an array, thereby increasing the length of the array. JavaScript allocates new memory as needed.

FORMAT

```
Arrayname.push(new elements);   // Appended to the array
```

EXAMPLE

```
myArray.push("red", "green", "yellow");
```

EXAMPLE 9.12

```
<html>
   <head><title>Array push() method</title></head>
   <body>
      <script type="text/javascript">
1         var names=new Array("Tom", "Dan", "Liz", "Jody");
2         document.write("<b>Original array: "+ names + "<br />");
3         names.push("Daniel","Christian");
4         document.write("New array: "+ names + "</b>");
      </script>
   </body>
</html>
```

EXPLANATION

1   An *Array* object called *names* is declared and initialized.

2   The contents of the array (i.e., all of its elements) are displayed.

3   The *push()* method appends two new elements, *"Daniel"* and *"Christian"*, to the end of the *names* array.

4   The array has grown. It is displayed in the browser window with its new elements (see Figure 9.15).

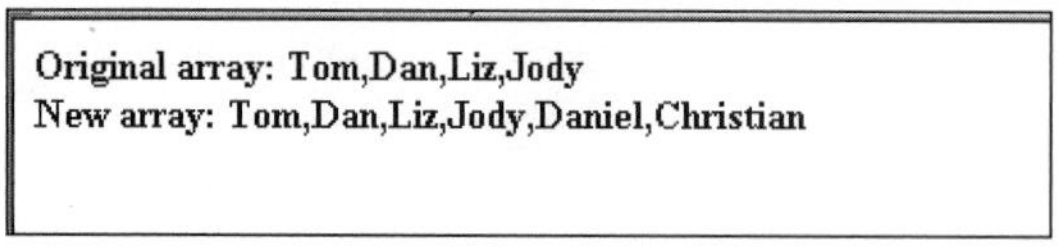

```
Original array: Tom,Dan,Liz,Jody
New array: Tom,Dan,Liz,Jody,Daniel,Christian
```

Figure 9.15   The Array *push()* method before and after.

The *shift()* and *unshift()* Methods.   The *shift()* method removes the first element of an array and returns the value shifted off; the *unshift()* method adds elements to the beginning of the array. These methods are just like *pop()* and *push()* except that they manipulate the beginning of the array instead of the end of it.

FORMAT

```
var return_value=Arrayname.shift();
Arrayname.shift( new elements);    // Prepended to the array
```

EXAMPLE

```
var shifted_off = myArray.shift();
myArray.shift("blue","yellow");
```

EXAMPLE 9.13

```
<html>
   <head><title>Array shift() and unshift() methods</title></head>
   <body>
      <script type="text/javascript">
1        var names=new Array("Dan", "Liz", "Jody" );
         document.write("<b>Original array: "+ names + "<br />");
2        names.shift();
         document.write("New array after the shift: " + names);
3        names.unshift("Nicky","Lucy");
         // Add new elements to the beginning of the array
         document.write("<br />New array after the unshift: " + names);
      </script>
   </body>
</html>
```

EXPLANATION

1   A new *Array* object called *names* is created.

2   The first element of the array is shifted off, shortening the array by 1.

3   The *unshift()* method will prepend to the beginning of the array the names *"Nicky"* and *"Lucy"*, thereby making it longer by two elements (see Figure 9.16).

```
Original array: Dan,Liz,Jody
New array after the shift: Liz,Jody
New array after the unshift: Nicky,Lucy,Liz,Jody
```

Figure 9.16   The Array *shift()* and *unshift()* methods.

The *slice()* Method.   The *slice()* method copies elements of one array into a new array. The *slice()* method takes two arguments: The first is the starting element in a range of elements that will be copied, and the second is the last element in the range, but this element is not included in what is copied. Remember that the index starts at zero, so that a beginning position of 2 is really element 3. The original array is unaffected unless you assign the result of the slice back to the original array.

FORMAT

```
var newArray = Arrayname.slice(first element, last element);
```

EXAMPLE

```
var ArraySlice = myArray.slice(2,6);    // ArraySlice contains elements
                                        // 2 through 5 of myArray.
```

EXAMPLE 9.14

```
<html>
  <head><title>Array slice() method</title></head>
  <body>
    <script type="text/javascript">
1       var names=new Array("Dan", "Liz", "Jody", "Christian",
                            "William");
        document.write("<b>Original array: "+ names + "<br />");
2       var sliceArray=names.slice(2, 4);
        document.write("New array after the slice: ");
3       document.write(sliceArray);
    </script>
  </body>
</html>
```

EXPLANATION

1　This is the original array of names.

2　The *slice()* method will start at position 2, copy *Jody* into the new array, then *Christian*, and stop just before position 4, *William*. The original array is not affected by the slice.

3　The new array created by the *slice()* method is displayed (see Figure 9.17).

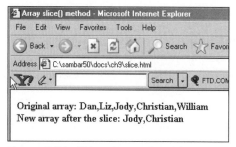

Figure 9.17　Using Array *slice()* to copy elements of an array.

The *splice()* Method.　The *splice()* method removes a specified number of elements from some starting position in an array and allows you to replace those items with new ones. (Don't confuse this method with the *slice()* method. The *slice()* method copies elements, the *splice()* method removes and/or replaces elements. Ropes, tapes, and films are spliced; bread, meat, and golf balls are sliced.)

FORMAT

```
Arrayname.splice(index position, number of elements to remove);
Arrayname.splice(index position, number of elements to remove,
                 replacement elements);
```

EXAMPLE

```
myArray.splice(3, 2);
myArray.splice(3, 2, "apples","oranges");
```

EXAMPLE 9.15

```
    <html>
      <head><title>Array splice() method</title></head>
      <body>
        <script type="text/javascript">
          // splice(starting_pos, number_to_delete, new_values)
1         var names=new Array("Tom","Dan", "Liz", "Jody");
          document.write("<b>Original array: "+ names + "<br />");
2         names.splice(1, 2, "Peter","Paul","Mary");
3         document.write("New array: "+ names + "</b>");
        </script>
      </body>
    </html>
```

EXPLANATION

1   An *Array* object called *names* is declared and initialized.

2   The *splice()* method allows you to delete elements from an array and optionally replace the deleted elements with new values. The first arguments to the splice method are *1, 2*. This means: start at element 1, and remove a length of 2 elements. In this example, element 1 starts with *"Dan"* (element 0 is *"Tom"*). *"Liz"* is the second element. Both *"Dan"* and *"Liz"* are removed. The next three arguments, *"Peter"*, *"Paul"*, and *"Mary"*, are then inserted into the array, replacing *"Dan"* and *"Liz"*.

3   The new *names* array is displayed in the browser window (see Figure 9.18).

```
Original array: Tom,Dan,Liz,Jody
New array: Tom,Peter,Paul,Mary,Jody
```

Figure 9.18   The *splice()* method to delete and insert elements of an array.

9.4 The *Date* Object

JavaScript provides the *Date* object for manipulating date and time.[2] Like the *String* and *Array* objects, you can create as many instances as you like.

As we'll see, the *Date* object provides a number of methods for getting or setting specific information about the date and time. The date is based on the UNIX date starting at January 1, 1970 (in Greenwich Mean Time[3] [GMT]), and doesn't support dates before that time. Figure 9.19 gives you an idea of the difference between GMT and local time. Time is measured in milliseconds (one millisecond is one thousandth of a second). Because client-side JavaScript programs run on a browser, the *Date* object returns times and dates that are local to the browser, not the server. Of course, if the computer is not set to the correct time, then the *Date* object won't produce the expected results. Figure 9.20 shows a typical date and time control panel.

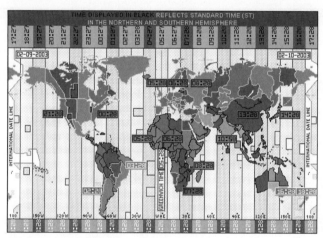

Figure 9.19   24-hour world time zones map with current time. Courtesy of *http://www.worldtimezone.com/index24.html.*

---

2. For more information about the time and date, see *http://www.timeanddate.com/worldclock/.*

3. Greenwich Mean Time (GMT) is now called Universal Coordinate Time (UTC). The current time in Greenwich, England is five hours + New York's present time, or eight hours + San Francisco's present time.

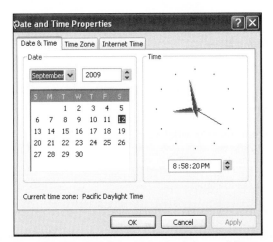

Figure 9.20   The computer's date and time settings.

If no arguments are passed to the *Date* object constructor, it returns the local date and time (based on the accuracy of the clock on your client machine). There are five formats that can be passed as arguments when creating a *Date* object; shown in Example 9.16.

EXAMPLE   9.16

```
new Date("Month dd, yyyy hh:mm:ss")
new Date("Month dd, yyyy")
new Date(yy,mm,dd,hh,mm,ss)
new Date(yy,mm,dd)
new Date(milliseconds)
```

Here are a few examples of instantiating a date:

```
mydate = new Date()
mydate = new Date("March 15, 2010 09:25:00")
mydate = new Date("March 15, 2010")
mydate = new Date(10,2,15)
mydate = new Date(10,2,15,9,25,0)
mydate = new Date(500);
```

9.4.1   Using the *Date* Object Methods

The *Date* object comes with a large number of methods (see Table 9.3) and only a *prototype* property. For browser versions supporting *Date* methods, see *http://www.w3schools.com/js/js_datetime.asp*.

Table 9.3   *Date* Object Methods

Method	What It Does
getDate	Returns the day of the month (1–31)
getDay	Returns the day of the week (0–6); 0 is Sunday, 1 is Monday, and so on
getFullYear	Returns the year with four digits
getHours	Returns the hour (0–23)
getMilliseconds	Returns the millisecond
getMinutes	Returns hours since midnight (0–23)
getMonth	Returns number of month (0–11); 0 is January, 1 is February, and so on
getSeconds	Returns the second (0–59)
getTime	Returns number of milliseconds since January 1, 1970
getTimeZoneOffset	Returns the difference in minutes between current time on local computer and UTC
getUTCDate()	Returns the day of the month
getUTCDay()	Returns the day of the week converted to universal time
get UTCFullYear()	Returns the year in four digits converted to universal time
getUTCHours()	Returns the hour converted to universal time
getUTCMilliseconds()	Returns the millisecond converted to universal time
parse()	Converts the passed-in string date to milliseconds since January 1, 1970
setDate(value)	Sets day of the month (1–31)
setFullYear()	Sets the year as a four-digit number*
setHours()	Sets the hour within the day (0–23)
setHours(hr,min,sec,msec)	Sets hour in local or UTC time
setMilliseconds	Sets the millisecond*
setMinutes(min,sec, msec)	Sets minute in local time or UTC
setMonth(month,date)	Sets month in local time
setSeconds()	Sets the second

Table 9.3   *Date* Object Methods (continued)

Method	What It Does
setTime()	Sets time from January 1, 1970, in milliseconds
setUTCdate()	Sets the day of the month in universal time
setUTCFullYear()	Sets the year as a four-digit number in universal time
setUTCHours()	Sets the hour in universal time
setUTCMilliseconds()	Sets the millisecond in universal time
setUTCMinutes()	Sets the minute in universal time
setUTCMonth()	Sets the month in universal time
setUTCSeconds()	Sets the second in universal time
setYear()	Sets the number of years since 1900 (00–99)
toGMTString()	Returns the date string in universal format
toLocaleString	Returns the string representing date and time based on locale of computer as 10/09/99 12:43:22
toSource()	Returns the source of the *Date* object
toString()	Returns string representing date and time
toUTCString()	Returns string representing date and time as 10/09/99 12:43:22 in universal time
UTC()	Converts comma-delimited values to milliseconds
valueOf()	Returns the equivalence of the *Date* object in milliseconds

EXAMPLE   9.17

```
    <html>
      <head><title>Time and Date</title></head>
      <body bgcolor="aqua"><h2>Date and Time</h2>
        <big>
        <script type="text/javascript">
1         var now = new Date();  // Now is an instance of a Date object
          document.write("<b>Local time:</b> " + now + "<br />");
2         var hours=now.getHours();
3         var minutes=now.getMinutes();
4         var seconds=now.getSeconds();
5         var year=now.getFullYear();
```

Continues

EXAMPLE 9.17 (CONTINUED)

```
            document.write("The full year is " + year +"<br />");
            document.write("<b>The time is:</b> " +
            hours + ":" + minutes + ":" + seconds);
        </script>
        </big>
      </body>
    </html>
```

EXPLANATION

1   A new *Date* object called *now* is created. It contains a string with the current date and time: Mon Aug 10 18:22:36 GMT-0700(Pacific Daylight Time).

2   The variable called *hours* is assigned the return value of the *getHours()* method.

3   The variable called *minutes* is assigned the return value of the *getMinutes()* method.

4   The variable called *seconds* is assigned the return value of the *getSeconds()* method.

5   The variable called *year* is assigned the return value of the *getFullYear()* method, *2010*. The output is shown in Figure 9.21.

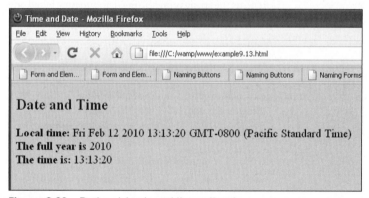

Figure 9.21   Date object and its methods.

9.4.2   Manipulating the Date and Time

JavaScript stores dates in milliseconds, so if you have more complicated calculations to perform, such as the number of days before a date, or between two dates, the information in Table 9.4 might be helpful in converting milliseconds to minutes, hours, days, and so forth.

Table 9.4 Basic Units of Time

Unit of Time	Milliseconds	
1 second	1,000	
1 minute	second * 60	(1,000 * 60)
1 hour	minute * 60	(1,000 * 60 * 60)
1 day	hour * 24	(1,000 * 60 * 60 * 24)
1 week	day * 7	(1,000 * 60 * 60 * 24 * 7)

EXAMPLE 9.18

```
    <html>
      <head><title>Countdown 'til Christmas</title></head>
      <body bgColor="#00FF99">
        <font face="arial" size="5" color="red">
        <script type="text/javascript">
1         var today = new Date();
2         var fullyear = today.getFullYear();
3         var future = new Date("December 25, "+ fullyear);
4         var diff = future.getTime() - today.getTime();
          // Number of milliseconds
5         var days = Math.floor(diff / (1000 * 60 * 60 * 24 ));
          // Convert to days
6         var str="Only <u>" + days + "</u>  shopping days left
                'til Christmas! ";
          document.write(str+"<br />");
        </script>
        </font>
      </body>
    </html>
```

EXPLANATION

1 A new *Date* object called *today* is created.

2 The *getFullYear()* method returns the year as 2010.

3 Another *Date* object called *future* is created. It will contain the future date, Christmas, passed as its argument.

4 The difference between the future time and the present time is calculated and returned in milliseconds with the *getTime()* method.

5 The *Math* object is used to round down the result of converting milliseconds to days.

6 This string contains the number of days between the present date and Christmas (see Figure 9.22).

Only 18 shopping days left 'til Christmas!

Figure 9.22 The number of days between two dates has been calculated.

9.4.3 Customizing the *Date* Object with the *prototype* Property

All objects have a *prototype* property that allows you to extend the capabilities of the object. With the *Date* object's *prototype* property, you can customize the time and the date by providing new methods and properties that will be inherited by all instances of this object. Because the *Date* object provides methods that return zero-based months, weeks, years, and other measures, you might want to create a prototype method where *"January"* is month number 1 instead of 0, and the day is *"Monday"* instead of 1, and so on.

EXAMPLE   9.19

```
    <html>
      <head><title>The Prototype Property</title>
        <script type = "text/javascript">
          // Customize the Date
1         function weekDay(){
2            var now = this.getDay();
3            var names = new Array(7);
             names[0]="Sunday";
             names[1]="Monday";
             names[2]="Tuesday";
             names[3]="Wednesday";
             names[4]="Thursday";
             names[5]="Friday";
             names[6]="Saturday";
4            return(names[now]);
          }
5         Date.prototype.DayOfWeek=weekDay;
        </script>
      </head>
      <body bgcolor="pink">
        <font face="arial">
        <big>
        <div align="center">
        <script type="text/javascript">
6         var today=new Date();
7            document.write("Today is " + today.DayOfWeek() + ".<br />");
        </script>
        </div>
        </big>
        </font>
      </body>
    </html>
```

1   The function called *weekDay()* is defined.

2   The variable *now* is assigned a number representing the day of the week, where 0 is Sunday.

3   A new *Array* object called *names* is created. It will contain seven elements. Each element will be assigned the name of the weekday (e.g., *"Sunday"*).

4   The value in *now*, a number between 0 and 6, will be used as an index in the *names* array. If *now* is 6, then the value of *names[6]*, *"Saturday"*, will be returned.

5   A *prototype* method called *DayOfWeek* is assigned the name of the function *week-Day*. Now the *Date* object has a new method that will be inherited by all objects created from the *Date()* constructor. The capabilities of the *Date* object have been extended to provide a method that will return the name of the weekday. (See Chapter 8 for more on prototypes.)

6   A new *Date* object is created with the *Date()* constructor function.

7   The new prototype method is called, and returns the string value of today's date, *"Saturday"* (see Figure 9.23).

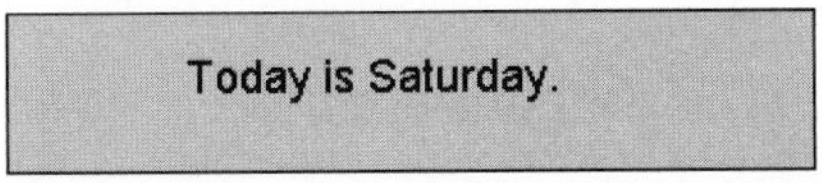

Today is Saturday.

Figure 9.23   The day is converted to a string using a prototype.

9.5   The *Math* Object

The *Math* object allows you to work with more advanced arithmetic calculations, such as square root, trigonometric functions, logarithms, and random numbers, than are provided by the basic numeric operators. If you are doing simple calculations, you really won't need it.

Unlike other objects, you don't have to create an instance of the *Math* object with the *new* keyword. It is a built-in object and has a number of properties (see Table 9.5) and methods (see Table 9.6). The *Math* object always starts with an uppercase M.

Table 9.5   *Math* Object Properties

Property	Value	Description
Math.E	2.718281828459045091	Euler's constant, the base of natural logarithms
Math.LN2	0.6931471805599452862	Natural log of 2
Math.LN10	2.302585092994045901	Natural log of 10

Continues

Table 9.5   *Math* Object Properties (continued)

Property	Value	Description
Math.LOG2E	1.442695040888963387	Log base-2 of E
Math.Log10E	0.4342944819032518167	Log base-10 of E
Math.PI	3.14592653589793116	Pi, ratio of the circumference of a circle to its diameter
Math.SQRT1_2	0.7071067811865475727	1 divided by the square root of 2
Math.SQRT2	1.414213562373985145	Square root of 2

Table 9.6   *Math* Object Methods

Method	Functionality
Math.abs(Number)	Returns the absolute (unsigned) value of *Number*
Math.acos(Number)	Arc cosine of *Number*, returns result in radians
Math.asin(Number)	Arc sine of *Number*, returns results in radians
Math.atan(Number)	Arctangent of *Number*, returns results in radians
Math.atan2(y,x)	Arctangent of *y/x*; returns arctangent of the quotient of its arguments
Math.ceil(Number)	Rounds *Number* up to the next closest integer
Math.cos(Number)	Returns the cosine of *Number* in radians
Math.exp(x)*	Euler's constant to some power
Math.floor(Number)	Rounds *Number* down to the next closest integer
Math.log(Number)	Returns the natural logarithm of *Number* (base E)
Math.max(Number1, Number2)	Returns larger value of *Number1* and *Number2*
Math.min(Number1, Number2)	Returns smaller value of *Number1* and *Number2*
Math.pow(x, y)	Returns the value of x to the power of $y (x^y)$, where x is the base and y is the exponent
Math.random()	Generates pseudorandom number between 0.0 and 1.0
Math.round(Number)	Rounds *Number* to the closest integer
Math.sin(Number)	Arc sine of *Number* in radians
Math.sqrt(Number)	Square root of *Number*

Table 9.6 *Math* Object Methods (continued)

Method	Functionality
Math.tan(Number)	Tangent of *Number* in radians
Math.toString(Number)	Converts *Number* to string

* Returns the value of E^x where E is Euler's constant and x is the argument passed to it. Euler's constant is approximately 2.7183.

Square Root, Power of, and Pi.   The *Math* object comes with a number of common mathematical constants (all uppercase), such as *PI* and natural log values, as well as methods to find the square root of a number, the power of a number, and so on. Example 9.20 demonstrates how to use some of these properties; the output is shown in Figure 9.24.

EXAMPLE   9.20

```
    <html>
       <head><title>The Math Object</title></head>
       <body>
         <h2>Math object Methods--sqrt(),pow()<br />
            Math object Property--PI
         </h2>
         <h3>
         <script type="text/javascript">
1           var num=16;
            document.write("The square root of " +num+ " is ");
            document.write(Math.sqrt(num),".<br />");
2           document.write("PI is ");
3           document.write(Math.PI);
            document.write(".<br />"+num+" raised to the 3rd power is " );
4           document.write(Math.pow(num,3) + ".");
         </script>
         </h3>
       </body>
    </html>
```

EXPLANATION

1   The number 16 will be manipulated by *Math* methods and constants.

2   The *Math* object's *sqrt()* method returns the square root of number 16, which is 4.

3   The *Math* object's PI constant produces the value of PI.

4   The *Math* object's *pow()* methods raises and returns number 16 to the 3rd power, which is 4096 (see Figure 9.24).

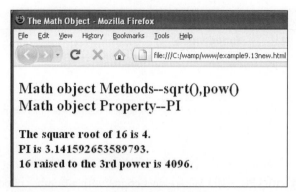

Figure 9.24 The *Math* object, some properties and methods.

9.5.1 Rounding Up and Rounding Down

There are three *Math* methods available for rounding numbers up or down. They are the *ceil()*, *floor()*, and *round()* methods (see Table 9.7 for examples). The differences among the methods might be confusing because all three methods truncate the numbers after the decimal point and return a whole number. If you recall, JavaScript also provides the *parseInt()* function, but this function truncates the number after the decimal point, without rounding either up or down.

The *ceil()* Method. The *ceil()* method rounds a number **up** to the next largest whole number and then removes any numbers after the decimal point; thus, 5.02 becomes 6 because 6 is the next largest number, and –5.02 becomes –5 because –5 is larger than –6.

The *floor()* Method. The *floor()* method rounds a number **down** to the next lowest whole number and then removes any numbers after the decimal point; thus, 5.02 now becomes 5, and –5.02 becomes –6.

The *round()* Method. The *round()* method rounds **up** only if the decimal part of the number is .5 or greater. Otherwise, it rounds **down** to the nearest integer; thus, 5.5 is rounded up to 6, and 5.4 is rounded down to 5.

Table 9.7 Rounding up and down

Number	ceil()	floor()	round()
2.55	3	2	3
2.30	3	2	2
–2.5	–2	–3	–2
–2.3	–2	–3	–2

EXAMPLE 9.21

```
<html>
    <head><title>The Math Object</title></head>
    <body>
        <h2>Rounding Numbers</h2>
        <p>
        <h3>
        <script type="text/javascript">
1           var num=16.3;
            document.write("<I>The number being manipulated is: ", num,
                        "</I><br /><br />");
2           document.write("The <I>Math.floor</I> method rounds down: "
                        + Math.floor(num) + "<br />");
3           document.write("The <I>Math.ceil</I> method rounds up: " +
                        Math.ceil(num) +"<br />");
4           document.write("The <I>Math.round</I> method rounds to\
                    the nearest integer: " + Math.round(num) + "<br />");
        </script>
        </h3>
    </body>
</html>
```

EXPLANATION

1   The number 16.3 will be manipulated by the *Math* object's methods.

2   The *Math* object's *floor()* method rounds the number down to the next lowest whole number. 16.3 rounds down to 16.

3   The *Math* object's *ceil()* method rounds a number up. 16.3 becomes 17.

4   The *Math* object's *round()* methods round 16.3 up only if the decimal part of the number is 5 or higher (see Figure 9.25).

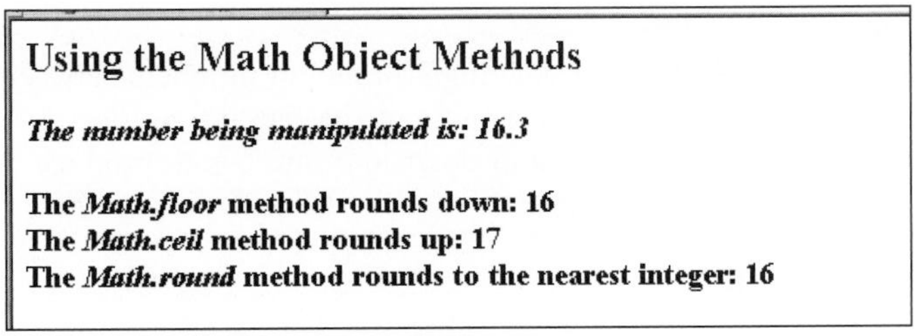

Using the Math Object Methods

The number being manipulated is: 16.3

The *Math.floor* method rounds down: 16
The *Math.ceil* method rounds up: 17
The *Math.round* method rounds to the nearest integer: 16

Figure 9.25   Output from Example 9.21.

9.5.2 Generating Random Numbers

Random numbers are frequently used in JavaScript programs to produce random images (such as banners streaming across a screen), random messages, or random numbers (such as for lotteries or card games). There are examples throughout this text where random numbers are used.

The *Math* object's *random()* method returns a random fractional number between 0 and 1 and is seeded with the computer's system time. (The seed is the starting number for the algorithm that produces the random number.) The *Math* object's *floor()* method truncates numbers after the decimal point and returns an integer.

EXAMPLE 9.22

```
        <html>
          <head><title>Random Numbers</title></head>
          <body bgcolor="darkblue">
            <p style="font-size:120%;color:white">
            <script type="text/javascript">
1             for(i=0; i < 10;i++){
                // Generate random numbers between 0 and 1
2               document.write(Math.random(),"<br />");
              }
              document.write("<br />");
              // Generate random numbers between 0 and 10
3             for(i=0; i < 20; i++){
4               document.write(Math.floor(Math.random() * 10 ) +" ");
              }
            </script>
            </p>
          </body>
        </html>
```

EXPLANATION

1   The *for* loop is entered and will cause the body of the block to be executed 10 times, thus producing 10 fractional random numbers between 0 and 1.

2   The *random()* method of the *Math* object produces random numbers between 0 and 1.

3, 4 This *for* loop will cycle 20 times producing 20 random numbers between 0 and 10, achieved by multiplying the return value of the random number by 10 and then using the *floor()* method to round down the number to produce a whole number. This will produce 0 but never 10 (see Figure 9.26 on page 247).

9.5.3 Wrapper Objects (String, Number, Function, Boolean)

A wrapper is an object bearing the same name as the primitive data type it represents. For each of the primitive data types (string, number, and Boolean), there is a *String* object, a *Number* object, and a *Boolean* object. These objects are called **wrappers** and

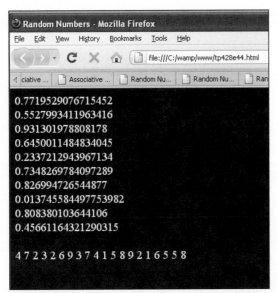

Figure 9.26 Producing random numbers (Example 9.22).

provide properties and methods that can be defined for the object. For example, the *String* object has a number of methods that let you change the font color, size, and style of a string; and the *Number* object has methods that allow you to format a number to a specified number of significant digits. Whether you use the object or literal notation to create a string, number, or Boolean, JavaScript handles the internal conversion between the types. The real advantage to the wrapper object is its ability to apply and extend properties and methods to the object, which in turn, will affect the primitive.

9.5.4 The *String* Object

We have used strings throughout this book. They were sent as arguments to the *write()* and *writeln()* methods, they have been assigned to variables, they have been concatenated, and so on. As you might recall, a string is a sequence of characters enclosed in either double or single quotes. The *String* object (starting with JavaScript 1.1) is a core JavaScript object that allows you to treat strings as objects. The *String* object is also called a wrapper object because it wraps itself around a string primitive, allowing you to apply a number of properties and methods to it.

You can create a *String* object implicitly by assigning a quoted string of text to a variable, called a string primitive (see "Primitive Data Types" on page 53 of Chapter 3, "The Building Blocks: Data Types, Literals, and Variables"), or by explicitly creating a *String* object with the *new* keyword and the *String()* object constructor method. Either way, the properties and methods of the *String* object can be applied to the new string variable.

FORMAT

```
var string_name = "string of text";
var string_name = new String("string of text");
```

EXAMPLE

```
var title="JavaScript by Example";
var title=new String("JavaScript by Example");
```

EXAMPLE 9.23

```
    <html>
      <head><title>The String Object</title></head>
      <body bgcolor="pink">
        <font face="arial">
        <big>
        <h2>Primitive and String Objects</h2>
        <script type="text/javascript">
1           var first_string = "The winds of war are blowing.";
2           var next_string = new String("There is peace in the valley.");
3           document.write("The first string is of type<em> "+
                        typeof(first_string));
            document.write(".</em><br />The second string is of type<em> "
4                       + typeof(next_string) +".<br />");
        </script>
        </big>
        </font>
      </body>
    </html>
```

EXPLANATION

1   This is the literal way to assign a string to a variable, and the most typical way. The
    string is called a string primitive. It is one of the basic building blocks of the lan-
    guage, along with numbers and Booleans. All of the properties and methods of the
    String object behave the same way whether you create a *String* literal or a *String*
    object as shown next. For all practical purposes, both methods of creating a string
    are the same, though this one is the easiest.

2   The *String()* constructor and the *new* keyword are used to create a *String* object.
    This is the explicit way of creating a string.

3   The *typeof* operator demonstrates that the first string, created the literal, implicit
    way, is a *String* data type.

4   The *typeof* operator demonstrates that this string, created with the *String()* con-
    structor, is an object type. Either way, when properties and methods are applied
    to a string, it is treated as a *String* object (see Figure 9.27).

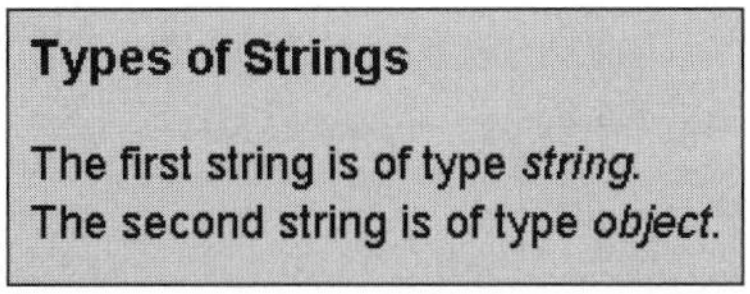

> **Types of Strings**
>
> The first string is of type *string*.
> The second string is of type *object*.

Figure 9.27   Output from Example 9.23.

The Properties of the *String* Object.   The string properties (see Table 9.8) describe the attributes of the *String* object. The most common string property is the *length* property, which lets you know how many characters there are in a string. The *prototype* property allows you to add your own properties and methods to the *String* object, that is, you can customize a string.

Table 9.8   *String* Object Properties

Property	What It Does
length	Returns the length of the string in characters.
constructor	Returns the function that created the *String* object.
prototype	Extends the definition of the string by adding properties and methods.

EXAMPLE 9.24

```
    <html>
      <head><title>The String Object</title></head>
      <body bgColor="lightblue">
        <font face="arial">
        <big>
        <h3>Length of Strings</h3>
        <script type="text/javascript">
1           var first_string = "The winds of war are blowing.";
            var next_string = new String("There is peace in the valley.");
2           document.write("\""+first_string +"\" contains "+
                        first_string.length + " characters.");
3           document.write("<br />\""+ next_string+"\" contains "+
                        next_string.length+" characters.<br />");
            document.write("<font size=-1><em>...not to imply that war
                        is equal to peace...<br />");
        </script>
        </big>
        </font>
      </body>
    </html>
```

EXPLANATION

1   Two strings are created, one the literal way (a string primitive) and the other with the constructor method (a *String* object).

2   The *length* property is applied to the first string. When the property is applied to a literal string, it is temporarily converted to an object, and then after the operation, it is reverted back to a string primitive.

3   The *length* property is applied to the second string, a *String* object. (It is just a coincidence that both strings are of the same length.) (See Figure 9.28.)

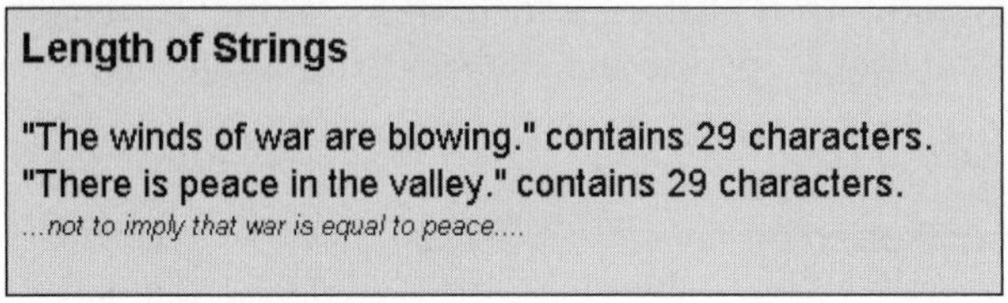

Length of Strings

"The winds of war are blowing." contains 29 characters.
"There is peace in the valley." contains 29 characters.
...not to imply that war is equal to peace....

Figure 9.28   Using the *String* object's *length* property.

Extending the String Object.   Because all objects have the *prototype* object, it is possible to extend the properties of a JavaScript built-in *String* object, just as we did for a user-defined object (see Chapter 8).

EXAMPLE 9.25

```
    <html>
      <head><title>The Prototype Property</title>
      <script type = "text/javascript">
        // Customize String Functions
1       function ucLarge(){
          var str=this.bold().fontcolor("white").
          toUpperCase().fontsize("22");
          return(str);
        }
2       String.prototype.ucLarge=ucLarge;
      </script>
    </head>
    <body bgcolor="black">
      <div align="center">
      <script type="text/javascript">
3       var str="Watch Your Step!!";
4       document.write(str.ucLarge()+"<br />");
      </script>
      <img src="high_voltage.gif">
      </div>
    </body>
    </html>
```

EXPLANATION

1   The *ucLarge()* function is defined. Its purpose is to generate and return an upper-case, bold, white font, with a point size of 22.

2   The *prototype* property allows you to customize an object by adding new properties and methods. The name of the customized method is *ucLarge*, which is the name of a new method that will be used by the *String* object. It is assigned the name (without parentheses) of the function *ucLarge()*, which performs the method's actions and returns a value. Using the same name for both the property and the function reduces the chance of mistakenly calling the method by the wrong name.

3   A new string is created.

4   The prototyped method, *ucLarge()*, is applied to the *String* object, *str*. It will modify the string as shown in the output in Figure 9.29.

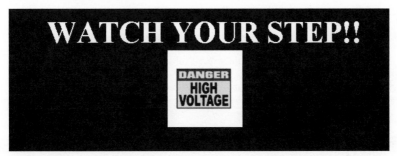

Figure 9.29   Using the *String* object's *prototype* property.

***String* Methods.**   There are two types of string methods: the string formatting methods that mimic the HTML tags they are named for, and the methods used to manipulate a string such as finding a position in a string, replacing a string with another string, making a string uppercase or lowercase, and the like.

Table 9.9 lists methods that will affect the appearance of a *String* object by applying HTML tags to the string, for example, to change its font size, font type, and color. Using these methods is a convenient way to change the style of a string in a JavaScript program, much easier than using quoted HTML opening and closing tags.

Table 9.9   *String* Object (HTML) Methods

Method	*Formats as HTML*
String.anchor(Name)	*<a name="Name">String</a>*
String.big()	*<big>String</big>*
String.blink()	*<blink>String</blink>*

Continues

Table 9.9   *String* Object (HTML) Methods (continued)

Method	Formats as HTML
String.bold()	*String*
String.fixed()	*<tt>String</tt>*
String.fontcolor(color)	*<font color="color">String</font>* e.g., *<font color="blue">String</font>*
String.fontsize(size)	*<font size="size">String</font>* e.g., *<font size="+2">String</font>*
String.italics()	*<i>String</i>*
String.link(URL)	*<a href="URL">String</a>* e.g., *<a href="http://www.ellieq.com">String</a>*
String.small()	*<small>String</small>*
String.strike()	*<strike>String</strike>* (puts a line through the text)
String.sub()	*_{String}* (creates a subscript)
String.sup()	*^{String}* (creates a superscript)

EXAMPLE   9.26

```
      <html>
        <head><title>String object</title></head>
        <body bgcolor="yellow">
          <big>
          <font face="arial">
          <h2>Working with String Objects:</h2>
          <script type="text/javascript">
1           var str1 = new String("Hello world!");
            // Use a String constructor
2           var str2 = "It's a beautiful day today.";
            document.write(str1) + "<br />";
3           document.write(str1.fontcolor("blue")+"<br />");
4           document.write(str1.fontsize(8).fontcolor("red").bold()+
                       "<br />");
5           document.write(str1.big()+ "<br />");
6           document.write("Good-bye, ".italics().bold().big() +
                       str2 + "<br />");
          </script>
          </font>
          </big>
        </body>
      </html>
```

EXPLANATION

1   A *String* object is created with the *String()* constructor.

2   A string primitive is created the literal way.

3   The *fontcolor()* method is used to change the color of the string to blue. This method emulates the HTML tag, *<font color="blue">*.

4   The *fontsize()*, *fontcolor()*, and *bold()* methods are used as properties of the string.

5, 6   The HTML method is concatenated to the string *"Good-bye, "* causing it to be displayed in italic, bold, large text (see Figure 9.30).

Working with String Objects:

Hello world!Hello world!

Hello world!

Hello world!

Good-bye, It's a beautiful day today.

Figure 9.30   Properties of the *String* object are used to change its appearance and determine its size.

There are a number of methods (see Table 9.10) provided to manipulate a string.

Table 9.10   Methods for String Manipulation

Method	*What It Does*
charAt(index)	Returns the character at a specified index position.
charCodeAt(index)	Returns the Unicode encoding of the character at a specified index position.
concat(string1, ..., stringn)	Concatenates string arguments to the string on which the method was invoked.
fromCharCode(codes)	Creates a string from a comma-separated sequence of character codes.
indexOf(substr, startpos)	Searches for the first occurrence of *substr* starting at *startpos* and returns the *startpos(index value)* of *substr*.
lastIndexOf(substr, startpos)	Searches for the last occurrence of *substr* starting at *startpos* and returns the *startpos (index value)* of *substr*.
replace(searchValue, replaceValue)	Replaces *searchValue* with *replaceValue*.

Continues

Table 9.10   Methods for String Manipulation (continued)

Method	What It Does
search(regexp)	Searches for the regular expression and returns the index of where it was found.
slice(startpos, endpos)	Returns string containing the part of the string from *startpos* to *endpos*.
split(delimiter)	Splits a string into an array of words based on *delimiter*.
substr(startpos, endpos)	Returns a subset of string starting at *startpos* up to, but not including, *endpos*.
toLocaleLowerCase()	Returns a copy of the string converted to lowercase.
toLocaleUpperCase()	Returns a copy of the string converted to uppercase.
toLowerCase()	Converts all characters in a string to lowercase letters.
toString()	Returns the same string as the source string.
toUpperCase()	Converts all characters in a string to uppercase letters.
valueOf	Returns the string value of the object.

Methods That Find a Position in a String.   A substring is a piece of an already existing string; thus *eat* is a substring of both *create* and *upbeat*, and *Java* is a substring of *JavaScript*. When a user enters information, you want to see if a certain pattern of characters exist, such as the @ in an e-mail address or a zip code in an address. JavaScript provides a number of methods to assist you in finding substrings.

The *indexOf()* and the *lastIndexOf()* methods are used to find the first instance or the last instance of a substring within a larger string. They are both case sensitive. The first character in a string is at index value 0, just like array indexes. If either of the methods finds the substring, it returns the position of the first letter in the substring. If either method can't find the pattern in the string, then a –1 is returned.

EXAMPLE   9.27

```
        <html>
          <head><title>Substrings</title></head>
          <body bgcolor="lightgreen">
            <font face="arial"
            <big>
            Searching for an @ sign
            <script type="text/javascript">
1             var email_addr=prompt("What is your email address? ","");
```

EXAMPLE 9.27 (CONTINUED)

```
2          while(email_addr.indexOf("@") == -1 ){
3            alert( "Invalid email address.");
             email_addr=prompt("What is your email address? ","");
           }
           document.write("<br />OK.<br />");
         </script>
         </big>
         </font>
      </body>
   </html>
```

EXPLANATION

1   The user is prompted for his or her e-mail address and the input is assigned to a
    string called *email_addr*.

2   The loop expression uses the *indexOf()* *String* method to see if there is an @ sym-
    bol in the e-mail address. If there isn't, the *indexOf()* method returns –1 and the
    body of the loop is executed.

3   If the *indexOf()* method didn't find the @ substring, the alert box appears and the
    user is prompted again (see Figures 9.31 and 9.32). The loop terminates when the
    user enters an e-mail address containing an @ sign. Of course, this is just a simple
    test for validating an e-mail address; more elaborate methods of validation are dis-
    cussed in Chapter 17, "Regular Expressions and Pattern Matching."

Figure 9.31   Using the *indexOf()* *String* method.

Figure 9.32   The user entered an e-mail address without the @ symbol.

EXAMPLE 9.28

```
  <html>
     <head><title>String Manipulation</title></head>
     <body>
        <h2>Working with String Manipulation Methods</h2>
        <script type="text/javascript">
           function break_tag(){
              document.write("<br />");
           }
           document.write("<h3>");
1          var str1 = new String("The merry, merry month of June...");
           document.write("In the string:<em> "+ str1 );
2          document.write("</em> the first 'm' is at position " +
                              str1.indexOf("m"));
           break_tag();
3          document.write("The last 'm' is at position " +
                              str1.lastIndexOf("m"));
           break_tag();
4          document.write("<em>str1.substr(4,5)</em> returns<em> " +
                              str1.substr(4,5));
           break_tag();
           document.write(str1.toUpperCase());
           document.write("</h3>");
        </script>
     </body>
  </html>
```

EXPLANATION

1. A new *String* object is created with the *String()* constructor.
2. The *indexOf() String* method returns the index value where "m" is first encountered in the string starting at the first character, position 0.
3. The *lastIndexOf()* method returns the index position of the last occurrence of "m" in the string starting from the left from position 0.
4. Starting at position 4, the *Substr* method returns 5 characters.

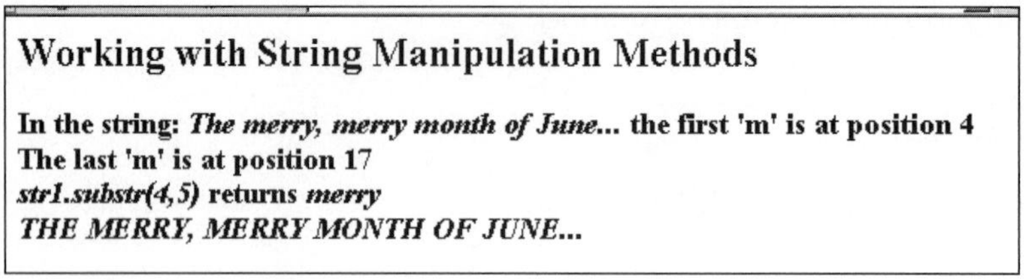

Figure 9.33 Output from Example 9.28.

Methods That Extract Substrings from a String. You might have to do more than just find a substring within a string; you might need to extract that substring. For example, we found the @ in the e-mail address, now we might want to get just the user name or the server name or domain name. To do this, JavaScript provides methods such as *splice()*, *split()*, *charAt()*, *substr()*, and *substring()*.

EXAMPLE 9.29

```
     <html>
        <head><title>Extracting Substrings</title></head>
        <body bgcolor="lightgreen">
           <font face="arial">
           <big>Extracting substrings</big>
           <small>
           <script type="text/javascript">
1             var straddr = "DanielSavage@dadserver.org";
              document.write("<br />His name is<em> " +
2             straddr.substr(0,6) + "</em>.<br />");
3             var namesarr = straddr.split("@" );
4             document.write( "The user name is<em> " + namesarr[0] +
                            "</em>.<br />");
5             document.write( "and the mail server is<em> " + namesarr[1]
                            + "</em>.<br />");
6             document.write( "The first character in the string is <em>"
                            + straddr.charAt(0)+ "</em>.<br />");
7             document.write( "and the last character in the string is <em>"
                            + straddr.charAt(straddr.length - 1)
                            + "</em>.<br />");
           </script>
           </small>
           </font>
        </body>
     </html>
```

EXPLANATION

1   A string is assigned an e-mail address.

2   The *substr()* starts at the first character at position 0, and yanks 6 characters from the starting position. The substring is *Daniel*.

3   The *split()* method creates an array, called *namesarr*, by splitting up a string into substrings based on some delimiter that marks where the string is split. This string is split using the @ sign as its delimiter.

4   The first element of the array, *namesarr[0]*, that is created by the *split()* method is *DanielSavage*, the user name portion of the e-mail address.

5   The second element of the array, *namesarr[1]*, that is created by the *split()* method is *dadserver.org*, the mail server and domain portion of the e-mail address.

Continues

EXPLANATION(CONTINUED)

6   The *charAt()* method returns the character found at a specified position within a string; in this example, position 0. Position 0 is the first character in the string, a letter *D*.

7   By giving the *charAt()* method the length of the string minus 1, the last character in the string is extracted, a letter *g* (see Figure 9.34).

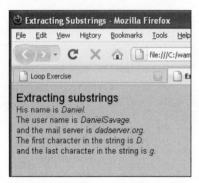

Figure 9.34   The *charAt()*, *split()*, and *substr()* methods: Output from Example 9.29.

Search and Replace Methods.   In word processing software you'll always find some mechanism to search for patterns in strings and to replace one string with another. JavaScript provides methods to do the same thing, using the *String* object. The *search()* method searches for a substring and returns the position where the substring is found first. The *match()* method searches a string for substrings and returns an array containing all the matches it found. The *replace()* method searches for a substring and replaces it with a new string. These methods are discussed again in Chapter 17, "Regular Expressions and Pattern Matching," in more detail.

EXAMPLE 9.30

```
     <html>
       <head><title>Search and Replace</title></head>
       <body bgcolor=lightgreen>
         <font face="arial" size="+1">
         Search and Replace Methods<br />
         <small>
         <script type="text/javascript">
1           var straddr = "DanielSavage@dadserver.org";
            document.write("The original string is "+ straddr
                       + "<br />");
            document.write( "The new string is "+
2           straddr.replace("Daniel","Jake")+"<br />");
3           var index=straddr.search("dad");
```

EXAMPLE 9.30 (CONTINUED)

```
        document.write("The search() method found \"dad\" at
                        position "+ index +"<br />");
4       var mysubstr=straddr.substr(index,3);
        document.write("After replacing \"dad\" with \"POP\" <br />");
5       document.write(straddr.replace(mysubstr,"POP")+"<br />");
    </script>
    </small>
    </font>
  </body>
</html>
```

EXPLANATION

1 An e-mail address is assigned to the string variable *straddr*.

2 The *replace()* method takes two arguments, the search string and the replacement string. If the substring *Daniel* is found, it is replaced with *Jake*.

3 The *search()* method takes a substring as its argument and returns the first position where a substring is found in a string. In this example the substring *dad* is searched for in the string *DanielSavage@dadserver.org* and is found at position 13.

4 The *substr()* method returns the substring found at position 13, 3 in the string, *DanielSavage@dadserver.org*: *dad*.

5 The substring *dad* is replaced with *POP* in the string (see Figure 9.35).

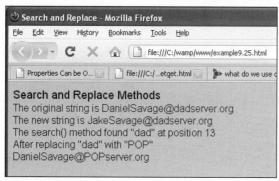

Figure 9.35 The *search()* and *replace() String* methods: Output from Example 9.30.

9.5.5 The *Number* Object

Now that we've travelled this far in JavaScript, have you wondered how to format a floating-point number when you display it, as you can with the *printf* function in C or Perl? Well, the *Number* object, like the *String* object, gives you properties and methods to handle and customize numeric data. The *Number* object is a wrapper for the primitive numeric values (see Chapter 2, "Script Setup"), which means you can use a primitive number type or an object number type and JavaScript manages the conversion back and forth as necessary. The *Number* object was introduced in JavaScript 1.1.

The *Number()* constructor takes a numeric value as its argument. If used as a function, without the *new* operator, the argument is converted to a primitive numeric value, and that number is returned; if it fails, *NaN* is returned. The *Number* object has a number of properties and methods, as listed in Tables 9.11 and 9.12.

FORMAT

```
var number = new Number(numeric value); //Object
var number = numeric value; // Primitive data type
```

EXAMPLE

```
var n = new Number(65.7);
var n = 65.7;
```

Table 9.11   The *Number* Object's Properties

Property	What It Describes
MAX_VALUE	The largest representable number, 1.7976931348623157e+308
MIN_VALUE	The smallest representable number, 5e–324
NaN	Not-a-number value
NEGATIVE_INFINITY	Negative infinite value; returned on overflow
POSITIVE_INFINITY	Infinite value; returned on overflow
prototype	Used to customize the *Number* object by adding new properties and methods

Table 9.12   The *Number* Object's Methods

Method	What It Does
toString()	Converts a number to a string using a specified base (radix)
toLocaleString()	Converts a number to a string using local number conventions
toFixed()	Converts a number to a string with a specified number of places after the decimal point
toExponential()	Converts a number to a string using exponential notation and a specified number of places after the decimal point
toPrecision()	Converts a number to a string in either exponential or fixed notation containing the specified number of places after the decimal point

Using Number Constants and Different Bases.   The constants *MAX_VALUE*, *MIN_VALUE*, *NEGATIVE_INFINITY*, *POSITIVE_INFINITY*, and *NaN* are properties of the *Number()* function, but are not used with instances of the *Number* object; thus, *var huge = Number.MAX_VALUE* is valid, but *huge.MAX_VALUE* is not. *NaN* is a special value that is returned when some mathematical operation results in a value that is not a number.

The methods provided to the *Number* object manipulate instances of number objects. For example, to convert numbers to strings representing different bases, the *toString()* method manipulates a number, either primitive or object. See Example 9.31.

EXAMPLE 9.31

```
        <html>
           <head><title>Number Contants</title></head>
           <body bgcolor="orange"><font color="black" size="+1">
              <h2>Constants</h2>
              <script type="text/javascript">
1                var largest = Number.MAX_VALUE;
2                var smallest = Number.MIN_VALUE;
3                var num1 = 20;    // A primitive numeric value
4                var num2 = new Number(13);    // Creating a Number object
                 document.write("<b>The largest number is " + largest
                             + "<br />");
                 document.write("The smallest number is "+ smallest
                             + "<br />");
5                document.write("The number as a string (base 2): "+
                             num1.toString(2));
6                document.write("<br />The number as a string (base 8): "+
                             num2.toString(8));
7                document.write("<br />The square root of -25 is: "+
                             Math.sqrt(-25) + "<br />");
              </script>
           </body>
        </html>
```

EXPLANATION

1   The constant *MAX_VALUE* is a property of the *Number()* function. This constant cannot be used with an instance of a *Number* object.

2   The constant *MIN_VALUE* is a property of the *Number()* function.

3   A number is assigned to the variable called *num1*.

4   A new *Number* object is created with the *Number()* constructor and assigned to *num2*. It is easier to use the literal notation: *num2 = 13*.

5   The number is converted to a string represented in binary, base 2.

6   The number is converted to a string represented in octal, base 8.

7   The square root of a negative number is illegal. JavaScript returns *NaN*, not a number, when this calculation is attempted (see Figure 9.36).

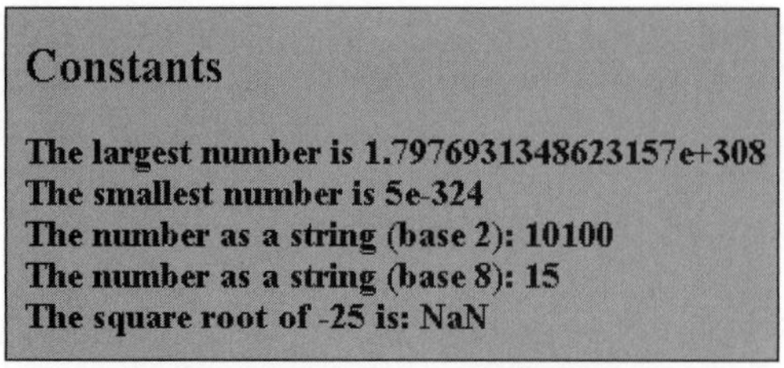

Constants

The largest number is 1.7976931348623157e+308
The smallest number is 5e-324
The number as a string (base 2): 10100
The number as a string (base 8): 15
The square root of -25 is: NaN

Figure 9.36   Constants, number conversion, and *NaN*: Output from Example 9.31.

Formatting Numbers.   To convert floating-point numbers to a string with a specified number of significant digits, JavaScript provides the *toFixed()* and *toExponential()* methods. You can apply these methods to a numeric variable whether it is created as a numeric literal or as an object.

EXAMPLE 9.32

```
      <html>
        <head><title>Number Object</title></head>
        <body bgcolor="orange">
          <font color="black" size="+1">
          <h2>Formatting Numbers</h2>
          <script type="text/javascript">
1            var n = new Number(22.425456);
             // var n = 22.425456;
2            document.write("<b>The unformatted number is " + n
                            + "<br />");
3            document.write("The formatted number is "+ n.toFixed(2) +
                            "<br />");
4            document.write("The formatted number is "+ n.toFixed(3) +
                            "</b><br />");
          </script>
          </font>
        </body>
      </html>
```

EXPLANATION

1   A new *Number* object is created and assigned to the variable *n*. It is a wrapper for the primitive number.

2   The value of the number is displayed as a large floating-point number, 22.425456.

3   The *Number* object's *toFixed()* method gets an argument of 2. This fixes the decimal point two places to the right and rounds up if necessary. The new value is 22.43.

4   This time the *toFixed()* method will format the number with three numbers to the right of the decimal point (see Figure 9.37).

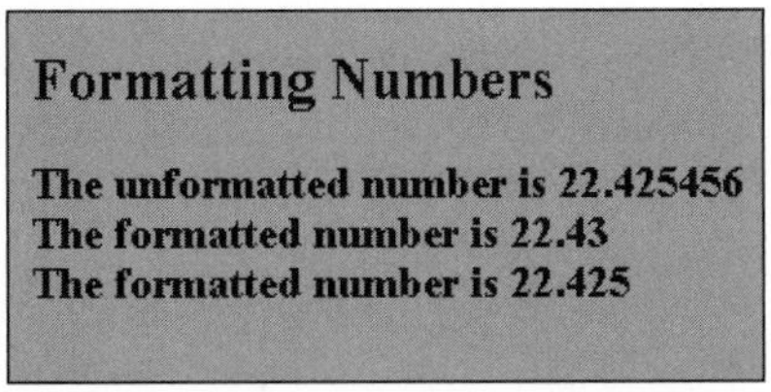

```
Formatting Numbers

The unformatted number is 22.425456
The formatted number is 22.43
The formatted number is 22.425
```

Figure 9.37   Using the *toFixed()* *Number* method: Output from Example 9.32.

9.5.6   The *Boolean* Object

The *Boolean* object was included in JavaScript 1.1. It is used to convert a non-Boolean value to a Boolean value, either *true* or *false*. There is one property, the *prototype* property, and one method, the *toString()* method, which converts a Boolean value to a string; thus, *true* is converted to *"true"* and *false* is converted to *"false"*.

FORMAT

```
var object = new Boolean(value);
```

EXAMPLE

```
var b1 = new Boolean(5);
var b2 = new Boolean(null);
```

EXAMPLE 9.33

```
      <html>
        <head><title>Boolean Object</title></head>
        <body bgcolor=aqua>
          <font face="arial" size="+1"><b>
          The Boolean Object<br />
          <small>
          <script type="text/javascript">
1            var bool1= new Boolean( 0);
             var bool2 = new Boolean(1);
             var bool3 = new Boolean("");
             var bool4 = new Boolean(null);
             var bool5 = new Boolean(NaN);
2          document.write("The value 0 is boolean " + bool1 + "<br>");
           document.write("The value 1 is boolean " + bool2 + "<br>");
           document.write("The value of the empty string is boolean " +
                          bool3 + "<br />");
           document.write("The value of null is boolean " + bool4 +
                          "<br />");
```

Continues

EXAMPLE 9.33 (CONTINUED)

```
            document.write("The value of NaN is boolean " + bool5
                    + "<br />");
        </script>
        </small>
        </font>
      </body>
    </html>
```

EXPLANATION

1   The argument passed to the *Boolean* object constructor is the initial value of the object, either *true* or *false*. If the initial value is *0*, the empty string *""*, *NaN*, or *null*, the result is *false*; otherwise, the result is *true*.

2   The *Boolean* object's values are displayed as either *true* or *false* (see Figure 9.38).

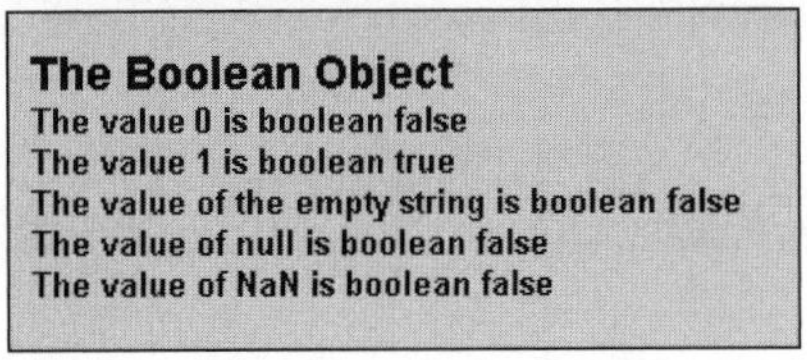

The Boolean Object
The value 0 is boolean false
The value 1 is boolean true
The value of the empty string is boolean false
The value of null is boolean false
The value of NaN is boolean false

Figure 9.38 *True* or *False*? Output from Example 9.33.

9.5.7 The *Function* Object

The *Function* object lets you define a function as an object. It allows a string to be defined at runtime and then compiled as a function. You can use the *Function*() constructor to create a variable that contains the function. Because the function has no name, it is often called an anonymous function and its arguments are passed as comma-separated strings. The last argument is the body of statements that will be executed when the function is called. If the *Function*() constructor does not require arguments, then the body of statements is treated as a string, and will be passed to the *Function*() constructor to define what the function is to do. Because functions are objects, they also have properties (see Table 9.13) and methods (see Table 9.14).

Function objects are evaluated each time they are used, causing them to be slower in execution than normal JavaScript functions.

Table 9.13 Properties of the *Function* Object

Property	What It Does
length	Returns the number of arguments that are expected to be passed (read only).
prototype	Allows the object to be customized by adding new properties and methods.

Table 9.14 Methods of the *Function* Object

Property	What It Does
apply()	Allows you to apply a method from one function to another.
call()	Allows you to call a method from another object.

FORMAT

```
var nameOfFunction = new Function (arguments, statements_as_string: }
```

EXAMPLE FUNCTION DEFINITION

```
var addemUp = new Function ( "a", "b", "return a + b;" );
```

EXAMPLE FUNCTION CALL

```
document.write(addemUp(10, 5));
```

EXAMPLE 9.34

```
        <html>
          <head><title>Function Object</title></head>
          <body bgcolor="lightgreen">
            <font face="arial" size="+1">
            <center>
            Anonymous Functions and the Function Constructor<p>
            <script type="text/javascript">
1              var sum = new Function("a","b", "return a + b; ");
2              window.onload =  new Function ( "document.bgColor='yellow';");
3              document.write( "The sum is " + sum(5,10)+ "<br />");
               document.write( "The background color is yellow<br />");
            </script>
            </font>
          </body>
        </html>
```

EXPLANATION

1. A variable called *sum* is a *Function* object, created by the *Function()* constructor. It has two arguments, "*a*" and "*b*". The function statements are the last string in the list. These statements will be executed when the function is called.

2. This *Function()* constructor only has one argument, the statement that will be executed when the function is called. Because the function is assigned to the *onload* event method for the *window* object, it will be invoked when the window has finished loading and cause the background color to be yellow.

3. The *sum* function is called with two arguments (see Figure 9.39).

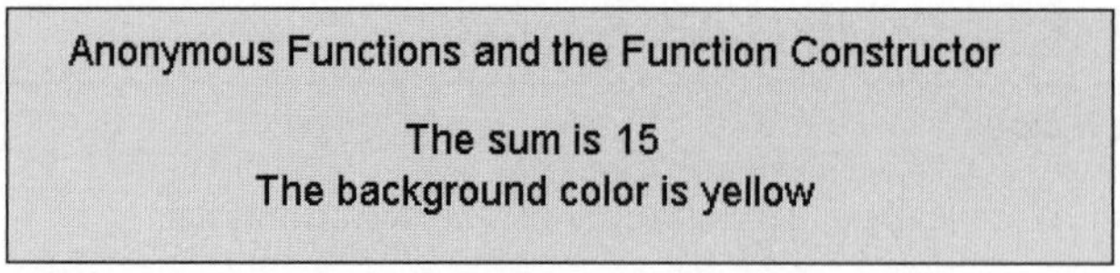

```
Anonymous Functions and the Function Constructor

            The sum is 15
      The background color is yellow
```

Figure 9.39   Output from Example 9.34.

9.5.8   The *with* Keyword Revisited

In Chapter 8, we used the *with* keyword with user-defined objects to make it easier to manipulate the object properties. Recall that any time you reference the object within the block following the keyword, you can use properties and methods without the object name. This saves a lot of typing and reduces the chances of spelling errors, especially when the properties have long names. The *String* object is used in the following example to demonstrate how *with* is used (see Figure 9.40).

EXAMPLE   9.35

```
        <html>
          <head><title>The with Keyword</title></head>
          <body>
            <h2>Using the <em>with</em> keyword</h2>
            <p>
            <h3>
            <script type="text/javascript">
              var yourname=prompt("What is your name? ","");
              // Create a string object
1             with(yourname){
              document.write("Welcome " + yourname +
                              " to our planet!!<br />");
2             document.write("Your name is " + length +
                              " characters in length.<br />");
3             document.write("Your name in uppercase: " + toUpperCase()
                              + ".<br />");
4             document.write("Your name in lowercase:  " + toLowerCase()
                              + ".<br />");
              }
            </script>
            </h3>
          </body>
        </html>
```

EXPLANATION

1   The *with* keyword allows the methods of an object (in this example a string object) to be called without the object's name and a dot.

EXPLANATION

2   The property *length* of the string object called *yourname* is printed. Because the object is enclosed within a block following the *with* keyword, the name of the object is omitted.

3   The to*UpperCase*() method caused the *str* object's character to be capitalized.

4   The *toLowerCase*() method caused the string to be lowercased.

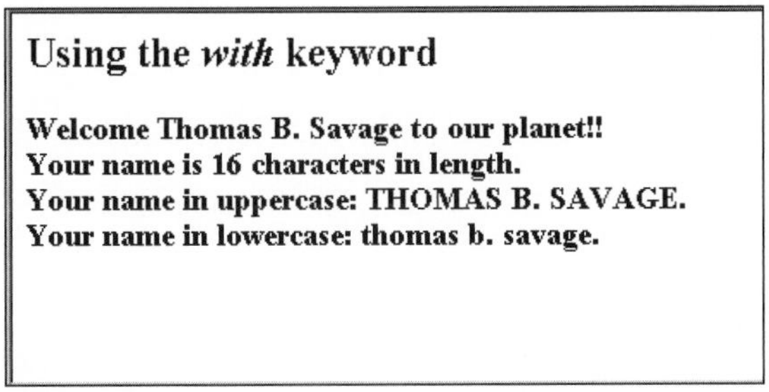

Using the *with* keyword

Welcome Thomas B. Savage to our planet!!
Your name is 16 characters in length.
Your name in uppercase: THOMAS B. SAVAGE.
Your name in lowercase: thomas b. savage.

Figure 9.40   The *with* keyword and strings.

9.6 What You Should Know

In the last chapter you learned how to create and manipulate your own objects, and in this chapter we concentrated on the built-in core objects of JavaScript and what properties and methods are provided for these objects. You learned about the Array object so that later you can create arrays of images and links, and so on. You learned how to manipulate time and dates and how to manage strings and numbers. All of these objects are vital to working with JavaScript as they are at the heart of all JavaScript programs. At this time you should know:

1. What JavaScript's core types are.
2. How to create an Array object with the *new* constructor.
3. How to find the size of an array.
4. How to create a literal array.
5. How to populate an array.
6. How to loop through an array.
7. How to create a two-dimensional array.
8. How to add and remove elements from an array.
9. The difference between slicing and splicing an array.
10. Five ways to instantiate a date object.
11. How JavaScript stores dates.
12. How to calculate the difference between two dates.
13. How to get the current year and month.
14. How to customize the Date object.

15. How to create a Math object.
16. How to use the properties of the Math object.
17. How to randomly select an array element.
18. How to control the number of decimal places in a number.
19. How to define a wrapper object.
20. How to find a character in a string.
21. How to find a substring in a string.
22. The meaning of *NaN*.
23. How to convert a number to a string.
24. How to get the square root of a number.

Exercises

1. Create an array of five animals. Use a *for* loop to display the values stored there. Now add two more animals to the end of the array and sort the array. (Use Java-Script's built-in array methods.) Display the sorted array.

2. Create an associative array called *colors*. Each element of the array is a string representing the color, for example, *red* or *blue*. Use the *for/in* loop to view each element of the array with a color of the font the same color as the value of the array element being displayed.

3. Create a function that will return the current month by its full name. Use the *Date* object to get the current month. Months are returned as 0 for January, 1 for February, 2 for March, and so on. Output should resemble this:

```
The current month is January.
```

   Hint: You can create an array, starting at index 0, and assign a month value to it; for example, *month[0]="January"* or use a *switch* statement, for example, *case 0: return "January"*.

4. An invoice is due and payable in 90 days. Write a function that will display that date.

5. How many days until your birthday? Write a function to calculate it.

6. To calculate the balance on a loan, the following formula is used:

$$PV = PMT * (\ 1 - (1 + IR\ )^{-NP}) / IR$$

   PV is the present value of the loan; *PMT* is the regular monthly payment of the loan; *IR* is the loan's interest rate; *NP* is the number of payments remaining. Write a JavaScript statement to represent this formula.

7. Using the formula to calculate the loan balance from the last exercise, write a function that will calculate the principal balance left on a loan where the monthly payments are \$600, the annual interest rate is 5.5 percent, and there are 9 years remaining on the loan. Use the *toFixed() Number* method to format the output.

8. Apply the *ceil()*, *floor()*, and *round()* methods to the number 125.5567 and display the results.

9. Create an array of 10 fortune cookies that will be randomly displayed each time the user reloads the page. The fortune will be a saying like: "Procrastination is the thief of time."

10. Create a string prototype that can be used to create italic, Verdana font, point size 26 text.

11. Calculate the circumference of a circle using the *Math* object.

12. Create a two-dimensional array consisting of numbers representing costs. After creating the array, print out the values with a sales tax of 9 percent added to each cost.

13. Write a JavaScript program that uses the *Array* and *Math* objects. Create an array of five sayings; for example, "*A stitch in time saves 9,*" or "*Too many cooks spoil the broth.*" Each time the Web page is visited, print a random saying.

14. a. Use the *Date* object to print today's date in this format:

    ```
    Today is Friday, December 17, 2010.
    ```

    b. Calculate and display the number of days until your next birthday.
    c. Create a prototype for the *Date* object that will print the months starting at 1 instead of 0.

15. a. Create a *String* object containing "*Jose lived in San Jose for many years.*"
    b. Find the index for the second *Jose*.

16. Print 58.5678567 in an alert box with only two numbers to the right of the decimal point. Use the *toFixed()* method.

chapter

10

It's the BOM!
Browser Objects

10.1 JavaScript and the Browser Object Model

JavaScript programs are associated with a browser window and the document displayed in the window. The window is a browser object and the document is an HTML object. In the browser object model, sometimes called BOM, the window is at the top of the tree, and below it are objects: *window*, *navigator*, *frames[]*, *document*, *history*, *location*, and *screen*. See Figure 10.1.

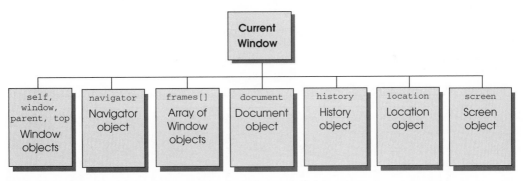

Figure 10.1 The hierarchy of the browser object model.

If you are writing a JavaScript program that needs to manipulate the window, then you would use the *window* object and properties and methods associated with it. For example, the *status* property of the *window* object is used when you want to display text in the status bar, and the window's *alert* method allows you to send a message to a dialog box.

The document object model refers to the HTML document and all the elements and attributes associated with it. Because your Web page is so closely linked to HTML (or XML), JavaScript uses the DOM to access the HTML elements and attributes within a page. The document is the root of this model. Each HTML element is assigned to an object: There are image objects, form objects, link objects, and so on (see Figure 10.2). (See Chapter 11, "Working with Forms and Input Devices," for more on document objects and the DOM.)

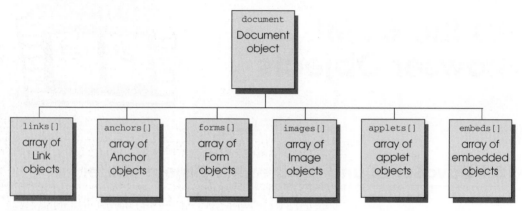

Figure 10.2   The hierarchy of the document object model.

By combining the browser and document object models, JavaScript allows you to manipulate all of the elements in a page as objects, from the window down the hierarchy, as shown in Figure 10.3.

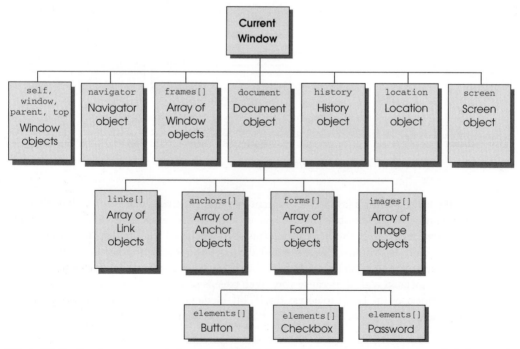

Figure 10.3   The browser and document object models combined (only a partial diagram).

10.1.1 Working with the *navigator* Object

The *navigator* object contains properties and methods that describe the browser. Netscape Navigator and Internet Explorer support the *navigator* object, but some browsers do not.

The *navigator* object can be used for platform-specific checking to determine the version of the browser being used, whether Java is enabled, what plug-ins are available, and so on.

Table 10.1 lists the properties that describe the *navigator* object.

Table 10.1 Properties of the *navigator* Object

Property	What It Describes
appCodeName	Code name for the browser.
appName	Name of the browser.
appVersion	Version of the browser.
mimeTypes	An array of MIME types supported by the browser.
platform	The operating system where the browser resides.
userAgent	HTTP user-agent header sent from the browser to the server.

EXAMPLE 10.1

```
<html>
<head><title>Navigator Object</title></head>
<body>
  <big>
    <script type="text/javascript">
1      for(var property in navigator){
2        str="navigator"+"."+ property;
3        document.write(property+ "  <em>"+
           eval(str)+"</em><br />");
       }
    </script>
  </big>
</body>
</html>
```

EXPLANATION

1   The special *for* loop assigns, in turn, each property of the *navigator* object to the variable called *property*.

2   A string is created by concatenating "navigator" with a dot and the *property* value.

3   Each property and its value of the *navigator* object is displayed in the browser window. See Figures 10.4 through 10.7.

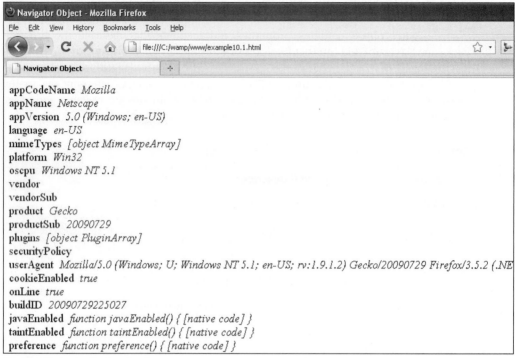

Figure 10.4 In Firefox the browser window displaying the properties of the *navigator* object: Output from Example 10.1. (Note that the *appName* property of Firefox is "Netscape.")

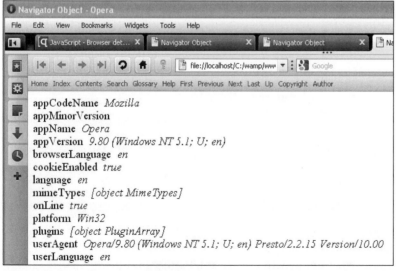

Figure 10.5 In Opera, the browser window displaying the properties of the *navigator* object: Output from Example 10.1.

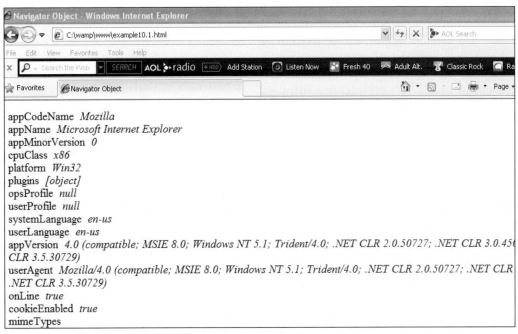

Figure 10.6 In Internet Explorer, the browser window displaying the properties of the *navigator* object: Output from Example 10.1.

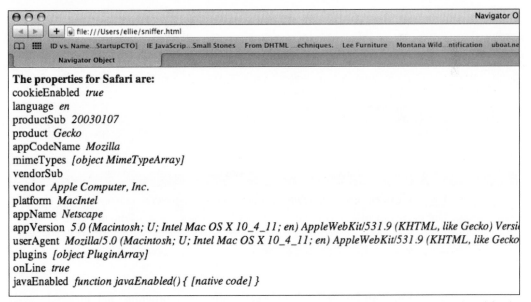

Figure 10.7 In Safari, the browser window displaying the properties of the *navigator* object: Output from Example 10.1.

What Is Your Browser's Name? Version Number?   Browsers support different features, properties, and methods; for example, Internet Explorer might display a page in a slightly different form than Firefox, one version of Mozilla might support a feature not supported by an older version, a version of Internet Explorer might not support a feature supported by Opera, and so on. If you take into consideration all the other browsers and their unique features, it can be tricky to please all of the browsers all of the time or even some of the browsers all of the time. Browser detection allows you to check for specific browser names, versions, whether cookies are enabled, what types of plug-ins are loaded, and so on. The *navigator* object contains a number of properties that allow you to detect information about the user's browser so you can customize your Web page in a way that is transparent to the user.

EXAMPLE 10.2

```
    <html>
        <head><title>The Navigator Object</title></head>
        <body>
            <h2>About The Browser</h2>
            <big>
            <script type="text/javascript">
1               var BrowserName= navigator.appName;
2               var BrowserVersion = navigator.appVersion;
3               var BrowserAgent= navigator.userAgent;
                var platform=navigator.platform;
                document.write("<b>The Browser's name  is:</b> " +
                            BrowserName + "<br />");
                document.write("<b>The Browser version is:</b> " +
                            BrowserVersion + "<br />");
                document.write("<b>The Browser's \"user agent\" is:</b> " +
                            BrowserAgent + "<br />");
                document.write("<b>The Browser's platform is:</b> " +
                            platform + "<br />");
            </script>
            </big>
        </body>
    </html>
```

EXPLANATION

1   The navigator object's *appName* property is the browser's name.

2   The navigator object's *appVersion* property is the version of the browser.

3   The *userAgent* property refers to the HTTP user-agent header sent from the browser to server.

What Is a Browser Sniffer?   A browser sniffer is a program that makes browser detection easy. Many Web sites provide free browser sniffers that determine the types of different browsers. Go to *http://www.quirksmode.org/js/detect.html*, where you will find a

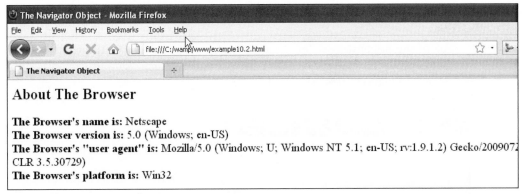

Figure 10.8   Browser properties (Example 10.2).

complete JavaScript program ready to copy and paste into your editor. Save it as a .js file and then include it in your JavaScript code as shown in Example 10.3. The script creates a literal JavaScript object called BrowserDetect and defines a number of methods to detect your browser's name, version, and operating system. The code is fully explained by the author. At this point in your JavaScript experience, you should be able to read the script and understand the explanations provided.

To display the results, the following function was added to the list of methods provided by the original script:

```
printResults: function display(){
   document.write("<b>This browser is "+BrowserDetect.browser);
     document.write( " version "+ BrowserDetect.version + ".<br />");
     document.write("The Operating System is "+ BrowserDetect.OS +
        "</b>.<br />");
   }
```

EXAMPLE 10.3

```
1 <script type="text/javascript" src="browser_sniffer_real.js">
  </script>
  <script type="text/javascript">
2     BrowserDetect.init();
3     BrowserDetect.printResults();
  </script>
```

EXPLANATION

1   The source file is a .js file, downloaded from *http://www.quirksmode.org/js/detect.html*.

2   The *init()* method for the *BrowserDetect* object sets the properties: *browser*, *version* and *OS* for the browser you are using to view the output.

Continues

EXPLANATION (CONTINUED)

3 The *printResults()* method, shown here, was added to this script, to show the value of the properties set for the *BrowserDetect* object; that is, the name of the browser, its version number, and the operating system. Output examples are shown in Figures 10.9, 10.10 and 10.11.

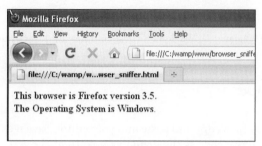

Figure 10.9   The output from Example 10.3 shown in Firefox.

Figure 10.10   The output from Example 10.3 shown in Opera.

Figure 10.11   The output from Example 10.3 shown in Internet Explorer.

Detecting Plug-Ins.   Plug-ins are special software programs that can be downloaded to add the ability to listen to audio, watch videos and movie clips, display animation, and create special image viewing files. Some examples of plug-ins are Macromedia

Shockwave or Flash player, Adobe Acrobat Reader, and RealNetworks RealPlayer. Plugins can be platform dependent and their MIME types can vary as well. If you are using Firefox, go to the Tools menu and select Addons to get more information about the plugins supported on your client. If using Internet Explorer, you will find the *plugins[]* array is empty. You can manage add-ons by going to the Internet Explorer Tools menu and clicking Manage Add-ons.

The *plugins[]* array of the *navigator* object (starting with Navigator 3) contains a complete list of installed plug-ins and can be numerically indexed to see all plug-ins installed for this browser. Each element of the *plugins[]* array represents a *plugin* object. The properties of the *plugin* object are shown in Table 10.2. When you use the HTML *<embed>* tag in a document, you are creating a *plugin* object. Each instance of the *<embed>* tag creates another object (see *<embed>* and *<object>* tags for embedding objects on page 281, Example 10.5).

Table 10.2 Properties of the *plugin* Object

Property	What It Describes
description	A description of the plug-in.
filename	The disk file name of the plug-in.
length	The number of elements in the *plugins[]* array.
name	The name of the plug-in.

EXAMPLE 10.4

```
<script type="text/javascript">
   // No plug-ins for Windows IE. Firefox uses this program.
1  var num_of_plugins = navigator.plugins.length;
2  for (var i=0; i < num_of_plugins; i++) {
      var number=i+1;
      document.write("<font color=red>Plug-in No." +
3     number + "- </font>"+navigator.plugins[i].name+"
         <br />[Location: " + navigator.plugins[i].filename + "]<p>");
   }
4  alert("\nYou have " + number + " plug-ins installed!")
</script>
```

EXPLANATION

1   The *length* property specifies the number of elements in the *plugins[]* array. If using Internet Explorer for Windows, then you will need to use the HTML *<object>* tag and identify a class ID.

2   The *plugins[]* array consists of a list of plug-ins that have been installed in this browser. The *for* loop is used to go through the array, one by one, listing each plug-in.

Continues

3   The plug-in is listed by name. The file name of the plug-in is displayed.

4   The alert lets you know how many plug-ins are installed (see Figure 10.12).

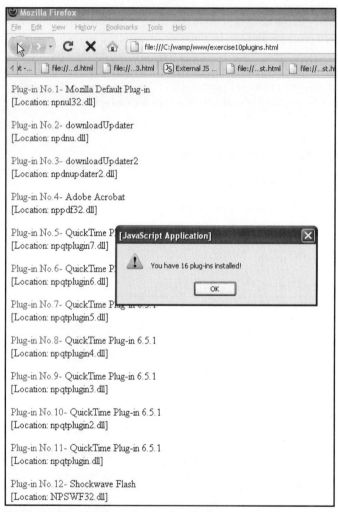

Figure 10.12   A list of plug-ins for Firefox.

What Is ActiveX?   Instead of plug-ins, Microsoft has something called ActiveX controls.[1] ActiveX controls are used as a means to embed objects or components into a Web

---

1. FF ActiveX Host can run ActiveX controls in Mozilla Firefox for Windows. Mozilla ActiveX Control was last updated in late 2005, and runs in Firefox 1.5.

page. Online spreadsheets, security updates, word processors, patches, and timers are examples of such components. The plug-ins we describe here are ActiveX controls and can be downloaded from vendor sites on the Internet. You can add ActiveX controls to your Web pages by using the standard HTML *<object>* tag. The *<object>* tag takes a set of parameters that specify which data the control should use and defines its appearance and behavior. For details, see the Active X Web page, Figure 10.13 (*http://msdn.microsoft.com*).

Figure 10.13 ActiveX Web page.

EXAMPLE 10.5

```
      <html>
        <body>
          <!--This file works with both Internet Explorer and Firefox -->
          <h2>Flash swf file As Object</h2>
1         <object
            width="250" height="100"
2           classid="clsid:d27cdb6e-ae6d-11cf-96b8-444553540000"
3           codebase="http://fpdownload.macromedia.com/pub/
                  shockwave/cabs/flash/swflash.cab#version=8,0,0,0" >
4           <param name="SRC" value="Spring.swf">
5           <embed src="Spring.swf"></embed>
6         </object>
        </body>
        <!--http://ptgmedia.pearsoncmg.coml/images/0201716143/
              files/files.htm -->
      </html>
```

EXPLANATION

1   The HTML *<object>* tag allows you to embed an Active X control directly with the HTML file.

2   The *classid* attribute uniquely identifies the Active X control. This is the unique ID for Shockwave Flash.

3   The *codebase* specifies the version number of the Active X control, in this example, Shockwave Flash is version 8. (This line was broken to fit the page. If you copy this file, put the codebase value on one line.)

4   The *param* attribute has the name/value pair to identify the source for the *.swf* (pronounced "swiff" or "swoof"), the Flash file that will be displayed on the page. The file is an animation with audio.

5   The *<embed>* tag gives the location of a data file that the plug-in should handle. It is included here for Mozilla type browsers because the *<object>* tag is only recognized by Internet Explorer.

6   The ActiveX control is closed with the *</object>* tag.
    (See *http://msdn.microsoft.com/library/default.asp?url=/workshop/components/activex/activex_ovw_entry.asp* for a tutorial on ActiveX.) See Figure 10.14.

Figure 10.14   Embedded Flash file and the *<Object>* tag.

What Are MIME Types?   MIME stands for Multipurpose Internet mail extensions.[2] It is a standard format for sending mail messages across the Internet. Now it is used to exchange all kinds of file types across the Internet, such as audio, video, and image files. All browsers have a list of MIME types. JavaScript 1.1 implemented the *mimeType* object

---

2. Available with NN3+ and IE5+ on the Mac, but not on Windows Internet Explorer.

(see Table 10.3). These objects are predefined JavaScript objects that allow you to access the *mimeTypes[]* array, a property of both the *navigator* object and the *plugin* object. (Note: The *mimeTypes[]* array will not produce output in IE.) *audio/x-pn-realaudio-plug-in* is an example of a MIME type for RealPlayer G2 LiveConnect-Enabled Plug-In.

Table 10.3   Properties of the *mimeType* Object

Property	What It Describes
description	A description of the MIME type.
enabledPlugin	A reference to the *plugin* object for this MIME type .
suffixes	A string of file name extensions allowed for this MIME type; e.g., jpeg, jpg, jpe, jfif, pjpeg, pjp object; e.g., *navigator.plugins["Shockwave"].length.*
type	The name of the MIME type; e.g., *image/jpeg.*

EXAMPLE   10.6

```
<html>
   <head><title>Mime Detection</title></head>
   <body bgcolor="lightgreen">
      <h3><u>Mime Types--Firefox</u></h3>
      <b>
      <script type="text/javascript">
         for ( var i=0;i < navigator.mimeTypes.length; i++){
1            if(navigator.mimeTypes[i].enabledPlugin != null){
               document.write ("<br /><font size='+1'>"+
2                 navigator.mimeTypes[i].type+"<br />");
               document.write("<font size='-1'>"+
                  "Enabled Plugin Name: <em>");
                  document.write("<font size='-1'>"+
3                 navigator.mimeTypes[i].enabledPlugin.name+"<br />");
               document.write("</em>Description: "+ "<em>"+
4                 navigator.mimeTypes[i].description+
                  "<br /></em>Suffixes: "+ "</em>"+
5                 navigator.mimeTypes[i].suffixes+"<br />");
            }
         }
      </script>
   </body>
</html>
```

EXPLANATION

1   If the MIME type for a plug-in is not null, the information about it is printed.

2   This is the MIME type of the plug-in, such as *application/x-mplayer2* or *application/x-shockwave-flash*.

3   This is the enabled plug-in referred to by this MIME type.

4   The MIME type is described, such as Acrobat (*.pdf) or Network Interface Plugin (*.nip).

5   The suffixes are the file name extensions that this MIME type supports, such as .rpm, .wav, .pdf, and so on. Partial output is shown in Figure 10.15.

Figure 10.15   MIME types: Output from Example 10.6 (partial list).

10.1.2   Working with the *window* Object

The *window* object is where all the action happens in a browser. It's at the top of the Java-Script hierarchy, and is automatically defined for each window that you open, as represented in Figure 10.12. When you start up your browser, you may stay in the current window until you exit the browser, or you may have any number of windows open at the same time. Within each window you browse the Internet, read e-mail, search for cheap airline tickets, and buy a new book. Each new page you bring up is a document within the current window. The window is often partitioned into independent display areas, called frames, which are windows within windows. (Frames are discussed in the section "Working with Frames" on page 303.)

The *window* object comes with a number of properties and methods. Because it is the basis of all objects, the name of the *window* object can be excluded when applying methods to it; for example, it is not necessary to specify *window.alert("Watch out!")* or *window.document.write("OK")*. You simply use *alert("Watch out!")* or *document.write("OK")*.

When a user clicks a button or rolls the mouse over a link, an event occurs that often affects the behavior of a window. Such user-initiated events are discussed in Chapter 13, "Handling Events."

Object's Properties and Methods.   The *window* object has a number of properties, which are also objects in their own right. Table 10.4 lists those properties and how they describe the attributes of the window.

Table 10.4   Properties of the *window* Object

Property	What It Describes
closed	True if the window is closed.
defaultStatus	The default status message displayed in the status bar at the bottom of the window.
document	The document object that is currently displayed in the window.
frames	An array of frame objects within the window.
history	The *history* object containing the URLs last loaded into the window.
length	The number of frames within the window.
location	The URL of the current window.
name	The name of the window.
offscreenBuffering	Used to draw new window content and then copy it over existing content when complete; controls screen updates.

Continues

Table 10.4   Properties of the *window* Object (continued)

Property	What It Describes
opener	The window that opened the current window.
parent	Indicates a window that contains another window (used with frames).
screen	Displays information about the screen, such as height, width (in pixels).
self	Refers to the current window. For all windows, the self and window properties of a window object are synonyms for the current window, and you can optionally use them to refer to the current window.
status	Specifies a temporary message in the status bar, resulting user interaction.
top	Topmost window containing a particular window (used with frames).
window	Identifies the current window being referenced, synonymous with self.

The *window* object also has a number of methods that define its behavior, listed in Table 10.5, such as how to open, close, scroll, and clear a window.

Table 10.5   Methods of the *window* Object

Method	What It Does
alert(text)	Creates a triangular dialog box with a message in it.
blur()	Removes focus from the window.
clearInterval(interval)	Clears a previously set interval timer.
clearTimeOut(timer)	Clears a previously set timeout.
close()	Closes a window.
confirm()	Creates a dialog box for user confirmation.
focus()	Gives the focus to a window.
open(url, name, [options])	Opens a new window and returns a new *window* object.
prompt(text, defaultInput)	Creates a dialog prompt box to ask for user input.

Table 10.5   Methods of the *window* Object (continued)

Method	*What It Does*
scroll(x, y)	Scrolls to a pixel position in a window.
setInterval(expression, milliseconds)	After a specified interval, evaluates an expression (see Examples 10.10 and 10.12).
setInterval(function, milliseconds, [arguments])	After a specified interval, evaluates a function (see Examples 10.10 and 10.12).
setTimeout(expression, milliseconds)	After a timeout period has elapsed, evaluates an expression (see Examples 10.10, 10.11, and 10.13).
setTimeout(function, milliseconds, [arguments])	After a timeout period has elapsed, evaluates a function (see Examples 10.10, 10.11, and 10.13).

Opening and Closing Windows.   You can open a new browser window by going to the *File* menu and selecting *New Window* (Netscape and Internet Explorer), or you can open a new window from a JavaScript program with the window's *open* method. These little windows are commonly called popups. When creating these windows, keep in mind that all major Web browsers now offer popup advertising filters, and your viewer might not even see the popup.

FORMAT

```
var window_object =  window.open("url", windowname, [options]);
```

EXAMPLE

```
var winObj= window.open("http://localhost/windows/winter.jpg",
    "winter","width=1150,height=350,resizable=yes,scrollbars=yes,
    location=yes");
```

EXAMPLE 10.7

```
     <html>
        <head><title>Opening a New Window</title>
          <script type="text/javascript">
1           function newWindow(){
2             var winObj=open("winter.jpg", "winter");
            }
          </script>
        </head>
        <body bgColor="lightblue">
          <h2>Winter Scene from the Old Country</h2>
```

Continues

EXAMPLE 10.7 (CONTINUED)

```
          <h3>Click here to see through my winter window<br />
3         <a href="JavaScript:newWindow()">Winter Scene</a></h3>
     </body>
</html>
```

EXPLANATION

1   The JavaScript function *newWindow* is defined.

2   The *open* method is called and returns a *window* object that is assigned to the variable, *winObj*. The first argument to the *open* method is the URL of the new window; in this case the document is an image file called *winter.jpg* located in the current directory. The name to be associated with this window is *winter*.

3   When the user clicks on the line *Winter Scene*, the JavaScript user-defined function, *newWindow*, is called (see Figure 10.16). This function is responsible for opening the new window. Instead of a URL, the HTML *<a href>* tag is assigned name of a JavaScript function. The *JavaScript:* label allows the function to be called when the user clicks the link. Without the *JavaScript:* label, the browser will try to find a URL address called *newWindow()* and fail.

Figure 10.16   A new popup window showing a winter scene is opened.

The *window* object's *open()* method has a number of options listed in Table 10.6 that allow you to further customize the new window.

Table 10.6 The *open()* Method and Its Options

Option	Values	Gives the Window
directories	Yes/no *or* 1/0	Directory buttons
height	Integer value	Height in pixels
location	Yes/no *or* 1/0	A location box
menubar	Yes/no *or* 1/0	A menu bar
resizable	Yes/no *or* 1/0	The ability to be resized
scrollbars	Yes/no *or* 1/0	Scrollbars along the side
status	Yes/no *or* 1/0	A status bar
toolbar	Yes/no *or* 1/0	A toolbar
width	Integer value	Width in pixels

EXAMPLE 10.8

```
    <html>
        <head><title>Opening a New Window with Parameters
                    and Closing It</title>
            <script type="text/javascript">
1           function newWindow(){
2               winObj=window.open("http://localhost/windows/winter.jpg",
                    "winter","width=1150,height=350,resizable=yes,
                    scrollbars=yes,location=yes");
3               winObj.focus();
4               //winObj.blur();
                }
5           function closeWindow(){
6               winObj.close();
                }
            </script>
        </head>
        <body bgColor="lightblue">
            <h2>Winter Scene from the Old Country</h2>
            <h3>Click the link to see my winter window<br />
7           <a href="JavaScript:newWindow()">Winter Scene</a>
                <p>When you are ready to close the window, click here<br />
8           <a href="JavaScript:closeWindow()">Close the window</a></h3>
        </body>
    </html>
```

EXPLANATION

1   The function *newWindow()* is defined.

2   The *open()* method is passed the URL of the JPEG image file that will be displayed in the new window called *winter*. The width and height of the new window are 1150 and 350 pixels, respectively. The window is resizable and has scrollbars. A location box appears in the top of the new window. The name of the *window* object created by the open method is *winObj*. It is important that you do not use any spaces or linebreaks between the commas in the list of parameters.

3   The *focus()* method brings the new window into focus: It appears in front of the parent window or any other windows.

4   The *blur()* method (commented out) would push the window behind any other windows that are open.

5   The user-defined function, *closeWindow()*, is defined.

6   The reference to the *window* object, *winObj*, will call the *close()* method to close the new window that was opened.

7   The *newWindow* function is called when the user clicks the link **Winter Scene**. The label, *JavaScript:*, prevents the link from trying to activate a URL, and instead goes to the JavaScript program and calls the function *closeWindow()*. See Figure 10.17.

8   When the user clicks this link, the new window will be closed. The original or parent window will remain in the browser. If the name of the new *window* object is not provided, the *close()* method will try to close the parent window.

Figure 10.17   Opening a new resizable window with a scrollbar and size dimensions in pixels: Output from Example 10.8.

Moving and Resizing a Window.   JavaScript provides several methods with which to resize and move a *window* object. The window can be moved or resized absolutely, or relative to its current position or size. The numbers, given as arguments, are the pixel coordinates, and are listed in Table 10.7.

Table 10.7   Move and Resize Methods

Method	Example	What It Does
moveBy()	*moveBy(20,20)*	Moves the window relatively by 20 pixels.
moveTo()	*moveTo(0,0)*	Moves to the top, left corner of the screen.
resizeBy()	*resizeBy(15,10)*	Resizes the window relatively by 15 × 10 pixels.
resizeTo()	*resizeTo(450,350)*	Resizes the window absolutely to 450 × 350 pixels.

EXAMPLE   10.9

```
        <html>
          <head><title>Move a New Window</title>
            <script type="text/javascript">
              function directions(){
1                 winObj=window.open("myplace.html","myplace",
                    "width=200,height=300,resizable=no");
2                 winObj.moveTo(0, 0); // Move window to top left corner
3                 winObj.focus();
4                 parent.window.moveTo(215, 0); // Move the parent window
5                 parent.window.resizeTo(400,400); // Resize browser window
              }
              function closeWindow(){
                winObj.close();
              }
            </script>
          </head>
          <body bgColor="lightblue">
            <h2>We've moved!</h2>
            For directions to our new place,
            <br />
            click the button
6           <form >
              <input type="button"
                value="Simple Directions"
7               onClick="directions();">
              <p>When you are ready to close the window, click here</p>
            </form>
            <a href="JavaScript:closeWindow()">Close the window</a>
          </body>
        </html>
```

EXPLANATION

1   A new *window* object is created. If the resizable option is turned off, the user will not be able to maximize the window. A maximized window cannot be moved with the *moveTo()* method.

2   The *moveTo()* method determines the position where the window will be moved. The arguments 0,0 represent the *x,y* coordinates (column,row) in pixels.

3   The new window will be put into focus, meaning it will be at the top of the window hierarchy, in front of all the other windows.

4   The parent window is the original window we started in. It is moved to coordinates 215 × 0 pixels.

5   The parent (original) window is resized to 400 × 400 pixels.

6   This is the start of a simple HTML form. It creates a simple input device called a button on the screen.

7   This is the *onClick* event handler. When the user presses the button, the event is triggered and a function called *directions()*, will be called. The new window is moved to the top left corner and put into focus. See Figure 10.18.

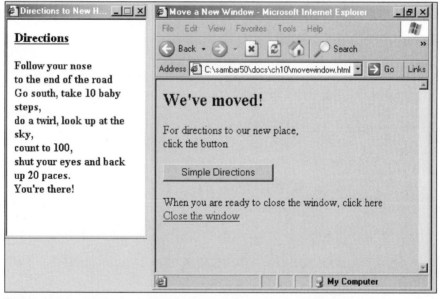

Figure 10.18   After moving, focusing, and resizing both the new window and the parent window: Output from Example 10.9.

10.1.3   Creating Timed Events

Timer Methods.   The *window* object provides two methods that act like an alarm clock so that you can time when you want certain things to happen in your program:

setTimeout() and *setInterval()* (see Table 10.8). The *setTimeout()* method evaluates an expression after a specified amount of time and quits. The *setInterval()* method automatically reschedules the execution of an expression at set intervals, continuing to repeat until the program ends or the *setInterval* is cancelled.

Table 10.8   Timers

Timing Methods	What They Do
setTimeout()	Invokes a function or evaluates an expression or a function when the number of milliseconds has passed.
setInterval()	Invokes a function or evaluates an expression or a function at set intervals in milliseconds.

Both methods have the same syntax, two arguments: a quoted expression or function reference, and the time in milliseconds to delay execution of the expression. (A minute contains 60,000 milliseconds, so 30 seconds would be 30,000 milliseconds.) Because JavaScript sees time in terms of milliseconds, Table 10.9 gives you a little conversion table to help determine the time in milliseconds.

Table 10.9   Basic Units of Time

Unit of Time	Milliseconds	
1 second	1,000	
1 minute	second * 60	(1,000 * 60)
1 hour	minute * 60	(1,000 * 60 * 60)
1 day	hour * 24	(1,000 * 60 * 60 * 24)
1 week	day * 7	(1,000 * 60 * 60 * 24 * 7)

If a function contains a *setTimeout()* or *setInterval()* method that in short intervals keeps invoking the function, the result can give the effect of continuous motion such as a scrolling panorama or message, or even animation.[3] Often, timers are used to scroll messages in the title or status bars or in containers within a window such as a div or textbox. You must decide what is tasteful on your Web page and what is annoying, but that aside, we use *setTimeout()* and *clearTimeout()* methods for scheduling something to happen in the future For a detailed explanation of how JavaScript internally handles the timers, see *http://www.howtocreate.co.uk/tutorials/JavaScript/timers*.

---

3. For an example of a timer to create animation, see Chapter 15, "The W3C DOM and JavaScript."

The *setTimeout()* and *setInterval()* methods are methods of the window object. They take two parameters:

1. The statements to execute: expressions in quotes or function references.
2. The time in milliseconds to wait before the statements are executed.

Which of the two timer functions should you use? It depends on what you are trying to do. If the function being called needs different parameters on each call or the content of the function itself decides whether or not to call itself again, then you would use *set-Timeout()* but if the function just needs to be called at regular intervals, then the *setInterval()* function would produce simpler and faster results.

You can cancel a timeout or interval by calling the *clearTimeout()* or *clearInterval()* method by passing it a reference to the return value of *setTimeout()* or *setInterval()*.

FORMAT

```
var timeout = setTimeout("expression", delaytime);
var timeout= setInterval("expression", intervaltime);
```

EXAMPLE

```
var timeout = setTimeout("timer()", 15000);   // In 15 seconds call the
                                              // function "timer()"
var timeout = setTimeout(timer,15000); //Use function reference
var timerId = setInterval("scroller()", 500);   // Every .5 seconds
                                              // call "scroller()"
var timerId = setInterval(scroller, 500);   //Use function reference
```

To clear the timed event use the *clearTimeout()* or *clearInterval()* methods:

```
clearTimeout(timeout);
clearInterval(timerID);
```

EXAMPLE 10.10

```
    <html>
    <head><title>The setTimeout method</title>
      <script type="text/javascript">
1         function changeStatusBar(){
2           window.status = "See me now before I disappear!";
3           timeout =setTimeout("window.status=''", 6000);
            // alert(timeout);   This value differs in Mozilla and IE
          }
      </script>
    </head>
      <body><div align="center">
        <font face="arial" size="3" color="blue">
        The timeout is set for 6 seconds.
```

EXAMPLE 10.10 (CONTINUED)

```
              <br />
4             <img src="alarm.jpg" border=2>
              <p>
              Watch the status bar
              <br />
5             <form>
                 <input type="button"
                   value="click here"
6                  onClick="changeStatusBar();">
              </form>
              </font>
              </div>
           </body>
        </html>
```

EXPLANATION

1 A JavaScript function, called *changeStatusBar()*, is defined. Its purpose is to print a message in the status bar of the window for six seconds.

2 A string value is assigned to the status property of the window. The string *"See me now before I disappear!"* will appear in the status bar at the bottom of the window.

3 The *setTimeout()* method is a window method. After six seconds, the status bar will be set to an empty string. Once the *setTimeout()* completes, it doesn't automatically start up again as *setInterval()* does.

4 This is an image of a clock that displays on the screen, just for decoration.

5 An HTML form starts here. The user will see a button, with the text *"click here,"* on the button.

6 When the user presses the button, the *onClick* event handler is triggered, causing the function *changeStatusBar()* to be invoked. See Figure 10.19.

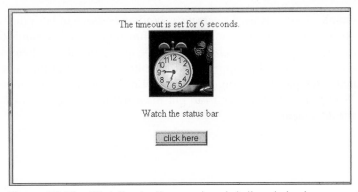

Figure 10.19 Click the button and watch the status bar.

Some might find meddling with the status bar annoying. In fact, JavaScript could be enabled, but the ability to change the status bar might have been disabled. For Firefox, take the following steps to enable or disable the window's features (see Figure 10.20):

1. Click Tools → Options.
2. When the Options dialog box appears, click Content.
3. Check Enable JavaScript if it is not already checked, and then click Advanced.
4. The Advanced JavaScript Settings dialog box appears. From here, you can enable or disable features as desired.
5. When done, click OK in the dialog boxes to close them.

Figure 10.20   Enable/Disable window and status bar options with Firefox.

In the next example, a timer is used to create a scrolling message in both the title and status bars of the window. This is done by calling a function every .3 seconds that will use JavaScript's *substring* function to change the value in a string of text. Removing the first character of a string and then appending that value to the end of the same string, all done repeatedly in rapid succession, gives the appearance of the text in motion. This example will be expanded in Chapter 15 to put the scrolling message in a *<div>* container within the document.

EXAMPLE 10.11

```
    <html>
        <!--  This script is a modification of a free script found at
              the JavaScript source.
              Author: Asif Nasir (Asifnasir@yahoo.com)
         -->
    <head>
        <script type="text/javascript">
1           var today = new Date();
2           var year=today.getFullYear();
3           var future = new Date("December 25, " + year);
4           var diff = future.getTime() - today.getTime();
                            // Number of milliseconds
5           var days =Math.floor(diff / (1000 * 60 * 60 * 24 ));
                            // Convert to days
6           var str=
                "Only " + days + "  shopping days left until Christmas!";
7           function scroller(){
8               str = str.substring(1, str.length) + str.substring(0,1);
9               document.title=str;
10              window.status=str;
11              setTimeout(scroller, 300);     // Set the timer
            }
        </script>
    </head>
12  <body onload = "scroller()">
        <b>
        <font color="green" size="4">
        Get Dizzy. Watch the title bar and the status bar!!
        <br />
        <image src="christmasscene.bmp">
        </font>
    </body>
    </html>
```

EXPLANATION

1   The *Date()* constructor creates an instance of a new *Date* object, called *today*.

2   The *getFullYear()* method returns the current year in four digits.

3   Another Date object is created with the date "*December 25, 2010*" assigned to the variable, called *future*, assuming the current year is 2010.

4   The difference in milliseconds between the future time and the current time is assigned to the variable called *diff*.

5   The milliseconds of time are converted into days, and the result is rounded down by the Math object's *floor()* method.

6   The string variable, "*Only (number of days goes here) shopping days left until Christmas!*", is assigned to *str*.

Continues

EXPLANATION(CONTINUED)

7   A function called *scroller()* is defined.

8   This looks kind of tricky, but here's what's happening. The *substr()* method extracts everything between the first character and the rest of the string *substr(1, str.length)*, resulting in *"nly 19 shopping days left until Christmas!"*. Next, another *subtsr(0,1)* method extracts the first character from the string, the *"O"*. The *"O"* is added onto the end of the new string, resulting in *"nly 19 shopping days left until Christmas!O"* and after .3 seconds the *scroll()* function will be called again. Then the string will become *"ly 19 shopping days left until Christmas!On"*, and then *"19 shopping days left until Christmas!Onl"* and so on. Because the *substr()* method is being called so rapidly, the effect is a scrolling banner.

9   The new string, *str*, created by the two *substr()* methods will appear in the document's title bar. Every time the function is called (i.e., every .3 seconds), the new string will appear, giving a scrolling effect.

10 The new string will also appear in the status bar of the window.

11 The timer is set here within the *scroller()* function. The first argument is a reference to a function that will be called, in this case, *scroller*, and the second argument is when it will be called, in this case, in 300 milliseconds or .3 seconds (300/1000). Because the *scroller()* function calls itself within the timer, it is recursive and will continue to call itself every .3 seconds until the program ends. The display is shown in Figure 10.21.

EXAMPLE 10.12

```
<html>
  <head><title><Timeout></title>
    <script type="text/javascript">
      var today = new Date();
      var year=today.getFullYear();
      var future = new Date("December 25,"+ year);
      var diff = future.getTime() - today.getTime();
                  // Number of milliseconds
      var days =Math.floor(diff / (1000 * 60 * 60 * 24 ));
                  // Convert to days
      var str=
        "Only " + days + "  shopping days left until Christmas! ";
1     function startup(){
2       setInterval(scroller,500);
      }
3     function scroller(){
        str = str.substring(1, str.length) + str.substring(0,1);
        document.title=str;
        window.status=str;
      }
    </script>
  </head>
```

EXAMPLE 10.12 (CONTINUED)

```
4     <body onLoad = "startup()">
       <h3>
          Get Dizzy. Watch the title bar and the status bar!!
       </h3>
       <image src="christmasscene.bmp">
     </body>
   </html>
```

EXPLANATION

1   This is the same program as Example 10.11 using the *setInterval()* method for set-
    ting a timer. The function called *startup()* contains the code to start the scrolling.

2   The *setInterval()* method is a window method and is executed and calls *scroller()* at
    intervals of 500 milliseconds (.5 seconds), and will continue to do so until the win-
    dow is exited or the *clearInterval()* method is called. In Example 10.11 we used *set-
    Timeout()* instead of *setInterval()*.

3   This is the *scroller()* function that creates the text in both the title bar and the sta-
    tus bar. It is executed at .5 second intervals.

4   When the page has finished loading, the *onLoad* event handler will call *startup()*.

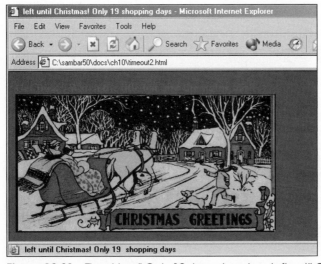

Figure 10.21 The string "*Only 19 shopping days left until Christmas!*" scrolls
continuously in the title bar and in the status bar. How annoying!

The *scrollTo()* Method.   This JavaScript method scrolls the content of a window to a
specified x/y coordinate pixel position. This method is only useful where there are areas of
the document not viewable within the current viewable area of the window. If you open
up another window, you might want to scroll to a particular place in the window based on
the user's selection from a menu in the main window, or you might want to use scrolling

to produce an animated effect. For example, if you have a large image that is too big to view in the new window, you can set up scrolling so that you start at the left side of the image and slowly move to a specified position at the right side and then back again, giving a panoramic effect. Scrolling might have different behavior on different browsers.[4]

The *scrollTo()* method takes two arguments, the horizontal and vertical pixel coordinates to represent the window position, where 0,0 would scroll to the left top corner of the window, and position 0,350 would scroll down 350 pixels from the starting position at the top left corner, and 350,0 would scroll to the right 350 pixels from the starting position, and so on.

FORMAT

```
window_object.scrollTo(horizontal_pixel_position,vertical_pixel_position);
```

EXAMPLE

```
parent.window.scrollTo(0,350);
```

EXAMPLE 10.13

```
      <html>
        <head><title>Scrolling through Autumn</title>
          <script type="text/javascript">
1         winObj=window.open("fallscene.gif","mysscene",
            "width=350,height=292,resizable=no"); // Create the new
                                                  //  window with an
                                                  //  image.
2         winObj.moveTo(0, 0);
3         winObj.focus();
4         var pixelpos=0;
5         var ImgWidth=1096;
6         var pixelstep = 2;
7         var timeout;
8         function startScroll(){
9            if (pixelpos <= (ImgWidth - 350)){
              // Check that scrolling is still within the
              // boundaries of the window.
10               pixelpos += pixelstep;
11               winObj.scrollTo(pixelpos,0);    // Go to that position
                                                 // in the new window
12               timeout=setTimeout(startScroll,20);
             }
          }
```

---

4. There might be browser compatibility issues with scrolling; for example, Example 10.13 works fine on a Mozilla browser, but does not work on Internet Explorer because the image is scaled to fit the window no matter what size it is. For this example to work in IE, go to Tools → Internet Options → Advanced → Multimedia, then clear the Enable Automatic Image Resizing checkbox.

EXAMPLE   10.13 (CONTINUED)

```
13        function scrollAgain(){
             pixelpos = 0;  // Reset the horizontal pixel position to 0
14           startScroll(); // Start scrolling again
          }
          function stopHere(){
15           clearTimeout(timeout); // Stop the clock to stop scrolling
          }
          function closeWindow(){
16           winObj.close();
          }
      </script>
   </head>
   <body bgColor="lightgreen">
      <font face="arial" size=4 >
      <b><br />
      <div align="center">
      A Window into an Autumn Day
      <form>
17       <input type="button"
            value="Start scrolling"
            onClick="startScroll();">
         <input type="button"
            value="Stop scrolling"
            onClick="stopHere();">
         <input type="button"
            value="Start over"
            onClick="scrollAgain();">
      </form></font>
      <font size=-1>
      <p>When you are ready to close the window, click here<br />
18    <a href="JavaScript:closeWindow()">Close the window</a>
      </font>
   </body>
</html>
```

EXPLANATION

1   A new *window* object is created. It will contain a .gif image of a fall scene.

2   The new *window* object is moved up to the top left corner of the browser (coordinates 0,0).

3   The *focus()* method puts the window on top of all other opened windows.

4   The initial pixel position that will be used for scrolling is set to 0.

5   The variable *ImgWidth* is assigned *1096*, which will be used to represent the size of the image in pixels.

6   Each time the image moves to the right, it will be moved 2 pixels in intervals of .02 seconds.

Continues

EXPLANATION(CONTINUED)

7   A variable called *timeout* is declared. It will hold the value returned from the *set-Timeout()* method.

8   A function called *startScroll()* is defined. It will start the image scrolling from the left of the screen to the right. If the scrolling is stopped before it reaches the end, this function will start scrolling where it left off.

9   If the value of the variable *pixelpos* is less than the width of the window, keep going.

10   Add one to the pixel position.

11   The *scrollTo()* method takes two arguments, the horizontal pixel position and the vertical pixel position. With vertical pixel position of 0, the image will move horizontally over one pixel to the right.

12   Set the *timeout* to 20 milliseconds: scroll the image to the right 50 times per minute.

13   A function called *scrollAgain()* is defined.

14   Scrolling starts again.

15   Stops the scrolling by clearing or turning off the timer.

16   This function closes the window.

17   Three buttons will be displayed. A function to start, stop, or restart the scrolling will be called depending on which button the user clicks.

18   If the user clicks this link, the window with the image will be closed. See Figures 10.22 and 10.23.

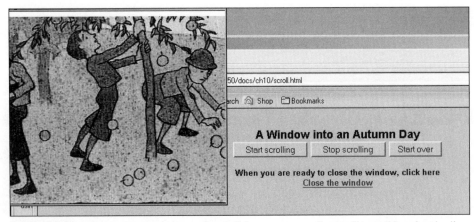

Figure 10.22   The new window on the left has a scene that will scroll by slowly; it can be stopped, and then restarted.

Figure 10.23 This is the scene that will be scrolling by in the small window above.

10.1.4 Working with Frames

When you look out the window in the room where you might be at the moment, it might be one big pane of glass like a picture window, or the window might be divided up into panes of squares or rectangles.

The browser is a virtual window that can be divided up into frames—independent windows, like panes, within the main window, where each frame is used to display different information. Invented by Netscape, frames allow you to display more than one Web page in the same window. Web designers have debated the merit of using frames because they are often misused but have some distinct disadvantages discussed later in this chapter.

The file that defines the layout of the frames is called the parent window, and each of the frames it describes is called a child (see Figure 10.24). Although you can't see the parent window, it will show up in the browser's source for the page.

Parent or Top Window

Child Frame	Child Frame
Child Frame	Child Frame

Figure 10.24 The parent window is divided into child frames.

To build frames in a Web page, you use the HTML *<frameset>* tags instead of the *<body>* tags (see Table 10.10). At least three files are needed to create frames. The first file defines the layout of the frames (or subwindows) by defining the size and position of the frames. The *rows* and *cols* attributes of each frameset specify how much room the frame will need within the window. These values use exact pixels as a default, although you can also use percentages to represent a section of the window, or an asterisk * to allocate leftover space. (These size values will be shown in Examples 10.15 and 10.16.)

Creating HTML Frames.   In Example 10.14 the window is divided into two frames: a left frame that takes up 25 percent (in columns) of the window and a right frame that takes up 75 percent (in columns) of the rest of the window. Because files are required to accomplish this, the main file defines the frameset, the second file contains the HTML code for the left frame, and the third file contains the HTML code for the right frame.

Table 10.10   HTML Frame Tags

Tag	Attribute	What It Does
<frameset>		Defines a collection of frames or other framesets.
	border	Sets frame border thickness (in pixels) between all the frames.
	frameborder	Draws 3D separators between frames in a frameset. A value of *1* or *yes* turns frame borders on; a value of *0* or *no* turns them off.
	rows	Defines the number and size of rows in a frameset.
	cols	Defines the number and size of columns in a frameset.
<frame>		Defines attributes of specific frames.
	name	Used by JavaScript to reference the frame by name.
	src	The URL or location of the frame.

EXAMPLE 10.14

```
      <html>
        <head><title>Frame Me!</title></head>
          <!-- Creating the framesets for two files -->
          <!-- This file is named: framesets.html -->
1     <frameset cols="25%,75%">
2       <frame src="leftframe.html" >
3       <frame src="rightframe.html" >
4     </frameset>
      </html>
```

EXAMPLE   10.14 (CONTINUED)

```
      <html>
         <head><title>Left Frame</title></head>
         <!--This file is named: leftframe.html -->
5     <body bgColor="yellow">
         <h2>
6            Just to show you that this is the left frame
         </h2>
         </body>
      </html>
```

```
      <html>
         <head><title>Right Frame</title></head>
7        <!--This file is named: rightframe.html -->
8     <body bgColor="lightgreen">
         <h2>
             Just to show you that this is the right frame
         </h2>
         </body>
      </html>
```

1   This is the parent file that defines how the window will be divided into frames. The first frame will take up 25 percent of the page in columns and the second frame will take up the rest of the page, 75 percent.

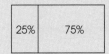

2   The frame *src* attribute is assigned the URL of the first HTML file, *leftframe.html,* that will be displayed in the window.

3   The frame *src* attribute is assigned the URL of the second HTML, *rightframe.html,* that will be displayed in the window.

4   The frameset definition ends with the *</frameset>* tag.

5   The background color of the left frame will be yellow.

6   This text appears in the left frame.

7   This section represents the right frame.

8   The background color of this frame is light green. See Figure 10.25.

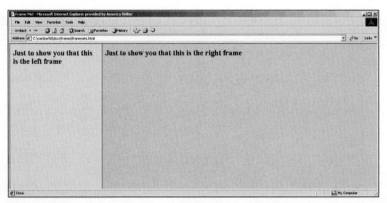

Figure 10.25 Two vertically positioned frames: Output from Example 10.14.

The next example shows a window partitioned into three horizontal frames.

```
   <html>
     <head><title>Frame Me!</title></head>
      <!-- This file simply defines the frames; it points to other
           HTML files (not shown) that comprise the HTML
           content  -->
1    <frameset rows="130,*,*" frameborder="yes"
         border="1" framespacing="0">
2      <frame src="topframe.html" >
3      <frame src="main.html" scrolling="no">
         <!--main.html is the middle frame -->
         <frame src="bottomframe.html" >
4    </frameset>
     </html>
```

EXPLANATION

1   This time the frameset will be divided up into three sections by rows. The first
    frame will be a horizontal frame consisting of 130 pixels in a row. Based on the
    amount of space taken up by the first frame, the remaining frames will be allocat-
    ed whatever space is left in the window. There are three frames that will be placed
    horizontally on the page (see Figure 10.26).

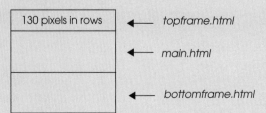

EXPLANATION (CONTINUED)

2   This is the URL to the first frame, *topframe.html*, which will be at the top of the window.

3   This is the URL to the second frame, *main.html*, which will be in the middle of the window.

4   This is the URL to the third frame, *bottomframe.html*, which will be at the bottom of the window.

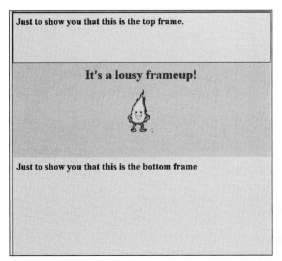

Figure 10.26   Three horizontal frames created in Example 10.15.

The *frame* Object.   HTML frames in JavaScript are represented as an array of frame objects. The *frames[]* array is a property of the *window* object and is referenced with the window's parent property. Each element of the array represents a frame in the order in which it appears in the document; thus, *window.parent.frames[0]* would reference the first frame defined in a frameset (see Figure 10.27). If you name the frame, then you can reference the frame element by its name. If the frame is named *leftframe*, it can be referenced as *window.parent.leftframe*.

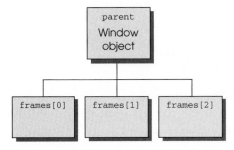

Figure 10.27   The JavaScript hierarchy.

Because frames are just little windows, they share many of the same properties and methods of the *window* object. See Table 10.11 for a list of properties and Table 10.12 for a list of methods.

Table 10.11   Properties of the *frame* Object

Property	What It Describes
document	The document currently loaded in the frame.
frames	An array of frames.
length	The number of elements in the frames array; that is, the number of frames.
name	The name of the frame assigned to the HTML name attribute.
parent	The main window from which the child frames are defined.
self	The current frame.
top	The window that started the script.
window	The current window or frame.

Table 10.12   Methods of the *frame* Object

Method	What It Does
blur()	Removes focus from the frame.
clearInterval()	Clears a timed interval.
clearTimeout()	Clears a timeout.
focus()	Puts focus into the frame.
print()	Invokes a print dialog box.
setInterval()	Sets a timed interval.
setTimeout()	Sets a timeout.
unwatch()	Unsets the watchpoint.
watch()	Sets a watchpoint on a frame property; if a property changes, calls a function.

Creating Menus and Navigation Bars.   Because frames can be used to divide a page, it is common to use one of the frames as a menu of items and the other as the main page where a page is loaded depending on the user's selection. If one frame contains a selection of links, then it can serve as a navigation bar. When the user clicks a link, the page at that URL will be loaded into the main frame.

In Example 10.16 the frames are defined for two frames. Example 10.17 displays the content of the two frame files. The left frame will represent a menu of links. The background color in the right frame will change when the user clicks a link in the left frame.

EXAMPLE 10.16

```
<html>
   <head><title>Frame Me!</title></head>
      <!--Creating the framesets for two frames -->
      <!--This HTML file is named: framedef.html -->

1     <frameset cols="25%,75%">
2        <frame src="leftmenu.html"  name=lframe>
3        <frame src="rightcolor.html" name=rframe>
4     </frameset>
   </html>
```

EXPLANATION

1   The HTML *<frameset>* tag replaces the *<body>* tag when working with frames. The size is determined by the *ROWS* and *COLS* attributes of the *<frameset>* tag. In this example, the first frame will occupy 25 percent of the window, and the second frame will occupy 75 percent of the window (in columns). The default is to set *ROWS* and *COLS* in pixels. (*ROWS* and *COLS* are not case sensitive.)

2   The first frame, named *lframe* occupies 25 percent of the left side of the window. Its content is in an *src* file called *leftmenu.html*.

3   This frame, called *rframe*, occupies 75 percent of the right side of the window. Its content is in an *src* file called *rightcolor.html*.

4   The HTML *</frameset>* tag ends the definition of the frames.

EXAMPLE 10.17

```
<html>
   <head><title>Left Frame</title>
      <!--This HTML file is named: leftmenu.html -->
      <script type="text/javascript">
1        function setBgColor(color){
2           parent.frames[1].document.bgColor=color;
            // Or use the frame's name: parent.rframe.document.bgColor
         }
      </script>
   </head>
```

Continues

EXAMPLE   10.17 (CONTINUED)

```
        <body bgColor="white">
          <h3>
            Pick a color:
            <br />
3           <a href="JavaScript:setBgColor('red')">red</a>
            <br />
            <a href="JavaScript:setBgColor('yellow')">yellow</a>
            <br />
            <a href="JavaScript:setBgColor('green')">green</a>
            <br />
            <a href="JavaScript:setBgColor('blue')">blue</a>
          </h3>
        </body>
    </html>
    -----------------------------------------------------------------
    <html>
      <head><title>Right Frame</title></head>
      <body>
        <h2>
          This is the frame where colors are changing.<br />
          In your JavaScript function, this is frame[1].
        </h2>
      </body>
    </html>
```

EXPLANATION

1   A function called *setBgColor()* is defined. It takes one parameter, a reference to a color being passed by the user.

2   Going down the document tree, start with the parent window, to the second frame, *frames[1]* (remember array subscripts start at 0), to the frame's document, and then the document's property, *bgColor*. Assign a color. This assignment will cause the background color in the right frame to change.

3   When the user clicks any of the following links, the JavaScript function *setBgColor()* will be called, with the color sent as an argument to the function. The *Java-Script:* pseudo URL prevents the link from going to a real URL. The display is shown in Figure 10.28 on page 311.

Using the *top* Property to Keep the Main Window Out of a Frame.   When the user loads your Web page into his or her browser, he or she may load it into a frame rather than in the main window. You might not want this, as framesets create states in the browser that are not addressable. For example the user might not be able to bookmark your page or reference it with the current URL once the frame content changes. See more on this at *http://htmlhelp.com/faq/html/frames.html#frame-problems*. You can use the location method to force your page to load in the main window by putting the

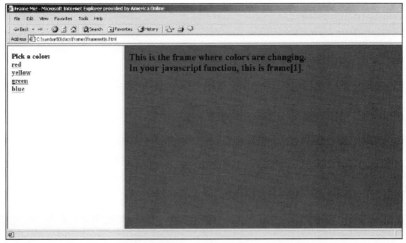

Figure 10.28 When the user clicks a link in the left frame, the background color in the right frame changes: Output from Example 10.17.

JavaScript code shown in Example 10.18 into the *<head>* portion of the page. Every window and frame has a *top* property, a reference to the topmost *window* object currently loaded in the browser.

EXAMPLE 10.18

```
     <html>
       <head><title>Forcing the Frame</title>
         <script type = "text/javascript">
1          if (window != top) {    // True if window is not the top
                                   // window in the hierarchy
2             top.location.href = location.href;
                                   // Put this window on top
           }
       </script>
3      <body bgcolor="lightblue">
         <h1>
           The important page that we're talking about
         </h1>
       </body>
     </html>
```

EXPLANATION

1   If the current window is not at the top of the window hierarchy in the browser, the statement in the block is evaluated. The *top* property references the highest object in the window hierarchy.

Continues

EXPLANATION(CONTINUED)

2   If the current window isn't at the top of the window hierarchy (if it's not the main window), this assignment forces the page, *location.href*, into the main window, *top.location.href*.

3   This is the body of the fictitious page that will be loaded into the main window of whoever views it.

Collapsing Toolbars and Menu Bars.   You don't always necessarily want to look at the toolbar or menu bar. It can be in the way of what you're viewing in the main page. Example 10.19 collapses the frame to bring the main frame to the foreground so that it will be viewed in the entire window.

EXAMPLE   10.19

```
<html>
  <head>
    <title>Untitled Document</title>
    <meta http-equiv="Content-Type"
          content="text/html; charset=iso-8859-1">
  </head>
  <frameset cols="117,450" rows="*">
    <frame src="toctoolbar.html" name="menu">
    <frame src="tocmain.html" name="main">
  </frameset>
  <noframes>
    <body bgcolor="#FFFFFF">
      Your browser needs to support frames to view this page.
    </body>
  </noframes>
</html>
------------------------------------------------------------------
(The Startup Main Page)
<html>
  <head>
    <title>Untitled Document</title>
    <meta http-equiv="Content-Type" content="text/html;
       charset=iso-8859-1">
  </head>
  <body bgcolor=yellow>
    <h1>This is the main page</h1>
  </body>
</html>
------------------------------------------------------------------
(The Menu Bar Page)
<html>
  <head>
    <title>Menu Bar</title>
```

EXAMPLE   10.19 (CONTINUED)

```
          <meta http-equiv="Content-Type" content="text/html;
              charset=iso-8859-1">
          <script type="text/javascript">
          var myUrl;
1         function openSite(url){
2             parent.main.location = url;
3             myUrl=url;
          }
4         function collapse(){
              if ( ! myUrl){
5                 parent.location = "tocmain.html";}
              else{
6                 parent.location=myUrl;        // Force this page into the
                                                 // parent location
              }
          }
          </script>
      </head>
      <body bgcolor="#FFFFFF">
7         <p><a href="JavaScript:openSite('tocmain.html')">Home</a><p>
          <p><a href="JavaScript:openSite('http://ellieq.com');">
              Page 1</a></p>
          <p><a href="JavaScript:openSite('http://prenticehall.com');">
              Page 2</a></p>
          <p><a href="JavaScript:openSite('http://google.com');">
              Page 3</a></p>
8         <p><a href="JavaScript:collapse();">Hide Menu</a><p>
      </body>
  </html>
```

EXPLANATION

1   A function called *openSite* is defined. It takes one parameter, the URL of the Web site.

2   The parent is the main window where the frames are defined. *main.location* is the frame on the right side of the toolbar. It was named *main* when the framesets were defined. The main frame is assigned the URL of one of the Web sites after the user clicks a link in the menu bar.

3   The global variable *myUrl* gets the URL of the current Web site shown in the right frame.

4   The function called *collapse()* is defined. Its function is to make the right frame fit into the whole window, hiding the menu bar.

5   If the user hasn't selected any page prior to selecting Hide Menu, the main frame will take up the whole window. The *location* property of the *window* object refers to the location of the parent window, the main window from where the frames were created.

Continues

EXPLANATION(CONTINUED)

6   The *location* property of the parent window is assigned the URL of the window currently being viewed in the right frame. This forces the right frame to take up the entire window. The menu bar is no longer displayed.

7   This list of links makes up the menu bar and is in the left frame (see Figure 10.29).

8   When the user clicks this link, the *collapse()* function is called, and the menu disappears, causing the right frame to take up the entire window (see Figure 10.30).

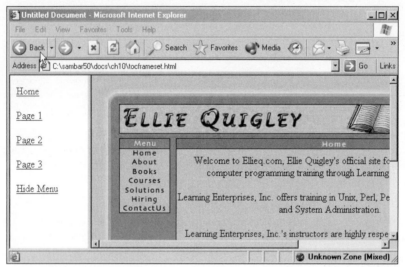

Figure 10.29   Two frames, a menu, and the main frame: The user clicked on Page 1.

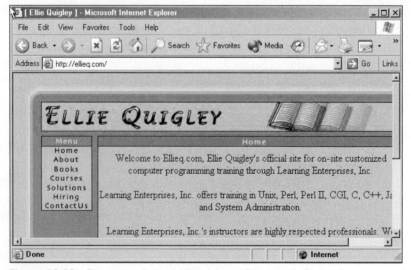

Figure 10.30   The user clicked *Hide Menu*. The larger frame has expanded to fill the entire page. Backpaging will take you back to the menu.

10.1.5   The *location* Object

The *location* object is a property of the *window* object and is used to access the URL of the document currently loaded in the window. In previous examples, we have seen *location* as a *window* property, but because it is really also an object itself, it also has properties used to describe the different parts of a URL (see Table 10.13).

If you are writing a page containing frames, the entire page might not be picked up by a search engine, such as Yahoo! or Google. Anyone linking to your page via the search engine will only get part of the page, not the complete frameset. Also, when a page is divided into frames, the visitor cannot bookmark the page if the browser is not pointing to the top frameset. The location object can be used to make sure the topmost window is the one currently viewed in the browser. (See the section "Using the top Property to Keep the Main Window Out of a Frame" on page 310.)

FORMAT

```
JavaScript: window.location.href = "URL";
JavaScript: window.location.replace("URL");
```

EXAMPLE

```
JavaScript: window.location.href = "http://www.legos.com/";
JavaScript: window.location.replace("http://www.legos.com/");
```

Table 10.13   Properties of the *location* Object

Property	What It Describes in the URL
hash	If it exists, the anchor part.
host	The hostname:port.
hostname	The hostname.
href	The entire URL.
pathname	The pathname.
port	The port number.
protocol	The protocol and colon.
search	The query string.

Table 10.14 *Methods of the location Object*

Method	What It Does
reload()	Reloads the current URL.
replace()	Replaces the current page with a new one.
unwatch()	Removes a watch point on the location property.
watch()	Sets a watch point on the *location* property; that is, calls a function if the property changes.

Two methods of interest (see Table 10.14) are *replace()* and *reload()*. The *replace()* method is used to change the location of the current page; that is, to point to another page. It is similar to the *href* property, but where *href* puts the new page at the top of the history list, the *replace()* method removes the current page from the history list and replaces it with the new page. The *reload()* method behaves like the browser's Reload button. It causes the window's current document to be reloaded.

Loading a New Page into a Frame with the *location* Object. In Example 10.20, the *location* object changes the location of the current page. By selecting a Web site, the user is taken to that site, which is displayed in the bottom frame of a frameset.

EXAMPLE 10.20

(The file defining the framesets called framefile.html)

```
<html>
   <head><title>Frames</title></head>
   <frameset rows="130,*" frameborder="yes" border="8"
            framespacing="0">
      <frame src="location.html" scrolling="no">
      <frame src="emptyframe.html" >
   </frameset>
</html>
```

(The empty file that will be the bottom frame called emptyframe.html)
```
<html>
   <head>
      <title>Empty Frame</title>
   </head>
   <body>
   </body>
</html>
```

EXAMPLE   10.20 (CONTINUED)

```
<html>
  <head>
    <title>The History Object</title>
    <script type="text/javascript">
1      function loadPage(urlAddress){
2        parent.frames[1].location.href = urlAddress;
       }
    </script>
  </head>
  <body bgcolor="F8C473">
    <big>
3    <form name="form1" id="form1">
      <input type="button"
        value="Amazon"
4        onClick="loadPage('http://amazon.com');">
      <input type="button"
        value="Borders"
        onClick="loadPage('http://borders.com');">
      <input type="button"
        value="Barnes&Noble"
        onClick="loadPage('http://barnesandnoble.com');">
    </form>
    </big>
  </body>
</html>
```

EXPLANATION

1   When the function *loadPage()* is called, it gets the URL address of the bookstore as its only parameter and assigns the address to the *location* object.

2   There are two frames in this document. The first frame contains the buttons with the names of bookstores to pick from—Amazon, Borders, and Barnes & Noble (see Figure 10.31). The second frame is empty until the user makes a selection. This statement assigns the URL of the chosen bookstore to the *location* object by traversing the JavaScript hierarchy, starting at the parent window, to the bottom frame, *frames[1]* and to the *href* property of the *location* object. By doing this, the browser will find the home page of the bookstore, and display it in the bottom frame.

3   The HTML form starts here. It is a form that displays three graphical buttons. When the user clicks one of the buttons, a function called *loadPage()* will be invoked and the bottom frame will display its Web page.

4   The JavaScript *onClick* event handler is triggered when the user clicks the button. The function called *loadPage()* will be called with the URL of the bookstore. The display is shown in Figure 10.32.

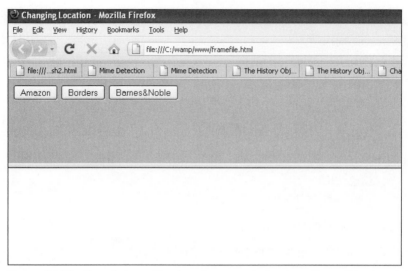

Figure 10.31   Two frames: The top frame puts the location of the bookstore in the bottom frame.

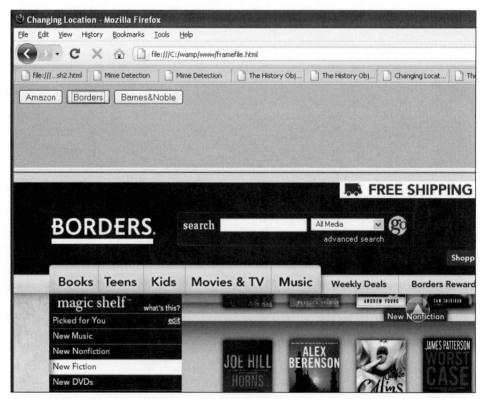

Figure 10.32   After the user clicks the Borders button, the bottom empty frame gets the page at that location.

10.1.6   The *history* Object

The *history* object is a property of the *window* object. It keeps track of the pages (in a stack) that the user has visited. The *history* object is most commonly used in JavaScript to move back or forward on a page, similar to the back button and forward button supported by your browser. The *history* object can reference only those pages that have been visited; that is, those pages on its stack. It has a *length* property and three methods called *go()*, *back()*, and *forward()*. See Tables 10.15 and 10.16.

Table 10.15   Properties of the *history* Object

Property	What It Describes in the URL
current	The current document URL.
length	The number of entries in the history object.
next	The URL of the next document in the history object.
previous	The URL of the previous document in the history object.
search	The query string.

Table 10.16   Methods of the *history* Object

Method	What It Does
back()	Goes to the previous URL entry in the history list; like the browser's back button.
forward()	Goes to the next URL entry in the history list; like the browser's forward button.
go()	The browser will go forward or back (if the value is negative) the number of specified pages in the history object.

EXAMPLE

```
history.go(-3)      // Go back three pages
history.go(2)       // Go forward three pages
back()              // Same as history.go(-1)
forward()           // Same as history.go(1)
```

EXAMPLE   10.21

```
1   (The file defining the framesets called framefile.html)
    <html>
       <head><title>Frames</title></head>
       <frameset rows="130,*" frameborder="yes" border="8"
              framespacing="0">
          <frame src="location.html" scrolling="no">
          <frame src="emptyframe.html" >
       </frameset>
    </html>
```

```
2   (The empty file will be the bottom frame called emptyframe.html)
    <html>
       <head>
          <title>Empty Frame</title>
       </head>
       <body>
       </body>
    </html>
```

```
    <html>
       <head>
          <title>The History Object</title>
          <script type="text/javascript">
             function loadPage(urlAddress){
3               parent.frames[1].location.href = urlAddress;
             }
          </script>
       </head>
       <body>
          <font size="+1" face=arial,helvetica>
          <form name="form1">
             <input type="button"
                value="Amazon"
                onClick="loadPage('http://amazon.com');" />
             <input type="button"
                value="Borders"
                onClick="loadPage('http://borders.com');" />
             <input type="button"
                value="Barnes&Noble"
                onClick="loadPage('http://barnesandnoble.com');" />
          </form>
          <form name="form2" id="form2">
             <input type="button"
                value="go back"
4               onClick="JavaScript: history.go(-1);">
             <input type="button"
                value="go forward"
5               onClick="JavaScript: history.go(1);">
          </form>
```

EXAMPLE 10.21 (CONTINUED)

```
        </font>
    </body>
</html>
```

EXPLANATION

1   This file defines the framesets that will be used to create the page seen in Figure 10.33.

2   This is the empty frame file seen at the bottom of the page.

3   When the user clicks one of the buttons, labeled Amazon, Borders, and Barnes & Noble, *parent.frames[1].location.href*, the bottom frame, will be assigned the URL of the selected page.

4   This button will be used if the user wants to go back to the previous page. If the *history* object's *go()* method takes a negative integer, such as *history.go(-1)*, the user will be sent back to the previous page just visited. (If nothing happens, the page is blank, and there is nothing in the history list to return to.)

5   This button will be used if the user wants to move to the next page. If you move forward and nothing happens, it's because you don't have anything on the history stack yet; you haven't gone anywhere. Once you load a new page, then go back, you will be able to move forward. Likewise if you go back and an empty page appears, it is because you haven't loaded a page yet. The *history* object's *go()* method, *history.go(1)*, will then move you forward one page. Output is shown in Figures 10.33 and 10.34.

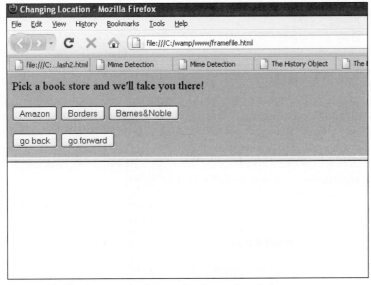

Figure 10.33 Frames before selecting a bookstore.

Figure 10.34   Bottom frame displays bookstore. If another bookstore is selected, then you can use history.

10.1.7   The *screen* Object

The *screen* object is a property of the *window* object and is automatically created when a user loads a Web page. It gives you access to the various properties of the user's screen such as its height, width, color depth, and so on. These are listed in Table 10.17. This can be helpful when designing pages that will require specific dimensions. For example, if the user's available screen width is less than 650 pixels (640×480), you might want to load a smaller image, whereas if it is over 1,000 pixels (1024×768), a larger image can be loaded. There are no event handlers for this object. Example 10.22 displays the properties of the screen object shown in Table 10.17.

Table 10.17   Properties of the *screen* Object

Property	What It Describes
availHeight	The pixel height of the screen, minus toolbars, and so on.
availLeft	The *x* coordinate of the first pixel, minus toolbars, and so on.

Table 10.17 Properties of the *screen* Object (continued)

Property	What It Describes
availTop	The *y* coordinate of the first pixel, minus toolbars, and so on.
availWidth	The pixel width of the screen, minus toolbars, and so on.
colorDepth	The maximum amount of colors that the screen can display.
height	The pixel height of the screen.
pixelDepth	The number of bits per pixel of the screen.
width	The pixel width of the screen.

EXAMPLE 10.22

```
   <html>
     <head><title>Screen Properties</title></head>
     <body bgcolor="orange"><font face="verdana">
       <b>The Screen</b><br />
       <table border=2>
         <tr><th>Screen Property</th><th>Value</th></tr>
         <tr>
           <td>Height</td>
           <td>
             <script type="text/javascript">
1              document.write(screen.height);
             </script>
           </td>
         </tr>
         <tr>
           <td>Available Height</td>
           <td>
             <script type="text/javascript">
2              document.write(screen.availHeight);
             </script>
           </td>
         </tr>
         <tr>
           <td>Width</td>
           <td>
             <script type="text/javascript">
3              document.write(screen.width);
             </script>
           </td>
         </tr>
```

Continues

EXAMPLE 10.22 (CONTINUED)

```
            <tr>
              <td>Available Width</td>
              <td>
                <script type="text/javascript">
4                   document.write(screen.availWidth);
                </script>
              </td>
            </tr>
            <tr>
              <td>Color Depth</td>
              <td>
                <script type="text/javascript">
5                   document.write(screen.colorDepth);
                </script>
              </td>
            </tr>
          </table>
          </font>
        </body>
      </html>
```

EXPLANATION

1 The *height* property of the *screen* object contains the height of the screen in pixels.
   (To see how to create a table dynamically with JavaScript, see Chapter 15, section
   "Creating a Table with the DOM" on page 644.)

2 The available height is the height minus any toolbars or other objects attached to
   the window.

3 The *width* property of the *screen* object contains the width of the screen in pixels.

4 The *availWidth* is the pixel width of the screen, minus toolbars, and so on.

5 The *colorDepth* refers to the maximum number of colors that the screen can display in bit format. The display is shown in Figure 10.35.

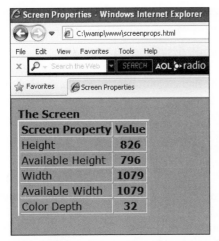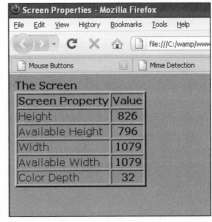

Figure 10.35 Tables showing properties of the *screen* object in Internet Explorer (left) and Firefox (right).

10.2 What You Should Know

They say windows are the eye of the soul and what would a browser be without them? This chapter was devoted to the BOM, and specifically the browser's window object. You learned how to open and close a window, and to divide it up into frames, how to time events within a window, create popups, navigation bars, and how to find the properties of your screen. You know the following about the browser and windows:

1. The appName and userAgent for your browser.
2. How to detect a plug-in.
3. What a browser sniffer does.
4. What MIME types are.
5. How to open and close a window.
6. How to give the window focus.
7. How to move a window to another part of the screen.
8. How to access the status bar.
9. How to access the title bar.
10. Two ways to set a timer.
11. How to create frames.
12. How to create a navigation bar.
13. How to use the location object.
14. How to use the history object to keep track of pages recently visited.
15. How to find the dimensions of your screen.

Exercises

1. In a new window, print all the properties of the *navigator* object.

2. Write a script that will display the name of your browser, the version, and the operating system you are using. (Use the *parseInt()* function to print just the version number.)

3. Does your browser support Shockwave Flash? Write a JavaScript program to show whether the plug-in is installed.

4. Create two links, one to open a new window and one to close it. The new window will display this message in a big font: *The eye is the window to your soul.* The new window will be positioned in the left corner of your screen, will be resizable, have a scrollbar, and it will have the focus.

5. Create an HTML document that contains four frames (i.e., four panes in a window, as in Figure 10.24). Each frame will display a different image. In another window, use JavaScript to display the number of frames in the original window and the name of the original window.

6. Create a program that produces a page containing frames. The first frame will span across the top of the page and contain a centered heading entitled *A Virtual Zoo.* A second frame will be used as a navigation bar at the left side of the screen. It will contain links to five animals. When the user clicks a link, an image of that animal will appear in a frame of its own to the right side of the navigation bar.

7. In an alert dialog box, display the pixel height, width, and color depth of your screen. Each value will be separated by a newline.

8. Create a program that will create a digital clock in the status bar. Use the *setInterval()* method to update the status bar once every minute with the current time.

chapter
11

Working with Forms and Input Devices

11.1 The Document Object Model and the Legacy DOM 0

If you recall from Chapter 1, "Introduction to JavaScript," a document object model is a way of conceptualizing a Web page where the document is represented as a tree structure. In Chapter 10, "It's the BOM! Browser Objects," we addressed the browser object model (BOM). The properties and methods of different browsers vary because there is no standard for defining what a browser does. The DOM, on the other hand, deals specifically with a document, and there are now standards that dictate how the objects in an HTML (or XML) page should be represented. The industry standard DOM is discussed in full in Chapter 15, "The W3C DOM and JavaScript." Before the W3C created a standard way to represent an XML/HTML document and all of its elements (DOM Levels 1, 2, and 3) there was a DOM, now called the Legacy Dom 0, invented by Netscape at the same time they created JavaScript. This DOM allowed developers to manipulate and query the content of a Web page, particularly forms and images, and it is still supported by all browsers even if they are DOM 1, 2, or 3 compliant. So if we have a better, newer, and more versatile DOM, why use the old DOM at all? Because the Legacy DOM is still more practical and easier to use when it comes to dealing with forms, images, links, and anchors. (In addition, DOM 0 is useful in searching for an element by its name with index values, removing and adding option elements from a select list, and using the *elements[]* array to work with input devices, such as buttons and textboxes.)

When an HTML document has been completely loaded, the browser represents it as a tree structure where all elements in the page are objects. When working with forms, JavaScript creates an array of all forms as it encounters them in the document, where *document.forms[0]* represents the first form and if there is another form, it is *document.forms[1]*. Similarly, all images, links, and anchors on the page are stored in a arrays representing their names, such as *document.images* and *document.links*, and so on. With JavaScript, you can go through these arrays in search of the exact image or form that you want to influence using the array syntax we discussed in Chapter 9, "JavaScript Core

Objects." The elements can be accessed in two ways: by name or by number. If, for example, you name the first form, "form1", then you can access it by name (associative array) as *document.forms["form1"]* or by numeric index value (numeric array) as *document.forms[0]*.

11.2 The JavaScript Hierarchy

We discussed the window as part of the BOM in the last chapter. The DOM is concerned only with those nodes that make up the document object. Documents contain text, images, forms, links, anchors, and so on. The most commonly used object is the ***document object***. Subordinate to the *document* object are another collection of objects, its children (see Figures 11.1):

1. The *anchors* object.
2. The *images* object.
3. The *forms* object.
4. The *links* object.

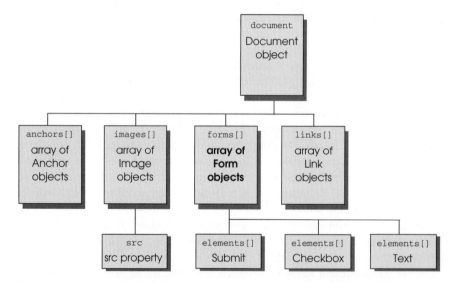

Figure 11.1   The document model.

Revisiting the Dot Syntax.   To refer to an object, you start with the *window* object (*parent*), followed by a dot, then the next object in the hierarchy, then another dot, and so on until you reach the desired object; for example, *window.location* or *window.document.forms[0]*. When referencing a child of the *window* object, it is not necessary to include the *window*, because JavaScript knows that the window is at the top of the tree. Instead of saying *window.document.bgcolor*, you can simply say *document.bgcolor*.

11.2.1 The Document Itself

The *document* object is a property of the *window* object, and if the window is partitioned into frames (subwindows), each frame is a property of the *window* object.

Every window (or frame) contains a *document* object that corresponds to the HTML document shown in the window. This object corresponds mainly to the body of the document—that is, what is inserted between the *<body></body>* tags. JavaScript programs manipulate this object to bring life to otherwise dead, static pages. Because the *document* object is below the *window* object, the *document* object can be represented as a property of the *window* by saying *window.document*. The *forms* object is an array of objects below the *document* object, so the *forms* object is a property of the *document* object and is represented as *window.document.forms[]*.

As stated before, because the *window* object is at the top of the hierarchy, any objects just below it, such as the *document* or *location* objects, are *window* properties and the word *window* is not required; thus, specifying *window.document.bgColor* is the same as *document.bgcolor*.

The syntax for describing the background color (*bgcolor*) property for a document object is shown in the following example:

```
document.bgcolor = "yellow";
```

Document Properties.   The *document* object is defined when the HTML *<body>* tag is encountered on the page and stays in existence until the page exits. The *<body>* tag has a number of attributes that define the appearance of the page. The *document* object has properties that correspond to the HTML *<body>* tag attributes, as shown in Tables 11.1 and 11.2. The properties of the *document* object are shown in the output of Example 11.2. (See Chapter 13, "Handling Events," for events that are associated with the *<body>* tag.)

Table 11.1   HTML *<body>* Tag Attributes

Attribute	What It Specifies
alink	Color of an active link; that is, while the mouse is on the link.
background	URL of a background image.
bgcolor	Background color of the page.
fgcolor	Text or foreground color.
link	Color of an unvisited link.
vlink	Color of a visited link.

Table 11.2 Some *document* Object Properties

Property	What It Describes
bgColor, fgColor	Determines the background color and text color, related to the HTML *<body>* tag.
cookie	Allows reading and writing HTTP cookies (see Chapter 16, "Cookies").
domain	A security property for Web servers in the same domain.
lastModified	A string with the date when the page was last modified.
linkColor, alinkColor, vlinkColor	Determines the color of unvisited links, active links, and visited links, respectively; related to link attributes of the HTML *<body>* tag.
location	The URL of the document (deprecated).
referrer	URL of the document that linked the browser to this document.
title	The title of the current document, related to the text between the *<title></title>* tags found in the head of the document.
URL	A string containing the URL of the document.

As shown in the output of Example 11.1 (see Figure 11.2), the document has a large assortment of properties. Most of these properties, those containing the word "Node," will be used with the standard W3C DOM Levels 1 and 2. The newer versions of the DOM give you the ability to get access to and manipulate all of the HTML/XML elements in the document.

EXAMPLE 11.1

```
      <html>
        <head><title>Looping through Object Properties</title></head>
        <body>
          <script type="text/javascript">
1            var props=new Array();
2            for ( var property in window.document){
3               props.push(property);
             }
4            for(i=0;i<props.length; i++){
5               document.write( props[i] + " " );
                if( i>0 && i%4 == 0 ){
                   document.write("<br />");
                }
             }
          </script>
        </body>
      </html>
```

EXPLANATION

1   A new array object called *props* is created with the *Array()* constructor.

2   The *for/in* loop allows you to enumerate (list one by one) the properties of an object, in this case the *document* object. The body of the *for/in* loop is executed once for each property of the *document* object.

3   Each time through the loop, a new property of the *document* object is pushed onto the *props* array.

4   This *for* loop iterates through the *props* array to list the properties that were assigned to it.

5   Each property of the *document* object is displayed in groups of three. The output differs somewhat on different browsers.

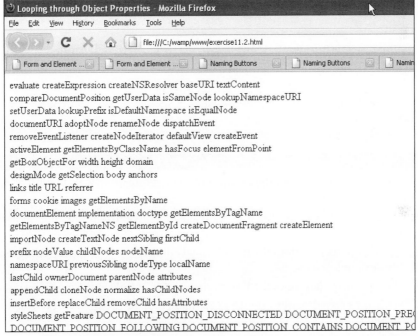

Figure 11.2   Partial output showing the document's properties.

Using the *document* Object Properties in JavaScript.   Example 11.2 demonstrates how the properties that describe the document are used in a JavaScript program. The *write()* method displays a description of each of these properties as they pertain to the current document. The background color is silver, the text is forest green, the unvisited link is blue, and the visited link is purple.

EXAMPLE 11.2

```
<html>
  <head><title>Document Object Properties</title></head>
  <body bgcolor="silver" text="forestgreen" link="blue"
             vlink="purple">
    <font face="arial" size="+2">
    <script type="text/javascript">
      var beg_tag="<em>"; end_tag="</em><br />";
      document.write("The location of the document"+ beg_tag +
1       document.location + end_tag);
      document.write("The document's title: "+ beg_tag+
2       document.title + end_tag);
      document.write("The background color: "+ beg_tag+
3       document.bgColor + end_tag);
      document.write("The link color is: "+ beg_tag+
4       document.linkColor + end_tag);
      document.write("The text color is: "+ beg_tag+
5       document.fgColor + end_tag);
      document.write("The document was last modified: "+ beg_tag +
6       document.lastModified + end_tag);
    </script>
7   <a href="thanks2.html">Thanks!</a>
    </font>
  </body>
</html>
```

EXPLANATION

1   This property contains the location of the document; that is, the full path name to the document.

2   This property contains the title of the document, shown in the title bar at the top of the window.

3   This property describes the hexadecimal color of the document's background, in this example, silver.

4   This property describes the hexadecimal color of links, blue in this example.

5   This property describes the hexadecimal color of the text, forest green in this example.

6   This displays the date and time when the document was last modified.

7   The link will change color from blue to purple once it has been visited. Complete output is shown in Figure 11.3. Clicking this link opens another page called "thanks2.html" displayed in Figure 11.4.

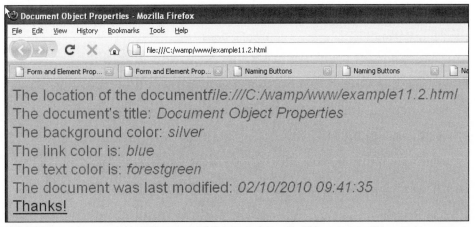

Figure 11.3 Document properties: Link turns purple after "thanks.html" has been visited.

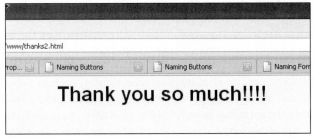

Figure 11.4 After the user clicks the link, this page is displayed.

The *document* Object Methods. The *document* object has methods to tell the object how to behave or what to do. Table 11.3 lists these methods. We have used the *write()* and *writeln()* methods throughout this text to send output to the screen dynamically, as shown here:

```
document.writeln("<h2>Welcome to the JavaScript World!</h1>");
```

Methods, like properties, use the dot syntax to define the object they are manipulating; for instance, *document.clear()* or *window.open()*. (The parentheses differentiate a method from a property.)

Table 11.3 Methods of the *document* Object

Method	What It Does
clear()	Clears the current document window.
close()	Closes the document window for writing.

Continues

Table 11.3   Methods of the *document* Object (continued)

Method	What It Does
focus()	Brings the document into focus.
getElementById()	Returns a reference to the first object with the specified ID.
getElementsByName()	Returns a collection of objects with the specified name.
getElementsByTagName()	Returns a collection of objects with the specified tag name.
open()	Begins a new document, erasing the old one.
write()	Writes and appends text into the current document.
writeln()	Same as *write()*, but appends a newline if in a *<pre>* tag.

11.3 About HTML Forms

At the heart of the Web is the form. It is used to pass information from the browser to the server. Anytime you go online and order a book, trade at an auction, fill out a survey, or send an e-mail using a Web browser, you are working with a form.

An HTML form offers you a number of ways to accept input, such as radio buttons, checkboxes, popup menus, hidden fields, and textboxes; these are called virtual input devices or controls. Once the form has been filled out by a user, it normally is sent to a server where the input is processed by a server-side program, such as a Java servlet, CGI, ASP.NET, or PHP application. It is important to understand how the form data is collected and sent to the server and then what role JavaScript has in this process.

11.3.1 Attributes of the *<form>* Tag

All forms are in HTML documents. They begin with a *<form>* tag and its attributes, followed by the input fields where the user enters form information, and end with a *</form>* tag.

```
<form name="form1" id="form1"
      action="URL to server program"
      method="post">
      <input type="text" name="town" id="town" />
            (continue here with body of the form
             including input devices for
             filling out the form;
             see Table 11.4 for a complete example).
</form>
```

The *action* Attribute. The *action* attribute is assigned the URL of the server program that will process the form data. After the user enters the information requested in the form, he or she will normally click a Submit button. That button might say "Order now," "Send Your Order!" or simply "Submit." When this button is clicked, the browser goes to the value in the *action* attribute to see where to send the data, which is normally the URL of a PHP, Perl CGI, or ASP script. The URL can be a relative or absolute URL (e.g., *http://localhost/cgi-bin/validate.pl* or simply *cgi-bin/validate.pl* or *validate.php*, etc.). When the form data is sent to the server program, it is processed further, validated, sent to a database or file, used in an e-mail, and so on.

Form data doesn't always get sent to a server program. It might be used by JavaScript to pass information to functions, cookies, and so on. To prevent the form from directing the page to a server, the *action* attribute can be assigned the empty string or simply be omitted, in which case the form data will not be sent.

The *method* Attribute. A *method* attribute can be assigned to the *<form>* tag. The *method* attribute indicates **how** the form data will be sent to the server. Simply put, for pure queries, the GET method is normally used, and for submitting form data, the POST method is used. (The method names are not case sensitive.)

The GET method is the default (does not need to be specified) and is used every time the browser requests a document. The GET method is preferable for operations that will not affect the state of the server; that is, simple document retrieval, queries, database lookups, bookmarking, and the like. It is the only method used for retrieving static HTML files and images. The GET method passes data to the server by appending the data to the URL (called the query string). The query string, prepended with a question mark, is a URL-encoded string consisting of name/value pairs. It can be seen in the Location bar of the browser as soon as the user clicks the Submit button in a form. In Figure 11.5 the name/value pairs being sent to the server are *color=yellow*.

You can also view HTTP headers of a page while browsing with a Firefox add-on called Live Headers (*http://livehttpheaders.mozdev.org/*). See Figures 11.5 and 11.6.

The POST method is preferred for handling operations that might change the state of the server, such as adding or deleting records from a database, uploading files, sending e-mail, and so on. The POST method is the most commonly used alternative when sending *form* data (see Figure 11.6). The post data is URL encoded in the same way it is with the *get* method, but it is posted to the server as a message body, similar to an e-mail message, rather than in a URL. The post method can be used when sending large amounts of data and is not shown in the Location bar of the browser, although it can be viewed as View Source under the browser's View option. If you try to backbutton post data, the browser normally sends you a warning so that you do not destroy or lose a previous transaction. This caution presumes that because the post method was used, there might be some permanent change to the state of the server.

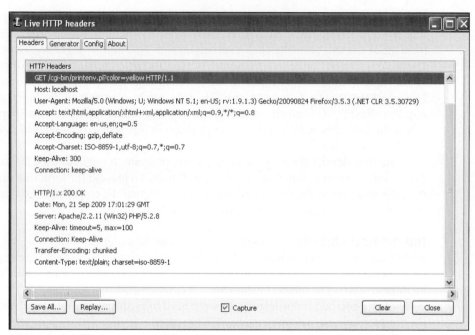

Figure 11.5   Firefox Live Headers shows how the GET method sends data in a query string appended to a URL and a question mark.

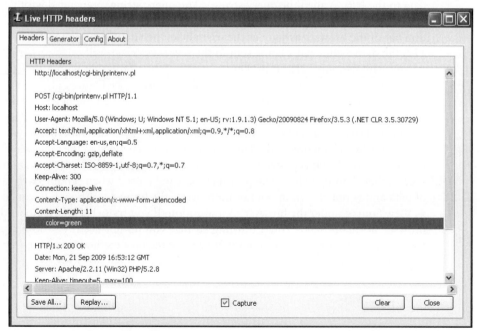

Figure 11.6   Firefox Live Headers shows Post data sent as part of the HTTP header.

A summary of the steps in producing a form follows:

1. START: Start the form with the HTML *<form>* tag.
2. ACTION: The *action* attribute of the *<form>* tag is the URL of the server-side (CGI) script that will process the data input from the form.
3. METHOD: Provide a method on how to process the data input. The default is the *get* method.
4. CREATE: Create the form with buttons, boxes, and whatever looks attractive using HTML tags and fields.
5. SUBMIT: Create a submit button so that the form can be processed. This will launch the PHP, ASP.NET, or CGI script listed in the *action* attribute.
6. END: End the form with the *</form>* tag.

Table 11.4 shows the various form input types.

Table 11.4   HTML Form Controls

Input Type	Attribute	Description
button	name, id	Creates a generic button for user input. It has no default action.
text	name, id, size, maxlength	Creates a textbox for user input. *size* specifies the size of the textbox. *maxlength* specifies the maximum number of characters allowed.
textarea	name, id, size, rows, cols	Creates a text area that can take input spanning multiple lines. *rows* and *cols* specify the size of the box.
password	name, id, value	Like textbox but input is hidden. Asterisks appear in the box to replace characters typed.
checkbox	name, id, value	Displays a square box that can be checked. Creates name/value pairs from user input. Multiple boxes can be checked.
radio	name, id, value	Like checkboxes, except only one button (or circle) can be checked.
select	name, id, option, size, multiple	Provides popup menus and scrollable lists. Only one can be selected. Attribute *multiple* creates a visibly scrollable list. A *size* of 1 creates a popup menu with only one visible box.
file	name, id	Specifies files to be uploaded to the server. MIME type must be *multipart/form-data*.
hidden	name, id, value	Provides name/value pair without displaying an object on the screen.

Continues

Table 11.4   HTML Form Controls (continued)

Input Type	Attribute	Description
submit	name, id, value	When clicked, executes the form; launches cgi.
image	src, name, id, value, align	Same as submit button, but displays an image instead of text. The image is in a file found at src.
reset	name, id value	Resets the form to its original position; clears all input fields.

First let's see how input gets into the form by looking at a simple document (see Figure 11.7) and the HTML code used to produce it (see Example 11.3). The user will be able to click a button or enter data in the textbox. The input in this example won't be processed when the Submit button is clicked. Nothing will be displayed by the browser.

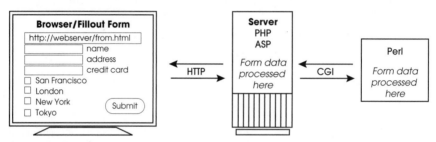

Figure 11.7   The life cycle of a fillout form.

```
      <html>
        <head><title>An HTML Form</title></head>
        <body>
          <big>
1         <form name="form1" id="form1"
                action="http://localhost/formtest.php"
                method="GET">
          <p><fieldset><legend> All About You</legend></p>
          Type your name here:
2         <input type="text" name="your_name" size="50" />
          <p>
            Talk about yourself here:<br />
3           <textarea name="comments" id="comments"
                  align="left" rows="5" cols="50">I was born...
            </textarea>
          </p>
```

EXAMPLE 11.3 (CONTINUED)

```
          <p>Choose your food:
          <strong>
4             <input type="radio" name="choice" id="choice1"
                      value="burger"/>Hamburger
              <input type="radio" name="choice" id="choice2"
                      value="fish"/>Fish
              <input type="radio" name="choice" id="choice3"
                      value="steak"/>Steak
              <input type="radio" name="choice" id="choice4"
                      value="yogurt"/>Yogurt
          </p>
          <p>Choose a work place:<br />
5             <input type="checkbox" name="place" id="place1"
                      value="LA"/>Los Angeles<br />
              <input type="checkbox" name="place" id="place2"
                      value="SJ"/>San Jose<br />
              <input type="checkbox" name="place" id="place3"
                      value="SF" checked />San Francisco
          </p>
          <p><b>Choose a vacation spot:</b><br />
6             <select multiple name="location" id="location">
                <option selected value="hawaii"> Hawaii </option>
                <option value="bali">Bali </option>
                <option value="maine">Maine </option>
                <option value="paris">Paris </option>
              </select>
          </p>
          <p></fieldset></p>
7         <input type="submit" value="Submit"/>
8         <input type="reset" value="Clear"/>
          </strong>
9      </form>
       </big>
     </body>
   </html>
```

EXPLANATION

1   This is the beginning of a *<form>* tag that specifies where the browser will send
    the input data and the method that will be used to process it. The default method
    is the GET method. When the data is submitted, a server-side program, in this ex-
    ample a PHP script, will be executed by the server on the local machine. (CGI
    scripts were the traditional way to process data submitted on a server.)

                                                                    Continues

EXPLANATION(CONTINUED)

2   The input type is a textbox that will hold up to 50 characters. When the user types text into the textbox, that text will be stored in the user-defined *name* value, *your_name*. For example, if the user types *Stefan Lundstrom*, the browser will assign to the query string, *your_name=Stefan Lundstrom*. If assigned a *value* attribute, the text field can display a default text string that appears in the textbox when it is first displayed by the browser. The *id* attribute can be used by JavaScript to manipulate the form element.

3   The user is asked for input. The text area is similar to the text field, but will allow input that scans multiple lines. The *<textarea>* tag will produce a rectangle named "comments" with dimensions in rows and columns (5 rows × 50 columns) and an optional default value (*I was born...*).

4   The user is asked to pick from a series of menu items. The first input type is a list of radio buttons. Only one button can be selected at a time. The input type has two attributes: a *type* and a *name*. The value of the *name* attribute *"choice"*, for example, will be assigned *"burger"* if the user clicks on the *Hamburger* option. *choice=burger* is passed onto the PHP program. And if the user selects *Fish*, *choice=fish* will be assigned to the query string. These name/value pairs are used to build a query string to pass onto the PHP program after the Submit button is clicked.

5   The input type this time is in the form of checkboxes. More than one checkbox can be selected. The optional default box is already checked. When the user selects one of the checkboxes, the value of the *name* attribute will be assigned one of the values from the *value* attribute; *place=LA* if *Los Angeles* is checked.

6   The user is asked for input. The *<select>* tag is used to produce a popup menu (also called a drop-down list) or a scrollable list. The *name* option is required. It is used to define the name for the set of options. For a popup menu, the *size* attribute is not necessary; it defaults to 1. The popup menu initially displays one option and expands to a menu when that option is clicked. Only one selection can be made from the menu. If a *size* attribute is given, that many items will be displayed. If the *multiple* attribute is given (as *<select multiple name="whatever">*), the menu appears as a scrollable list, displaying all of the options and the user can select more than one option by holding down the Ctrl key while clicking the option.

7   If the user clicks the Submit button, the PHP script listed in the form's *action* attribute will be launched. The form data will be URL encoded and sent to the server program assigned to the form's *action* attribute.

8   If the reset button (*"Clear"*) is pressed, all input boxes are reset to their defaults.

9   This tag ends the form. The output is shown in Figure 11.8.

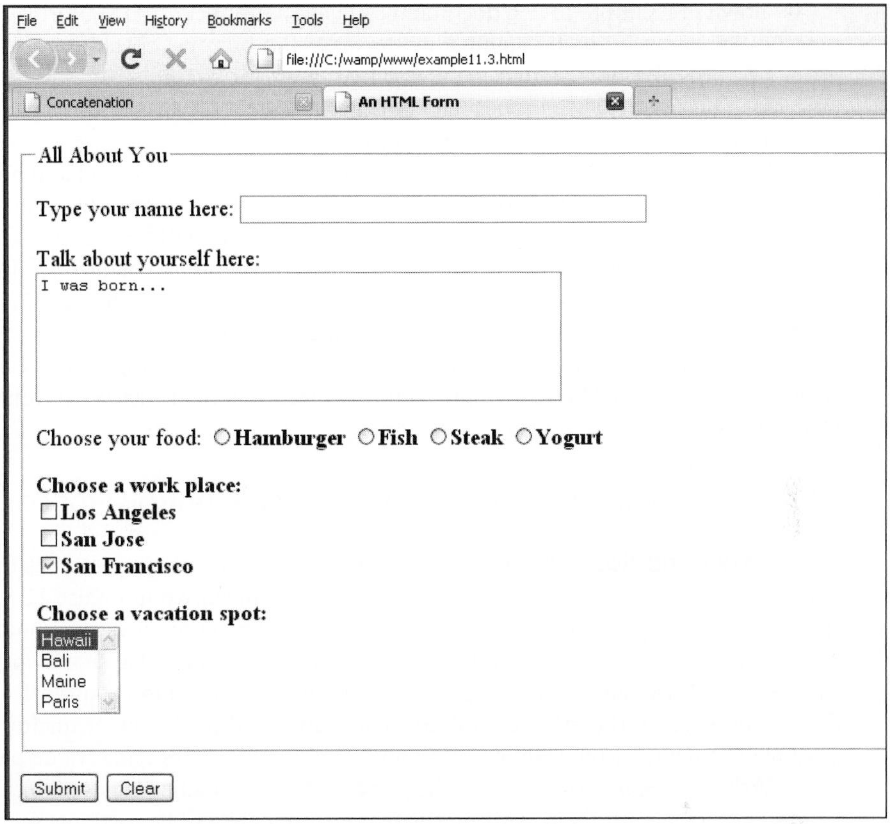

Figure 11.8 An HTML form.

11.4 JavaScript and the *form* Object

In the previous example, the HTML form had nothing to do with JavaScript. After a form has been filled out, the user clicks a Submit button and the information is normally sent from the browser to a server in a URL-encoded format. The server then calls a server helper application such as PHP or CGI to handle the information. So where does Java-Script come into all of this? Well, before sending the form information to the server, JavaScript can check to see if the form was filled out properly; for example, every input field can be validated by JavaScript. It can check for empty fields or improperly filled out fields. For example, it can check for the correct format of a credit card number, e-mail address, zip code, and so on. In addition, rather than having the user submit the form, submission can be controlled by JavaScript with its own *submit()* method. And by naming the forms, JavaScript can handle multiple forms and input types, respond to user-initiated events, and call functions to handle the data that was submitted.

As shown in Example 11.3, a document can have a number of HTML forms and input types, called controls, such as simple textboxes, radio buttons, checkboxes, and so on. JavaScript provides objects that parallel HTML tags; for example, the JavaScript *form* object parallels the HTML *<form>* tag and the JavaScript *elements* object parallels the input devices such as radio buttons or checkboxes.

In this section we focus on the structure of the JavaScript *form* object and how to use it in terms of the Legacy DOM 0, but because DOM 1 is a standardized version, some of the examples will include that version. In this chapter you will be introduced to event handling and forms, but events will be covered in more depth in Chapter 13. This chapter also includes a section on how to validate input data, but in Chapter 17, "Regular Expressions and Pattern Matching," you will learn how to check all the input fields of a form, using the magic of regular expressions and pattern matching and in Chapter 15 we will use the W3C DOM to manipulate form objects and fields (as well as other HTML elements).

11.4.1   Naming Forms and Input Types (Controls) for Forms

The *name* Attribute.   The HTML 4.01 specification calls the input types for forms, controls. The controls are listed in Table 11.4. The form shown in Figure 11.8 displays the controls in the browser as textboxes, checkboxes, select menus, radio buttons, etc. The controls are created by the HTML *<input type=name/value/>* tag shown in Example 11.3. After the user enters data into the form or clicks a button to make a selection, the data is collected by the browser and normally submitted to the server for further processing. The name of the form control and its value are sent as name/value pairs (e.g., *choice=fish* or *city=San Francisco*), to the server, where the names are used to extract the values associated with them. This means that if form data will be used in a server script such as PHP, ASP.NET, or CGI, the *name* attribute is required.

The *id* Attribute.   Before the server-side program is called, JavaScript can be used to validate the data that was entered into a form, manipulate the data, collect the form data and display in another window, send it in an e-mail, and so on. So why the *id* attribute? Java-Script uses the unique *id* attribute and its associated *document.getElementById()* method to identify all XML/HTML elements (nodes) within the document, including form controls. If the form data is not going to be sent to the server for processing, then the *name* attribute is not necessary. Because the form control can be referenced either by its name or a unique ID, when creating form fields, it is customary to use both and give them the same value when possible:[1]

```
<form>
   <input type="text" id="your_name" name="your_name" />
   <input type="text" id="cell_phone" name="field2" />
</form>
```

---

1. The ability to reference all of the HTML elements by unique ID was introduced by the W3C DOM, covered in depth in Chapter 15.

Normally the *id* and *name* attribute should match but this is not always possible. For example, when creating radio buttons, one name suffices for all the buttons, because only one of the buttons can be selected, but if you use the *id* attribute, each *id* has to be unique as shown here:

```
<input type="radio" name="color" id="rbutton1" value="red" />
<input type="radio" name="color" id="rbutton2" value="green" />
<input type="radio" name="color" id="rbutton3" value="yellow" />
```

In Example 11.4 the radio buttons are named using the same name, but with different IDs. After the user clicks a radio button, based on his or her choice, the *name/value* pairs from the form are collected by the browser and sent to the server-side program (see Figure 11.9). If the method attribute is GET, the name/value pairs will be assigned to a query string and if the method attribute is assigned POST, the pairs will be sent in an HTTP message body. When the PHP server script called color.php is executed, it receives the name/value pair "color=green". The PHP program can process the data, send it to a file or database, send it in an e-mail, respond to the user, and so on. The output for the server program is shown in Figure 11.10. Notice that the *id* attribute values are not sent to the server, but are retrieved via the *getElementById()* methods so that JavaScript can utilize them. *Name* attributes do not have to be unique; *id* attributes do.

EXAMPLE   11.4

```
    <html>
      <head><title>Id and Name Attributes</title></head>
      <body>
        <big>
1       <form name="form1" id="form1"
              method="GET" action="http://localhost/color.php">
          Pick a color: <br />
2         <input type ="radio" name="color" id="rbutton1"
              value="green"/>
          <label for="rbutton1">Green</label>
          <br />
          <input type ="radio" name="color" id="rbutton2"
              value="blue"/>
          <label for="rbutton2">Blue</label>
          <br />
          <input type ="radio" name="color" id="rbutton3"
              value="yellow"/>
          <label for="rbutton3">Yellow</label>
          <br />
          <br />
3         <input type="submit" value="Send to Server" />
4       </form>
```

Continues

EXAMPLE 11.4 (CONTINUED)

```
5        <script type="text/javascript">
6          var rb1=document.getElementById("rbutton1");
           var rb2=document.getElementById("rbutton2");
           var rb3=document.getElementById("rbutton3");
7          document.write("Using the id Attribute:<br />");
           document.write(rb1.value+"<br />");
           document.write(rb2.value+"<br />");
           document.write(rb3.value+"<br />");
         </script>
         </big>
       </body>
     </html>
```

EXPLANATION

1   The form is an object. It has a name and an ID. When this form is submitted, it will use the GET method to send the data to the Web server. You will be able to see the input data as name/value pairs right in the location box of your browser, the name of the input device being the key and the user input, the value.

2   The input type is a radio button. The name for all radio buttons is the same for all the buttons because only one button can be selected by the user. But the *id* attribute must be unique. Therefore, each radio button has the same name but a different ID. If input data is going to be sent to a server program, the name attribute is necessary to create the name/value pairs. If the input data is going to be used by JavaScript then the *getElementById()* method can use the unique value to get a reference to the input device.

3   When the submit button is selected, the data input by the user is collected in name/value pairs and sent by the browser to the server.

4   The HTML form ends here.

5   In the following script, JavaScript utilizes the *id* attribute to access the data for each of the radio buttons.

6   The *getElementById()* method returns a reference to the first radio button by using its unique *id*. The variable *rb1* contains the reference.

7   Once you have a reference to the button, you can use its properties with the dot syntax.

Figure 11.9   The form from Example 11.4 using both the *name* and *id* attribute.

Figure 11.10   The PHP program responds. Note the name/value pair after the ? in the Location box.

11.4.2   The Legacy DOM with Forms

The *forms[]* Array.   Because the document contains forms, the *form* object is a property of the *document* object. Every time you create a form in a given document, the browser creates a unique form object and assigns it as an element of an array, called the *forms[]* array. The index value of the array, starting at 0, corresponds to the order in which the form occurs in the document; the first form is assigned to *forms[0]*, and each successive form would get the next index value. When accessing a form from JavaScript, the first form to appear in the page would be referred to as *document.forms[0]* and the next form *document.forms[1]*, and so on. See Figure 11.11.

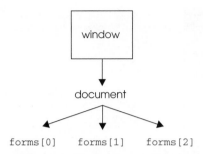

Figure 11.11   The JavaScript *forms()* array parallels the HTML form elements.

If you name the form with the *name* attribute of the HTML *<form>* tag, you can use that name to reference the JavaScript *forms* object. Rather than saying *document.forms[0]* or *document.forms[1]*, you can reference the form by its name. For example, if the first HTML form is named *myform1*, the corresponding JavaScript object, *document.forms[0]*, can now be referenced as *document.myform1*. Even better, you can use the name of the form as the index in an associative array, *document.forms["myform1"]* where the name of the form is the index value rather than a number.

The *elements[]* Array.   HTML forms contain input devices like buttons and text-boxes, also called fields. Similarly, the JavaScript *form* object consists of a property called *elements*. This is a JavaScript array that parallels all of the HTML fields within the form. Each of the input types in the *elements[]* array is also an object in its own right. See Figure 11.12.

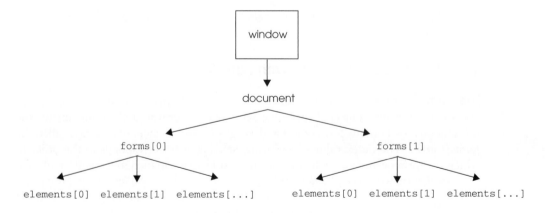

Figure 11.12   How the *elements[]* array parallels the HTML input devices.

When going down the DOM hierarchy, *document.forms[0].elements[0]* refers to the first field in the first form. The *element* objects also contains properties, such as the *name*, *type*, and *value* of the field. For example, *document.forms[0].elements[0].name* references the name of the field and *document.forms[0].elements[0].type* references the type of the field, such as *submit, reset, button, text, radio,* or *checkbox.*

If you name the field or input types, those names can be used to reference the corresponding JavaScript object. For example, *document.forms["myform1"].elements["your-name"].value* is easier to decipher than *document.forms[0].elements[0].value*, although they reference the same field value. Furthermore if the forms on the page are reordered, using the name of the form element as an associative array value makes it easier to move the object by name rather than by resetting the index values. When you start using DOM 1 and 2 in Chapter 15 the form and its elements can be assigned an *id* attribute. The *id* attribute must be unique for each element. It is used with the *getElementById()* method to retrieve a reference to the form or its fields, and in fact it can be used to retrieve any other element on the page as well.

The following example contains two forms, each containing input types. The name of the first form is *form1* and the name of the second form is *form2*. Each form is an element of the *forms[]* array.

Properties and Methods

EXAMPLE 11.5

(Two Forms)

```
<form name="form1" id="form1">
    <input type="text"
        name="yourname": Type your name here /><br />
    <input type="button"
        name="button1" id="button1"
        value="Push Button" />
</form>

<form name="form2" id="form2">
    <input type="radio"
        name="veggie" id="veggie1"
        value="bean" />Beans
    <input type="radio"
        name="veggie" id="veggie2"
        value="carrot"/>Carrots
</form>
```

Continues

EXAMPLE 11.5 (CONTINUED)

(Object Hierarchy using the array notations and the "name" attribute)

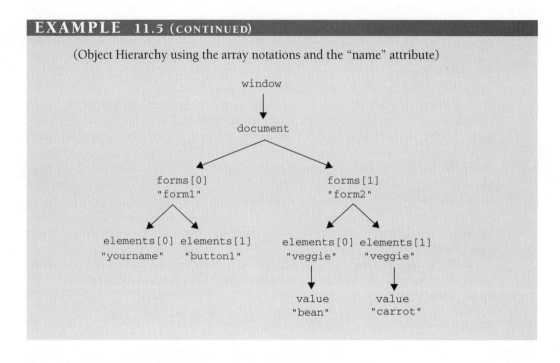

The *form* object is a property and child of the *document* object. Each form is an element of the *forms[]* array and each form has properties that correspond to the HTML attributes of the form as well as properties that describe the form. As discussed previously, these properties might be objects in their own right; for example, the *button* property of the form is also an object with its own properties. Some of the properties of the *form* object are listed in Table 11.5 and methods are listed in Table 11.6. Properties of the *elements* object are listed in Table 11.7.

Table 11.5   Properties of the *forms* Object

Property	What It Describes
action	The URL to the server (where the form is sent).
button	An object representing a generic button.
checkbox	An object representing a checkbox field.
elements	An array containing an element for each form field (radio button, checkbox, button, etc.) defined within a form.
encoding	MIME type (*application/x-www-urlencoded* or *multipart/form-data*).
FileUpload	An object representing a file-upload form field.
hidden	An object representing a hidden field in a form.
length	The number of fields defined within the form.
method	*get* or *post* (how the form is sent to the server).
name	The name of the form.
password	An object representing a password field.
radio	An object representing a radio button field.
reset	An object representing a reset button.
select	An object representing a selection list.
submit	An object representing a submit button.
target	References the HTML target tag attribute, the name of the frame where the user's response to the submitted form will be displayed.
text	An object representing a text field.
textarea	An object representing a text area field.

Table 11.6   Methods of the *forms* Object

Method	What It Does
reset()	Resets the form fields to their default values.
submit()	Submits a form.

Table 11.7 Properties of the *elements* Object

Property	What It Describes
form	The name of the form object where the element was defined (read-only).
name	The name of the input device as specified in the HTML *name* attribute (read-only).
type	The type of input device, such as radio, checkbox, password, and so on (read-only).
disabled	A Boolean value; if true the element is disabled so that it can't be modified; even if it contains a value, data from a disabled form field is not sent back to the server.
value	The text that is associated with the input device, such as the text entered into the text area or textbox, the text that appears in a button, and so on (read/write).

11.4.3 Naming Forms and Buttons

How JavaScript References a Form by *name* or *id*.   The *<form>* tag has a *name* attribute that allows you to give your form a name. It is somewhat easier and more readable to reference a form by its name than by using the array syntax, such as *forms[0]* and *forms[1]*. You will need the *name* attribute if you are submitting the form to a server-side program as discussed in Section 11.4.1.

Any object, including the form, can also be referenced by using its unique ID and the *getElementById()* method of the document, standardized by the W3C DOM.

In Example 11.6, two HTML forms are created: One contains a textbox, and the other a button. Each of the forms is given a name with the *name* attribute and an *id*. In the JavaScript program, the two forms are accessed by using the *name* and the *id* of the form and its elements.

EXAMPLE 11.6

```
    <html>
      <head><title>Naming Forms object</title></head>
      <body>
1       <form  name="form1" id="first_form">
          Enter your name:
2         <input type="text"
            id="namefield"
            name="namefield"
            value="Name:  " />
3       </form>
```

EXAMPLE 11.6 (CONTINUED)

```
4       <form  name="form2" id="second_form">
5         <input type="button" value="Press here">
6       </form>
        <big>
7       <script type="text/javascript">
          // DOM Level 0. How do we reference the form in JavaScript?
          // Go down the document tree: window/document/form.property
          // The window object can be left off, because it is at the top
          document.write( "The first form is named: " +
8           window.document.forms["form1"].name);
          document.write( ".<br />The second form is named: " +
9           document.forms["form2"].name);
          document.write(".<br />Also can be referenced as: <em>" +
            'document["form2"].name'+".</em><br />");
          document.write("Another way to reference a form: <em>" +
            'document.form2.name' +".</em><br />");
10        // DOM Level 1. The standardized W3C DOM way
          document.write("<br />Using the id attribute to get the form \
            name,<br />");
11        var f1 = document.getElementById("first_form");
          // define variables
          var f2 = document.getElementById("second_form");
12        document.write("The first form is named " + f1.name +
            ".<br />");
          document.write("The first form is named " + f2.name +
            ".<br />");
        </script>
        </big>
      </body>
    </html>
```

EXPLANATION

1   The *name* of the first HTML form in the document is *form1*. The *id* attribute is assigned *first_form*.

2   The input type for this form is a text field with a default value *"Name: "*.

3   This tag ends the first form.

4   The name of the second form is *form2*. Its *id* is *second_form*.

5   The input type for this form is a button with the value *"Press here"*, which will appear as text in the button.

6   This tag ends the second form.

7   The JavaScript program starts here.

Continues

EXPLANATION

8   To display the name of the first form, descend the JavaScript tree, starting at the *window*, to the *document*, to the first *form* object named *form1*, to its *name* property. We could write *document.forms[0].name* or *document.form1.name*, but by using the *form* object as a property of the document and the associative array notation with its name in square brackets, it is easier to identify the object as a form object by name if there are a number of forms on the page.

9   To display the name of the second form, descend the JavaScript tree as in line 8. This time we left out the *window* object, which is fine because JavaScript knows that the *window* is always at the top of the tree. See Figure 11.13.

10 Although this chapter focuses on the JavaScript legacy DOM 0 when working with forms, all HTML elements are accessible via the DOM Level 1, the standardized DOM, which all modern browsers should support. Navigating forms, images, and links with JavaScript has always been supported by DOM 0 and is still widely used.

11 The *getElementById()* method returns a reference to the HTML element by the *id* that was assigned to it on line 1. In most of the examples, the *name* and *id* are the same, but in this example, they are different to make it clear that the *id*, not the *name*, is used to get a reference to the element. The variable, *f1*, is a reference to the first form.

12 Now that we have a reference to the form, we can use it and the dot notation to get its name.

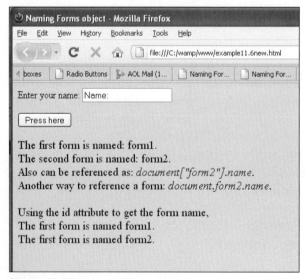

Figure 11.13   Name those forms!

The elements and properties of the HTML *<form>* tag are shown in Table 11.8.

Table 11.8   *<form>* Tag Elements and Properties

Object	*Property*	*Purpose*
button	*name, type, value*	A general-purpose GUI button.
checkbox	*checked, defaultChecked, name, type, value*	A set of (or one) clickable boxes allowing multiple selections.
FileUpLoad	*name, type, value*	A field allowing a file to be submitted as part of a form.
hidden	*name, type, value*	A field where the content is not shown in the form.
password	*defaultValue, name, value*	A field for entering a password, masking the real characters typed.
radio	*checked, defaultChecked, name, type, value*	A set of (or one) clickable boxes allowing only one selection.
reset	*name, type, value*	A button that clears and resets the form fields.
select	*length, name, options, selectedIndex, type, value*	A popup or scrolling list of items from which to choose.
submit	*name, type, value,*	A button used for submitting form data.
text	*defaultValue, name, type, value*	A rectangular field allowing one line of input.
textarea	*defaultValue, name, type, value*	A rectangular box allowing multiple lines of input value.

How JavaScript References the Form Elements by Name.   Each form object is an element of the *forms[]* array and each form contains input types such as buttons, textboxes, checkboxes, and so on. Each of the input types is also stored in an array called *elements[]* in the order in which the input device is found in the document. In the following example, there is one form, called *myform*. It contains two elements, button input types, named *button1* and *button2*, respectively. The JavaScript program gets access to the form and button properties by using names to reference them. An object can be referenced by using the numeric array notation, or referenced by its name with the dot notation; that is, object first, then dot and name, or by putting the name as a string in square brackets (associative array). If there are a number of forms and buttons, using the associative array notation, rather than the numerically indexed array notation, might make it easier to locate the object. For instance, if one of the forms or input devices has been moved or deleted, the numeric index values for all of the objects on the page would need to be changed. Writing *document["form3"]["button2"]* in place of *document.forms[2].elements[1]* would make the change easier.

If the first form on the page is named "myForm", there are several ways to reference it:

```
document.forms[0]
document.forms.myForm
document.forms["myForm"]
```

And to name a form's input element:

```
document.forms[0].elements[0]
document.myform.button1
document["myForm"]["button1"]
```

EXAMPLE 11.7

```
   </html>
     <head><title>Naming Buttons</title></head>
     <body bgcolor="cyan"><font face="arial">
       <strong>Naming Forms and Buttons<br />
       <big>
1      <form name="myform">
2         <input type="button" name="button1" id="button1"
                 value="red" />
3         <input type="button" name="button2" id="button2"
                 value="blue" />
4      </form>
       <script type="text/javascript">
         document.write("<b><br />Form name is: </b><em>" +
5           document.myform.name + "</em>");
         document.write("<b><br />Form name is: </b><em>" +
6           document["myform"].name +"</em>");
         document.write("<b><br />Name of first button is:</b><em> " +
7           document["myform"]["button1"].name
            + "</em>and its type is<em>"
            + document.myform.button1.type);
         document.write("</em><b><br />Value of button1 field:</b><em> " +
8           document["myform"]["button1"].value);
         document.write("</em><b><br />Name of second button is:</b><em> "
            + document.myform.button2.name);
         document.write("</em><b><br />Value of button2 field:</b><em> "
            + document.myform.button2.value);
       </script>
       </big>
       </strong>
     </body>
   </html>
```

EXPLANATION

1   The HTML form starts here. It is named *myform*. JavaScript can now reference the form by its name.

2   The input type is a button named *button1* and assigned a value of *red*. JavaScript can now reference the button by its name. The *id* attribute will not be used in this example. It is here because it is common to use both a *name* and *id* for the form and its elements. The *id* gives JavaScript another way to get access to the object, which will be covered in detail in later chapters.

3   The input type is a button named *button2* and assigned a value of *blue*.

4   The form ends here.

5   Within the JavaScript program the form is referenced by its name. It is a property of the *document* object. Without naming the form, it would be referenced as *document.forms[0].name*.

6   The name assigned to the first button is displayed. Putting the name as a string in square brackets (associative array) is a common approach to naming forms and their elements. Without naming the form or the button, it would be referenced as *document.forms[0].elements[0].value*. It is easy to make typos here. Spelling *myform.name* as *myform1.name* causes the output to be *myform1 is undefined*. See Figures 11.14 and 11.15.

7   Using the associative array notation, the name for the form is a string inserted in the first set of brackets, and the second element, a string name for *button1* is inserted in the second set of square brackets. We use the dot notation to retrieve the value of the *type* property for the form's button.

8   Using the two-dimensional associative array notation, we retrieve the value that was assigned to *button1*, which is *red*.

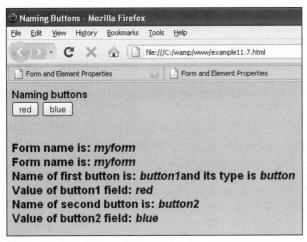

Figure 11.14 Name that button!

Figure 11.15 What went wrong? Watch your spelling! We tried to reference a form by the wrong name!

11.4.4 Submitting Fillout Forms

Submitting an HTML Form *Without* JavaScript. When the user clicks a submit button, the form is normally sent to the server for further processing by another application such as a PHP, ASP.NET, or CGI script. Before the server gets the form, its content is gathered by the browser, URL encoded, and then sent to the address supplied in the *action* attribute of the form. (In the previous examples, the *action* attribute was not used because there was no reason to process the user input in the sample forms.) The application on the server side decodes and processes the form information. From there, an acknowledgment can be sent back to the user, an e-mail delivered, the processed information sent to a database, or whatever else we define. Now let's look at an example of an HTML form and how it is submitted to a server application. After the user fills out the form, he or she will click the Submit button. The form data will be collected by the browser as name/value pairs and sent to the server. The *method* attribute determines how the data is sent (as a query string or message body) and the *action* attribute determines where it will be sent (the URL of a server).

EXAMPLE 11.8

```
  <html>
     <head><title>An HTML Form</title></head>
     <body><big><strong>
1    <form action="/cgi-bin/bookstuff/form1.cgi" method="post"><p>
        <fieldset><legend>All About You</legend>
        <p>
        Type your name here:
2       <input type="text" name="namestring" size="50" />
        </p>
        <b>Choose a work place:</b><br />
3       <input type="checkbox" name="place"
                value="LA">Los Angeles<br />
        <input type="checkbox" name="place" value="SJ">San Jose<br />
        <input type="checkbox" name="place"
                value="SF" checked>San Francisco <br />
```

EXAMPLE 11.8 (CONTINUED)

```
                    <br />
                    <input type="radio" name="status"
                            value="senior" id="senior" />
                    <label for="senior">senior</label>
                    <br />

                    <input type="radio" name="status" value="adult" id="adult" />
                    <label for="senior">adult</label>
                    <br />

                    <input type="radio" name="status" value="child" id="child" />
                    <label for="senior">child</label>
                    <br />
                    <br />Choose a vacation spot:<br />
    4               <select multiple name="location" />
                       <option selected value="hawaii"> Hawaii </option>
                       <option value="bali">Bali </option>
                       <option value="maine">Maine </option>
                       <option value="paris">Paris </option>
                    </select>
                    <p>
                    </fieldset>
    5               <input type="submit" value="Submit" />
    6               <input type="reset" value="Clear" />
                    </p>
                </form>
    7           </big>
                </strong>
            </body>
        </html>
```

EXPLANATION

1 The form starts here. The *action* attribute contains the URL of the server program that will get the form. The method being used (how the form will be sent) is the *post* method. This is the most common method used with forms.

2 The user is asked to type something into a text field box.

3 The user is asked to check a box for his or her place of work.

4 The user is asked to select a vacation spot from a select menu, or drop-down list. Because this is set to multiple, it allows more than one option to be chosen.

5 When the user clicks the Submit button, the form is sent to the URL (server program) assigned to the *action* attribute of the *<form>* tag.

6 If the user clicks the Clear button, all fields will be reset to their defaults.

7 This tag marks the end of the form. See Figure 11.16.

Figure 11.16   An HTML form.

Submitting a Form with an Image Button.   The image input type gives you another way to submit a form. You can replace the standard Submit button with a graphical image. The *src* attribute must be included to specify the location (URL) of the image. As with other image tags, the *alt* attribute (HTML 4.0) should be used to give replacement text for browsers that cannot load the image. Many browsers rely on either the *name* or *value* attribute as alternate text, so if there is any doubt, all three attributes for the same purpose should be used.

EXAMPLE 11.9

```
    <html>
      <head><title>An Image Input Type</title></head>
      <body bgcolor="magenta"> <big>
        <div align="center">
        Enter your name:
        <br />
1       <form action="http://localhost/cgi-bin/example.cgi"
              method="post">
2         <input type="text" id="textfield" size=50 />
          <p>
```

EXAMPLE 11.9 (CONTINUED)

```
3           <input type="image" name="submitbutton" src="submit.gif"
                alt="submit" />
            <br />
4           <input type="reset">
5         </form>
          </div>
          </big>
        </body>
      </html>
```

EXPLANATION

1   The HTML form starts here using the POST method to send the form input.

2   The input type is text. The user enters his or her name here.

3   The input type is a GIF image submit button. When the user clicks on the image, the form will be submitted and sent to the CGI program assigned to the form's *action* attribute. The *src* attribute is assigned the URL of the *submit.gif* image. If the image can't be loaded, the *alt* attribute will cause the word "submit" to appear where the image should go.

4   When the user clicks the Reset button (see Figure 11.17), the textbox will be cleared.

5   The HTML form ends here.

Figure 11.17 An image as a submit button (IE).

Submitting a Form *with* JavaScript (Event Handlers). A discussion of forms would be incomplete without mentioning how JavaScript implements form events (see Chapter 13 for a complete discussion). Events are triggered by a user when he or she initiates some action, like pressing a key, clicking the mouse on a button, or moving the mouse over a link. When such an action occurs, the browser detects it, and depending on what event is triggered, something will be done in response. A function might be called, a form can be validated—something happens. See Figure 11.18.

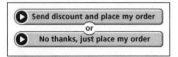

Figure 11.18   The user initiates an action, and an event is triggered.

With a form, an event handler allows you to control whether the form is submitted or cleared. For example, after the user has filled out the form, normally it is sent right off to a CGI, PHP, or ASP program on the server side to be processed. But if a JavaScript event handler is set up, then when the user clicks the submit button, the handler can check the input data, and based on what comes in, determine whether to go ahead with the submission of the form data or reject it without refreshing the page. That way, the user doesn't have to wait for the form to go to the server, have it validated there, and then sent back for mistakes that could have been corrected right away. (See section "Form Validation with Regular Expressions" on page 765 in Chapter 17 for a complete discussion.) Likewise, before clearing all the values typed into the form, an event handler can confirm with the user that this is really what he or she wants to do, before resetting all the input devices to their default values.

With forms there are two event handlers that allow you to catch the form before it goes to the server. They are the *onClick* event handler and the *onSubmit* event handler. The *onReset* event can be used to clear the form's input devices or to stop them from being cleared.

The *onClick* Event Handler.   One way to either accept or reject the submission is to use the *onClick* event handler. The *onClick* event handler is an attribute of the HTML *submit* or *button* input type. When the user clicks the button, the event is triggered, and if the handler function returns *true*, the form will be submitted; otherwise, it will be rejected.

EXAMPLE 11.10

```
       <html>
          <head><title>onClick Event Handler and Forms</title>
            <script type="text/javascript">
1             function readySubmit(){
                if(confirm("Are you ready to submit your form? ")){
                  return true;
                }
                else{
                  return false;
                }
              }
            </script>
          </head>
```

EXAMPLE   11.10 (CONTINUED)

```
        <body>
2           <form action="http://cgi-bin/testform.cgi"
                method="post">
            Enter your user id:
3           <input type="text"
                name="textbox"
                value="" />
            <br />
            Type your password:
            <input type="password"
                name="secret" />
            <p></p>
4           <input type="submit"
            onClick="readySubmit();" />
            </form>
        </body>
    </html>
```

EXPLANATION

1   The JavaScript function called *readySubmit()* is defined. It will display a confirm dialog box. If the user clicks OK, a *true* value will be returned and the form will be submitted. If the user clicks Cancel, *false* will be returned, and the form will be stopped (see Figure 11.19).

2   The form starts here. When submitted, it will go to the server-side CGI program. The URL of the CGI program is assigned to the *action* attribute of the HTML *<form>* tag.

3   The input types for this form are a text field and a password field.

4   When the user clicks the submit button, the *onClick* event handler is triggered. It will handle the event by invoking the JavaScript function called *readySubmit()*.

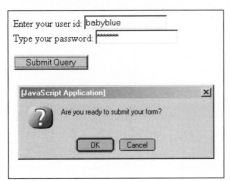

Figure 11.19   Submitting a form and the *onClick* event.

The *onSubmit* Event Handler.   Another important form event handler, called *onSubmit*, will also be triggered when the user clicks the submit button or presses the Enter key, just before the form is submitted. The *onSubmit* event handler is added as an attribute of the *<form>* tag (and **only** the *<form>* tag), to control what happens when the user clicks the submit button. When a function is assigned to the *onSubmit* event handler, if the value returned by the function is *true*, the form will be submitted to the server, but if it returns *false*, the form will be stopped and the user will be given a chance to reenter data in the form. Example 11.11 produces the same output as the previous one, but notice the placement of the handler. Instead of being associated with a button, it is associated with the form and set as an attribute of the *<form>* tag.

EXAMPLE 11.11

```
      <html>
         <head><title>onSubmit Event Handler and Forms</title>
            <script type="test/JavaScript">
1            function readySubmit(){
                if(confirm("Are you ready to submit your form? ")){
                   return true;}
                else{
                   return false;}
             }
            </script>
         </head>
         <body>
            <form action="cgi-bin/testform.cgi"
                method="post"
2               onSubmit="return(readySubmit());" >
            Enter your user id:
            <input type="text"
               name="textbox"
               value="" />
            <br />
            Type your password:
            <input type="password"
               name="secret" />
            <p>
3           <input type="submit" />
            </form>
         </body>
      </html>
```

EXPLANATION

1   The JavaScript function called *readySubmit()* is defined. It will display a confirm dialog box. If the user clicks OK, a *true* value will be returned and the form will be submitted. If the user clicks Cancel, *false* will be returned, and the form will be stopped.

2   The *onSubmit* event handler is an attribute of the HTML *<form>* tag. It will catch
     the form just before it is sent off to the server. When the user clicks the submit
     button, the event handler *readySubmit()* will be invoked. If the event handler is
     called by the *onSubmit* attribute of the *<form>* tag, an explicit *return* must be used
     (see Figure 11.20).

3   The input type is a submit button. When the user clicks this button, the JavaScript
     onSubmit event is triggered. (See line 2.)

Figure 11.20   Submitting a form and the *onSubmit* event handler.

The *onReset* Event Handler.   The HTML reset button allows the user to clear the
form fields and set them back to their default values. JavaScript will let you set up an
onReset event handler to either accept or reject this action. This event handler can be
used to make sure that clearing an entire form is really what you want to do before it's
too late, especially if you've done a lot of typing and don't want to reenter all that data.
It is an attribute of the *<form>* tag.

EXAMPLE   11.12

```
    <html>
      <head><title>The onReset Event</title>
        <script type="text/javascript">
1         function resetAll(){
2           if(confirm("Do you want to reset the form to its default "
                     + " values? ")){
3             return true;
            }
            else{
4             return false;
            }
          }
        </script>
      </head>
```

Continues

EXAMPLE 11.12 (CONTINUED)

```
        <body>
5         <form action="http://cgi-bin/testform.cgi"
              method="post"
              onReset="return resetAll();" />
          Enter your user id:
6         <input type="text"
                  name="textbox"
                  value="Name? "
                  id="textbox" />
                  value="Name? " />
          <p>Type your password:
7         <input type="password"
                  name="secret"
                  id="secret" />
          </p><p>
          <input type="submit"/>
8         <input type="reset"
                  value="Reset Form"/>
          </p>
        </form>
      </body>
    </html>
```

EXPLANATION

1   The function called *resetAll()* is defined. It is invoked when the *onReset* event handler is triggered.

2   If the user clicks the Reset button on line 8, he or she sees this confirm dialog box, a *true* value will be returned by this function, allowing the reset to clear all the input fields and set them back to their original values.

3   If a value *true* is returned, the fields will be cleared.

4   If a value of *false* is returned by this function, the reset action will be dismissed.

5   The form starts here. The *onReset* event handler is an attribute of the <form> tag.

6, 7   The input types for this form are a text field and a password field.

8   The reset button is used to reset the form fields back to their original values. When this button is clicked, the *onReset* event handler will be triggered. See Figure 11.21.

Figure 11.21 The user clicked the Reset Form button. The dialog box confirms the choice before the input boxes are reset to their default values.

11.4.5 The *this* Keyword

The *this* keyword is especially helpful when dealing with forms. We used the *this* word when working with objects as a reference to the current object. For forms containing multiple objects, such as checkboxes, radio buttons, and textboxes, it is easier to refer to the object with the *this* keyword than by using its full name when calling a function.

When using an event handler, the *this* keyword always refers to the object that triggered the event. If the event is triggered from within the *<form>* tag, *this* refers to the current form, but if it is triggered by an element within the form, such as an input device, then it references that element. Each element has a *form* property that references the form in which it was created. In the following segment of an HTML document, note that when the *onClick* event handler is triggered within the first *button* input type, the *form* property is used to reference the form itself, whereas in the second button, the *this* keyword refers to the current button.

FORMAT

```
<form>                                 <-- The JavaScript form object
<input type="button"                   <-- This a JavaScript element
   value="Print Form Stuff"
   onClick="display_formval(this.form);" />  <-- this keyword references the
                                                 form object by using the
                                                 element's form property

<input type="button"
   value="Print Button Stuff"
   onClick="display_buttonval(this);" />   <-- this keyword references the
                                               current object, the button
</form>
```

EXAMPLE 11.13

```
<html>
    <head><title>An HTML form and the "this" keyword and
           Event Handler</title>
        <script type="text/javascript">
1           function checkForm(form1){
2               if(form1.your_name.value == ""){
                    // Check for an empty string
3                   alert("Please type in your name");
                    return(false);
                }
                else{
                    return(true);
                }
            }
        </script>
    </head>
    <body><b>
4       <form method="post"
               action="http://localhost/cgi-bin/check.pl"
               onSubmit="return checkForm(this)"><p>
        <big><p>
        Type your name here:
5       <input type="text" name="your_name" size="50" />
        <br /><br />
6       <input type="submit" value="Submit" />
        <input type="reset" value="Clear" />
        </form>
    </body>
</html>
```

EXPLANATION

1   The function called *checkForm()* is assigned to the *onSubmit* event. When the user clicks the submit button, the event is triggered and as a result, the *checkForm* function is called. The *this* argument is a reference to this form. In *checkForm*, the parameter is called *form1*, called on line 4 with the *this* keyword, which is a reference to the form.

2   When following the DOM hierarchy, *form1* refers to *document.forms[0]*. The text field was named *your_name* on line 5. Now it can be referenced as *document.form1.your_name*. The *value* property refers whatever was entered in the text field. We are checking to see if the text field is the empty string, in which case we will alert the user.

3   The user is alerted to enter his or her name in the text field.

4   The *onSubmit* handler sends one argument, *this*, to the function *checkForm()*. The keyword *this* is a shorthand name for the current object; in this example the current object is a form, *document.forms[0]*.

5   The HTML input type is a text field named *your_name*, which will display up to 50 characters.

6   The HTML input type is a submit button. When the user clicks this button, the *onSubmit* handler in line 4 is triggered. If the return value from the function *check_Form* is *true*, the form will be submitted to the server, located at the URL shown in the *action* attribute of the form named *info*.

Using the *button* Input Type Rather than *submit*.   As shown in the previous examples, before the browser sends data to the server, an *onSubmit* or *onClick* event handler is triggered when the user clicks the submit button or presses the Enter key. But what if you don't want the form to go off to the server? Then you will have to reject the submission or the browser will reset all the field values to their defaults.

If the form is **not** going to submit data to a server, the *button* input type can be used instead of the *submit* button. The *button* object has no default behavior and is used as a triggering device so that when the user clicks the button, it causes something to happen. The *onClick* event handler is commonly used with buttons and is set as an attribute of the *button* input type. The *onClick* event handler is triggered when the user clicks the button associated with it.

EXAMPLE   11.14

```
    <html>
       <head><title>button input type</title>
        <script type="text/javascript">
1           function greetme(){
               alert("Why did you click me like that? ");
            }
        </script>
      </head>
      <body>
2        <form name="form1">
            <!-- event handler for a button is an attribute for its
                input type -->
3           <input type="button"
              value="Click me!"
4           onClick="greetme()" />
         </form>
      </body>
    </html>
```

EXPLANATION

1   This function called *greetme()* is called when the user clicks the button device.

2   A form called *form1* is started.

Continues

EXPLANATION(CONTINUED)

3   The input type is a simple graphical *button* containing the text *"Click me!"*

4   When the user clicks the button, the *onClick* event handler is triggered and the function called *greetme()* is called. It will send an alert dialog box to the screen, as shown in Figure 11.22.

Figure 11.22   Using a button to call a function.

11.4.6 The *submit()* and *reset()* Methods

In addition to event handlers (fully discussed in Chapter 13), JavaScript provides two methods for the *forms* object, the *submit()* and the *reset()* methods. These methods emulate the event handlers of the same name: The *submit()* method submits the form just as though the user had clicked the submit button, and the *reset()* method resets the form elements to their defaults just as if the user had clicked the reset button. Neither of these methods trigger the *onSubmit* or *onReset* event handlers. (Note that the methods must be spelled with lowercase letters.) These methods allow you to ask for user confirmation, check input data, and so on, before sending the form to the server for processing.

EXAMPLE   11.15

```
      <html>
        <head><title>An HTML Form</title></head>
        <body>
          <b>
1         <form name=myForm
                action="http://localhost/cgi-bin/environ.pl"
                method="post">
          <p>
          <fieldset><legend><big> All About You</legend>
          <p><font size=3 color="blue">
          Type your name here:
2         <input type="text"
                  name="namestring"
                  size="50" />
```

EXAMPLE 11.15 (CONTINUED)

```
          <p>
          Talk about yourself here:<br />
3         <textarea name="comments"
                  align="left"
                  rows="5" cols="50">I was born...
          </textarea>
          <p>
          <b>Choose a work place:</b><br />
4         <input type="checkbox"
                  name="place"
                  value="LA" />Los Angeles
          <br />
          <input type="checkbox"
                  name="place"
                  value="SJ" />San Jose
          <br />
          <input type="checkbox"
                  name="place"
                  value="SF"
                  checked />San Francisco
          <p></fieldset>
      </form>
      <p>
5     <a href="#" onClick="JavaScript: myForm.submit();" />
      Click here to submit this form</a>
      <p>
6     <a href="#" onClick="JavaScript: myForm.reset();" />
      Click here to reset this form</a>
   </body>
</html>
```

EXPLANATION

1   The form called *myForm* starts here. When the form is submitted, it will go to the address assigned to the *action* attribute, and the method—how the form is sent—is the *post* method.

2   The text field input type will accept a line of text from the user.

3   The text area box will accept up to 5 rows of text from the user.

4   The user can select any of the checkboxes. The default, *San Francisco*, is checked.

5   The link has been deactivated with the #. When the user clicks the link, the *onClick* event will be triggered and cause the JavaScript *submit()* method to be invoked (see Figure 11.23). The form data will be sent to the URL assigned to the *action* attribute of the form. The URL is a CGI program residing on the local server. Note that there is no need for the submit button here.

6   The link has been deactivated with the #. When the user clicks the link, the *onClick* event will be triggered and cause the JavaScript *reset()* method to be invoked. The input boxes will all be cleared and set back to their default values.

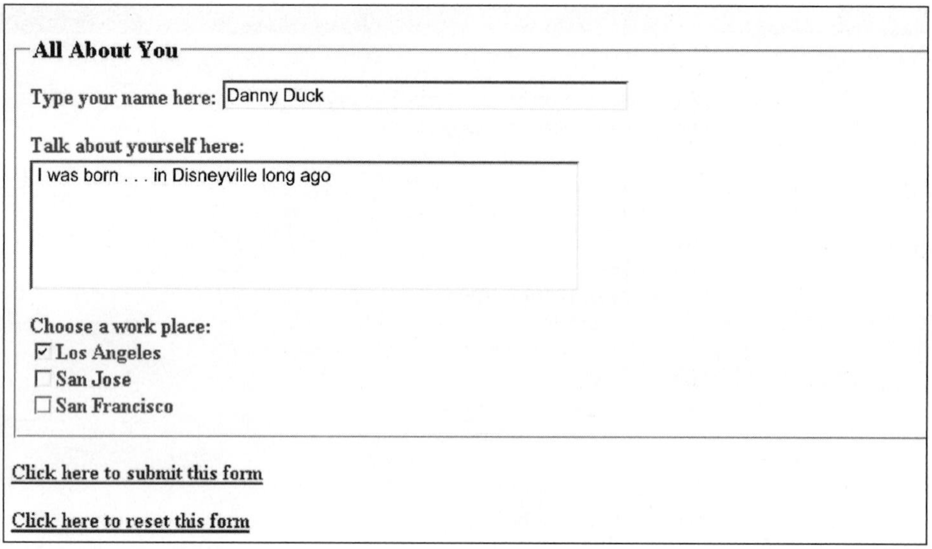

All About You

Type your name here: Danny Duck

Talk about yourself here:

I was born . . . in Disneyville long ago

Choose a work place:
☑ Los Angeles
☐ San Jose
☐ San Francisco

Click here to submit this form

Click here to reset this form

Figure 11.23 When the user clicks one of the links, either the *submit()* or the *reset()* method will be invoked.

Displaying a Form's Content in a Popup Window. After filling out a form, you might want to display the form content for confirmation before submitting it to a server. This can be done by creating another window, called a popup, and outputting the form data dynamically into that window. Example 11.16 uses JavaScript to open a new window to display the gathered form data from another file.

EXAMPLE 11.16

```
    <html>
      <head><title>Display Form Input</title>
        <script type="text/javascript">
1         function showForm(myform) {
2           NewWin=window.open('','','width=300,height=200');
3           name_input="<b>Your name: " + myform.user_name.value
                + "</b><br />";
4           NewWin.document.write(name_input);
            phone_input="<b>Your phone: " + myform.user_phone.value
                + "</b><br />";
5           NewWin.document.write(phone_input);
          }
6         function close_window(){
            NewWin.window.close();
          }
        </script>
    </head>
```

EXAMPLE 11.16 (CONTINUED)

```
      <body><hr><h3> Display form data in a little window</h2><p>
7         <form name="formtest">
8           Please enter your name: <br />
            <input type="text" size="50" name="user_name" />
            <p>
            Please enter your phone: <br />
            <input type="text" size="30" name="user_phone" />
            </p><p>
9           <input type="button"
                    value="show form data"
                    onClick="showForm(this.form)"; />
          </form>
          </p>
          <big>
10          <a href="JavaScript:void(0)" onClick="close_window()">
            Click here to close little window</a>
          </big>
      </body>
    </html>
```

EXPLANATION

1   A JavaScript function called *showForm()* is defined. Its only parameter is a refer-
    ence to the name of the form; in this example, *myform*.

2   A new *window* object is created with the window's *open()* method.

3   The variable called *name_input* is assigned a string that will contain HTML tags
    and the value that was assigned to the form's text field.

4   The document of the new window will display the string value assigned to the
    variable *name_input* in line 3.

5   The document of the new window will display the string value assigned to
    phone_input.

6   This function will close the new window.

7   The HTML form called *formtest* starts here.

8   The input type for this form consists of two text fields that will be used to obtain
    the name and the phone of the user.

9   When the *button* input device is clicked, the *onClick* handler will be invoked. This
    is when you will see the new little window appear on the screen with all the form
    data.

10 The JavaScript *void(0)* operator has the effect of deactivating the link so that it will
    not try to go to some URL when clicked (like the # in Example 11.17). Instead,
    event handler *close_window()* will be invoked and the little window that was
    opened to display the form data will be closed. See Figure 11.24.

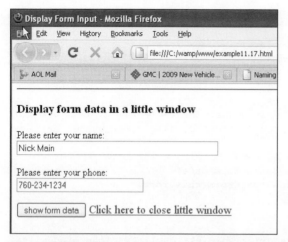

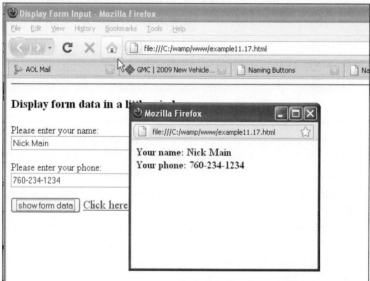

Figure 11.24 Form data is displayed in another window, called a popup window.

11.5 Programming Input Devices (Controls)

With JavaScript, you can alter the contents of the form's input devices dynamically (also called controls or elements). Because each input device is an object, each has properties and methods, and can be manipulated like any other JavaScript object (i.e., it can be assigned to, changed, deleted, etc.). You can program checkboxes, assign values to text areas and textboxes, change the value in fields, add choices to drop-down menus, verify password entries, and do all of this on the fly. The following section shows you how to program input devices.

The *text* Object.   The *text* object represents the HTML text field *<input type="text">* and also has name and value fields. To reference a text field from JavaScript, go down the document tree, starting at the *document*, then to the *form*, and then the *text* element. To get a value in the text field, for example, you would use the following syntax:

```
document.form1.textbox1.value,
```

where *form1* is the name of the form and *textbox1* is the name of the text field. Shown in Figure 11.25 is the JavaScript object hierarchy for the *text* object. Table 11.9 lists its properties and Table 11.10 lists its methods.

Figure 11.25   The *text* object within the JavaScript hierarchy.

Table 11.9   Properties of the *text* Object

Property	What It Describes
accessKey	By default, pressing an access key sets focus to the text object. The object receives focus when the user simultaneously presses the Alt key and the access key assigned to an object.
alt	Sets or returns alternate text to display if a browser does not support text fields.
defaultValue	The value assigned to the *value* attribute, and the default value the user sees in the textbox when it first appears.
disabled	Sets or returns whether or not a text field should be disabled.
form	The name of the form where the textbox is defined.
id	Sets or returns the *id* of a text field.
name	The name used to reference the textbox.

Continues

Table 11.9   Properties of the *text* Object (continued)

Property	What It Describes
type	The type of the input device; for example, *text*.
readOnly	Sets or returns whether or not a text field should be read-only.
size	Sets or returns the size of a text field.
tabIndex	Sets or returns the tab order for a text field.
type	Returns the type of form element a text field is.
value	The value attribute that will be assigned whatever the user types in the textbox.

Table 11.10   Methods of the *text* Object

Method	What It Describes
blur()	Removes focus away from the object.
focus()	Puts focus on the object.
handleEvent(event)	Invokes the handler for a specified event.
select()	Selects or highlights text in the box.
unwatch()	Turns off the watch for a particular property.
watch()	Watches, and when a property is changed, calls a function.

EXAMPLE 11.17

```
   <html>
     <head><title>Text Boxes</title></head>
     <body bgcolor="azure">
1       <form name="form1"
            id="form1">
         Enter your name:<br />
2         <input type="text"
            name="namefield"
            id="namefield"
            size=30 value="Name: "
3           onFocus="document.form1.namefield.select()" />
4           <!-- onFocus="this.select()">  -->
       </form>
```

EXAMPLE   11.17 (CONTINUED)

```
            <br />
            <font face=arial>
            <big>
            <script type="text/javascript">
            // How do we reference the form's text field in JavaScript?
            // Go down the document tree: document.form[].element.property
               document.write( "The type of the input device is:<em> "+
5                  document.form1.namefield.type);
            // document.write( "The type of the input device is:<em> "+
6            //    document["form1"]["namefield"].type);
               document.write( "<br /></em>The textbox is named:<em> "+
                  document.form1.namefield.name);
               document.write("<br /></em>The value in the text field is:<em>"
                  + document.form1.namefield.value);
               document.write("<br /></em>The size of the text field is:<em>"
                  + document.form1.namefield.size);

            // Using the id attribute of the element
               var tfield=document.getElementById("namefield");
               document.write("<br />The id of the textbox is "+tfield.id);
               document.write("<br />The  name of the textbox is "+
                  tfield.name+"<br />");

            </script>
            </big>
            </font>
         </body>
      <html>
```

EXPLANATION

1   The form starts here in the body of the document.

2   The input type is a textbox, named *namefield* with a default value *"Name: "*.

3   When the mouse cursor is clicked in this box, the *onFocus* event is triggered and the *select()* method causes the value in the textbox to be highlighted.

4   Instead of using the long, drawn-out, DOM hierarchy, the *this* makes it easier to reference this input type.

5   The property for the textbox, named *namefield*, is accessed using the DOM hierarchy. The output is shown in Figure 11.26.

6   An alternate way to access the property of the textbox is to shed the array format, in this case a two-dimensional associative array.

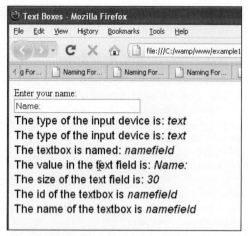

Figure 11.26   The textbox and its properties.

EXAMPLE 11.18

```
        <html>
          <head>
            <title>Assigning Value on the Fly to a Text Field</title>
          </head>
          <body bgcolor="aquamarine">
            <font face=arial>
            <big>
1           <form name="form1" id="form1">
              Enter your name
2             <input type="text"
3               name="yourname"
                id="yourname"
                size="60"/>
              <p></p>
              Click in the box
4             <input type="text"
5               name="message"
                id="message"
                size="60"
6               onClick="this.value='Greetings and Salutations, '+
                  document.forms["form1"]["yourname"].value+ '!';"
                />
              <p>
              <input type="reset" />
              </p>
7           </form>
            </big></font>
          </body>
        </html>
```

EXPLANATION

1 An HTML form called *form1* is started.

2 The input type for this form is a textbox that will hold up to 60 characters.

3 The name of the textbox is *yourname*.

4 The second input type is also a textbox.

5 The name of this textbox is *message*.

6 The *onClick* event handler is triggered when the user clicks inside this textbox. It concatenates the message "*Greetings and Salutations*" to whatever was typed in the first box, and assigns that value to this textbox, called *message*.

7 To clear all the boxes, the user can click the Reset button. See Figures 11.27 and 11.28.

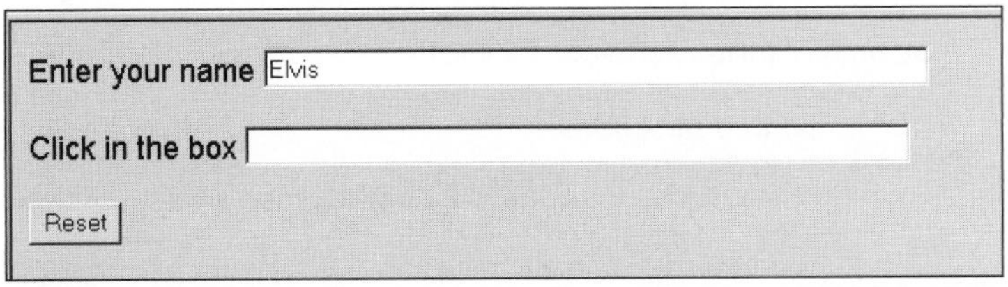

Figure 11.27   The user enters his or her name in the first text field.

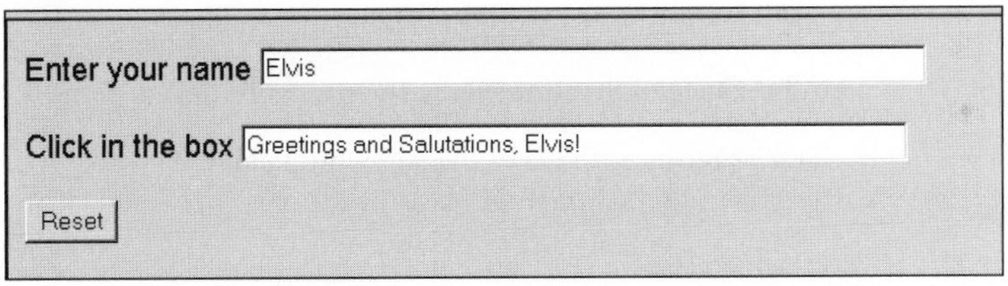

Figure 11.28   When the user clicks in the second textbox, a message appears.

The *password* Object.   The *password* object is much like the *text* object except that the input does not appear as text, but as asterisks or bullets, depending on the browser. The idea is to prevent a snoopy onlooker from seeing what is being typed in the box, but this is hardly a safe or secure type of password. If you look at the source of the HTML document, anywhere the actual password is spelled out, it appears in plain text for the viewer of the source.

The *password* object parallels the HTML password field *<input type="password">* and also has name and value fields. To reference a text field from JavaScript, you go down the document tree, starting at the *document*, the *form*, and then the *text* element. To get a value in the text field, for example, you would use *document.form1.passwd.value*, where *form1* is the name of the form and *passwd* is the name of the password field. Figure 11.29 shows the JavaScript object hierarchy for the *password* object. Tables 11.11 and 11.12 show properties and methods of the *password* object.

Figure 11.29   The *password* object within the JavaScript hierarchy.

Table 11.11   Properties of the *password* Object

Property	What It Describes
accessKey	Sets or retrieves the keyboard key to access a password field.
alt	Sets or retrieves an alternate text to display if a browser does not support password fields.
defaultValue	The value assigned to the *value* attribute, and the default value the user sees in the password field when it first appears.
form	A reference to the form where the password field is defined.
id	Sets or retrieves the *id* of the password field. Used with *getElementById()* method.
name	The name used to reference the password box. Used by the browser to set name/value pairs sent to a server when the form is submitted.
maxLength	Sets or retrieves the maximum number of characters in the password field.
readOnly	Sets or retrieves whether or not the password field should be read-only.
size	Sets or retrieves the size of the password field.
tabIndex	Sets or retrieves the tab order for the password field.
type	The type of the input device (i.e., *password*).
value	The value attribute that will be assigned whatever the user types in the password field.

Table 11.12 Methods of the *password* Object

Method	What It Describes
blur()	Removes focus from the password box.
focus()	Puts focus on the password box.
handleEvent()	Invokes the handler for a specified event (JavaScript 1.2).
select()	Selects or highlights text in the box.
unwatch()	Turns off the watch for a particular property.
watch()	Watches, and when a property is changed, calls a function.

EXAMPLE 11.19

```
1   <html>
        <head><title>Password Boxes</title>
            <script type="text/javascript">
2               function verify(pw){
                    if ( pw.value == "letmein" ){
                        alert("The chamber door will open now!");
                    }
3                   else{
                        alert("Sorry, you cannot enter. Please leave.");
                    }
                }
            </script>
        </head>
        <body bgcolor="#330033"><font color="FFCCFF">
            <div align="center">
            <h2> Welcome To The Secret Chamber</h2>
            <img src="wizard.jpg"><br />
            To enter, a password is required:<br />
4           <form name="form1" id="form1">
5               <input type="password"
                    name="passwfield"
                    size="30"
6                   onBlur="return verify(this)"/>

7               <input type=button value="Knock to verify"/>
            </form>
            </div>
        </body>
    </html>
```

EXPLANATION

1   The function called *verify()* is defined with one parameter, a reference to a *password* object.

2   If the value of the password box is equal to the string *letmein*, the user is told he can enter.

3   If the user didn't type in the correct password, he or she will be sent a message in an alert box.

4   The HTML form named *form1* starts here.

5   The input type is a password box. When the user types something into the box, a series of dots appears.

6   The *onBlur* event handler function, called *verify()*, is invoked when the user leaves the box and clicks his or her cursor anywhere else on the page. The purpose of the handler is to check that the user typed in a correct password.

7   When the user clicks the button, the *onBlur* event handler is triggered. See Figures 11.30 and 11.31.

Figure 11.30   The *password* object.

Figure 11.31 The user enters a password that isn't correct and receives the alert message.

The *textarea* Object.   If you don't have enough room to say it all in a text field, then you can use the text area box for multiple lines of input. The *textarea* object parallels the HTML *<textarea>* tag. The number of characters in a line is specified with the *cols* attribute of the *<textarea>* tag, and the number of rows in the box is specified by the *rows* attribute. If the *wrap* attribute is defined, when the user reaches the end of a line, a newline will be inserted and the input will start on the next line; otherwise a scrollbar will appear. The *textarea* object, like the *text* object, has a number of properties and methods that make it possible to access and change the text area from within a JavaScript program. These are shown in Tables 11.13 and 11.14.

To reference a text area box from JavaScript, you go down the document tree, starting at the *document*, then to the *form*, and then the *textarea* element. To get a value in the text area box, for example, you would use *document.form1.textarea1.value*, where *form1* is the name of the form, and *textarea1* is the name of the text area. Figure 11.32 shows the JavaScript object hierarchy for the *textarea* object.

Table 11.13   Properties of the *textarea* Object

Property	What It Describes
accessKey	Sets or returns the keyboard key to access a *textarea*.
cols	Sets or returns the width of a *textarea*.
defaultValue	The value assigned to the *value* attribute, and the default value the user sees in the text area when it first appears.
disabled	Sets or returns whether or not a *textarea* should be disabled.
form	The name of the form where the text area is defined.
id	Sets or returns the *id* of a *textarea*.
name	The name used to reference the text area.
readOnly	Sets or returns whether or not a *textarea* should be read-only.
rows	Sets or returns the height of a *textarea*.
tabIndex	Sets or returns the tab order for the *textarea*.
type	The type of the input device; i.e., *textarea*.
value	The value attribute that will be assigned whatever the user types in the text area.

Table 11.14   Methods of the *textarea* Object

Method	What It Describes
blur()	Removes focus from the text area box.
focus()	Puts focus on the text area box.
handleEvent()	Invokes the handler for a specified event (JavaScript 1.2).
select()	Selects or highlights text in the text area box.
unwatch()	Turns off the watch for a particular property.
watch()	Watches, and when a property is changed, calls a function.

Figure 11.32 How the *textarea* object is created within the JavaScript hierarchy.

EXAMPLE 11.20

```
   <html>
      <head><title>Text Area Boxes</title></head>
      <font face="verdana">
      <body bgcolor="lightgreen">
        <font face="verdana">
        <form name="form1">
          <strong>
             Finish the story
          </strong><br />
1         <textarea name="story" rows="8" cols="60" >
             Once upon a time, there were three little ...
          </textarea>
        </form>
        <script type="text/javascript">
          document.write( "The type of the input device is:<em> "+
2           document.form1.story.type);
          document.write( "<br /></em>The text area is named:<em> "+
3           document.form1.story.name);
          document.write("<br /></em>The number of rows in the "+
4           "text area is:<em> "+document.form1.story.rows);
          document.write("<br /></em>The value in the text area is:<em>"
5           + document.form1.story.value);
          document.write( "<br /></em>The number of cols in the text "
6           + "area is:<em>"+ document.form1.story.cols);
        </script>
        </font>
      </body>
   </html>
```

EXPLANATION

1 An HTML text area is defined. Its name is *story* and it consists of 8 rows and 60 columns. The text, *"Once upon a time, there were three little..."* appears in the text area.

2 The name of the text area is *story*. It is a *textarea* object. Its type is *textarea*.

3 The value of the *name* property is displayed.

4 The *rows* property of the text area contains the number of rows that were assigned in the *rows* attribute of the text area.

5 This is the value of the text that appears inside the box.

6 The *cols* property of the text area contains the number of columns that were assigned in the *cols* attribute of the text area. The output is shown in Figures 11.33 and 11.34.

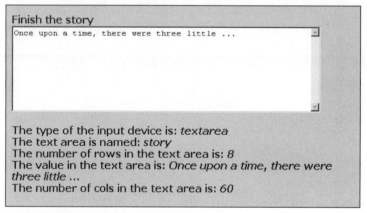

Figure 11.33   The *textarea* object.

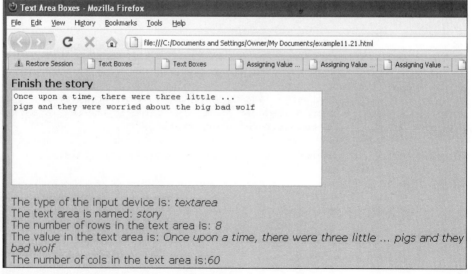

Figure 11.34   Output from Example 11.20.

Selection Lists (Drop-Down Menus).   The HTML *<select>* tag defines a field for display as a drop-down or a scrolling box. A select list consists of menu items called options. JavaScript supports a *select* object. The *select* object can be named but the options cannot. However, the *select* object has an *options* property (unique to DOM 0) that is an array of all the option items, so that if you have to get access to one of the options, remove or add options, you can use the *options* array. The *selectedIndex* property contains a number that represents the index number of the option that has been selected. If, for example, the first option in the menu is selected, then the value of the *selectedIndex* property is 0 (because array elements start at 0). To get a value in the selection list, you could use, for example, *document.form1.select1.options[0].value*, where *form1* is the name of the form, *select1* is the name of the *select* object, and *options[0]* is the first option in the list. Tables 11.15 and 11.16 list the properties and methods of the *select* object. Figure 11.35 shows the JavaScript object hierarchy for the *select* object.

Table 11.15   Properties of the *select* Object

Property	What It Describes
disabled	Sets or retrieves a value that indicates whether the user can interact with the drop-down list.
form	The name of the form where the select is defined.
id	Sets or retrieves the *id* of a drop-down list.
length	The number of items in the select list; same as *options.length*.
multiple	Sets or retrieves whether or not multiple items can be selected.
name	The name used to reference the select menu.
options[]	An array of option objects describing each of the selection options. Can modify select options (JavaScript 1.1). The *options* object has properties: *index length, text, selected, value*.
selectedIndex	The integer index value of a selected option, –1 if no option is selected. This value can be modified. If set to an index value, that option is *selected*, and all others *deselected*.
size	Sets or retrieves the number of visible rows in a drop-down list.
tabIndex	Sets or retrieves the index that defines the tab order for the select object.
type	Two possible values for the select object; if *multiple* is on, the value is *select-one* and if not, *select-multiple*.

Table 11.16   Methods of the *select* Object

Method	What It Does
blur()	Removes focus from the select box.
focus()	Puts focus in the select box.
handleEvent()	Invokes the handler for a specified event (JavaScript 1.2).
unwatch()	Turns off the watch for a particular property.
watch()	Watches, and when a property is changed, calls a function.

Figure 11.35   How the *select* object is created within the JavaScript hierarchy.

EXAMPLE **11.21**

```
        <html>
          <head><title>Drop-Down Menus</title></head>
          <body bgcolor="lightgreen">
            <font face="arial">
            <strong>Select a Course
1           <form name="form1">
2             <select name="menu1" size="4" >
3                 <option name="choice1" value="Perl1">Intro to
                      Perl</option>
                  <option name="choice2" value="Perl2">Advanced
                      Perl</option>
```

EXAMPLE   11.21 (CONTINUED)

```
                    <option name="choice3" value="Unix1">Intro to
                        Unix</option>
                    <option name="choice4" value="Shell1">Shell
                        Programming</option>
4           </select>
            <br /><br />
        </form>
5       <script type="text/javascript">
            document.write("The name of the selection list is ",
6               document.form1.menu1.name);
            document.write("<br />The number of items in the selection"+
7               "list is ", document.form1.menu1.length);
            document.write("<br />The item currently selected is option["+
8               document.form1.menu1.selectedIndex + "]");
            document.write("<br />The text in the first selection is "+
9               document.form1.menu1.options[0].text);
            document.write("<br />The text in the second selection is "+
                document.form1.menu1.options[1].text);
        </script>
        </strong>
        </font>
    </body>
</html>
```

EXPLANATION

1   The HTML form named *form1* starts here. The *action* and *method* attributes are not included here because this form is not being sent to a server.

2   The *select* tag starts a drop-down list named *menu1*; it has four options.

3   The options that will appear in the menu are listed.

4   This ends the select list.

5   The JavaScript program starts here. It displays the properties of the *select* object.

6   The name of the *select* object is displayed.

7   The number of options in the select list is displayed.

8   The index value of the option selected by the user is displayed. If no option has been selected, the value of *selectedIndex* is −1. If one has been selected, the index value of the option is displayed. The options are in an array where the index starts at 0. The first option is at index 0, the second option is index 1, and so on.

9   The actual text shown in the list for the first option is displayed, followed by the text in the second selection. The output is shown in Figures 11.36 and 11.37.

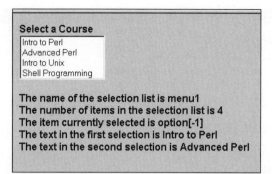

Figure 11.36   A selection list's properties before anything has been selected.

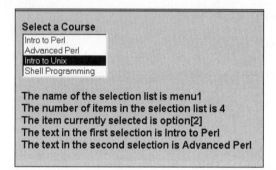

Figure 11.37   A selection list's properties after an item has been selected.

EXAMPLE 11.22

```
    <html>
      <head><title>Drop-Down Menus</title>
        <script type="text/javascript">
1         function schedule(f){
2           if(f.menu1.selectedIndex == 0){
              // Could also say: document.form1.menu1.selectedIndex
3             f.text1.value="PL100, Feb 3-7, 9am to 5pm, Room 2133,
                  Dr. Baloney "
              // Could also say: document.form1.text1.value
            }
            if(f.menu1.selectedIndex == 1){
              f.text1.value="PL200 Feb 10-13 9am to 5pm, Room 209B,
                  Ms. Eclectic";
            }
            if(f.menu1.selectedIndex == 2){
              f.text1.value="UX101 Mar 2-6 9am to 5pm, Room 209,
                  Mr. Nerdly";
            }
```

EXAMPLE 11.22 (CONTINUED)

```
                if(f.menu1.selectedIndex == 3){
                    f.text1.value="SH201 Apr 10-13 9am to 5pm, Room 209B,
                        Miss Bashing";
                }
            }
        </script>
    </head>
    <body bgcolor="lightgreen">
        <font face="arial">
        <b>
4       <form name="form1">
            Select a Course<br />
5           <select name="menu1" size="4"
                    onChange="schedule(this.form)">
6               <option name="choice1" value="Perl1">Intro to
                    Perl</option>
                <option name="choice2" value="Perl2">Advanced
                    Perl</option>
                <option name="choice3" value="Unix1">Intro to
                    Unix</option>
                <option name="choice4" value="Shell1">Shell
                    Programming</option>
            </select>
            <br /><br />
7           <input type="text" name="text1" size=60 />
        </form>
        </font>
    </body>
</html>
```

EXPLANATION

1   A function called *schedule()* is defined. The parameter, *f*, represents the *form* object; that is, *document.form1*.

2   If the first item in the select menu is checked, the *selectedIndex* value is 0. The number represents the index into the *options[]* array, where *options[0]* is the first option.

3   If the first option was selected in the menu, then the value of the textbox, called *textbox1*, is assigned a string describing the "*Intro to Perl*" course. This assignment updates the textbox field dynamically.

4   The form, named *form1*, starts here.

5   The select menu called *menu1* will contain a list of four options. The *onChange* event will be triggered for this event as soon as something is entered in one of the options.

6   An option list for the select input device is created. This will produce a menu with choices.

7   An input textbox device, named *text1*, is created. The output is shown in Figures 11.38 and 11.39.

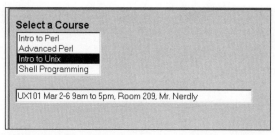

Figure 11.38   After the user selected the third option in the menu, the textbox is updated dynamically.

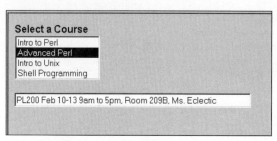

Figure 11.39   The user selects another menu item.

Multiple Selects.   If you use the *multiple* attribute of a select list, more than one option can be selected. To select more than one item, hold down the Control key while clicking on an item. If more than one item is chosen, the *selectedIndex* value will indicate only the first one that was selected. To test whether more than one option has been selected, you can use the *selected* property of the *options* object. This property will result in *true* if an option has been selected; *false* otherwise. See Example 11.23.

EXAMPLE   11.23

```
      <html>
        <head><title>Drop Down Menus</title>
          <script type="text/javascript">
1           function showme(form){
2              var choices="";
3              for (i=0;i< form.vacation.options.length;i++){
4                 if( form.vacation.options[i].selected == true){
5                    choices += form.vacation.options[i].text+"\n";
                  }
               }
6              alert(choices);
            }
          </script>
        </head>
```

EXAMPLE 11.23 (CONTINUED)

```
           <body bgcolor="lightgreen">
             <font face="arial">
             <b>
7            <form name="form1" onSubmit="showme(this);" />
               Where do you want to go? <br />
8            <select name="vacation" size=4 multiple>
               <option>Maui</option>
               <option>Jamaica</option>
               <option>Bali</option>
               <option>Virgin Islands</option>
             </select>
             <p></p>
             </b>
             <input type="submit" />
             <input type="reset" />
           </form>
           </font>
         </body>
      </html>
```

EXPLANATION

1   The function called *showme()* is defined. It is passed one parameter, a reference to a *form* object.

2   The variable called *choices* is declared and assigned an empty string.

3   The *for* loop is entered. The initial value, *i*, is set to 0. As long as the value of *i* is less than the length of the options array, the body of the loop will be entered; thus, as long as we haven't looped through all the options in the menu, the loop will be entered.

4   If the option from the menu was selected, the *selected* property will evaluate to *true*.

5   If an option was selected, the variable, called *choices*, will be assigned the text value of the option; perhaps *Maui* or *Bali* will be assigned to *choices*. Each time through the *for* loop, if an option is selected, it will be appended to the variable, resulting in a string that contains all of the selected options.

6   The alert dialog box will display the string value containing all the options that were selected.

7   The HTML form called *form1* starts here.

8   The HTML select menu called *vacation* starts here. It will contain four menu options, and allow multiple selections. See Figure 11.40.

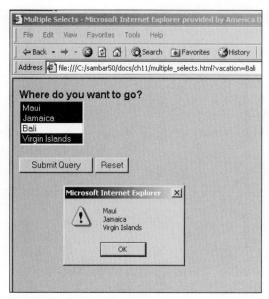

Figure 11.40   Multiple selections were made by the avid traveller.

Radio Buttons.   Like the buttons on an old-fashioned radio, you can only push one button when using HTML radio buttons. When a radio button is checked, it is selected, and when another button is checked, the previously checked one is deselected. In short, only one button at a time can be checked. This type of button is useful if you want a user to be able to select only one of a list of items.

Radio buttons are created with the HTML *<input type="radio">* and are represented in JavaScript as a *radio* object with specific properties and methods used to manipulate the object. Each button is a property of the *radio* object and assigned to an array of elements in the order in which they are placed in the form. The *checked* property of the *radio* object specifies whether a button was checked. It returns Boolean *true* if the button was selected, and *false* if not.

Figure 11.41   How the *radio* object is created within the JavaScript hierarchy.

To reach a value in the radio list, for example, you would use *document.form1.radio1*, where *form1* is the name of the form, and *radio1* is the name of the *radio* object.

Figure 11.41 shows the JavaScript object hierarchy for the *radio* object. Tables 11.17 and 11.18 list the properties and methods of the *radio* object.

Table 11.17 Properties of the *radio* Object

Property	What It Describes
accessKey	Sets or retrieves the keyboard key to access a radio button.
alt	Sets or returns alternate text to display if a browser does not support radio buttons.
checked	Is true if the radio button was selected, false if not.
defaultChecked	Refers to the checked attribute of the radio input tag—what the user sees as a default checked box when the buttons first appear.
form	The name of the form where the radio buttons are defined.
id	Sets or retrieves the *id* of a radio button.
name	The name used to reference the radio input tag.
tabIndex	Sets or retrieves the tab order for a radio button.
type	Refers to the type attribute of the radio input tag.
value	Refers to the value attribute of the radio input tag.

Table 11.18 Methods of the *radio* Object

Method	What It Does
blur()	Removes focus from the select box.
click()	Simulates a mouse being clicked on the button.
focus()	Puts focus in the select box.
handleEvent()	Invokes the handler for a specified event (JavaScript 1.2).
unwatch()	Turns off the watch for a particular property.
watch()	Watches, and when a property is changed, calls a function.

EXAMPLE 11.24

```
      <html>
        <head><title>Radio Buttons</title>
          <script type="text/javascript">
1            function changeBg(f){
2              for (var i = 0; i < f.color.length;i++){
3                if(f.color[i].checked){
4                  document.bgColor= f.color[i].value;
                 }
               }
             }
          </script>
        </head>
        <body bgcolor="#CCFFFF">
          <font face="arial"><b>
5          <form name="formradio">
           Pick a background color:<p>
6          <input type=radio
                   name="color"
                   value="#0099CC" />dark cyan<br />
           <input type=radio
                   name="color"
                   value="#339966" />teal<br />
           <input type=radio
                   name="color"
                   value="#FF00FF" />magenta<br />
           <input type=radio
                   name="color"
                   value="#FFFF66" />light yellow<br />
           <input type=radio
                   name="color"
                   value="#FF9933" />light orange<br />
           <p>
           <input type=button
7             value="Click for Color" onClick="changeBg(this.form);" />
           <input type="reset" />
          </form>
          </font>
        </body>
      </html>
```

EXPLANATION

1   A function called *changeBg()* is defined. It will take one parameter, a reference to the
    form where the radio buttons are defined. The parameter *f* could also be written us-
    ing the DOM hierarchy: *document.form[0]* or *document.formradio* (the form's name).

2   The *for* loop is entered. The variable, *i*, will be used to index through each of the
    elements of the *radio* object. The name *color* is a reference to each object in the
    forms *elements[]* array. The *length* property specifies how many radio buttons were
    created in the form. When all of the buttons have been tested, the loop will exit.

EXPLANATION(CONTINUED)

3   If a radio button was checked, the *checked* property will return *true*.

4   If checked, the color of the background will be changed by assigning the value of the radio button's *value* attribute to the *bgColor* property of the document.

5   The form is defined. It is named *formradio*.

6   The input type is a radio button, named *color*. Only one button can be selected (see Figure 11.42). The value is a hexadecimal color code.

7   When the user clicks this button, the *onClick* event handler is triggered and the handler function *changeBg()* is called, using the *this* keyword and the *form* object as its argument.

Figure 11.42   Using radio buttons; only one can be checked.

Checkboxes.   Although radio buttons can only be checked once, a user can check as many checkboxes as he or she wants. When a checkbox is clicked, it is on, and when it is not, it is off.

Checkboxes are created with the HTML *<input type="checkbox">* and are represented in JavaScript as a *checkbox* object with specific properties and methods used to manipulate the object. Each checkbox is a property of the *checkbox* object and assigned to an array of elements in the order in which they are placed in the form. The *checked* property of the *checkbox* object specifies whether a box was checked. It returns true if checked, and false if not.

To reach a value in the checkbox list, you could use, for example, *document.form1.check1*, where *form1* is the name of the form, and *check1* is the name of the *checkbox* object. Figure 11.43 shows the JavaScript object hierarchy for the *checkbox* object. Tables 11.19 and 11.20 list the properties and methods of the *checkbox* object.

Figure 11.43   How the *checkbox* object is created within the JavaScript hierarchy.

Table 11.19   Properties of the *checkbox* Object

Property	What It Describes
accessKey	Sets or returns the keyboard key to access a checkbox.
alt	Sets or returns an alternate text to display if a browser does not support checkboxes.
checked	Returns true if the checkbox is checked.
defaultChecked	Returns true if the <input> tag includes the *checked* attribute, a default box that is initially checked; otherwise, returns false.
disabled	Sets or returns whether or not a checkbox should be disabled.
form	The name of the form where the checkbox is defined.
id	Sets or returns the *id* of a checkbox.
name	A string that names the checkbox.
tabIndex	Sets or returns the tab order for a checkbox.
type	The type of input device; i.e., *checkbox*.
value	The text assigned to the value attribute.

Table 11.20 Methods of the *checkbox* Object

Method	What It Does
blur()	Removes focus from the checkbox.
click()	Simulates a mouse being clicked in the checkbox.
focus()	Puts focus in the checkbox.
handleEvent()	Invokes the handler for a specified event (JavaScript 1.2).
unwatch()	Turns off the watch for a particular property.
watch()	Watches, and when a property is changed, calls a function.

EXAMPLE 11.25

```
    <html>
      <head><title>Checkboxes</title>
        <script type="text/javascript">
1          function check(f){
             var str="";
2           for (var i = 0; i < f.topping.length;i++){
3             if(f.topping[i].checked){
4               str += f.topping[i].value + "\n";
              }
            }
5           f.order.value=str;      // Put str value into the text area
          }
6          function OK(myForm){
             var result= confirm("Are you sure you
                                 are ready to order?  ");
             if(result == true){
7              document.myForm.submit();
             }
             else { return false;}
           }
        </script>
      </head>
      <body bgColor="#CCFF33">
        <font face="verdana">
        <table border="2">
          <tr><td><b>Checkboxes</b></td></tr>
        </table>
```

Continues

EXAMPLE   11.25 (CONTINUED)

```
        <strong>
 8      <form name="formchbox"
                    method="post"
                    action="http://localhost/pizza.php">
        Pick your pizza toppings:<p></p>
 9      <input type="checkbox"
                name="topping"
                value="tomatoes" />Tomatoes
        <br />
        <input type="checkbox"
                name="topping"
                value="salami" />Salami
        <br />
        <input type=checkbox
                name="topping"
                value="pineapple" />Pineapple
        <br />
        <input type=checkbox
                name="topping"
                value="Canadian bacon" />Canadian bacon
        <br />
        <input type=checkbox
                name="topping"
                value="anchovies" />Anchovies
        <br />
        <input type=checkbox
                name="topping"
                value="extra cheese" />Extra Cheese
        <br />
        <p><small>
        Pizza Toppings
        <br />
10      <textarea name="order" rows=6 cols=35
11        onFocus="JavaScript:check(this.form);">
          Click here to check your order!!
        </textarea>
        <p></p>
        Press the pizza man to order!
        <br />
12      <input type=image src="pizzaguy.jpg"
          onClick="JavaScript:return OK(this.form);" />
        <br />
        <input type=reset value="Clear the form" />
        </small>
        </form>
        </strong></font>
      </body>
    </html>
```

EXPLANATION

1   A JavaScript function called *check()* is defined. It takes one parameter, a reference to a form. Instead of *f*, the form could also be referenced as *document.forms[0]* or *document.formchbox.*

2   A *for* loop is entered to go through each of the checkboxes in the form. The name of the checkbox object is *topping*. The *length* property refers to how many checkboxes were defined. After all of the checkboxes have been inspected, the loop exits.

3   If the checkbox element, called *topping[i]*, is checked, the *check* property has a value *true*; otherwise *false*.

4   A string called *str* is assigned the value stored in the checkbox, and for each box that is checked, its value will be appended to the string.

5   After all of the checkboxes have been tested, their values will be found in the *str* variable. These values are assigned to the text area box, called *order*.

6   A function, called *OK()*, is defined. Its purpose is to confirm that the user is ready to submit his or her order.

7   If the user clicks OK in the confirmation box, the checkbox's *submit()* method is invoked. Otherwise, nothing happens.

8   The HTML form called *formchbox* is defined.

9   The input type is a checkbox, named *topping*. Each of the checkbox choices is created for this form.

10 An HTML text area, named *order*, is defined. It consists of 6 rows and 35 columns.

11 When the text area gets focus (that is, when the user clicks his or her mouse anywhere in the text area box), the handler *check()* is invoked. A reference to this form is passed as an argument.

12 This is an image input type used instead of a submit button. When the user clicks the image of the pizza man, the *OK()* handler will be invoked (see Figures 11.44 and 11.45).

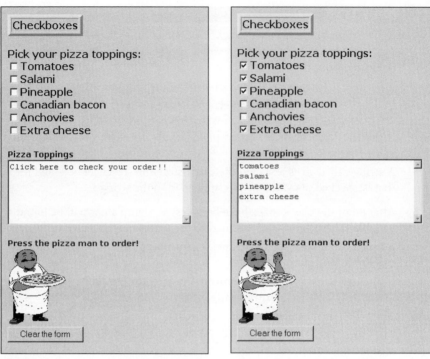

Figure 11.44   The initial form with empty checkboxes (left) and after the user has clicked on some of the checkboxes (right).

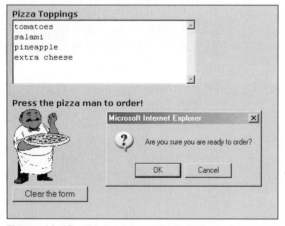

Figure 11.45   When the user clicks the pizza man, a confirmation box appears.

11.5.1   Simple Form Validation

Have you ever filled out a form to buy something, clicked the submit button, waited, waited, and then received a big red message saying that the card number you entered was invalid? And then after all that waiting, you had to retype the entire form because all of the fields were reset? By letting JavaScript do some preliminary checking of the form input for obvious mistakes and erroneous information, you can save the user a lot of time and aggravation. Then, after the preliminary checking is done, the form is ready to go off to a server program, such as Perl or PHP, where it can be further validated and processed. This section will show you a little about validating forms: doing preliminary checking to see if a password is the correct length, making sure a field isn't empty, checking for unwanted characters, and more. Chapter 17, "Regular Expressions and Pattern Matching," shows you how to validate the format for e-mail addresses, credit cards, zip codes, names, phone numbers, Social Security numbers, and the like by using regular expressions, a powerful pattern matching tool provided by JavaScript.

Checking for Empty Fields.   Forms often have mandatory fields that must be filled out before the form can be submitted. The following example checks for empty fields.

EXAMPLE 11.26

```
    <html>
        <head><title>An HTML Form and the onSubmit Event Handler</title>
        <script type="text/javascript">
1           function checkForm(yourinfo){
2               if(yourinfo.namestring.value == "" ||
                    yourinfo.namestring.value == null){
                            // Check for an empty string or null value
3                   alert("Please type in your name");
4                   return(false);
                }
                else{
5                   return(true);
                }
            }
        </script>
    </head>
    <body>
        <b>
6           <form name="info" action="http://cgi-bin/bookstuff/form1.cgi"
                method="post"
7               onSubmit="return checkForm(this);">
            <big><p>
```

Continues

EXAMPLE 11.26

```
          Type your name here:
8         <input type="text" name="namestring" size="50">
          </p>
9         <input type="submit" value="Submit" />
          <input type="reset" value="Clear" />
          </big>
        </form>
      </body>
    </html>
```

EXPLANATION

1   The function called *checkForm()* has one parameter, *yourinfo*, which is a reference to the form defined on line 6.

2   If the user didn't enter anything into the textbox, the value of the input type will be null. The expression *if(yourinfo.namestring.value == "")* checks for an empty field.

3   The user didn't enter anything into the textbox, an alert dialog box will appear on the screen, and after he presses OK, he will have a chance to fill out the form again.

4   If *false* is returned from this function, the form will not be submitted to the server.

5   If *true* is returned from this function, the form will be submitted to the server.

6   The HTML form starts here. The form, *document.forms[0]*, is named *info*. The *action* attribute contains the URL of the program that will process the form, a CGI script on the server. The *method* attribute defines the HTTP method that determines how the data will be sent to the server.

7   The *onSubmit* event is an attribute of the HTML *<form>* tag. It is triggered when the user clicks the Submit button. The event handler is a function called *checkForm()*. Its argument is *this*, same as *document.forms[0]*). The *return* keyword is required when using the *onSubmit* event handler. One of two values will be returned: either *true* or *false*.

8   The input type for this form is a text field box. Its name is *namestring* and it can hold a string of up to 50 characters.

9   The input type is the Submit button. When the user clicks this button, the *onSubmit* event handler on line 7 is activated. See Figure 11.46.

Figure 11.46 Using the *onSubmit* event handler to stop a form if the user didn't enter anything in the field.

Checking for Alphabetic Characters. If checking input fields for alphabetic characters, such as a user name, the following example will go through a loop evaluating each character in a string to guarantee it is an alphabetic. See Chapter 17 for more on this type of validation.

EXAMPLE 11.27

```
    <html>
      <head><title>Verifying a Name</title>
        <script type="text/javascript">
1         function validate(form){
2           if(alpha(form.first) == false){
              alert ("First name is invalid");
              return false;
            }
3           if(alpha(form.last) == false){
              alert("Last name is invalid");
              return false;
            }
            return true;
          }
4         function alpha(textField ){
5           if( textField.value.length != 0){
6             for (var i = 0; i < textField.value.length;i++){
7               var ch= textField.value.charAt(i);
                /* alert(ch);  Using alert to see what characters
                              are coming in
                */
8               if((ch < "A" || ch > "Z") && (ch< "a" || ch >"z")){
                  return false;
                }
              }
            }
```

Continues

EXAMPLE 11.27 (CONTINUED)

```
               else {
9                   return true;
                   }
               }
           </script>
       </head>
       <body bgcolor="lightgreen">
           <font face=verdana>
           <strong>
10         <form name="alphachk" onSubmit="return validate(this);">
           Enter your first name:
           <br />
11         <input name="first"
                   type="text"
                   size=60>
           <p>
           Enter your last name:
           <br />
12         <input name="last"
                   type="text"
                   size=60>
           <p>
13         <input type=submit value="Check it out">
           <input type=reset>
       </form>
       </strong></font>
   </body>
</html>
```

EXPLANATION

1   A JavaScript function called *validate()* is defined. It takes one parameter, a reference to a *form* object.

2   The *if* expression invokes a function, called *alpha()*, and passes the text object to it. The first name is validated by the *alpha()* function. If *false* is returned, the block is entered and the user is alerted that he or she did not enter a valid first name. If this function returns *false* to the *onSubmit* handler that invoked it, on line 10, the form will not be submitted.

3   As in line 2, the *alpha()* function is being called, only this time to verify the last name of the user.

4   The function called *alpha()* is defined. All the validation work is done here. This function will validate that the user entered something in the textbox, and that what he or she entered is alphabetic characters, and only alphabetic characters, either uppercase or lowercase.

5   If the length of characters entered in the text field is not equal to 0, then the block is entered.

EXPLANATION

6   The *for* loop is used to check each character, one at a time, that was entered in the text field.

7   The *charAt()* string method returns a character at a specified position in the string. Each time through the loop, a new character is assigned to the variable, *ch.*

8   This is the test for alphabetic characters. Because each character is represented internally as an ASCII number, ("A" is ASCII 65, "B" ASCII 66, etc.), any character outside the range "A" to "Z" and "a" to "z" is not an alphabetic character.

9   If *true* is returned by the *alpha()* function, the form will be submitted.

10 The name of the form is *alphachk.* The *onSubmit* event is triggered when the user clicks the Submit button on line 13.

11 The input type is a text field, called *first.* This is where the user will enter his or her first name.

12 The input type is a text field, called *last.* This is where the user will enter his or her last name.

13 The input type is a Submit button. When the user clicks this button, the *onSubmit* event is triggered, and if the form was valid, it will be submitted to the server. (In this example, it isn't going anywhere, because the *action* attribute of the form wasn't specified.) See Figure 11.47.

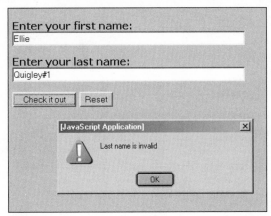

Figure 11.47   The user enters a valid first name and an invalid last name.

Checking E-Mail Addresses.   You are frequently asked to include your e-mail address when filling out a form. There are some requirements for a valid e-mail address such as *TommyTucker@somewhere.com.* One requirement is that there is an @ symbol after the user name, and that there is at least one dot (.) in the address. The following example is a preliminary check for the existence of both of those characters, but it is far from a complete check. See Chapter 17 for a much more robust version of e-mail validation using regular expressions.

EXAMPLE   11.28

```
   <html>
     <head><title>Checking Email</title>
       <script type="text/javascript">
1        function email(form){    // Validate the address
2          if(form.address.value.indexOf("@") != -1 &&
             form.address.value.indexOf(".") != -1){
               alert("OK address!");
3              return true;
           }
           else {
             alert("Invalid address");
4            return false;
           }
         }
       </script>
     </head>
     <body bgcolor="lightgreen">
       <font face=verdana>
       <b>
       <div align="center">
5      <form name="mailchk"
             action="http://cgi-bin/ml.pl"
             method="post"
             onSubmit="return email(this);">
         Enter your email address:
         <p>
6        <input name="address"
                 type="text"
                 size=60 />
         </p><p>
7        <input type=submit value="Check it out" />
         <input type=reset />
         </p>
       </form>
       </div></b></font>
     </body>
   </html>
```

EXPLANATION

1   A JavaScript function called *email()* is defined. It takes one parameter, a reference to a form.

2   If the string method, *indexOf*, does not return a −1, then the @ character and a dot (.) were found in the value entered by the user in the textbox, and an alert message will let the user know his or her e-mail address is okay. This is where the validation takes place.

3   If *true* is returned, the form will be submitted.

EXPLANATION

4   If *false* is returned, the form is stopped, and will not be submitted.

5   The HTML form, called *mailchk*, starts here. The *onSubmit* event will be triggered when the user clicks the submit button on line 7.

6   The form's input type is a textbox named *address* that will hold up to 60 characters.

7   When the user clicks the submit button, the *onSubmit* handler on line 5 is triggered. It invokes the handler function, called *email*, and passes a reference to the form as an argument. See Figures 11.48 and 11.49.

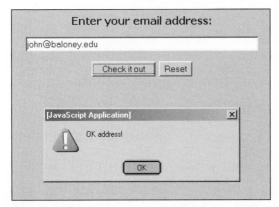

Figure 11.48   The user enters a valid e-mail address.

Figure 11.49   The user enters an invalid e-mail address. A dot is missing in the address.

Checking Password Fields.   There are a number of checks made on password entries. Does it have the right number of characters? Does it contain one numeric character? Can it contain upper and lowercase characters? The following example is a simple validation routine to check for alphanumeric characters and that the number of characters in the password field is not less than six.

EXAMPLE 11.29

```
<html>
  <head><title>Verifying a Password</title>
    <script type="text/javascript">
1      function valid(form){
2        if( form.pass.value.length == 0 ){
            alert("Please enter a password");
            return false;
         }
3        if( form.pass.value.length < 6 ){
            alert("Password must be at least 6 characters");
            return false;
         }
         for (var i = 0; i < form.pass.value.length;i++){
            var ch= form.pass.value.charAt(i);
4        if((ch < "A" || ch > "Z") && (ch< "a" || ch >"z")
            && (ch < "0" || ch > "9")){
               alert("Password contains illegal characters");
               return false;
            }
         }
5        alert("OK Password");
         return true;
       }
    </script>
  </head>
  <body bgcolor="red">
    <font face="verdana">
    <b><div align="center">
6    <form name="passchk" onSubmit="return valid(this);">
       Enter your password:
       <br />
7      <input name="pass"
              id="pass"
              type="password"
              size=33 />
       <p>
       <input type=submit value="Submit Password" />
       <input type=reset />
       </p>
    </form>
    </div>
    </font>
  </body>
</html>
```

EXPLANATION

1   A JavaScript function called *valid()* is defined. It takes one parameter, a reference to a form.

2   If the password entered by the user has a length of 0 characters, an alert message is sent.

3   If the password entered by the user has a length of less than 6 characters, an alert message is sent.

4   If the value of the password entered by the user contains any character that is not an alphabetic character and not a number, an alert message is sent.

5   If the password was at least 6 characters and contained only alphanumeric characters (letters and numbers), then the validation test was passed, and the user is alerted. A value of *true* is returned to the *onSubmit* handler, allowing the form to be submitted.

6   The HTML form called *passchk* is started here. Its *onSubmit* handler is triggered when the user clicks the submit button.

7   The input type is a password box, called *pass*. This is where the user will enter his or her password. See Figure 11.50.

Figure 11.50   The user enters a password of less than 6 characters (left) or enters a password that contains illegal characters (right).

11.6 What You Should Know

Any Web site that is trying to sell you something will have a form. They are at the heart of Web commerce. This chapter focused on how to create forms and different input devices used to collect the data, textboxes, checkboxes, drop-down menus, and so on. You learned how JavaScript can access this data and manipulate it; for example, how to change the text in a box, verify that there was any input, stop a submission, open up

another window and display the form data, do some simple validation, and so on. After
going through this chapter, you should know:

1. What the DOM tree looks like to JavaScript.
2. Why we use the Legacy DOM with forms.
3. How to create HTML forms and input devices.
4. What two methods are used to send data to a server.
5. How the browser bundles up the input data.
6. What name/value pairs represent in forms.
7. What a server-side program does.
8. How the *form* object and the *elements* object are used.
9. When to use the *name* and the *id* attributes. How do they differ?
10. How to catch a form before it is submitted to a server.
11. How to reference the input devices in a JavaScript function.
12. How to stop form data from being submitted.
13. How to program input devices/controls.
14. How the *this* keyword is used with forms.
15. How the button input device differs from the submit button.
16. How to use an event handler with a form.
17. How the form's *submit()* method differs from the *onSubmit* event handler.
18. How to change the text in a textbox with JavaScript.
19. What the *blur()* and *focus()* methods do.
20. How to use multiple selects.
21. How the *selectedIndex* property works with drop-down menus.
22. How to test for input that does not contain alphabetic data.
23. How JavaScript can tell which button was selected in a list of radio buttons.

1. What's a BOM? What's a DOM? What is the Legacy DOM and why is it used with forms?

2. How does the *name* attribute differ from the *id* attribute of an input device?

3. Create an HTML document that contains two forms. One form consists of a text field, the other a text area. Name the forms and the input devices. Use JavaScript to print out the names and values in the forms.

4. Add a button to the last example. If the user clicks it, display the form content in another window.

5. Create two text fields. In one text field, the user will enter his or her birth month and day. Write a JavaScript program that will print the number of days until his or her birthday in the second text field.

6. Write a JavaScript function that will finish the story in Example 11.20.

7. Write a multiple-choice quiz. It has five questions and the user can only select one answer. After the user selects an answer, alert him or her if he or she is wrong, and show the user the correct answer in a separate textbox field.

8. Change Example 11.36 so that a confirmation box will appear, asking the user to confirm his or her vacation choices. The vacation choices will be listed in a popup window.

9. Create a form that uses a text input type. Ask the user to type his or her name in uppercase letters. The submit button will be an image. Validate that the form is not empty and that the user typed his or her name in only uppercase letters. Send the form to a server program if it is valid.

10. Create a form with radio buttons representing different colors. Use the *id* attribute for each radio button. In a JavaScript program, *the getElementById()* will return a reference to the radio button that was selected. Change the background color to the color that was selected.

chapter

12

Working with Images
(and Links)

12.1 Introduction to Images

A picture is worth a thousand words. Whether it's a slide show, banner, movie, or photo album, the Web contains a huge collection of images. Any time you buy something online, there is usually an image associated with the item, maybe a small image, and then a bigger image if you want more detail. Whatever it is, a book, a house, a pair of shoes, or a toy, we like to see it before we put it in our virtual shopping cart and pay the money. Although the focus of this chapter is on JavaScript and images, hypertext links are so closely intertwined with images and navigation, they are also discussed here.

Images can be links, clickable image maps, banners, marquees, billboards, or roll-overs—you name it. With HTML, the images you load are static, and just sit on the page. They cannot be changed without loading a brand new page, and loading a lot of images takes time. JavaScript brings a new dimension to working with images. Instead of view-ing a static image on the page, you can create dynamic images that can be changed on the fly, adding animation and drama to your Web page. For example, you can create effects such rollovers, slide shows, cycling banners, dynamic menus, and more. Just as with forms, JavaScript has access to every image on you page. Before getting into the fun of images, we will look at how JavaScript accesses them. In Chapter 13, "Handling Events," and Chapter 15, "The W3C DOM and JavaScript," you utilize what you learn here to see the full potential of image manipulation with JavaScript.

12.1.1   HTML Review of Images

Before using images with JavaScript, the following section reviews the basics of using images in a static Web page. Table 12.1 lists HTML image tags.

Table 12.1   HTML Image Tags

Tag	Attributes	Description
IMG		Starting tag for loading an image.
	ALIGN	Floats the image either to the left or right side of the page, or aligns the image with text in directions, *texttop*, *top*, *middle*, *absmiddle*, *bottom*, or *absbottom*.
	ALT	Alternative text in case the image doesn't appear.
	BORDER	The width in pixels of an image border.
	HEIGHT	Height of the image in pixels.
	HSPACE	Adds space, in pixels, to both the right and left sides of the image.
	SRC	Contains the URL, location of the image relative to the document root of the Web page.
	VSPACE	Adds space, in pixels, to both the top and bottom of the image.
	WIDTH	Width of the image in pixels.
MAP		Starting tag for an image map. Image maps link areas of an image with a set of URLs. Clicking on an area of the map sends the user to that page.
	ID	The name of the image map.
	NAME	Also the name of the image map.
AREA		Defines the clickable areas of the image map.
	ALT	Describes what happens when the user clicks.
	COORDS	Determines the shape of a rectangle, circle, or polygon in *x,y* pixel coordinates.
	HREF	The address of the page that will appear when the user clicks in a particular area.
	SHAPE	Assigned a *type*, where *type* represents the shape of the area.

Using an Image in an HTML Web Page.   Example 12.1 is an HTML file linked to an image. In this example, we review the way inline images are created in a document.

EXAMPLE   12.1

```
  <html>
     <head><title>HTML Images</title></head>
     <body bgcolor="lightblue">
1    <img src="baby.jpg" alt="baby" border=2 align="left"
2        hspace="10" width="220" height="250" />
3    <pre>
     Father calls me William,
         sister calls me Will,
     Mother calls me Willie,
         but the fellers call me Bill!
     Mighty glad I ain't a girl--
         ruther be a boy,
     Without them sashes, curls, an' things
         that's worn by Fauntleroy!
     Love to chawnk green apples
         an' go swimmin' in the lake--
     Hate to take the castor-ile
         they give for belly-ache!
     Most all the time, the whole year round,
         there ain't no flies on me,
     But jest 'fore Christmas
         I'm as good as I kin be!
     </pre>
     </body>
  </html>
```

Eugene Field, *Jest 'Fore Christmas*, in *Childcraft*, Vol. 2, (Chicago: Field Enterprises, Inc., 1949).

EXPLANATION

1   The image *src* attribute defines where the image is located. This image, *baby.jpg*, is located where the HTML file called *image.html* is found, normally under the document root of your browser. If the image can't be loaded, the *alt* attribute specifies text that will appear in its place. The image will be aligned at the left side of the page and will have a thin black border around it. There will be 10 pixels of space on both the left and right sides of the image. This keeps the text from jamming up too close to the picture.

2   The *width* and *height* attributes of the *img* tag allow you to specify the size of your image in pixels. If you right-click on an image (Windows), a popup window will appear where you can select Properties to obtain info about your image.

3   This is a *<pre>* tag that is followed by all the text that appears at the right side of the image. See Figure 12.1.

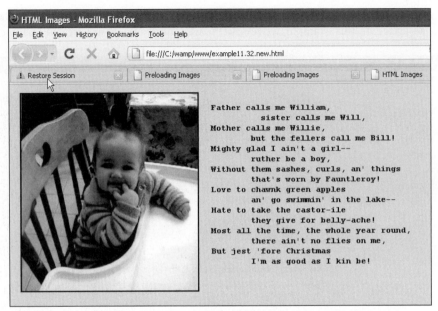

Figure 12.1   Using images in an HTML page: Output from Example 12.1.

12.1.2   The JavaScript *image* Object

With the Legacy DOM, JavaScript provided the *image* object as a property of the *document* object, giving you easy access to the images that have been loaded into a document. Although you can use the W3C versions of the DOM, the Legacy DOM is supported by all modern browsers and is commonly used when working with images. Just like the *form* object, the *image* object corresponds to the HTML *<img>* tag and each image is assigned to the *images[]* array[1] in the order in which the image appears within the document. The first image would be represented as *document.images[0]*, the next as *document.images[1]*, and so on (see Figure 12.2). As with forms, images can also be named and given an *id*. The properties for the *image* object correspond to the HTML attributes of the *<img>* tag, such as *src, width, height, border, vspace,* and *hspace,* and are shown in Table 12.2.[2] It is possible to assign values to these properties to dynamically change the size, shape, and border of the image. There are no common methods for the *image* object unless you use the *id* attribute and methods such as *getElementById()* and *getElementsByTagName()* provided by the W3C DOM.

JavaScript also provides event handlers that are triggered when an image is loaded, a mouse crosses the image, or when the user clicks on an image. Although we use event handling in this chapter, Chapter 13 provides a more complete discussion.

---

1. Implemented starting in JavaScript 1.1.

2. These properties are common to both Mozilla/Firefox and Internet Explorer. Internet Explorer, however, supports many more than those listed here.

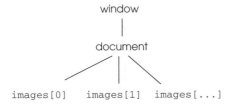

Figure 12.2 Document object and images.

For preloading offscreen images, JavaScript provides an image constructor (see Example 12.6). The constructor is used if you have large images that will take time to download or images that are being replaced dynamically within the page. The images are preloaded into memory (but not displayed) and available from the cache when the user requests them, thus making the response time much faster (see Example 12.4).

Table 12.2 *image* Object Properties

Property	HTML <img> Attribute	Description
border	border	An integer value determining the width of an image border in pixels.
complete		A Boolean value returning true if Navigator has finished downloading the image.
height	height	An integer representing the height of the image in pixels.
hspace	hspace	An integer representing the horizontal space (pixels) around the image.
lowsrc	lowsrc	Specifies an optional image to display for a low-resolution device.
name	name	A string containing the name of the image.
prototype		Used to add user-specified properties to an *image* object.
src	src	A string containing the path and name of the image.
vspace	vspace	An integer representing the vertical space (pixels) around the image.
width	width	An integer representing the width of the image in pixels.

12.2 Reviewing Links

Links are fundamental to the Web. They are primarily used to navigate you from page to page. We have been using links in many examples so far. There are a number of ways to execute JavaScript from a link such as navigating to another page, opening a link in a popup window, calling a function from a link, submitting a form from a link, and so on. This chapter focuses on how links are used with images.

As you know, HTML hypertext links are usually created by assigning a Web address or a file name to the HTML *<a href>* tag, for example:

```
<a href="http://www.ellieq.com">Go Home</a>
```

If a JavaScript function is assigned to the *<a href>* tag, when the user clicks the link, the function will be executed (see Example 12.4).

```
<a href="JavaScript:greetings()"><big>Click here for salutations</big>
<a href="JavaScript: function_name(arguments);">  Do Something </a>
```

And you can use an event handler with a link (see Chapter 13):

```
<a href="newpage.htm" onClick="newwindow();return false">Click Here!</A>

<a href=JavaScript: onClick="return handler(arguments)" >

<A HREF="JavaScript:newwindow()" ><IMG SRC="mypic.jpg" border="0"></A>
```

12.2.1   The JavaScript *links* Object

Like the form object and image object, the *link* object is a property of the *document* object and gives you access to the hypertext links that have been loaded into a document (see Figure 12.3). It corresponds to the HTML *<a href>* tag. As each HTML form is a JavaScript element of the *forms[]* array, and each image is assigned to the *images[]* array, so each link is assigned to the *links[]* array in the order in which the link appears within the document.

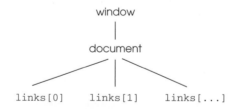

Figure 12.3   Document object and links.

The first link would be represented as *document.links[0]*. The properties for the *links* object are shown in Tables 12.3 and 12.4.[3] There are no common methods for the *links* object.

---

3. These properties are common to both Netscape and Internet Explorer. Internet Explorer, however, supports many more than are listed here.

A *links* object contains a URL, similar to the window's *location* object, and shares the same properties. A full URL takes the following form:

<protocol>//<host>[:<port>]/<pathname>[<hash>][<search>]

There are nine events that can be triggered by a link: *onClick, onDblClick, onKey-Down, onKeyPress, onKeyUp, onMouseDown, onMouseUp, onMouseOver,* and *onMouse-Out.* (For details, see Chapter 13.)

Table 12.3 Properties of the W3C *links* Object

Property	What It Describes
charset	Sets or returns the character encoding of the target URL.
disabled	Sets or returns whether or not the target URL should be disabled.
href	The entire URL.
hreflang	Sets or returns the base language of the target URL.
id	Sets or returns the *id* of a *<link>* element.
media	Sets or returns on what device the document will be displayed.
name	The name of the *<link>* element.
rel	Sets or returns the relationship between the current document and the target URL.
rev	Sets or returns the relationship between the target URL and the current document.

Table 12.4 Properties of the JavaScript *links* Object

Property	What It Describes
hash	The anchor part of the URL (if any).
host	The hostname port part of the URL.
hostname	The hostname part of the URL.
href	The entire URL.
pathname	The pathname part of the URL.
port	The port part of the URL.

Continues

Table 12.4   Properties of the JavaScript *links* Object (continued)

Property	What It Describes
protocol	The protocol part of the URL, including the colon.
search	The query part of the URL.
target	The HTML target attribute of the link.

EXAMPLE 12.2

```
     <html>
       <title>Using Links </title></head>
       <body>
         <h2>Links and their Properties</h2>
         <big>
1        <a href="http://search.yahoo.com/bin/search?p=JavaScript
                                                    tutorial">
         Search for JavaScript Stuff</a>
         <p>
2        <a href="http://google.com?" >Go to google</a>
         </p><p>
3        <a href="http://www.bing.com">Go to bing</a>
         </p>
         <script type = "text/javascript">
           document.write("<br /><b>This document contains "
               +document.links.length + " links.<br /></b>");
4          for (i = 0; i< document.links.length; i++){
5            document.write("<u>document.links["+i+"]:</u><br />");
5            document.write("<b>hostname:</b> "
                 +document.links[i].hostname +"<br />");
6            document.write("<b>href: </b>"
                 +document.links[i].href +"<br />");
7            document.write("<b>pathname:</b>"
                 +document.links[i].pathname +"<br />");
8            document.write("<b>port:</b> "
                 +document.links[i].port +"<br />");
9            document.write("<b>query string:</b> "
                 +document.links[i].search +"<br />");
10           document.write("<b>protocol:</b> "
                 +document.links[i].protocol +"<br /><br />");
           }
         </script>
         </big>
       </body>
     </html>
```

EXPLANATION

1   This link goes to the Yahoo! search engine's main site and searches for the word "JavaScript tutorial." Note: The browser inserted a %20 for the space between "JavaScript"and "tutorial", an example of URL encoding.

2   This link goes to the Google search engine's main site.

3   This link goes to the Bing search engine's main site.

4   The size of the *links[]* array is determined by the *length* property. It displays the number of links in the document.

5–10   The *for* loop is used to iterate through the links array and display some of its properties. The output is shown in Figures 12.4 and 12.5.

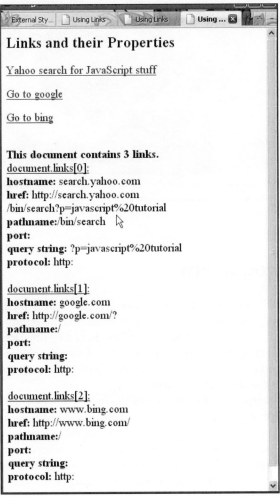

Figure 12.4 Viewing the properties of the *links* object.

Figure 12.5   After clicking on a hyperlink: Output from Example 12.2.

12.3 Working with Imagemaps

An imagemap is an image with clickable areas where each area is represented by a link, also called a hotspot. An imagemap makes it possible to make one image link to several pages depending on the area or pixel coordinate positions clicked by the user. A simple example would be an image of the map of the United States. If the user clicks on Maine, for example, then a link would navigate the user to another page with information about that state, a closer image of the state, and so forth.

In the HTML page you simply specify the area of the image (hotspot) and the link that will be associated with that part of the image. The most time-consuming and boring part of this process is determining the coordinate positions for the hotspot. This can be done manually or by an image mapping program. There are a number of programs on the Web to help you (see Figure 12.6), and many are free. In fact, most HTML editors have image mapping as a built-in function (see Figures 12.7 and 12.8).

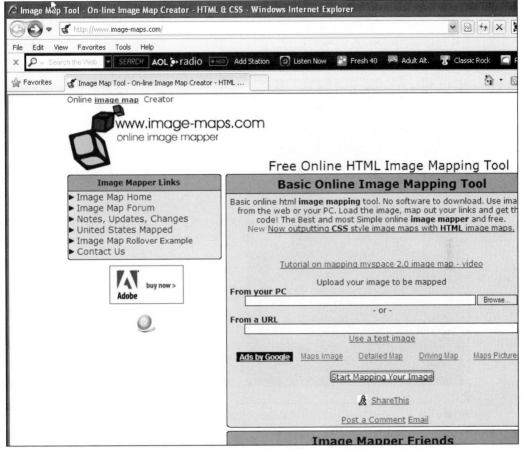

Figure 12.6 A free online image mapping tool.

Figure 12.7 Using the tool to map a rectangular hotspot.

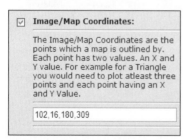

Figure 12.8 Using the image mapping tool to get the coordinates of the hotspot. Coordinates are for the highlighted rectangular shape.

In Example 12.3, if you click on the face of any of the people in the family, you are linked to a page with information about that family member. In the HTML page the *<area>* tag and its attributes represent the coordinates and the shape of the image map (see Table 12.5) as well as a link to the navigation page where the user will be directed when he or she clicks on the hotspot. Example 12.3 demonstrates how to create an image map.

In Example 12.3 the coordinates are plotted with rectangular image mappings, but there are other shapes that can be used: the circle and polygon. (The polygon shape can be used to customize the area of the link.) Note: All coordinate values are relative to the top left corner of the image (0,0).

Table 12.5 Shape Coordinates for an Imagemap

Shape	Coordinates–coords
rect	"x1,y1,x2,y2" Top left and bottom right corners of the rectangle.
circle	"x.y,r" Center and radius of the circle.
poly	"x1,y1,x2,y2,x3,y3,..." Corners of the polygon.
default	The remaining area of the image, not defined by any coordinates.

EXAMPLE

```
<area shape=rect coords= x1,y1, x2,y2 href="http://www.domain.com">

<area shape=circle coords= x1,y1, x2,y2 href="http://www.domain.com">

<area shape=polygon coords= x1,y1, x2,y2, .., xn,yn
       href="http://www.domain.com">
```

EXAMPLE 12.3

```
    <html>
      <head><title>Using Links </title>
1     <map name="my_image_map">
2       <area shape="rect" href="nicky.html" coords="68,41,159,190">
        <area shape="rect" href="daniel.html" coords="202,28,287,133">
        <area shape="rect" href="jake.html" coords="273,20,358,125">
        <area shape="rect" href="kimmy.html" coords="350,76,431,185">
        <area shape="rect" href="uncledan.html"
            coords="403,10,491,98">
        <area shape="rect" href="jessica.html" coords="485,8,573,96">
3       <area shape="default" href="family.gif">
      </map>
```

Continues

EXAMPLE   12.3 (CONTINUED)

```
      </head>
      <body>
        <div align="center">
        <h2>The Family</h2>
4       <img src="family.gif" usemap="#my_image_map" />
      </body>
   </html>


------------The file: nicky.html------------------------

   <html>
      <head><title>Nicky</title></head>
      <body>
        <script type="text/javascript">
            var age = 14;
            alert("Nicky, age "+ age);
5           window.location="example12.12.html";
        </script>
      </body>
   </html>
```

EXPLANATION

1   The HTML *<map>* tag defines the client-side image map. The *name* attribute is required to make an association with the name and the *usemap* attribute of the image. See line 4. In this definition, you tell the browser where the hotspots are in the image, and what the hotspots need to link to.

2   The *<area>* tag defines the hotspot for a rectangular shape; that is, the top left and bottom right corners of the rectangle. The rectangular shape for each area of the map is drawn around each of the family members in the picture (see Figure 12.9).

3   The default represents the remaining area of the image not defined by any area tags. It has no coordinates.

4   This is the image that will be displayed on the screen. The attribute *usemap="#my_image_map"* attribute associates the image map with this image. The image map could also be placed in another file as *usemap="imagefile.map#my_image_map"* where "imagefile.map" is the name of a file that defines the areas.

5   When the user clicks on the area around the image of the girl at the far left, the link goes to this page, nicky.html. After displaying information about Nicky, the user is directed back to the original page.

The user clicks his or her mouse on one of the faces and will be redirected to another file (see Figure 12.10).

Figure 12.9 The image has hotspot areas defined for each of the family members.

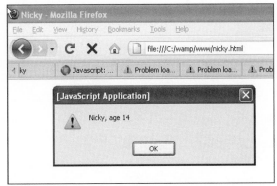

Figure 12.10 User clicked the mouse on Nicky's face. A link to nicky.html is opened.

12.3.1 Replacing Images Dynamically with the *src* Property

By changing the value assigned to the *src* property of an image, it is possible to dynamically replace one image with another. You can create an array of images with the *Array()* constructor, and assign any one of these images to the *src* property of the JavaScript *images[]* array.

EXAMPLE 12.4

```
        <html>
          <head><title>HTML Images</title>
            <script type="text/javascript">
1               var myImages=new Array("baby1.jpg", "baby2.jpg",
                                       "baby3.jpg", "baby4.jpg");
2               index_val=0;
3               function next_image(){
4                  index_val++;
5                  if (index_val < myImages.length){
6                     document.images["babypic"].src = myImages[index_val];
                      // could say document.babypic.src or
                      // document.images[0].src
                   }
7                  else{
                      index_val=0;
                      document.images["babypic"].src = myImages[index_val];
                   }
                }
8               function previous_image(){
                   index_val--;
9                  if (index_val >= 0){
                      document.images["babypic"].src = myImages[index_val];
                   }
10                 else{
                      index_val=myImages.length - 1;
                      document.images["babypic"].src = myImages[index_val];
                   }
                }
            </script>
          </head>
          <body>
            <div align="center">
            <h2>Baby Gallery</h2>
11          <img name="babypic" id="babypic" src="baby1.jpg"
                 width="329" height="440" >
            <br />
```

EXAMPLE   12.4 (CONTINUED)

```
12      <a href="JavaScript:next_image()">
           View next baby<br />
        </a>
13      <a href="JavaScript:previous_image()">
           View previous baby<br />
        </a>
        </div>
     </body>
   </html>
```

EXPLANATION

1   The array *myImages* consisting of four images is created by the *Array()* constructor.

2   The index value for the array is assigned to a variable called *index_val*.

3   A function called *next_image()* is defined. When called, the function will cause the next image in the array to be displayed.

4   By increasing the value of the index, the next image in the array will be accessed.

5   As long as the end of the array hasn't been reached, the block will be entered and the new image displayed.

6   The name of the image, *babypic*, is used as an index into the *images[]* array to reference the default image by name. By assigning a new image (from the *myImages* array) to the image's *src* property, the current image will be replaced by the new image.

7   If the end of the array has been reached, the statements within the *else* block will be executed, resetting the array index back to the beginning, index 0.

8   A function called *previous_image()* is defined. When called, it will go backward in the array and cause the previous image to be displayed.

9   If the index value is still ≥0, we are still within the boundaries of the array.

10 If by subtracting one from the index value, we have ended up with a value of –1, we are out of the bounds of the array, and will set the index value back to the size of the array, its length –1.

11 This is the initial image displayed on the screen before the user initiates an action.

12 When this link is clicked, the JavaScript function called *next_image()* is invoked.

13 When this link is clicked, the JavaScript function called *previous_image()* is invoked. See Figure 12.11.

Figure 12.11   Image replacement. Each time a link is pressed, one image is replaced with another.

```
<html>
  <head><title>HTML Replacing Images</title></head>
  <body bgcolor="cornflowerblue">
```

```
          <h2>  This Is Baby William</h2>
1         <img name="display" src="baby1.jpg" width="220" height="250" >
          <script type="text/javascript">
2           var myImages=new Array("baby1.jpg", "baby2.jpg",
                                   "baby3.jpg");
3           var n = prompt("Pick a number between 1 and 3","");
4           n--;
5           document.images["display"].src = myImages[n];
            // document.images[0].src = myImages[n]
          </script>
      </body>
  </html>
```

EXPLANATION

1 An HTML inline image called *display* is created. Its source is a file called *baby1.jpg* with the width and height defined in pixels.

2 An array object called *myImages* is created with the *Array()* constructor. The elements of the array are three *.jpg* files.

3 The user is prompted to pick a number between 1 and 3, which will determine which image will be displayed. The user input is assigned to variable *n*.

4 Array indexes start at 0. The user entered a number between 1 and 3, and because *n* will be used as an index into the array, it must be decremented to produce an index number ranging from 0 to 2.

5 The *images* array can be indexed by number or name. In this example, *display* is the name given to the default image shown on the screen, *baby.jpg*. By changing the *src* property, the default image will be replaced by any one of the images listed in the *myImages* array. See Figure 12.12.

Figure 12.12 Another example of image replacement: Output from Example 12.5 (left) after the user picks a number (right).

12.3.2 Preloading Images and the *Image()* Constructor

If you assign a new image to the *src* property of an *image* object, there might be some lag in the time it takes to download the image from the server. And if you have a slow connection, this can be a real turnoff, to the point that you don't even bother to wait for the image to load. To solve this problem, the *Image()* constructor allows you to preload an offline image; this puts the image in the browser's cache before it is used. This technique of caching the image makes the response time much faster, especially when you have large images, animation, rollovers, and the like. The *Image()* constructor can also define the size (height and width, in pixels) of the cached image. Be sure to put the *Image()* constructor in the *<head>* portion of the document so that the images are put in the cache before the script starts to run. For seamless transition when replacing one image with another, both images should be of the same size, accomplished by cropping or scaling the image. To use the *Image()* constructor, see next.

FORMAT

```
var newImage = new Image();
var newImage = new Image(height, width)
newImage.src = "image.gif";
```

EXAMPLE

```
var myImage = new Image(200,300);
myImage.src = "baby.gif";
```

It is possible, but unlikely, the viewer is using a browser that doesn't support the image object. We can add a little snippet of code to detect if the image object exists and then continue with preloading the images:

```
if(document.images){
        pic1=new Image(100,25);
        pic1.src="http://someplace.com/image1.gif";
}
```

A Simple Rollover with a Mouse Event.   We talked about event handlers with the *form* object and now we will demonstrate the use of an event handler with the *image* object. For a complete discussion, see Chapter 13. The objective of the next example is to change the image when the mouse rolls over a link, and to change it back when the mouse moves away from the link. There are two images involved: the image that initially appears on the page and the image that replaces it when the mouse rolls over the link associated with it. Both of the images are preloaded with the *Image()* constructor. The JavaScript *onMouseOver* event is triggered when the user's mouse moves onto the link, and the *onMouseOut* event is triggered when the mouse moves away from the link.

EXAMPLE 12.6

```
      <html>
         <head><title>Preloading Images</title>
            <script type="text/javascript">
1              function preLoadImages(){
2                  baby = new Array();  // global variable
3                  baby[0]=new Image();
4                  baby[0].src="baby1.jpg";
                   baby[1]=new Image();       // Preload an image
5                  baby[1].src="baby2.jpg";
               }
            </script>
         </head>
6         <body bgcolor="cornflowerblue" onLoad="preLoadImages();">
            <h2>This Is Baby William</h2>
7            <a href="#" onMouseOver="document.willy.src=baby[1].src;"
8               onMouseOut="document.willy.src=baby[0].src;">
9              <img name="willy"  src="baby1.jpg" width=190 height=200 />
            </a>
         </body>
      </html>
```

EXPLANATION

1   A function called *preLoadImages()* is defined in the head of the document. It will define a list of images that will be loaded before anything else. With this technique (unless the images are large or great in number), the viewer will have the necessary images in his browser's cache before the script starts to run, reducing waiting time. For a small example, such as this, there will be no noticeable difference.

2   The new array, called *baby*, is declared.

3   The *Image()* constructor creates and preloads a new *image* object and assigns it to the first element of the *baby* array.

4   The *src* property is assigned the name of the external image file called *baby1.jpg*.

5   The *src* property is assigned the name of the external image file called *baby2.jpg*.

6   When the page has loaded, the *onLoad* event is triggered causing the *preLoadImages()* function to be called.

7   The # (hash mark) disables the link so that the browser does not try to go to a URL when clicked. The link is an image. The *onMouseOver* event is triggered when the user's mouse moves onto the link, and the *onMouseOut* event is triggered when the user's mouse moves away from the link (image). When the mouse moves over the image, the baby image changes from the first image to the second one. When the mouse is moved away from the image, the original image is displayed. Going down the JavaScript hierarchy, we start with the *document*, then to *document.willy* or *document.images[0]* or *document.images["willy"]*), then to the *src* property that is assigned the *image* object. One image is replaced with another. Note: *document.images["willy"]* is an associative array. Any object, not just the *Array* object, can use the square bracket notation to reference its properties. See Chapter 9, "JavaScript Core Objects."

Continues

EXPLANATION (CONTINUED)

8   When the mouse is moved away from the link, the initial image *baby1.jpg* will re-appear on the screen.

9   The initial external image called *baby1.jpg* is named *willy* and is aligned on the left side of the screen. The output is shown in Figure 12.13.

  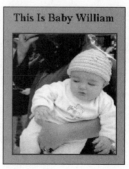

Figure 12.13   Before the mouse rolls over the image (left), as the mouse hovers over the image (middle), and when the mouse moves away from the image (right).

12.3.3   Randomly Displaying Images and the *onClick* Event

By using the *Math* object's *random()* method, it is sometimes fun to randomly generate pictures from a list of images. Example 12.7 demonstrates how to change the *src* attribute of an *image* object by using a random number as the index of an element in an image array. All of the images are preloaded by using the *Image()* constructor, greatly improving the time it takes to load the images.

EXAMPLE 12.7

```
    <html>
      <head><title>Preloading Images</title></head>
        <script type="text/javascript">
1         ImageHome=new Array(3);
2         for(var i=0; i<3; i++){
              ImageHome[i]=new Image();
          }
3         ImageHome[0].src="baby1.jpg";
          ImageHome[1].src="baby2.jpg";
          ImageHome[2].src="baby3.jpg";
4         function myRandom(){
5           var n=ImageHome.length - 1;
6           var randnum=Math.floor(Math.random() * (n + 1));
7           document.images["display"].src = ImageHome[randnum].src;
          }
        </script>
```

EXAMPLE   12.7 (CONTINUED)

```
      </head>
      <body bgcolor="cornflowerblue"><center>
         <h2>  This Is Baby William</h2>
8     <img name="display" id="display"
          src="baby.jpg"
          border=5
          width="200" height="250" />
      <p>
      <form>
9        <input type="button"
                value="Click Here for Baby Picture"
10               onClick="myRandom()" />
      </form>
      </center>
      </body>
   </html>
```

EXPLANATION

1   The *Array()* constructor creates an *array* object to consist of three elements. This array will be used to hold three images.

2   The *Image()* constructor will preload and cache three images and assign them to the array created in line 1.

3   The *src* property of the first element of the *image* array is assigned an image called *baby1.jpg*. Each array element is assigned a different image.

4   The function called *myRandom()* is defined. It produces a random number that will be used as the index into the image array, causing a random picture to be displayed on the screen.

5   The variable called *n* is assigned the value of the length of the image array minus 1.

6   The variable called *randnum* is assigned a random whole number between 1 and 3, the value returned from the *Math* object's random method.

7   Instead of using a number to access the image array, a string is used. The string is the name given to the HTML image defined on line 8. This is the image that initially appears in the browser window. In the JavaScript tree, this image is represented as *document.images[0].src* or *document.display.src* or d*ocument.images["display"].src*. Either way, this image will be replaced with the value of the image in the array *ImageHome[randnum].src*.

8   The inline image, called *baby.jpg* is displayed on the screen when the program starts. It is named *display*.

9   This form input type creates a button on the screen.

10 When the user clicks the button, the *onClick* event is fired up, and the event is handled by calling *myRandom()*, which displays a random image. See Figure 12.14.

Figure 12.14   Each time the user clicks the button, a random picture is displayed.

12.3.4   Links with an Image Map and JavaScript

You might want to associate more than one link with an image. This can be done by using an HTML image map. The image map is used to list the links associated with the image and an event handler will activate some action when the user clicks the link or rolls the mouse over it, and so on. In Example 12.8, an image map is created with a number of links associated with an original image entitled "Spring in San Francisco." When JavaScript handles the page, it creates a links array where each element of the array is a link in the order in which it was placed in the document. There is an *onClick* event handler associated with each link. When the user clicks on a link, he or she is redirected to another image of "Spring in San Francisco" (see *http://www.tutorialspoint.com/java-scritpt/javascript_image_map.htm*).

EXAMPLE 12.8

```
    <html>
      <head><title>Using Links </title>
1     <map name="my_image_map">
2       <area shape="rect" href="spring5.jpg"onclick=
            "this.href='JavaScript:void(0)';this.disable=true">
        <area shape="rect" href="spring2.jpg"onclick=
            "this.href='JavaScript:void(0)';this.disable=true">
        <area shape="rect" href="spring3.jpg"onclick=
            "this.href='JavaScript:void(0)';this.disable=true">
        <area shape="rect" href="spring4.jpg"onclick=
            "this.href='JavaScript:void(0)';this.disable=true">
        <area shape="rect" href="spring5.jpg" onclick=
            "this.href='JavaScript:void(0)';this.disable=true">
```

EXAMPLE 12.8 (CONTINUED)

```
            <area shape="rect" href="spring6.jpg" onclick=
                "this.href='JavaScript:void(0)';this.disable=true" />
3           <area shape="default" href="spring1.jpg" />
        </map>
    </head>
    <body>
        <div align="center">
        <h2>Spring in San Francisco</h2>
        <img src="spring1.jpg" height=257 width=343
            usemap="#my_image_map" />
        <script type="text/javascript">
4           var lstr = "<ul>";  // tag to create a bulleted list
            var len = document.links.length - 1;
5           for ( var i = 1; i < len; i++ ){  // Create links
                lstr += "<li><a href=" + document.links[i].href;
                lstr += ">spring" + i +" </a>\n";
            }
6           lstr += "</ul>";
7           document.write(lstr);
        </script>
        </div>
    </body>
</html>
```

EXPLANATION

1   The image map starts here. It can be used to allow multiple links to be associated with one image. For each HTML hyperlink created in the document, JavaScript creates a corresponding links array, the first link being *links[0]*.

2   The links are deactivated to prevent the user from being surprised if he or she clicks on one of the images. The disabled property of JavaScript is a Boolean property; it can take two possible values: *true*, or *false*. The image map is used to create links, shown under the picture, so that the user can click on one of the links and be redirected to another image. The image map makes it possible to have one image with multiple links, rather than a single link with a single image. Because there will be no "hotspots" in this image, there is no need to use coordinates (see Figure 12.15).

3   This is the image that is displayed on the screen.

4   The string *lstr* will contain a bulleted list of each hyperlink in the links array.

5   The *for* loop will cycle until all the links have been assigned to *lstr*. JavaScript makes use of the *href* property of the link object to create the string.

6   The string of bulleted list items is completed with a closing *</ul>* tag.

7   When the list is displayed, it will consist of links to images associated with the one originally displayed; that is, more images of spring in San Francisco (see Figure 12.16).

Figure 12.15   Creating links with JavaScript and an image map.

Figure 12.16   Thumbnails of pictures in the image map for "Spring in San Francisco."

12.4 Resizing an Image to Fit the Window

If you resize a window and the image remains the same size, you might want to resize the image as well so that it is proportional to the window; that is, as the window gets bigger or smaller, so does the image. By using the *onLoad* event handler, each time the page loads, a function will be called to reset the dimensions of the image, but to see the change, you will have to refresh the page.

Because the image size will be based on the height and width of the client's window, it is better to base the size of the image on the height of the window rather than the width, as vertical positioning is less flexible in most browsers. The width of the image will be scaled automatically as long at the browser knows its height. Example 12.9 demonstrates how to resize the window and to see its actual dimensions once it has been resized.

EXAMPLE 12.9

```
      <html>
        <head>
          <title>Planet Earth</title>
          <script type="text/javascript">
1           function alert_me(){
              alert("This window's outer width is: "
2                    +window.outerWidth+" and the outer height is: "
                     +window.outerHeight);
            }
3           function resizeEarth() {
4             document.images["earth"].style.height =
5                  (document.body.clientHeight - 75) * 0.9;
            }
          </script>
        </head>
6     <body onload="resizeEarth();">
7         <div style="margin-top:75px; text-align:center">
          <img name="earth"
          src="http://recycle4acause.files.wordpress.com/2009/12/earth.jpg"
          alt="earth"images/Earth.jpg" alt="earth picture"
          onclick="alert_me();"/>
          </div>
        </body>
      </html>
```

EXPLANATION

1 This is a test to find the dimensions of the window's dimensions before resizing it.

2 The properties of the window object are used to get the height and width of the window.

3 If the user resizes his browser window, this function will scale the image down to be proportional to the size of the screen.

4 The *style* property of the object will be used to resize the height of the image. Because the image was initially given a margin of 75 pixels from the top of the page, 75 is subtracted from the total height of the browser window (clientHeight - 75), and multiplied by 90 percent.

5, 6 Now resize your browser window manually. The image will not be proportioned properly, but if you refresh/reload the page, the *onLoad* event handler is triggered and the *resizeEarth()* function will be called.

7 This style for the image of the earth is defined. If the user clicks the image, a function called *alert_me()* will be called to display the window dimensions in an alert dialog box. The results are shown in Figures 12.17, 12.18, and 12.19.

Figure 12.17 The image before changing the size of the window.

Figure 12.18 After resizing the window and clicking the Refresh button.

Figure 12.19 After clicking on the image, this alert box displays the window's dimensions.

12.5 Introduction to Slideshows

Figure 12.20 A carousel slideshow
(*http://www.dynamicdrive.com/dynamicindex14/carousel.htm*).

JavaScript slide shows are great for creating photo albums, auction listings, digital presentations, art galleries, 3D carousels, and so on (see Figure 12.20). Once you get a basic slide show working, you can reuse the code to create other slide shows and change the images accordingly. There are numerous sites on the Web where you can get excellent JavaScript slideshow libraries that have already been created and free for reuse. The examples provided in this text are to give you some insight on how a simple JavaScript slideshow is created, how to control the start and stop of the slideshow, how to create clickable images, and simple animation. Once you understand the basics, understanding and debugging existing code will be much easier.

When you build a slide show, the visitor of your site must be a first consideration; for example, what is the bandwidth and type of browser, or will the load time be too slow if you are loading a large number of images? Navigation is another important consideration. Will the visitor be able to control the slideshow manually or will it automatically start when the page loads and stop when it exits or when it has completed a specified number of cycles? You might want to create buttons to control the slideshow such as start, pause, go back, forward, speed up, slow down, stop, and so on. You might want to create optional hyperlinks or clickable images where each frame leads to a different URL. You might want to randomly display the images or show them in a certain sequence.

The size of the images also weighs into a well-constructed slideshow. When you have a series of images coming from different sources, they will probably not have the same height and width. When the slideshow starts, images of different sizes will give the page a jumpy appearance. You might want to crop the images to make them all the same size. Because the first image you load will be followed or overlaid by the next series of images, the dimensions of that image will determine the size of the rest of the images giving the page a smooth transition as each one loads. However, if you have images of varying dimensions, forcing all the images to be of the same size, might distort the image objects if not proportionally scaled. You might also want to get a sleek fade-in effect when one image replaces the previous image, or get persistence so that when the user reloads the page, he or she picks up in the slideshow where it left off.

Figure 12.21 on page 443, called "Ultimate Fade-in slideshow (v2.1) located at *dynamicdrive.com*, demonstrates a sophisticated, cross-browser, fade-in slideshow script, and the site offers free code to build your own slideshow similar to the demos shown later, saving lots of time and energy. Before downloading sophisticated scripts from the Web, this chapter describes a very basic slideshow to help you understand how JavaScript slideshows work, which will help you later when you are debugging, updating, revising, and maintaining more complicated scripts.

Note: To disable the viewer from right-clicking the mouse to get a menu for saving images from your page, go to *http://www.dynamicdrive.com/dynamicindex9/noright2.htm* for free Java-Script code.

12.5.1   A Simple Slideshow with Controls

Example 12.10 is a JavaScript program that cycles through a selection of images. It makes use of image replacement, a timer function, and buttons that serve as controls to give the user the ability to start and stop the slideshow. See Chapter 13 for an example (Example 13.11) of a slideshow using a mouse rollover.

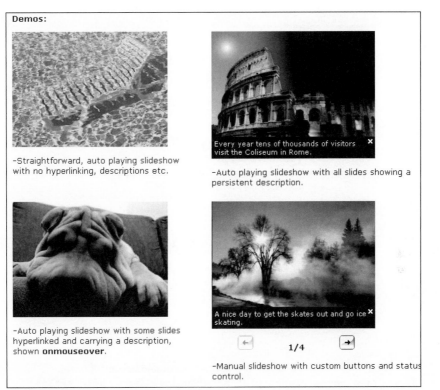

Figure 12.21   *http://www.dynamicdrive.com/dynamicindex14/fadeinslideshow.htm* (see page 442).

EXAMPLE   12.10

```
      <html>
        <head><title>Slide Show</title>
          <script type="text/javascript">
            var i=0;
            var timeout;
1           function preLoadImages(){
              if(document.images){
2               planet = new Array();   // global variable
3               planet[0]=new Image();
                planet[0]="/images/Venus.jpg";
                planet[1]=new Image();
                planet[1]="/images/Neptune.jpg";
                planet[2]=new Image();
                planet[2]="/images/Earth.jpg";
                planet[3]=new Image();
                planet[3]="/images/Mars.jpg";
```

Continues

EXAMPLE 12.10 (CONTINUED)

```
               planet[4]=new Image();
               planet[4]="/images/Jupiter.jpg";
            }
            else{
               alert("There are no images to preload");
            }
         }
4        function startSlideShow(){
5           if(i < planet.length){
6              document.images["planet_pic"].src = planet[i];
               i++;
            }
            else{
               i=0;
7              document.images["planet_pic"].src = planet[i];
            }
8           timeout = setTimeout('startSlideShow()',1500);
         }
9        function stopSlideShow(){
            clearTimeout(timeout);
         }
      </script>
   </head>
   <body bgColor="black" onload = "preLoadImages()">
10    <img name="planet_pic" src="Jupiter.bmp"  height="348"
         width="545px" />
      <form>
         <br /><br />
         <input type=button value="Start Show"
               onClick="return startSlideShow();"/>
         <input type=button value="Stop Show"
               onClick="return stopSlideShow();"/>
      </form>
   </body>
</html>
```

EXPLANATION

1   A function called *preLoadImages()* is defined in the head of the document. It will define a list of images that will be loaded before anything else.

2   A new array called, *planets*, will is declared. It will be assigned the images of the planets.

3   The *Image()* constructor creates and preloads a new *image* object called *planet[0]*.

4   The function called *startSlideShow()* allows the user to determine when to start the slideshow.

5   The variable *i* is initially set to 0 and is used as an index in the array called *planets*. As long as the index value is less than the size of the array, the statements in the *if* condition will be executed.

6   The *src* property of the image object is assigned a new picture. By using the name of the image as an index value of the images array, JavaScript can determine which image object to use. (Another way to get to the image: *document.planet_pic.src* or *document.images[0].src*.)

7   Once the index value exceeds the length of the array, the index value, *i*, is reset to 0 and the slideshow begins again.

8   The timer is set so that once every 1.5 seconds a new picture is displayed.

9   When the user clicks the button labeled "Stop Show," the *clearTimeout()* function is called, causing the timer to stop. The argument, *timeout*, is a reference to the timer set on line 8.

10   The initial image is a picture of the planet Jupiter (see Figure 12.22). It is given size dimensions, which will determine the size of all images in the slideshow. If the images are of different dimensions, they will have to be scaled to this size. Not properly sizing images will give them a distorted appearance.

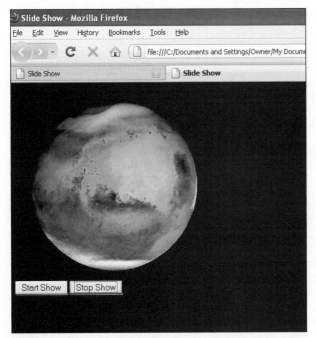

Figure 12.22 Planet slideshow with two control buttons.

12.5.2 A Clickable Image Slideshow

In Example 12.11 a set of planet images is displayed as a slideshow. If the viewer clicks one of the planets, he or she is redirected to a Web page that describes that planet. This is accomplished by assigning the image to a link; that is, a link that is assigned a Java-Script user-defined function and triggered when the user clicks the image.

EXAMPLE 12.11

```
      </html>
        <head><title>Planet Slide Show</title>
          <script type="text/javascript">
1           var timeout;
            var step=0
            var whichimage=0;
2           var planet=new Array();
            function preLoadImages(){
3             planet[0]=new Image();
              planet[0]="/images/Jupiter.bmp";
              planet[1]=new Image();
              planet[1]="/images/Neptune.bmp";
              planet[2]=new Image();
              planet[2]="/images/Earth.jpg";
              planet[3]=new Image();
              planet[3]="/images/venus.jpg";
              planet[4]=new Image();
              planet[4]="/images/http:/mars.jpg";
            }
4           function slideShow(){
5             document.images["planet_pic"].src=planet[step];
6             whichimage=step;
7             if (step < planet.length){
                step++;
              }
              else{
8               step=0;
              }
9             setTimeout("slideShow()",1800);
            }
10          function slideLink(){
11          switch(whichimage){
            case 0:
12            window.location=
              "http://www.nasa.gov/worldbook/jupiter_worldbook.html";
              break;
            case 1:
              window.location=
              "http://www.aerospaceguide.net/planet/planetneptune.html"
              break;
            case 2:
              window.location=
          "http://www.windows.ucar.edu/tour/link=/earth/earth.html";
              break;
```

EXAMPLE   12.11 (CONTINUED)

```
                    case 3:
                        window.location=
                "http://csep10.phys.utk.edu/astr161/lect/venus/venus.html";
                        break;
                    case 4:
                        window.location=
                        "http://www.nasa.gov/worldbook/mars_worldbook.html";
                        break;
                }
            }
        </script>
    </head>
13  <body bgColor="black" onLoad = "preLoadImages(); slideShow()">
        <font color="white">
        <big>
        Click on a Planet<br /><br />
14      <a href="JavaScript:slideLink()">
        <img src="Jupiter.bmp" name="planet_pic"
            border="0" width="120" /></a>
        </big>
        </font>
    </body>
</html>
```

EXPLANATION

1   Global variables that will be used by the functions in this program are declared in the head of the document.

2   The *Array()* constructor creates an *array* object, called *planets*.

3   The *Image()* constructor will preload and cache four images and assign them to the array created in line 2.

4   This function starts the slideshow. It displays an array of images one at a time at selected intervals of 1.8 seconds.

5   The *src* property of the first element of the *image* array is assigned an image called *Jupiter.bmp*. Each array element is assigned a different image. Every 1.8 seconds an image is replaced with a new image in the array, until all the planets have been displayed, at which time the index value, called *step*, is set back to 0.

6   The variable, *whichimage*, is used to get the index value of the image that was just clicked by the user. This value will be used in the *switch* statement on line 11.

7   As long as the value of *step* is less than the size of the *planets* array, the *step* value will be incremented by 1, taking us to the next image in the array.

8   When the index value is greater than the size of the array, it will be reset to 0.

9   Here the JavaScript time is set to call *slideShow()* every 1.8 seconds.

10 The function *slideLink()* is defined. Its purpose is to redirect the user to a page describing the planet when he or she clicks its image.

Continues

EXPLANATION

11 The *whichimage* variable is set to the index value of the current image. After the user clicks the link in the current image, the *switch* statement is used to match on the index value of that image and then redirect the user to a page describing the planet. By using the back button, the slideshow will continue.

12 The *location* property of the *window* object is assigned a Web page describing the planet that the user clicked during the slideshow.

13 Once the page has loaded, the functions *preLoadImages()* sand *StartShow()* are called to preload the images and then start the slide show. In this example, there are no controls to start or stop the slideshow.

14 The first image, Jupiter.bmp, is assigned to a link, that when clicked, will call the function, *slideLink()* to bring up another page with a description of Jupiter. Output is shown in Figures 12.23 and 12.24. Figure 12.25 shows an open source Web site that includes example slideshows.

Figure 12.23   A clickable image slideshow.

Figure 12.24   After the user clicks on the planet Neptune, he or she is redirected to the URL shown here.

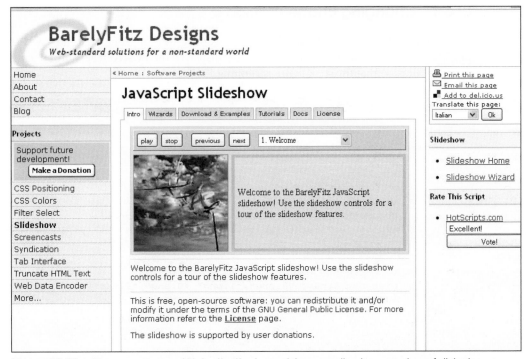

Figure 12.25 An open source Web site that provides excellent examples of slideshows.

12.6 Animation and Timers

On a small but thick pad of paper a boy has drawn a stick man on each page. For each page he draws his stick man in a sightly different position, maybe moving one leg up and an arm down. After filling the pad with as many little stick man pictures as he wants to draw, he goes to his friend and starts rapidly flipping the pages. Voila! He has made a little movie! Although seemingly primitive, this is the idea behind JavaScript animation. Instead of flipping through a pad of drawings, the stick man drawings can be scanned into your computer as a set of images as shown in Figure 12.26. JavaScript can load the images and then give them the appearance of animation by using a timer that will be set to put a new image on the page at short repeating intervals, similar to flipping the pages of the small pad of paper. With JavaScript, a number of DOM elements (*<img />*, *<div>*, etc.) can be moved in the document according to a looping mechanism or an expression tied to a timer.

Two JavaScript functions used as timers are *setTimeout()* and *setInterval()*, which allow JavaScript code to be executed at set intervals. (We have seen the use of both of these functions throughout this text.)

```
setTimeout(someFunction,500);
        // calls someFunction() 500 milliseconds from now
setInterval(someFunction,500);
        // calls someFunction() every 500 milliseconds until stopped
```

12.6.1   Changing Image Position

In Example 12.12, two stick figures have been scanned into the computer and saved as .png files. The figures are loaded and alternately displayed on the screen at short intervals giving the illusion that the stick figure is running.

EXAMPLE   12.12

```
      <html>
        <head><title>animation</title>
          <script type="text/javascript">
1           var pics;
2           function animate(whichone){
3              whichone %= pics.length;
4              document.images["stickman"].src=pics[whichone];
5              window.setTimeout("animate(" + (whichone + 1)+");",500);
            }

6           window.onload=function(){
7              pics=new Array( "0.png","1.png","0.png","1.png");
8              animate(0);
            }

        </script>
      </head>

      <body bgcolor=lightgreen>
9        <img src="0.png"  name="stickman" />
      </body>
    </html>
```

EXPLANATION

1   A global variable called *pics* is declared, which will be available to all the functions in this JavaScript code.

2   The function called *animate()* is called the first time on line 8. The initial value of *pos* is 0. On line 5 the window's *setTimeout()* function calls *animate()* repeatedly every .5 sec. Each time *animate()* is called the *whichone* value is incremented by 1.

3   The value of *whichone* is changed each time the function is called by using the modulus operator. The remainder will be a number between 0 and 4, not including 4. This number is used as an index in the *pics* array to select an image.

4   The source file for the stick man image file changes each time the function is called, so rapidly that the stick man appears to be running.

5   This is where the timer is set to cause the animation of the stick man.

6, 7, 8   When the page has loaded this anonymous function will create an array of images, and then call the *animate()* function on line 2 with an initial value of 0.

9   The initial stick man image is displayed in the document.

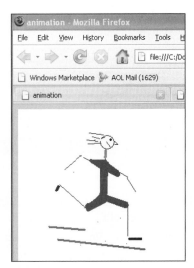

Figure 12.26 Animated stick man appears to be running.

12.6.2 Changing Image Height and Width Properties

In Example 12.13 the width and height properties of the image object allow us to change the size of an image dynamically. By increasing the width of a black bar image at set time intervals, the bar appears to be lengthening as it is displayed.

EXAMPLE 12.13

```
    <html>
      <head><title>Progress Bar</title>
        <script type="text/javascript">
1         function progress(){
            // Set the width of the image every .5 second
2           if(document.images["bar"].width < 300){
3             document.images["bar"].width += 5;
              document.images["bar"].height = 10;
              // Setting the height keeps the bar from getting taller
              // as the image is widened.
            }
            else{
4             clearInterval(timer);
            }
          }
5         var timer;
6         window.onload = function(){
            timer = setInterval("progress();",500);
            // Image is stretched every .5 seconds
          }
        </script>
```

Continues

EXAMPLE 12.13

```
       </head>
       <body bgColor="aquamarine">
7        <img src="blackbar.bmp" height="10" name="bar"/>
         <p>Watching your Progress</p>
       </body>
     </html>
```

EXPLANATION

1   This user-defined function will cause the image to be stretched horizontally every .5 seconds.

2   As long as the length of the bar is less than 300 pixels, we enter this *if* block. If not, the interval timer is stopped.

3   The width of the image is increased by 5 pixels every .5 seconds.

4   The height of the bar is at a constant 10; otherwise the browser will attempt to increase the height of the bar to be proportional to the increase in the length.

5   The variable, *timer*, will be assigned the return value of the *setInterval()* function.

6   The window's *onload* method is assigned an anonymous function. When the page has finished loading, this function starts the timer, *set Interval()*, which in turn calls the *progress()* function every .5 seconds.

7   The image of a black bar will be displayed when the page is loaded (see Figure 12.27).

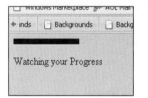 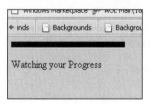

Figure 12.27   Making an image grow!

12.7 What You Should Know

A story book without pictures is like a Web page without images: Doable, but not much fun. This chapter demonstrated some of the ways you can animate a Web page using JavaScript to manipulate images. Now you should know:

1. How JavaScript stores the images from a Web page.
2. How JavaScript stores the hyperlinks from a Web page.
3. How to draw the document tree with images and links using the Legacy DOM.
4. How to figure out how many links and images are on the page.

5. How the image name is used to reference a particular image.
6. How to replace images with the *src* property.
7. How to create a simple rollover.
8. What considerations contribute to how you set up a slideshow.
9. What preloading accomplishes.
10. About the Image constructor.
11. How event handlers work with images.
12. How links work with images.
13. How to use the *link* object and imagemaps.
14. How to create a simple slideshow.
15. How timers work with animation.
16. How to resize an image.
17. How to randomly display a set of images.

1. Create an array of different sports images so that each time the page loads, a random image is displayed. Center the image on the page, and specify width and height. Choose a background color.

2. Create a document entitled "Our Universe." The page will consist of three frames. The top frame will be a horizontal frame to contain the title, "Our Universe," The left frame will contain a form with radio buttons representing the names of planets and a textbox. The background image in the second frame will be a sky filled with stars. When the user clicks a radio button, a picture of the selected planet will appear in the second frame. A description of the planet will appear in a textbox under the form in the left frame.

3. Create a JavaScript program that will produce a slideshow. It will contain an array of four images. Preload the images. A timer will be set so that a new image replaces another image every 10 seconds. If the user clicks a button labeled *Start*, the timer starts the image replacement. If the user clicks a button labeled *Stop*, the timer stops it.

4. When the page is loaded, call a function that will preload two images, each associated with a link. When the mouse rolls over an image, replace the first image with the second image. When the mouse moves away from the image, the first image appears.

5. Create the illusion of a car driving across the screen using animation. Move the car to the right a certain number of pixels using a timer. Create two buttons to start and stop the car.

6. Use a program such as Windows Paint to draw three traffic lights. Preload the three images. Every 30 seconds change the light. When the light turns green, say "Go" in a little box under the light, for yellow "Slow down," and for red, "Stop."

7. Find a picture of the major planets in our solar system. Create an imagemap so that when the user clicks one of the planets, a popup window is opened describing that planet.

chapter

13

Handling Events

13.1 Introduction to Event Handlers

JavaScript reacts to events. We have been talking about events since Chapter 1, "Introduction to JavaScript," because events are inherently part of almost all Web pages and they make the pages interactive and dynamic. JavaScript events are asynchronous, meaning that they can happen at any time. They are actions that are initiated by a user visiting a Web page; for example, if the user submits a form or moves the mouse over a link or an image, he or she might trigger an event. When an event occurs, your browser has some default actions it takes; for example, if you click on a link, it opens up the location in the *href*. JavaScript can also respond to a user's action and execute code in response. The event itself may be blur, click, change, keystroke, and so on. We have seen many examples using event handlers in previous examples. This chapter explains how each of the event handlers responds when events occur on different objects.

JavaScript has three event models for programming events: the inline model, the scripting model, and the DOM 2 model. In this chapter we discuss the inline model and the scripting model. In Chapter 15, "The W3C DOM and JavaScript," we describe the way events are handled by the W3C DOM Level 2 model and its pros and cons.

13.2 The Inline Model for Handling Events

This is the oldest and easiest way to handle events. With the inline model, the event handlers are attributes of an HTML tag and are used to handle the event for which they are named. For example the *onClick* handler will handle the click event, the *onSubmit* handler will handle the submit event, and so on. Although a very popular way of dealing with events, the disadvantage of using the inline model is that JavaScript is intrusive; that is, it is not separated from the HTML markup. The inline model will be used here to show you what the many event handlers do, and how they affect the objects in a document. Later in this chapter, we discuss the JavaScript scripting method for handling events.

As shown in previous examples, if the user clicks the submit button, JavaScript can check to see if a form was filled out properly; or if the mouse moves over a link, Java-Script can replace one image with a new one. JavaScript's response to one of these user-initiated events is called **event handling**. If the user clicks a button, for example, Java-Script might handle the event by calling a function that will perform some designated task, such as to open a new window or bring a window into focus, perform a calcula-tion, or submit a fillout form. Here is a list of some of the kinds of events that Java-Script can handle:

- Mouse actions.
- Keyboard actions.
- Actions on form fields.
- When the page is first loaded or unloaded.
- After a specified time has passed.
- When an error has occurred.

13.2.1 HTML and the Event Handler

JavaScript event handlers are **not** enclosed between *<script></script>* tags. Event han-dlers are attributes of HTML tags (specified in the HTML 4 specification). If the event is associated with a form tag, then it will be an attribute of the *<form>* tag, and if associated with a link, it will be an attribute of the *<a href>* tag, and so on. Once you have decided what event you want to handle, you normally assign a function to the event handler. This is called registering the event.

To register an event, a string representing a command is assigned to the event handler. The command, usually a JavaScript function, will be executed when the event is trig-gered by the user. Whereas a property or method might be associated with a single object, events are usually associated with more than one object. The *onClick* event han-dler, for example, may be associated with a form's input tag, but it could also be associ-ated with a link tag, or an image map area, or a simple button. There is an order in which events are handled. See the section "Capturing and Bubbling (Trickle Down and Bubble Up)" on page 500.

(Note the spelling convention used for the event handlers. The first word, *on*, is all lowercase, and the first letter of each subsequent word is capitalized. Unless the event is being used as a method in a JavaScript program (see the section "JavaScript Object Meth-ods and Events" on page 462), it is not case sensitive. Using *onClick* or *onclick* is fine.)

Consider the following example:

```
<form>
   <input type="button"
          value="Wake me"
          onClick="wakeUpCall()" />
</form>
```

The HTML *<form>* tag contains an input tag with three attributes: *type*, *value*, and *onClick*. The input type is a *"button"*; it has a value of *"Wake me"*, and a JavaScript event handler called *onClick*. The *onClick* event handler is assigned a function called *"wake-UpCall()"*. When the user clicks the button labeled *Wake me*, a *click* event occurs, the *onClick* event handler is triggered, and the *wakeUpCall()* function will be executed, as demonstrated in Example 13.1 and shown in Figure 13.1.

EXAMPLE 13.1

```
    <html>
       <head><title>Wake up call</title>
1       <script type="text/javascript">
2         function wakeUpCall(){     // Function is defined here
3           setTimeout('alert("Time to get up!")',5000);
          }
4       </script>
5     </head>
      <body bgcolor="lightblue">
6       <form>
7         <input type="button"
8                 value="Wake me"
9                 onClick="wakeUpCall()">
        </form>
      </body>
    </html>
```

EXPLANATION

1   The start of the JavaScript program.

2   The *wakeUpCall()* function is defined in the JavaScript program, between the *<script></script>* tags. When the user clicks the form button, the function assigned to the event handler is called; that is, *wakeUpCall()* is called. The function itself is defined in a JavaScript program, even though it is called from outside the program.

3   The timer is set for 5,000 milliseconds. The alert dialog box will pop up on the screen 5 seconds after the user clicks the button.

4   End of the JavaScript program.

5   End of the HTML *<head>* tag.

6   This is the start of an HTML *<form>* tag.

7   The type of form uses a *"button"* input type.

8   The value is shown in the button as the text, *"Wake me"*.

9   The *onClick* event is assigned the name of a function. When the user clicks the button, the *onClick* event handler, *wakeUpCall()*, will be called.

Figure 13.1   Before clicking the button (left); after clicking and waiting five seconds (right).

A list of JavaScript event handlers and their uses is given in Table 13.1.

Table 13.1   JavaScript Event Handlers and What They Do

Event Handler	*What It Affects*	*When It Happens*
onAbort	Images	When image loading has been interrupted.
onBlur	Windows, frames, all form objects	When focus moves out of this object except *hidden*; e.g., when the cursor leaves a textbox.
onChange	Input, select, and text areas	When a user changes the value of an element and it loses the input focus. Used for form validation.
onClick	Links, buttons, form objects, image map areas	When a user clicks on an object. Return false to cancel default action.
onDblClick	Links, buttons, form objects	When a user double-clicks on an object.
onDragDrop	Windows	When a user drops an object, such as a file, onto the browser window.
onError	Script	When an error in the script occurs; e.g., a syntax error.
onFocus	Windows, frames, all form objects	When a mouse is clicked or moved in a window or frame and it gets focus; except *hidden*.
onKeyDown	Documents, images, links, forms	When a key is pressed.
onKeyPress	Documents, images, links, forms	When a key is pressed and released.
onKeyUp	Documents, images, links, forms	When a key is released.
onLoad	Body, framesets, images	After the document or image is loaded.
onMouseOut	Links (and images within links)	When the mouse moves away from a link.

Table 13.1   JavaScript Event Handlers and What They Do (continued)

Event Handler	What It Affects	When It Happens
onMouseOver	Links (and images within links)	When the mouse moves over a link. Return true to prevent link from showing in the status bar.
onMove	Windows	When the browser window is moved.
onReset	Forms reset button	When the form's Reset button is clicked. Return false to stop reset.
onResize	Windows	When the browser window changes size.
onSelect	Form elements	When a form element is selected.
onSubmit	Forms	When you want to send a form to the server. Return false to stop submission to the server.
onUnload	Body, framesets	After the document or frameset is closed or reset.

13.2.2   Setting Up an Event Handler

There are two parts to setting up an event handler:

1. The event handler is assigned as an attribute of an HTML tag such as a document, form, image, or link. If you want the event to affect a document, then it would become an attribute of the *<body>* tag; if you want the event to affect a button, then it would become an attribute of the form's *<input>* tag; and if you want the event to affect a link, then it would become an attribute of the *<a href>* tag. For example, if the event is to be activated when a document has finished loading, the *onLoad* event handler is used, and if the event happens when the user clicks an input device, such as a button, the *onClick* event handler is fired up.

```
<body onLoad="alert('Welcome to my Web site');">
   <form>
      <input type="button"
             value="Tickle me "
             onClick="alert('Hee hee ho hee');" />
   </form>
</body>
```

2. The next step is to register or assign a value to the event handler. The value can be a built-in method such as *alert()* or *confirm()*, a user-defined function, or a string of JavaScript statements. Although the event handler is an attribute of an HTML tag, if a user-defined function is assigned to the event handler, then that function must be defined either in a JavaScript program or as direct script statements (separated by semicolons).

   And be careful with quotes! The handling function must be enclosed within either double or single quotes. If you have double quotes within the function, surround the whole thing in single quotes, and if you have single quotes within the function, either escape the single quote with a backslash, or surround the whole thing in double quotes.

```
built-in method    -->    onClick="window.open('myhome.html', 'newWin')"

user-defined function -->  onUnLoad="timeOver();"

group of statements -->    onChange="if (!checkVal(this.value, 1, 10)){
                                        this.focus();  this.select();}"
```

EXAMPLE   13.2

```
   <html>
     <head><title>An event</title></head>
1    <body bgcolor="magenta" onUnload="alert('So long, stranger!')";>
       <center>
2        <form>
3          <input type="button"
4                  value="Click here to be alerted"
5                  onClick='alert("Watch out! An asteroid is approaching
                            earth!")' />
6          </form>
       </center>
     </body>
   </html>
```

EXPLANATION

1   The *<body>* tag contains the *onUnload* event handler. When the user browses to another page or exits the page, the *alert()* method will be triggered. Normally you would use this event for a quick cleanup or exit function, such as closing a window or clearing a page. Starting some time-consuming process at this point would be annoying to the user, because he or she is trying to leave this page without silly delays. The only purpose for this example is to demonstrate when the event happens.

2   The form starts here with the *<form>* tag.

3   The input type for this form is *"button"*.

4   The value on the button is *"Click here to be alerted"*.

5   The *onClick* event is an attribute of the HTML form's input tag. When the user clicks the mouse on the button (the *onClick* event), the *alert()* method is called. See Figure 13.2.

6   The HTML form tag ends here.

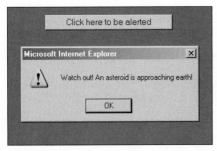

Figure 13.2   When the user clicks the button, the *onClick* event is activated (left); when the page is refreshed or exits, the *onUnload* event is activated (right).

13.2.3   Return Values

Sometimes the event handler's return value is necessary if a certain action is to proceed. The browser's default actions can be suppressed by returning a *false* value, or a form's submission can be completed by sending back a *true* value. For example, if the *onSubmit* handler gets a true value back from a function or method, then a form may be submitted to the server, and if not, the form will be stopped. In Chapter 11, "Working with Forms and Input Devices," we saw that when validating a form, return values are used. Example 13.3 illustrates these return values.

EXAMPLE 13.3

```
      <html>
        <head><title>An HTML Form and the onSubmit Event Handler</title>
          <script type="text/javascript">
1           function checkForm(yourinfo){
2             if(yourinfo.namestring.value == "" ||
                 yourinfo.namestring.value == null){
                 // Check for an empty string or null value
3               alert("Please type in your name");
4               return(false);
              }
              else{
5               return(true);
              }
            }
          </script>
        </head>
        <body><big>
          <b>
6         <form name="info" action="/cgi-bin/bookstuff/form1.cgi"
              method="post"
7             onSubmit="return checkForm(document.info)">
            <br /><br />
```

Continues

EXAMPLE 13.3 (CONTINUED)

```
             Type your name here:
8            <input type="text" name="namestring" size="50" />
             <br /><br />
9            <input type="submit" value="Submit" />
             <input type="reset" value="Clear" />
         </form>
         <big>
      </body>
   </html>
```

EXPLANATION

1   The function called *checkForm()* has one argument, *yourinfo*, which is a reference to the form defined on line 6.

2   If the user didn't enter anything into the textbox, the value of the input type will be null. The expression *if(yourinfo.namestring.value == "")* checks for an empty field.

3   The user didn't enter anything into the textbox. An alert dialog box will appear on the screen, and after the user clicks OK, he or she will have a chance to fill out the form again.

4   If *false* is returned from this function, the form will not be submitted to the server.

5   If *true* is returned from this function, the form will be submitted to the server.

6   The HTML form starts here. The form, *document.forms[0]*, is named *"info"*. The *action* attribute contains the URL of the program that will process the form, a CGI script on the server. The *method* attribute defines the HTTP method that determines how the data will be sent to the server.

7   The *onSubmit* event handler is an attribute of the HTML *<form>* tag and is triggered when the user clicks the submit button. The event handler is a function called *checkForm()*. Its parameter is the name of the form, *document.info* (also could use its array name: *document.forms[0]*). The *return* keyword is required when using the *onSubmit* event handler. One of two values will be returned: either *true* or *false*.

8   The input type for this form is a text field box. Its name is *"namestring"* and it can hold a string of up to 50 characters.

9   The input type is the submit button. When the user clicks this button, the *onSubmit* event handler on line 7 is activated. See Figure 13.3.

13.2.4   JavaScript Object Methods and Events

JavaScript event methods can be used to simulate the event attributes. (See the section "Unobtrusive JavaScript" in Chapter 15.) An event handler is an attribute of an HTML

Figure 13.3 Using the *onSubmit* event and return values. If the return value is *true* the form is submitted; otherwise, it is stopped.

tag, whereas an event method is applied to an object. Because HTML elements are also treated as objects (e.g., the window, form, or button are also JavaScript objects), there are several methods that can be applied to these objects to simulate events (see Table 13.2). When an object uses an event method, the method behaves as though the event has happened; for example, the *click()* method behaves like the *onClick* event, the *blur()* method behaves like the *onBlur* event, and so on.[1] The event method is applied to the object with the dot syntax, as are all other methods; for example, in a JavaScript program you might see something like the following:

```
document.test.button1.click(), window.focus(),
document.myform.submit();
```

Table 13.2 Event Object Methods

Event Method	Event Handler It Simulates	The Object It Can Affect
blur()	*onBlur*	Removes focus from windows, frames, form fields.
click()	*onClick*	Simulates a mouse click in form fields (buttons).
focus()	*onFocus*	Puts focus in a window, frame, form field.
reset()	*onReset*	Clears the form fields.
select()	*onSelect*	Selects or highlights text in a form field.
submit()	*onSubmit*	Submits a form.

---

1. Event methods behave as though the event has happened but in themselves do not trigger an event handler. For example, the *click()* method does not trigger the *onClick* event handler.

EXAMPLE 13.4

```
   <html>
      <head><title>Simulation Methods</title></head>
      <body bgcolor="yellow">
1     <form name="myform"
2           action="http://localhost/cgi-bin/doit.pl"
            method="post">
         Enter your name:<br />
         <input type="text"
                name="namefield"
                id="namefield"
                size="30"
                value="Name: "
3               onFocus="this.select()" />
         <p>
         Enter your address:<br />
4         <input type="text"
                name="addressfield"
                id="namefield"
                size="30"
                value="Address: "
5               onFocus="this.select()" />
         </p><p>
      </form>
6     <a href="#" onClick="JavaScript: document.myform.submit();">
         Click here to submit your form</a>
      </p><p>
7     <a href="#" onClick="JavaScript:document.myform.reset();">
         Click here to reset your form</a>
      </p>
      </body>
   </html>
```

EXPLANATION

1 A form named *myform* is started.

2 This is the URL where the form will be processed after it is submitted.

3 The *onFocus* event handler is assigned an event method called *select()*. For *this* textbox, when the mouse cursor is clicked in the box, the *onFocus* event is triggered and the event is handled by highlighting or selecting the text in the box.

4 Another textbox is defined to hold the user's address.

5 When the cursor is moved into this field, the textbox gets focus and the *select()* method is called to highlight this box, as in line 3.

6 A deactivated link is assigned an *onClick* event handler. When the user clicks the link, the JavaScript code is executed. The pseudo *JavaScript:* protocol is followed by a reference to the form and a *submit()* method, which causes the form to be submitted when the user clicks the link. A JavaScript function could also have

been called here such as: *<a href="#" onClick="validateForm(this)">* and the *submit()* method used within the function if the form is OK. (See the section "Form Validation with Regular Expressions" on page 765 in Chapter 17.)

7   A deactivated link is assigned an *onClick* event handler. When the user clicks the link, the JavaScript code is executed. The pseudo *JavaScript:* protocol is followed by a reference to the form and a *reset()* method, which clears the form fields. See Figure 13.4.

Figure 13.4 The focus is in the first box and the field is selected (highlighted).

13.3 Handling a Window or Frame Event

A window is the main Web page, unless it is divided up into frames. There are a number of events that will affect windows and frames; these are described in Table 13.3. The following examples illustrate some of the events that affect windows and frames.

Table 13.3 Window and Frame Events

Event Handler	When It Is Triggered
onBlur	When the mouse moves away from the window or frame and it loses focus.
onFocus	When the mouse is clicked or moved in a window or frame and it gets focus.
onLoad	When a document or image has finished loading.
onMove	When a window is moved.
onUnLoad	When a page is exited or reset.

13.3.1 The *onLoad* and *onUnLoad* Events

The *onLoad* event handler is invoked on the occurrence of a *Load* event; that is, when a document, its frameset, or images have completely finished loading. This includes the point at which all functions have been defined and scripts have been executed, and all forms are available. This event can be helpful in synchronizing the loading of a set of frames, particularly when there might be large images that need to be loaded or all of the frame data hasn't arrived from the server.

The *onUnLoad* event handler is invoked when the page is exited or reset.

EXAMPLE 13.5

```
    <html>
      <head><title>load and unload Events</title>
1       <script type="text/javascript">
2         var sec=0;
3         function now(){
            var newdate= new Date();
            var hour=newdate.getHours();
            var minutes=newdate.getMinutes();
            var seconds=newdate.getSeconds();
            var timestr=hour+":"+minutes+":"+seconds;
4         window.setInterval("trackTime()", 1000);
5         alert("Your document has finished loading\n"+
                "The time: "+timestr);
          }
6         function trackTime(){
7           sec++;
          }
8         function howLong(){
            alert("You have been browsing here for "+ sec+" seconds");
          }
        </script>
      </head>
9   <body background="blue hills.jpg" onLoad="now();"
10        onUnLoad="howLong();">
        <font face="arial,helvetica" size=5>
        When you leave or reload this page, <br />an alert dialog box
        will appear.
        </font>
      </body>
    </html>
```

EXPLANATION

1   The JavaScript program starts here.

2   A global variable called *sec* is declared.

3   The user-defined function *now()* contains several of the *Date* object's methods to calculate the time. This function is used to keep track of how long the user browses from the time the page is loaded until it is exited.

4   The *window* object's *setInterval()* method is set to call the function *trackTime()* every 1,000 milliseconds (1 second) starting when the document is loaded until it is unloaded.

EXPLANATION (CONTINUED)

5 The alert dialog box pops up when the page finishes loading.

6 This is a user-defined function that keeps track of the number of seconds that have elapsed since the page was loaded.

7 The variable called *sec* is increased by one each time *trackTime()* is called.

8 This function is called when the page is exited or reloaded. It is the event that is triggered by the *onUnLoad* handler on line 10.

9 When the document has finished loading, the *onLoad* event handler is triggered. The *onLoad* event handler is an attribute of the *<body>* tag. The event handler is assigned a function called *now()* that sets up a timer that will go off every second while the page is opened. After a second passes another function called *trackTime()* will keep updating a variable that stores the number of seconds that have elapsed. The background attribute of the HTML *<body>* tag is set to an image of blue hills.

10 The *onUnLoad* event handler is triggered when the user either leaves or reloads the page. See Figure 13.5.

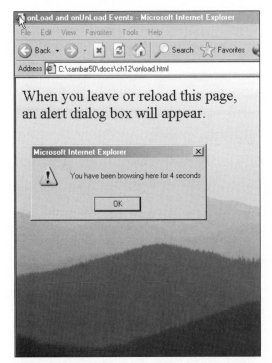

Figure 13.5 If you exit or click the reload button, this alert box appears.

13.3.2 The *onFocus* and *onBlur* Event Handlers

When an object has the focus, it is waiting for the user to do something, such as click a button, click a link, or start or stop an animation. If you are moving between frames, the frame where the mouse is pointing has the focus, and when the cursor moves out of the frame, it loses focus or is "blurred." The *onFocus* event handler is triggered by the user clicking on the current window, frame, or form element, or by using the Tab key to cycle through different elements on the screen. The *onFocus* event handler allows you to initiate a window or frame type function when the mouse is moved into a window, and the *onBlur* event handler is triggered when you leave a window or frame. This can be caused by the user clicking outside of the current window, frame, or form element. It's exactly the opposite of *onFocus*.

When a window has focus, it becomes the top window in a stack of windows. Example 13.6 changes the background color of the left frame to pink when it goes into focus and to yellow when it goes out of focus. The status bar at the bottom of the window reflects what frame has the focus.

EXAMPLE 13.6

```
    <html>
      <head><title>Frame Me!</title></head>
1     <frameset cols="25%,75%">
2       <frame src="leftfocus.html" name="left">
3       <frame src="rightfocus.html" name="right" >
      </frameset>
    </html>
----------------------------------------------------------------------
    <!-- The right frame file -->
    <html>
4   <head><title>Right Frame</title></head>
5   <body bgColor="lightblue">
      <font face="arial" size=4> right frame<br />
    </body>
    </html>
----------------------------------------------------------------------
    <html>
      <head><title>Left Frame</title>
6       <script type="text/javascript">
7       function focus_on_me(){
            document.bgColor="pink";  // Current doc is the left frame
8           window.status="focus leftframe";
          }
9       function defocus_me(){
            parent.left.document.bgColor="yellow";   // Another way to
                                                      // reference
10          window.status="focus rightframe";   // See the status bar
          }
      </script>
```

EXAMPLE 13.6 (CONTINUED)

```
       </head>
  11   <body onFocus="focus_on_me()"      // Event handlers
  12       onBlur="defocus_me()"
           bgColor="lightgreen">
           <image src="signs.jpg">
       </body>
     </html>
```

EXPLANATION

1   In this example, there are three files involved with frames. This is the HTML file that defines the frameset. It consists of a main window divided into two frames, a left frame consisting of 25 percent of the window, and right frame consisting of 75 percent of the window.

2   The left frame's source code is in a file called *leftfocus.html*.

3   The right frame's source code is in a file called *rightfocus.html*.

4   This HTML document is the content for the right frame.

5   The background color of the right frame is *lightblue*.

6   This is the start of the JavaScript program found in the file called *leftfocus.html*.

7   This user-defined function, called *focus_on_me()*, is called when the *onFocus* event handler is triggered; that is, when the user's cursor has focus in that window. It assigns a pink background color to the left frame by going down the JavaScript hierarchy: *parent.left.document.bgcolor*.

8   The status bar in the window is assigned the string *"focus leftframe"*. Look in the status bar.

9   This user-defined function, called *defocus_me*, is called when the *onBlur* event handler is triggered; that is, when the user's cursor loses focus in that window. It assigns a yellow background color to the right frame by going down the JavaScript hierarchy: *parent.right.document.bgcolor*.

10 The status bar in the window is assigned the string *"focus rightframe"*. Look in the status bar. (If the status bar doesn't show anything, it could be that the "Hide the status bar" feature has been enabled for your browser. For Firefox, see Tools→Options→ Enable JavaScript→Advanced JavaScript Settings).

11 An *onFocus* event handler is assigned to the *<body>* tag for the file called *leftfocus.html*. As soon as focus goes into this window (frame), the handler's function called *focus_on_me()* is called.

12 An *onBlur* event handler is assigned to the *<body>* tag for *leftfocus.html*. When focus leaves this frame (i.e., the user clicks the mouse in another window), the function called *defocus_me()* is called. The output is shown in Figure 13.6.

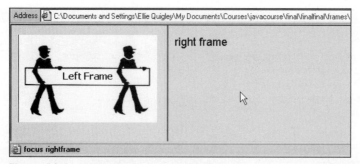

Figure 13.6   When focus is on the left frame, it turns pink. When focus leaves the left frame, it turns yellow. Notice the mouse pointer is in the right frame. That's where the focus is. Check the status bar.

The *focus()* and *blur()* Methods.   The *focus()* and *blur()* methods behave exactly the same as their like-named events. These methods are applied to an object, such as a window or form object, and are called from the JavaScript program. When the *focus()* method is applied to an object, it will cause that object to be in focus and when the *blur()* method is applied to an object, it will lose its input focus.

EXAMPLE   13.7

```
        <html>
        <head><title>The focus and blur methods</title>
          <script type="text/javascript">
1             function newWindow(){
2                 winObj=window.open("summertime.jpg",
                  "summer","width=650,height=200,resizable=yes,
                  scrollbars=yes,location=yes");
3                 winObj.moveTo(0,0);    // Move to left corner of screen
4                 winObj.focus();        // New window gets the focus
                  //windObj.blur();
                  }
5             function closeWindow(){
6                 winObj.close();        // Close the new window
                  }
          </script>
        </head>
        <body bgColor="lightgreen">
          <h2>Summer Scene from the Old Country</h2>
          <form>
            <input type=button
                   value="Open Window"
7                  onClick="JavaScript:newWindow();" />
            <input type=button
                   value="Close Window"
8                  onClick="JavaScript:closeWindow();" />
```

EXAMPLE 13.7 (CONTINUED)

```
        </form>
      </body>
   </html>
```

EXPLANATION

1   A user-defined function, called *newWindow()*, will create a new *window* object with the *window* object's *open()* method, specified with a number of options to further define the window.

2   The new *window* object contains an image called *summertime.jpg*.

3   The new window is moved to the left corner of the screen, pixel position (0,0).

4   The new window gets focus. It will be on top of all the other windows.

5   This user-defined function is responsible for closing the new window.

6   The *close()* method of the *window* object causes the new window to be closed.

7   When the user clicks this button, the *onClick* event handler is triggered, and a new window will be opened.

8   When the user clicks this button, the *onClick* event handler is triggered, and the new window will be closed. The output is shown in Figures 13.7 and 13.8.

Figure 13.7   The parent window.

Figure 13.8   The new window is in focus and will appear on top of its parent window.

13.3.3 The *onResize* Event Handler

The *onResize* event handler fires when the size of an object has changed.[2] In Firefox, Opera, and Safari, the *onResize* event handler is fired only when the size of the browser window changes and can be an attribute or property of the body, frameset, document, and window objects. In Internet Explorer, the *onResize* event handler is fired when the size of the browser window or the size of a body element is changed (although Internet Explorer can be quirky and lock up at times; new problems with this handler were reported with Internet Explorer 8).

```
<body onResize="JavaScript:resizeTo(400,400);">
```

This event handler can be used as an attribute of the window object but is not a valid attribute for the XHTML body tag. When the size of the document or window changes, the *onResize* event is fired on the body element in Internet Explorer. In Firefox, Opera, and Safari, an *onResize* event handler is fired on the body element when the browser window is resized.

EXAMPLE 13.8

```
    <html>
       <head><title>Test window.onresize</title>
         <script type="text/javascript">
1           function shrinkScreen() {
2              var newWidth=screen.availWidth/2;
               var newHeight=screen.availHeight/2;
3              window.resizeTo(newWidth,newHeight);
4              alert("The screen's width is: " +
                     newWidth+ " and the height is: "+ newHeight);
            }
5           function getDimensions() {
6              if (window.outerWidth){   // Firefox
                  alert("OnResize event: the original screen dimensions
                        are: " +
                     screen.availWidth+" x "+ screen.availHeight+
                       "new dimensions are: \n" + window.outerWidth + " "+
                       window.outerHeight);
               }
               else{ // Internet Explorer
7                 alert("OnResize event: the original screen dimensions
                        are: "+
                     screen.availWidth+" x "+ screen.availHeight+
                       "\nnew dimensions are: " + document.body.clientWidth +
                       " "+ document.body.clientHeight);
               }
            }
```

_____

2. This event does not fire for files with embedded controls.

EXAMPLE 13.8 (CONTINUED)

```
        </script>
    </head>
8   <body onResize="getDimensions();">
        <form>
            <input type="button" value="Click to change window size"
9                  onClick="JavaScript:shrinkScreen()" />
        </form>
    </body>
</html>
```

EXPLANATION

1   The function *shrinkScreen()* will cause the screen to be made half its size, if it is within the lower limit of 100 pixels.

2   The available screen width, *screen.availWidth*, and the available screen height, *screen.availHeight*, specify the current width or height of the screen, in pixels, minus features such as the taskbar in Windows. The variables *newWidth* and *newHeight* will get the available screen width and height divided by two.

3   The window will be resized to the new dimensions created on the previous two lines.

4   The alert box displays the dimensions of the screen in pixels after it has been resized.

5   The function, *getDimensions()*, is called whenever the window is resized.

6   If the *outerWidth* property exists, the browser is not Internet Explorer. The original screen dimensions and the new window dimensions will be displayed in the alert box. The *outerWidth* property determines the width of the window (including taskbars, etc.); using the *innerWidth* property determines the width excluding the text decoration.

7   Internet Explorer uses the *clientWidth* property of the document object to get the width of the window.

8   The *onResize* handler is associated with the body of the document. When the window changes in size, this handler is triggered.

9   When the *onClick* event handler is triggered, the *shrinkScreen()* function will be called and the screen will be resized to half its size. The output is shown in Figure 13.9.

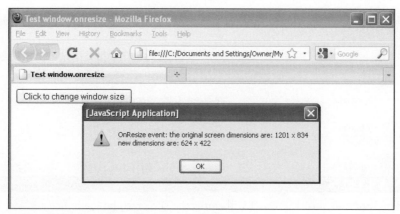

Figure 13.9   Window was resized manually by the user. The *onResize* event handler was triggered.

13.4 Handling Mouse Events

In many previous examples, we've seen uses of the *onClick* event handler to initiate an action when a user clicks the mouse in a button or on a link. There are a number of other events that can be fired due some action of the mouse. When the user moves the mouse pointer over a link, image, or other object, the *onMouseOver* event handler is triggered, and when he or she moves the mouse pointer away from an object, the *onMouseOut* event is triggered. Table 13.4 lists events that are triggered when mouse movement is detected.

Table 13.4   Mouse Events

Event Handler	When It Is Triggered
onClick	When the mouse is clicked on a link and on form objects like button, submit.
onDblClick	When the mouse is double-clicked on a link, document, form object, image.
onMouseDown	When the mouse is pressed on a link, document.
onMouseMove	When the mouse is moved when it is over a link, form object, or most elements.
onMouseOut	When a mouse is moved out of a link, imagemap.
onMouseOver	When a mouse is moved over or enters a link, imagemap, or most elements.
onMouseUp	When the mouse is released from a link, document.

13.4.1   How to Use Mouse Events

The *onMouseOver* and *onMouseOut* event handlers occur when the user's mouse pointer is moved over or out of an object. The *onMouseMove* event occurs when the mouse just touches the object. In Example 13.9, every time the user touches the button labeled *onMouseMove* with his or her mouse, a function called *counter()* is invoked to keep track of the number of mouse moves that have taken place. That number is displayed in an alert dialog box, as shown in Figure 13.10. If the user double-clicks the mouse anywhere on the page, the a message will appear, and if OK is clicked, the window will be closed.

EXAMPLE   13.9

```
    <html>
      <head><title>Mouse Events</title>
1       <script type="text/javascript">
2         var counter=0;
3         function alertme(){
            alert("I'm outta hea!");
4           window.close();
          }
5         function track_Moves(){
6           counter++;
            if(counter==1){
              alert(counter + " mouse moves so far!");
            }
            else{
              alert(counter + " mouse moves so far!");
            }
          }
        </script>
      </head>
7     <body bgColor="CCFF00" onDblClick="alertme()";>
        <p><font face="arial" size=3>
        Double click anywhere on this page to get out!
        </p><p>
        When the mouse moves over the link, an event is triggered.
8       <a href="#" onMouseOver="alert('Event:onMouseOver');" />
          onMouseOver
        </a></p><p>
        When the mouse moves away from a link, an event is triggered.
9       <a href="#" onMouseOut="alert('Event:onMouseOut');" />
          onMouseOut
        </a></p><p>
        When the mouse moves in or out of the button, a function<br />
        is called that keeps track of how many times the mouse touched
        the button.
```

Continues

EXAMPLE 13.9 (CONTINUED)

```
10      <form>
          <input type="button"
                value="onMouseMove"
11                onMouseMove="track_Moves();" />
        </form>
        </p>
      </body>
   </html>
```

EXPLANATION

1   A JavaScript program starts here.

2   A global variable called *counter* is initialized.

3   If the user double-clicks the mouse anywhere on the page, an alert dialog box will appear; if the user clicks OK in the alert dialog box, the window will be closed.

4   The *window*'s *close* method causes the current window to be closed.

5   This function is called when the *onMouseOver* event handler is triggered. This event happens when the user touches the mouse on an object, in this case, a button object.

6   The counter is incremented by one every time the user touches the button.

7   The *onDblClick* event handler is an attribute of the HTML *<body>* tag. When the user double-clicks the mouse, the *alertme()* function will be called, and the window closed.

8   The *onMouseOver* event handler is an attribute of the *<a href>* link tag. It is triggered anytime the user moves the mouse over the link. (The link has been deactivated by using the # sign.) When this event occurs, the *alert* method is called.

9   The *onMouseOut* event handler is an attribute of the *<a href>* link tag. Any time the user moves the mouse away from this link, the event is triggered, and the *alert* method is called.

10 The form starts here. The input type is a button.

11 When the user's mouse touches the button, the *onMouseMove* event handler is triggered, and the *track_Moves()* function is called. This function will simply increment a counter by one each time it is called, and then alert the user.

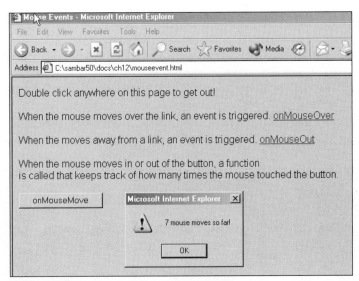

Figure 13.10 Links and mouse events.

13.4.2 Mouse Events and Images—Rollovers

The *onMouseOver* and *onMouseOut* event handlers are commonly used to create a rollover, an image that is replaced with a different image every time the mouse moves over a link or image. (See section "A Simple Rollover with a Mouse Event" on page 432 in Chapter 12.) In the following example, if the user touches the first link, the picture of the first mouse will be replaced with a new picture, giving the illusion that the mouse's eyes are moving.

EXAMPLE 13.10

```
    <html>
      <head><title>Mouse Events</title></head>
      <body bgColor="orange">
1       <a href="#" onMouseOver="document.mouse.src='mouse.gif'">
          onMouseOver </a><p>
2       <a href="#" onMouseOut="document.mouse.src='mouse2.gif';">
          onMouseOut</a><p>
3       <img src="mousestart.gif" width=300 height=150 name="mouse">
      </body>
    </html>
```

EXPLANATION

1   The *onMouseOver* event handler is assigned to a deactivated link (# causes the link to be inactive). When the mouse rolls onto the link, the event is triggered, and a new image called *mouse.gif* will replace the original image, *mousestart.gif*.

Continues

2   The *onMouseOut* event handler is assigned to another deactivated link, this time with another image of the mouse. When the mouse rolls away from the link, the event is triggered, and a new image called *mouse2.gif* will replace the last image, *mouse.gif*. By rolling the mouse back and forth, the mouse's eyes seem to move. The words "*hi*" and "*bye*" also keep changing.

3   This is the original image that is displayed before the links are touched. See Figure 13.11.

Figure 13.11   Original display (left), as the mouse moves over the link (middle), and as the mouse moves away from the link (right).

13.4.3 Creating a Slideshow with Mouse Events

By using a timer with an event, you can do all sorts of fun things with images. You can create scrolling banners, rotating billboards, button rollovers, and more. Example 13.11 is a simple slideshow. Four images are preloaded and each image is assigned to an array element. When the user moves the mouse onto one of the pictures, a new picture will replace the previous one every 2 seconds, and when he or she moves the mouse away from the image, the show stops. Any time the mouse moves over the image, the show starts again.

EXAMPLE 13.11

```
      <html>
        <head><title>The Four Seasons</title>
          <script type="text/javascript">
1             var season = new Array();
2             var indx = 0;
3             var timeDelay=2000;
```

EXAMPLE 13.11 (CONTINUED)

```
4        season[0]=new Image();
5        season[0].src="winter.jpg";
         season[1]=new Image();
         season[1].src="summer.jpg";
         season[2]=new Image();
         season[2].src="fall.jpg";
         season[3]=new Image();
         season[3].src="spring.jpg";
6        function changeSeason(){
7           var size= season.length - 1;
            if( indx < size ) {
               indx++;
            }
            else {
               indx = 0;
            }
8           document.times.src= season[indx].src;
9           timeout=setTimeout('changeSeason()', timeDelay);
         }
10       function stopShow(){
11          clearTimeout(timeout);
         }
      </script>
   </head>
   <body bgcolor="cornflowerblue">
      <div align="center"><font face="arial">
         <h2>The 4 Seasons</h2><b>
         To see slide show, put your mouse on the image.<br />
         Move your mouse away from the image, to stop it.
12       <a href="JavaScript:void(null);"
               onMouseOver="return changeSeason();"
               onMouseOut="return stopShow()">
            <img name="times" src="winter.jpg" align="left"
               border=8  hspace="10" width="700" height="200">
         </a>
         <br />
      </div>
   </body>
</html>
```

EXPLANATION

1 A new *Array* object called *season* is declared. It will be used to store an array of images.

2 A global variable called *indx* is declared and initialized to 0.

3 The value 2000 is assigned to another global variable, called *timeDelay*.

4 Using the *Image()* constructor preloads and caches the images. Each new image object is assigned to an element of the *season* array.

Continues

EXPLANATION

5   The first element of the *season* array gets a *new Image* object. The *src* property (the location and name of the image) is *winter.jpg*, located in the present working directory.

6   A user-defined function called *changeSeason()* is defined. It is called when the *onMouseOver* event handler is triggered by the user moving the mouse onto the image. Its purpose is to replace one image with another image in the *season* array, every 2 seconds, for as long as the user's mouse is on the image. (It might be nice to add a little Vivaldi audio clip here to enhance the show!)

7   The size of the array is its length − 1 because array indexes start at 0. As long as the array size isn't surpassed, the index value will keep being incremented by 1.

8   This is where image replacement happens. The name of the original image is *times* (line 14) and it is referenced by JavaScript using the DOM hierarchy: *docment.times.src* is assigned a new image from the *season* array, *season[indx].src*. The new image will be displayed.

9   The *window* object's *setTimeout()* method will be set to call the *changeSeason()* function every 2,000 milliseconds (2 seconds). Every 2 seconds a new image is displayed as long as the user keeps the mouse on an image.

10   The user-defined function called *stopShow()* is defined. It is called when the *onMouseOut* event is triggered by the mouse moving away from the image. It turns off the timer, stopping the slideshow.

11   The *setTimeout()* method is cleared.

12   The link has two mouse event handlers, *onMouseOver* and *onMouseOut*. The pseudo URL, *JavaScript:void(null)*, deactivates the link and ensures that if there is a return value from the event, it will be nullified. Because neither of the events returns anything, it would be enough to just use the protocol as *JavaScript:*. The display is shown in Figures 13.12 and 13.13.

Figure 13.12   Watch the seasons change every 2 seconds.

Figure 13.13 Spring image (top), summer image (middle), and fall image (bottom) are all part of the slideshow created in Example 13.11.

13.5 Handling Link Events

In many of the previous examples, links have been used to trigger events. When the user clicked or moved the mouse over a link, a link event was triggered. One link event, *onClick*, gets sent whenever someone clicks on a link. As we saw with mouse events, *onMouseOver* and *onMouseOut* also cause a link event to occur. The link events are listed in Table 13.5.

Table 13.5 Link Events

Event Handler	*When It Is Triggered*
onClick	When the mouse is clicked on a link
onMouseOut	When a mouse is moved out of a link
onMouseOver	When a mouse is moved over a link

13.5.1 JavaScript URLs

We have seen JavaScript code in a *JavaScript:* URL throughout this text. In the example using mouse events, the event handler was assigned to a link and the link was deactivated by assigning a quoted hash mark to the link *href* attribute:

```
<a href="#" onClick='alert("This hotlink is out of service!");
   return false;'>Click here</a>
```

or by using the *JavaScript*: protocol followed by the *void* operator to guarantee that any return value from the function will be discarded:

```
<a href="JavaScript:void(0);" onMouseOver="return changeSeason();"
```

In either case, the link was not supposed to take the user to another location, but instead to handle an event or call a function. (Make sure that any function calls in the URL have been defined.) Another note: If the "#" causes the browser to jump to the top of the page when the link is clicked, you can add a return *false* statement inside the *onClick* handler to keep the browser from checking the content of the *href*.

The following simple example uses the *onClick* event handler with a deactivated link and the return statement; the display is shown in Figure 13.14.

EXAMPLE 13.12

```
<html><head><title>Deactivate the hotlink</title></head>
<body>
<center>
<a href="#" onClick='alert("This hotlink is out of service!");
   return false;'>Click here</a>
</center>
</body>
</html>
```

Figure 13.14   The user clicked a deactivated link.

13.6 Handling a Form Event

As discussed in Chapter 11, the *document* object has a *form* property. It contains an array of all the forms that have been defined in the document. Each element of the array is a *form* object and the number in the index of the array represents the order in which the form appeared on the page. The first form would be *document.forms[0]*. Each form contains elements, also represented as an array. The elements represent the input types of the form, such as a checkbox, radio button, or text field. By naming each of the forms and its respective elements, it is much easier to work with them in JavaScript. (See Chapter 11 for a complete discussion of the *forms[]* array.) There are a number of events associated with the form's elements. Many of them were also covered in Chapter 11. They are listed in Table 13.6.

Table 13.6 Event Handlers for the Form's Elements

Object	*Event Handler*
button	onClick, onBlur, onFocus
checkbox	onClick, onBlur, onFocus
FileUpLoad	onClick, onBlur, onFocus
hidden	none
password	onBlur, onFocus, onSelect
radio	onClick, onBlur, onFocus
reset	onReset
select	onFocus, onBlur, onChange
submit	onSubmit
text	onClick, onBlur, onFocus, onChange
textarea	onClick, onBlur, onFocus, onChange

13.6.1 Buttons

One of the most common GUI form elements is the button. The button object has no default action and is normally used to trigger an event such as the *onClick* event. HTML 4 allows you to create a *<button>* tag without the *<input>* tag.[3] There are several buttons associated with a form; the buttons are called:

- *submit*
- *reset*
- *button*

If an event handler, such as *onSubmit* or *onChange* is an attribute of a form tag, then the event occurs when the user clicks one of the buttons associated with the form object. Form event handlers are listed in Table 13.7.

---

3. The *<button> </button>* tags give greater flexibility to the appearance of the button by allowing HTML content to be displayed instead of plain text that is assigned to the value attribute of a button created using the *<input type="button">*.

Table 13.7 Form Event Handlers

Event Handler	When It Is Triggered
onBlur	When a form's select, text, or textarea field loses focus.
onChange	When a select, text, or textarea field loses focus and its value has been changed.
onClick	When an object on a form is clicked.
onFocus	When a field receives input focus by tabbing with the keyboard or clicking with the mouse in the field.
onReset	When the user resets the form.
onSelect	When a user selects some of the text within a text or textarea field.
onSubmit	When a user submits a form.

13.6.2 *this* for Forms and *this* for Buttons

The *this* keyword refers to the current object and is especially helpful when dealing with forms. In forms that contain multiple items, such as checkboxes, radio buttons, and textboxes, it is easier to refer to the item with the *this* keyword than by using its full name when calling a function or an event handler. (Examples of the *this* keyword are shown in Chapter 11.)

In a form, *this* could be the form itself or one of the input devices. With an event handler, the *this* keyword by itself references the current object, such as an input device, whereas *this.form* references the form object where the input device was created.

EXAMPLE 13.13

```
      <html>
        <head><title>The this keyword</title>
          <script type="text/javascript">
1           function display_formval(myform){
                alert("text box value is: " + myform.namestring.value );
            }
2           function display_buttonval(mybutton){
                alert("button value is: " + mybutton.value);
            }
          </script>
        </head>
        <body><b>
          <hr>
3         <form name="simple_form">
            <p>
            Type your name here:
            <input type="text" name="namestring" size="50" />
```

EXAMPLE 13.13 (CONTINUED)

```
           <p>
4          <input type="button"
                   value="Print Form Stuff"
5                  onClick="display_formval(this.form);" />
           <input type="button"
                   value="Print Button Stuff"
6                  onClick="display_buttonval(this);" />
           <input type="reset" value="Clear">
        </form>
      </body>
   </html>
```

EXPLANATION

1   The function called *display_formval()* is defined. Its only parameter is a reference to a form; in this example the form started on line 3. The purpose of this function is to display the text that the user typed in a text box, called *"namestring"*. The function is called when the *onClick* event handler is triggered on line 5.

2   The function called *display_buttonval()* is defined. Its only parameter is a button input type, defined on line 4. It displays the value in the button.

3   This is the start of a form named *simple*.

4   The input type is a button in the form named *simple*.

5   The *onClick* event handler is triggered when the user clicks this button. The argument sent to the *display_formval()* function, *this.form*, is a reference to the form object. Without the *form* property, the *this* keyword would refer to the current object, the button. See line 6. Rather than using the full JavaScript hierarchy to reference a form, the *this* keyword simplifies the process.

6   The *onClick* event is triggered when the user presses this button. Because the handler is assigned to the button, the *this* keyword is a reference to the button object. The display is shown in Figure 13.15.

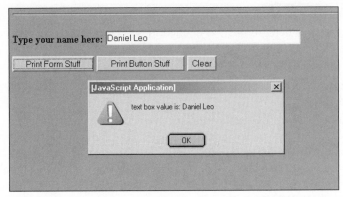

Figure 13.15   The user clicked the Print Form Stuff button.

13.6.3   Forms and the *onClick* Event Handler

The *onClick* event handler is used most often in forms. The click event occurs when a button in a form, such as a radio or checkbox, is pressed. It also happens when an option is selected in a Select menu. In Chapter 11, we used many examples of the *onClick* event handler. Here are a few more.

EXAMPLE 13.14

```
        <html>
          <head>
            <title>Event Handling and Forms</title>
            <script type="text/javascript">
1             function greetme(message){
                alert(message);
              }
            </script>
          </head>
          <body bgcolor="white">
            <h2>
              Greetings Message
            </h2>
            <hr>
2           <form>
3             <input type="button" value="Morning"
4                   onClick="greetme('Good morning. This is your wakeup
                                      call!')" />
              <input type="button" value="Noon"
                    onClick="greetme('Let\'s do lunch.')" />
              <input type="button" value="Night"
                    onClick="greetme('Have a pleasant evening.\nSweet
                                      dreams...')" />
            </form>
          </body>
        </html>
```

EXPLANATION

1   A simple function called *greetme()* is defined. It will be called each time the user clicks one of three buttons and will send an alert message to the screen.

2   The HTML form starts here.

3   The input type for this form is three buttons, respectively labeled *"Morning"*, *"Noon"*, and *"Night"*. See Figure 13.16.

4   When the user clicks a button, the *onClick* event is fired up, and the *greetme()* function is called with a string. See Figure 13.17. Watch the quotes in the string. Because the outside quotes are double quotes, the inner quotes are single. And if the outer set of quotes had been single quotes, the inner set would be double. It's very easy to ruin a program just because the quoting is off, as you well know by now if you've gone this far in the book.

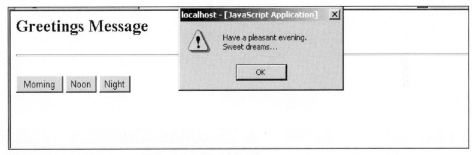

Figure 13.16   Three buttons waiting for a user to click one of them.

Figure 13.17   The user clicked the Night button.

13.6.4   Forms and the *onFocus* and *onBlur* Event Handlers

The *onFocus* event handler is triggered when a form element has focus: The cursor is sitting in the box, waiting for key input or in the case of a button, for the Enter key to be pressed. The *onBlur* event is triggered when the form element loses focus, when the cursor is moved away from the input device.

EXAMPLE   13.15

```
      <html>
        <head><title>Using the onFocus Event Handler</title>
          <script type="text/javascript">
1           function handler(message){
2             window.status = message;    // Watch the status bar
            }
          </script>
        </head>
        <body bgcolor="magenta"><b>The onFocus Event Handler
          <i>(When you click in one of the boxes, focus goes
             to the status bar)</i>
```

Continues

EXAMPLE 13.15 (CONTINUED)

```
3          <form name="form1">
              <p>Type your name:
4          <input type="text"
                     name="namestring"
                     size="50"
5                    onFocus="handler('Don\'t forget to enter your name')">
              <br />Talk about yourself here:<br />
6          <textarea name="comments"
                     align="left"
7                    onFocus="handler('Did you add comments?')"
                     rows="5" cols="50">I was born...
              </textarea><p>
              <input type="button"
                     value="submit">
              <input type="reset"
                     value="clear">
           </form>
          </body>
         </html>
```

EXPLANATION

1   A user-defined function called *handler()* is defined. It takes a string as its only parameter.

2   The string message, *"Don't forget to enter your name"* (or *"Did you add comments?"*) is passed to the function and assigned to the window's status bar. (If you don't see anything in the status bar, the feature has been disabled for your browser. For Firefox go to the View option and click Status bar. For Safari, View, and click Hide Status Bar.)

3   The HTML form starts here.

4   The first input type is a textbox.

5   The textbox contains the attribute for the *onFocus* event handler. When this box has focus, the event will be fired up and call the *handler()* function.

6   A text area is defined to hold user comments.

7   The text area contains the attribute for the *onFocus* event handler. When this box has focus, the event will be fired up and call the *handler()* function. See Figure 13.18.

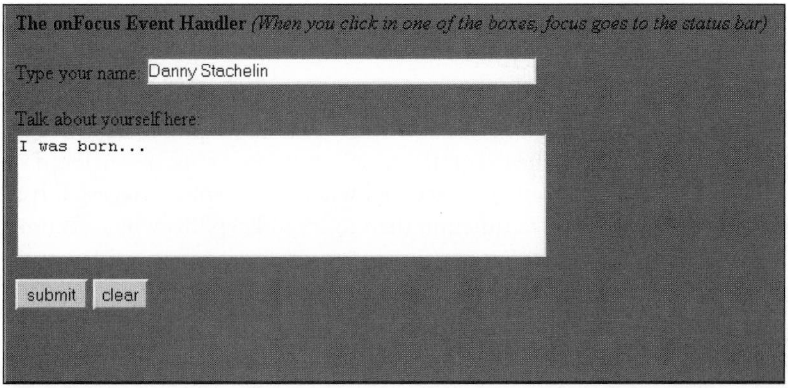

Figure 13.18   Look at the status bar. You might have to enable the View Status Bar feature for your browser.

13.6.5   Forms and the *onChange* Event Handler

The *onChange* event handler is triggered after the user modifies the value or contents of an HTML input, select, or text area element in a form, and then releases the mouse. This is another event handler that can be useful in checking or validating user input.

EXAMPLE 13.16

```
   <html>
      <head><title>onChange Event Handler</title></head>
      <body>
1      <form>
         Please enter your grade:
2         <input type="text" onChange="
               grade=parseInt(this.value);   //Convert to integer
3            if(grade < 0 || grade > 100){
               alert('Please enter a grade between 0 and 100');
            }
4            else{
               confirm('Is '+ grade + ' correct?');
            }
5         " />
6      </form>
      </body>
   </html>
```

EXPLANATION

1   The HTML form starts here.

2   The input type is a text field. The *onChange* event is triggered when something changes in the text field box, such as a user entering input. Instead of assigning a function to the handle the event, the JavaScript statements are enclosed in double quotes and will be parsed and executed when the event is triggered. It might be less error prone to write a function than to try to keep this whole section of code enclosed in quotes.

3   If the input assigned to grade is less than 0 or greater than 100, it is out of the legal range, causing an alert box to appear.

4   If the input was within the limits, then the *else* block is executed. A confirm box will appear to verify that this is what the user meant to type.

5   This quote marks the end of the JavaScript statements, and the > marks the end of the input type tag.

6   The HTML form ends here. The actions of the handler are shown in Figures 13.19 through 13.21.

Figure 13.19   The user enters no value at all: There is no change.

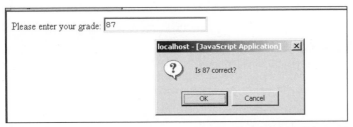

Figure 13.20   The user enters a value. A change has taken place within the textbox. The *onChange* handler is invoked.

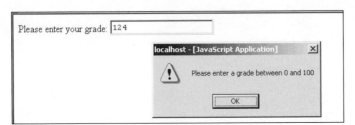

Figure 13.21   The user enters a value. The *onChange* handler is invoked. The value entered was out of range, causing the alert box to appear.

13.6.6 Forms and the *onSubmit* Event Handler

When you submit an online order for a purchase you made at a Web site like Amazon or iTunes, once you have submitted the order, you can't back out. It's too late. You have your e-mail confirmation before you can blink an eye, your new tune or movie ready to play, and your payment has already been processed. You pressed the submit button, maybe with a different label, like "Order now," but pressing that button triggered an event that caused your order to be processed.

The *onSubmit* event handler was discussed in detail in Chapter 11, but it is included again in this chapter because it is such an important form event. You will see this event again in Chapter 17. If you recall, the *onSubmit* event is an attribute of the HTML *<form>* tag and is triggered when the user presses the submit button after filling out a form. This event allows the programmer to validate the form before sending it off to the server. If the return value from the event handler is true, the form will be submitted; if false it won't be submitted. The following examples demonstrate two different programs using an *onSubmit* event handler. Example 13.17 creates two text fields for the user's name and address. The *onSubmit* event handler is triggered when the user clicks the submit button, causing a function to be called that will produce a little popup window with the user's input data. By allowing the user to view the data entered, the submission can be delayed for further validation, and so on. Example 13.18 is a snippet of code that could be used after a shopping cart has been filled and the user is ready to go to the checkout page. When the user clicks the submit button labeled "Go to Checkout" a function will be called. It returns true if the user has checked a checkbox and false if he or she hasn't. By checking the small checkbox, the user is confirming that he or she is ready to submit the form data. Then a server side program will perform further validations and calculations, send e-mail, open a database, and so on. Both of the examples show the value of having an *onSubmit* handler to catch the form before it is submitted to allow the user to change a field, go back to another page, confirm that he or she has finished and is ready to order, and so on.

EXAMPLE 13.17

```
<html>
   <head><title>The onSubmit Event Handler</title>
     <script type="text/javascript">
1        function popUp(){
2           newWin=window.open('','NewWin','toolbar=no,
                        status=no,width=500,height=200');
3           newWin.document.write("<body bgcolor='yellow'>
                        <h3>Form data</h3>");
            newWin.document.write("<b>Your name is:</b> " +
            document["form1"].namestring.value);
            newWin.document.write("<br /><b>Your address is:
                        </b></body>" +document["form1"].address.value);
            newWin.document.close();
         }
     </script>
```

Continues

EXAMPLE 13.17 (CONTINUED)

```
        </head>
        <body bgcolor="yellow">
4       <form name="form1" onSubmit="return popUp();">
          <p>
          <table>
            <tr>
              <td>
                <b>Type your name:</b>
              </td>
              <td>
5                <input type="text"
                        name="namestring"
                        size="50">
              </td>
            </tr>
            <tr>
              <td>
                <b>Type in your address:</b>
              </td>
              <td>
6                <input type="text"
                        name="address"
                        size="80">
              </td>
            </tr>
          </table>
          <p>
          <input type="submit" value="Submit form" />
          <input type="reset" value="Clear" />
        </form>
      </body>
</html>
```

EXPLANATION

1   A function called *popUp()* is defined. It will cause a popup window to appear with
     data that was entered into a form. (Your browser might not allow popup windows
     unless you change a setting.)

2   This is where the new *window* object is created and assigned properties. (In this
     example, the line is broken to make it fit on the page, but if you do this in a script,
     make sure there are no spaces between any of the window options.)

3   The *write()* method will send its output to the new window.

EXPLANATION(CONTINUED)

4   The HTML form starts here. When the submit button is clicked, the *onSubmit* event handler will be triggered and call the *popUp()* function, causing a new pop-up window to appear containing the information that the user typed into the form. At this point the program could ask the user if the data is valid and continue to process the information by sending it to a server. Because the *action* attribute for the HTML form hasn't been defined, nothing will happen.

5   The input types for the form are defined here as two textboxes, one for the user's name and one for the address.

6   The submit button is created here. When the user submits the form, the *onSubmit* handler on line 4 will be triggered. The action is shown in Figures 13.22 and 13.23.

Figure 13.22   The fillout form.

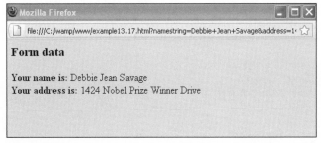

Figure 13.23   Popup window with form data after submit.

EXAMPLE 13.18

```
      <html>
        <head><title>Check it Out!</title>
          <script type="text/javascript">
            // Script modified from original found at
            // http://JavaScript.internet.com
1           function okForm(form){
              if (form.accept.checked == true){
                return true;}
              else{
                alert("Please check the box!");
                form.accept.focus();
                return false;}
            }
          </script>
        </head>
        <body bgcolor="#CCCCFF">
          <font face="arial,helvetica" size=2>
2         <form action="http://localhost/phpexamples/processform.php"
              method="post"
3             onSubmit="return okForm(this)">
          <b>Your name:</b><br />
4         <input type="text" name="yourname">
          <p>
            <b>What will you purchase today?</b><br />
          </p>
          <input type="radio" name="choice"
                value="burger">Burger, fries and coke
          <br />
          <input type="radio" name="choice"
                value="veggie">Veggies and Vitamin water
          <p>
          <b>Thank you for your order.
            Check the box and then "Go to Checkout".</b></p>
5         <input type="checkbox"
                name="accept"
                value="0" />
6         <input type="submit"
                value="Go to checkout" />
          </p>
7         <input type="button"
                value="Go back to Home Page"
                onClick="window.location.replace('http://localhost';)">
          </font>
          </form>
        </body>
      </html>
```

EXPLANATION

1   A function called *okForm()* is defined. The function is called by the *onSubmit* event handler. Its purpose is to ensure that a checkbox has been checked before allowing the user to submit the form. If it has, the return value is *true*, and the form will be submitted. If not, the user will be reminded to check the box, *false* will be returned, and the form will not be submitted. See Figure 13.24. Once the checkbox has been checked, and the submit button labeled "Go to Checkout" clicked, the form will be submitted to the URL address assigned to the form's action attribute; in this case a PHP script called "processform.php" (see Figure 13.25).

2   The *action* attribute is the URL of the server where the form data will be sent for processing, once it has been submitted.

3   The *onSubmit* event handler is triggered when the user clicks the submit button for this form.

4   This is the part of the form where the user enters data to be sent to the server-side program for processing.

5   This is the checkbox that must be clicked before the user can submit the form. The *okForm()* checks to see if this box was checked before allowing the form to be submitted.

6   When this submit button, labeled "Go to Checkout" is pressed, the *onSubmit* handler on line 3 is triggered.

7   When the user presses this button, the *onClick* handler will be fired up, and cause the page to be redirected to the shopping cart page for the site.

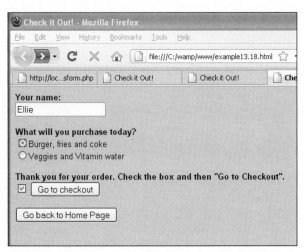

Figure 13.24 The user cannot go to checkout (i.e., submit the form) until he or she clicks the little box at the left.

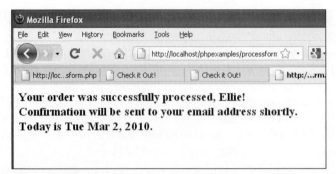

Figure 13.25   After the user checks out, the PHP script processes the input data from the form.

13.6.7   HTML Event Handlers and JavaScript Event Methods

You'll find that many JavaScript programs use a combination of event handlers and event methods, especially when working with forms. Example 13.19 uses event handlers and event methods. It creates a random number between 1 and 10, and asks the user to guess what the number is. As soon as the document is loaded, the *onLoad* event handler is triggered, and when the user clicks the button, the *onClick* handler is fired up. The *focus()* method is used to put focus in the textbox where the user will enter his or her guess.

EXAMPLE   13.19

```
    <html>
       <head><title>Event Handling</title>
         <script type="text/javascript">
           var tries=0;
1          function randomize(){
             // Random number is set when the document has loaded
             var now=new Date();
             num=(now.getSeconds())%10;
             //modulus-remainder after division
             num++;
           }
2          function guessit(form){
             // Function is called each time the user clicks the button
             if (form.tfield.value == num){
               alert("Correct!!");
3              form.tfield.focus();
               n=0;
               randomize();
             }
```

EXAMPLE   13.19 (CONTINUED)

```
                else{
                    tries++;
4                   alert(tries + " Wrong. Try again.");
                    form.tfield.value=""; // Clear the textbox
                    form.tfield.focus();   // Put the cursor in the textbox
                }
            }
            // End hiding from old browsers -->
        </script>
    </head>
    <body bgcolor="lightgreen"
5       onLoad="randomize()">  <!--Call function when page is loaded-->
        <center>
        <b>Pick a number between 1 and 10</b>
        <form name="myform">
6           <input type="textbox" size=4
                    name="tfield" />
            <p>
7           <input type="button"
                    name="button1"
8                   value="Check my  guess"
                    onClick="guessit(this.form)" /> </p>
        </form>
    </body>
</html>
```

This script was modified from one written by Andree Growney originally available at *http://www.htmlgoodies.com/primers/jsp/.*

EXPLANATION

1   A function called *randomize()* is defined. It will create a random number by dividing the number of seconds by 10 and returning the remainder (modulus); for example, 59/10 would return the number 9. Then, by adding 1 to that, we get 10.

2   The function called *guessit* will take one argument, a reference to the form. Its purpose is to see if the number entered by the user, *form.tfield.value*, matches the value of the random number calculated in the *randomize()* function.

3   The *focus()* method puts the cursor in the text field.

4   If the user guessed wrong, the alert dialog box appears and tells him or her so, the text field is cleared, and focus is put there.

5   Once the document has loaded, the *onLoad* event handler is triggered, causing the function *randomize()* to be called. This sets the initial random number for the program.

Continues

EXPLANATION(CONTINUED)

6   The form's input type is a textbox. This is where the user will enter his or her guess.

7   This input type is a button.

8   When the user clicks this button, the *onClick* event handler is triggered, causing the *guessit()* function to be called with *this* form as an argument. The display is shown in Figures 13.26 and 13.27.

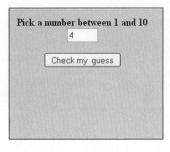
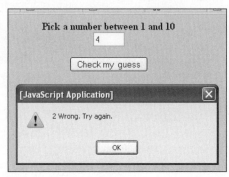

Figure 13.26   The user makes a guess (left), but is told he or she guessed wrong (right).

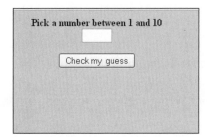

Figure 13.27   Focus returns to the form field.

13.6.8   The *onError* Event

The error event fires when a JavaScript error has occurred (window) or when an image cannot be found (image elements).

EXAMPLE 13.20

```
<html>
   <head><title>Wake up call</title>
      <script type="text/javascript">
         function wakeupCall(){    // Function is defined here
            timeout=setTimeout('alert("Time to get up!")',2000);
         }
```

EXAMPLE 13.20 (CONTINUED)

```
        </script>
    </head>
    <body bgcolor="white">
        <form>
            <div align="center">
            <p>
1           <image src="Image/java_steam.gif"
2                   onError="alert('Image is having trouble loading!')">
            </p>
            <input type="button"
                    value="Wake me"
                    onClick="wakeupCall()" />
            </div>
        </form>
    </body>
</html>
```

EXPLANATION

1   The *<image>* tag identifies the *src* of a *.gif* image to be loaded from a subdirectory called *Image*.
2   The *onError* event handler is triggered when an error occurs while loading the image. See Figure 13.28.

Figure 13.28   The *onError* event handler was triggered because the image *src* was wrong (left), and after the image loads (right).

13.7 The *event* Object

As we have seen throughout this text, events are happening all the time with JavaScript. Event objects are sent to an event handler with each event that occurs within a document; for example, when the user clicks on the left mouse button, JavaScript registers the event, what key was pressed, its coordinates (pixel positions of where it was pressed on the screen), and so on. To learn more about what happened so that you can track problems, get pixel coordinates, find out what button was pushed or what key was released, and so on, the event object provides specific information about the event. This topic can be very confusing because W3C, Mozilla/Firefox type browsers, and Microsoft Internet Explorer differ in how events should be handled. Like economists argue over taxes, trickle-up or trickle-down economics, browser companies argued over the order in which events are handled, also called event propagation. Does the event bubble up from its target or does it trickle down to its target?

13.7.1 Capturing and Bubbling (Trickle Down and Bubble Up)

The way that the events are handled differs by the browser and is based on how Netscape and Internet Explorer dealt with events back in the 1990s. Suppose you have used an *onClick* event handler in the button of a form. The user clicks the button. What happens? Netscape said that the event is captured, that is, it comes to life at the window level and trickles down the document to the form object until it finally reaches the button, its target: When it reaches its target, the button, the event is fired. An analogy could be water trickling down a mountain stream until it reaches a lake at the bottom. Internet Explorer says the event springs to life for the target for which it was intended; (i.e., the button) and then sends information about the event back up from the button to the form to the document, then window, like the bubbling up effect of soda water in a glass (see Figure 13.29).

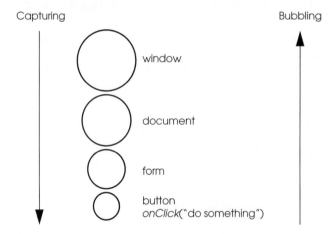

Figure 13.29 Bubbling and capturing.

Fortunately, the W3C DOM Level 2 provides an Events module that allows the DOM nodes to handle events with a combination of these methods, but defaults to the bubble-up model. We will see later how to use event handling with the DOM, how to specifically program the event to use one model or the other, cancel the bubbling effect, and so on. For now we will assume the browser is W3C compliant and defaults to bubbling. If you want to check what model your browser is using, the last exercise in this chapter provides the JavaScript code for testing. We discuss bubbling and capturing again in Chapter 15.

13.7.2 Event Object Properties

Now we will look at some of the properties of the event object and how they are used to glean information about an event that has occurred. Many of the examples listed on different Web sites might not work when you try them because they were written for a specific client. You might be using Opera or Safari and think, "This doesn't work at all. I give up." But if you bring up Internet Explorer, the program seems to work fine. To see what does or doesn't apply to your browser go to "Events Compatibility Table" at *http://www.quirksmode.org/dom/events/index.html*. Although the DOM provides a standard model, not all browsers are compliant. We discuss the DOM in Chapter 15.

Tables 13.8 and 13.9 provide a list of the event properties for Internet Explorer and Firefox.

Table 13.8 Properties of the *event* Object: Internet Explorer

Property	*What It Describes*
altKey, ctrlKey, shiftKey	Set to true or false to test if Alt, Shift, or Control keys were pressed when the event occurred.
button	An integer indicating which mouse button was pressed or released, 1 = left, 2 = right, 4 = middle. If multiple buttons are pressed, the value is the sum of both buttons, such as 3 (1+2) for left and right.
cancelBubble	Set to true or false to cancel or enable event bubbling. To cancel across browsers, the *stopPropagation()* method is supported.
clientX and *clientY*	The cursor's horizontal and vertical position in pixels, relative to the upper-left corner Web page in which the event occurred. Also good for the Mozilla/Firefox and W3C event model.
fromElement, toElement	Used to indicate the elements where a mouse is (mouseout and mouseover) leaving from or moving into. See *relatedTarget* for W3C/Firefox.
keyCode	The Unicode key code associated with a keypress event. Use *String.fromCharCode(keyCode)* to convert keycode code to a string.
offsetX and *offsetY*	The cursor's horizontal and vertical position in pixels, relative to the container in which the event occurred, or if outside the container returns the upper left corner of the document.
returnValue	The return value of the event handler, either *true* or *false*. For W3C/Firefox use *preventDefault()* method.
srcElement	The element from where the event originated, not necessarily the element where it was assigned due to bubbling. Use *target* for Firefox.

Continues

Table 13.8   Properties of the *event* Object: Internet Explorer (continued)

Property	What It Describes
srcFilter	Specifies the filter object that caused an *onfilterchange* event.
x and y	The cursor's horizonal and vertical position in pixels, relative to the document in which the event occurred.
reason	Used to indicate the status of a data transfer for data source objects.

Table 13.9   Properties of the *event* Object: Mozilla Firefox

Property	What It Describes
altKey, ctrlKey, metaKey, shiftKey	Set to true or false to test if Alt, Shift, Control, or Meta keys were pressed when the event occurred (Internet Explorer doesn't support metaKey).
pageX and pageY	Horizontal and vertical cursor position within a Web page, relative to the document, not supported by Internet Explorer.
bubbles	Set to Boolean value indicating whether or not the event bubbles.
button	An integer indicating which mouse button was pressed or released, 0 = left, 2 = right, 1 = middle. Slightly different in Internet Explorer, as described earlier.
cancelable	A Boolean value indicating whether or not the event can be canceled.
charCode	Indicates the Unicode for the key pressed. Use *String.fromCharCode(which)* to convert code to string.
clientX, clientY	Returns the mouse coordinates at the time of the event relative to upper-left corner of the window.
currentTarget	The node that this event handler is currently being run on.
eventPhase	An integer value indicating which phase of the event flow this event is being processed in. One of CAPTURING_PHASE (1), AT_TARGET (2) or BUBBLING_PHASE (3).
layerX and layerY	Returns the horizontal and vertical cursor position within a layer, not standard.
relatedTarget	On a mouseover event it indicates the node that the mouse has left. On a mouseout event it indicates the node the mouse has moved onto.
screenX and screenY	Returns the coordinates of the mouse relative to the screen when the event fired.

Table 13.9 Properties of the *event* Object: Mozilla Firefox (continued)

Property	What It Describes
target	The node from which the event originated.
timestamp	Returns the time (in milliseconds since the epoch) the event was created. Not all events return a timestamp.
type	A string indicating the type of event, such as "mouseover", "click", and so on.
which	Netscape legacy property indicating the Unicode for the key pressed. Identical to *charCode*.
modifiers	The bitmask representing modifier keys such as Alt, Shift, Meta, and so on.
data	Array of URLs for dragged and dropped.
height and *width*	Height and width of the window.

13.7.3 Using Event Object Properties

The *srcElement/target* and *type* Properties.   The *srcElement* (Internet Explorer) and the *target* properties (Firefox) return the element that fired the event. The *srcElement* also has a *tagName* property: *event.srcElement.tagName* will return "IMG" if you click on an image object. And we can also read styles, so if the image has a style height of 100px, then *event.srcElement.style.height* will return "100px".

The *type* property contains the event name (e.g., *click*, *mouseover*, *keypress*, and so on). This is the same for nonphysical events. If we capture and handle an *onload* event, type will be "load", and so on.

EXAMPLE 13.21

```
      <html>
        <head><title>Event Properties</title></head>
        <body bgcolor="yellow"
          <!--Internet Explorer has srcElement property-->
          <!--Firefox has target property-->
          <!--Opera has both-->
1         <form name="form1">
2           <input type=button
                  value="Internet Explorer"
3                 onClick="alert( event.type + ' ' + event.srcElement);">
            <input type=button
                  value="Firefox"
4                 onClick="alert( event.type + ' ' + event.target);" />
```

Continues

EXAMPLE 13.21 (CONTINUED)

```
    </form>
   </body>
</html>
```

EXPLANATION

1   The HTML form starts here.

2   When the user clicks the first button in this form, the *onClick* event is triggered. It will cause an alert message to appear displaying two event properties: the *type* of the event and the HTML element where it came from (*srcElement* (Internet Explorer) property of the object). The type of event is cross-browser compliant.

3   The input type for this form is a button. When the user clicks the button for Internet Explorer, an alert box displays the type of the event and the source or object from when it originated.

4   When the *onClick* event is triggered, an alert message will appear displaying two event properties: the *type* of the event and the *target* (Firefox) property or object from which the event originated. See Figures 13.30, 13.31, and 13.32. W3C and Firefox both use the *target* property. Internet Explorer uses *srcElement*.

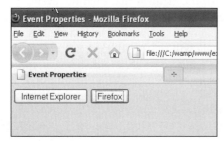

Figure 13.30   Displaying the event object's property in Internet Explorer (left), and Firefox (right).

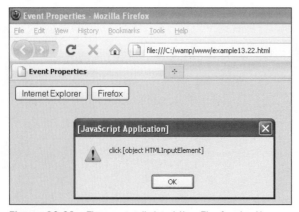

Figure 13.31   The user clicked the Firefox button.

Figure 13.32 The user clicked the Internet Explorer button.

13.7.4 Passing Events to a JavaScript Function

As stated earlier, JavaScript registers events as they occur within the document and registers information about that event such as what key was pressed, what mouse button clicked, and so on. You can pass this information directly to a JavaScript function. The problem is that Internet Explorer has its own way of tracking events and the other major browsers use the W3C standard (e.g., Firefox and Opera). With the W3C method, the *event* object is sent as a parameter to the JavaScript function, but with Internet Explorer the event is a property of the window object (*window.event*). It is easy enough to check for both without interrupting the flow of your program by testing for both conditions. The following line uses the ternary operator to test for both events and for null. (The ternary operator was described in detail in section "The Conditional Operator" on page 108, Chapter 5.)

```
function testEvent(e){
   var evt = (e) ? e: ((window.event)? window.event: null)
}
```

EXAMPLE 13.22

```
<html>
   <head><title>Event Object and Incompatible Browsers</title>
   <script>
1       function whichEvent(e) { // passing e is for Firefox
2          if(!e){ var e=window.event;} // Microsoft IE
```

Continues

EXAMPLE 13.22 (CONTINUED)

```
3                if(e.target) {targ=e.currentTarget; targ=targ.id;}
                              // Firefox
4                else if(e.srcElement) {targ=e.srcElement.id;}
                              // Microsoft IE
5                alert(targ +" has recieved a "+e.type);
             }
          </script>
       </head>
6       <body id="main" onload="whichEvent(event);">
          <br />
7          <div style="background-color:lightgreen">
          <form id="form1" onclick="whichEvent(event);">
             <br />
             <input type="text" id="textbox1"
                    onkeypress="whichEvent(event);" />
             <br /><br />
             <input type="button" value="rollover me" id="button1"
                    onmouseout="whichEvent(event);" />
             <br />
          </form>
          </div>
       </body>
    </html>
```

EXPLANATION

1   Four types of events will be sent to this user-defined function: the *load*, *keypress*, *mouseout*, and *click* events. The purpose of the function is to show you how to make a cross-compliant script to handle events on different browsers.

2   Unless the browser is Microsoft Internet Explorer, a reference to the *event* object is passed as an argument to *whichEvent()* and called *e* as a parameter to the *whichEvent()* function. If not, Internet Explorer uses the *event* property of the window object to get the value of *e*.

3   If the *target* property is applied to the object, then a Mozilla type browser is being used. The *currentTarget* property returns the object from where the click originated. (To understand the flow of events, see the section "Capturing and Bubbling (Trickle Down and Bubble Up)" on page 500.)
    Using the *id* attribute of the object where the event occurs allows us to identify what object received the event. For example, if the user clicks the form, with the *id* of *form1*, then we can see that the click originated in *form1*.

4   If the *srcElement* property is defined, then we are using Internet Explorer

5   The *id* of the element and the type of event that was fired are displayed.

6   When the page has loaded, the user-defined function, *whichEvent*, is triggered. If this is a Mozilla type browser, the *event* object is passed to the function.

EXPLANATION (CONTINUED)

7   Each object, the form, the textbox, and the button have an event attribute that will be triggered if the user clicks any of those objects. The argument to this function, *event*, is a reference to the particular event that was triggered when the user clicked it. Output examples are shown in Figures 13.33, 13.34, 13.35, and 13.36.

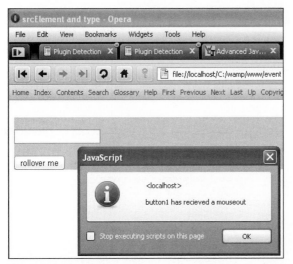

Figure 13.33   Opera—the mouse has left the button.

Figure 13.34   Microsoft IE—The mouse was clicked in the textbox—bubble up.

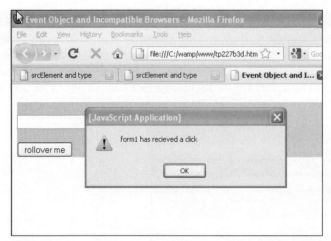

Figure 13.35   Firefox—The mouse was clicked in the textbox but captured first in the form.

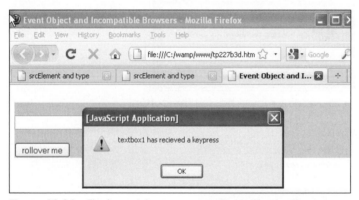

Figure 13.36   Firefox—A key was pressed in the textbox.

13.7.5 Mouse Positions

We devoted a whole section of this chapter to handling mouse event handlers and what happens if the mouse rolls over a link or an image. In this section we discuss how to find out what event the mouse triggered and where the mouse was positioned when it fired. For browser compatibility tables see *http://www.quirksmode.org/dom/w3c_cssom.html*.

Mouse Position.   The *client X* and *clientY* properties (Internet Explorer) and *pageX* and *pageY* properties (Firefox) are used to get the coordinate positions of the mouse pointer in the document when the event is triggered. If you want to get the coordinate positions of the mouse within an element, then you would use the *offsetX* and *offsetY* properties (Internet Explorer) and nonstandard *layerX* and *layerY* (Firefox).

EXAMPLE 13.23

```html
<html>
    <head><title>Mouse Coordinates</title>
        <script type="text/javascript">
            function getCoords(e) {
1               var x = 0;  // x and y positions
                var y = 0;
2               if (!e) var e = window.event;  // Internet Explorer
3               if (e.pageX || e.pageY){        // Firefox
                    x = e.pageX;
                    y = e.pageY;
                }
4               else if (e.clientX || e.clientY) {
5                   x = e.clientX + document.body.scrollLeft
                        + document.documentElement.scrollLeft;
                    y = e.clientY + document.body.scrollTop
                        + document.documentElement.scrollTop;
                }
                // x and y contain the mouse position
                // relative to the document
                alert(x +", "+ y);
            }
        </script>
    <head>
    <body>
        <div style="background-color:aqua;position:absolute;top:50px"
            onMouseover="return getCoords(event);">
        <h1>Mouse positions are relative to the document, not the
            &lt;div&gt; container</h1>
        </div>
    </body>
</html>
```

EXPLANATION

1 Variables *x* and *y* are declared. They will hold the pixel coordinates of the mouse.

2 If using Mozilla/Firefox, the value of *e* will be sent to the function; if using Internet Explorer, the value of *window.event* will be assigned to *e*. In this way both browsers will get a reference to the event triggered when the mouse event is fired.

3 The *pageX,pageY* pair represents the coordinates of a page regardless of scrollbars, but this pair is not supported by Internet Explorer. See an excellent demo at *http://www.java2s.com/Code/JavaScriptDemo/EventpageYandpageX.htm*.

4 The *clientX,clientY* pair represents the coordinates of a page and accounts for scrollbars.

5 The *clientX* and *clientY* pair return the position of the mouse pointer in the document, whereas *offsetX* and *offsetY* return the position of the mouse pointer on the element (see Figure 13.37).

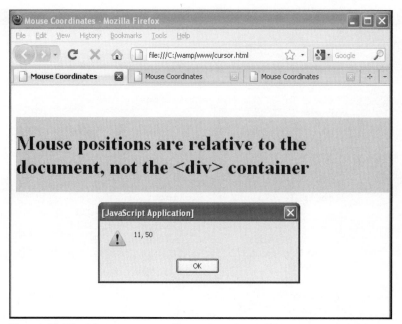

Figure 13.37 Mouse was positioned on the left top corner of the *div* box, 11 px from left, 50 px from top.

Mouse Buttons.   Here we go again with more incompatibilities among browsers! And the mouse might only have one button, such as the Mac's mouse, or two buttons and a wheel, or maybe the mouse button properties don't work for all of the buttons. You will have to work with these properties for the particular browser you are using or make adjustments to your program to allow for multiple conditions; for example:

```
if( browser == "Opera" ) {
   do this;
}
else if ( browser == "IE") {
   do that;
} .....
```

In Example 13.24 the mouse used was a Microsoft mouse and then a Targus mouse with a left and right button and wheel in the middle. The browsers used were Firefox and Internet Explorer. Firefox returned a 3 for the right click and a 1 for the left click. Internet Explorer was consistent with Table 13.10. Could it be that running a virtual window OS on a Mac could make the difference? This is where the confusion really sets in! The only option is to test all possible button values in your script.

The *which* (Firefox) and the *button* (Internet Explorer) properties are used to find out which mouse button was clicked: the left button, the middle button, or the right button.

Table 13.10 Button Values

Microsoft Internet Explorer *event.button*	*W3C/Mozilla/Firefox* *event.which*
Left button = 1	Left button = 0
Middle button = 4	Middle button = 1
Right button = 2	Right button = 2

EXAMPLE 13.24

```
<html>
    <head><title>Mouse Buttons</title>
        <script>
            function whichButton(e) {
                var button;
1               if (!e) {var e = window.event;}
2               if(e.which){ button = e.which;}
3               else if(e.button){ button=e.button; }
                alert(button);
4               switch(button){
                    case 0:
                        return("FF leftclick");
                        break;
                    case 1:
                        return("leftclick");
                    case 2:
                    case 3:  // Firefox returned 3 on the Mac
                        return("rightclick");
                        break;
                    case 4:
                        return("IE middleclick");
                }
            }
        </script>
    </head>
    <body>
          Click the mouse in the green box
        <div onMousedown="alert(whichButton(event));"
            style="position:absolute;top:100;left:20;
                    height:200;width:200;background-color:green">
        </div>
    </body>
</html>
```

EXPLANATION

1   Unless the browser is Microsoft Internet Explorer, a reference to the *event* object is passed as a parameter called *e*. Internet Explorer uses the *event* property of the window object to get the value of *e*.

2   If not Internet Explorer, the *which* property contains a value representing the mouse button.

3   If Internet Explorer, the button property contains that value.

4   The *switch* statement is used to determine which button was clicked. See Figures 13.38 and 13.39.

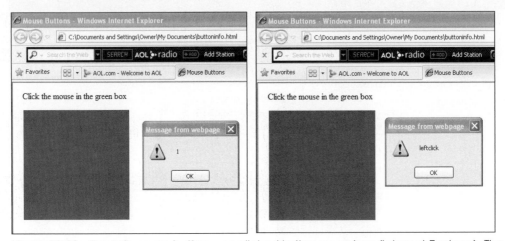

Figure 13.38   The **left mouse button** was clicked in the green box (Internet Explorer). The value was 1.

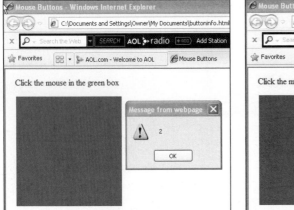

Figure 13.39   The **right mouse button** was clicked in the green box (Internet Explorer). The value was 2.

13.7.6 Key Events

The Handlers.   As of JavaScript 1.2, keyboard actions, not just mouse actions, can be detected in JavaScript programs. Now that we have discussed the event object, we will look at how to detect keyboard actions. This is useful, for example, in creating widgets or certain types of game programs where keyboard entry must be detected to determine the next action. The *onKeyPress, onKeyDown,* and *onKeyUp* event handlers are triggered when the user presses a key and releases it. The *onKeyPress* event is a combination of two actions: After you press down on the key, the event happens just at the point you release it. The other two key events happen as soon as you press a key down (*onKey-Down*) and then when you release it (*onKeyUp*). The *onKeyDown* and *onKeyPress* events keep firing continuously as long as the user keeps a key depressed, whereas the *onKeyUp* event fires once when the user releases the key. Detecting a user's keystrokes might give you problems as all browsers are not compatible in how they handle the keys and the event properties.

Properties for the *key* Event.   The two main properties for the *key* event are *key-Code* and *charCode*. The *keyCode* property describes the actual key that was pressed, for example, the B key. The *charCode* property provides the ASCII value for that key. If it is a lowercase b, it will return 98 and if it is an uppercase B, it will return 66. The problem is that Windows Internet Explorer and Opera do not support *charCode*, but they do support *keyCode* when the *onKeyPress* event is triggered. For tables showing which browsers support these properties and a selection of other tables dealing with punctuation keys, special keys, and so on, see *http://www.quirksmode.org/js/keys.html.*

Browser Incompatibilities.   Figures 13.40 and 13.41 were taken from a site where a test can be run from your browser by performing keystrokes. The output shows what properties are supported for keydown, keypress, keyup, and so on. Go to *http://unixpapa.com/js/test-key.html* to run the test. Go to *http://www.JavaScriptkit.com/jsref/eventkeyboardmouse.shtml* for an excellent reference with examples.

Figure 13.40 Checking Opera key events at *http://unixpapa.com/js/testkey.html.*

Figure 13.41 Checking Firefox key events.

EXAMPLE 13.25

```
      <html>
        <head><title>keypress event</title>
1         <script type="text/javascript" src="browser_info.js"></script>
        </head>
2       <body onKeyPress="
3             if(browserName =='Firefox'){
4               alert('The key pressed:'+ event.which +
5                 ' ASCII= '+ String.fromCharCode(event.which));
              }
6             else if(browserName == 'Microsoft Internet Explorer'  ||
                    browserName=='Opera') {
                alert('The key pressed:'+ event.keyCode +
                    ' ASCII='+ String.fromCharCode(event.keyCode));
              }
            ">
        <font face = "verdana">
          <b>Press any key on your keyboard and see what happens!</b>
        </font>
      </body>
    </html>
```

EXPLANATION

1 An external file is loaded here. It contains the code to determine what browser is being used. See *http://www.JavaScripter.net/faq/browsern.htm* for source code.

2 The body tag is assigned an *onKeyPress* event handler. If the user presses a key anywhere in the body of the document, the event is triggered, causing an *alert* method to appear and display the value of the key.

3 First we check to see if the browser being used is Firefox. Firefox and Internet Explorer use different properties to describe the numeric value of the key being pressed.

4 The *which* property of the event object describes the numeric ASCII value for the key that was pressed. (See more of the event object on page 499.)

5 The *String* method *fromCharCode()* converts the ASCII value of the key to the character value that is shown on the key (e.g., ASCII 65 is character "A").

6 If the browser isn't Firefox, the alternative for this example is Internet Explorer or Opera. They use the *keyCode* property to represent the numeric value of the key being pressed. The *fromCharCode() String* method converts the number to a character. The output is displayed for both browsers in Figures 13.42 and 13.43.

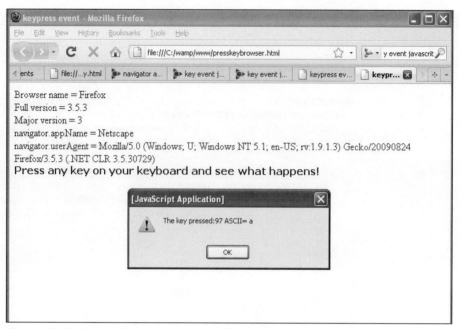

Figure 13.42 The 'a' key was pressed (Firefox).

Figure 13.43 Internet Explorer and the *onKeyPress* event (Shift+a).

13.8 The Scripting Model for Handling Events

We have been using event handlers like *onClick*, *onSubmit*, and *onMouseOver*, throughout this text. So far, this chapter has described in detail all of the different event handlers and how to use them as inline HTML attributes. Inline event handling is the oldest and simplest way to handle events and is browser compatible. The following example uses the *onClick* handler as an attribute of the button element. When the user clicks the button, the function *movePosition()* will be called.

```
<input type="button" value="move text"
       onClick="movePosition()" />
```

But using this type of handler violates the principle of separation of the layers; that is, the separation of markup/presentation from behavior/ JavaScript. To solve this problem, we can handle events within the JavaScript code itself. All of the HTML attributes used as event handlers can also be used as DOM properties. These properties can be used in JavaScript to simulate the event that they are named for. If, for example, you want to trigger a window event, JavaScript views the window as an object and any event associated with it as a property. If you want to use the *onload* event with the window object, you would say *window.onload*. The main difference is that unlike using HTML attributes, which take a string value, a function reference is assigned to an event handler. All JavaScript event properties must be in lowercase, such as *window.onload* or *window.ununload*. (The event handlers, used as HTML attributes, are **not** case sensitive, so *ONUNLOAD*, *onUnLoad*, and *onunload* are all acceptable.)
Here's an example:

```
window.unload=some_function;
```

13.8.1   Getting a Reference to the Object

To assign an event property to an object, JavaScript will need a reference to the object. For example, if the click event is to be triggered when the user clicks a button, then JavaScript will need to use a reference to the button. By assigning an *id* to the HTML button, JavaScript can use the DOM's *getElementById()* method to get the reference it needs.
In the HTML part of the document:

```
input type button id="button1">
```

In the JavaScript script:

```
var b1=document.getElementById("button1");
```

Now *b1* in the script is a reference to "button1" from the HTML document.
After JavaScript has a reference to the HTML element, the name of the event, such as *click* or *onmouseover* can be used as a property:

```
b1.click
b1.mouseover
```

The next step is to assign a value to the event property. The value will be a reference to either a named function or an anonymous function. Note: When used as a reference, the function name is not enclosed in quotes and does not have parentheses!

```
b1.click=greetings;

function greetings(){
   alert("Welcome!");
}
```
     or an anonymous function

```
b1.click=function(){alert("Welcome!");}
```

Now when the user clicks "button1" in the document, the JavaScript event handler will be triggered and the greeting displayed in an alert box.

Another example of using JavaScript event handling is with the *onload* event. This event is used to guarantee that the entire page has been loaded before an event is fired. When a function is assigned to *onload*, the function will not be executed until the page has loaded:

```
window.onload = init;
function init() {
   do_something
}
```

You can also assign an anonymous function to the *onload* property as follows:

```
window.onload = function(){ do something; }
```

See Example 13.26. When the page has loaded, the function that was registered to the event will be called. If you want to assign more than one function to the event, there are several ways to do this. One method is to place several function calls in a chain, using one onload event handler.

```
function start() {
   func1();
   func2();
}
window.onload = start;
```

Like the inline model, each event can only have one event handler registered. To remove an event handler, simply set the property to null. Object event properties are shown in Table 13.11.

For a more elegant examples of how to use onload go to *http://www.site-point.com/blogs/2004/05/26/closures-and-executing-JavaScript-on-page-load/*.

Table 13.11   Object Event Properties

Event Handler Property	Event
onblur	blur
onfocus	focus
onchange	change
onmouseover	mouseover
onmousemove	mousemove
onmousedown	mousedown
onmouseup	mouseup
onclick	click
ondblclick	dblclick
onkeydown	keydown
onkeyup	keyup
onkeypress	keypress
onsubmit	submit
onload	load
onunload	unload

EXAMPLE   **13.26**

```
        <html>
          <head><title>Event Handling and Forms</title>
            <script type="text/javascript">
1               var b1,b2,b3;
2               window.onload=function(){
3                 b1=document.getElementById("button1");
                  b2=document.getElementById("button2");
                  b3=document.getElementById("button3");
4                 b1.onclick=morning;
                  b2.onclick=noon;
                  b3.onclick=night;
                }
```

Continues

EXAMPLE 13.26 (CONTINUED)

```
5          function morning(){
              alert ("Good Morning");
           }
           function noon(){
              alert("Let's have lunch.");
           }
           function night(){
              alert("Good-night!");
           }
        </script>
     </head>
     <body>
        <h2>
           Greetings Message
        </h2>
        <hr />
        <form>
6          <input type="button" id="button1" value="Morning" />
           <input type="button" id="button2" value="Noon" />
           <input type="button" id="button3" value="Night" />
        </form>
     </body>
  </html>
```

EXPLANATION

1   Some global variables are defined to be used later in the script.

2   The *onload* event property of the *window* object mimics the behavior of the HTML *onLoad* event handler of the body element. The function defined will be called when a document or frameset is completely loaded into its window or frame.

3   The *document.getElementById()* method takes the *id* of each of the HTML buttons and returns a reference to each of them. Now JavaScript has access to the buttons.

4   Using the *onclick* property with the button reference allows JavaScript to react to the click event when the user clicks one of the buttons. The function called *morning* is assigned to this property and will be called when "button1" is clicked. Note that this is a reference to the function and there are no quotes or parentheses. The actual function it references is on line 5.

5   This is the actual function that will be called when the user clicks the "Morning" button.

6   Three HTML buttons are defined in the document. Each is given a unique *id* to be used in the JavaScript program as an argument to the *document.getElementById()* method. See Figures 13.44 and 13.45.

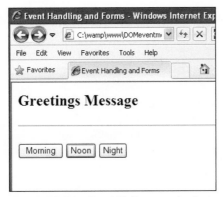

Figure 13.44 The HTML page before clicking one of three buttons.

Figure 13.45 The user clicked the first button.

In Example 13.27, an image is assigned to the HTML *<a>* tag. When the user rolls the mouse over the initial image, the image is replaced with a new image. Rather than have the *onMouseOver* and *onMouseOut* event handlers used as attributes to the HTML link tag, they will be properties to the link object in the JavaScript code. This allows the program to separate the structure (HTML) from the behavior (JavaScript).

EXAMPLE 13.27

```
     <html>
        <head><title>Preloading Images</title>
          <script type="text/javascript">
1             window.onload=preLoad;
2             function preLoad(){
3                var linkId=document.getElementById("link1");
                 baby = new Array();  // global variable
                 baby[0]=new Image(); // Preload an image
                 baby[0].src="babysmile.jpg";
                 baby[1]=new Image();
                 baby[1].src="babygoo.jpg";

4                linkId.onmouseover=firstBaby;   // Event property on a link
5                linkId.onmouseout=secondBaby;
              }
6             function firstBaby(){
                 document.images["willy"].src=baby[1].src;
              }
7             function secondBaby(){
                 document.images["willy"].src=baby[0].src;
              }
          </script>
        </head>
        <body>
          <h1>This is Baby William</h1>
8         <a id="link1"><img name="willy" src="babygoo.jpg"
                          width="220" height="250">
          </a>
        </body>
     </html>
```

EXPLANATION

1   The *onload* property of the window object simulates the HTML *onLoad* event handler of the body element. The function *preLoad()* will be called when a document or frameset is completely loaded into its window or frame.

2   This function will be called as soon as the document has loaded. It will preload the images and set up the event handling.

3   To apply a property to a link, we need to get a reference. The *getElementById()* method returns a reference, *linkID*, to the link object identified on line 8 with a unique *id*.

4   The *mouseover* event handler property is assigned to *linkId*. Its value is a reference to a function, called *firstBaby()*, and defined on line 6. The function will be called when the *mouseover* event happens.

5   The *mouseout* event is a property of *linkId*. When the *mouseout* event happens the function *secondBaby()* will be called.

EXPLANATION (CONTINUED)

6, 7   These are the functions that are called when the mouse events are triggered.

   8   The HTML *<a>* tag is given an *id* of "link1" and assigned an initial image. The output is shown in Figure 13.46.

Figure 13.46   Mouse rolls over first baby. Image is replaced with second baby.

13.9 What You Should Know

The day the music died ... the day events died, is when JavaScript ceased to exist. It would be a challenge to find a JavaScript program that doesn't have an event handler. Events are the basis for interactivity and without them, a Web page is dead. This chapter focused on all the major event handlers you can use in JavaScript, what triggers them, and how to register them. We saw that event handlers can be assigned to objects such as buttons, links, windows, and forms and that when a user rolls the mouse over an object, clicks a button, presses a key, resizes the window, submits a form, or changes a value, JavaScript can react and do something based on those actions. The simplest way to use the handlers is as attributes of HTML tags, but in doing so, JavaScript is made part of the HTML markup. To keep the structure (markup) and the behavior (JavaScript) separate, the event handlers can be used as properties of objects. In Chapter 15, we will take this to the next level, working with event handlers and the DOM. So far, you should know:

1. How to create an inline event handler.
2. What it means to register an event.
3. When the return value from the event handling function is necessary.
4. How to use JavaScript event methods.
5. How the *onblur* and *onfocus* event handlers are used.
6. What event handlers are used with windows and frames.

7. How to use mouse events.
8. How mouse events are used with a rollover.
9. What event handlers are used with links.
10. How a button input device differs from a submit input device.
11. What events are used with forms.
12. How to prevent a form's submission.
13. What the event object is.
14. The difference between capturing and bubbling.
15. How you can tell what element fired the event: Internet Explorer? Firefox?
16. How to pass an event to a JavaScript function.
17. How to get the coordinate positions of a mouse within an element.
18. How to handle key events.
19. How to use the scripting model for handling events.

Exercises

1. Create three buttons, labeled *Shoot movies*, *Shoot guns*, and *Shoot basketballs*. When the user clicks any button, use the *onClick* event handler to call a function that will send a message based on which button was pressed.

2. Create a form that contains two text fields to receive the user's name and address. When the user leaves each text field, use the *onBlur* event handler to check if the user entered anything in the respective field. If the user didn't, send an alert telling him or her so, and use the *focus()* method to return focus back to the text field the user just left.

3. Make a link that changes the background color to light blue when the mouse pointer is rolled over it.

4. Create a form that will contain a textbox. After the user enters text, all the letters will be converted to lowercase as soon as he or she clicks anywhere else in the form. (Use the *onChange* event handler.)

5. Write a script that will detect what event occurred and the pixel positions of a mouse when it rolls over a hotspot in an image map.

6. Create a text field in a form. When the user clicks on a button, a function will be called to make sure the field is not empty. In a JavaScript program use the *document.getElementById()* method to get a reference to the button object. Use the *onclick* event property.

7. Write the HTML part of this script to test capturing and bubbling for your browser. Explain the order of event handling.

```
document.onclick = function(){
   alert("Document clicked!");
};

function buttonClick(){
   alert("Button clicked!");
}

function formClick(){
   alert("Form clicked!");
}
```

8. Rewrite Example 13.5 (p.467) using the scripting method. The *onload* event handler will be used as a property of the window object. The definition of the *now()* function will be the value assigned to the event handler; it will be anonymous.

The *onunload* event handler will also be made part of the JavaScript code. After you have tested your program, put the JavaScript program in an external .js file. In the HTML file, use the *src* attribute of the script tag to include the .js file and run your program. All JavaScript is now separated from the HTML markup.

chapter

14

Introduction to CSS (Cascading Style Sheets) with JavaScript

14.1 What Is CSS?

Cascading Style Sheets (CSS) was a standard introduced by the World Wide Web Consortium (W3C) in 1995 to help designers get more control over their Web pages by enhancing what HTML can do—it is used to stylize the content of a Web page. Whereas HTML is concerned with the structure and organization of a document, CSS is concerned with its layout and presentation, or formatting the document. In the old days, HTML tags were used to set up the structure and style of a page. If you wanted to create an H1 tag with an Arial blue font, point size 22, you would have to set the same attributes for each H1 tag in the entire document, To apply these changes to an entire Web site could be a daunting task. With CSS you can set the style once for all H1 tags and put that style definition in its own .css file. When the page is loaded the CSS style will be applied to all H1 tags in the page in one sweeping change.

Because the initial style of the content of a page is done with CSS, we'll start there. The goal is to use CSS with the DOM and JavaScript (Chapter 15) together to dynamically change the style of the page, often called Dynamic HTML (DHTML). For a complete discussion of CSS (both CSS1 and CSS2), see *http://www.w3org/Style/CSS*. If you are a designer and already have a good CSS foundation, you can skip this chapter and go directly to Chapter 15, "The W3C DOM and JavaScript."

14.2 What Is a Style Sheet?

Webster's Dictionary defines "style" as a manner of doing something very grandly; elegant, fashionable. Style sheets make HTML pages elegant by allowing the designer to create definitions to describe the layout and appearance of the page. This is done by creating a set of rules that define how an HTML element will look in the document. For example, if you want all *H1* elements to produce text with a green color, set in an Arial 14-point font centered on the page, normally you would have to assign these attributes

527

to each *H1* element as it occurs within the document, which could prove quite time consuming. With style sheets you can create the style once and have that definition apply to all *H1* elements in the document. If you don't have a lot of time to learn how to create style sheets, an excellent alternative is Macromedia's Dreamweaver MX. For more on authoring tools, see *http://www.w3.org/Style/CSS/#editors*.

Style sheets are called cascading because the effects of a style can be inherited or cascaded down to other tags. This gets back to the parent/child relationship we have talked about since Chapter 1, the DOM. If a style has been defined for a parent tag, any tags defined within that style may inherit that style. Suppose a style has been defined for a *<p>* tag. The text within these tags has been set to blue and the font is set to a sans serif font. If within the *<p>* tag, another set of tags is embedded, such as *<b>* or *<em>*, then those tags will inherit the blue color and the "sans serif" font. The style has cascaded down from the parent to the child. But this is a simplistic definition of cascading. The rules can be very complex and involve multiple style sheets coming from external sources as well as internal sources. And even though a browser might support style sheets, it might render the CSS information differently. For example, the DOCTYPE declaration used at the start of the document might allow a document to be displayed with nonstandard rendering rules (Quirks mode) or follow the W3C strict standard, and older browsers may have a limited or a buggy implementation of the CSS standard. For more on this topic, see *https://developer.mozilla.org/en/Common_CSS_Questions*.

The good news is that all modern browsers support CSS.

14.2.1   What Is a CSS-Enhanced Browser?

A CSS-enhanced browser supports CSS and will recognize the style tag *<style>* as a container for a style sheet, and based on the definition of the style, will produce the document accordingly. Modern browsers, such as Internet Explorer, Mozilla Firefox, Netscape, Opera, and Safari support CSS, and the majority of Web users are running a CSS-enhanced browser. However, just because a browser is CSS enhanced doesn't mean that it is flawless or without limitations. And just because a browser is not CSS enhanced, doesn't mean that it can't see the content of a page.[1]

Traditionally, browsers have silently ignored unknown tags, so if a browser does not support CSS, when it encounters a *<style>* tag, its content will be treated simply as part of the document. To hide the *<style>* tag content, one method is to enclose it within HTML comments as shown here:

```
<style type="text/css"><!--
    p.largetext/* */ { font-size: 200% ; }
--></style>
```

Example from: *http://www.thesitewizard.com/css/excludecss.shtml*

---

1. For an updated overview of available browsers, see the W3C overview page: *http://www.w3.org/Style/CSS/#browsers*.

(See the section "CSS Program Structure" on page 530 for more on this.) If you are contending with an older version of your browser, it might just be a good time to upgrade to a newer model!

14.2.2 How Does a Style Sheet Work?

A style sheet consists of the style rules that tell your browser how to present a document. The rules consist of two parts: a selector—the HTML element you are trying to stylize—and the **declaration block**—the properties and values that describe the style for the selector.

FORMAT

```
selector { property: value }
           declaration block
```

EXAMPLE

```
H1 { color: blue }
```

This rule sets the color of the *H2* element to blue:

```
H2 { color: blue }
```

A rule, then, consists of two main parts: the **selector** (e.g., *H2*) and the declaration block (e.g., *color: blue*). Example 14.1 demonstrates this simple rule.

EXAMPLE 14.1

```
   <html>
      <head><title>First Style Sheet</title>
1     <style type="text/css">
2        h1 { color: saddlebrown } /* rule */
         h2 { color: darkblue  }
      </style>
   </head>
   <body bgcolor=silver>
3     <h1>Welcome to my Stylin' Page</h1>
4     <h2>What do you think?</h2>
   </body>
   </html>
```

EXPLANATION

1   The style sheet starts with the HTML *<style>* tag and specifies that the style sheet consists of text and CSS. The purpose of this style sheet is to customize HTML tags, thus giving them a new style.

2   A selector is one of any HTML elements, such as *h1, h2, body, li, p,* or *ul.* In this example, the *h1* and *h2* elements are selectors. The declaration has two parts: property (*color*) and value (*saddlebrown*). Every time an *<h1>* tag is used in the document, it will be saddle brown, and every time an *<h2>* tag is used, it will be blue. (There are approximately 50 properties beyond the color property that are defined in the CSS specification!)

3   The *<h1>* tag will be displayed in saddle brown, based on the rule in the style sheet.

4   The *<h2>* tag will be displayed in blue, based on the rule in the style sheet. Output is shown in Figure 14.1.

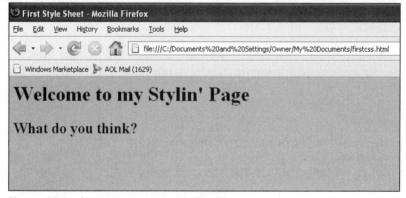

Figure 14.1   Style sheet output in Firefox.

14.3 CSS Program Structure

14.3.1 Comments

CSS comments, like C language comments, are enclosed in /* */. They are the textual comments that are ignored by the CSS parser when your style is being interpreted, and are used to clarify what you are trying to do. They cannot be nested.

```
H1 { color: blue }     /* heading level 1 is blue */
```

14.3.2 Grouping

Grouping is used to reduce the size of style sheets. For example, you can group selectors in comma-separated lists, if you want the same rule to apply to all of the elements:

```
H1, H2, H3 { font-family: arial; color: blue }
```

Now all three heading levels will contain blue text in an Arial font.

You can also group a set of declarations to create the style for a selector(s). The following rule combines a number of declarations describing the font properties for an *H1* element:

```
H1 {
    font-weight: bold;
    font-size: 12pt;
    line-height: 14pt;
    font-family: verdana;
}
```

And you can group the values for a particular property as follows:

```
h2 {font: bold 24pt arial}
```

EXAMPLE **14.2**

```
    <html>
      <head><title>Grouping Properties</title>
        <style type="text/css">
1         h1,h2,h3 { color: blue }   /* grouping selectors */
2         h1 {                       /* grouping declarations */
            font-weight: bold;
            font-size: 30pt;
            font-family: verdana;
          }
3         h2 {                       /* grouping a property's values */
            font: bold 24pt arial
          }
        </style>
      </head>
      <body bgcolor=silver>
4       <h1>Welcome to my Stylin' Page</h1>
5       <h2>What do you think?</h2>
6       <h3>Groovy!</h3>
      </body>
    </html>
```

EXPLANATION

1   Three selectors, *h1*, *h2*, and *h3*, are grouped together. The declaration block enclosed in curly braces sets the color property to *blue*. Whenever any one of the *h1*, *h2*, or *h3* elements is used in the document, its text will be blue.

2   The declaration block for the *h1* selector consists of a group of properties and values to further define the font style for this heading.

3   The *font* property, in this example, groups the font values as a list, rather than creating individual property/value pairs as done on line 2.

4   Now the *h1* tag is tested to see if the style was applied, and it is!

5   The style for the *h2* tag is tested and it has been applied.

6   The only style set for the *h3* tag is a blue font, and that's all we get, as shown in Figure 14.2.

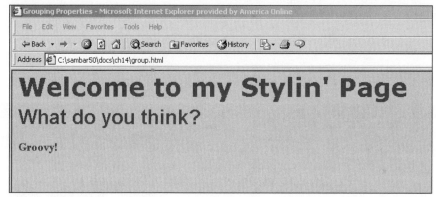

Figure 14.2   Grouping selectors and declarations for *h1*, *h2*, and *h3* HTML elements.

14.4 Common Style Sheet Properties

In the previous examples, *font-family* and *color* are properties (also called attributes), and assigning values to them defines the style of the document. Listed in Table 14.1 are some of the properties commonly used in style sheets. Many of these properties are used in the style sheets defined throughout this chapter and later as properties of the style object used with JavaScript. The Web Design Group provides a complete listing of this information at *http://www.htmlhelp.com/reference/css/properties.html*.

Table 14.1   Style Sheet Properties

Property	Value/Example	Tags Affected
Fonts		
font	12pt/14pt sans-serif, 80% sans-serif, x-large/110% arial, normal small-caps	All
font-family	serif, sans-serif, cursive, fantasy, monospace; or any specific font typeface name may be used	All
font-size	12pt, larger, 150%, 1.5em	All
font-size-adjust	xx-small, x-small, small, medium, large, x-large, xx-large, smaller, larger, 12pt, 25%	All
font-stretch	normal, wider, narrower, ultra-condensed, extra-condensed, condensed, semi-condensed, semi-expanded, expanded, extra-expanded, ultra-expanded	All
font-style	normal, italic, oblique	All
font-variant	normal, small-caps	All
font-weight	normal, bold, bolder, lighter,100, 200...900	All
Colors and Background		
background-attachment	scroll, fixed	All
background-color	red, blue, #F00, transparent	All
background-image	URL (bay.gif), none	All
background-position	right top, top center, center, bottom, 100% 100%, 0% 0%, 50% 50%	Block-level and replaced elements
background-repeat	repeat, repeat-x (horizontally), repeat-y (vertically), no-repeat	All
color	red, green, #F00, rgb(255,0,0)	All
Text Alignment		
letter-spacing	normal, 0.1em	All
line-height	normal, 1.2, 1.2em, 120%	All
text-decoration	underline, overline, line-through, blink	All
text-transform	capitalize, uppercase, lowercase, none	All

Continues

Table 14.1 Style Sheet Properties (continued)

Property	Value/Example	Tags Affected
Text Alignment *(Continued)*		
text-align	left, right, center, justify	All
text-indent	3em, 15%	Block-level elements
vertical-align	baseline, sub, super, top, text-top, middle, bottom, text-bottom, 50%	Inline elements
word-spacing	normal, 2em	All
Margins and Borders		
border-bottom	<border-bottom-width> or <border-style> or <color>	All
border-bottom-width	thin, medium, thick, 2em	All
border-color	red, green, #0C0	All
border-left	<border-left-width> or <border-style> or <color>	All
border-left-width	thin, medium, thick, 3em	All
border-right	<border-right-width> or <border-style> or <color>	All
border-right-width	thin, medium, thick, 1cm	All
border-style	[none], dotted, dashed, solid, double, groove, ridge[inset,outset]{1,4}	All
border-top	<border-top-width> or <border-style> or <color>	All
border-top-width	thin, medium, thick, 3em	All
border-width	thin, medium, thick, .5cm	All
clear	none, left, right, both (allows or disallows floating elements on its sides)	All
float	left, right, or none (wraps text around an element, such as an image)	All
height	12em, auto	Block-level and replaced element
margin	5em, 3em, 2em, 1em (top, right, bottom, left)	All
margin-bottom	100px, 50%	All
margin-left	.5in, 40%	All

Table 14.1   Style Sheet Properties (continued)

Property	Value/Example	Tags Affected
Margins and Borders *(Continued)*		
margin-right	20em,45%	All
margin-top	1cm, 20%	All
padding	2em, 4em, 6em (right, bottom, left)	All
padding-bottom	2em, 20%	All
padding-left	.25in, 20%	All
padding-right	.5cm, 35%	All
padding-top	20px, 10%	All
width	12em, 30%, auto (initial width value)	Block-level and replaced element[a]

a.   A replaced element has set or calculated dimensions, such as *img, select, textarea.*

14.4.1   Units of Measurement

You can express the size of a given property in different units of measurement; for example, a font size can be expressed in pixels or ems or points (the default is pixels). Colors can also be expressed in combinations of red, green, and blue, either by the name of the color, or its hexadecimal value.

Measurement is used in three categories: absolute units, relative units, and proportional units. For example, a point size measurement (e.g., *14pt*) would be the actual size (absolute) of a particular font; a value (e.g., *5em*) could be relative to the size of the current font; and a color (e.g., *50%80%100%*) could represent red, green, and blue as a percentage value of the original color. Relative sizes *larger* and *smaller* (relative to the parent font) can be used when defining a font. These sizes are determined by browsers or other user agents.[2] Tables 14.2 and 14.3 introduce the types of measurements that are often used in style sheets.

Table 14.2   Font Size Units

Absolute Font Size Unit
inches (in)
centimeters (cm)

Continues

---

2.   User agents include Web browsers, search engine crawlers (spiders), cell phones, screen readers, and Braille browsers used by people with disabilities.

Table 14.2 Font Size Units (continued)

millimeters (mm)
points (pt) 1/72th of an inch
picas (pc) 12 points

Table 14.3 User Agent Determined Font Sizes

CSS Absolute Sizes	HTML Font Size
xx-small	1
x-small	2
small	3
medium	4
large	5
x-large	6
xx-large	7

Here are some examples:

- `font-size: 10pt`
- `top: 20px`
- `margin: 1em`
- `margin-right: 20%`
- `font-size: xx-large`
- `font-size: 150%`

14.4.2 Working with Colors

What is style without color? Tables 14.4 and 14.5 give information for managing color. You can use these properties to create color for the document's background and fonts, margins, borders, and more. The colors can be expressed with real names (e.g., *red*, *blue*, *yellow*, *magenta*) or their corresponding hexadecimal values (e.g., *#FF0000*, *#0000Ff*, *#ffff00*, *#ff00FF*).

Table 14.4 Color Properties

Property	Value/Example	Elements Affected
background-color	red, blue, #F00	All
color	red, green, #F00, rgb(255,0,0)	All

Table 14.5 Common Color Names and Hexadecimal Values

Color Names

As mentioned, there are 16 color names. The chart below shows these names and their corresponding hexadecimal value.

Color	Color Name	Hexadecimal Value	Color	Color Name	Hexadecimal Value
	Black	#000000		Green	#008000
	Silver	#c0c0c0		Lime	#00ff00
	Gray	#808080		Olive	#808000
	White	#ffffff		Yellow	#ffff00
	Maroon	#800000		Navy	#000080
	Red	#ff0000		Blue	#0000ff
	Purple	#800080		Teal	#008080
	Fushia	#ff00ff		Aqua	#00ffff

Example of Color Usage

```
<h3 style="color:#ff00ff">HTML Colors</h3>
```

Color Depth.   Sometimes colors don't look as crisp and bright as you would expect; pink might look like red, or some of the colors in a field of flowers might be pale. In Chapter 10, "It's the BOM! Browser Objects," we discussed the *screen* object. It has a property called *colorDepth* that will tell you how many distinct colors (bits per pixel) a computer can handle. For example, a color-bit depth of 4 will display 16 colors and a color-bit depth of 24, represented as 2 to the 24th power, will provide 16.7 million colors. How many colors can your computer display?

There are a number of color charts available on the Web that provide Web-safe color palettes.[3] See *www.lynda.com, www.paletteman.com, or www.visibone.com*

Hexadecimal Codes.   These are the codes that define colors. They are groups of three hexadecimal (base 16) numbers. The first number is red, the second green, and the third blue. Each hexadecimal number is an RGB triplet. 00 is the lowest hue, and FF is the highest. For example, red is ff0000, blue is 0000ff, green is 00ff00, and purple is 990099. For a complete list of CSS colors, their names, hex values, shades, and color mixer, go to *http://www.w3schools.com/css/css_colornames.asp*. These colors are supported by all major browsers.

---

3. "Browser-Safe Palette only contains 216 colors out of a possible 256. That is because the remaining 40 colors vary on Macs and PCs. By eliminating the 40 variable colors, this palette is optimized for cross-platform use." —Lynda Weinman (*http://www.lynda.com/resources/webpalette.aspx*).

EXAMPLE 14.3

```
      <html>
        <head><title>Colors</title>
          <style type="text/css">
1           body {
                font-family:cursive;
                background-color: blue; }
2           h1 {color: #FFFF33;}  /* yellow */
3           p { color: white ;  }
          </style>
        </head>
4       <body>
          <font size="+2">
5         <h1>Welcome to my Stylin' Page</h1>
6         <p>This paragraph is all white text on a blue background.<br />
              Do you like it? I think it has potential.
          </p>
        </body>
      </html>
```

EXPLANATION

1   A style is defined for the background of the document. It will be blue.

2   The text for all *<h1>* tags will be yellow (*#FFFF33* is yellow).

3   Paragraphs will have white text.

4   The body color of the page was defined in the CSS style sheet to be blue.

5   The heading level *<h1>* is displayed in its yellow style.

6   Any text enclosed in *<p> </p>* will be white against a blue body. The font was also set by CSS. See Figure 14.3 for output.

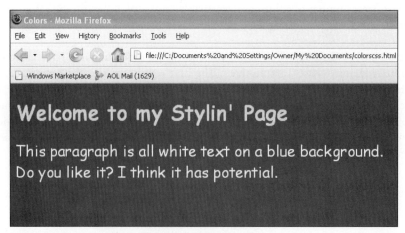

Figure 14.3   Colored text and background.

14.4.3   Working with Fonts

The presentation of a document would be quite boring if you only had one font face and size available. CSS lets you specify a style for the fonts in a document in a variety of ways—by family, size, color, and others (see Table 14.6). There are a huge number of fonts to pick from, although it's a good idea to specify fonts that users are likely to have installed. Like the HTML *<font>* tag, CSS lets you specify several font families (see Table 14.7), and will go from left to right, selecting the one available on your computer. See Figure 14.5 to sample different font styles for your operating system.

Table 14.6   Font Properties

Property	Value/Example	Elements Affected
font	12pt/14pt sans-serif, 80% sans-serif, x-large/110% arial, normal small-caps	All
font-family	serif, sans-serif, cursive, fantasy, monospace; or any specific font family typeface name may be used	All
font-size	12pt, larger, 150%, 1.5em	All
font-style	normal, italic, oblique	All
font-variant	normal, small-caps	All
font-weight	normal, bold, bolder, lighter, 100, 200...900	All

Table 14.7   Font Families

Family Names	Specific Family Typeface Names
Serif	Times, Palatino, Bookman
Sans serif	Arial, Helvetica, GillSans
Monospace	Courier, OCRB, WALLSTREET
Cursive	ZapfChancery, Mural Script, Vivante
Fantasy	Celtic, Impact, Marriage

EXAMPLE 14.4

```
        <html>
          <head><title>Fonts</title>
            <style type="text/css">
              body { background-color: darkblue; }
1             h1 { color: yellow; font-size:x-large;
                  font-family: lucida, verdana, helvetica; }
2             h2 { color:lightgreen; font-size:large;
                  font-family:courier; }
3             h3 { color:lightblue; font-size:medium;
                  font-family:helvetica; }
4             p { color:white; font-size: 22pt;
                  font-style: italic;
                  font-family: arial;
                  font-variant:small-caps; }
            </style>
          </head>
          <body>
            <font size="+2">
            <h1>My name is Papa Bear</h1>
5           <h2>My name is Mama Bear</h2>
            <h3>and I'm the Baby Bear</h3>
            <p>Once upon a time, yaddy yaddy yadda...</p>
          </body>
        </html>
```

EXPLANATION

1   The *h1* element will have yellow text and an extra-large font size from the Lucida family of fonts. If that font is not available in this browser, Verdana will be used, and if not Verdana, then Helvetica.

2   The *h2* element will have a light green, large, Courier font.

3   The *h3* element will have a light blue, medium, Helvetica font.

4   Paragraphs will have white text, with an italic, Arial font size of 22 points, all in small caps.

5   The *<h2>* tag is displayed in its big style. See Figure 14.4.

Figure 14.4 Changing fonts.

Figure 14.5 CSS font sampler and survey at *www.codestyle.org*.

14.4.4 Working with Text

If you want to make a business card, how do you put extra space between each of the letters of your company name? If you're writing a science term paper, how do you deal with exponents, equations, or subscripts? And how do you make it double-spaced? If you're writing a cool poem and want your text in the shape of an hourglass or a circle to give it visual appeal, or you just want to emphasize certain words to make your point for a presentation, then what to do? The CSS controls listed in Table 14.8 could be your answer.

Table 14.8   Text Alignment Properties

Property	Value/Example	Elements Affected
letter-spacing	normal, 0.1em	All
line-height	normal, 1.2, 1.2em, 120%	All
text-align	left, right, center, justify	All
text-decoration	underline, overline, line-through, blink	All
text-indent	3em, 15%	Block-level elements
text-transform	capitalize, uppercase, lowercase, none	All
vertical-align	baseline, sub, super, top, text-top, middle, bottom, text-bottom, 50%	Inline elements
word-spacing	normal, 2em	All

EXAMPLE 14.5

```
    <html>
      <head><title>First Style Sheet</title>
        <style type="text/css">
1         #title{
2             word-spacing: 10px;
              letter-spacing: 4px;
              text-decoration: underline;
              text-align: center;
              font-size: 22pt ;
              font-family:arial;
              font-weight: bold;
          }
```

EXAMPLE 14.5 (CONTINUED)

```
3          p { line-height: 2;
                text-indent: 6%;
                font-family:arial;
                font-size:18; }
           }
        </style>
      </head>
      <body bgcolor="coral">
4        <p id=title>The Color Palette</p>
5        <p>The world is a colorful place. Web browsers display
         millions of those colors every day to make the pages seem
         real and interesting. Browser colors are displayed in
         combinations of red, green, and blue, called RGB. This is a
         system of indexing colors by assigning values of 0 to 255 in
         each of the three colors, ranging from no saturation (0) to
         full saturation (255). Black has a saturation of 0 and
         white has a saturation of 255. In HTML documents these
         colors are represented as six hexadecimal values, preceded
         by a # sign. White is #FFFFFF and black is #000000.</p>
6        <p>
         Although there are millions of different combinations of color,
         it is best when working with Web pages to use what are
         called Web-safe colors.</p>
      </body>
   </html>
```

EXPLANATION

1   *#title* is called an ID selector, a way in the style sheet that we can allow any selector to use a style. In this example, the title of the page is going to be distinct from the text in the rest of the page. For example, if the *<p>* tag is used, it can identify itself with this ID selector to produce the text style described in the declaration block (see line 4). If the ID is not used, the rest of the paragraphs will display text as defined by the rule in line 3. More discussion on ID selectors is presented in the section "The ID Selector and the ID Attribute" on page 564.

2   Text controls are defined in the rule. The text will be centered, underlined, with a 22-point, bold Arial font. The spacing between each letter and each word is defined in pixels.

3   When the *<p>* tag is used, a line height of 2 will produce double-spaced lines. The first line of each paragraph will be indented by 6% from the left margin.

4   This paragraph is identifying itself with the *title* ID. This means that for this paragraph, the style will follow the rule defined after line 1.

5, 6   Both of these paragraphs take on the style provided by the rule in line 3. The results is shown in Figure 14.6.

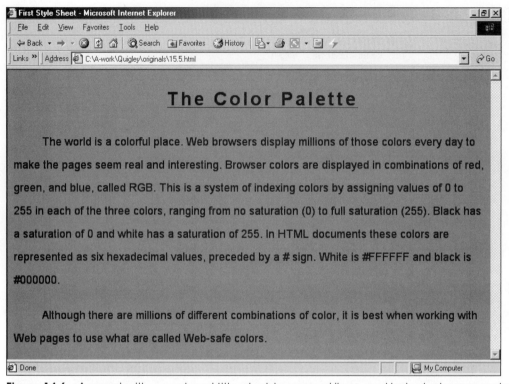

Figure 14.6   A report with a centered title, double-spaced lines, and indented paragraphs.

14.4.5 Working with Backgrounds and Images

The same way that wallpaper in a guest room can create a sense of warmth or calm, background images can add decoration and design to an otherwise blah page. CSS gives you a number of ways to control the appearance of background images. Refer to Table 14.9.

Table 14.9   Image and Background Properties

Property	Value/Example	Elements Affected
background-attachment	scroll, fixed	All
background-image	URL (bay.gif), none	All
background-position	right top, top center, center, bottom, 100% 100%, 0% 0%, 50% 50%	Block-level and replaced elements
background-repeat	repeat, repeat-x (horizontally), repeat-y (vertically), no-repeat	All

EXAMPLE 14.6

```
<html>
   <head><title>Backgrounds</title>
      <style type="text/css">
1         body {
             background-image: url('Moonbeams.jpeg');
             background-repeat: no-repeat;
             background-attachment: fixed;
             background-color: #ccccff;
             background-position:center 80px;
          }
2         h2 {
             color:white;
             font-family:cursive;
             font-variant:small-caps;
          }
      </style>
   </head>
3  <body>
4     <h2 align='center'>Looking at Moonbeams</h2>
   </body>
</html>
```

EXPLANATION

1 CSS rules are defined for an HTML selector, the *body* element. The declarations define the background style of an image called Moonbeams.jpg.

2 The HTML selector is an *h2* element styled to have a white, cursive, font in small caps.

3 The body of the document reflects the CSS rules laid out on line 1.

4 The *h2* tag reflects the font style set by CSS. See Figure 14.7.

Figure 14.7 Background image positioned and nonrepeating.

EXAMPLE 14.7

```
      <html>
         <head><title>Backgrounds</title>
            <style type="text/css">
1              body {background-color:"pink" ;
2              background-image: url(greenballoon.gif);
3              repeat-x }
4              h1 {font-size: 42pt;text-indent: 25%;
                     color:red; margin-top: 14%;
                     font-family:fantasy;}
            </style>
         </head>
5        <body>
6           <h1>Happy Birthday!!</h1>
            <h1>Happy Birthday!!</h1>
         </body>
      </html>
```

EXPLANATION

1   The rule for the *body* element is to give it a pink background color.

2   The background image will come from a file called *greenballoon.gif*, in the current directory. The URL specifies the location of the image.

3   The image will repeat itself horizontally across the screen.

4   The rule for the *h1* element is a red 42-point fantasy font, indented 25% from the left of the block, where the margin is 14% from the top.

5   The body of the document reflects the style that was set for it in line 1.

6   The *<h1>* tag reflects the rule set for it in line 4. The result shown in Figure 14.8.

Figure 14.8   Background color and a repeating image.

14.4.6 Working with Margins and Borders

Containers.   When you look at your document, it is composed of a number of containers. The *<body>* tag is a container and it may contain a heading, a paragraph, a table, or other elements. Each of these elements also can be thought of as a container. The *<div>* tag is another special type of container used to define logical divisions with the content of a page. You can use the *<div>* tag to center a block of content or position a content block in a specific place on the page.

Margins, Padding, and Borders.   Each container has an outer margin, and the margin can have some padding (space between it and the next container). The padding is like the CELLPADDING attribute of a table cell. On the inside of the padding is a border that separates the container from its contents. The border is normally invisible. You can change the margin, create colorful borders, or increase or decrease the padding, to give the page more style. See Figure 14.9 for a graphic representation, and Table 14.10 for a list of margin and border properties. Different browsers might handle the borders differently. Margins and borders will behave better if enclosed within *<div>* tags.

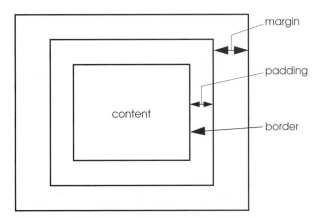

Figure 14.9   How an element is contained.

Table 14.10   Margin and Border Properties

Property	Value/Example	Elements Affected
border-bottom	<border-bottom-width> or <border-style> or <color>	All
border-bottom-width	thin, medium, thick, 2em	All
border-color	red, green, #0C0	All
border-left	<border-left-width> or <border-style> or <color>	All

Continues

Table 14.10   Margin and Border Properties (continued)

Property	Value/Example	Elements Affected
border-left-width	thin, medium, thick, 3em	All
border-right	<border-right-width> or <border-style> or <color>	All
border-right-width	thin, medium, thick, 1cm	All
border-style	[none], dotted, dashed, solid, double, groove, ridge [inset,outset]{1,4}	All
border-top	<border-top-width> or <border-style> or <color>	All
border-top-width	thin, medium, thick, 3em	All
border-width	thin, medium, thick, .5cm	All
margin	5em, 3em, 2em, 1em (top, right, bottom, left)	All
margin-bottom	100px, 50%	All
margin-left	.5in, 40%	All
margin-right	20em, 45%	All
margin-top	1cm, 20%	All
padding	2em, 4em, 6em (right, bottom, left)	All
padding-bottom	2em, 20%	All
padding-left	.25in, 20%	All
padding-right	.5cm, 35%	All
padding-top	20px, 10%	All

EXAMPLE 14.8

```
    <html>
      <head><title>Margins and Borders</title>
        <style type="text/css">
1         body { margin-top: 1cm; margin-left: 2cm ;
2                margin-bottom: 1cm; margin-right: 2cm;
3                border-width: thick;
                 border-style:solid;
                 border-color: red blue green yellow; padding:15px;
        }
```

EXAMPLE 14.8 (CONTINUED)

```
            h1{ /* grouping properties */
                font-weight: bold;
                font-size: 30pt;
                font-family: verdana;
            }
            h2 { /* grouping a property's values */
4               border-style:dotted; border-color:purple;
                font: bold 24pt arial
            }
        </style>
    </head>
    <body bgcolor=silver>
        <h1>Crossing the Border!</h1>
        <h2>Welcome!</h2>
        <h3>Nice country.</h3>
    </body>
</html>
```

EXPLANATION

1   The margins and borders are defined for the body of this document.

2   The margin bottom is 1 centimeter up from the bottom of the document and 2 centimeters in from the left. There will be more whitespace around the headings, paragraphs, and other elements within the body because of the increased margin sizes.

3   A thick, multicolored border is placed on the inside of the margin.

4   The border style for *h2* elements is purple dots. See Figure 14.10.

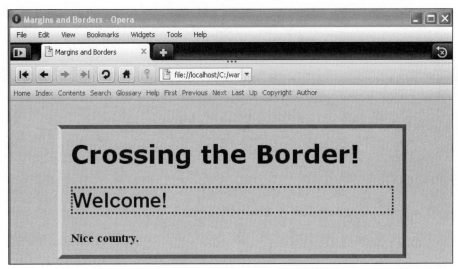

Figure 14.10 Playing with margins and borders. This is how the colorful border appears in Opera. (The border looks different in Internet Explorer 6: It surrounds the entire window.)

14.5 Types of Style Sheets

There are several ways to define style sheets within a document:

1. **Embedded**—The style is defined within the *<style>* tags for the HTML document.
2. **Inline**—The style is defined for a specific HTML element.
3. **External**—The style is defined in an external file.

14.5.1   The Embedded Style Sheet and the *<style>* Tag

A style sheet that is created with the HTML *<style></style>* tags right in the current document is called an embedded style sheet.

The *<style>* Tag.   The *<style></style>* tags were introduced into HTML to allow the style sheets to be inserted right into an HTML document. They are used to create a set of rules to define the style of an HTML element(s). The *<style></style>* tags are placed between the *<head></head>* tags in the document, as shown here:

```
<html><title>CSS Example</title>
   <head>
     <style>
        h1 { color: blue ; }
     </style>
   </head>
```

The *type* Attribute.   Because it is possible to have more than one style sheet language, you can tell the browser what type of style sheet you are using with the *type* attribute of the HTML *<style>* tag. When the browser loads the page, it will ignore the style sheet if it doesn't recognize the language; otherwise it will read the style sheet.

The following example specifies that the type is *text/css*; that is, text and CSS.

FORMAT

```
<style type="style sheet language">
```

Example:

```
<style type="text/css">
```

EXAMPLE   14.9

```
       <html>
       <head><title>Cascading Style Sheets</title>
1         <style type="text/css">
          <!--
2             body { background-color: lightblue; }
3             p { background:yellow;
                  text-indent:5%;
                  margin-left: 20%;
                  margin-right: 20%;
                  border-width:10px;
                  border-style:groove;
                  padding: 15px;
                  font-family: times,arial;
                  font-size:150%;
                  font-weight:900 }
4             h1, h2, h3 {
                  text-align: center;
                  background:blue;
                  border-width:5px;
                  border-style:solid;
                  border-color:black;
                  margin-left:20%;margin-right:20%;
                  font-family:courier, arial;
                  font-weight:900;
                  color: white; }
5             h2,h3 { font-size:24; }
6             em { color: green;font-weight: bold }
          -->
7         </style>
       </head>
       <body>
8      <div align="center"><h1>Stylin' Web Page</h1></div>
9      <p>HTML by itself doesn't give you much other than structure in
       a page and there's no guarantee that every browser out there
       will render the tags in  the same way. So along came style
       sheets. Style sheets enhance HTML as a word processor enhances
       plain text. <p>But... no guarantees what a browser might do
       with a style sheet, any more than what a stylist might do to
       your hair, but we can hope for the best.
10     <h2><center>An H2 Element</center></h2>
       <h3><center>An H3 Element</center></h3>
11     <p>This is not a <em>designer's dream style</em>, but it
       illustrates the power.</p>
       </body>
       </html>
```

EXPLANATION

1   The HTML *<style>* tag belongs within the *<head></head>* tags. The is the start of an embedded CSS.

2   A rule is defined for the HTML *body* element. The background color of the document will be light blue.

3   A rule is defined for the HTML *p* (paragraph) element. The left and right margins are set at 20%, meaning that they will be moved inward 20% from their respective edges. They will be surrounded by a grooved border, with the text given a 15-pixel size padding. The font is Times or Arial (whichever works on your browser), point size 150% bigger than its default, and weight 900 is the boldest of the bold.

4   A rule is defined for a group of selectors (heading levels *h1*, *h2*, and *h3*). They will be centered on the page, and the text will be white against a blue bordered background in a Courier or Arial font.

5   The rule for the *<h2>* and *<h3>* tags sets the font size to 24 points.

6   A rule is defined for an *em* element. Text will be green and bold.

7   This marks the end of the HTML header that encloses the style sheet.

8   As shown in the output (see Figure 14.11), the heading level is displayed according to the style defined in the style sheet, line 4.

9   This paragraph is displayed according to the rule set in the style sheet, line 3. Notice how both the left and right margins have moved toward the center.

10 The heading level is displayed according to the rule set in the style sheet, lines 4 and 5, and the first paragraph is indented.

11 The *<em>* tag is embedded within the *<p>* tag. It inherits from the *<p>* tag everything but the font color and weight. These paragraph properties were overridden in the style sheet defined on line 6 for the *em* element.

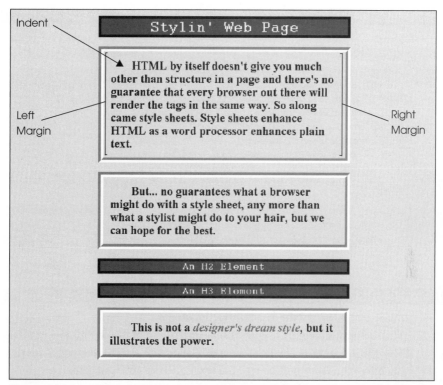

Figure 14.11   HTML and CSS—An embedded style sheet.

14.5.2   The Inline Style and the *<style>* Attribute

Inline style sheets are also embedded within an HTML document, but are assigned as an attribute of the *<style>* tag in the **body** of the document and are useful for overriding an already existing style for a particular element in a linked style sheet. On the negative side, they have to be redefined for any element that requires that style, element by element. For example, if the *h1* element has been defined to be blue and you want to temporarily change it to red, you can define the style as an attribute of the style tag for that element:

```
<h1 style= "color: red; "> This is red text</h1>
```

EXAMPLE   14.10

```
    <html>
      <head><title>Inline Style Sheets</title>
1       <style type="text/css">
2         body { background-color: orange;
              color:darkblue;  /* color of text */ }
```

Continues

EXAMPLE   14.10 (CONTINUED)

```
            </style>
         </head>
         <body>
3           <h1 style="color:darkred;
               text-align:center;
               text-decoration:underline;">Inline Stylin'</h1>
4           <p style="color:black;
               background:white;
               font-family:sans-serif;font-size:large">
            This paragraph uses an inline style. As soon as another
            paragraph is started, the style will revert back to its
            default.
5           <p> This paragraph has reverted back to its default style,
            and so has the following heading.</p>
            <h1>Default heading</h1>
         </body>
      </html>
```

EXPLANATION

1   A CSS starts here in the head of the document.

2   The background color is set to orange and the color of the font is set to dark blue.

3   This *h1* uses an inline style, an attribute of the *<h1>* tag and effective for this heading only. The color will be red, the text centered and underlined.

4   This is an inline style for the paragraph tag. It is an attribute of the *<p>* tag and is only good for this paragraph. The text of the paragraph will be black, the background color of the paragraph will be white, and the font family, sans serif, large. The next time a *<p>* tag is used, the style will revert to its former style.

5   This paragraph has reverted to its former style. See Figure 14.12.

Inline Stylin'

This paragraph uses an inline style. As soon as another paragraph is started, the style will revert back to its default.

This paragraph has reverted back to its default style, and so has the following heading.

Default heading

Figure 14.12   Inline styles are temporary.

14.6 The External Type with a Link

14.6.1 The *<link>* Tag

In Chapter 1, we talked about the three layers of a Web page: HTML/XHTML, CSS, and JavaScript. The CSS layer can be separated from the HTML document by placing style sheets in external files. In fact, external style sheets are the most powerful type if you want the style to affect more than one page; in fact, you can use the same style for hundreds, thousands, or millions of pages. The file name for the external style sheet has a *.css* extension, just as the HTML file has an *.html* or *.htm* extension, and a JavaScript external file has a *.js* extension.

To link the external file to the existing HTML file, a link is created as shown here:

```
<link rel=stylesheet href="style_file.css" type="text/css">
```

The following examples demonstrate the use of external style sheets. Example 14.11 is the HTML file containing a link to the external file and Example 14.12 is the *.css* file. It contains the style sheet, but notice it does not contain *<style></style>* tags.

EXAMPLE 14.11

```
      <html>
         <head><title>External Style Sheets</title>
1         <link rel=stylesheet type="text/css"
               href="extern.css" media="all">
          <!-- Name of external file is extern.css. See Example 14.12 -->
2         </head>
3         <body>
             <h1><u>External Stylin'</u></h1>
             <h2>Paragraph Style Below</h2>
             <p>The style defined for this paragraph is found in an external
                CSS document. The filename ends with <em>.css</em>. Now
                we can apply this style to as many pages as we want to.</p>
             <h2>An H2 Element</h2>
             <h3>An H3 Element</h3>
             <p>This is not a <em>designer's dream style</em>, but it
                illustrates the power. Don't you think so?</p>
         </body>
      </html>
```

EXPLANATION

1   The *link* tag is opened within the *<head>* tags of your HTML document. The *link* tag has a *rel* attribute that is assigned *stylesheet*. This tells the browser that the link is going to a style sheet type document. The *href* attribute tells the browser the name of the CSS file containing the style sheet. This is a local file called *extern.css*. If necessary, use a complete path to the file.

Continues

EXPLANATION(CONTINUED)

2   The *<head>* tag ends here.

3   In the body of the document, each of the HTML tags will be affected by the style defined in the external CSS file. See Figure 14.13 for output.

EXAMPLE 14.12

```
(The external extern.css file)
1 body { background-color: pink; }
2 p {
    margin-left:20%;
    margin-right:20%;
    font-family: sans-serif;
    font-size: 14
3 }
  h1, h2, h3 { text-align: center;
               font-family: sans-serif;
               color: darkblue
  }
4 em { color: green;
      font-weight: bold
  }
```

EXPLANATION

1   This is the external CSS file that will be linked to the file in Example 14.12. Using an external CSS file keeps the main file size smaller and allows the style sheet to be shared by multiple files. First use the *<link>* tag, then the *rel* attribute tells the browser that this is a link to a style sheet, the *href* specifies the location of the CSS file, and *type* specifies the type of information that will be linked (i.e., text in this example). You may also specify a media type. If you add *media="all"* then all media types will be included.

2   The paragraph *<p>* style is set to have a margin in 20% from the left and right, the text in size 14, and font family sans serif.

3   The heading levels 1, 2, and 3 styles are set to be centered with a dark blue font, from the sans serif family.

4   The *<em>* style will be a bold, green font.

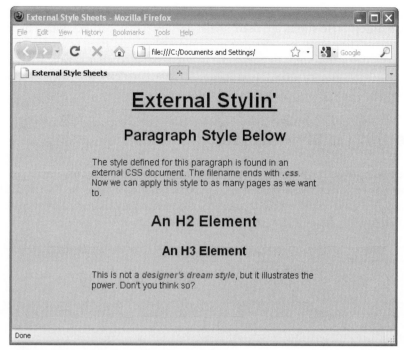

Figure 14.13   External style sheets.

14.6.2   Importing with @import

You can also import CSS files with the @import rule. This rule allows you to import one external CSS file into another by adding the @import rule in other external CSS files. The format for doing this is:

FORMAT

```
@import url(externalfile.css);
```

EXAMPLE

```
<style type="text/css">
        @import url(http://www.mystyles.com/style.css);
        @import url(/stylesheets/.css);
        h1 { color: blue }
</style>
```

Cascading Order.   You can import as many files as you want, but keep in mind that when multiple style sheets are used, the style sheets may conflict over which selector has control. There must be rules that determine what style sheet's rule has precedence. The order that determines the outcome of the type of conflict is called the cascading order. A full discussion can be found at *http://www.w3.org/TR/CSS2/cascade.html#cascading-order.*

14.7 Creating a Style Class

Rather than globally defining a style for an element, you can customize the style by defining a class. The class style can be applied to individual tags when needed. The class name, called the **class selector**, is preceded by a period and followed by the declaration enclosed in curly braces.

FORMAT

```
.classname { style rules; }
```

EXAMPLE

```
.header { font-family: verdana, helvetica ; }
```

Once you have defined a class, it can be used on any of the HTML elements in the body of the document as long as that element understands the style you have applied to it. To apply the class, you use the **class attribute**. The class attribute is assigned the name of the class; for example, for the *<p>* tag, you would stipulate *<p class=name>* where *name* is the name of the class.

EXAMPLE 14.13

```
    <html>
1   <head><title>CSS Class Name</title>
2     <style>
3       p { margin-right: 30%;font-family: arial;
            font-size: 16pt;
            color:forestgreen; }
4        .bigfont { font-size: x-large; color:darkblue;
                    font-style:bold;}
5        .teenyfont { font-size:small;
                      font-style: italic;color:black;}
      </style>
    </head>
```

EXAMPLE 14.13 (CONTINUED)

```
        <body>
6           <p>The text in this paragraph is green and the point size
            is 16. The font family is <em>arial</em>.</p>
7           <p class="bigfont"> This paragraph has a bigger font and is
            dark blue in color.</p>
8           <p>The font style is specified as a class called
            <em>.bigfont</em>.</p>
9           <h1 class="bigfont">Testing the Class on an H1 Element</h1>
10          <p class="teenyfont">Is this a small font?"</p>
            <p>Let's start a new paragraph. This is green with a font
            size of 16. What style is in effect here?</p>
        </body>
    </html>
```

EXPLANATION

1   The style is defined in the *<head>* of the document.

2   The CSS starts here.

3   A rule is defined for the paragraph (*p* selector). All paragraphs will have a right margin, 30% in from both left and right. The Arial font will be 12 point and forest green.

4   A class selector called *.bigfont* is defined. Class names start with a period. When used on an HTML element, the font will be extra large, dark blue, and bold.

5   The class selector called *.teenyfont* is defined. All HTML elements that use this class will have a small, italic, black font.

6   The paragraph is styled according to the rule on line 3.

7   This paragraph is assigned the *bigfont* class. The text will be in the style defined for this class on line 4.

8   This paragraph reverts to the style rule on line 3.

9   The *<h1>* tag is using the *bigfont* class defined on line 4.

10 The *<p>* tag is using the *teenyfont* class defined on line 5. See Figure 14.14.

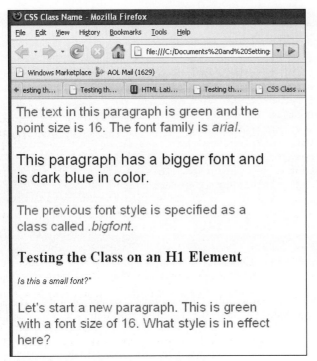

Figure 14.14 Testing the CSS classes.

14.7.1 Styling a Simple Table with Class

A class can be applied to tables as with any other element. By default the browser determines the size of the table cells based on the elements and text they contain and expands the cells accordingly. With images, the edge of the image will be the edge of the cell. The browser will not shrink the image to fit the text, but will stretch the text to fit the image. Text is stretched out until the first line break or until a paragraph ends. You can specify table width with the CSS width property. Example 14.14 uses both a table and an image width class.

EXAMPLE 14.14

```
      <html>
        <head><title>Bengaluru, India</title>
1         <style type="text/css">
2              table, td{ border:groove darkgreen; }
3              .size{ width:200px; }   /* class */
4              .caption { font-size: .8em;font-style:italic; }
        </style>
      </head>
```

EXAMPLE 14.14 (CONTINUED)

```
        <body>
5       <table border=0 class="size">
6           <tr><td><img src="indiacows.jpg" width="200"
                        height="150" alt="Cows Rule"></td></tr>
7           <tr><td class="caption">Some cows take a leisurly stroll
                    down the Jayanagar Block after a morning rain in
                    Bengaluru, India.</td></tr>
        </table>
        </body>
    </html>
```

EXPLANATION

1   The CSS style sheet starts here.

2   The *table* and the *td* elements are given a grooved dark green border.

3   This is a class to define the width of an HTML element.

4   This style defines a class called *.caption* defining font size and style of an HTML element.

5   The class attribute of the HTML table defines the width of the table.

6   The first row and cell of the table is the image. Its border was defined as grooved and dark green in the CSS on line 2.

7   The second row of the table contains a class called "caption" to style the text font in the cell. This cell also uses the style for a grooved, green border. The output is shown in Figure 14.15.

Figure 14.15   A table with an image and text from Example 14.14.

14.7.2 Using a Specific Class Selector

In previous examples we have defined a class style that can be used by all HTML elements. The following class can be applied to all HTML elements:

```
.center {text-align: center;}
```

With a class selector you can define different styles for a specific HTML element. For example, if you want different styles for just the *<p>* tag, you can specify a class description by appending a dot to the element followed by the class name:

```
p.right {text-align: right}
p.center {text-align: center}
/* These classes apply only to the paragraph element */
```

When the class selector is applied to a style, then you use the class attribute in your HTML document as follows:

```
<p class="right">
  This paragraph will be right-aligned.
</p>
<p class="center">
  This paragraph will be center-aligned.
</p>
```

Note: To apply more than one class per given element, the syntax is:

```
<p class="center bold">
  This is a paragraph.
</p>
```

This paragraph will be styled by a class called "center" and a class "bold".

EXAMPLE 14.15

```
    <html>
      <head>
        <style type="text/css">
1         p.normal-cursive {
              font-variant: normal;
              font-family: cursive
          }
2         p.small { font-variant: small-caps }
        </style>
      </head>
      <body bgcolor=tan>
3       <p class="normal-cursive">This is a paragraph</p>
4       <p class="small">This is a paragraph</p>
      </body>
    </html>
```

EXPLANATION

1   A specific class selector is defined to describe the style of a paragraph's font, and only a paragraph.

2   Another class selector is defined for a paragraph's font.

3   Now to use the class with the *<p>* tag, the class name is specified and the text will be printed in cursive.

4   The class for this paragraph will style the text in small capital letters. Output is shown in Figure 14.16.

Figure 14.16   Using the *class* selector to style a paragraph.

EXAMPLE 14.16

```
<html>
  <head>
    <style type="text/css">
1        ul.disc {list-style-type: disc}
         ul.circle {list-style-type: circle}
         ul.square {list-style-type: square}
         ul.none {list-style-type: none}
    </style>
  </head>
  <body bgcolor="aquamarine">
2    <ul class="disc">
        <li>Coffee</li>
        <li>Tea</li>
        <li>Beer</li>
     </ul>
     <ul class="circle">
        <li>red</li>
        <li>blue</li>
        <li>yellow</li>
     </ul>
```

Continues

EXAMPLE   14.16 (CONTINUED)

```
        <ul class="square">
          <li>circle</li>
          <li>square</li>
          <li>triangle</li>
        </ul>
        <ul class="none">
          <li>Thanks</li>
          <li>Tack</li>
          <li>Gracias</li>
        </ul>
      </body>
  </html>
```

EXPLANATION

1   A CSS class is defined for a list with different styles.
2   This is an HTML list item using the "disc" class. The output shown in Figure 14.17.

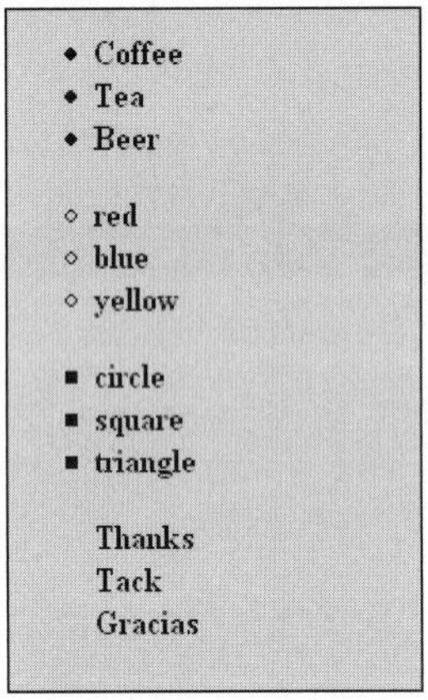

Figure 14.17   Using a CSS class to create different styles for lists.

14.8 The ID Selector and the ID Attribute

The ID Selector.   The ID selector is another way to create a style that is independent of a specific HTML tag. By using the ID selector, you can choose the style for the element by assigning it a unique ID. The name of the ID selector is always preceded by a hash mark (also called a pound sign, #). The declaration block, consisting of properties and values, follows the ID selector and is enclosed in curly braces.

```
#IDselector { declaration ; }
```

```
#menu1 { font-family: arial;
         font-size: big;
         color: blue; }
```

To apply an ID to an HTML tag, use the *id* attribute. The attribute will be assigned the same name given to the ID selector; so, to apply an ID selector to a *<p>* tag, you would stipulate *<p id=name>* where *name* is the name of the ID selector (see Example 14.17).

The *id* Attribute.   When JavaScript enters the picture, the *id* attribute is used to identify each element as a unique object so that it can be manipulated in a JavaScript program. The *id* should be unique for an element and not used more than once on a page. If you need to use the style more than once for multiple elements, it would be better to use the class selector instead. The ID selector can be used with a class selector of the same name, as *#big, .big { }*.

```
      <html>
        <head><title>ID's</title>
1        <style type="text/css">
2           p{ font-family:arial,sans-serif,helvetica;
               font-style:bold;
               font-size:18
            }
3           #block { /* The ID selector */
               color: red;
               text-decoration:underline;
            }
         </style>
      </head>
      <body >
4        <p>When making my point, I will get quite red and underline
            what I say!!</p>
5        <p id="block">This text is red and underlined!!</P>
6        <p>and now I am somewhat appeased.
         </body>
      </html>
```

1   This is the start of a style sheet; it is placed between the *<head></head>* tags in the document.

Continues

EXPLANATION(CONTINUED)

2   The style of the paragraph element is defined. This style will take effect anywhere in the document where the *<p>* tag is used. Note that point sizes may be different on different browsers. Pixels will give you more accuracy.

3   The ID selector is called *block* and must be preceded by a hash mark. It can be used by any HTML element to produce red, underlined text. ID selectors should only be used once on a page to serve as a unique ID for the element.

4   A paragraph containing text will be displayed according to the style defined in the style sheet on line 2.

5   By adding the ID called *block*, the style for this paragraph will be changed to red, underlined text.

6   The *<p>* tag will revert to the style defined on line 2. See Figure 14.18.

When making my point, I will get quite red and underline what I say!!

This text is red and underlined!!

and now I am somewhat appeased.

Figure 14.18   Using the ID selector in style sheets.

14.9 Overriding or Adding a Style with the *<span>* Tag

The *<span></span>* tags are used if you want to change or add styles to only a selected portion of text (see Table 14.11). By doing so, you can create an inline style that will be embedded within another element and apply only to that portion of the content. In this way you can add or override a style to an element for which a style has already been defined. Carriage returns and breaks in the text will not occur with these tags.

Table 14.11   Attributes of the HTML *span* Tag

Attribute	Definition
class	Sets a class for a specific element or elements.
id	Used to apply settings to specific HTML elements.
style	Used to apply style settings for the specific element included in the *span* tags.
title	Used to give specific elements a title that might appear as a tooltip when the mouse is held over the element.

14.9.1   The *<span>* Tag and the *style* Attribute

In Example 14.18, the paragraph style has been defined in a CSS. But later in the body of the document, the *<span>* tag is used to override the font size and to add margins to the text.

EXAMPLE   14.18

```
        <html>
          <head><title>Margins</title></head>
            <style type="text/css">
 1            body { margin:10%;
                    border-width: 10px; border-style:solid;
                    border-color: white; padding:5px;}
 2            p { color=black;
                  font-size: 22pt;
                  margin-left:10;
                  margin-right:10;
                  padding:5px;
                  border-style:groove;
                  border-color:white;
                  background-color:cyan;}
            </style>
          <body bgcolor=blue>
            <p>
 3            <span style="margin-left:10%;font-size:26pt;">The Three
                Little Bears</span>
 4          </p>
            <p>
                Once upon a time there were three little bears,
                Mama bear, Papa bear, and Baby bear.
                They lived very happily in the deep woods.
            </p>
            <p>And then there was Goldilocks!</p>
          </body>
        </html>
```

EXPLANATION

1   The style rule for the *body* element is defined. It will have a margin distance increased by 10% on all sides and a solid, white border with a padding of 5 pixels between the margin and the border. Margin borders will differ in appearance depending on your browser.

2   The style rule for the paragraph defines black text of a 22-point font, with both right and left margins of 10 pixels, contained within a grooved, white border, against a cyan background.

Continues

EXPLANATION

3   The *<span>* tag defines a left margin increased by 10% relative to this paragraph, and changes the font size to 26 points. The only part of the document to be affected is the paragraph in which the *<span></span>* tags are enclosed. The text *The Three Little Bears* will be displayed according to this style.

4   The *<span>* tags have no effect on this paragraph. The style reverts to the rule in the style sheet. See Figure 14.19.

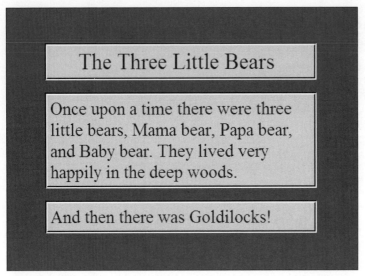

Figure 14.19   The *<span>* tag only affects a specific portion of the text.

14.9.2   The *<span>* Tag and the *class* Attribute

The *<span>* tag provides no visual change by itself. It allows you to change or modify the appearance of a selected portion of a document within the tags based on a CSS class rule. Example 14.19 highlights specific portions of text between the *<span></span>* tags.

EXAMPLE   14.19

```
      <html>
        <head>
          <style type="text/css">
1           span.highlight { background-color:yellow }
          </style>
        </head>
        <body>
```

EXAMPLE 14.19 (CONTINUED)

```
     <p>
2        <span class="highlight">This is a text.</span> Highlighting
             text is a nice idea.<br>Whenever you apply a span style
             to this paragraph, you'll see what happens.
3        <span class="highlight">This is the highlighted text.</span>
     </p>
   </body>
</html>
```

EXPLANATION

1 This is a dependent class selector rule. The class *highlight* can only be applied to *<span> </span>* tags.

2 The class attribute is assigned the name of a class called "highlight". The class will be in effect for only the portion of text between the *<span></span>* tags. The background color of the text is changed to yellow as shown in Figure 14.20.

3 The text between the *<span></span>* tags will be highlighted based on the class rule.

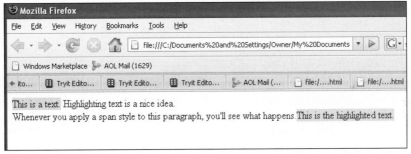

Figure 14.20   Highlighting text between *<span></span>* tags using the *class* attribute.

14.9.3 Inheritance and Contextual Selectors

Virtually all selectors that are nested within selectors will inherit the property values assigned to the outer selector unless otherwise modified. For example, a color defined for the "body" will also be applied to text in a paragraph. Contextual selectors have an inheritance basis. For example, if a *<b>* tag is nested within a *<p>* tag, then the *<b>* tag takes on the characteristics assigned to its parent. If the *<p>* is green, then the bold text will also be green. If a bullet list *<ul>* has *<li>* tags nested within it, the bullets take on the characteristics of its parent. If the *ul* element is red, then all the bullets and the accompanying text will be red.

EXAMPLE 14.20

```
      <html>
        <head><title>Contextual Selector</title>
          <style type="text/css">
1           table td { color: blue; /* Table cells will take this style */
                      font-size: 18pt;
                      font-family: verdana; }
          </style>
        </head>
        <body bgcolor="silver">
          <div align="center">
            <h1><em>The Three Bears</em></h1>
            <table cellspacing="20" cellpadding="20%" border="3">
              <tr>
2                 <td>Mama Bear</td>
              </tr>
              <tr>
3                 <td>Papa Bear</td>
              </tr>
              <tr>
4                 <td>Baby Bear</td>
              </tr>
            </table>
          </div>
        </body>
      </html>
```

EXPLANATION

1   A rule is defined for a table cell. The table's data will be blue, the font size 18
     points, and the font family, Verdana. Whenever you create a table, each of the table
     cells, defined by the *<td>* tag, will have this style.

2–4 The table data in these cells will take on the style described in line 1. The output
     is shown in Figure 14.21.

Figure 14.21   A table with stylized cells.

When you create a contextual selector, the last element in the selector list is the one that is affected by the style when it is used in context of the elements preceding it. For example, if you have a selector list: *table td em { color: blue ;}*, then the *em* element, the last in the list, will be affected by the style only when it is inside a table cell at which point the table cell will be contain blue italic text. This doesn't define the style for the *<td>* tag, only the *<em>* tag if it is used in the context of *<td>*; as in *<td><em>*. See Example 14.21

```
EXAMPLE   14.21

      <html>
        <head><title>Contextual Selector</title>
          <style type="text/css">
1           table td em { color: blue; /* Table cells take this style */
                           font-size: 18pt;
                           font-family: verdana; }
          </style>
        </head>
        <body bgcolor=silver>
          <div align="center">
2           <h1><em>The Three Bears</em></h1>
            <table cellspacing="20" cellpadding="20%" border="3">
              <tr>
3                 <td><em>Mama Bear</em></td>
              </tr>
              <tr>
4                 <td>Papa Bear</td>
              </tr>
              <tr>
```

Continues

EXAMPLE   14.21 (CONTINUED)

```
5                    <td>Baby Bear</td>
                  </tr>
               </table>
            </div>
         </body>
      </html>
```

EXPLANATION

1   When a table is defined, the data cells will take on this style only if the *<em>* tag is used within the cell. See line 3.

2   The *<em>* tag used within this *<h1>* tag is not affected by the contextual selector because it is not within a table cell; that is, it is out of context.

3   The *<em>* tag is embedded within a *<td>* tag. The table's data will follow the style defined on line 1; it is in context.

4   This table cell is not using the *<em>* tag, so will not be affected by the style rule on line 1. It can only be affected if in context.

5   This table cell will not be affected by the style rule either because it doesn't use the *<em>* tag. See Figure 14.22.

Figure 14.22   A table cell is defined by the contextual selector.

14.10 Positioning Elements and Layers

One of the most important features of CSS is the ability to position objects on a page, to size them, and to make them either visible or invisible. This feature makes it possible to move objects to different sections of a page, move text and images, create animation, create tooltips, scrolling text, and more. Normally when you place tags in an HTML document, the flow is from top to bottom. Now, with style sheets, you can set the position of an element, even layering one on top of the other (see Table 14.12).

A note about Netscape layers. Netscape 4 introduced layer (*<layer></layer>*) tags, a prototype of CSS positioning, to control the position and visibility of elements on a page, and then with Netscape 6 abandoned the whole thing. This book does not address the Netscape layer technology because it is really a thing of the past. However, the term "layer" is still in use, and is used to refer to objects using the *id* attribute.

Table 14.12 Positioning Styles

Property	*What It Specifies*
bottom, right	The placement of the bottom, right edges of an element.
clip	A specified region of the element that will be seen.
display	Whether an element is displayed.
overflow	What to do if there is an overflow; that is, there isn't enough space for the element.
position	How to position the element on the page.
top, left	The placement of the top, left edges of an element.
visibility	Whether an element can be seen.
width, height	The size in width and height of an element's content, not additional padding, margins, borders, and so forth.
z-index	The third dimension in a stack of objects.

14.10.1   Absolute Positioning

Absolute positioning places an element in a specific location on the page and can be used to achieve full animation; for instance, moving an image across a page. It is used to specify the absolute coordinates (x,y) of the element in terms of the browser window itself. The *top* and *left* properties are used to determine the coordinates (see Figure 14.23). If not specified, the browser will assume the top left corner of the browser window, where x is 0 and y is 0. The top left corner of the window is position 0,0 and the bottom right corner depends on the resolution of the screen. If the screen resolution is set to 800 pixels in width and 600 pixels in height, the bottom right corner is positioned at coordinates 800, 600.

If an absolutely positioned element is nested within another absolutely positioned element, it will be positioned relative to that element.

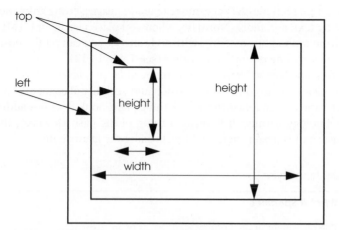

Figure 14.23   Absolute positioning.

EXAMPLE 14.22

```
   <html>
     <head>
       <title>layers</title>
       <style type="text/css">
1        #first{
           background-color: red;
           border-style: solid;
           font-weight:bold;
           top: 20;
2          position: absolute;
           left: 20;
           height: 100;
           width: 100;
         }
3        #second{
           background-color: blue;
           border-style: solid;
           font-weight:bold;
           top: 30 ;
           position: absolute;
           left: 60;
           height: 100;
           width: 100;
         }
```

EXAMPLE   14.22 (CONTINUED)

```
4          #third{
               background-color: orange;
               border-style: solid;
               font-weight:bold;
               top: 40 ;
               position: absolute;
               left: 100;
               height: 100;
               width: 100;
           }
        </style>
5       <body>
6          <p id="first">
               First position
           </p>
7          <p id="second">
               Second position
           </p>
8          <p id="third">
               Third position
           </p>
        </body>
     </html>
```

EXPLANATION

1   An ID selector called *#first* sets the pixel positions for a red block that will be absolutely positioned 20 pixels from the top of the window, 20 pixels from the left side, and have a size of 100 × 100 pixels (width × height).

2   The *position* attribute is specified as absolute. It is independent of all other elements in the body of this document.

3   An ID selector called *#second* sets the pixel positions for a blue block that will be absolutely positioned 30 pixels from the top of the window, 60 pixels from the left side, and have a size of 100 × 100 pixels (width × height). The blue box will appear to be layered over the red one.

4   An ID selector called *#third* sets the pixel positions for an orange block that will be absolutely positioned 40 pixels from the top of the window, 100 pixels from the left side, and have a size of 100 × 100 pixels (width × height). The orange box will appear to be layered over the blue one.

5   The *<body>* serves as the container for three objects. The red, blue, and orange boxes will appear in the window at the absolute positions assigned to them in relationship to their container, the body of the document.

Continues

EXPLANATION(CONTINUED)

6   The paragraph element is positioned and styled according to the rule for the *first* ID selector.

7   The paragraph element is positioned and styled according to the rule for the *second* ID selector.

8   The paragraph element is positioned and styled according to the rule for the *third* ID selector. See Figure 14.24.

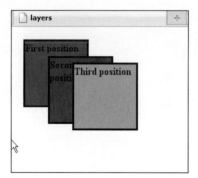

Figure 14.24   Three layers based on absolute positioning (Internet Explorer 8, Firefox).

Top, Left, Bottom, Right—Absolute Positions.   As shown in Example 14.22, once the position has been set, the *left*, *top*, *right*, and *bottom* attributes can be used to specify exactly where on the page the element should be located. Although we used *left* and *top* to define the position of the element within the body of the document, *right* and *left bottom* can also position the element on the page. In the following example, four elements are placed in different fixed positions in the document. If you change the size of the window, the boxes will appear to be located in different places than shown in the output of this example, Figure 14.25. That is because the fixed positions are relative to the dimensions of the document's window. For example, if you shrink the window horizontally, and the boxes are positioned 10 pixels from the bottom, they are still 10 pixels from the bottom of the document, and the boxes at the top are still 10 pixels from the top, giving the appearance that they have moved much closer together. If the window is shrunk enough either vertically or horizontally, the boxes might even overlap to maintain their absolute positions, as shown in Figure 14.26.

EXAMPLE   14.23

```
<html>
  <head>
    <title>layers</title>
    <style type="text/css">
      <!--
```

EXAMPLE 14.23 (CONTINUED)

```
1        #first{
             background-color: red;
             border-style: solid;
             font-weight:bold;
             position: absolute;
             top: 10;
             right: 100;
             height: 100;
             width: 100;
         }
2        #second{
             background-color: blue;
             border-style: solid;
             font-weight:bold;
             position: absolute;
             top:10;
             left:400;
             height: 100;
             width: 100;
         }
3        #third{
             background-color: orange;
             border-style: solid;
             font-weight:bold;
             position: absolute;
             top: 10;
             left: 200;
             height: 100;
             width: 100;
         }
4        #fourth{
             background color: yellow;
             border-style: solid;
             font-weight:bold;
             position: absolute;
             bottom: 10 ;
             right: 40;
             height: 100;
             width: 100;
         }
     </style>
   </head>
5  <body>
6    <p id="first">
       First position
     </p>
```

Continues

EXAMPLE   14.23 (CONTINUED)

```
7        <p id="second">
           Second position
         </p>
8        <p id="third">
           Third position
         </p>
9        <p id="fourth">
           Fourth position
         </p>
      </body>
   </html>
```

EXPLANATION

1   An ID selector called *#first* sets the pixel positions for a red block that will be absolutely positioned 10 pixels from the top of the current window, 100 pixels from the right side, and have a size of 100 × 100 pixels (width × height).

2   An ID selector called *#second* sets the pixel positions for a blue block that will be absolutely positioned 10 pixels from the top of the window, 400 pixels from the left side, and have a size of 100 × 100 pixels (width × height).

3   An ID selector called *#third* sets the pixel positions for an orange block that will be absolutely positioned 10 pixels from the top of the window, 200 pixels from the left side, and have a size of 100 × 100 pixels (width × height).

4   An ID selector called *#fourth* sets the pixel positions for a yellow block that will be absolutely positioned 10 pixels from the bottom of the window, 40 pixels from the right side, and have a size of 100 × 100 pixels (width × height).

5   The body is called the container for the elements within it. The red, blue, orange, and yellow boxes will appear in the window at the absolute positions assigned to them in relationship to their container, the body of the document. If you change the size of the window, the boxes are fixed to the absolute positions, making it seem as though the boxes have moved. They are aligned to the fixed pixel positions from the top, bottom, right, and left sides of the current sized window.

6   The paragraph element is positioned and styled according to the rule for the *first* ID selector, the top, right corner.

7   The paragraph element is positioned and styled according to the rule for the *second* ID selector, the left, bottom corner.

8   The paragraph element is positioned and styled according to the rule for the *third* ID selector, the top, left corner.

9   The paragraph element is positioned and styled according to the rule for the *fourth* ID selector, the bottom right corner. See Figure 14.26.

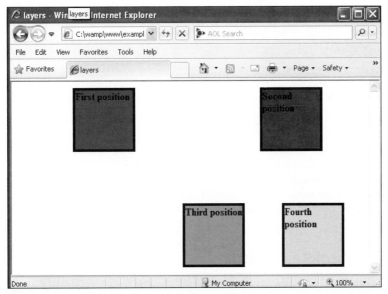

Figure 14.25 Blocks are absolutely positioned based on pixels from top, bottom, left, and right.

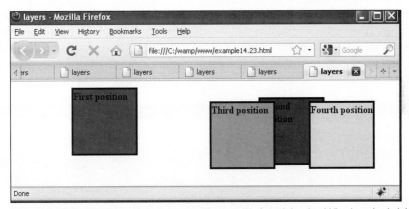

Figure 14.26 Firefox: Absolute positions with four blocks. Window height is changed and boxes overlap.

14.10.2 The *<div>* Container

One of the most important containers is the *<div>* It serves as a generic block-level container where you can put other elements and give them color, borders, margins, and so forth. It is most useful when used with CSS, allowing you to easily change the contents of the *div* for an entire site. A site, for example, is often divided up into a header, navigation bars, content, and a footer. Each of these sections could be placed in its own *div* container and all of those *divs* enclosed in one main *div*.

```
(CSS Class Declaration)
.bigblue {
      border-style: solid;
      border-width:1px;
      color: blue;
      font-family:arial, times, serif;
      font-size:32pt;color: blue;
 }
------------------------------------
(The HTML <div> tags)
<div class="bigblue">
  This is the text in a container.
</div>
```

14.10.3   Absolute Positioning

The *div* container is not only used to change colors, borders, fonts, and so on, but it is used for absolute or relative positioning of a block of text. For example, it allows you to create a paragraph style independent of the *<p>* tag. Within the block, the *<span>* tags can be used to introduce other styles.

   In the following example, the *<div>* tag is used to create a block. It is absolutely positioned in the window at position 0,0, which is the top, left corner. Absolute positioning allows you to place an element anywhere on the page separate from the rest of the document. The top left corner of the document or the elements' parent originate at coordinates 0,0.

EXAMPLE 14.24

```
    <html>
      <head><title>Positioning</title>
1     <style>
2        .divStyle {background-color:blue;
3                    position: absolute;
                     width: 250px; height: 150px;
         }
         p { color: white;
             font-size:18pt;
             position: absolute;
             left:10px; height:5px;
         }
      </style>
    </head>
    <body>
4     <div class="divStyle">
5        <p>
```

EXAMPLE 14.24 (CONTINUED)

```
              This is a paragraph.
          </p>
       </div>
    </body>
  </html>
```

EXPLANATION

1   The style sheet starts here with the *<style>* tag.

2   A class called *divStyle* is defined.

3   This style will produce a blue box, 250 pixels wide and 150 pixels high. It will be positioned at the top, left corner of the window (0,0) because the *top* and *left* properties are undefined.

4   The *div* element will use the style defined by the *divStyle* class.

5   The paragraph element is embedded within the *<div>* tags. The *div* box is like a mini window. It will placed at the top, left corner of the window, because its position has not been defined. See Figure 14.27.

Figure 14.27   The *div* block is absolutely positioned in the window.

14.10.4   Relative Positioning

Relative positioning places the element in a position relative to the element where it is defined within the document. This type of positioning is used to control the way elements appear in relation to other elements in the document. In the following example the *.ParaStyle* class is positioned relative to where it should be placed within its container, a *div* block.

EXAMPLE 14.25

```
     <html>
       <head><title>Positioning</title>
1        <style>
2          .divStyle { background-color:lightblue;
3                      position: absolute;
4                      width: 250px; height: 150px;
                       border-style: solid;
                       border-color: darkblue;
           }
5          .paraStyle { color:darkblue;
6                       position: relative;
                        font-size:18pt;
           }
         </style>
       </head>
       <body>
7        <div style="left:50px; top:50px" class="divStyle">
8          <p style="left:15%; top:20%" class="paraStyle">
             This is a paragraph.
           </p>
         </div>
       </body>
     </html>
```

EXPLANATION

1   The style sheet starts here.

2   A style class called *divStyle* is defined for the *div* element.

3   The *div* box will be absolutely positioned in terms of the browser window.

4   The dimensions of width and height of the *div* box are set. The border around the *div* container is a solid, dark blue border.

5   A style class called *paraStyle* is defined for the paragraph (*p*) element. The color of the text will be dark blue.

6   The position will be relative to the *div* box where the paragraph is contained. If *top* and *left* properties are not defined, the paragraph will be in the top, left corner of the box, position 0,0 relative to the *div* container where it is placed.

7   An inline style is set for the *div* element, placing the box 50 pixels from both the top and the left side of the browser window.

8   An inline style is set for the *p* element, placing the paragraph at a percentage of 15% from the left and 30% from the top based on the dimensions of the *div* box. See Figure 14.28.

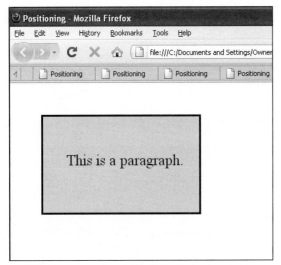

Figure 14.28 The paragraph is positioned relative to the *div* style.

14.10.5 The *z-index* and Three Dimensions

The last type of position sets the precedence of a stack of overlapping elements. The absolute position properties include three coordinates: x, y, and z, where x is the left side of an object, y is the right side, and z is the value of the stacking position. If you have three containers layered on top of each other, the z position of the bottom layer is 0; the next layer, 1; and the top layer in the stack is layer 2. In the next section, JavaScript will allow us to move these objects around, rearranging the stacking order dynamically, by manipulating the z-position.

EXAMPLE 14.26

```
    <html>
      <head><title>layers</title></head>
      <body bgcolor="lightgreen">
1        <span style="position: absolute; z-index:0;
             background-color: red; width: 200;height:250;
             top: 50px; left:160px;"></span>
2        <span style="position: absolute; z-index:1;
             background-color:yellow; width: 90;height:300;
             top: 20px; left:210px;"></span>
3        <span style="position: absolute; z-index:2;
             background-color: blue; width: 250;height:100;
             top: 125px; left:134px;"></span>
```

Continues

EXAMPLE   14.26 (CONTINUED)

```
4         <span style="position: absolute; z-index:3;
              background-color: white; width: 50;height:50;
              top: 140px; left:230px;"></span>
     </body>
</html>
```

EXPLANATION

1   A *span style* is used to create a red rectangle, size 200 pixels × 250 pixels, in the top, left corner of the screen. A *z-index* of 0 means that this rectangle will be the bottom layer in a stack.

2   A *span style* is used to create a yellow rectangle, size 90 pixels × 300 pixels, positioned above the red rectangle, *z-index* of 1, or on top of it in the stacking order.

3   A *span style* is used to create a blue rectangle, size 250 pixels × 100 pixels, positioned above the yellow rectangle, *z-index* of 2, or on top of it in the stacking order.

4   A *span style* is used to create a white square, size 50 pixels × 50 pixels, positioned above the blue rectangle, *z-index* of 3, or on top of it in the stacking order. See Figure 14.29.

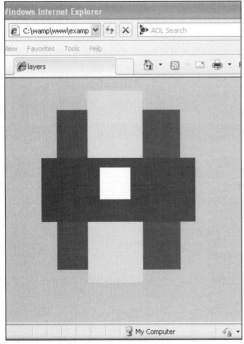

Figure 14.29   Using the z-index for overlapping elements.

14.11   Where Does JavaScript Fit In?

14.11.1   What Is DHTML?

DHTML stands for Dynamic HTML. It is not a programming language, but a technique used when HTML/XHTML, CSS, and JavaScript (and Ajax) work together to make up a dynamic interactive Web page. With CSS we were able to control the style (i.e., color, font, margins, etc.) of the HTML elements and store the style sheets in separate files. All by itself, CSS is presenting a style for your page, but now we need JavaScript to bring the Web page to life, to make it dynamic. Throughout this text we have been using event handlers and functions with JavaScript to create rollovers, slideshows, animation, submit forms, and so on. In the next chapter we discuss how to access every element on a Web page with the DOM. Then you can apply CSS styles and JavaScript to the DOM elements to create what will effectively make it possible to manipulate, create, and delete any part of your page on the fly.

14.11.2   How JavaScript Views Style Sheets

Sometimes a page consists of more that one style sheet. When the page is loaded, all external and embedded style sheets are stored in an array in the order in which they are placed within the document, just as are images, forms, and links. The array is called *styleSheets*, a property of the document object, so *document.styleSheets[0]* is the first style sheet, normally the general style sheet for the entire page. The next style sheet, maybe one that uses the *@import* rule, would be *document.styleSheets[1]*, and if you embedded another style within the document, that would be *document.styleSheets[2]*. Because each of the elements of the *styleSheets* array has a disabled property that can be turned on and off, you can dynamically toggle between styles, allowing a user to select a style suited to his or her own taste. It is also possible to access a specific rule within a style sheet by using the W3C *cssRules* array or the Microsoft *rules* array. Both arrays work with index numbers. The first rule is *cssRules[0]*, the second one *cssRulse[1]*, and so on. Example 14.27 contains two style sheets, one that is imported and one that is embedded. By using JavaScript the user can toggle between two styles. When reverting to the first style, one of the rules is changed; that is, the rule for the *h1* selector is changed to purple.

EXAMPLE 14.27

```
    <html>
      <head><title>Stylesheets</title>
        <style type="text/css">
1         @import url("pstyle.css");
        </style>
```

Continues

EXAMPLE 14.27 (CONTINUED)

```
          <script type="text/javascript">
2             function changeStyle(){
                  // alert(document.styleSheets.length);
3                 document.styleSheets[0].disabled=false;   // now visible
4                 document.styleSheets[1].disabled=true;
              }
5             function enableOldStyle(){
                  document.styleSheets[0].disabled=true;
6                 if(document.styleSheets[1].cssRules){   // W3C
                     document.styleSheets[1].cssRules[1].style.color="purple";
                  }
                  else{ //Microsoft Internet Explorer
7                    document.styleSheets[1].rules[1].style.color="purple";
                     document.styleSheets[1].disabled=false;
                  }
                  document.styleSheets[1].disabled=false; // now visible
              }
          </script>
8         <style type="text/css">
              p { background-color:darkblue;
                  font-weight:bold ;
                  font-size: 12pt;
                  font-family:arial;
                  color:yellow; }
              h1{color:red;}
          </style>
      </head>
      <body>
          <h1>Hello</h1>
9         <form>
              <input type="radio"
                  onclick="JavaScript:changeStyle()">new style<br />
              <input type="radio"
                  onclick="JavaScript:enableOldStyle()">old style<br />
          </form>
          <p>
10        This is the changing style sheet. Notice when we click on
          the radio button,how the style for the whole page changes.
          That's because we disabled one stylesheet and replaced it
          with another.
          </p>
          <h1>Goodbye</h1>
      </body>
  </html>
```

EXPLANATION

1   The first style sheet is imported. This will be *styleSheets[0]* in the JavaScript array. The second style sheet is defined on line 8.

2   This user-defined function will be called when the user clicks the first radio button.

3   By setting the *disabled* property of the *styleSheet* object to *false*, *styleSheets[0]* will become visible. In this example the style for the whole page will be changed according to the rules in the first style sheet that was imported.

4   Setting the second style sheet, *styleSheets[1]* to *true*, makes this style sheet invisible.

5   This function sets *styleSheets[1]* to *false*, making it visible. This style is defined on line 8.

6   The *cssRules[]* array contains all the rules set for the style sheet. In the style sheet defined on line 8, the second rule, *cssRules[1]*, defines a rule for an *h1* element. For this rule, the rule is changed to a different color using the document's *styleSheet* array and the *cssRules* array with the *style* property, and the color is reset to purple.

7   To change the rule of a style sheet with Microsoft, use the *rules[]* array as shown here.

8   This is an embedded style sheet that styles the *p* and *h1* selectors.

9   The form gives the user two radio buttons, one to make the first style visible, and one to make the second style visible and change one of the rules.

10 This is the paragraph that will be given a new style if the "change style" option in the radio button is selected by the user. See Figures 14.30, 14.31, and 14.32.

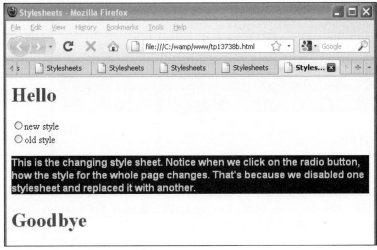

Figure 14.30   The page as it first appears.

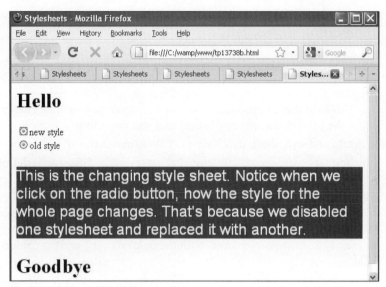

Figure 14.31   After the user clicks the "new style" radio button, a new style is made visible.

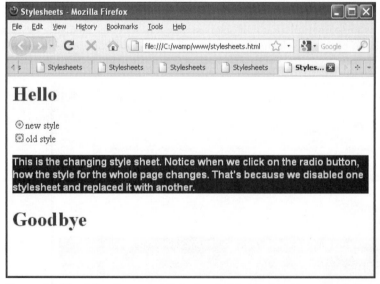

Figure 14.32   After the user clicks the "old style" button, the first stylesheet becomes visible. H1 text is now purple.

14.11.3 The *style* Object

The style object contains a set of properties corresponding to the CSS attributes supported by your browser. Each HTML object has a *style* property used to access the CSS style attributes assigned to it; for example, an *h1* element might have been defined with a CSS *font-style*, *color*, and *padding*. The *style* object has properties to reflect each of the CSS attributes. See Table 14.13.

Many of the CSS style attributes, such as *background-color*, *font-size*, and *word-spacing*, contain hyphens in their names. Like all objects we have seen in JavaScript, there is a convention for spelling the name of the object. The name would not contain a hyphen, and multiple words after the first word are usually capitalized. Therefore, the CSS naming convention is different with the properties of the *style* object. The hyphen is removed and the first letter of each word after the hyphen is capitalized. For example, the CSS attribute, *background-color*, when used as a style property, is spelled *backgroundColor*, *font-size* is *fontSize*, and *border-right-width* is *borderRightWidth*.

FORMAT

```
elementname.style.property="value";
```

EXAMPLE

```
div2.style.fontFamily = "arial";
```

Table 14.13 *style* Object Properties

Property	Example CSS Value	HTML Tags Affected
Fonts		
font	12pt/14pt sans-serif, 80% sans-serif, x-large/110% arial, normal small-caps	All
fontFamily	serif, sans-serif, cursive, fantasy, monospace	All
fontSize	12pt, larger, 150%, 1.5em	All
fontStyle	normal, italic, oblique	All
fontVariant	normal, small-caps	All
fontWeight	normal, bold, bolder, lighter, 100, 200...900	All

Continues

Table 14.13 *style* Object Properties (continued)

Property	Example CSS Value	HTML Tags Affected
Colors		
backgroundColor	red, blue, #F00	All
color	red, green, #F00, rgb(255,0,0)	All
Images		
backgroundAttachment	scroll, fixed	All
backgroundImage	URL (bay.gif), none	All
backgroundPosition	right top, top center, center, bottom, 100% 100%, 0% 0%, 50% 50%	Block-level and replaced elements
backgroundRepeat	repeat, repeat-x (horizontally), repeat-y (vertically), no-repeat	All
Text Alignment		
letterSpacing	normal, 0.1em	All
lineHeight	normal, 1.2, 1.2em, 120%	All
textAlign	left, right, center, justify	All
textDecoration	underline, overline, line-through, blink	All
textIndent	3em, 15%	Block-level elements
textTransform	capitalize, uppercase, lowercase, none	All
verticalAlign	baseline, sub, super, top, text-top, middle, bottom, text-bottom, 50%	Inline elements
wordSpacing	normal, 2em	All
Margins and Borders		
align		All
borderStyle	none, solid, 3D	All
borderWidth	thin, medium, thick, 2em	All
margin	5em, 3em, 2em, 1em (top, right, bottom, left)	All
marginBottom	100px, 50%	All
marginLeft	.5in, 40%	All

Table 14.13 *style* Object Properties (continued)

Property	Example CSS Value	HTML Tags Affected
Margins and Borders (*Continued*)		
marginRight	20em, 45%	All
marginTop	1cm, 20%	All
padding	2em, 4em, 6em (right, bottom, left)	All
paddingBottom	2em, 20%	All
paddingLeft	.25in, 20%	All
paddingRight	.5cm, 35%	All
paddingTop	20px, 10%	All
length		Block-level elements
width	12em, 30%, auto (initial width value)	Block-level element

For a complete list of properties, see *http://www.w3.org/TR/REC-CSS2/propidx.html*.

EXAMPLE 14.28

```
    <html>
     <head><title>Changing Background Color Dynamically</title>
1      <script type="text/javascript">
2       function bodyColor(){
3         var i = document.form1.body.selectedIndex;
4         bodycolor = document.form1.body.options[i].value;
5         document.getElementById("bdy").style.backgroundColor=
                                                       bodycolor;
        }
     </script>
    </head>
6   <body id="bdy">
     <p>
       Pick a background color for this page.
     </p>
7   <form name="form1">
      <b> Color </b>
8     <select name="body" onChange="bodyColor();">
        <option value="pink">pink</option>
        <option value="lightblue">blue</option>
```

Continues

EXAMPLE   14.28 (CONTINUED)

```
                <option value="yellow">yellow</option>
                <option value="lightgreen">green</option>
            </select>
            <br />
        </form>
        <p>
            This is a test.
        </p>
    </body>
</html>
```

EXPLANATION

1   The JavaScript program starts here.

2   A JavaScript user-defined function called *bodyColor()* is defined.

3   The number, *selectedIndex*, of the option chosen from a select list is assigned to variable *i*.

4   The value of the selected option is one of the colors listed in the select list on line 8.

5   The *getElementById()* method returns a reference to the *body* tag, whose *id* is *bdy*. By using the *style* property with the reference to the body, the background color of the document is changed with this statement.

6   The *body* tag is given an *id* attribute by which to identify it.

7   An HTML form called *form1* starts here.

8   A select menu is defined to give the user options to change the background color of the document on the fly. The *onChange* event is triggered when one of the options is selected, and is handled by invoking the function *bodyColor()*. The output is shown in Figure 14.33.

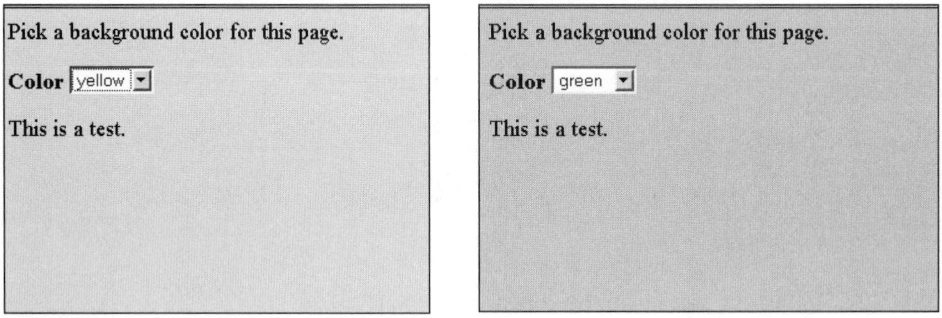

Pick a background color for this page.

Color yellow ▾

This is a test.

Pick a background color for this page.

Color green ▾

This is a test.

Figure 14.33   Changing the background color dynamically (left); now the color is green (right).

EXAMPLE 14.29

```
<html>
  <head><title>The onload() method</title>
    <script type="text/javascript">
1     window.onload=setBorder;
2     function setBorder(){
3       document.getElementById("bdy").style.border=
                                              "2px solid blue";
      }
4     /* window.onload=function(){    // Anonymous function
           document.getElementById("bdy").style.backgroundColor=
                                              "lightgreen";
         }
      */
5     function getToday(){
        var d=new Date();
        var weekday=new Array(7);
        weekday[0]="Sunday";
        weekday[1]="Monday";
        weekday[2]="Tuesday";
        weekday[3]="Wednesday";
        weekday[4]="Thursday";
        weekday[5]="Friday";
        weekday[6]="Saturday";
        return (weekday[d.getDay()]);
      }
    </script>
  </head>
6 <body id="bdy">
    <div align="center">
      <script type="text/javascript">
7       document.write("<h1>Today it is " + getToday() +"!</h1>");
      </script>
    </div>
  </body>
</html>
```

EXPLANATION

1   When the page has completely loaded, JavaScript will execute the user-defined function called *setBorder*. Notice that there are no parentheses or quotes when *setBorder* is assigned to the event handler. That is because *setBorder* is being assigned as a reference to the function defined on line 2.

2   The function *setBorder()* will be called when the onload event is fired on line 1.

3   The purpose of this function is to use the *getElementById()* method to retrieve a reference to the body of the document and with the reference create a solid blue border in the body of the document.

Continues

EXPLANATION(CONTINUED)

4   This is another way to use the *onload* property to call a function. An anonymous function is assigned to onload and will be called after the page has loaded and the *onload* event has been fired.

5   The user-defined function *getToday()* returns the current day of the week.

6   This is the HTML body tag with the *id* attribute. The *id* will be used on line 2 with the *getElementById()* method to get a reference to this body element.

7   You can see in the display (see Figure 14.34) that the blue border was created for the document once the page was loaded.

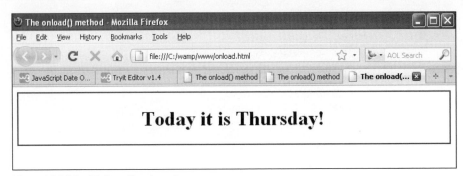

Figure 14.34   Styling the border.

Positioning Text with the *style* Property.   By assigning a position to the *style* property it is possible to place an element in different sections of the page. In Example 14.30, by assigning positions, the text is moved after the document has been loaded.

EXAMPLE 14.30

```
     <html>
        <head><title>Positioning</title>
          <style type="text/css">
             body { background-color: aliceblue;}
             div {   font-size:larger;
                    color: white;
                    border: solid;
                    border-color:aqua;
                 }
 1           .pos1 {position:absolute; top:50px;left:10px;
                    background-color:blue;
                 }
```

EXAMPLE   14.30 (CONTINUED)

```
        .pos2 {position:absolute; top:100px;left:10px;
                background-color:teal;
        }
        .pos3 {position:absolute; top:150px;left:10px;
                background-color:darkblue;
        }
    </style>
    <script type="text/javascript">
2       var div1,div2,div3;
3       window.onload=function(){
4           div1=document.getElementById("first");
            div2=document.getElementById("second");
            div3=document.getElementById("third");
        }
5       function startPosition(){
            div1.style.top = 50;
            div1.style.left=10;
            div2.style.top = 100;
            div2.style.left=10;
            div3.style.top = 150;
            div3.style.left=10;
        }
6       function movePosition(){
7           div1.style.left = 50;
            div1.style.top = 150;
8           div2.style.left = 100;
            div2.style.top = 100;
9           div3.style.left = 150;
            div3.style.top = 50;
        }
    </script>
    </head>
    <body>
10      <div id="first"   class="pos1">one</div>
        <div id="second" class="pos2">two</div>
        <div id="third"   class="pos3">three</div>
        <form>
11          <input type="button" value="move text"
                    onClick="movePosition()">
            <input type="button" value="put it back"
                    onClick="startPosition()">
        </form>
    </body>
    </html>
```

EXPLANATION

1   The CSS style sheet creates classes that will be used to position the first three *div* elements.

2   These variables will be used by the functions in the JavaScript code.

3   After the document has been loaded, the window's *onload* event will be triggered and the anonymous function called.

4   The *getElementById()* method returns references to three *div* block objects.

5   A function called *startPosition()* is defined. It will put the *div* elements back in their original positions after they have been moved.

6   A function called *movePosition()* is defined. It is responsible for moving the text to different positions on the screen.

7   The first block of text will be positioned at 50 pixels from the left side of the screen and 150 pixels from the top.

8   The second block of text will be positioned at 100 pixels from the left side of the screen and 100 pixels from the top.

9   The third block of text will be positioned 150 pixels from the left side of the screen and 50 pixels from the top.

10 The *div* containers are given an *id* and a class that will assign absolute positions on the page. Each *div* block will contain a string of text.

11 When the user clicks the button labeled "move text", the *onClick* event will be triggered, causing the text to be moved to a different location on the page. See Figure 14.35.

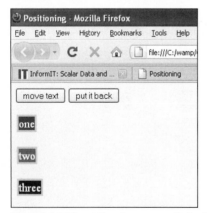
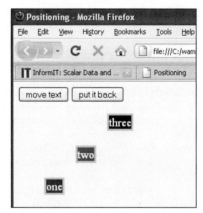

Figure 14.35   After the user clicks the "move text" button, the *div* containers are moved.

Revisiting the *z-index* and Dynamic Positioning.   On page 583 of this chapter, the *zIndex* property was described to create a three-dimensional effect with a stack of <div> containers. In Example 14.31 a JavaScript program manipulates the containers so that they can be moved into different positions.

EXAMPLE 14.31

```
      <html>
        <head><title>layers</title>
          <script type="text/javascript">
1             function moveUp(id){
2                 var box= document.getElementById(id);
3                 if(box.style.zIndex == 100){ //Can't stack higher than 100
4                    box.style.zIndex=2;
                  }
5                 else if(box.style.zIndex != 3){
                     box.style.zIndex=100;
                  }
                  else{
6                    box.style.zIndex=0;
                  }
              }
          </script>
        </head>
        <body bgcolor=lightgreen>
7         <span id="red" style="position: absolute;z-index:0;
                background-color:red; width:200; height:250;
                top:50px; left:160px;"
8             onClick="moveUp(id);"></span>

9         <span id="yellow" style="position: absolute;z-index:1;
                background-color:yellow; width:90; height:300;
                top:20px; left:210px;"
              onClick="moveUp(id);"></span>

10        <span id="blue" style="position: absolute;z-index:2;
                background-color:blue; width:250; height:100;
                top:125px; left:134px;"
              onClick="moveUp(id);"></span>

11        <span id="white" style="position: absolute;z-index:3;
                background-color:white; width:50; height:50;
                top:140px; left:230px;"
              onClick="moveUp(id);"></span>

        </body>
      </html>
```

EXPLANATION

1   The JavaScript user-defined function called *moveUp()* is defined. It has one pa-
    rameter, the *id* of the tag from where it was called.

2   The *getElementById()* method returns a reference to the object that called this
    function and assigns it to the variable called *box*.

Continues

EXPLANATION

3   If the *zIndex* of the object evaluates to 100, it must be at the top of the stack, because that is as high as the stack gets.

4   This sets the stack level of the *zIndex* to 2, causing it to move toward the bottom of the stack.

5   If the *zIndex* for the object is not 3, it is not at the top. Its *zIndex* will be set to 100, moving it to the top of the stack.

6   The object is moved to the bottom of the stack with a *zIndex* of 0.

7   The *<span>* tag is used to create a rectangular red box on the screen. With a *zIndex* of 0, it will be positioned at the bottom of the stack.

8   When the user clicks the button, the *onClick* event is triggered, and the handler function, *moveUp(id)*, is called.

9   A yellow rectangular box is created with the *<span>* tag. With a *zIndex* of 1, it will be positioned above the last block in the stack.

10   A blue square box is created with the *<span>* tag. With a *zIndex* of 2, it will be positioned above the last block in the stack.

11   A small white rectangular box is created with the *<span>* tag. With a *zIndex* of 3, it will be positioned at the top of the stack. See Figure 14.36.

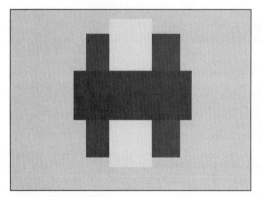 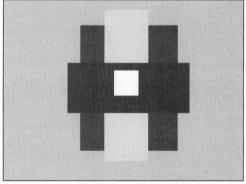

Figure 14.36 The original configuration of the four rectangles (left); after manipulating the rectangles by reassigning the *z-index* (right).

14.11.4   The *className* Property

The *className* property is used to reference a CSS class. The *className* property is defined for all HTML elements. With the *className* property, you can change an element dynamically by assigning it the name of a class defined in a CSS. Example 14.32 contains a CSS with three classes.

EXAMPLE 14.32

```
      <html>
        <head><title>Coloring Text</title>
          <style type="text/css">
            body { background-color: yellow;
                   font-size: 22pt;
                   font-weight: bold;
            }
1         .red { color:rgb(255,0,0);    /* Defining classes */
                   font-style: verdana;
                   font-size: 32;
            }
2         .blue { color:blue;
                   font-style: verdana;
                   font-size: 36;
            }
3         .green { color: green;
                   font-style: verdana;
                   font-size: 40;
            }
          </style>
          <script type="text/javascript">
4         window.onload=init;
          function init(){
              div1=document.getElementById("first");
              div2=document.getElementById("second");
              div3=document.getElementById("third");
          }
5         function colorText(){
              div1.style.left = 50;
              div1.style.top = 50;
6             div1.className="red";
              div2.style.left = 100;
              div2.style.top = 100;
7             div2.className="blue";
              div3.style.left = 150;
              div3.style.top = 150;
8             div3.className="green";
          }
          </script>
        </head>
        <body>
9         <div id="first"  style="position:absolute; top:50px">It's a
          one,</div>
          <div id="second"  style="position:absolute; top:100px">and a
          two,</div>
```

Continues

EXAMPLE 14.32 (CONTINUED)

```
            <div id="third"  style="position:absolute; top:150px">and
               three!</div>
            <form>
               <input type="button" value="move and color text"
10                 onClick="colorText()">
            </form>
         </body>
      </html>
```

EXPLANATION

1   A CSS class for a style is defined. Text will be a red, Verdana font, point size 32. The rgb (red, green, blue) color is used here for demonstration. It would be easier to just assign *red* to the *color* property.

2   A CSS class for another style is defined. The text will be a blue, Verdana font, point size 36.

3   A CSS class for a third style is defined. The text will be a green, Verdana font, point size 40. Notice that each class not only changes the color of the font, but increases its point size.

4   When the *onload* event handler is triggered, just after the document has been loaded, the user-defined *init()* function is called. The *getElementById()* method returns references to three *div* objects.

5   A function called *colorText()* is defined. It sets the position of the *div* containers and defines the color for the text in each container.

6   The *className* property is used to reference the CSS class named *red*, defined in the document.

7   The *className* property is used to reference the CSS class named *blue*, defined in the document.

8   The *className* property is used to reference the CSS class named *green*, defined in the document.

9   The positions for each of the *div* containers are defined.

10 When the user clicks this button, the *onClick* event is triggered. It invokes the *colorText()* function, which will move and change the text in each of the *div* containers. The output is displayed in Figures 14.37 and 14.38.

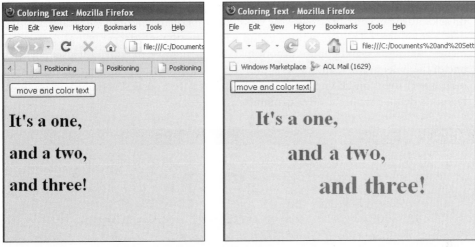

Figure 14.37   The initial appearance of the document (left); after clicking the button, the color, position, and size of the text is changed (right).

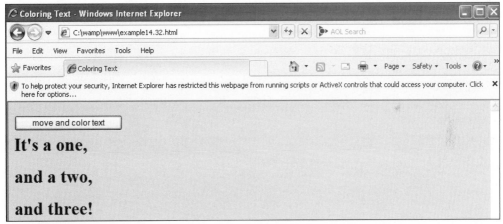

Figure 14.38   If text will not move in Internet Explorer and you see the security warning, click the *x* and turn it off.

14.11.5   Drop-Down Menus and Tooltips

Drop-down menus are commonly used in Web pages to create submenus that appear and then disappear when no longer needed. A tooltip is a small box of text that appears near an object when the mouse moves over the object. The text in the box (which can also contain an image) usually contains a brief text message pertaining to the object. Both drop-down menus and tooltips use the *visibility* property to bring the object into view and then make it disappear depending on a user-initiated event.

The *visibility* Property.   The *visibility* property lets you hide an object and then bring it back into view. You can also use the visibility property to determine the state: Is it "visible" or "hidden"? This property is useful when creating interfaces such as drop-down menus, slideshows, and popups or tooltips.[4] In Example 14.34, when the user clicks on one of the links in the main menu, a drop-down menu will appear. If the user rolls the mouse over the drop-down menu, it will be hidden from view. Each of the drop-down menus is defined within a *<div>* container.

EXAMPLE 14.33

```
     /* this style sheet is in a file called dropdown.css */
1    a {  font-family: verdana, arial;
          text-decoration: none;
          font-weight: bold;
          margin-left: 4px; } /*link style for main menu*/
     .linkstyle { color: #f33;}

2    #menu, .menu { font-stye: verdana;
                    font-size:10pt;
                    color:black; }
                    /* link style for drop-down menu */
3    #menu { position:absolute;
             text-decoration:underline;
             top:40px;
             border-style:solid;
             border-width:1px;
             padding: 5px;
             background-color:yellow;
             width:75px;
             color: black;
             font-size: 12pt;
4            visibility:hidden; }
5    #menu2 { position:absolute;
              text-decoration:underline;
              top:40px;
              left:3.2cm;
              border-style:solid;
              border-width:1px;
              padding: 5px;
              background-color:orange;
              width:80px;
              color: black;
              font-size: 12pt;
              visibility:hidden;
     }
```

---

4. The *visibility* property applies to an entire object. The *clip* property allows you to designate how much of an element will be visible.

EXAMPLE 14.33 (CONTINUED)

```
6        #menu3 { position:absolute;
                  text-decoration:underline;
                  top:40px;
                  left:6.2cm;
                  border-style:solid;
                  border-width:1px;
                  padding: 5px;
                  background-color:pink;
                  width:80px;
                  color: black;
                  font-size: 12pt;
                  visibility:hidden;}
7        /* End of style sheet */
```

EXAMPLE 14.34

```
     <html>
       <head><title>Drop-Down Menu</title>
         <link rel="stylesheet" href="dropdown.css"type="text/css"/>
         <script type="text/javascript">
8          function showMenu(id){
9            var ref = document.getElementById(id);
10           ref.style.visibility = "visible";   // Make the drop-down
                                                  // menu visible
           }
11         function hideMenu(id){
12           var ref = document.getElementById(id);
13           ref.style.visibility = "hidden"; //Hide the drop-down menu
           }
         </script>
       </head>
       <body bgColor="lightblue">
14       <table width="350" border="2" bgcolor="lightgreen"
                cellspacing="1" cellpadding="2">
           <tr>
15           <td width="100">
16             <div id="menu" onClick="hideMenu('menu');">
                 <a class="menu" href="#">US</a><br />
                 <a class="menu" href="#">World</a><br />
                 <a class="menu" href="#">Local </a><br />
               </div>
17             <a href="#" onMouseOver="showMenu('menu');">News</a>
             </td>
```

Continues

EXAMPLE 14.34 (CONTINUED)

```
                 <td width="100">
                     <div id="menu2" onClick="hideMenu('menu2');">
                         <a class="menu" href="#">Basketball</a><br />
                         <a class="menu" href="#">Football</a><br />
                         <a class="menu" href="#>">Soccer</a><br />
                     </div>
18                   <a href="#" onMouseOver="showMenu('menu2');">Sports</a>
                 </td>
                 <td width="100">
                     <div id="menu3" onClick="hideMenu('menu3');">
                         <a class="menu"
                             href="http://www.imdb.com/">Movies</a><br />
                         <a class="menu" href="#">Plays</a><br />
                         <a class="menu" href="#>">DVD's</a><br />
                     </div>
19                   <a href="#"
                         onMouseOver="showMenu('menu3');">Entertainment</a>
                 </td>
20           </tr>
         </table>
     </body>
 </html>
```

EXPLANATION

1 The *a* selector is followed by the style definition for the links that appear in the main menu.

2 An ID selector and a class are defined. This style will be used on links in the drop-down menus.

3 This ID selector defines the style of the first drop-down menu. When the user clicks the News link, this yellow drop-down menu will appear directly under the table cell containing the News link.

4 Initially, the first drop-down menu is *hidden* from view.

5 This ID selector defines the style of the second drop-down menu. It will be orange and drop down directly under the Sports link.

6 This ID selector defines the style of the third drop-down menu. It will be pink and drop down directly under the Entertainment link.

7 The CSS ends here, and the JavaScript program begins on the next line.

8 A function called *showMenu* is defined. Its only parameter is the *id* attribute of a *div* object, that is, the ID of one of the three drop-down menus.

EXPLANATION (CONTINUED)

9   The *getElementById()* method returns a reference to the *div* object that contains the drop-down menu.

10   The *visibility* property is set to *visible*. The drop-down object comes into view, right below the main menu item where the user clicked the link.

11   A function called *hideMenu()* is defined. Its only parameter is the *id* attribute of a *div* object. When this function is invoked, the drop-down menu being referenced will be *hidden* from view.

12   The *getElementById()* method returns a reference to the *div* object that contains the drop-down menu.

13   The *visibility* property is set to *hidden*. The object being referenced disappears from view.

14   An HTML table is defined. It will be light green, 350 pixels wide, and contain one row and three data cells.

15   The first cell of the table contains a *<div>* container that is positioned and styled by the CSS *#menu* ID selector. If the user clicks from within this tag, it will be hidden from view. If he or she clicks a link in the drop-down menu, the user will be directed to a Web site.

16   The links within the *<div>* container are described by the CSS *.menu* class. The links are deactivated for this example.

17   When the user rolls the mouse onto this link called News, the *onMouseOver* event will be triggered. A function called *showMenu* will be invoked, causing the drop-down menu to appear.

18   The second drop-down menu is created and will be made visible when the user rolls the mouse over the Sports link.

19   Like the other two links, the Entertainment link also has a drop-down menu associated with it, which will be made visible when the user rolls the mouse over it, and made invisible when the user clicks on the drop-down list.

20   The table row and table are closed. See Figure 14.39.

Figure 14.39   A drop-down menu controlled by mouse actions.

Tooltips.   The following example uses the visibility property to hide the text in the tooltip until the user rolls the mouse over the image.

EXAMPLE 14.35

```
      <html>
        <head><title>A tool tip</title>
          <style type="text/css">
            body { background-color:black;}
1         #divclass { font-size:12pt;
                      font-family: arial;
                      font-weight: bold;
                      background-color:aqua;
                      border:thin solid;
                      width: 210px;
                      height:40px;
2                     visibility: hidden; /* Can't see the container */
                      position:absolute;
                      top: 50px;
                      left: 175px;
3                     z-index: 1; /* Put the div container on top */
            }
```

EXAMPLE 14.35 (CONTINUED)

```
4          a { font-family: cursive;
               font-size: 18pt;
               font-weight: bold;
               color:white;
               position: absolute;
               left: 60px;
           }
5          img { position:absolute; top: 50px; z-index:0; }
        </style>
        <script type = "text/javascript">
           var div1;
6          function init(){
              div1=document.getElementById("divclass");
           }
7          function showHideTip(e) {
8             if(e.type == "mouseover"){
                 div1.style.visibility="visible";
              }
9             else if(e.type == "mouseout"){
                 div1.style.visibility="hidden";
              }
           }
        </script>
     </head>

10   <body onLoad="init();">
11      <a href="http://www.servant.xxx"
12         onMouseover="showHideTip(event);"
13         onMouseout="showHideTip(event);"
           >At Your Service!
        </a>
        <br />
14      <img src="waiter.gif">
15      <div id="divclass">Always tip me at least 20%!</div>
     </body>
  </html>
```

EXPLANATION

1   A CSS style is defined for the ID selector, *#divclass* to create a tooltip.

2   The *visibility* property for this style is set to *hidden*; it will not be seen.

3   The *z-index* property is set to 1, putting it above the image that is set to *z-index* 0. Remember, the higher the *z-index* number, the higher the element is placed on the stack.

4   The style for a link is defined.

5   A style for positioning an image is defined. Its *z-index* is 0, placing it below any other elements.

Continues

EXPLANATION(CONTINUED)

6   The *init()* function is defined to get the ID of a *div* element. In this example, this will be the ID for the tooltip.

7   The *showHideTip()* function is defined. It takes one parameter, a reference to an event object. It contains information about the event that caused this function to be called.

8   If the event was caused by the mouse going over the link, a *mouseOver* event, then the tooltip will be made visible.

9   If the event was caused by the mouse moving away from the link, a *mouseOut* event, then the tooltip will be hidden from view.

10   As soon as the document has finished loading, the *onLoad* event is triggered, and the *init()* function invoked.

11   This is the link that displays as "At Your Service!". Rolling the mouse over it will cause the tooltip to appear.

12   The *onMouseOver* event is triggered when the user puts the mouse on the link. The tooltip will be shown.

13   When the user moves the mouse away from the link, the tooltip disappears.

14   The image for the waiter is below the tooltip, because its *z-index* is 0, whereas the tooltip's *z-index* is 1.

15   The *<div>* container is used to hold the tooltip text and style defined by the CSS ID selector called *divclass*. The output is shown in Figure 14.40.

Figure 14.40   Before the mouse moves over the link (left), and after (right) when tooltip appears.

14.12 **What You Should Know**

Adding a touch of style to your site, such as colors, fonts, borders, and so on, is what CSS is all about. This chapter was designed to introduce the way style sheets work, how to define different styles for HTML elements, and how to store these styles in a file so that they can be applied to all the pages in a Web site at once. JavaScript enters the picture to allow for dynamic enhancement of pages, changing styles on the fly based on some user interaction. In the next chapter, we will use the W3C DOM to access every element in a page. With CSS, JavaScript, and the DOM, all of these technologies will be used together to create DHTML. By now you should know:

1. What cascading means to a style.
2. What a CSS-enhanced browser means.
3. The meaning of a selector and a declaration block.
4. How to group selectors.
5. The syntax for style sheet properties.
6. What units of measurement can be used for fonts and margins.
7. How colors are represented.
8. How to designate one or more fonts.
9. How to align text.
10. What kinds of text decorations are available.
11. How to create a repeating background image.
12. Types of containers and how to set borders and padding.
13. Three types of style sheets.
14. How to use the style attribute.
15. How to store CSS styles in an external file.
16. How to create a class.
17. How to create an *id* selector.
18. How to override a style.
19. The difference between absolute and relative positioning.
20. What *z-index* is.
21. What DHTML is.
22. How style sheets are stored in JavaScript.
23. How the style object is used.
24. How to use the *className* property.
25. How to create a tooltip.
26. How to create a drop-down menu.

Exercises

1. Create a CSS style sheet that makes all *h1* elements italic and blue.

2. Define a class called *title* that can be used on an element to make the font Arial, extra large, and bold.

3. Create a style for a paragraph with a unique ID that will define a style for a font family, font size, and font color.

4. Create a style that will affect all the cells in an HTML table.

5. Create a style that be used with a *<div>* tag to produce a light green box, positioned in the left corner of the screen, with a solid, dark green border. The *<div>* container will contain a paragraph of italic text.

6. Create a colored *div*. Each time the user clicks the *div* it will grow longer by 10 pixels.

7. Create two paragraphs in a *div* container. When the user clicks the *div*, change the background color of the *div* with JavaScript.

8. Create an animation of a stick man running. You will need to draw several stick men of the same size in different running positions. Your program will give the illusion of the stick man running.

9. Find a picture of a ghost. When the user rolls the mouse over the ghost, make it invisible. When the user moves it back, the ghost will reappear.

10. Find an image of our planetary system. Create an image map. When the user rolls the mouse over a planet, a tooltip will appear with the name of the planet and a brief description of it.

11. Use CSS to create a page consisting of *div* containers: one for a header at the top of the page, another with a navigation bar at the left side of the page, the body content, and a footer at the bottom of the page.

chapter

15

The W3C DOM and JavaScript

15.1 The W3C DOM

The W3C DOM provides JavaScript applications a standard way to access all the elements of the document. Although the DOM was designed to help developers navigate an XML document, HTML documents can be navigated in the same way. For JavaScript to change the style of a document dynamically, the HTML elements must be represented as objects. We have already discussed the way JavaScript views the hierarchical tree-like structure of the document object model (DOM Level 0) in Chapter 11, "Working with Forms and Input Devices." The W3C DOM, starting with DOM 1, expanded the DOM to include every XML/HTML element of the page. With this DOM (see Figure 15.1), all HTML elements, attributes, and text become objects and the DOM provides methods and properties allowing not only access to all these objects, but the ability to use CSS to style them on the fly. With the W3C DOM, a Web page can be restructured by creating, adding, modifying, and deleting any item on the page. An excellent source describing the DOM objects and methods is *http://www.howtocreate.co.uk/tutorials/JavaScript/domstructure*.

Today the term unobtrusive JavaScript shows up in tutorials, blogs, books, and discussion groups when discussing Web development techniques. The goal is to completely, if possible, separate JavaScript code from the other two layers of a Web page by putting all the JavaScript functionality in separate .js files independent of the markup and CSS. This allows the programmer to make updates in one place, and to avoid interfering with those using unsupported browsers or those who have disabled JavaScript. The DOM Level 1 provided a way to do this by turning every element of a Web page into an object.

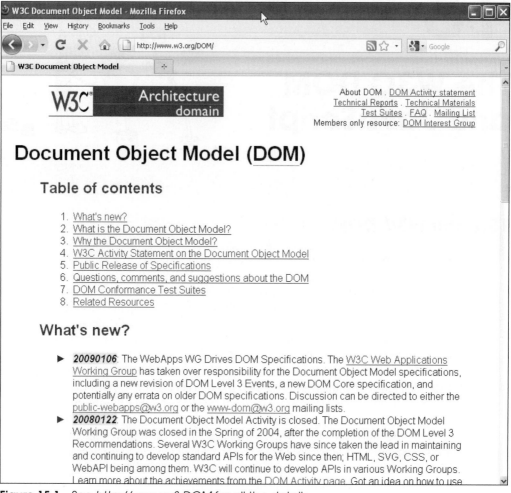

Figure 15.1   See *http://www.w3.DOM* for all the details.

15.2 How the DOM Works with Nodes

Just as we used the DOM to access forms, images, links, and events as objects, we can use the DOM to access every element in an HTML document. The standard W3C DOM currently consists of three parts: the DOM core, the XML DOM, and the HTML DOM (see *http://www.w3.org/TR/REC-DOM-Level-1/introduction.html*). The DOM core specifies a standard way to manipulate document structures, elements, and attributes; the DOM XML and HTML just extends that functionality to XML and HTML, respectively. In this chapter we discuss the HTML DOM.

Recall that the DOM represented an HTML document as a tree: With the DOM, every HTML element can be defined as part of the tree, as shown in Figure 15.2.

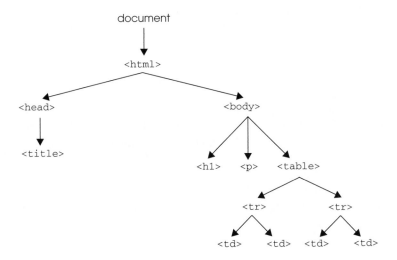

Figure 15.2 An HTML document as a tree.

The purpose of the hierarchal tree is to provide a logical structure to represent a document and a way to navigate that structure, and to add, modify, or delete elements and content from it. Starting with the document at the top of the tree, called the *root*, you can traverse down the tree to every element until you reach the element, attribute, or text you are seeking. The core DOM identifies each element in the tree as a **node** object. There are parent and child nodes, sibling nodes, and more (see Table 15.1).

Table 15.1 Some DOM Objects

Object	Definition
Node	The primary data type that represents an HTML element.
Document	The root of the document tree.
Element	An element within an HTML document.
Attribute	Attributes of an HTML tag.
Text	The text between markup tags, such as the text between *<h1>* and *</h1>*.

15.3 Nodes

Every time you load an HTML page, the Web browser generates an internal representation of the page as an upside-down tree structure. The DOM views the trees as a set of nodes where every HTML element shown in Figure 15.3 is a node. In the tree, the top node is the *<html>* tag, called the **root node** of the document. Below it are the *<head>* and *<body>* tags, which are called **child nodes** of the HTML element. In the *<title>* is the text *My Title,* which is also a node, called a **text node**. Because it is the last node, the tree-like structure terminates at that node, also called a **leaf node**. The nodes are divided into three types of nodes: the **element node**, **attribute node**, and the **text node**. These types are numbered 1, 2, and 3, for element, attribute, and text node, respectively. In the example, the *<p> and <h1>* tags are element nodes, *title="para1"* is an attribute node, and the text between the *<title>* tags, *My Title,* is an example of a text node. An attribute node is represented as a property of the HTML element to which it is assigned; for example, the *<a>* tag has an *href* attribute. In the example, *<a href="http://www.prenhall.com">, a* is an element node, *href* is an attribute node and the URL is called its *nodeValue.* (The text nodes are not supported on all browsers.)

Refer to Tables 15.2 and 15.3 for a list of node properties and node methods.

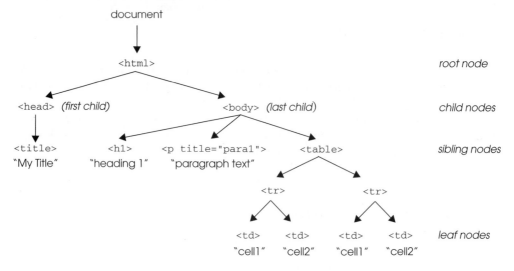

Figure 15.3 A tree of nodes.

Table 15.2 Node Properties

Property	What It Does
firstChild	Returns the first child node of an element.
lastChild	Returns the last child node of an element.
nextSibling	Returns the next child node of an element at the same level as the current child node.

Table 15.2 Node Properties (continued)

Property	What It Does
nodeName	Returns the name of the node.
nodeType	Returns the type of the node as a number: 1 for element, 2 for attribute, 3 for text.
nodeValue	Sets the value of the node in plain text.
ownerDocument	Returns the root node of the document that contains the node.
parentNode	Returns the element that contains the current node.
previousSibling	Returns the previous child node of an element at the same level as the current child node.

Table 15.3 Node Methods

Method	What It Does
appendChild(new node)	Appends a new node onto the end of the list of child nodes.
cloneNode(child option)	Makes a clone of a node.
hasChildNodes()	Returns *true* if the node has children.
insertBefore(new node, current node)	Inserts a new node in the list of children.
removeChild(child node)	Removes a child node from a list of children.
replaceChild(new child, old child)	Replaces an old child node with a new one.

15.3.1 Parents and Children

When looking at the structure of the tree hierarchy, some nodes are above others. A node above another node is a parent node, and the ones below the parent node are its children. See Figure 15.4. Any HTML tags that have both an opening and a closing tag are always parent nodes, for example, *<p>* and *</p>*.

Attributes of an element are considered to be separate nodes in their own right. For example, the *href* attribute of the *<a>* tag is an attribute node, not a child of the *<a>* tag, and the *title* attribute of the *<p>* tag is also an attribute node. The other type of node is a text node, which represents the text of an element or an attribute, such as *<a href="http//w3schools.com"*>, where the quoted string of text (URL) is a text node.

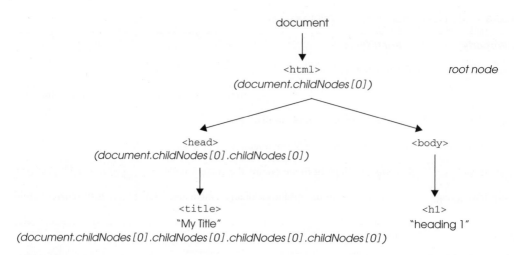

Figure 15.4   Tree hierarchy of nodes.

15.3.2   Siblings

A sibling, like a brother or sister, is a node on the same level as another node. In the example,

```
<p>
  <em>this is </em>some <b>text</b>
</p>
```

the parent node is *<p>* and has two children, the *<em>* node and the *<b>* node. Because the *<em>* and *<b>* tags are at the same level within the text, they are called siblings, brother or sister nodes.

15.3.3   The *nodeName* and *nodeType* Properties

When walking down the DOM tree, you can find out the name of a node and the type of the node with the *nodeName* and *nodeType* properties. Table 15.4 gives the value for each of the properties. Dealing with all these nodes can be confusing to say the least, so the DOM provides methods for quick retrieval of elements: *getElementById()* and *getElementsByTag Name()*, discussed in the next section.

Table 15.4   The *nodeName* and Its Type

Node	nodeName Property	nodeType Property
Element	Name of the element (*h1*, *p*)	1
Attribute	Name of the attribute (*id*, *href*)	2
Text	#text	3

15.3.4 The Whitespace Bug

When testing a document's nodes, be careful of the whitespace bug! If you break lines, for example, between the *<head>* and *<title>* tags, the whitespace is considered a text node and your output might not be consistent. There are a number of Web sites that deal with the whitespace bug and offer programmatical ways to solve the problem when traversing the DOM tree. See *https://developer.mozilla.org/en/Whitespace_in_the_DOM* (see Figure 15.5).

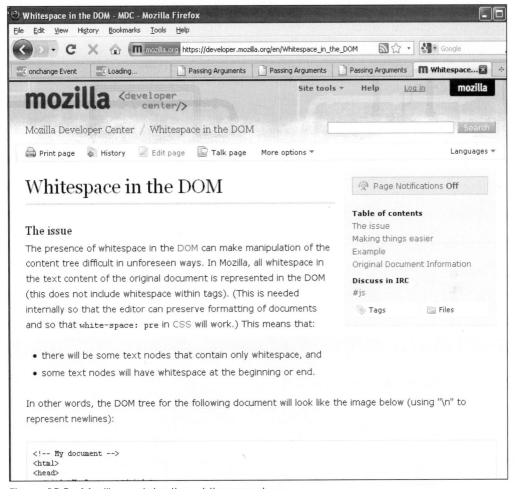

Figure 15.5 Mozilla explains the whitespace bug.

15.4 Walking with the DOM

In Example 15.1, we will take a walk down the DOM tree, one step at a time, using the parent/child/sibling nodes to represent each element in the document. The simple layout of the HTML page is drawn in Figure 15.6. You can quickly see that using DOM properties to navigate the tree can get confusing, and if in any way the structure of the document changes, then all the nodes properties will have to be reset. We discuss a quicker more efficient way to get around in the next section.

Because every element in the tree has a parent (other than the root node), a relationship can be established going up or down the tree as long as you know which node and which children will lead you to the target element you want. The five properties for each node in the tree are *parentNode*, *firstChild*, *lastChild*, *previousSibling*, and *next Sibling*.

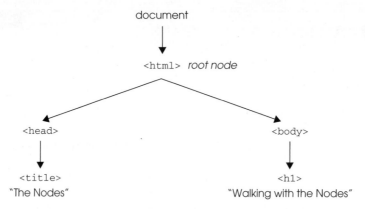

Figure 15.6   The DOM tree for Example 15.1.

EXAMPLE 15.1

```
1  <html>
     <head><title>The Nodes</title>
       <style>
         p{font-size: x-large; color:darkblue;
           font-style:bold;
         }
       </style>
     </head>
     <body>
       <h1>Walking with Nodes</h1>
       <p>Who knows what node?</p>
       <p>
```

EXAMPLE   15.1 (CONTINUED)

```
          <script type="text/javascript">
2             var Parent=document.childNodes[0];
                              // First child node is HTML
3             var Child=Parent.childNodes[0];
                              // Parent's first child is HEAD

          document.write("The parent node is: ");
4         document.write(Parent.nodeName+"<br />");
                              // Get the name parent node
          document.write("The first child of the parent node is: ");
5         document.write(Child.nodeName+"<br />");
          document.write("The node below the child is: ");
6         document.write(Child.childNodes[0].nodeName+"<br />");
          document.write("The text node below title is: ");
7         document.write(Child.childNodes[0].childNodes[0].nodeName +
              "<br />");
          document.write("The value of the text node is: " +
8             Child.childNodes[0].childNodes[0].nodeValue+"<br />");
          document.write("The first child of the parent is: ");
9         document.write(Parent.firstChild.nodeName+"<br />");
          document.write("The last child of the parent is: ");
10        document.write(Parent.lastChild.nodeName+"<br />");
          document.write("The node below the body is: ");
11        document.write(Parent.lastChild.childNodes[0].nodeName+
              "<br />");
          document.write("The next sibling of the h1 element is: ");
12
document.write(Parent.lastChild.childNodes[0].nextSibling.nodeName+
              "<br />");
          document.write("It's value is " +
              "Parent.lastChild.childNodes[0].nextSibling.nodeValue);
13        document.write("<br />The last child's type is: ");
          document.write(Parent.lastChild.nodeType);
      </script>
      </p>
    </body>
  </html>
```

EXPLANATION

1   The JavaScript program will access the HTML elements through the DOM
    where each element is viewed as a node. This line cannot be broken for format-
    ting due to the **whitespace bug**. If you break up this line, the whitespace created
    will be considered a text node, and the rest of the script will not display the
    nodes as expected.

Continues

EXPLANATION(CONTINUED)

2   The first node, *childNodes[0]*, is the first node in the HTML hierarchy, the parent node. This node is assigned to a variable, *Parent*. The only reason to create the variable is to cut down on the amount of typing and propensity for errors when we go further down the document tree. Note: Watch your spelling when working with the DOM in JavaScript.

3   The parent node's first child is *document.childNodes[0].childNodes[0]*. This portion of the tree is assigned to the variable *Child*.

4   The name of a node is found in the *nodeName* property. The parent node is *HTML*, the highest element in the HTML hierarchy.

5   The *nodeName* of the first child of the parent node is *HEAD*.

6   The next node in the hierarchy is the child of the *HEAD* element. It is the *title* element:

```
<html>
   <head>
      <title>
```

7   Continuing the walk down the DOM tree, we come to the text node. It contains the text between the *<title> </title>* tags. The name of the text node is preceded by a # mark.

8   The actual text between the *<title></title>* tags is found in the *nodeValue* property of the node.

9   Using the *firstChild* property to simplify things, the first child of the parent again shows to be the *HEAD* element.

10 The last child of the HTML parent is the *BODY* element:

```
<html>
   <head>
   <body>
```

11 The node directly below the body is the *h1* element:

```
<body><h1>Walking with the Nodes</h2>
```

12 The node below the body (i.e., the last child of the body element), *document.child-Nodes[0].lastChild.nodeName*, is the *h1* element.

13 The parent's last child node's type is 1. An element node type is type 1, an attribute type is type 2, and a text node is type 3. See Figure 15.7.

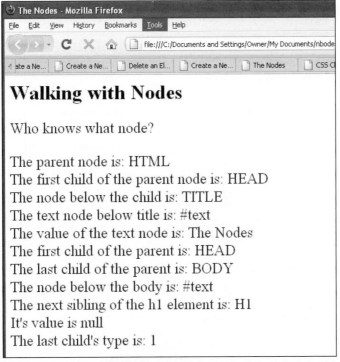

Figure 15.7   The node properties.

15.5 DOM Inspectors

A DOM inspector is a browser tool that lets you dynamically traverse the DOM tree and check CSS styles, in a two-paned window as shown in Figure 15.8. Now you can view the markup in your Web page and all the nodes and their types for those parts of the page that are of interest to you.

For Firefox: see *https://developer.mozilla.org/en/dom_inspector*.
For Internet Explorer see: *http://www.ieinspector.com/dominspector/*.
For Opera go to the menu: Tools→Advanced→Developer Tools.

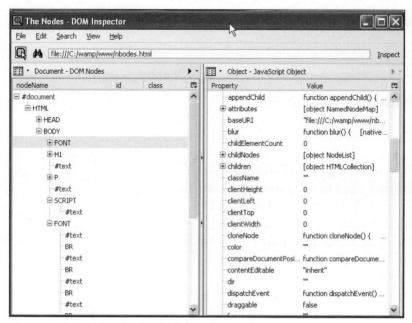

Figure 15.8   The Firefox DOM Inspector.

15.6 Methods to Shorten the DOM Walk

In the previous example, walking with the nodes was like walking through a maze in a palace garden. Although the DOM is represented as a hierarchal tree of elements, where each element is represented as a node, walking with the nodes can be daunting, so the W3C provides additional methods and properties to help make the walk easier.

The DOM provides two methods, *getElementById()* and *getElementsByTag()*, to directly access the target element you are trying to reach. It also provides properties to represent attributes of an element listed in Table 15.5.

15.6.1   The *document.getElementById()* Method

Using the *id* attribute is not a new idea. We have been using it throughout this text. All browsers that comply with the W3C's DOM1+ should implement the *id* attribute for accessing the elements in a document. It uniquely identifies any HTML element in a Web document. Note: This is not the same as the *name* attribute discussed in Chapters 11 and 12. If you recall, the *name* attribute is used with forms, images, links, and anchors. The *name* attribute does not have to be unique and is used by the browser to create *name/value* pairs to be submitted to a server program as part of the URL (GET method) or HTTP header (POST).

The HTML element's *id* attribute must be assigned a unique value that is used as a CSS selector to identify a style rule or to get a reference to that element in a JavaScript program. In Chapter 11 when working with forms, we used both the *name* and *id* attributes. When working with DOM nodes, the *id* attribute allows you to specify a specific node and retrieve a reference to it with the *document.getElementByID()* method, a DOM1 method.

Although all major browsers are DOM1 compliant, here is a little test code you can run to check your browser:

```
if (document.getElementById){
        alert("DOM compliant!");
}
```

Go to *http://www.webreference.com/tools/browser/JavaScript.html* to see examples of "browser sniffer" programs—programs that can tell what browser is being used.

All that node stuff can be really tricky, but by combining the HTML *id* attribute with the *getElementById()* method of the *document* object, it is much easier to get a handle on any HTML object. The *getElementById()* method takes the *id* of an HTML element as its argument and returns a reference to that element. (Remember that *getElementById()* is a method of the document object and must be written as *document.getElementById()*). With the reference you can manipulate the element in your JavaScript code. Suppose you have a paragraph tag defined with an *id* attribute, as:

```
<p id="para1">This is the paragraph.</p>
```

Now in JavaScript you can get a reference to the *p* element with the *getElementById()* method as follows:

```
p_element = document.getElementById("para1");
```

Rather than descending the entire DOM tree, *p_element* is a reference to the *p* element identified as "para1" and can be used with the DOM properties:

```
alert(p_element.nodeName);   // Name of the element
alert(p_element.childNodes[0].nodeValue); // Text between tags
```

Example 15.2 demonstrates the use of the *id* attribute on several HTML elements. After getting a reference to the element, the DOM node properties can be applied to the reference.

EXAMPLE 15.2

```
<html>
    <head><title>The Dom and Id's</title></head>
1   <body id="body1">
2       <h1 id="head1">Shortening the DOM Walk</h1>
3       <p id="para1">This is the paragraph!<p/>
        <p><big>
```

Continues

EXAMPLE   15.2 (CONTINUED)

```
            <script name="text/javascript">
4               var h1tag=document.getElementById("head1");
5               var bodytag=document.getElementById("body1");
6               var paratag = document.getElementById("para1");
7               h1tag.style.fontFamily="verdana";
                h1tag.style.fontSize="32";
                h1tag.style.color="darkgreen";
                paratag.style.fontSize="125%";
                paratag.style.color="blue";
                bodytag.style.backgroundColor="silver";

8               document.write(h1tag +"<br />");
                document.write(paratag+"<br />");
                document.write(bodytag+"<br /><br />");

                //Let's get the text between the tags
                document.write("<h2>This is the text within
                                    the tags:</h2>");
9               document.write(h1tag.childNodes[0].nodeValue+"<br />");
                document.write(paratag.childNodes[0].nodeValue+"<br />");
            </script>
          </big>
          </p>
        </body >
    </html>
```

EXPLANATION

1   The *<body>* tag is given an *id* called *"body1"*.

2   The *<h1>* tag is given an *id* called *"head1"*.

3   The *<p>* tag is given an *id* called *"para1"*.

4   In the JavaScript program, the *getElementById()* method returns a reference to an *h1* element, and assigns that value to the variable called *h1tag*.

5   The *getElementById()* method returns a reference to a *BODY* element, and assigns that value to the variable called *bodytag*.

6   The *getElementById()* method returns a reference to a *p* element, and assigns that value to the variable called *paratag*.

7   Now, by using the *style* property, the elements are assigned new values for font size and color, causing them to change dynamically.

8   The value returned by the *getElementById()* method is displayed for each of the elements. As shown in the output, each one of these HTML elements is an object. See Figure 15.9.

9   Rather than starting at the top of the DOM tree to obtain the text between the HTML tags, it is easier to get a reference to the tag and then add the DOM properties to the reference as shown here. An even easier way to fetch the text value between the tags is to use the *innerHTML* property described later in this chapter.

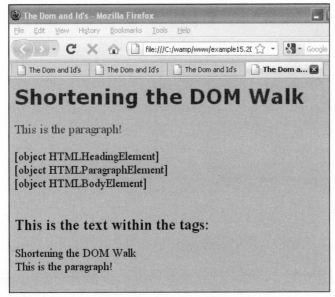

Figure 15.9   HTML elements are objects.

15.6.2   The *document.getElementsByTagName()* Method

To reference a collection of elements in a document, such all the *<p>* tags, *<h1>* tags, or *<a>* tags in your document, you can use the *getElementsByTagName()* method. This method takes the name of the element as its argument and returns a list of all the nodes of that name in the document. If you need to collectively change the values of a particular element, such as all the links in an *<a>* tag, do this by manipulating the reference returned by the *getElementsByTagName()*. Use the DOM nodes to continue walking down the tree from the point of reference retrieved from *document.getElementsByTag-Name()* method as shown in Example 15.3.

EXAMPLE   15.3

```
<html>
  <head><title>Working with Tags</title>
    <style type="text/css">
      body {background-color:aliceblue;color:green;
           font-size:larger;}
      h1{color:darkblue; }
    </style>
  </head>
  <body>
1     <h1> First</h1>
      <h1> Second</h1>
      <h1> Third</h1>
2     <script type="text/javascript">
3       var heading1=document.getElementsByTagName("h1");
        document.write(heading1 + "<br />");
        document.write("There are "+
4       heading1.length+ " H1 tags.<br />");
5       for(i=0; i< heading1.length; i++){
6          document.write( heading1[i].nodeName+": <em>"+
7                  heading1[i].childNodes[0].nodeValue+"</em><br />");
        }
      </script>
  </body>
</html>
```

EXPLANATION

1   Three *<h1>* tags are used in this document.

2   Because of the top-down processing by the HTML renderer, be sure to put the JavaScript program at the end of the document. This way, the tags will already have been identified before they are put into the HTML collection returned by the *getElementsByName()* method.

3   The HTML collection of h1 tags is stored as an array of nodes in the variable, *heading1*.

4   The length of the array is 3 in this example because there are three H1 elements in the document. See Figure 15.10.

5   The *for* loop will iterate through each of the *heading1* tag objects in the HTML collection.

6   The *nodeName* property contains the name of the HTML element.

7   The child of the h1 element, *childNodes[i]*, (where *i* is the index value) is the text between the *<h1>* tags. The *nodeValue* property contains the actual text.

Figure 15.10 Getting elements by tag name: Mozilla Firefox (left), Internet Explorer (right).

15.6.3 JavaScript Properties to Represent HTML Attributes

The attributes of an HTML element are accessible as properties in JavaScript. Table 15.5 lists the properties available to JavaScript to test an attribute.

Table 15.5 Properties to Represent HTML Attributes

Property	Description	Example
className	Represents the class of a CSS element	`div2.className "color";` *div2* refers to an HTML element. It is being assigned the CSS class called *blue* (see Example 15.17)
dir	Specifies the text direction for a document; for example, read left to right (English), or right to left (Hebrew); ltr (left to right) or rtl (right to left)	`element.dir="ltr";`
id	Value of the unique *id* of the current element	(see Section 15.6.1)
lang	Specifies the language in which the text of the document is written; for example, *en* for English, *ja* for Japanese, and *sp* for Spanish	`if(document.lang=="ja")`

Continues

Table 15.5   Properties to Represent HTML Attributes (continued)

Property	Description	Example
style	Value of the CSS inline style attribute (CSS2)	`div.style.color="green";` (see Section 14.5.2)

title	Returns the title of the document found between the *<title>* and *</title>* tags	`<title>My Book</title>`
		`strTitle = document.title`
		strTitle contains "My Book"

EXAMPLE 15.4

```
      <html>
        <head><title>Properties</title>
1         <style>
            .color { color:darkblue; background:aqua;}
          </style>
        </head>
        <body>
2         <p id="paraid1" dir="ltr" class=color
            style="font-size:x-large">
            This is an English style.
          </p>
3         <p id="paraid2" dir="rtl" class="color" style="font-
            family:cursive">
            This is Hebrew style.
          </p>
          <big>
            <script type="text/javascript">
4             p1=document.getElementById('paraid1');
5             document.write("The text direction is "+ p1.dir +
                      "and the font size is "+ p1.style.fontSize);

6             p2=document.getElementById('paraid2');
              document.write("<br />The text direction is "+p2.dir+
                      " and the class name is "+ p2.className);
            </script>
          </big>
        </body>
      </html>
```

EXPLANATION

1   A CSS style contains a class called *.color* to be used by elements within the HTML page.

2   The *p* element is assigned a number of attributes: *id*, *dir*, *class*, and *style*, all available in a JavaScript program to either change or display values.

EXPLANATION (CONTINUED)

3   This *p* element is also assigned attributes. The *dir* attribute with *rtl* means the text will be displayed from the right side of the screen to the left, as would be used with Arabic or Hebrew.

4   The *getElementById()* method uses the *id* of the first paragraph and returns a reference to it.

5   The first paragraph has a *dir* and *style* attribute. Using *dir* and *style.fontSize*, Java-Script can get access to these attributes.

6   The second paragraph has also been assigned attributes. Using the *dir* and *class-Name* properties, JavaScript can find the direction of the text, right to left, and the name of the class that is used to style this paragraph. The *className* property can also be assigned the name of a different class to change the style of the object. The output is shown in Figure 15.11.

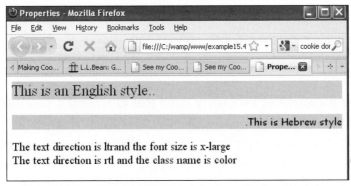

Figure 15.11   Displaying HTML attributes with JavaScript properties.

15.7 Modifying the DOM (Appending, Copying, and Removing Nodes)

You can create new nodes, make a clone of an existing node, insert a new node before an existing node, remove a node, or replace a node. All of this is possible because the W3C DOM introduced methods to modify the DOM. Table 15.6 lists the DOM methods. For a complete list of DOM methods and an excellent resource, go to the JavaScript Kit page at *http://www.JavaScriptkit.com/domref/elementmethods.shtml*. For another great resource on how to modify the DOM, go to *http://www.howtocreate.co.uk/tutorials/Java-Script/dombasics*.

Table 15.6 The DOM Methods

Method	What It Does
appendChild(new node)	Appends a new node onto the end of the list of child nodes.
cloneNode(child option)	Makes a clone of a node.
hasChildNodes()	Returns *true* if the node has children.
getAttribute(attributeName)	Returns the value of the attribute of the current node.
hasAtrributes()	Returns a Boolean value if the node has defined attributes.
hasChildNodes()	Returns a Boolean value if the node has defined child nodes.
insertBefore(new node, current node)	Inserts a new node in the list of children.
removeChild(child node)	Removes a child node from a list of children.
setAttributeNode(attributereference)	Sets or creates an attribute for the current node.
replaceChild(new child, old child)	Replaces an old child node with a new one.

15.7.1 The *innerHTML* Property and the Element's Content

The easiest way to get or modify the content of an element is by using the *innerHTML* property. Although the *innerHTML* is not a part of the W3C DOM specification, it is supported by all major browsers. The *innerHTML* property is useful for inserting or replacing the content of HTML elements; that is, the code and text between the element's opening and closing tag. It can also be used to view the source of a page that has been dynamically modified (including *<html>* and *<body>*). Interactive pages are created by simply changing the value of the element's *innerHTML* property. Because it is a property, not a method, *innerHTML* doesn't return a reference to the content it inserts. If you need to do more than simply get or set content, then you can use specific DOM methods instead.

In Example 15.5 the *innerHTML* property is used to retrieve the contents of two paragraphs. First we will give the paragraphs an *id* so that we can easily identify a particular paragraph. Next, with the *id* of the element, the *getElementById* method returns a JavaScript reference to the specified paragraph, and finally the *innerHTML* property contains the text between the *<p></p>* tags. With this property we can easily modify the paragraph's text and style on the fly.

EXAMPLE 15.5

```
<html>
   <head>
      <title>innerHTML</title>
```

EXAMPLE 15.5 (CONTINUED)

```
       <style type="text/css">
         body{ background-color:blue;}
1        p { background: white;
             font-style: bold;
             font-family: courier,arial;
             text-indent: 5%;
             margin-left:20%;
             margin-right:20%
         }
       </style>
     </head>
     <body>

2      <p id="para1">Today is Sunday and there is a sailing festival
         going on in the Ferry Park. The tall ships are docked in the
         bay for tourists to visit. The fog is rolling in.</p>

3      <p id="para2">I'm trying to figure out how to grab the text
         from this paragraph with JavaScript using the innerHTML
         property. I may take a break now and go to the park.</p>

       <script type="text/javascript">
         document.write("<p>JavaScript's innerHTML property</p>");
4        ptxt1=document.getElementById("para1").innerHTML;
5        ptxt2=document.getElementById("para2").innerHTML;
         document.write("<p style='background:yellow'>"+
6                        ptxt1.toUpperCase()+ "</p>");
         document.write("<p style='background:yellow'>" +
7                        ptxt2.toUpperCase()+ "</p>");
       </script>
     </body>
   </html>
```

EXPLANATION

1   This is the CSS code to style paragraphs in this document.

2   The first HTML paragraph element is given an *id* with the *id* attribute.

3   The second HTML paragraph element is also given an *id*.

4   The *getElementById()* uses the *id* of the paragraph to get a reference to the paragraph. By applying the *innerHTML* property to this reference, all the text between *<p></p>* tags is assigned to the variable, *ptext1*.

5   By applying the *innerHTML* property to this reference, all the text between *<p></p>* tags is assigned to the variable, *ptext2*.

6, 7   The text in both paragraphs is displayed in uppercase letters by applying the *toUpperCase()* method to the variables, *ptxt1* and *ptxt2*. Figure 15.12 shows the result.

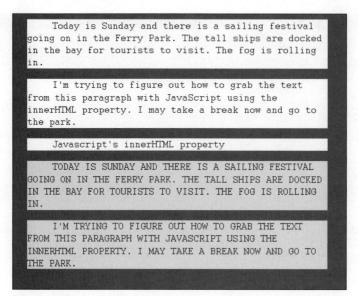

Figure 15.12 JavaScript grabs the two paragraphs at the top of the page and displays them at the bottom.

15.7.2 Modifying the Content of an Element

By changing an element's *innerHTML* property, after some user interaction, you can change the text that occurs between that element's opening and closing tag.

EXAMPLE 15.6

```
<html>
   <head><title>Modify Text</title>
      <style type="text/css">
         body{background-color:aliceblue;}
         .divStyle {
                     background-color:green;
                     margin-left:20%
                     margin-right:20%
                     border-style:solid;
                     color:white;
                     font-size:150%
         }
      </style>
```

EXAMPLE 15.6 (CONTINUED)

```
          <script type="text/javascript">
1             window.onload=function(){
2                var divObj = document.getElementById("divtest");
3                alert(divObj);
4                divObj.innerHTML="Inserting new text in the
                                  div container.";
              }
          </script>
        </head>
        <body>
5         <div id="divtest" class="divStyle">
6            Original text in div container.
          </div>
        </body>
      </html>
```

EXPLANATION

1   When the page has finished loading the statements in the anonymous function are executed.

2   The variable, *divObj*, is assigned a reference to the *div* element identified by its *id*, *divtest*.

3   By adding this *alert*, you will be able to see what was in the original *div* container before it is overwritten by the new text. After the user clicks the alert's OK button, the new text will be displayed. If the alert box is removed, the original text will be overwritten before you can see it. The only output will be what you see in Figure 15.13.

4   The *innerHTML* property is used to change the text within the *<div></div>* tags.

5   The *id* and *class* attributes are assigned to the *<div>* tag.

6   This is the original text that is modified by JavaScript on line 4. See Figure 15.14.

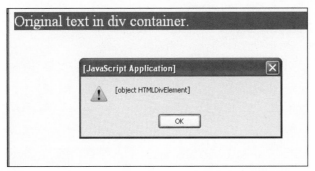

Figure 15.13 The original text before it is modified.

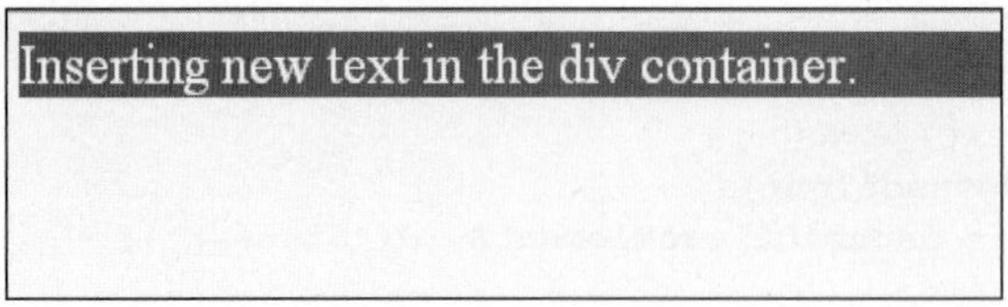

Inserting new text in the div container.

Figure 15.14   Original text is modified using the *innerHTML* property.

15.7.3   Creating New Elements with the DOM

To create new elements on the fly, the DOM provides the *createElement()* method, and for new text, the *createTextNode()* method. Once you get a reference to the new element, you must insert or append it to the document. If, for example, you have created a *p* element as follows:

```
var pref = document.body.createElement("p");
```

you can now append the new element to the body as follows:

```
document.body.appendChild(pref);
```

Now we can add text to the new paragraph by using the *createTextNode()* method and the *appendChild()* method as follows:

```
txt = document.createTextNode("Hello, new paragraph!");
```

And finally, we will append this text to the new paragraph as:

```
new_pref.appendChild(txt);
```

EXAMPLE 15.7

```
    <html>
      <head><title>Creating a New Element</title>
        <style type="text/css">
          .divStyle { background-color:blue;
                      border-style:solid;
                      color:white;
          }
          p{ color:yellow; font-size:150%;}
        </style>
        <script type="text/javascript">
          // Create a new p element and append it to a div
1         window.onload=function(){
2           var para = document.createElement("p");
3           var divObj = document.getElementById("divtest");
```

EXAMPLE   15.7

```
4              divObj.appendChild(para);
5              var txt = document.createTextNode("Wow! Hope this works!");
6              para.appendChild(txt);
            }
         </script>
      </head>
      <body>
7         <div id="divtest" class="divStyle">
            <p>Original text in div container.</p>
         </div>
      </body>
   </html>
```

EXPLANATION

1   After the page has completely loaded this anonymous function will be called.

2   A new paragraph is created with the DOM's *createElement()* method.

3   Now we get a reference to the *div* element defined on line 7.

4   The paragraph is appended to the *div* element with the DOM's *appendChild()* method (see Figure 15.15).

5   The DOM's *createTextNode()* method will return a reference to the text that will be placed within the new paragraph node.

6   The text created on line 5 is appended to the paragraph.

7   A *div* container is created with an *id* attribute, *divtest*, to be used on line 3 to get a reference to the *div* element.

Figure 15.15   Creating a new *p* element with the DOM and appending it to a *div* container.

15.7.4 Inserting Before a Node

The *insertBefore()* method allows you to insert a child node before the specified node, called the reference node, and if the reference node is null, this will insert the node at the end of a list of child nodes.

FORMAT

```
insertBefore(newElement, targetElement)
```

EXAMPLE

```
document.body.insertBefore(newPara, firstPara);
```

Example 15.8 demonstrates how to insert a new paragraph node into a DOM before another node.

EXAMPLE 15.8

```
      <html>
        <head><title>Inserting Before</title>
          <style type="text/css">
            p { font-style:arial;
                color:darkblue;
                font-size:18;
              }
          </style>
          <script type="text/javascript">
1           function insertMessage() {
2             var newPara = document.createElement("p");
3             var newText = document.createTextNode("I am inserting
                                                myself above you!");
              // If you copy this, don't break the lines.
4             newPara.appendChild(newText);
5             var firstPara = document.getElementById("firstp");
6             document.body.insertBefore(newPara, firstPara);
            }
          </script>
        </head>
7       <body onload="insertMessage()">
          <p id="firstp">I was supposed to be first.</p>
        </body>
      </html>
```

EXPLANATION

1   Once the page has loaded, this function will be called.

2   With the *createElement()* method, a new paragraph is created. A reference to it is assigned to a variable, *newPara*.

EXPLANATION

3   Now we are going to insert some text into the paragraph with the *createTextNode()* method.

4   After creating a reference to the new text, it is appended to the paragraph with the *appendChild()* method.

5   The *document.getElementById()* returns a reference to the first paragraph. This will be the reference node, or the node in which the second paragraph will be inserted.

6   The new paragraph is inserted above the first paragraph (see Figure 15.16).

7   When the page is loaded, this function will be called. It will cause a new paragraph to be inserted above the paragraph identified below this line, with the *id*, *firstp*.

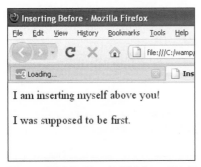

Figure 15.16   The DOM *insertBefore()* method.

15.7.5   Creating Attributes for Nodes

The *setAttribute()* method creates a new attribute for an element. If an attribute with that name (*nodeName*) already exists in the element, it is replaced by the new one. See the section "Cloning Nodes" later in this chapter for more examples.

FORMAT

```
reference_to_element.setAttribute(attributeName, value);

reference_to_element.setAttribute(attributeName, value, boolean);
// boolean 0 turns off case-sensitivity, 1 is on the default
// Internet Explorer only
```

EXAMPLE

```
var headings = document.getElementsByTagName("h1")
headings[0].setAttribute("id", "firsth1")
```

EXAMPLE 15.9

```
<html>
  <head><title>Create Elements and Attributes with the DOM</title>
    <style type="text/css">
      p { font-style:arial;
          color:darkblue;
          font-size:18
        }
    </style>
  </head>
  <body>
    <script type="text/javascript">
1     window.onload=function(){
        // Create three paragraphs with text
2       for(var i=1; i <= 3; i++){
3         var aPara=document.createElement("p");
4         var aBR = document.createElement("br");
5         var theTXT1=document.createTextNode("Hello, world. ");
          var theTXT2=document.createTextNode("I hope you're
                                  enjoying this DOM stuff! ");
          var theTXT3=document.createTextNode("I am paragraph " +
                                  i +".");

6         aPara.setAttribute("id","aPara" + i);
            //set id attribute for the p element

          document.body.appendChild(aPara);
          aPara.appendChild(theTXT1);
          aPara.appendChild(aBR);
          aPara.appendChild(theTXT2);
          aPara.appendChild(aBR);
          aPara.appendChild(theTXT3);

        }
7       alert(document.getElementById("aPara1"));

      }
    </script>
  </body>
</html>
```

EXPLANATION

1 When the page has completely been loaded, this anonymous function will be called. Its function is to create three paragraphs with unique *ids* and text (see Figure 15.17).

2 The *for* loop will iterate three times to create the three paragraphs.

3 A reference to a new *p* element is created.

EXPLANATION

4   A reference to a new *br* element is created.

5   A new text node is created to be placed in each paragraph.

6   A unique *id* attribute is set for each paragraph.

7   The *getElementById()* method returns a reference to the paragraph identified as "aPara1". The alert method displays the value of the reference.

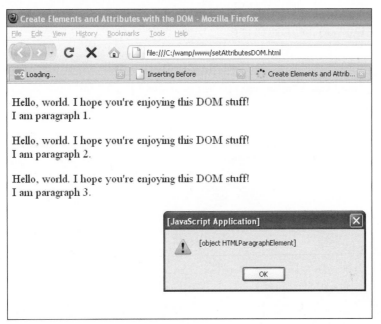

Figure 15.17   Creating new elements and attributes with the DOM.

15.7.6 DOM Review: Creating a Blog

The next example, Example 15.10, is a program demonstrating how to use the DOM methods and properties we have covered thus far. The idea is to dynamically add new text entries, called blogs, into a Web page. The user will be presented with an area in which to write his or her blog. After the user clicks the "Add a blog" button, JavaScript will create a blog object and use DOM methods to define the structure of the new entry in the document.[1] Each blog entry will be appended to the previous one with the blogger's name, the date the blog was posted, and the blog message.

---

1. To save the blogs in a database or file, you will need a server-side program such as PHP or ASP.NET.

EXAMPLE 15.10

```
   <html>
     <head><title>Creating a Blog</title>
1      <style type="text/css">
         body{ background-color:#7fffd4;}
         div#div1{ background: white;
                   border-width:1px;
                   margin-left:20%;
                   margin-right:20%;
         }
         p  { margin-left:1%;
              font-family: arial;}
       </style>
       <script type="text/javascript">
2        function BlogEntry(){  //Create a blog class
           var date;          //Properties
           var message;
           var name;
           this.setDate=setDate;    // Methods
           this.setBlogger=setBlogger;
           this.setMessage=setMessage;
           this.showBlog=showBlog;

3          function setDate(){    // Get the current date
             var d=new Date();
             var year=d.getFullYear();
             var month=d.getMonth() + 1;
             var day=d.getDate();
             date=month + "/" + day + "/" + year;
           }

4          function setBlogger(nameVal){
             name=nameVal;
           }
           function setMessage(messageVal){
             message=messageVal;
           }
5          function showBlog(){
             // Create HTML elements
6            var para = document.createElement("p");
             var count=document.getElementsByTagName("p").length;
             // Get number of paragraphs
7            para.setAttribute("id","para" + count); // Set id for P
              // alert("There are " + count+ " paragraphs so far.");
8            var aBR = document.createElement("br");
             var aBold = document.createElement("b");
9            var divObj = document.getElementById("div1");
             //Get a reference to the div
```

EXAMPLE 15.10 (CONTINUED)

```
10              divObj.appendChild(para);   // Append a paragraph
                                            // Create nodes
11              var txt1=document.createTextNode("Posted by "+ name
                                                + " on ")
                var txt2=document.createTextNode(date);
                var txt3=document.createTextNode(message);
12              para.appendChild(txt1);
13              para.appendChild(txt2);
                aBold.appendChild(aBR);
                para.appendChild(aBold);
                aBold.appendChild(txt3);
                para.appendChild(aBold);
14              // alert(document.getElementById("para"
                                              +count).innerHTML);
            }
15      } // End class
16      function addBlog(){  /* Add a blog entry using the DOM
                                and get form data */
17          message=document.getElementById("text").value;
            bloggername=document.getElementById("name").value;
18          var blog = new BlogEntry();  // Create a new blog object
            blog.setMessage(message);      // Call object's methods
            blog.setBlogger(bloggername);
            blog.setDate();
            blog.showBlog();
        }
      </script>
    </head>
    <body>
      <div align="center">
        <img src="images/sunny.gif">
        <img src="images/rain.gif">
        <img src="images/partlycloudy.gif">
        <img src="images/mostlycloudy.gif">
        <img src="images/snow.gif">
      </div>
      <h2 align="center">MoodyWedderBlog</h2>
19    <div id="div1">
      </div >
      <br />
      <div align="center">
        <form method="post">
          Enter your name (optional) <br />
          <input type="text" id="name" />
          <br /><br />
20        <textarea id="text" name="text" rows="5" cols="40"
                    onfocus="this.value=''">
          </textarea><br />
```

Continues

EXAMPLE 15.10 (CONTINUED)

```
21              <input type="button" value="Add a blog"
                   onclick="addBlog();"/>
           </form>
        </div>
      </body>
    </html>
```

EXPLANATION

1   This is the CSS style sheet for the page.

2   The function *BlogEntry()* defines a class consisting of the properties and methods for each new blog object that is created.

3   This method will get and format the current date with JavaScript's *Date()* constructor. It will be assigned to the date property of the object.

4   These next two methods will set the properties for the name of the blogger and the message the blogger typed into the form.

5   The *showBlog()* method is where we make good use of the DOM by creating elements and text nodes. Each blog message will be placed in a paragraph appended to a *div* container. It will contain the blogger name and date on one line and the blogger's message in bold text on the next lines. Every time a new blog is entered it will be appended in a paragraph to the previous paragraph.

6   A new paragraph element is created and a reference to it is assigned to *para*.

7   A unique *id* attribute is set for each paragraph after it is created. Every time a new paragraph is added the *document.getElementsByTagName("p")* method returns the number of *p* elements in the document, causing the count to go up by one. This *count* value is concatenated to the string "para" producing a new *id* for each new paragraph created on line 6.

8   A reference to an HTML *br* (break line) element is created and assigned to *aBR*. On the next line, a reference to an HTML *b* (bold) element is created.

9   The *document.getElementById()* method returns a reference to a *div* object identified as *div1* on line 19. This is where the paragraphs will be added and the blog messages displayed.

10 Now a *p* element (paragraph) is appended to the *div* object.

11 Three text nodes are created with values that will be inserted into the paragraph. The properties of the blog object, *name*, *date*, and *message*, contain the text values that will be assigned to the text nodes.

12 The text for the paragraph is now appended as a child node.

13 The next line of text is appended followed by the *br* element and the *b* element.

14 This *alert()*, when uncommented, will display the text (*innerHTML*) for each paragraph after it has been created, for example: *Posted by Ellie Quigley on 3/21/2010
This is a hazy day and I'm in a hazy mood.*

15 The *BlogEntry* class ends here.

EXPLANATION(CONTINUED)

16 The function *addBlog()* is a user-defined function, not part of the class. Its function is to create a new *blog* object and assign it properties.

17 The form data (the blogger's name and blog message) is retrieved with the *document.getElementById()* method.

18 An instance of a new *BlogEntry* object is created and a reference to it is assigned to the variable, *blog*. The methods for the object are called to set the properties for the *blog* object.

19 After setting up all the weather images, this is the *div* container where the blog messages will be stored and displayed.

20 The user will write his or her blog in a *textarea* input device. After writing the message, if the user leaves the text area and then clicks in the box, the *onfocus* event handler will be triggered and the box will be cleared by setting its value to an empty string.

21 When the user clicks this button, the *onclick* event hander will call the *addBlog()* function to create a new blog object and set its properties with the form data retrieved on line 17. The results are shown in Figures 15.18 and 15.19.

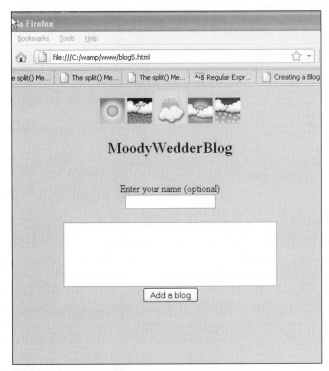

Figure 15.18   Before adding a blog entry.

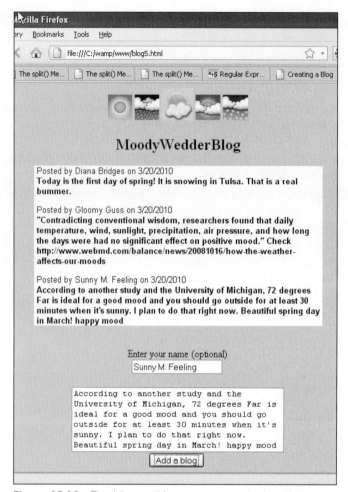

Figure 15.19   The blog entries are appended as they are added.

15.7.7   Creating a Table with the DOM

Creating a table with the DOM can be a little confusing to say the least. Just as we have seen in previous examples, the DOM requires two steps: first, to create an empty element with the *createElement()* method, and then to insert the element into the document tree with the *appendChild()* or *insertChild()* method. That means for the table element, the table heading, captions, rows and table data, and so on. you must create an empty element and then place it in the tree. Forgetting a step will lead to a partial table or an empty page. Using a DOM inspector can be very helpful when laying out a table, as shown in Figure 15.20.

Firefox does not require either a *tBody* or a *tFoot*. Internet Explorer requires that you create a *tBody* element and insert it into the table when using the DOM. Without it, you will get a blank page. Because you are manipulating the document tree directly, Internet

Explorer does not create the *tBody*, which is automatically implied when using HTML. See *http://msdn.microsoft.com/en-us/library/ms532998(VS.85).aspx#TOM_Struct*.

Example 15.11 demonstrates the steps needed to create a table dynamically with the DOM. The CSS and JavaScript could now be placed in their own respective files, leaving the HTML document unobstructed. This is unobtrusive JavaScript at play!

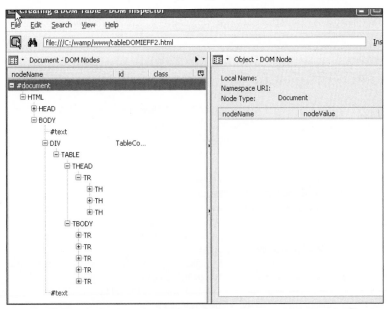

Figure 15.20   Looking at a table with the Firefox DOM Inspector.

EXAMPLE 15.11

```
     <html>
       <head><title>Creating a DOM Table</title><head>
         <style type="text/css">
1          table { width:380px;
                 border: 2px solid darkgreen;
                 background-color:#8fbc8f; }
           th { font-size: larger;
               font-family:arial}
           td { border: 1px solid #888878;
               padding: 5px;
               background-color:#fff8dc;
               font-family:arial;
           }
         </style>
```

Continues

EXAMPLE 15.11 (CONTINUED)

```
    <script type="text/javascript">
2     window.onload = function(){
3       // Create the table elements
        var Table = document.createElement("table");
        Table.setAttribute("id","myTable");   // Create id
        var THead = document.createElement("thead");
        var TBody = document.createElement("tbody");
        var Row, Cell;
        var i, j;
        // Declare two-dimensional array of table data
4       var header=new Array( "State","Capital","Abbr");
5       var state =[ ["Arizona","Phoenix","AZ"],
                     ["California","Sacramento","CA"],
                     ["Maine","Augusta","ME"],
                     ["Montana","Helena","MT"],
                     ["New York","Albany","NY"]
                   ];
        // Insert the created elements into Table
6       Table.appendChild(THead);
        Table.appendChild(TBody);
        // Insert a row into the header
7       Row = document.createElement("tr");
8       THead.appendChild(Row);
        // Create and insert table cells into the header row.
9       for (i=0; i<header.length; i++){
10        Cell = document.createElement("th");
11        Cell.innerHTML = header[i];
          Row.appendChild(Cell);
        }
        // Insert rows and cells into bodies.
12      for (i=0; i<state.length; i++){
13        Row = document.createElement("tr");
          TBody.appendChild(Row);
14        for (j=0; j<state[i].length; j++){
15          Cell = document.createElement("td");
16          Cell.innerHTML = state[i][j];
            Row.appendChild(Cell);
          }
        }
        // Insert the table into the document tree
17      Tcontainer=document.getElementById("TableContainer");
        Tcontainer.appendChild(Table);
      }
    </script>
```

EXAMPLE   15.11 (CONTINUED)

```
         </head>
         <body>
18          <div id="TableContainer"></div>
         </body>
     </html>
```

EXPLANATION

1   The CSS style sheet will create the style for the table we are creating, including the table itself, its heading, and cells.

2   When the page loads, the *startUp()* function will be called.

3   The next statements create the table, its header, and body for the DOM tree.

4   This array will contain the header values for the table.

5   This two-dimensional array contains the values that will go into the table cells.

6   Now that the table node has been created, we insert the table nodes into the main DOM tree, at which point the browser can display it.

7   Next a row is created for the header in the table and a reference returned.

8   The row is inserted into the DOM tree for the header of the table.

9   This *for* loop will iterate for each cell needed to create the header of the table.

10   The cell for the header data is created.

11   From the array of data for the header ("State', "Capital", and "Abbr"), the *innerHTML* property will be assigned the data for a cell each time through the loop. Next the data is appended to each of the cells.

12   This *for* loop will iterate until all the rows and cells have been filled for the table.

13   The table rows are created, one by one, and appended to the DOM tree.

14   This nested *for* loop will iterate through each of the cells in a row so that we can access the data in the two-dimensional array created on line 5 and put it in the table cells.

15   First we need to create a table cell for each row.

16   Once the table cell is created, the actual data from the two-dimensional array, called *states*, must be inserted in each table cell and appended to the DOM structure.

17   A reference to the *div* container (line 18) is returned by the *getElementID()* method, and the entire completed table is appended to the *div*.

18   The HTML portion of this page is very small. It consists of *<div></div>* tags that will hold the table built with the DOM methods and JavaScript. See Figure 15.21 the result.

Figure 15.21   Creating a table with the DOM from Example 15.11.

15.7.8   Cloning Nodes

To make a copy of a node you can use the *cloneNode()* method.[2] The *cloneNode()* method returns a duplicate of the current node with all of its attributes. It does not become part of the document; that is, it does not have a parent node, until it is appended to another node. This method takes only one argument of Boolean type, true or false, which is not mandatory. If the value is *false*, then only the node and its attributes are cloned but not any child nodes (which means any of its text is not cloned). If set to *true* (deep copy) then the cloning will include all of its child nodes as well. Caveat: If you clone an element and it has an *id* attribute, you will have to give the cloned node its own *id*, because *ids* must be unique. See Example 15.14.

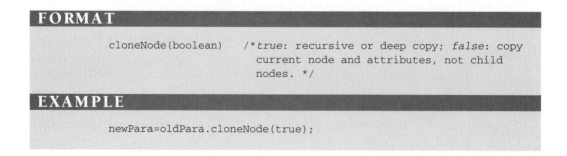

FORMAT

```
cloneNode(boolean)    /*true: recursive or deep copy; false: copy
                        current node and attributes, not child
                        nodes. */
```

EXAMPLE

```
newPara=oldPara.cloneNode(true);
```

2.To see how cloning can be used effectively with XML documents, see
http://www.w3schools.com/dom/tryit.asp?filename=try_dom_clonenode.

EXAMPLE 15.12

```
        <html>
           <head><title>Cloning Nodes</title>
              <style>
                 p { font-family: cursive ;
                     background-color: yellow;
                     border-style:solid;
                     border-width:2px;
                     border-color:blue;
                 }
              </style>
              <script type="text/javascript">
1                function addPara(mode){
2                   var p1 = document.getElementById("para1");
3                   var oldPara=p1.firstChild;
4                   newPara=oldPara.cloneNode(mode);
5                   p1.appendChild(newPara);
                 }
              </script>
           <head>
           <body>
6              <p id="para1">
                 The news is so fabulous, I need to shout it out again! You
                 won the lottery!<br />
              </p>
7              <input type="button" onClick="addPara(true);"
                     value="Clone me" />
           </body>
        </html>
```

EXPLANATION

1   The purpose of the *addPara()* function is to clone the text in a paragraph.

2   We get a reference to the paragraph that will be cloned.

3   The *firstChild* contains the contents or text of the paragraph.

4   Now a new paragraph is created, an exact replica of the old paragraph. It is a recursive copy, so all child nodes will be copied as well.

5   To make the clone a real part of the document, it is appended to the first paragraph.

6   This is the paragraph that will be cloned. It is given an *id* to reference it in the function on line 2.

7   When the button is clicked, the *addPara()* function is called with the Boolean value *true*, which will be used to make a deep copy of the first paragraph. See Figures 15.22 and 15.23.

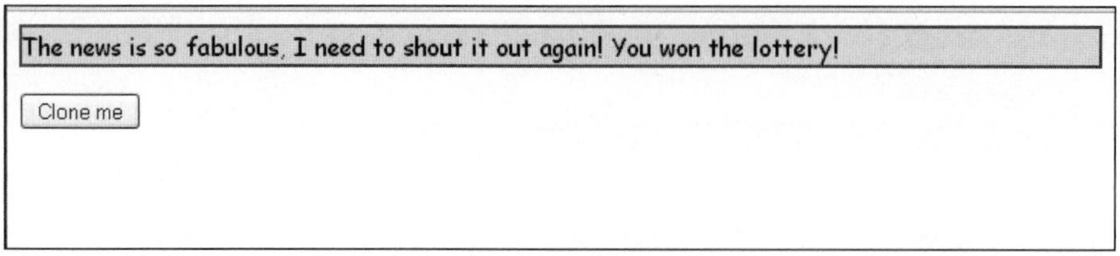

> The news is so fabulous, I need to shout it out again! You won the lottery!
>
> [Clone me]

Figure 15.22 Before the cloning takes place.

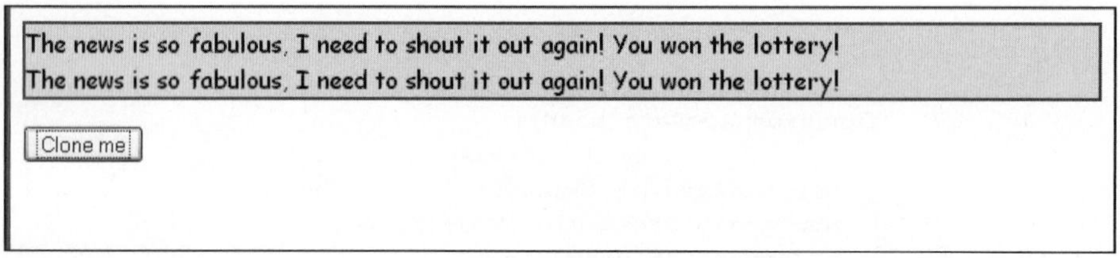

> The news is so fabulous, I need to shout it out again! You won the lottery!
> The news is so fabulous, I need to shout it out again! You won the lottery!
>
> [Clone me]

Figure 15.23 The user clicks the button and the first paragraph has been cloned.

Cloning a Node Attribute. The next example uses cloning to set an attribute for an element, in this case the *style* attribute. If the same attribute already exists for that node, it will be replaced with the new attribute.

FORMAT

```
setAttributeNode(referenceToAttribute)
```

EXAMPLE

```
var p1Style=p1.getAttributeNode("style");
var cloneP1Style=p1Style.cloneNode(mode);
p2.setAttributeNode(cloneP1Style);
```

EXAMPLE 15.13

```
      <html>
        <head><title>Attributes and Nodes</title>
          <script type="text/javascript">
1           function stylePara(mode){
2             var p1 = document.getElementById("para1");
              var p2 = document.getElementById("para2");
3             var p1Style=p1.getAttributeNode("style");
4             var cloneP1Style=p1Style.cloneNode(mode);
5             p2.setAttributeNode(cloneP1Style);
            }
```

EXAMPLE 15.13 (CONTINUED)

```
        </script>
    </head>
    <body>
6       <p id="para1" style="font-family: cursive ;
                          background-color: yellow;
                          border-style:solid;
                          border-width:2px;
                          border-color:blue;">
        The news is so fabulous, I need to shout it out again! You
        won the lottery!<br />
        </p>
        <p id="para2">I like your style, not what you say.
        </p>
7       <input type="button" onClick="JavaScript:stylePara(false);"
            value="Clone me" />
    </body>
</html>
```

EXPLANATION

1   The purpose of the *stylePara()* function is to copy the style of a paragraph where *style* is an attribute of the first paragraph. (To set the class attribute use the *className* property.)

2   First we need to get a reference to both paragraphs, the one with the *style* attribute set, and the one without it.

3   Next we use the *getAttributeNode()* method to get a reference to the *style* attribute for the first paragraph. The returned reference is assigned to *p1Style*.

4   This cloning step creates a replica of the *style* attribute of the first paragraph.

5   The *setAttributeNode()* method sets the *style* attribute for the second paragraph.

6   The style for the first paragraph is assigned to the *style* attribute. This is the attribute that will be cloned and set for the second paragraph.

7   When the user clicks this button, the function *stylePara()* will be called with an argument of false. In this example the program works the same way whether you send true or false as the mode. Figures 15.24 and 15.25 show the results.

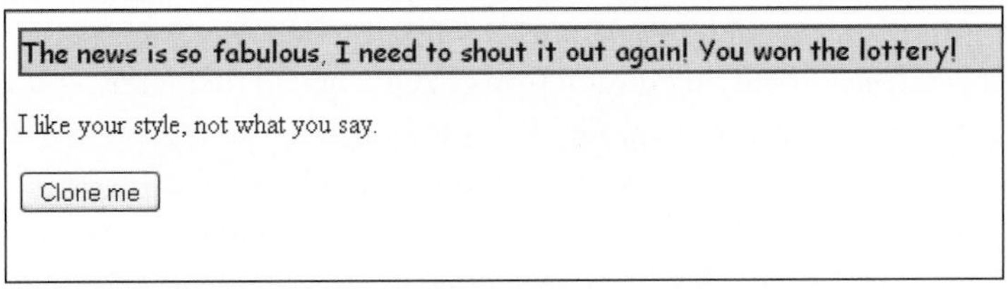

Figure 15.24 Cloning a style attribute—before clone.

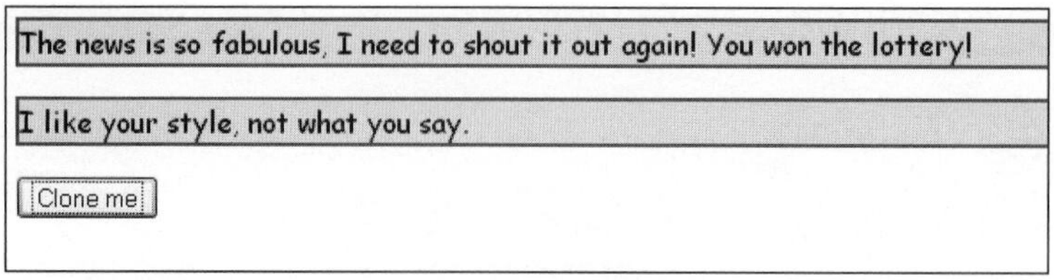

The news is so fabulous, I need to shout it out again! You won the lottery!

I like your style, not what you say.

[Clone me]

Figure 15.25   After clone, style is applied to the text in the second paragraph.

Cloning a Table with a Unique *id*.   In the next example we clone a table, the same table created in Example 15.13. Rather than copying all the code, this example shows the steps necessary to clone the table and then give the new table a unique *id*.

EXAMPLE 15.14

```
        <Continued from Example 15.11 at line 17.>

        // Insert the table into the document tree—line 17
        // in Example 15.11
        Tcontainer=document.getElementById("TableContainer");
        Tcontainer.appendChild(Table);
        // Let's make a copy of the table
1       var tableCopy = document.getElementById("myTable");
2       var newTable = tableCopy.cloneNode(true);
3       newTable.id = "newtable_id";
4       newDiv = document.getElementById("NewTableContainer");
5       newDiv.appendChild(newTable);
        }
    </script>
  </head>
  <body>
    <div id="TableContainer"></div>
    <br />
6   <div id="NewTableContainer"></div>
  </body>
</html>
```

EXPLANATION

1   The *id* attribute for the table created in Example 15.11 is *myTable*. The *document.getElementById()* method returns a reference to that table.

2   The original table created in Example 15.11 is cloned with the *cloneNode()* method. It is a replica of the original table including all of its attributes.

3   Because the clone includes the *id* attribute, a new unique *id* is assigned to the cloned table. The rule is that HTML *ids* must be unique or the program cannot identify another element with the same *id*.

4   A reference to a new *div* is returned.

5   The cloned table is appended to the *div* just below the original table (see Figure 15.26).

6   This is the *div* container for the cloned table.

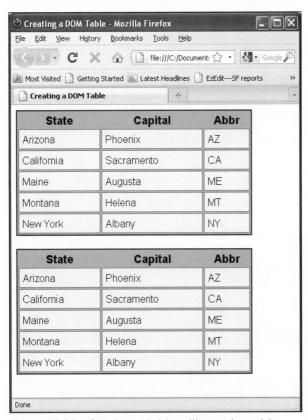

Figure 15.26   Cloning a table with a unique *id*.

15.7.9   Removing a Node

If you want to dynamically remove a post from a blog or an ingredient from an online recipe, it can be done with the DOM. To delete an element or node from the DOM tree, we use the *removeChild()* method. This method must be called from the parent node because you will be removing a child. It takes a reference to the child it will remove as its only argument. The following examples demonstrate how to dynamically remove nodes with JavaScript and the DOM. The first example, Example 15.15, removes a *div* and its contents; the second example, Example 15.16, removes paragraphs.

FORMAT

```
removeChild(referenceToChild)
```

EXAMPLE

```
parentDiv1.removeChild(div2);
```

EXAMPLE 15.15

```
    <html>
      <head><title>Removing a Child with the DOM</title>
        <script type="text/javascript">
1         function removeDiv() {
2            var divMid = document.body.getElementsByTagName("div")[1];
3            divMid.parentNode.removeChild(divMid);
             // Remove the middle div
             // alert((document.body.getElementsByTagName("div")).length
             //         + " divs left");  prints 2
          }
        </script>
      </head>
      <body onload="removeDiv()">
4         <div>this is div1</div>
5         <div>this is div2</div>
6         <div>this is div3</div>
      </body>
    </html>
```

EXPLANATION

1   The function called *removeDiv()* will remove a *div* element from the DOM tree.

2   The *getElementsByTagName()* method returns a reference to the second *div* tag in the document. The *[1]* index is applied to the *<div>* reference returned by *getElementsByTagName()*, and retrieves the second *div*. *[0]* would be the first *div* in the list of *<div>* tags.

3   Using the reference to the second *<div>*, we go to the parent *<div>* and remove its child, the second *div* (see Figure 15.27).

4   Three *divs* are defined in this document.

Figure 15.27   A *div* container is removed.

EXAMPLE   15.16

```
      <html>
          <head><title>Delete an Element with the DO</title>
              <style type="text/css">
                  p { font-style:arial;
                      color:darkblue;
                      font-size:18
                  }
              </style>
              <script type="text/javascript">
1                 function remove(f){
2                     for(var i=0; i<f.choice.length; i++){
3                         if(f.choice[i].checked){
                              //Find the paragraph that was checked
4                         var p_element=document.getElementById(f.choice[i].value);
5                         document.body.removeChild(p_element)
                          }
                      }
                  }
              </script>
          </head>
          <body>
              <script type="text/javascript">
                  // Create three paragraphs with text
6                 for(var i=1; i <= 3; i++){
                      var aPara=document.createElement("p");
                      var aBR = document.createElement("br");
                      var aTXT1=document.createTextNode("Hello, world. ");
                      var aTXT2=document.createTextNode("I really don't
                                                      want to be deleted! ");
                      var aTXT3=document.createTextNode("I am paragraph " + i);
7                     aPara.setAttribute("id","aPara" + i);
                      document.body.appendChild(aPara);
                      aPara.appendChild(aTXT1);   //Put paragraph in the doc
                      aPara.appendChild(aBR);
```

Continues

EXAMPLE 15.16 (CONTINUED)

```
            aPara.appendChild(aTXT2);
            aPara.appendChild(aBR);
            aPara.appendChild(aTXT3);
        }
    </script>
    <form>
        Which paragraph do you want to remove? <br />
8       <input type="radio" name="choice"
                value="aPara1">Paragraph 1 /><br />
        <input type="radio" name="choice"
                value="aPara2">Paragraph 2 /><br />
        <input type="radio" name="choice"
                value="aPara3">Paragraph 3 /><br />

        <input type=button value="click for paragraph to remove"
9               onClick="remove(this.form);" />
    </form>
    </body>
</html>
```

EXPLANATION

1 This user-defined function is responsible for removing a paragraph based on the user's choice. The parameter, *f*, is a reference to the form object passed when the button was clicked on line 9.

2 The *for* loop will iterate three times, one for each radio button.

3 The radio button's property, *checked*, returns true for the button if it was selected.

4 Based on the choice of the user (i.e., the radio button that was checked), the *getElementById()* method will return a reference to the value attribute of the radio button that happens to be the unique *id* of the paragraph.

5 The paragraphs are children of the *body* element. Now that we have a reference to the paragraph, it can be removed from the body of the document with the *removeChild()* DOM method.

6 This *for* loop cycles three times. For each iteration of the loop a new paragraph is dynamically created using the DOM.

7 Each paragraph is assigned a unique *id* attribute to be used by JavaScript to get a reference to the paragraph to be removed.

8 The user can click a radio button to remove one of the paragraphs.

9 When the user clicks this button, a reference to this form, *this.form*, is sent to the function called *remove()*. This process is shown in Figures 15.28, 15.29, and 15.30.

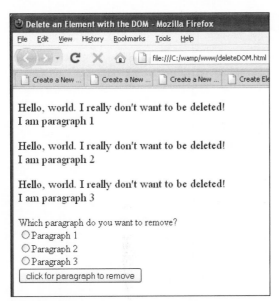

Figure 15.28   Three paragraphs have been created.

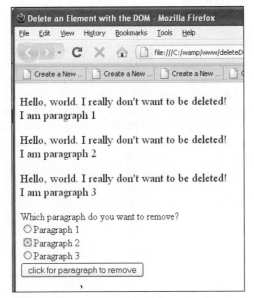

Figure 15.29   The user clicks on paragraph 2 for removal.

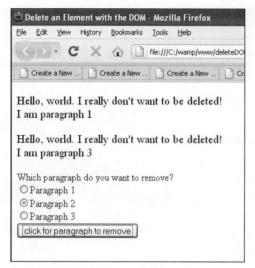

Figure 15.30   Paragraph 2 has been removed.

15.7.10   Scrolling with the Nodes

In the following example, all three layers of a a Web page are represented: the HTML content layer, the CSS presentation layer, and the JavaScript behavioral layer. By using the *getElementById()* method and a little node knowledge, a scrolling marquee is created in Example 15.17. In Chapter 10, Example 10.11 we saw scrolling in the window's status and title bar. Now we can scroll within the body of the document. The program creates a message that will continuously scroll across the screen. The original message is placed within a *<div>* container. By first identifying the HTML *div* element—*getElement-ById()*—JavaScript can then reference its child node, which is the text of the message (*firstChild*). This is depicted in Figure 15.31.

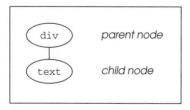

Figure 15.31   Referencing a child node requires first identifying the *div* element.

EXAMPLE 15.17

```
   <html>
     <head><title>Scrolling Text</title>
       <style type="text/css">
1        #div1 { background-color:darkgreen;
               color: white;
               font-family:courier;
               font-weight: bold;
               position:absolute;
               border-style:groove;
               border-color:white;
               padding-left:10px;
               top:20px;
               left:10px;
2              width: 595px; height: 6%;
3              overflow: hidden;
         }
4        img { position: absolute; top: 10px;left:60px;
               border-style:solid;border-color:"darkgreen";}
         body { background-color:#669966;}
       </style>
       <script type="text/javascript">
5        /*Modification of text box marquee by Dave Methvin,
           Windows Magazine */
6        var scroll_speed = 200;    // 200 milliseconds
         var chars = 1;
         var divElement;
7        window.onload=function() {
             divElement=document.getElementById("div1");
         }
8        function scroller() {
9            window.setTimeout('scroller()',scroll_speed);
10           var msg=divElement.firstChild.nodeValue;
11           divElement.firstChild.nodeValue = msg.substring(chars)
                       + msg.substring(0,chars);
         }
12       scroller();
       </script>
     </head>
     <body>
       <img src="BubyanIsland.JPG" width="450" length="500">
13     <div id="div1">
         The latest news from Baghdad is not good tonight. Sand and
         rain are hindering our troops. The number of refugees
         continues to increase in the north...
       </div>
     </body>
   </html>
```

EXPLANATION

1   An ID selector is defined with a style for the *div* element on line 13.

2   The size of the *div* container is defined.

3   If the text within the *div* container will not fit within the dimensions of the box, the *overflow* property will adjust it to fit.

4   The image is fixed at this absolute position on the screen and has a dark green, solid border.

5   The *scroller()* routine (line 8), modified from the original, was found at the Java Planet Web site and submitted by Dave Methvin. (Thank you Dave, wherever you are!)

6   The initial values used for the *scroller()* function are assigned values. One is the speed for the timer, the other the value of an argument to the *substr()* method.

7   This anonymous function is called after the document has been loaded. Its purpose is to get a reference to the *div* element. The *getElementById()* method returns a reference to the *div* element.

8   The function called *scroller()* is defined. Its function is to cause the text found in the *<div>* container to scroll continuously from the right side of the container.

9   The window's *setTimeout()* method is used to call the *scroller()* function every 200 milliseconds (.2 seconds). It's the timer that creates the action of actually scrolling.

10 The *div* element is a parent node. It has a child node. The value of its first child, *divElement.firstChild.nodeValue*, is the textual content of the message; that is, the text found between the *<div></div>* tags. The variable *msg* gets the value of the child node.

11 The value returned by *msg.substr(1)* is "*he latest news from Baghdad is not good tonight. Sand and rain are hindering our troops. The number of refugees continues to increase in the north...*" Notice that the first character in the message has been removed. The next substring method will return the first character—*substring(0,1)*—and append it to the first value resulting in "*he latest news from Baghdad is not good tonight. Sand and rain are hindering our troops. The number of refugees continues to increase in the north...T*". All of this is assigned back to the value of the child node. In 200 milliseconds, the *scroller()* function is called again, and the message becomes "*e latest news from Baghdad is not good tonight. Sand and rain are hindering our troops. The number of refugees continues to increase in the north...Th*", and so on.

12 The *scroller()* function is called for the first time here.

13 The *<div>* tags contain the text of the message that will be scrolled. Its id, "*div1*", defines the CSS style that will be used, and is the unique identifier that will be used by JavaScript to get a reference to it. See the output in Figure 15.32.

o increase in the north. The latest news from Baghdad is

Figure 15.32 A scrolling marquee continues to print news across the image.

15.8 Event Handling and the DOM

15.8.1 The HTML Inline Way

We have been using event handlers like *onClick*, *onSubmit*, *onMouseOver*, throughout this text. In fact, Chapter 13, "Handling Events," described in detail all of the different event handlers and how to use them. They are the oldest and simplest way that is browser compatible. The following example uses the *onClick* handler as an attribute of the button element. When the user clicks the button, the function *movePosition()* will be called.

```
<input type="button" value="move text"
onClick="movePosition()" />
```

But using this type of handler violates the principle of separation of the layers; that is, the separation of markup from JavaScript.

15.8.2 The Scripting Way

To keep the markup and the JavaScript separate, the JavaScript provided a way for programmers to apply properties to any object in the HTML tree. In the following example, the *onLoad* event property is applied to the window object so that when the document has completed loading the function assigned to that object will be triggered. In this example the background color will be changed to light green. See Chapter 13 for details if you need to be refreshed on this traditional model for handling events.

```
window.onload=function(){
    document.getElementById("bdy").style.backgroundColor="lightgreen";
}
```

15.8.3 The DOM Way

The W3C Dom Level 2 standardized the event model to solve compatibility problems between browsers. Most modern browsers (Mozilla, Opera, Safari, Chrome and Konqueror) are W3C compliant, except Microsoft Internet Explorer which has its own model.

DOM objects can be registered as event listeners. This feature can be used to assign multiple handlers for a given event which is the main difference from the traditional model. To achieve this, event listeners are no longer stored as HTML attribute values but are registered with an event listener method.

The W3C supports event bubbling described below, but has a *useCapture* option can be used to specify that the handler should be called in the capture phase. Browser).

15.8.4 Bubbling and Capturing

When we discussed events in Chapter 13 we introduced capturing and bubbling to describe the flow of events in a program. The way that the events are captured differs in different browsers. In Mozilla Firefox, for example, the event comes to life at the window level and is sent down the tree of nodes until it finally reaches the target object for which it was intended, whereas with Internet Explorer the event springs to life for the target it was intended to affect, and then sends information about the event bubbling back up the chain of nodes. Handling the way events propagate has been another browser compatibility issue. The W3C DOM Level 2 allows the DOM nodes to handle events with a **combination** of these methods, but defaults to the **bubble up** propagation model.

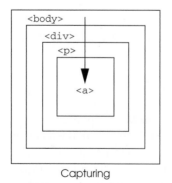
Capturing

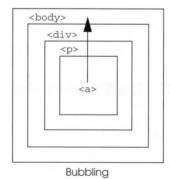
Bubbling

Figure 15.33 Event capturing and bubbling.

How Bubbling Works.   In Figure 15.33, the document contains a *<body>* that contains a *<div>* that contains a *<p>* that contains an *<a>* tag. Now assume that a click event handler has been assigned to all four of them. When a user clicks the link, the events bubble up. The click's original target, the *<a>*, gets to see the event first, and then passes it upward to the *<p>* for further processing, which passes it on to the *<div>*, which finally passes it up to the body of the document. This program was executed in three browsers, Firefox, Opera, and Internet Explorer. All of them use bubbling

How Capturing Works.   With capturing, when the user clicks the link, the link doesn't get the event first. Instead, the event listener attached to the document grabs the event first and processes it. (That is, it captures the event before it gets to its intended target.) The event is then passed down to the *<div>*'s event handler. The event then goes to the *<p>*, and finally to the *<a>*. That is, all of the clicked-on object's "ancestors" higher up in the document capture the event for processing before sending it down the chain to its intended target.

See event listeners for setting event capturing.

EXAMPLE   15.18

```html
<html>
    <title>Bubbling</title><head>
        <script type="text/javascript">
            /* This program behaves the same way in both Firefox and
               Internet Explorer and Opera. The W3C states bubbling as
               the default. */
1           var d1,p1,p2,a1;
2           window.onload=function(){
3               b1=document.getElementById('bdy1');
                d1=document.getElementById('div1');
                p1=document.getElementById('para1');
                p2=document.getElementById('para2');
                a1=document.getElementById('link1');

4               b1.onclick=iam;
                d1.onclick=iam;
                p1.onclick=iam;
                p2.onclick=iam;
                a1.onclick=iam;
            }
5           function iam(){
                alert(this.id);
            }
        </script>
    </head>
6   <body id="bdy1">
        <h2>Bubble bubble...</h2>
        <div id="div1">
```

Continues

EXAMPLE 15.18 (CONTINUED)

```
                <p id="para1">Some text in a paragraph element.</p>
                <p id="para2">Another paragraph element with text.
7                   <a id="link1" href="#">link</a>
                </p>
            </div>
        </body>
    </html>
```

EXPLANATION

1   Global variables are declared for the script.

2   Once the page has loaded, the onload event is triggered and the anonymous function is called.

3   The *getElementById()* method is used to get a reference to on the elements in the page: the body, the *div*, the paragraph, and the link.

4   For each element an *onclick* event is registered. The *iam()* function will be called when the event happens. When the user clicks the link, the function will be called and then bubble up to the parent of the link, its grandparent, and so on. If you start at say "para1" and click on that paragraph, the bubbling starts from there and ignores those events for "para2" and "link1".

5   This function will be called when the *click* event happens on each of the elements listed above. See the output to see when this function is called.

6   The body of the page is given a unique *id*.

7   In this example, the user clicked the link, which started a chain of events bubbling up from there, as shown in Figures 15.34 and 15.35.

Figure 15.34   The page before any event occurs.

Figure 15.35 The user clicked on the link first, and it bubbled up from there for each element. The body element was last and at the top of the bubbling chain.

Stopping or Cancelling the Event Flow.   The W3C event model allows you to cancel or stop the flow of a set of events from happening. In the last example, once you clicked on the link, the next click event happened, and so on, until the last element, the *body*, was reached. In the next example, the bubbling is stopped with the *stopPropagation()* event method, a method provided to stop bubbling in W3C compliant browsers. Some event methods are given in Table 15.7.

Table 15.7 Event Methods

stopPropagation()	Prevent further propagation of an event during event flow.
preventDefault()	Cancels the event if it is cancelable, meaning that any default action normally taken when the event happens, will not occur.
initEvent(eventType, isBubble, isCancelable)	Event type such as click, mousedown, and so on. Boolean true or false to determine event's default event flow, bubble or cancel.

The *cancelBubble* Property (Internet Explorer).   If using Internet Explorer, this is how you would cancel the bubbling in Example 15.19 with the *cancelBubble* property. If set to *true* this property disables bubbling for this event, preventing the next event in the hierarchy from receiving the event.

```
event.cancelBubble = true;
```

EXAMPLE 15.19

```
    <html>
       <title>Bubbling Cancelled</title><head>
         <script type="text/javascript">
1           var d1,p1,p2,a1;
2           window.onload=function(){
3             b1=document.getElementById('bdy1');
```

Continues

EXAMPLE 15.19 (CONTINUED)

```
            d1=document.getElementById('div1');
            p1=document.getElementById('para1');
            p2=document.getElementById('para2');
            a1=document.getElementById('link1');

4           b1.onclick=iam;
            d1.onclick=iam;
            p1.onclick=iam;
            p2.onclick=iam;
            a1.onclick=iam;
        }
5       function iam(e){
        if (!e){
            e = window.event;
6           e.cancelBubble = true; /* Microsoft IE* /
        }
        else{
7           e.stopPropagation(); /* W3C */
        }
        // stop all other targets with event listeners from
        // triggering this event
        }
    </script>
    </head>
8   <body id="bdy1">
    <h2>Bubble bubble...</h2>
    <div id="div1">
9       <p id="para1">Some text in a paragraph element.</p>
        <p id="para2">Another paragraph element with text.
10          <a id="link1" href="#">link</a>
        </p>
    </div>
    </body>
</html>
```

EXPLANATION

1   Global variables are declared that will be used in the function that follows.

2   Once the page has loaded the onload event handler is triggered, causing the anonymous function to be executed.

3   The *document.getElementById()* method returns references to all of the HTML elements with *id* attributes.

4   Each of the element references is assigned the *onclick* event property and its value, a function called *iam()*.

EXPLANATION(CONTINUED)

5   When the click event is triggered, the function called *iam()* is called and sent to the event. The event object is received as a parameter. It contains data about the event, in this case the *click* event and the object that was clicked. (See Chapter 13.)

6   The *cancelBubble* property (Internet Explorer) returns or sets a Boolean that represents whether the current event should bubble up the hierarchy of event handlers. If set to *true*, event bubbling is canceled, preventing the next event handler in the hierarchy from receiving the event.

7   The *stopPropagation()* method is used to prevent further propagation of an event during event flow. If this method is called by any event listener or handler, the event will stop bubbling up the DOM tree. The event will complete dispatch to all listeners on the current EventTarget before event flow stops. This method may be used during any stage of event flow so if you click the link, the bubbling will stop there or if you click on the *div* element, it will stop at that point and go no further. See *http://www.w3.org/TR/DOM-Level-2-Events/events.html#Events-flow-cancelation.*

8   An *id* attribute is assigned to the *body* element.

9   Two paragraphs within the *div* container are also given *ids*.

10   Within the second paragraph, an *id* is assigned to the *<a>* tag. If bubbling starts at the link, it will propagate upward through its ancestor tree to the all of those elements that are waiting for a *click* event to happen, but in this example the bubbling will stop right away because it is being canceled when the *iam()* function is called. See the results in Figures 15.36 and 15.37.

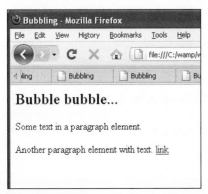

Figure 15.36   The initial page before clicking on the link.

Figure 15.37   Further bubbling stops after a user clicks the link.

15.9 Event Listeners with the W3C Model

15.9.1 Adding an Event

The *addEventListener* Method.   The W3C event model adds the *addEventListener()* method, which registers a single event listener on a document, a window, a DOM node or X(HTML), or an Ajax XMLHttpRequest (see Chapter 18, "An Introduction to Ajax (with JSON)"). This method takes three arguments:

1. The event type to listen for (mouseover, click, etc.).
2. A function to be executed when the event is fired.
3. A Boolean (called *useCapture*) of true or false to specify the event propagation type: *true* to turn on event capturing and *false* to turn on event bubbling (the most cross-browser-compliant way is false).

FORMAT

```
        target.addEventListener(type, listener, useCapture);
```

EXAMPLE

```
        var div1 = document.getElementById("mydiv");
        div1.addEventListener('click',sayWelcome,false);
```

You can register more than one event for a target if the events or capture parameters are different. Now we register another event listener to the same element as follows:

```
var div1 = document.getElementById("mydiv");
div1.addEventListener("click",bigFont,false);
div1.addEventListener("click",smallFont, true);
```

So which event takes place first? The W3C model does not state which event handler is fired first so we will check in Example 15.21. However, if multiple identical event listeners are registered on the same target with the same parameters, the event listener will only be called once and the duplicate instances discarded.

Using *this* within the Handler.   As we have seen in many examples throughout this text, the *this* keyword normally represents a reference to an object passed to a function, but the *this* keyword, when used with W3C event handlers, is a reference to the HTML element from which the event handler was fired, giving you easy access to the element.

```
function changeStyle() {
    this.style.backgroundColor = '#cc0000';
}
```

EXAMPLE   15.20

```
    <html>
      <head><title></title>
        <script type="text/javascript">
          window.onload=function(){
1           var paraHandle = document.getElementById("mypara");
2           paraHandle.addEventListener('click',alterText, false);
            function alterText(){
3               this.style.backgroundColor ="tan";
                this.style.fontFamily ="fantasy";
                this.style.fontWeight ="bold";
            }
          }
        </script>
      </head>
      <body>
4       <p id="mypara">
          There was an old lady who lived
          in a shoe.<br />
          She had so many children, she
          didn't know what to do.<br />
        </p>
      </body>
    </html>
```

EXPLANATION

1   The *getElementById()* method returns a reference to the paragraph identified on line 4.

2   The *addEventListener()* method takes three arguments, the event that will be registered for the paragraph, the name of a function that will be called when the *click* event is triggered, and a Boolean value of false, indicating the bubbling is the method of event propagation.

3   When the user clicks on the paragraph, the paragraph will be styled using the *style* property of the current object, *this*. Because *this* refers to whatever object was affected by the click, it could be used by more than one event listener.

4   The *p* element is assigned an *id* attribute that will be used to identify the paragraph in line 1. See the results in Figures 15.38 and 15.39.

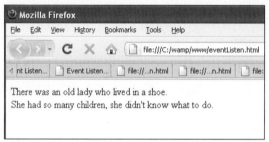

Figure 15.38   Before clicking on the paragraph.

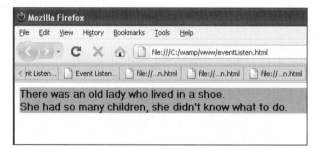

Figure 15.39   After clicking on the paragraph.

15.9.2   Registering More Than One Event

The W3C model allows you add as many event listeners as you want to an element. In Example 15.21, the second paragraph is registered with two event handlers. If the mouse is rolled over the element, the text is highlighted. If the click event occurs, the font is enlarged.

EXAMPLE 15.21

```
        <html>
            <head><title>Register Multiple Events</title>
                <script type="text/javascript">
1               window.onload=function(){
2                   var paraHandle = document.getElementById("para1");
                    var paraHandle2 = document.getElementById("para2");
3                   paraHandle.addEventListener('mouseover',highLight, false);
4                   paraHandle2.addEventListener('click', function(){
5                       this.style.fontSize="x-large"},false);
6                   paraHandle2.addEventListener('mouseover', highLight,false);
7                   function highLight(){
8                       this.style.backgroundColor ="tan";
                        this.style.fontFamily ="fantasy";
                        this.style.fontWeight ="bold";
                    }
                }
                </script>
            </head>
            <body>
9               <p id="para1">
                    There was an old lady who lived in a shoe.<br />
                    She had so many children, she didn't know what to do.</p>
10              <p id="para2">She gave them some broth,<br />
                    without any bread,<br />
                    Whipped them all soundly <br /> and sent them to bed.
                </p>
            </body>
        </html>
```

EXPLANATION

1   When the page has loaded the inline anonymous function will be called.

2   In the next two lines, JavaScript's *getElementById()* method will return references to two paragraphs in the HTML document.

3   The *addEventListener()* method takes three arguments, the event that will be registered for the paragraph, the name of a function, *highLight*, that will be called when the *mouseover* event is triggered, and a Boolean value of false, indicating the bubbling is the method of event propagation.

4   Another *addEventListener()* method registers the *click* event for the second paragraph, the inline function, that when called will dynamically change the font in the paragraph to extra large.

5   The *this* keyword when used with event handlers references the object on which the event fired, in this case, the second paragraph.

Continues

EXPLANATION(CONTINUED)

6   A second event listener registers another event, *mouseover*, to the second paragraph. Now if the user clicks the mouse on the second paragraph or rolls the mouse over, two events will be fired and their respective functions called, one to highlight the text and the other to make the font larger.

7   The function *highLight* is called when the *mouseover* event is triggered on the first paragraph. This function is nested within the anonymous function defined on line 1 that was called when the onload event was triggered on line 1.

8   The function has access to the object through the *this* keyword. (A function defined within another function is called a closure. See Chapter 7, "Functions."

9   This is the first paragraph that will be changed when the *mouseover* event is triggered.

10 This is the paragraph for which two events are registered, both the *click* and the *mouseover* events, and demonstrates that more than one event can be registered for the same object. This process is shown in Figures 15.40, 15.41, and 15.42.

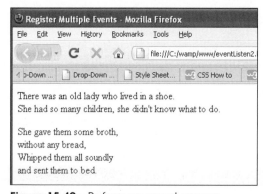

Figure 15.40   Before an event occurs.

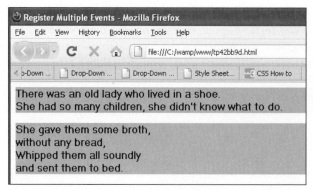

Figure 15.41   After clicking on both of the paragraphs.

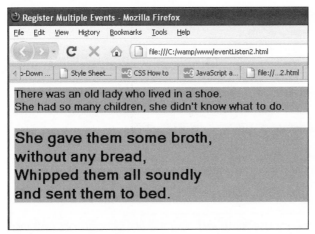

Figure 15.42   After the *mouse* event is fired on the second paragraph.

15.9.3   Removing an *EventListener*

To remove an event handler, the W3C provides the *removeEventListener()* method. With this function you can choose which event listeners to remove. The method takes three arguments: the name of the event, the function that will handle the event, and the Boolean flag, *useCapture*, which specifies the event flow: *true* for event capturing and *false* for event bubbling, the default. Note: The keyword "on" is not used with the event type, whereas with the Internet Explorer model it is required.

FORMAT

```
element.removeEventListener(eventType, function, useCapture);
```

EXAMPLE

```
element.addEventListener("mouseover", highlight, false);
element.removeEventListener("mouseover", highlight, false);
```

Note that you must specify the same *useCapture* value when removing a listener exactly as you used it when adding the event listener. To remove the event handler, simply make the *onclick* method empty. The results is shown in Figure 15.43.

Another way to remove the event handler is to set its value to null as:

```
element.onclick = null;
```

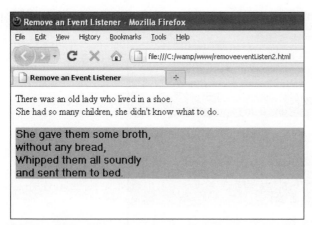

Figure 15.43 When the mouse is moved over the first paragraph, nothing happens. The event listener was removed.

EXAMPLE 15.22

```
     <html>
       <head><title>Register Multiple Events</title>
         <script type="text/javascript">
1          window.onload=function(){
2            var paraHandle1 = document.getElementById("para1");
             var paraHandle2 = document.getElementById("para2");
3            paraHandle1.addEventListener('mouseover',highLight, false);
4            paraHandle2.addEventListener('click', function(){
                this.style.fontSize="x-large"},false);
5            paraHandle2.addEventListener('mouseover', highLight,false);
6            paraHandle1.removeEventListener('mouseover',
                                            highLight,false);
7            function highLight(){  //Closure
8              this.style.backgroundColor ="tan";
               this.style.fontFamily ="fantasy";
               this.style.fontWeight ="bold";
             }
           }
         </script>
       </head>
       <body>
9        <p id="para1">
           There was an old lady who lived
           in a shoe.<br />
```

EXAMPLE 15.22 (CONTINUED)

```
           She had so many children, she
           didn't know what to do.</p
10         <p id="para2">She gave them some broth,<br />
           without any bread,<br />
           Whipped them all soundly <br />
           and sent them to bed.
         </p>
      </body>
   </html>
```

EXPLANATION

1   When the page loads, this anonymous function is activated. It will be used to change the style of two paragraphs.

2   The *document.getElementById()* method returns a reference to the first paragraph, and in the next line it returns a reference to the second paragraph.

3   The *addEventListener()* method is waiting for a *mouseover* event to occur on the first paragraph, at which time it will call the *highLight()* function. The Boolean false flag indicates that event bubbling is turned on.

4   The *addEventListener()* method is waiting for a *click* event to occur on the second paragraph, at which time it will call the inline anonymous function that will enlarge the font. The Boolean false flag indicates that event bubbling is turned on.

5   The *addEventListener()* method is waiting for a *mouseover* event to occur on the second paragraph, at which time it will call the *highLight()* function that will cause the text in the paragraph to be highlighted in a tan color. The Boolean false flag indicates that event bubbling is turned on.

6   The event listener that was added on line 3 is now removed with the *removeEventListener()* method. When the user moves the mouse over the first paragraph, it will no longer be highlighted (see Figure 15.44).

7   This is a function defined within a function. This function is on standby waiting for an event to be fired.

8   The JavaScript *this* keyword refers to the HTML element on which the event was fired. If it was fired on reference to a *p* element, then it refers to a paragraph. The style property will be used with CSS properties to highlight the text when the event occurs.

9   The first paragraph has a unique id, *para1*, with which to identify it in the JavaScript program.

10 The second paragraph has a unique id, *para2*, with which to identify it in the JavaScript program.

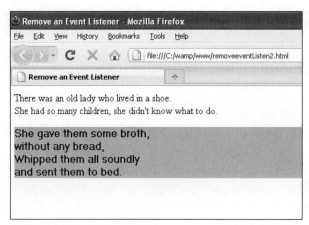

Figure 15.44   The event listener was removed. The mouse event doesn't occur.

15.9.4   Event Listeners with Microsoft Internet Explorer

Microsoft, too, has developed an event registration model. It looks similar to W3C's, but has some important differences. To write cross-platform compatible code, you can test for both. See Example 15.23.

The *attachEvent()* Method.   The *attachEvent()* method is an IE5+ proprietary equivalent of *addEventListener()*. The method is attached to the object for which the event is intended. The parameters include the event type and a function. Unlike the W3C model, the event type parameter must include the *on* prefix (i.e., *onload*, *onclick* etc.). If you forget this little, but important point, the method will not work!

FORMAT

```
            object.attachEvent(eventType, function)
```

EXAMPLE

```
if (window.attachEvent){
    myDiv=document.getElementById("div1");
    myDiv.attachEvent("onclick", changeColor);
}
```

The detachEvent() Method.   The *detachEvent()* method removes an event handler and its function and is the IE5+ proprietary equivalent of the DOM's *removeEventListener()*.

FORMAT

```
object.detachEvent(eventType, function);
```

EXAMPLE

```
if (window.detachEvent)
    object.detachEvent("onload", init)
```

There are differences you should be aware of when comparing the W3C model and the Internet Explorer model:

1. Events always bubble. There is no capturing feature.
2. The *this* keyword cannot be used to represent the event handling function. The *this* keyword refers to the global window object.

See Example 15.23 for examples of Internet Explorer handling.

EXAMPLE 15.23

```
      <html>
        <head><title>Internet Explorer Event Handling</title>
          <script type="text/javascript">
1           function greetings(){
              alert( "Hello World" );
            }
            // Add an event handler
2           window.attachEvent( "onload", greetings );

            // Add another event handler
3           document.attachEvent( "onclick", greetings );

            // Add another event handler
            document.attachEvent( "onmouseover", greetings);

4           // Remove an event handler just added
5           document.detachEvent( "onmouseover", greetings );
          </script>
        </head>
        <body>
          <p>IE has its own way of listening.</p>
        </body>
      </html>
```

EXPLANATION

1   This function will be called when a series of events are fired.

2   The *attachEvent()* method (IE) causes the onload event to fire when the page has loaded. The *onload* event is a window event, and the function defined on line 1, called *greetings()* will be called when that event is fired. This method requires that you use the *on* prefix with the event handler (see Figure 15.45).

3   The *attachEvent()* method (IE) causes the *click* event to fire when the user clicks anywhere on the document (i.e., Web page). When that happens the *greetings()* function will be called.

4   The *attachEvent()* method (IE) causes a *mouseover* event to fire when the user moves the mouse in the document. Two different events are tied to the document.

5   The *detachEvent()* method (IE) causes the mouse event created on line 4 to be removed.

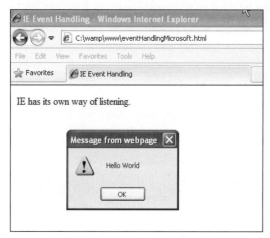

Figure 15.45   When the page loads an event is fired and when the user clicks anywhere on the document another event is fired.

15.9.5   Event Properties Revisited

In Chapter 13 we discussed the event object. There are a number of event types defined by the DOM HTML Events module, as shown in Table 15.8.

In Example 15.24, event listeners for both the DOM and Internet Explorer model are listening for *mouseOver* and *mouseOut* events. The function parameter of the event listeners change the style of a block of text to give it emphasis. When the mouse rolls over a specific block of text, the event handler invokes a function that can check to see what block of text the mouse is on and detect when it leaves the box. The node where the event occurred can be found in the *currentTarget* property (Firefox) or the *srcElement* property (Internet Explorer).

Table 15.8   Event Properties: DOM and Internet Explorer

Name	What It Describes
bubbles	Boolean to test whether an event can bubble up the document tree.
canceleable	Boolean to test whether the event can be cancelled.
currentTarget	The node currently being processed by a handler (Internet Explorer doesn't support this).
eventPhase	A number specifying the phase of the event propagation.
fromElement	Refers to the object where the mouse was pointing before the *mouseover* event was triggered (Internet Explorer).
srcElement	Refers to the object of the tag that caused the event to fire (Internet Explorer).
target	The node on which the event occurred, not necessarily the same as *currentTarget*.
timeStamp	When the event occurred (a *Date* object).
type	The type of the event that occurred, such as *click* or *mouseOut*.

EXAMPLE   15.24

```
/* File: externstyle.css */
  body { background-color: silver;
        font-size: 22pt;
        font-weight: bold;
  }
  .red { color:rgb(255,0,0);    /* Defining classes */
        font-style: verdana;
        font-size: 32;
  }
  .blue { color:blue;
          font-style: verdana;
          font-size: 36;
  }
  .green { color: green;
           font-style: verdana;
           font-size: 40;
  }
```

Continues

EXAMPLE 15.24 (CONTINUED)

```
    --------------------------------------------------
    <html>
      <head><title>Positioning</title>
1       <link rel=stylesheet type="text/css" href="externstyle.css">
        <script type="text/javascript">
          var div1,div2,div3;
2         window.onload=function (){
3           div1=document.getElementById("first");
            div2=document.getElementById("second");
            div3=document.getElementById("third");
4           if(div1.addEventListener!= undefined){
              //W3C Firefox Opera
5             div1.addEventListener('mouseover',unColorText,false);
              div1.addEventListener('mouseout', colorText,false);
              div2.addEventListener('mouseover',unColorText,false);
              div2.addEventListener('mouseout', colorText,false);
              div3.addEventListener('mouseover',unColorText,false);
              div3.addEventListener('mouseout', colorText,false);
            }
6           else{  // Internet Explorer
              div1.attachEvent('onmouseover',unColorText);
              div1.attachEvent('onmouseout', colorText);
              div2.attachEvent('onmouseover',unColorText);
              div2.attachEvent('onmouseout', colorText);
              div3.attachEvent('onmouseover',unColorText);
              div3.attachEvent('onmouseout', colorText)
            }
          }
7         function colorText(e){
8           var evt = e || window.event;  //Browser differences
9           var evtTarget= evt.target   || evt.srcElement;
10          if(evtTarget.id=="first"){
              div1.className="red";
            }
            else if(evtTarget.id == "second"){
              div2.className="blue";
            }
            else{ div3.className="green";}
          }
11        function unColorText(e){
            var evt = e || window.event;// use e.srcElement.id (IE)
            var evtTarget= evt.currentTarget   || evt.srcElement;
            if(evtTarget.id == "first"){
              div1.className="black";
            }
            else if(evtTarget.id == "second"){
              div2.className="black";
            }
```

EXAMPLE   15.24 (CONTINUED)

```
                else{
                    div3.className="black";
                }
            }
        </script>
    </head>
    <body>
12      <div id="first"
            style="position:absolute; top:50px">Roll over me! </div>
        <div id="second"
            style="position:absolute; top:100px">and then me,</div>
        <div id="third"
            style="position:absolute; top:150px">and me too.</div>
    </body>
</html>
```

EXPLANATION

1   The style for this document is coming from an external style sheet. It's the same style used in the previous example.

2   When the *onload* event is fired (when the page has been fully loaded) this anonymous function will be called, its purpose to color the text.

3   Now we get a reference to all three of the *divs* by their unique *ids*, assigned in the HTML document on line 12.

4   If using Internet Explorer, the *addEventListener()* method is undefined. If it's not undefined (i.e., the browser supports the DOM method), then this block of text will be entered.

5   The event listeners are waiting for a *mouseover* or a *mouseout* event to occur on each of the *divs* in the document. When the mouse rolls over a *div*, the *unColorText()* function will be called, and when the mouse moves out of a *div*, the *ColorText()* function is called.

6   Internet Explorer has its own method for event listening, called the *attachEvent()* method. The event listed as an argument, *onmouseover* or *onmouseout*, must have the prefix *on* or an error will occur.

7   The function *colorText()* takes one argument, a reference to the object where the event occurred. It is called when the user rolls the mouse away from the text in the *div*.

8   The type of the event is either passed to the function as a parameter, *e*, (W3C) or is a property of the global window object, *window.event* (Internet Explorer).

9   The target refers to the HTML element for which the event occurred. W3C uses the *currentTarget* property and Microsoft Internet Explorer uses the *srcElement* property.

Continues

EXPLANATION (CONTINUED)

10 By using the *id* of the target, we get the value of the unique *id* that was assigned to the object where the event occurred. The first *div* container is defined with an *id* name *"first"*. The *className* property defines the class for this object. When the mouse rolls over this *div*, it will turn "red".

11 The function, *unColorText()*, is triggered when the mouse moves over the text in one of the *divs*. This function works like the *ColorText()* function, but turns the text black when the mouse moves over the text, rather than coloring it. (It also changes the font size.) The results are shown in Figure 15.46.

12 The three *div* containers are set up and positioned for the document.

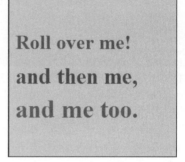

Figure 15.46   Before the mouse rolls over the first *<div>* block (top left); after the mouse has left all three containers (right). The font has changed in size and color for each *div*.

15.10 Unobtrusive JavaScript

In Chapter 1 we started talking about the three layers that make up a complete Web page:

1. The content or structural layer consisting of the HTML/XML markup.
2. The style or presentation layer consisting of the CSS style sheets.
3. The behavior layer consisting of JavaScript.

Although there is often a blurred line among these layers, the concept of separating content structure and style from behavior has become the goal for many developers building accessible and yet easy-to-maintain Web sites. The idea of keeping JavaScript completely separate from the other two layers is commonly called unobtrusive Java-Script. Developers have been keeping the structure and style of the document separate by placing the HTML/XML in one file and the CSS styles in a separate file, making it easy to change the layout throughout a Web page simply by changing the style sheet. Next comes JavaScript. Because JavaScript functions can be placed in separate files, the goal is to remove the inline JavaScript code, such as event handlers, from the HTML page, leaving the markup clean and yet still keeping the JavaScript accessible. Another function of the separation is for better practices such as adhering to the W3C standards and DOM scripting to avoid problems with nonstandard browser extensions and inconsistencies. Finally comes another important aspect of unobtrusive JavaScript, a strategy called "progressive enhancement" coined by Steve Champeon in 2003. The idea was that the content of the page would be made available to the browsers with the least capabilities, even those without JavaScript support. Aaron Gustafson describes in his article "Progressive Enhancement" the three layers of a Web page by using the analogy of a peanut M&M where the content layer is the peanut, the presentation layer is the chocolate layer surrounding the peanut, and the client-side scripting layer is the hard candy on the outside. He explains, "Then there are folks who can't handle the chocolate and candy layers on top of the peanut (diabetics, for example). Like them, people on mobile devices or older browsers may not be able to see your pretty design or interact with your slick Ajax-driven interface." The idea is to make the content as rich as possible so that everyone gets the best possible experience, no matter what browser they are using, rather than being forced to upgrade or just go without any experience at all. (See *http://www.alistapart.com/articles/understandingprogressiveenhancement/* for more on this subject.) There are a number of articles and forums on the Web offering guidelines on how to accomplish this "unobtrusiveness" both for and against it (see Figure 15.47). It is definitely a topic worth investigating if you are planning a serious Web project that will affect many users.

Now that we have discussed how to use the DOM to manipulate the HTML elements, to handle events without using HTML tags, and how to use CSS styles, it is time to put all the pieces together to illustrate the separation of the layers. Example 15.25 is an .html file that describes the HTML content layer, Example 15.26 is a .css file representing the CSS layer, and Example 15.27 is the .js file, the JavaScript program that provides interactivity and behavior. Together, these three files make up a simple Web page with a slideshow of images. The HTML markup is defined in the .html file; the colors, borders, and *div* positions are defined in the .css file; and the JavaScript program provides the behavior and interactivity with functions that respond to user-initiated events (see Figure 15.48). These files are intentionally kept small for demonstration purposes so that you can see the forest for the trees, rather than getting lost in long files cluttered with detail.

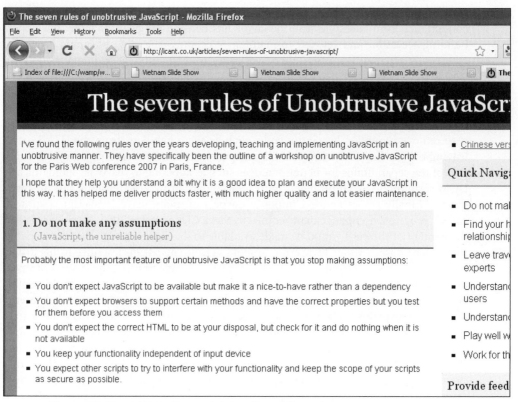

Figure 15.47   A Web site explaining the philosophy.

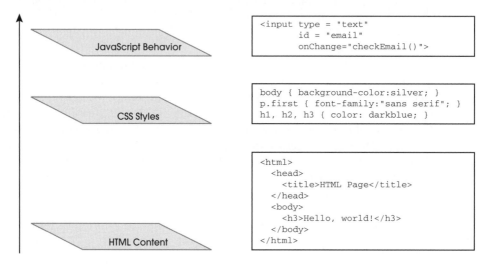

Figure 15.48   Three layers that make up a Web page.

Step 1: The HTML File—Structure and Content

EXAMPLE 15.25

```
    <html>
      <head><title>Vietnam Slide Show</title>
1       <link rel="stylesheet" type="text/css" href="vietnam_trip.css" />
2       <script type="text/javascript" src="vietnam_trip.js"></script>
      </head>
      <body>
        <div class="title">Vietnam Trip Gallery</div>
3       <img class="mainpic"
             id="vietnam_pic"
             src='file:///C:/wamp/www/images/DSCN1232.jpg'
             alt="vietnam travelog"
             width='492' height='370'/>
4       <div class="caption" id="description">
          Tour boats in the Mekong Delta<br />
        </div>
5       <div class="divbuttons">
          <form>
            <input type=button id="startButton"
                   value="Start Slideshow"/>
            <input type=button id="stopButton"
                   value="Stop Slideshow"/>
          </form>
        </div>
      </body>
    </html>
```

EXPLANATION

1   The external CSS style sheet is linked to the HTML document.

2   The external JavaScript program is included in this document.

3   This is the image that is initially displayed on the page.

4   The <*div*> uses a class defined in the external CSS file to display a caption under the image.

5   Two buttons are defined to start and stop the slideshow. Their positions on the page are defined by the *divbuttons* class in the external style sheet. Figure 15.49 shows the result.

Figure 15.49 The Web page.

Step 2: The CSS File: Presentation and Style

EXAMPLE 15.26

```
   /*Style for the Vietnam Trip Gallery */
1  .mainpic {  position:absolute; top: 50px;left:60px;
               border-style:solid;border-color:darkgreen;}
2  .title { position: absolute; left:165px; top: 8px;font-size:160%;
            color:darkgreen;font-family:cursive;}
3  .divbuttons { position:relative; top: 465px;left:60px;}
4  .caption { position:absolute; top: 430px;left:60px;
               font-family:cursive;font-style:bold;
               font-size:16pt;color:darkgreen;}
5  body{background-color:silver;}
```

1   A class defines the style of the first picture that appears in the document.
2   A class defines the style for the title at the top of each image in the slideshow.
3   A class defines the *div* position containing the start and stop buttons.
4   A class defines the title attribute of the *img* object that will serve as a caption under each image as it is displayed.
5   The body selector sets the background color of the window.

Step 3: The JavaScript File: Behavior and Interactivity

EXAMPLE 15.27

```
1  var i=0;
   var timeout;
   var hochimin;
2  window.onload=function(){
3     start=document.getElementById("startButton");
      stop=document.getElementById("stopButton");
4     hochimin=new Array();
5     var jpegs=["DSCN1211.jpg", "DSCN1212.jpg","DSCN1239.jpg",
                 "DSCN1257.jpg", "DSCN1202.jpg", "DSCN1264.jpg",
                 "DSCN1218.jpg", "DSCN1266.jpg","DSCN1200.jpg",
                 "DSCN1232.jpg"];
6     var picfile="file:///C:/wamp/www/images/";
7     var title = [ "Sidewalk food of noodles, chicken, fish, etc.",
                    "Balloon lady in Hochiminh City",
                    "Water buffalo pops his head up from the mud.",
                    "Sundown along the Mekong Delta",
                    "Some very colorful and hairy fruit",
                    "Meat vendor in Ben Hanh market",
                    "Single proprietor selling goods",
                    "Preparing food at dawn",
                    "No thanks. No Moped. We're walking",
                    "Tour boats in the Mekong Delta"
                  ];
8     for(var i=0; i<jpegs.length;i++){  //Preload images
         hochimin[i]=new Image();
         hochimin[i].src=picfile + jpegs[i];
         hochimin[i].title=title[i];  // Assign title to each image
      }
9     if(window.attachEvent){ // Is this Microsoft IE?
         start.attachEvent("onclick", startSlideShow);
         stop.attachEvent("onclick", stopSlideShow);
      }
```

Continues

EXAMPLE   15.27 (CONTINUED)

```
        else{ // W3C standard
10          start.addEventListener("click", startSlideShow, false);
            stop.addEventListener("click", stopSlideShow, false);
        }
    }
11  function startSlideShow(){
12      picture=document.getElementsByTagName("img").item(0);
13      divCaption=document.getElementById("description");
        if(i < hochimin.length){
14          picture.src=hochimin[i].src; //Image replacement
            divCaption.innerHTML=hochimin[i].title
            i++;
        }
        else{i=0;}
15      timeout = setTimeout('startSlideShow()',5000);
    }
16  function stopSlideShow(){
        clearTimeout(timeout);
    }
```

EXPLANATION

1   Global variables will be used by the functions.

2   When the page has finished loading the *onload* event handler is triggered, causing the anonymous function to be activated.

3   The next two lines get a reference to each of the buttons in the HTML page, one to start the slideshow and one to stop it.

4   This array will be used to preload all the images and to assign the location and title to each image (see Figure 15.50).

5   All of the JPEG images used in the Web page are assigned to the literal array called *jpegs*.

6   The variable, *picfile*, is assigned the directory path to the image files.

7   The literal array, *title*, is a list of all the captions that will appear under the pictures. They will be assigned as attributes of the image object.

8   The *for* loop is used to preload each image in the list of JPEGS and to assign both an *src* attribute with the path and name of the image, and a title for the image.

9   If using Microsoft's event model, then we go into the block and attach an *onclick* handler to the object called *start*. When the user clicks the button, the *startSlide-Show()* function will be called. Then we do the same for the *stop* object.

10   If using the DOM event model, the *addEventListener()* method will be attached to the objects called *start and stop*. When the user clicks one of the buttons, the event will be triggered to either start or stop the slideshow.

11   This is the function that will be called when the user clicks the "Start Slideshow" button in the form.

EXPLANATION (CONTINUED)

12 The *getElementsByTagName()* method returns a reference to the first *img* element in the document and assigns the reference to *picture*.

13 The *getElementById()* method returns a reference to the *div* element that will hold the caption for an image.

14 Every 5 seconds, an image replacement takes place by changing the value assigned to the *src* attribute of the image.

15 Every 5 seconds, the timer will call the *startSlideShow()* function.

16 The *stopSlideShow()* function turns off the timer, allowing the user to stop the slideshow at any time.

Figure 15.50 A sample of the slideshow thumbnails.

15.10.1 JavaScript Libraries

Although the code used in this book has been written from scratch, beginning with the very basic JavaScript, once you get going you might want to download some of the useful and free unobtrusive JavaScript code found in libraries on the Web. See *http://JavaScriptlibraries.com/* for a list of libraries and their links, and for a description of the ten most popular libraries, go to *http://www.ajaxline.com/10-most-popular-JavaScript-frameworks*. They are:

1. jQuery
2. Prototype

3. script.aculo.us
4. MooTools
5. ExtJS
6. Qooxdoo
7. Yahoo! UI Library (YUI)
8. MochiKit
9. Midori
10. The Dojo Toolkit

The libraries are compared for different features such as purpose, speed, event handling, animation, Ajax support, documentation, and more.

15.11 What You Should Know

One's first time looking at a JavaScript program that uses the DOM, a person could get very turned off with the upside-down tree, its parent and child nodes, the children of the child node, siblings, first node, last node, and the different event propagation models, and just let someone else deal with it. This chapter introduced that "DOM DOM" and we stepped through the W3C standard DOM methods used to manipulate the tree so that JavaScript could get a handle on very element of a Web page. We also discussed how to use the DOM for event handling and the differences between the standard W3C model and Microsoft's model. We talked about unobtrusive JavaScript, the strategy of separating JavaScript code from the HTML content and CSS presentation when developing Web pages. Now that you have reached the end of this chapter, the DOM should not be such a mystery, and you should be able to:

1. Traverse the document tree from node to node.
2. Understand the parent/child/sibling relationship.
3. Manipulate the tree using the DOM methods.
4. Create a new element and insert it into the DOM tree.
5. Delete an item from a list using the DOM.
6. Change the text in a paragraph using the DOM.
7. Create a list and table on the fly.
8. Clone an attribute.
9. Use event listeners.
10. Register more than one event for an object.
11. Turn on and off bubbling and capturing.
12. How Microsoft differs from the W3C implementation of handling events.
13. Use events to change the style of a document.
14. Cancel an event.
15. Why using the DOM event handling model is better than using the HTML inline or scripting model.
16. What is meant by unobtrusive JavaScript.
17. Find JavaScript libraries.

Exercises

1. Looking at the following markup, draw a model demonstrating the element and text nodes as a tree.

   ```
   <p>This is the <em>content</em> of my paragraph.</p>
   ```

2. Create an HTML document based on the following DOM tree. Check your DOM tree with a DOM inspector.

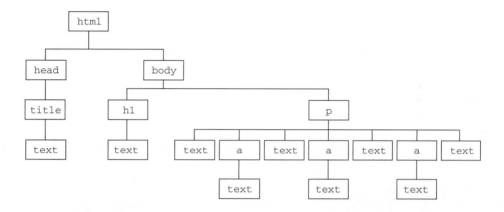

3. Using the DOM properties and methods, and using the markup in Exercise 1, create a JavaScript function that will be called when the document is loaded. Start with an HTML document containing *<div>* tags with an *id* attribute called *testdiv*. The function should be set up as follows:

   a. Create an element node *p* assigned to a variable called *para*.
   b. Create a text node assigned to a variable called *txt1*.
   c. Append *txt1* to *para*.
   d. Create an element node *em* assigned to a variable called *emphasis*.
   e. Create a text node assigned to a variable called *txt2*.
   f. Append *emphasis* to *para*.
   g. Append *txt2* to *emphasis*.
   h. Append *emphasis* to *para*.
   i. Create a text node assigned to a variable called *txt3*.
   j. Append *txt3* to *para*.
   k. Append *para* to the element *testdiv* in the document.

4. Create an HTML document with a list of vegetables styled with square bullets. Write a JavaScript function that will use the *getElementsByTagName()* function to retrieve the list items. Append a new vegetable to the list using the DOM.

5. Use the following JavaScript function in a .js file and create an HTML document
   to produce the output shown here:

```
function get_fortune() {
   today = new Date();
   sayings = new Array(
     "Carpe Diem.",
     "Silence is golden but duck tape is silver.",
     "An apple a day keeps the doctor away.",
     "To each his own.",
     "If at first you don't succeed, try again.",
     "Never settle for mediocrity, strive for success",
     "Live and let live."
   );
   n=sayings.length;
   number = Math.floor(Math.random()*n);
   fortune = "Today is "+today+ ".<br /><br />Today's fortune:
           <br /><br /><em>" +sayings[number] +"</em>";
   document.getElementById('divsaying').innerHTML = fortune;
}
```

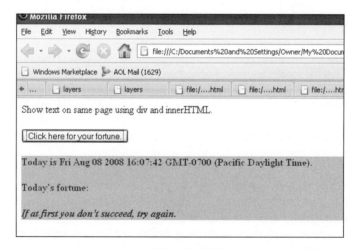

6. Create a document that contains a table with at least two rows and columns.
   Put text in the table cells using the DOM.

7. Write a function that can be used to add and remove an event listener. The
   function will be cross-browser compliant. It will take three arguments: a reference to the object, the event (*click, onclick*), and the function that will handle
   the event. The W3C Boolean value will be set to *false*. You can rewrite Example
   15.23 using your functions.

8. Write a JavaScript program that will use an event listener to modify a table as shown here. When the user clicks the first table cell the second one is changed.

9. Use the DOM to dynamically create a link and set its attributes. Use the DOM to get the attribute and display its value in an alert box.

10. How would you remove one of the blogs in Example 15.10? Write a function to demonstrate.

chapter
16

Cookies

16.1 What Are Cookies?

The Web protocol, HTTP, was designed to be stateless to keep transactions between a browser and server brief and cut down on the overhead of keeping connections open. **Stateless** means that after a transaction takes place between the browser and server, the connection is lost and neither the browser nor server have any recollection of what transpired between one session and the next. But as the Internet grew and people started filling up shopping carts with all kinds of goodies, ordering everything from groceries to music, books, prescription drugs, and even cars and homes, it became necessary for merchants to remember what their customers purchased, their preferences, registration numbers, user IDs, and so on. Enter Netscape way back in 1994 with the cookie. A **cookie** is a local file used to store information, and it is persistent; that is, it is maintained between browser sessions and remains even when the user shuts down his or her computer. The cookie idea became very popular and is now supported by all major browsers.

The term "cookie" comes from an old programming trick for debugging and testing routines in a program. A text file called a "magic cookie" was created. It contained text that was shared by two routines so that they could communicate with each other. The cookie feature started by Netscape[1] is also just a little piece of textual data that is stored in a file (often called the cookie jar) on the hard drive of the client (browser). It contains information about the viewer as he or she navigates different pages on a Web site or returns to the Web site at a later time. The information might be as simple as to welcome the viewer to your site, and based on past visits, show him or her a new book by a favorite author, display the latest stock quotes, or take the user to CNN Europe when he or she wants to view the news. It could save billing and shipping information to be retrieved at a later time to save retyping it over again.

There are two kinds of cookies: session cookies and persistent cookies. The session cookies are stored in memory on the server, whereas persistent cookies are stored in a

---

1. See *www.netscape.com/newsref/std/cookie_spec.html* for cookie specification.

cookie file on the client. We will be talking about persistent cookies in this chapter. The HTTP server sends the cookie to the browser when the browser connects for the first time and from then on, the browser returns a copy of the cookie to the server each time it connects. The information is passed back and forth between the server and browser via HTTP headers. Figure 16.1 demonstrates how the Firefox add-on, called Live HTTP Headers, displays the back-and-forth transaction between a browser and server with cookies (server site is Amazon.com).

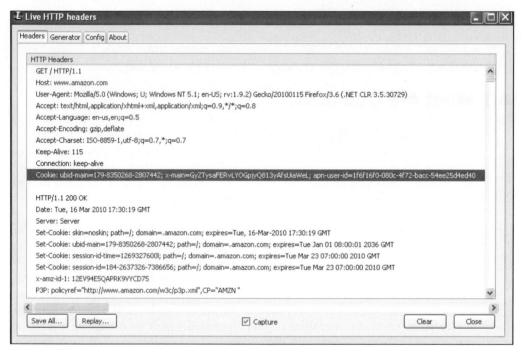

Figure 16.1   Watching cookies with Firefox Live HTTP Headers add-on.

Cookies can make a Web page personal and friendly, and store important information about the user's language, reading, or music preferences, and how many times he or she has visited your site; track items in a shopping cart; and more. However, some companies use cookies to track you across various Web sites, even if you aren't aware of the company or didn't give them permission to do so. Modern browsers take care of this by giving you control over what sites are allowed or not allowed to set cookies. Cookies can also be annoying, and some question the security of putting unknown data on their hard drive.[2] Love 'em or hate 'em, they're an intrinsic part of the Web. But you do have a say about whether or not to

---

2. When a cookie is set in the set-Cookie HTTP response header as HttpOnly, the Web browser should not allow client-side scripts such as JavaScript to have access to the cookie. This can help mitigate the effects of cross-site scripting attacks. Both Firefox and Internet Explorer support this feature.

use them. If you don't like cookies, you can turn them off, and remove all of them from your hard drive. For example, if using Firefox, go to the Tools→Options→Privacy and from there you can block all cookies for this site (see Figure 16.2).

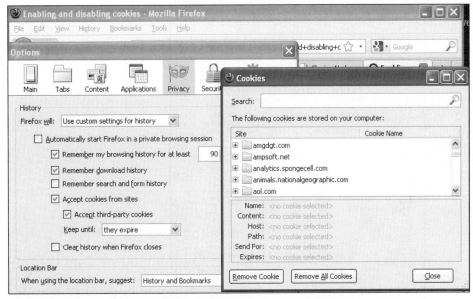

Figure 16.2   Firefox and cookies options.

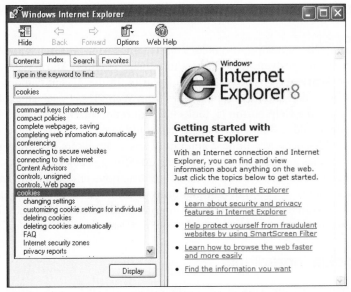

Figure 16.3   Internet Explorer Help on cookies.

If you are using Internet Explorer (see Figure 16.3), you can restrict cookies by going to the Tools menu and then to Internet Options→Privacy (see Figure 16.4).

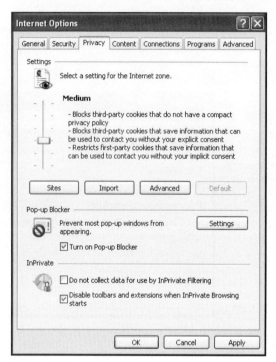

Figure 16.4   Internet Explorer: Move slider to select what cookie types are restricted.

If you are using Opera, it supports cookies in the same format as Firefox and Internet Explorer. Go to Tools→Advanced→Cookies to manage cookies. And if Safari is your browser, choose Safari→Preferences and click Security. In the Accept cookies section, specify if and when Safari should accept cookies from Web sites. To see an explanation of the options, click the Help button (it looks like a question mark).

Unlike Grandma's old-fashioned cookie jar that could be packed full of sugar cookies, Web browser cookies occupy a limited amount of space. Browsers usually can't store more than 300 cookies and servers not more than 20. Storage is usually limited to only 4 kilobytes per cookie, so you can't store a lot of information. The actual file name that holds the cookie data varies on different platforms. Mozilla Firefox stores cookies in a file named *cookies.txt* in the system directory; Internet Explorer stores them in the Window\Cookies directory, and for the Mac in /Users/YourUserName/Library/Cookies.

16.1.1   Cookie Ingredients

Cookies are often sent from a program on the server side (PHP, Java Servlet) to the browser through HTTP request and response headers, but with JavaScript you can set cookies on the local browser, eliminating the need for the server-side program to handle them, and thereby cutting down on server activity. The cookie's default lifetime is the length of the current session; then they are destroyed. See the expiration attribute discussed later.

Cookies are composed of text in the form of name/value pairs, often nicknamed "crumbs," and up to 20 pairs can be stored in a single cookie string. The browser stores only one cookie per page.

When making cookies, the crumbs consist of *name=value* pairs, called attributes, that must be terminated with a semicolon. Within the string, semicolons, commas, or whitespace characters are not allowed. The HTTP *Set-Cookie* header has the following format:

FORMAT

```
Set-Cookie: name=value; [expires=date};[path=path];
[domain=domainname]; [secure];
```

EXAMPLE

```
Set-Cookie: id="Bob";expires=Monday, 21-Oct-05 12:00:00
GMT;domain="bbb.com"; path="/"; secure;
```

16.1.2 The Attributes of a Cookie

When setting the cookie, it is important to understand the components of a cookie. It has a name and a value and another set of optional attributes to determine the expiration date, the domain, path, and whether the cookie must be sent over a secure communications channel (HTTPS). All of these attributes are assigned as strings.

Name.   The actual cookie text consists of the name of the cookie and the value stored there. It can be a session ID, a user name, or whatever you like.

FORMAT

```
nameofcookie=value;
```

EXAMPLE

```
id=456;
email=joe@abc.com;
name=Bob;
```

Don't confuse the value with what the cookie is named. The name of the cookie is on the left side of the = sign and the cookie text that gets stored there is on the right side. The value assigned is a string. With JavaScript you can also use the built-in *escape()*

method, which returns URL encoding for a string, acceptable to the browser. (See the section "Assigning Cookie Attributes" on page 702.)

Expiration Date.   The cookie normally expires when the current browser session ends, which gives it little value, but you can specify an expiration date that will let it persist, by using the following format:

FORMAT

```
;expires=Weekday, DD-MON-YY  HH:MM::SS GMT
```

EXAMPLE

```
;expires= Friday, 15-Mar-04 12:00:00 GMT
```

The day of the week is specified by *Weekday*, the day of the month by *DD*, the first three letters of the month by *MON*, and the last two numbers of the year by *YY* (e.g., *03* or *04*). The hour, minutes, and seconds are specified in *HH:MM:SS* and the GMT time zone is always used. Some cookies last for days, but it's possible for them to even last for years. It's up to the designer to decide how long a cookie should live. If sensitive information is contained in a cookie, setting the expiration date also can limit a potential attacker from intercepting the cookie as it is transported back and forth across the network (see *http://en.wikipedia.org/wiki/HTTP_cookie#Cookie_hijacking*).

Once the cookie has expired it is called stale and is automatically destroyed.

Domain Name.   The domain name, not commonly used, specifies a general domain name to which the cookie should apply. Each cookie has a domain and a path, if not set, the page that set the cookie. The domain tells the browser to which domain the cookie should be sent. The purpose of setting the domain is to allow cookies to cross subdomains; it allows the cookie to be shared among multiple servers instead of just the one you're on. If you don't use the full *http://domain* syntax, then a leading dot must precede the domain name.

FORMAT

```
; domain=.domain_name
; domain=http://somedomain.com
```

EXAMPLE

```
; domain=.kajinsky.com
; domain=http://kajinksy.com
```

Path.   The path is used to specify where the cookie is valid for a particular server. Setting a path for the cookie allows other pages from the same domain to share a cookie.

FORMAT

```
; path=pathname
```

EXAMPLE

```
; path=/home
```

Secure.   If a cookie is secure, it must be sent over a secure communication channel (HTTPS server).

FORMAT

```
; secure
```

16.2 Creating a Cookie with JavaScript

In the following examples, we will create a cookie, view the cookie, and then destroy it. It is important to note when you are setting cookies that they are stored in the browser's memory and not written to the hard drive until you exit the browser.

16.2.1   The Cookie Object

The cookie is stored by JavaScript as a document object for both reading and writing cookie data. Cookies are made by assigning attributes to the *cookie* property. When you start your browser, if there are cookies, they pertain to the current document. The *document.cookie* property contains a string of *name=value* pairs representing the names of all the cookies and their corresponding values, such as a session ID number or a user ID. All the other attributes set for the cookie, such as expiration date, path, and secure, are not visible. In a JavaScript program, if you execute the statement shown in Figure 16.5, you will see all the cookies set for this page.

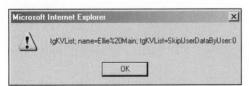

Figure 16.5   Using *alert(document.cookie);*

When you reload the page, the *document.cookie* property will contain all the cookie text saved for that page.

16.2.2   Assigning Cookie Attributes

To create a cookie, assign the *name=value* pairs to the *document.cookie* property. Be careful with quotes, making sure the variables you use are not quoted, but the text that the cookie needs, such as the word *"name"*, and *"="* are quoted. Also, this will be a big string where the different parts are concatenated together with the + operator. The following format sets a cookie using all possible attributes. Those attributes enclosed in square brackets are optional:

FORMAT

```
name=value;[expires=date];[path=path];[domain=somewhere.com];[secure]
```

EXAMPLE

```
document.cookie="id=" + form1.cookie.value ";expires=" +
expiration_date+";path=/";
```

The *escape()* and *unescape()* Built-In Functions.   It is important to know that when assigning string *name=value* attributes to a cookie, you cannot use whitespace, semicolons, or commas. The *escape()* function will encode the string object by converting all nonalphanumeric characters to their hexadecimal equivalent, preceded by a percent sign; for example, *%20* represents a space and *%26* represents an ampersand. To send information back and forth between browser and server, the browser encodes the data in what is called URI encoding. You can see this encoding in the location bar of your browser; when you go to Google and search for something, you will see the search string in the location bar of the browser all encoded. Because the browser handles cookies, the cookie strings can be encoded with JavaScript's built-in *escape()* function to ensure that the cookie values are valid.

The *unescape()* function converts the URI-encoded string back into its original format and returns it. The *encodeURI()* and *decodeURI()* built-in functions are a more recent version of *escape()* and *unescape()* and do not encode as many characters.

EXAMPLE   16.1

```
<html>
   <head>
      <title>The escape() Method</title>
      <script type="text/javascript">
```

EXAMPLE 16.1 (CONTINUED)

```
1          function seeEncoding(form){
               var myString = form.input.value;
2              alert(escape(myString));
           }
3          function seeDecoding(form){
               var myString = form.input.value;
4              alert(unescape(myString));
           }
        </script>
     </head>
     <body background="cookebg.jpg" >
        <div align="center"><h2>URL Encoding </h2>
           <form name="form1">
              Type in a string of text:
              <p>
                 <input type="text" name="input" size=40 />
              </p><p>
                 <input type="button"
                        value="See encoding"
5                       onClick="seeEncoding(this.form);" />
              </p><p>
                 <input type="button"
                        value="See decoding"
6                       onClick="seeDecoding(this.form);" />
              </p>
           </form>
        </div>
     </body>
  </html>
```

EXPLANATION

1   A function called *seeEncoding()* is defined. It takes a reference to a form as its only parameter.

2   The built-in *escape()* function is used to URI encode the string that was entered as input by the user.

3   A function called *seeDecoding()* is defined. It takes a reference to a form as its only parameter.

4   The built-in *unescape()* function is used to convert the URI encoded string back into its original ASCII format.

5   When the user clicks this button, the *onClick* event is triggered and the encoded string will appear in an alert dialog box.

6   When the user clicks this button, the *onClick* event triggers a function that will decode the encoded string. See Figures 16.6 and 16.7.

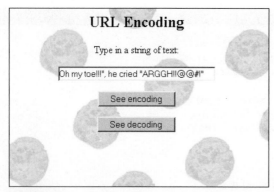

Figure 16.6 Using the *escape()* and *unescape()* functions.

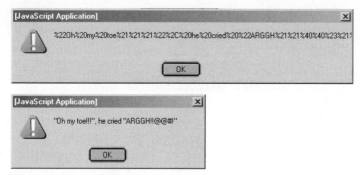

Figure 16.7 The user pressed the "See encoding" button (top); the user pressed the "See decoding" button (bottom).

16.2.3 Let's Make Cookies!

Now that we have all the ingredients, let's put them together and make a cookie, then pull it out of the oven (your program) and enjoy a delicious cookie for your browser. The following example creates two cookies called *"visitor"* and *"color"*. The value assigned to it will be the visitor's name and his or her favorite color. You will see this *name=value* pair in the *document.cookie* property. Once this page has been viewed, the cookie values are saved on the browser in a cookie file. The next time a user views a page on this site, the cookie values are available. In Example 16.2 we will retrieve the cookies on a different page and use the user preferences gleaned from a cookie to change the background color of the page.

EXAMPLE 16.2

```
      <html>
        <head><title>Making Cookies</title>
          <script type="text/javascript">
1           function makeCookie(form){
2              var when = new Date();
               when.setTime(when.getTime() + 24 * 60 * 60 * 1000);
                                       // 24 hours from now
3              when.setFullYear(when.getFullYear() + 1);
                                       // One year from now
               yname=form.yourname.value;
               favcolor=form.yourcolor.value;
4              document.cookie=escape("visitor")+"="+escape(yname)+
                                   ";expires="+when.toGMTString();
               document.cookie=escape("color")+"="+escape(favcolor)+
                                   ";expires="+when.toGMTString();
               alert(document.cookie);
            }
5           function welcome(myForm){
               you=myForm.yourname.value;
6              var position=document.cookie.indexOf("name=");
               if ( position != -1){
                  var begin = position + 5;
                  var end=document.cookie.indexOf(";", begin);
                  if(end == -1){ end=document.cookie.length;}
7                 you= unescape(document.cookie.substring(begin, end));
8                 alert("Welcome " + you);
               }
               else{ alert("No cookies today");}
            }
          </script>
        </head>
        <body onLoad="document.form1.reset()" >
          <div align="center">
            <h2> Got milk?</h2>
            <form name="form1">
               What is your name?
               <br />
9              <input type="text" name="yourname" />
               <br />
               What is your favorite color?
               <br />
               <input type="text" name="yourcolor" />
               <br />
               <p>
10                <input type="button" value="Make cookie"
                        onClick="makeCookie(this.form);" />
               </p>
```

Continues

EXAMPLE 16.2 (CONTINUED)

```
           <p>
11             <input type="button"
                   value="Get Cookie" onClick="welcome(this.form);" />
           </p>
         </form>
       </div>
     </body>
   </html>
```

EXPLANATION

1   A function called *makeCookie()* is defined. It takes a reference to a form as its only parameter. This is the function that creates the cookie.

2   A new *Date* object is created and assigned to the variable called *when*.

3   The *Date* object creates a date a year from now. This will be the expiration date for the cookie.

4   Two cookies are created. The first cookie's name is *"visitor"* and its value is the user's name, stored in *yname*. The second cookie's name is *"color"* and its value stored in *favcolor*. Both values came from the form input. The attributes are escaped just in case the user added unwanted characters, such as spaces, commas, or semicolons. The expiration date is set to a year from now and is converted to GMT time, the required format for the *"expires"* attribute. Notice the quotes. If the text is literal for the attribute it must be quoted; if it is a variable value, then it is not quoted or JavaScript can't interpret it—very tricky getting these right.

5   A function called *welcome()* is created. It takes a reference to a form as its only parameter. Its purpose is to greet the user based on the cookie value.

6   The following statements are used to parse out the *value* attribute of the cookie. The beginning index position is set to where the *"name="* string starts in the cookie string. It will be at position 5 in this example. Starting at index position 0, position 5 takes us to the character directly after the = sign. The end position is either at the first semicolon or at the end of the string, whichever applies.

7   After getting the substring, the *value* part of the cookie, the *unescape()* function, will convert the URI-encoded string back into its original ASCII format.

8   The user is welcomed, all based on the value extracted from the cookie. The cookie lets this Web site know who you are so that you can get a personal greeting when you return to the site.

9   The user will enter his or her name in a textbox field. See Figure 16.8.

10 When the user clicks this button, the *onClick* event is triggered, and the cookie will be made. See Figure 16.9.

11 When the user clicks this button, the *onClick* event is triggered, and the user will be welcomed by the name he or she entered in the textbox. See Figure 16.10.

Figure 16.8 Creating a cookie with user preferences.

Figure 16.9 Contents of a cookie.

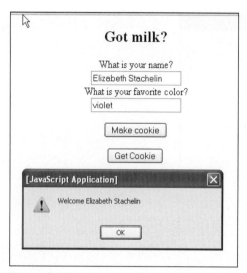

Figure 16.10 Retrieve the cookie and welcome the user.

16.2.4 Retrieving Cookies from a Server

When retrieving cookies, you can only get those that were written for the server you are on and written by you. You cannot read and write cookies that belong to someone else or reside on a different server. In the last example, we got one cookie; in Example 16.3 all the cookies for this page are displayed.

EXAMPLE 16.3

```
      <html>
        <head><title>See my Cookies</title>
          <script type="text/javascript">
1            function seeCookie(){
               if(document.cookie == ""){
                 document.write("No cookies");
               }
               else{
                 var cookiestr="";
2                var myCookie = document.cookie.split("; ");
3                for(var i=0;i<myCookie.length; i++){
                   /* document.write("<b>Cookie: " +
                                myCookie[i].split("=")[1] +"<br />"); */
4                  cookiestr+=myCookie[i] + " ";
5                  var cookieData=myCookie[i].split("=");
6                  if (cookieData[0] == "color"){
7                    document.bgColor=cookieData[1];
                     //Visitor preference to change color
                 }
```

EXAMPLE   16.3 (CONTINUED)

```
                    }
                }
8               alert(cookiestr);
            }
        </script>
    </head>
9   <body onLoad="document.form1.reset()" >
        <div align="center"><h2> Got milk?</h2>
            <form name="form1">
                Click to see document.cookie property
                <p>
10                  <input type="button" value="See Cookie"
                        onClick="seeCookie();" />
                </p>
            </form>
        </div>
    </body>
</html>
```

EXPLANATION

1   A function called *seeCookie()* is defined. It will list out all the cookies that have been set. First, we check to see if there are any cookies at all. If not, the alert box will say so.

2   The *split* function splits up the cookie string by semicolons and returns an array called *myCookie*.

3   The *for* loop iterates through each element of the *myCookie* array until the end of the array, *myCookie.length*, is reached.

4   Each time we get a cookie it is appended to this string, called *cookiestr*.

5   The name/value pairs of the cookie string are split by "=" signs. An array is returned.

6   If the name assigned to the cookie is "color", that name is stored in *cookieData[0]* and the color choice of the user is stored in *cookieData[1]*.

7   Based on the user's preference of color, the background color of the page is changed.

8   The alert box displays all the cookies that were retrieved.

9   When the document is loaded and every time the user refreshes the page, the *on-Load* event is triggered and the values in the form are cleared with the *reset()* method.

10   When the user clicks the button, the *onClick* event is triggered, and the *seeCook-ie()* function will be called to display all the cookies for this page. The process is shown in Figures 16.11 and 16.12.

Figure 16.11   When the user clicks the "See Cookie" button, all cookies are retrieved.

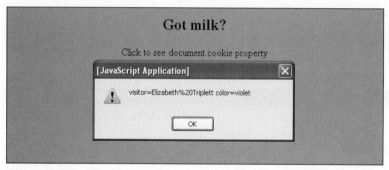

Figure 16.12   After the user clicks the button, the color of the page changes based on the cookie that was sent.

16.2.5   Deleting a Cookie

If you want to delete a cookie for the current page, set the expiration date of the cookie to a date earlier than the current date. This will cause the cookie to be deleted when the session ends.

EXAMPLE 16.4

```
    <html>
      <head><title>Delete Cookie</title><head>
        <script type = "text/javascript">
          var i = 0;
1         function delCookie (cookieName){
2           document.cookie = cookieName + "="
                          +"; expires=Thu, 01-Jan-1970 00:00:01 GMT";
          alert("Cookie was deleted!");
          seeCookie();
        }
```

EXAMPLE   16.4 (CONTINUED)

```
3          function seeCookie(){
               if(document.cookie == ""){
                 alert("No cookies");
                 return false;
               }
               else{
4                var myCookie = document.cookie.split("; ");
                 if ( i < myCookie.length ){
5                  document.form1.cookietype.value =
                                        myCookie[i].split("=")[0];
                     i++;   // Increase the index value
                            // to see the next cookie
                 }
                 else{alert("No more cookies");}
               }
           }
       </script>
   </head>
6  <body onLoad="seeCookie()" >
     <div align="center">
       <h2> Got milk?</h2>
7      <form name="form1">
         Is this the cookie you want to delete?
         <br />
         <input type="text" name="cookietype" >
         <p>
8          <input type="radio"
                   name="radio"
                   value="choice"
9                  onClick=
                   "delCookie(document.form1.cookietype.value);" />Yes
           <input type="radio"
                   name="radio"
                   value="choice"
10                 onClick="seeCookie();" />No
         </p>
       </form>
     </div>
   </body>
   </html>
```

EXPLANATION

1   The function called *delCookie*() will remove a requested cookie. The name of the
     cookie, *cookieName*, is passed as a parameter to the function.

Continues

EXPLANATION(CONTINUED)

2   The expiration date of the cookie is set to the beginning of UNIX time, also called epoch time—January 1, 1970. Certainly this date has passed and the cookie will be deleted. After the cookie has been deleted, the *seeCookie()* function will be called, and the user will be presented with another cookie. If he or she clicks the Yes radio button, that cookie will be removed.

3   The function called *SeeCookie()* will check to see if there are any cookies remaining in the *document.cookie* property. If not, the program is over. To actually see if the cookies were deleted, close this session, and then reopen it.

4   By splitting up the *document.cookie* property by semicolons, an array is created consisting of a *name* and *value* attribute of the cookie.

5   The first element of the array, the name of the cookie, is assigned to the textbox represented as *document.form1.cookietype.value*. It will appear in the textbox for the user to see. Each time the function is called, the next cookie will be assigned to the textbox, giving the user the option to delete that cookie.

6   When the document has finished loading, the *onLoad* event is triggered, and calls the *seeCookie()* function. The first cookie name will appear in the textbox.

7   The HTML form starts here.

8   The textbox input type will be used to hold the cookie name.

9   This radio button, when clicked, will called the *delCookie()* function. The user wants to remove this cookie. See Figures 16.13 and 16.14.

10   This radio button, when clicked, means the user doesn't want to delete this cookie but would like to see the next cookie. When the user clicks No, the *seeCookie()* function will be called. After all the cookies have been shown, the alert message will say "*No more cookies.*"

Figure 16.13 The cookie's name is *visitor*. If the user clicks Yes (top), the cookie will be removed (bottom).

Figure 16.14   The cookie has been deleted after user clicked the "Yes" button.

16.2.6   Using the Browser to Remove Cookies

Another way to delete cookies is to go in your browser and select Help and search for Delete cookies. In Internet Explorer go to the Tools menu and Internet Options (see Figure 16.15). Then you can remove all or some cookies from the hard drive.

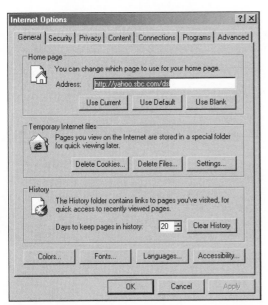

Figure 16.15   Internet Options in Internet Explorer.

16.3 What You Should Know

Now you know what cookies are and why commercial sites like to use them. You should know:

1. A little about the history of the cookie.
2. How to make a cookie.
3. How to use a cookie.
4. What escaping a cookie value means.
5. When the cookie normally expires if an expiration date is not set.
6. How to delete a cookie.
7. How to delete cookies using your browser.
8. How to enable or disable cookies on your browser.
9. How JavaScript views a cookie.

Exercises

1. Create a form that contains a set of checkboxes with different types of coffees—espresso, cappuccino, mocha, and so on. Ask the user for his or her name and room number and to select a type of coffee. Tell the user you will be sending the coffee to that room number. Create a cookie to remember the user's preference. The next time the user brings up the page, tell him or her there is a special rate for his or her (use the cookie value) favorite coffee.

2. Create a form that asks for the user's shipping address. The next time the user brings up the page, fill in the address using a cookie value.

chapter
17

Regular Expressions and Pattern Matching

17.1 What Is a Regular Expression?

A user is asked to fill out an HTML form and provide his or her name, address, and birth date. Before sending the form off to a server for further processing, a JavaScript program checks the form to make sure the user actually entered something, and that the information is in the requested format. We saw in Chapter 11, "Working with Forms and Input Devices," some basic ways that JavaScript can check form information, but now with the addition of regular expressions, form validation can be much more sophisticated and precise. Regular expressions are also useful for searching for patterns in input data, and replacing the data with something else or splitting it up into substrings. This chapter is divided into two main parts: (1.) how to create regular expressions and regular expression metacharacters, and (2.) how to validate form input data with regular expressions. If you are savvy with Perl regular expressions (or the UNIX utilities, *grep*, *sed*, and *awk*), you can move rapidly through the first section, because JavaScript regular expressions, for the most part, are identical to those found in Perl.

A regular expression is really just a sequence of characters that specify a pattern to be matched against a string of text when performing searches and replacements. A simple regular expression consists of a character or set of characters that matches itself. The regular expression is normally delimited by forward slashes; for example, /abc/.

Like Perl, JavaScript[1] provides a large variety of regular expression metacharacters to control the way a pattern is found. A metacharacter is a special character that represents something other than itself, such a a ^, $,*, and so on. They are placed within in the regular expression to control the search pattern; for example, /^abc/ means look for the pattern *abc* at the beginning of the line. With the help of metacharacters, you can look for strings containing only digits, only alphas, a digit at the beginning of the line followed by any number of alphas, a line ending with a digit, and so on. When searching for a pattern of characters, the possibilities of fine-tuning your search are endless.

---

1. JavaScript 1.2, NES 3.0 JavaScript 1.3 added *toSource()* method. JavaScript 1.5, NES 6.0 added *m* flag, nongreedy modifier, noncapturing parentheses, look-ahead assertions. ECMA 262, Edition 3.

Again, JavaScript regular expressions are used primarily to verify data input on the client side. When a user fills out a form and presses the submit button, the form is sent to a server, and then often to a server script such as PHP, ASP.NET or a JavaServlet for further processing. Although forms can be validated by a server program, it is more efficient to take care of the validation before sending the script to the server. This is an important function of JavaScript. The user fills out the form and JavaScript checks to see if all the boxes have been filled out correctly, and if not, the user is told to reenter the data before the form is submitted to the server. Checking the form on the client side allows for instant feedback, and less traveling back and forth between the browser and server. It might be that the server-side program does its own validation anyway, but if JavaScript has already done the job, it will still save time and inconvenience for the user. With the power provided by regular expressions, the ability to check for any type of input, such as e-mail addresses, passwords, Social Security numbers, and birthdates is greatly simplified. This chapter will teach you how regular expressions and their metacharacters are used so that you will be able to read expressions even as complicated as the one shown in Figure 17.1. There are a number of regular expression validators and libraries on the Web. An excellent source is at *http://www.regexlib.com*.

Figure 17.1 A regular expression library. The user types "email" in the Search box. See Figure 17.2 for results.

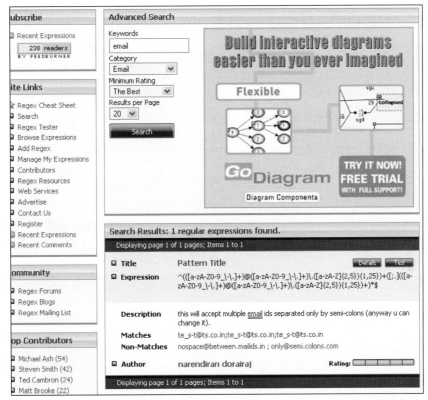

Figure 17.2 The result of searching for the email regular expression considered to be the best.

17.2 Creating a Regular Expression

A regular expression is a pattern of characters. It shouldn't be any surprise by now. JavaScript regular expressions are objects. When you create a regular expression, you test the regular expression against a string. For example, the regular expression /green/ might be matched against the string "The green grass grows". If green is contained in the string, then there is a successful match.

Building a regular expression is like building a JavaScript string. If you recall, you can create a *String* object the literal way or you can use the *String()* constructor method. To build a regular expression object, you can assign a literal regular expression to a variable, or you can use the *RegExp* constructor to create and return a regular expression object.

17.2.1 The Literal Way

To create a regular expression object with the literal notation, you assign the regular expression to a variable. The regular expression is a pattern of characters enclosed in forward slashes. After the closing forward slash, options may be provided to modify the search pattern. The options are *i*, *g*, and *m*. See Table 17.1.

Table 17.1 Options Used for Modifying Search Patterns

Option	Purpose
i	Used to ignore case.
g	Used to match for all occurrences of the pattern in the string.
m	Used to match over multiple lines.

FORMAT

```
var variable_name = /regular expression/options;
```

EXAMPLE

```
var myreg = /love/;
var reobj = /san jose/ig;
```

If you are not going to change the regular expression, say, if it is hard-coded right into your script, then this literal notation is faster, because the regular expression is evaluated at runtime.

17.2.2 The Constructor Method

The constructor method, called *RegExp()*, creates a *RegExp* object. The *RegExp()* constructor takes one or two arguments. The first argument is the regular expression; it is a string representing the regular expression, for example, *"green"* represents the literal regular expression */green/*. The second optional argument is called a **flag** such as *i* for case insensitivity or *g* for global. The constructor method is used when the regular expression is being provided from some other place, such as from user input, and can change throughout the run of the program. This method is handled at runtime.

FORMAT

```
var variable_name = new RegExp("regular expression", "options");
```

EXAMPLE

```
var myreg = new RegExp("love");
var reobj = new RegExp("san jose", "ig");
```

17.2.3 Testing the Expression

The *RegExp* object has two methods that can be used to test for a match in a string, the *test()* method and the *exec()* method, which are quite similar. The *test()* method searches for a regular expression in a string and returns *true* if it matched and *false* if it didn't. The *exec()* method also searches for a regular expression in a string. If the *exec()* method succeeds, it returns an array of information including the search string, and the parts of the string that matched. If it fails, it returns *null*. This is similar to the *match()* method of the *String* object. Table 17.2 summarizes the methods of the *Reg-Exp* object.

Table 17.2 Methods of the *RegExp* Object

Method	*What It Does*
exec	Executes a search for a match in a string and returns an array.
test	Tests for a match in a string and returns either *true* or *false*.

The *test()* Method.   The *RegExp* object's *test()* method is used to see if a string contains the pattern represented in the regular expression. It returns a *true* or *false* Boolean value. After the search, the *lastIndex* property of the *RegExp* object contains the position in the string where the **next** search would start. (A string starts at character position 0.) If a global search is done, then the *lastIndex* property contains the starting position after the last pattern was matched. (See Example 17.4 to see how the *lastIndex* property is used.)

Steps to test for a match:

1. Assign a regular expression to a variable.
2. Use the regular expression *test()* method to see if there is a match. If there is a match, the *test()* method returns *true*; otherwise, it returns *false*. There are also four string methods that can be used with regular expressions. (See section "String Methods Using Regular Expressions" on page 727.)

FORMAT

```
var string="String to be tested goes here";
var regex = /regular expression/;            // Literal way
var regex=new RegExp("regular expression");   // Constructor way
regex.test(string);                // Returns either true or false

or

/regular expression/.test("string");
```

EXAMPLE

```
var myString="She wants attention now!";
var regex = /ten/          // Literal way
var regex=new RegExp("ten");    // Constructor way
regex.test(myString);       // Looking for "ten" in  myString
```

or

```
/ten/.test("She wants attention now!");
```

EXAMPLE 17.1

```
<html>
  <head><title>Regular Expression Objects the Literal Way</title>
    <script language = "JavaScript">
1      var myString="My gloves are worn for wear.";
2      var regex = /love/;     // Create a regular expression object
3      if (regex.test(myString)){
4        alert("Found pattern!");
       }
       else{
5        alert("No match.");
       }
    </script>
  </head>
  <body></body>
</html>
```

EXPLANATION

1   *"My gloves are worn for wear."* is assigned to a variable called *myString*.

2   The regular expression */love/* is assigned to the variable called *regex*. This is the literal way of creating a regular expression object.

3   The *test()* method for the regular expression object tests to see if *myString* contains the pattern, *love*. If *love* is found within *gloves*, the *test()* method will return *true*.

4   The alert dialog box will display *Found pattern!* if the *test()* method returned *true*.

5   If the pattern */love/* is not found in *myString*, the *test()* method returns *false*, and the alert dialog box will display its message, *No match*.

EXAMPLE 17.2

```
<html>
  <head>
    <title>Regular Expression Objects with the Constructor</title>
    <script language = "JavaScript">
1      var myString="My gloves are worn for wear.";
```

EXAMPLE   17.2 (CONTINUED)

```
2          var regex = new RegExp("love");       // Creating a regular
                                                  // expression object
3          if ( regex.test(myString)){
4             alert("Found pattern love!");
           }
           else{
5             alert("No match.");
           }
        </script>
      </head>
      <body></body>
    </html>
```

EXPLANATION

1   The variable called *myString* is assigned *"My gloves are worn for wear."*

2   The *RegExp()* constructor creates a new regular expression object, called *regex*. This is the constructor way of creating a regular expression object. It is assigned the string *"love"*, the regular expression.

3   The *test()* method for the regular expression object tests to see if *myString* contains the pattern, *love*. If it finds *love* within *gloves*, it will return *true*.

4, 5   The alert dialog box will display *Found pattern!* if the *test()* method returned *true*, or *No match.* if it returns *false*. See Figure 17.3.

Figure 17.3   *My gloves are worn for wear."* contains the pattern *love*.

The *exec()* Method.   The *exec()* method executes a search to find a match for a specified pattern in a string. If it doesn't find a match, *exec()* returns null; otherwise it returns an array containing the string that matched the regular expression.

FORMAT

```
array = regular_expression.exec(string);
```

EXAMPLE

```
list = /ring/.exec("Don't string me along, just bring me the goods.");
```

EXAMPLE 17.3

```html
<html>
   <head><title>The exec() method</title>
      <script type="text/javascript">
1        var myString="My lovely gloves are worn for wear, Love.";
2        var regex = /love/i;    // Create a regular expression object
3        var array=regex.exec(myString);
4        if (regex.exec(myString)){
            alert("Matched! " + array);
         }
         else{
            alert("No match.");
         }
      </script>
   </head>
   <body></body>
</html>
```

EXPLANATION

1   The string *"My gloves are worn for wear."* is assigned to *myString*.
2   The regular expression */love/* is assigned to the variable *regex*.
3   The *exec()* method returns an array of values that were found.
4   If the *exec()* method doesn't return *null*, then there was a match. See Figure 17.4.

Figure 17.4   The array returned by *exec()* contains *love*.

17.2.4   Properties of the *RegExp* Object

There are two types of properties that can be applied to a *RegExp* object. The first type is called a **class property** (see Table 17.3) and applies to the *RegExp* object as a whole, not a simple instance of a regular expression object. The *input* property is an example of a class property. It contains the last string that was matched, and is applied directly to the *RegExp* object as *RegExp.input*.

The other type of property is called an **instance property** and is applied to an instance of the object (see Table 17.4); for example, *mypattern.lastIndex* refers to the position within the string where the next search will start for this instance of the regular expression object, called *mypattern*. These properties will be explained in examples throughout this chapter.

Table 17.3   Class Properties of the *RegExp* Object

Property	*What It Describes*
input	Represents the input string being matched.
lastMatch	Represents the last matched characters.
lastParen	Represents the last parenthesized substring pattern match.
leftContext	Represents the substring preceding the most recent pattern match.
RegExp.$*	Boolean value that specifies whether strings should be searched over multiple lines; same as the multiline property.
RegExp.$&	Represents the last matched characters.
RegExp.$_	Represents the string input that is being matched.
RegExp.$ `	Represents the substring preceding the most recent pattern match (see the *leftContext* property).
RegExp.$ '	Represents the substring following the most recent pattern match (see the *rightContext*property).
RegExp.$+	Represents the last parenthesized substring pattern match (see the *lastParen* property).
RegExp.$1,$2,$3...	Used to capture substrings of matches.
rightContext	Represents the substring following the most recent pattern match.

Table 17.4   Instance Properties of the *RegExp* Object

Property	*What It Describes*
global	Boolean to specify if the *g* option was used to check the expression against all possible matches in the string.
ignoreCase	Boolean to specify if the *i* option was used to ignore case during a string search.
lastIndex	If the *g* option was used, specifies the character position immediately following the last match found by *exec()* or *test()*.
multiline	Boolean to test if the *m* option was used to search across multiple lines.
source	The text of the regular expression.

EXAMPLE 17.4

```
       <html>
         <head>
           <title>The test() method</title>
         </head>
         <body bgcolor="silver">
           <font face="arial" size="+1">
           <script type = "text/javascript">
1            var myString="I love my new gloves!";
2            var regex = /love/g;    // Create a regular expression object
3            var booleanResult = regex.test(myString);
             if ( booleanResult != false ){
4              document.write("Tested regular expression <em>"+
                               regex.source + ".</em> The result is <em>"
                               + booleanResult + "</em>");
               document.write(".<br>Starts searching again at position " +
5                              regex.lastIndex + " in string<em> \"" +
6                              RegExp.input + "\"<br />");
               document.write("The last matched characters were: "+
7                              RegExp.lastMatch+"<br />");
               document.write("The substring preceding the last match is:
8                              "+ RegExp.leftContext+"<br />");
               document.write("The substring following the last match is:
9                              "+ RegExp.rightContext+"<br />");
             }
             else{ alert("No match!"); }
           </script>
           </font>
         </body>
       </html>
```

EXPLANATION

1   The string object to be tested is created.

2   A regular expression object, called *regex*, is created.

3   The *test*() method returns *true* or *false* if the regular expression is matched in the string.

4   The *source* property is applied to *regex*, an instance of a *RegExp* object. It contains the text of the regular expression, */love/*.

5   The *lastIndex* property is applied to an instance of a *RegExp* object. It represents the character position right after the last matched string.

6   The *input* class property represents the input string on which the pattern matching (regular expression) is performed.

7   *lastMatch* is a class property that represents the characters that were last matched.

8   *leftContext* is a class property that represents the leftmost substring pattern that precedes the last pattern that was matched; here, whatever string comes before */love/*.

9   *rightContext* is a class property that represents the rightmost substring pattern that follows the last pattern that was matched; here, whatever string comes after */love/*. Output is shown in Figure 17.5.

Tested regular expression *love*. The result is *true*.
Starts searching again at position 6 in string *"I love my new gloves!"*
The last matched characters were: love
The substring preceding the last match is: I
The substring following the last match is: my new gloves!

Figure 17.5   Regular expression properties.

17.3 String Methods Using Regular Expressions

In addition to the *RegExp* object's *test()* and *exec()* methods, the *String* object provides four methods that also work with regular expressions, as shown in Table 17.5.

Table 17.5   *String* Object Regular Expression Methods

Method	What It Does
match(regex)	Returns substring in *regex* or *null*.
replace(regex, replacement)	Substitutes *regex* with replacement string.
search(regex)	Finds the starting position of *regex* in string.
split(regex)	Removes *regex* from string for each occurrence.

17.3.1   The *match()* Method

The *match()* method, like the *exec()* method, is used to search for a pattern of characters in a string and returns an array where each element of the array contains each matched pattern that was found. If no match is found, returns *null*. With the g flag, *match()* searches globally through the string for all matching substrings.

FORMAT

```
array = String.match(regular_expression);
```

EXAMPLE

```
matchList = "Too much, too soon".match(/too/ig);
```

EXAMPLE 17.5

```
       <html>
         <head>
           <title>The match() Method</title>
         </head>
         <body>
           <big><font face="arial, helvetica">
           <script type = "text/javascript">
1              var matchArray = new Array();
2              var string="I love the smell of clover."
3              var regex = /love/g;
4              matchArray=string.match(regex);
5              document.write("Found "+ matchArray.length
                              +" matches.<br />");
           </script>
           </font></big>
         </body>
       </html>
```

EXPLANATION

1 A new array object is created.

2 The variable called *string* is assigned *"I love the smell of clover."*

3 The regular expression called *regex* is assigned the search pattern *love*. The *g* modifier performs a global search: multiple occurrences of the pattern will be returned.

4 The *match()* method is applied to the string. The regular expression is passed as an argument. Each time the pattern */love/* is found in the string it will be assigned as a new element of the array called *matchArray*. If the g modifier is removed, only the first occurrence of the match will be returned, and only one element will be assigned to the array *matchArray*.

5 The length of the array, *matchArray*, tells us how many times the *match()* method found the pattern */love/*. See Figure 17.6.

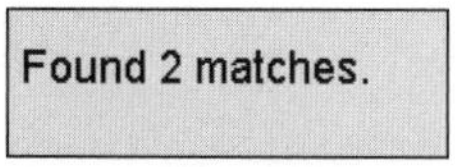

Found 2 matches.

Figure 17.6 The pattern *love* was found twice in the string.

17.3.2 The *search()* Method

The *search()* method is used to search for a pattern of characters within a string, and returns the index position of where the pattern was found in the string. The index starts at zero. If the pattern is not found, –1 is returned. For basic searches, the *String* object's *indexOf()* method works fine, but if you want more complex pattern matches, the *search()* method is used, allowing you to use regular expression metacharacters to further control the expression. (See the section "Getting Control—The Metacharacters" on page 733.)

FORMAT

```
var index_value = String.search(regular_expression);
```

EXAMPLE

```
var position = "A needle in a haystack".search(/needle/);
```

EXAMPLE 17.6

```
    <html>
      <head>
        <title>The search() Method</title>
      </head>
      <body bgcolor="yellow">
        <big>
        <font face="arial, helvetica">
        <script type="text/javascript">
1         var myString="I love the smell of clover."
2         var regex = /love/;
3         var index=myString.search(regex);
          document.write("Found the pattern "+ regex+ " at position "
                        +index+"<br />");
        </script>
        </font></big>
      </body>
    </html>
```

EXPLANATION

1   The variable called *myString* is assigned the string, *"I love the smell of clover."*

2   The variable called *regex* is assigned the regular expression */love/*. With the *search()* method, using the g modifier is irrelevant. The index position of the pattern where it is first found in the string, is returned.

3   The *String* object's *search()* method returns the index position, starting at zero, where the regular expression, *regex*, is found. See Figure 17.7.

> Found the pattern /love/ at position 2

Figure 17.7   The *search()* method found the pattern starting at character position 2, where 0 is the beginning character.

17.3.3 The *replace()* Method

The *replace()* method is used to search for a string and replace the string with another string. The *i* modifier is used to turn off case sensitivity and the *g* modifier makes the replacement global; that is, all occurrences of the found pattern are replaced with the new string. The *replace()* method is also used with the grouping metacharacters. (See the section "Grouping or Clustering" on page 761.)

FORMAT

```
string = oldstring.replace(regular_expression, replacement_value);
```

EXAMPLE

```
var str1 = "I am feeling blue".replace(/blue/, "upbeat");
   ( str1 is assigned: "I am feeling upbeat.")
```

EXAMPLE 17.7

```
      <html>
        <head>
          <title>The replace() Method</title>
        </head>
        <body bgcolor="yellow">
          <script type = "text/javascript">
1             var myString="Tommy has a stomach ache."
2             var regex = /tom/i;   // Turn off case sensitivity
3             var newString=myString.replace(regex, "Mom");
              document.write(newString +"<br />");
          </script>
        </body>
      </html>
```

EXPLANATION

1   The variable called *myString* is assigned the string *"Tommy has a stomach ache."* Note that the pattern *Tom* or *tom* is found in the string twice.

2   The variable called *regex* is assigned the regular expression */tom/i*. The *i* modifier turns off the case sensitivity. Any combination of uppercase and lowercase letters in the pattern *tom* will be searched for within the string.

3   The *String* object's *replace()* method will search for the pattern, *regex*, in the string and if it finds the pattern will replace it with *Mom*. If the *g* modifier were used, all occurrences of the pattern would be replaced with *Mom* (see Figure 17.8). For example, */tom/ig* would result in *"Mommy has a sMomach ache."*

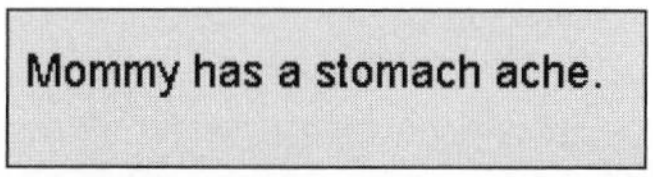

Mommy has a stomach ache.

Figure 17.8   The first occurrence of *Tom,* uppercase or lowercase, is replaced with *Mom.*

17.3.4   The *split()* Method

The *String* object's *split()* method splits a single text string into an array of substrings. In a real-world scenario, it would be like putting little crayon marks at intervals on a piece of string and then cutting the string everywhere a mark appeared, thus ending up with a bunch of little strings. In the JavaScript world, the crayon mark is called a **delimiter**, which is a character or pattern of characters that marks where the string is to be split up. When using the *String* object's *split()* method, if the words in a string are separated by commas, then the comma would be the delimiter and if the words are separated by colons, then the colon is the delimiter. The delimiter can contain more complex combinations of characters if regular expression metacharacters are used.

FORMAT

```
array = String.split( /delimiter/ );
```

EXAMPLE

```
splitArray = "red#green#yellow#blue".split(/#/);
   (splitArray is an array of colors. splitArray[0] is "red")
```

EXAMPLE 17.8

```
<html>
  <head><title>The split() Method</title></head>
  <body>
    <script type = "text/javascript">
1       var splitArray = new Array();
2       var string="apples:pears:peaches:plums:oranges";
3       var regex = /:/;
```

Continues

EXAMPLE 17.8 (CONTINUED)

```
4              splitArray=string.split(regex);  // Split the string by colons
5              for(i=0; i < splitArray.length; i++){
                   document.write(splitArray[i] + "<br />");
               }
           </script>
         </body>
     </html>
```

EXPLANATION

1   A new array object is created.

2   The variable called *string* is assigned a colon-delimited string of text.

3   The variable called *regex* is assigned the regular expression */:/*.

4   The *String* object's *split()* method splits the string using colons as the string delimiter (marks the separation between words), and creates an array called *splitArray*.

5   Each of the array elements is displayed in the page. See Figure 17.9.

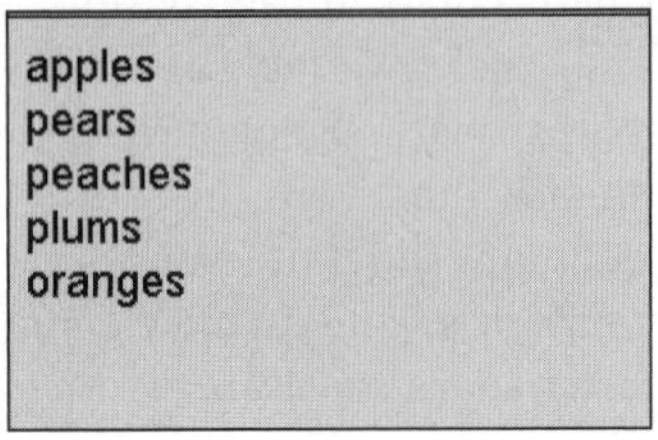

```
apples
pears
peaches
plums
oranges
```

Figure 17.9   The string is split on colons.

EXAMPLE 17.9

```
     <html>
       <head>
         <title>The split() Method</title>
       </head>
         <script type = "text/javascript">
1          var splitArray = new Array();
2          var myString="apples       pears,peaches:plums,oranges";
3          var regex = /[\t:,]/;   // Delimeter is a tab, colon, or comma
4          splitArray=myString.split(regex);
           for(i=0; i < splitArray.length; i++){
5              document.write(splitArray[i] + "<br />");
           }
         </script>
       </body>
     </html>
```

1   A new array object is created.

2   The string *"apples   pears,peaches:plums,oranges"* is assigned to the variable called *myString*. The delimiters are a tab, comma, and colon.

3   The regular expression */[\t:,]/* is assigned to the variable called *regex*.

4   The *String* object's *split()* method splits up the string using a tab, colon, or comma as the delimiter. The delimiting characters are enclosed in square brackets, which in regular expression parlance is called a character class. (See the section "Getting Control—The Metacharacters" on page 733.) In simple terms, any one of the characters listed within the brackets is a delimiter in the string. The *split()* method will search for any one of these characters and split the string accordingly, returning an array called *splitArray*.

5   Each of the array elements is displayed in the page. See Figure 17.10.

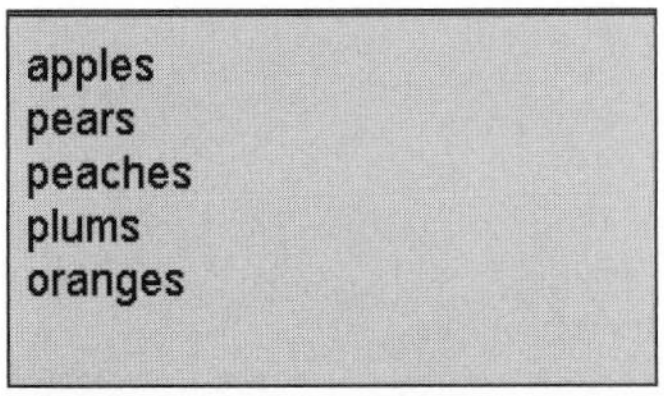

```
apples
pears
peaches
plums
oranges
```

Figure 17.10   The string is split on tabs, colons, and commas.

17.4 Getting Control—The Metacharacters

Regular expression metacharacters are characters that do not represent themselves. They are endowed with special powers to allow you to control the search pattern in some way (e.g., find the pattern only at the beginning of line, or at the end of the line, or if it starts with an upper- or lowercase letter, etc.). Metacharacters will lose their special meaning if preceded with a backslash. For example, the dot metacharacter represents any single character, but when preceded with a backslash it is just a dot or period.

If you see a backslash preceding a metacharacter, the backslash turns off the meaning of the metacharacter, but if you see a backslash preceding an alphanumeric character in a regular expression, then the backslash is used to create a metasymbol. A metasymbol provides a simpler form to represent some of the regular expression metachacters. For example, *[0-9]* represents numbers in the range between 0 and 9, and *\d*, the metasymbol, represents the same thing. *[0-9]* uses the bracketed character class, whereas *\d* is a metasymbol (see Table 17.6).

```
/^a...c/
```

EXPLANATION

This regular expression contains metacharacters (see Table 17.6). The first one is a caret (^). The caret metacharacter matches for a string only if it is at the beginning of the line. The period (.) is used to match for any single character, including a whitespace. This expression contains three periods, representing any three characters. To find a literal period or any other character that does not represent itself, the character must be preceded by a backslash to prevent interpretation.

The expression reads: Search at the beginning of the line for an *a*, followed by any three single characters, followed by a *c*. It will match, for example, *abbbc, a123c, a   c, aAx3c*, and so on, but only if those patterns were found at the beginning of the line.

Table 17.6 Metacharacters and Metasymbols

Metacharacter/Met asymbol	What It Matches
Character Class: Single Characters and Digits	
.	Matches any character except newline
[a–z0–9]	Matches any single character in set
[^a–z0–9]	Matches any single character **not** in set
\d	Matches one digit
\D	Matches a nondigit, same as [^0–9]
\w	Matches an alphanumeric (word) character
\W	Matches a nonalphanumeric (nonword) character
Character Class: Whitespace Characters	
\0	Matches a null character
\b	Matches a backspace
\f	Matches a formfeed
\n	Matches a newline
\r	Matches a return
\s	Matches whitespace character, spaces, tabs, and newlines
\S	Matches nonwhitespace character
\t	Matches a tab

Table 17.6   Metacharacters and Metasymbols (continued)

Metacharacter/Met asymbol	What It Matches
Character Class: Anchored Characters	
^	Matches to beginning of line
$	Matches to end of line
\A	Matches the beginning of the string only
\b	Matches a word boundary (when not inside [ ])
\B	Matches a nonword boundary
\G	Matches where previous $m//g$ left off
\Z	Matches the end of the string or line
\z	Matches the end of string only
Character Class: Repeated Characters	
$x?$	Matches 0 or 1 of x
$x*$	Matches 0 or more of x
$x+$	Matches 1 or more of x
$(xyz)+$	Matches one or more patterns of xyz
$x\{m,n\}$	Matches at least m of x and no more than n of x
Character Class: Alternative Characters	
was|were|will	Matches one of *was*, *were*, or *will*
Character Class: Remembered Characters	
(string)	Used for backreferencing (see the section "Remembering or Capturing" on page 762)
\1 or $1	Matches first set of parentheses
\2 or $2	Matches second set of parentheses
\3 or $3	Matches third set of parentheses

Continues

Table 17.6   Metacharacters and Metasymbols (continued)

Metacharacter/Met asymbol	What It Matches
New with JavaScript 1.5	
(?:x)	Matches *x* but does not remember the match. These are called noncapturing parentheses. The matched substring cannot be recalled from the resulting array's elements *[1], ..., [n]* or from the predefined *RegExp* object's properties *$1, ..., $9*.
x(?=y)	Matches *x* only if *x* is followed by *y*. For example, */Jack(?=Sprat)/* matches *Jack* only if it is followed by *Sprat*. */Jack(?=Sprat|Frost)/* matches *Jack* only if it is followed by *Sprat* or *Frost*. However, neither *Sprat* nor *Frost* are part of the match results.
x(?!y)	Matches *x* only if *x* is not followed by *y*. For example, */\d+(?!\.)/* matches a number only if it is not followed by a decimal point. */\d+(?!\.)/.exec("3.141")* matches *141* but not *3.141*.

If you are searching for a particular character within a regular expression, you can use the **dot** metacharacter to represent a single character, or a **character class** that matches on one character from a set of characters. In addition to the dot and character class, Java-Script has added some backslashed symbols (called metasymbols) to represent single characters. See Table 17.7 for the single-character metacharacters, and Table 17.8 on page 742 for a list of metasymbols.

Table 17.7   Single-Character and Single-Digit Metacharacters

Metacharacter	What It Matches
.	Matches any character except newline.
[a–z0–9_]	Matches any single character in set.
[^a–z0–9_]	Matches any single character **not** in set.

17.4.1   The Dot Metacharacter

The dot metacharacter matches for any single character with the exception of the newline character. For example, the regular expression */a.b/* is matched if the string contains an *a*, followed by any one single character (except the \n), followed by *b*, whereas the expression */.../* matches any string containing at least three characters.

EXAMPLE   17.11

```
        <html>
          <head><title>The dot Metacharacter</title></head>
          <body>
            <script type="text/javascript">
1               var textString="Norma Jean";
2               var reg_expression = /N..ma/;

3               var result=reg_expression.test(textString);  // Returns true
                                                             // or false
                document.write(result+"<br />");
4               if ( reg_expression.test(textString)){        // if (result)
                   document.write("<b>The reg_ex /N..ma/ matched the
                                  string\""+ textString +"\".<br />");
                }
                else{
5                  document.write("No Match!");
                }
            </script>
          </body>
        </html>
```

EXPLANATION

1   The variable *textString* is assigned the string *"Norma Jean"*.

2   The regular expression */N..ma/* is assigned to the variable *reg_expression*. A match is found if the string being tested contains an uppercase *N* followed by any two single characters (each dot represents one character), and an *m* and an *a*. It would find *Norma*, *No man*, *Normandy*, and so on.

3   The *test* method returns *true* if the string *textString* matches the regular expression and *false* if it doesn't. The variable *result* contains either *true* or *false*.

4   If the string *"Norma Jean"* contains regular expression pattern */N..ma/*, the return from the *test* method is true, and the output is sent to the screen as shown in Figure 17.11.

5   If the pattern is not found, *No Match!* is displayed on the page.

Figure 17.11   The user entered *Norma Jean,* an *N* followed by any 2 characters, and *ma.*

17.4.2 The Character Class

A character class represents **one** character from a set of characters. For example *[abc]* matches either an *a*, *b*, **or** *c*; and *[a-z]* matches one character from a set of characters in the range from *a* to *z*; and *[0-9]* matches one character in the range of digits between *0* to *9*. If the character class contains a leading caret, ^, then the class represents any one character not in the set; thus, *[^a-zA-Z]* matches a single character **not** in the range from *a* to *z* or *A* to *Z*, and *[^0-9]* matches a single digit not in the range between 0 and 9.

JavaScript provides additional symbols, called metasymbols, to represent a character class. The symbols *\d* and *\D* represent a single digit and a single nondigit, respectively; the same as *[0-9]* and *[^0-9]*; whereas *\w* and *\W* represent a single word character and a single nonword character, respectively; same as *[A-Za-z_0-9]* and *[^A-Za-z_0-9]*.

EXAMPLE 17.12

```
<html>
  <head><title>The Character Class</title></head>
  <body>
    <script type="text/javascript">
1       var reg_expression = /[A-Z][a-z]eve/;
2       var textString=prompt("Type a string of text","");
3       var result=reg_expression.test(textString);  // Returns true
                                                      // or false
        document.write(result+"<br />");
        if ( result){
           document.write("<b>The reg_ex /[A-Z][a-z]eve/ matched the
                          string\""+ textString +"\".<br />");
        }
        else{
           alert("No Match!");
        }
    </script>
  </body>
</html>
```

EXPLANATION

1   The variable is assigned a bracketed regular expression containing alphanumeric characters. This regular expression matches a string that contains at least one uppercase character ranging between A and Z, followed by one lowercase character ranging between a and z, followed by *eve*.

2   The variable *textString* is assigned user input, in this example *Steven lives in Cleveland* was entered.

3   The regular expression *test()* method will return *true* because *Steven* contains an uppercase character, followed by a lowercase character, and *eve*. *Cleveland* also matches the pattern. The variable *result* contains either *true* or *false*. See the output in Figures 17.12 and 17.13.

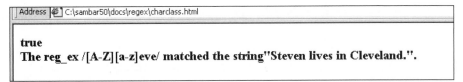

Address 📄 C:\sambar50\docs\regex\charclass.html

true
The reg_ex /[A-Z][a-z]eve/ matched the string"Steven lives in Cleveland.".

Figure 17.12 The user entered *Steven lives in Cleveland*, one uppercase letter *(A-Z)*, followed by one lowercase letter *(a-z)*, followed by *eve*. This matches both *Steven* and *Cleveland*.

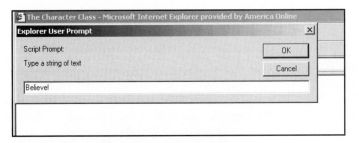

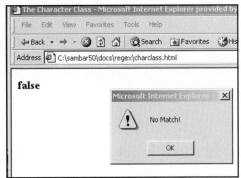

Figure 17.13 When the user entered *Believe!* (top), it didn't match (bottom). Would it have matched if he or she had entered *BeLieve*. Why?

EXAMPLE 17.13

```html
<html>
  <head><title>The Character Class</title></head>
  <body>
    <script type="text/javascript">
      // Character class
      var reg_expression = /[A-Za-z0-9_]/;// A single alphanumeric
                                          // word character
      var textString=prompt("Type a string of text","");
      var result=reg_expression.test(textString);  // Returns true
                                                    // or false
```

Continues

EXAMPLE   **17.13** (CONTINUED)

```
            document.write(result+"<br />");
            if (result){
               document.write("<b>The reg_ex /[A-Za-z0-9_]/ matched the
                               string\""+ textString +"\".<br />");
            }
            else{
               alert("No Match!");
            }
         </script>
      </body>
</html>
```

EXPLANATION

1   A regular expression object, an alphanumeric character in the bracketed character
    class *[A-Za-z0-9_]* is assigned to the variable called *reg_expression*. This regular
    expression matches a string that contains at least one character in the character
    class ranging between *A* and *Z*, *a* and *z*, *0* and *9*, and the underscore character, *_*.

2   User input is entered in the prompt dialog box and assigned to the variable *text-
    String*. In this example the user entered *Take 5*.

3   The regular expression test method will return *true* because this string *Take 5* con-
    tains at least one alphanumeric character (see Figure 17.14).

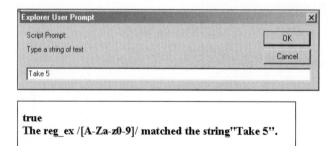

true
The reg_ex /[A-Za-z0-9]/ matched the string"Take 5".

Figure 17.14   User entered *Take 5* (top). The string contained at least one
alphanumeric character (bottom).

EXAMPLE   **17.14**

```
<html>
   <head><title>The Character Class and Negation</title></head>
   <body>
```

EXAMPLE 17.14 (CONTINUED)

```
        <script type="text/javascript">
        // Negation within a Character Class
1       var reg_expression = /[^0-9]/;
2       var textString=prompt("Type a string of text","");
3       var result=reg_expression.test(textString);  // Returns true
                                                      // or false
        document.write(result+"<br />");
        if (result){
           document.write("<b>The reg_ex /[^0-9]/ matched the
                          string\""+ textString +"\".<br />");
        }
        else{
           alert("No Match!");
        }
        </script>
     </body>
   </html>
```

EXPLANATION

1   The caret inside a character class, when it is the first character after the opening bracket, creates a negation, meaning any character not in this range. This regular expression matches a string that **does not** contain a number between 0 and 9.

2   User input is assigned to the variable *textString*. In this example, *abc* was entered.

3   The regular expression *test()* method will return *true* because the string *abc* does not contain a character ranging from 0 to 9 (see Figure 17.15).

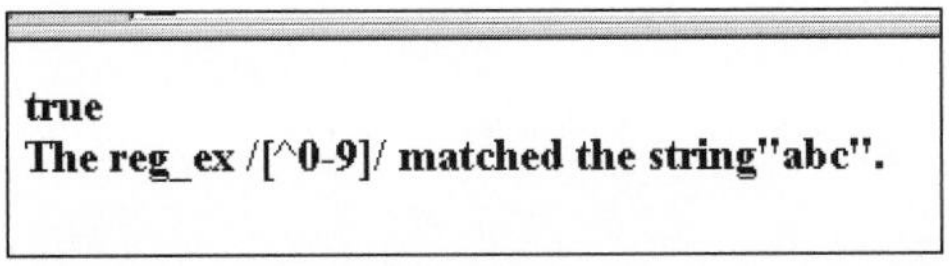

---

true
The reg_ex /[^0-9]/ matched the string"abc".

Figure 17.15   The user entered *abc*. It contains a character that is **not** in the range between 0 and 9.

17.4.3   Metasymbols

Metasymbols offer an alternative way to represent a character class. For example, instead of representing a number as *[0-9]*, it can be represented as \d, and the alternative for representing a nonnumber *[^0-9]* is \D. Metasymbols are easier to use and to type than metacharacters.

Table 17.8 Metasymbols

Symbol	What It Matches	Character Class
\d	One digit	[0-9]
\D	One nondigit	[^0-9]
\s	One whitespace character (tab, space, newline, carriage return, formfeed, vertical tab)	
\S	One nonspace character	
\w	One word character	[A-Za-z0-9_]
\W	One nonword character	[^A-Za-z0-9]

EXAMPLE 17.15

```
      <html>
        <head><title>The Digit Meta Symbol</title></head>
        <body>
          <script type="text/javascript">
1             var reg_expression = /6\d\d/;
2             var textString=prompt("Type a string of text","");
3             var result=reg_expression.test(textString);   // Returns true
                                                             // or false
              document.write(result+"<br />");
              if (result){
                 document.write("<b>The regular expression /6\\d\\d/ matched
                             the string\""+ textString +"\".<br />");
              }
              else{
                 alert("No Match!");
              }
          </script>
        </body>
      </html>
```

EXPLANATION

1   The variable is assigned a regular expression containing the number 6, followed by two single digits. The metasymbol \d represents the character class [0-9].

2   The variable *textString* is assigned user input; in this example, *126553* was entered.

3   The regular expression *test()* method will return *true* because this string, *126553*, contains a 6 followed by any two digits. See Figure 17.16.

Address   C:\sambar50\docs\regex\metasymbol.html

true
The regular expression /6\d\d/ matched the string"126553".

Figure 17.16   The user entered *126553*. It contains a 6 followed by any two digits.

```
<html>
  <head><title>The Digit Meta Symbol Negated</title></head>
  <body>
    <script type="text/javascript">
1     var reg_expression = /[a-z]\D\D/;
2     var textString=prompt("Type a string of text","");
3     var result=reg_expression.test(textString);   // Returns true
                                                     // or false
      document.write(result+"<br />");
      if (result){
         document.write("<b>The regular expression /[a-z]\\D\\D/
                    matched the string\"" + textString +"\".<br />");
      }
      else{
         alert("No Match!");
      }
    </script>
  </body>
</html>
```

EXPLANATION

1   The variable is assigned a regular expression containing a letter, followed by two single nondigits. The metasymbol \D represents the character class *[^0-9]*.

2   The variable *textString* is assigned user input; in this example, *Hello!* was entered.

3   The regular expression *test()* method will return *true* because this string *Hello!!* matches a lowercase letter, followed by two nondigit characters. See Figure 17.17.

Address   C:\sambar50\docs\regex\metasymbolnegation.html

true
The regular expression /[a-z]\D\D/ matched the string"Hello!!".

Figure 17.17   The user entered a lowercase letter followed by two nondigits.

EXAMPLE 17.17

```
        <html>
           <head><title>Word and Space Metasymbols</title></head>
           <body>
              <script type="text/javascript">
1                 var reg_expression = /\w\s\w\W/;
2                 var textString=prompt("Type a string of text","");
3                 var result=reg_expression.test(textString);  // Returns true
                                                               // or false
                  document.write(result+"<br />");
                  if (result){
                     document.write("<b>The regular expression /\\w\\s\\w\\W/
                             matched the string\""+ textString +"\".<br />");
                  }
                  else{
                     alert("No Match!");
                  }
              </script>
           </body>
        </html>
```

EXPLANATION

1   The variable is assigned a regular expression containing an alphanumeric word character \w, followed by a space \s, followed by another alphanumeric word character, followed by a nonalphanumeric word character \W. The metasymbol \w represents the character class *[A-Za-z0-9_]*. The metasymbol \W represents the character class *[^A-Za-z0-9_]*, and the metasymbol \s represents a whitespace character (tab, space, newline, carriage return, formfeed).

2   The variable *textString* is assigned user input; in this example, *ABC D%* was entered first.

3   The regular expression *test()* method will return *true* because the string *ABC D%* matches an alphanumeric character (*C*), followed by a space, another alphanumeric character (*D*) and a nonalphanumeric character (*%*) (see Figure 17.18). An example of output where the pattern failed is shown in Figure 17.19.

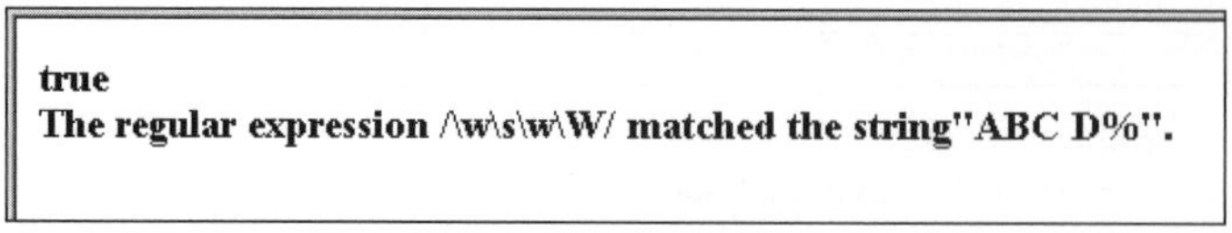

---

true
The regular expression /\w\s\w\W/ matched the string"ABC D%".

Figure 17.18   The user entered *ABC D%*. It contained a word character, followed by a whitespace, another word character, and a nonwhitespace.

Figure 17.19   The user entered *ABCD#*. To match, the string needs a space between the *C* and *D*.

17.4.4   Metacharacters to Repeat Pattern Matches

In the previous examples, the metacharacter matched on a single character. What if you want to match on more than one character? For example, let's say you are looking for all lines containing names and the first letter must be in uppercase, which can be represented as *[A-Z]*, but the following letters are lowercase and the number of letters varies in each name. *[a-z]* matches on a single lowercase letter. How can you match on one or more lowercase letters, or zero or more lowercase letters? To do this you can use what are called **quantifiers**. To match on one or more lowercase letters, the regular expression can be written */[a-z]+/* where the + sign means "one or more of the previous characters"; in this case, one or more lowercase letters. JavaScript provides a number of quantifiers as shown in the Table 17.9.

Table 17.9   Quantifiers: The Greedy Metacharacters

Metacharacter	What It Matches
x?	Matches 0 or 1 of *x*.
(xyz)?	Matches zero or one pattern of *xyz*.
x*	Matches 0 or more of *x*.
(xyz)*	Matches zero or more patterns of *xyz*.
x+	Matches 1 or more of *x*.
(xyz)+	Matches one or more patterns of *xyz*.
x{m,n}	Matches at least *m* of *x* and no more than *n* of *x*.

The Greed Factor.   Normally quantifiers are "greedy"; that is, they match on the largest possible set of characters starting at the left of the string and searching to the right, looking for the last possible character that would satisfy the condition. For example, given the string:

```
var string="ab123456783445554437AB"
```

and the regular expression:

`/ab[0-9]*/`

If the *replace()* method were to substitute what is matched with an *"X"*:

`string=string.relace(/ab[0-9]/, "X");`

the resulting string would be:

`"XAB"`

The asterisk is a greedy metacharacter. It matches for zero or more of the preceding characters. In other words, it attaches itself to the character preceding it; in the preceding example, the asterisk attaches itself to the character class *[0-9]*. The matching starts on the left, searching for *ab* followed by zero or more numbers in the range between 0 and 9. It is called greedy because the matching continues until the last number is found; in this example, the number 7. The pattern *ab* and all of the numbers in the range between 0 and 9 are replaced with a single *X*.

Greediness can be turned off so that instead of matching on the maximum number of characters, the match is made on the minimal number of characters found. This is done by appending a question mark after the greedy metacharacter. See Example 17.18.

EXAMPLE 17.18

```
<html>
   <head><title></title></head>
   <body>
      <script type="text/javascript">
1        var reg_expression = /\d\.?\d/;
2        var textString=prompt("Type a string of text","");
3        var result=reg_expression.test(textString);  // Returns true
                                                       // or false
         document.write(result+"<br />");
         if (result){
            document.write("<b>The regular expression /\\d\\.?\\d/
                    matched the string\""+textString +"\".<br />");
         }
         else{
            alert("No Match!");
         }
      </script>
   </body>
</html>
```

EXPLANATION

1   The variable is assigned a regular expression containing a decimal character \d, and followed by either one or zero literal periods, \.?. The question mark (zero or one) controls the character preceding it, in this case a period. There is either one period or no period at all in the string being matched.

2   The variable *textString* is assigned user input; in this example, *3.7* was entered.

3   The regular expression *test* method will return *true* because the string *3.7* matches a decimal number, 3, followed by a period (or not one) and followed by another decimal number, 7. See the examples in Figure 17.20.

---

true
The regular expression /\d\.?\d/ matched the string"3.7".

---

true
The regular expression /\d\.?\d/ matched the string"456".

false

Figure 17.20   The user entered *3.7*, or number, period, number (top); the user entered *456*, or number, no period, number (middle); the user entered *5A6*, but there must be at least two consecutive digits for a match (bottom).

EXAMPLE   17.19

```
<html>
  <head><title></title></head>
  <body>
    <script type="text/javascript">
      // Greediness
```

Continues

EXAMPLE 17.19 (CONTINUED)

```
1          var reg_expression = /[A-Z][a-z]*\s/;
2          var textString=prompt("Type a string of text","");
3          var result=reg_expression.test(textString);  // Returns true
                                                          // or false
           document.write(result+"<br />");
           if (result){
             document.write("<b>The regular expression /[A-Z][a-z]*\\s/
                     matched the string"+ textString +"\".<br />");
           }
           else{
             alert("No Match!");
           }
        </script>
     </body>
  </html>
```

EXPLANATION

1   The variable is assigned a regular expression containing an uppercase letter, *[A-Z]*, followed by zero or more lowercase letters, *[a-z]**, and a space, *\s*. There are either zero or more lowercase letters.

2   The variable *textString* is assigned user input; in this example, *Danny boy* was entered.

3   The regular expression test method will return *true* because the string *Danny boy* matches an uppercase letter *D*, followed by zero or more lowercase letters *anny*, and a space. See Figure 17.21.

> **true**
> The regular expression /[A-Z][a-z]*\s/ matched the string"Danny boy".

> **true**
> The regular expression /[A-Z][a-z]*\s/ matched the string"DANNY BOY".

Figure 17.21   The user entered *Danny boy*, consisting of one uppercase letter, zero or more lowercase letters, and a space (top); the user entered *DANNY BOY*, consisting one uppercase letter, zero lowercase letters, and a space (bottom). Note: the "Y" is followed by a space.

EXAMPLE 17.20

```
<html>
  <head><title></title></head>
  <body>
    <script type="text/javascript">
1     var reg_expression = /[A-Z][a-z]+\s/;
2     var textString=prompt("Type a string of text","");
3     var result=reg_expression.test(textString);  // Returns true
                                                   // or false
      document.write(result+"<br />");
      if (result){
        document.write("<b>The regular expression /[A-Z][a-z]+\\s/
                matched the string\""+ textString +"\".<br />");
      }
      else{
        alert("No Match!");
      }
    </script>
  </body>
</html>
```

EXPLANATION

1   The regular expression reads: Search for an uppercase letter, followed by one or more lowercase letters, followed by a space.

2   The user is prompted for input.

3   The regular expression *test()* method checks that the string *textString* entered by the user matches the regular expression and returns *true* or *false* (see Figure 17.22).

---

true
The regular expression /[A-Z][a-z]+\s/ matched the string"Danny Boy".

false

Figure 17.22 The user entered *Danny Boy* or one uppercase letter, one or more lowercase letters, and a space (top); the user entered *DannyBoy* and gets no match, because there was not a space in the search string (bottom).

EXAMPLE 17.21

```
<html>
  <head><title></title></head>
  <body>
    <script type="text/javascript">
1     var reg_expression = /abc\d{1,3}\.\d/;
2     var textString=prompt("Type a string of text","");
3     var result=reg_expression.test(textString);   // Returns true
                                                     // or false
      document.write(result+"<br />");
      if (result){
        document.write("<b>The regular expression
                        /abc\\d{1,3}\\.\\d/ matched the string\""+
                        textString +"\".<br />");
      }
      else{
        alert("No Match!");
      }
    </script>
  </body>
</html>
```

EXPLANATION

1   The variable is assigned a regular expression containing the pattern *abc\d{1,3}\.\d*, where *abc* is followed by at least one digit, repeated by up to three digits, followed by a literal period, and another digit, *\d*.

2   The variable *textString* is assigned user input; here, *abc456.5xyz* was entered.

3   The regular expression contains the curly brace {} metacharacters, representing the number of times the preceding expression will be repeated. The expression reads: Find at least one occurrence of the pattern *\d* and as many as three in a row. See Figure 17.23.

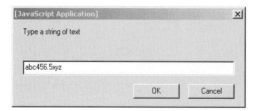

Figure 17.23   The user entered *abc* followed by between one and three numbers, followed by a literal period, and *xyz* (top); the entered string matched *true* (bottom).

EXAMPLE 17.22

```html
<html>
   <head><title></title></head>
   <body>
      <script type="text/javascript">
         //Repeating patterns
1        var reg_expression = /#\d{5}\.\d/;
2        var textString=prompt("Type a string of text","");
3        var result=reg_expression.test(textString);  // Returns true
                                                       // or false
         document.write(result+"<br />");
         if (result){
            document.write("<b>The regular expression /#\\d{5}\\.\\d/
                    matched the string ""+ textString +"\".<br />");
         }
         else{
            alert("No Match!");
         }
      </script>
   </body>
</html>
```

EXPLANATION

1 The variable is assigned a regular expression that reads: Find a # sign, followed by exactly five repeating digits \d{5}, a period, and another digit \d.

2 The user is prompted for input.

3 The *test()* method returns *true* if the regular expression pattern was found in the input string. See Figure 17.24.

---

true
The regular expression /#\d{5}\.\d/ matched the string"#34234.6".

---

true
The regular expression /#\d{5}\.\d/ matched the string"abac#12345.56789".

false

Figure 17.24 The user entered *#34234.6*, or a # sign, followed by five repeating digits, a period, and a number (top). This returns *true*. The user entered *abac#12345.56789* (middle). This returns *true*; but when the user entered *#234.555* (there are not five repeating digits after the # sign), no match was madVtse (bottom).

EXAMPLE 17.23

```
    <html>
      <head><title></title></head>
      <body>
        <script type="text/javascript">
          //Repeating patterns
1         var reg_expression = /5{1,}\.\d/;
          var textString=prompt("Type a string of text","");
2         var result=reg_expression.test(textString);  // Returns true
                                                        // or false
          document.write(result+"<br />");
          if (result){
            document.write("<b>The regular expression #\\5{1,}\\.\\d/
matched the string\" " + textString + "\".<br />");
          }
          else{
            alert("No Match!");
          }
        </script>
      </body>
    </html>
```

EXPLANATION

1   The variable, called *reg_expression*, is assigned a regular expression. The regular expression reads: Search for the number 5, followed by at least 1 or more of them (the curly braces determine how many consecutive 5s to look for), followed by a literal period and a digit.

2   The *test*() method returns *true* if the regular expression pattern was found in the input string. See Figure 17.25.

---

true
The regular expression #\5{1,}\.\d/ matched the string" abc5555555.2".

---

true
The regular expression #\5{1,}\.\d/ matched the string" 5.6".

Figure 17.25 The user entered *abc5555555.2*, or the number 5 at least 1 time, followed by a literal period, and any digit, \d (top). This returns *true*; the user entered *5.6* (bottom). This also returns *true*.

Metacharacters That Turn off Greediness. By placing a question mark after a greedy quantifier, the greed is turned off and the search ends after the first match, rather than the last one.

EXAMPLE 17.24

```
<html>
   <head><title>Greed</title></head>
   <body bgcolor="lightblue">
      <script type="text/javascript">
1        var myString="abcdefghijklmnopqrstuvwxyz";
         document.write("<b>Old string:</b>"+myString+"<br />");
2        myString=myString.replace(/[a-z]+/, "XXX");
3        document.write("<b>New string:<b> "+  myString+"<br />");
      </script>
   </body>
</html>
```

EXPLANATION

1   The variable, called *myString*, is assigned a string of lowercase letters.

2   The regular expression reads: Search for one or more lowercase letters, and re-
    place them with *XXX*. The + metacharacter is greedy. It takes as many characters
    as match the expression; that is, it starts on the left side of the string, grabbing as
    many lowercase letters as it can find until the end of the string.

3   The value of *myString* is printed after the substitution, as shown in Figure 17.26.

Old string: **abcdefghijklmnopqrstuvwxyz**
New string: **XXX**

Figure 17.26 The + sign is greedy. One or more lowercase letters are replaced with
XXX; that is, the whole string.

EXAMPLE 17.25

```
<html>
   <head><title></title></head>
   <body>
      <script type="text/javascript">
1        var myString="abcdefghijklmnopqrstuvwxyz";
         document.write("<font size='+1'>Old string: <b>"
                        +myString+"<br />");
2        myString=myString.replace(/[a-z]+?/, "XXX");
         document.write("</b>New string: <b>"+myString+"<br />");
      </script>
   </body>
</html>
```

EXPLANATION

1   The variable called *myString* is assigned a string of lowercase letters, just exactly like the last example.

2   The regular expression reads: Search for one or more lowercase letters, but after the + sign, there is a question mark. The question mark turns off the greed factor. Now instead of taking as many lowercase letters as it can, this regular expression search stops after it finds the first lowercase character, and then replaces that character with *XXX*. See Figure 17.27.

Old string: **abcdefghijklmnopqrstuvwxyz**
New string: **XXXbcdefghijklmnopqrstuvwxyz**

Figure 17.27   This is not greedy: Output from Example 17.25.

17.4.5 Anchoring Metacharacters

Often it is necessary to anchor a metacharacter down, so that it matches only if the pattern is found at the beginning or end of a line, word, or string. These metacharacters are based on a position just to the left or to the right of the character that is being matched. Anchors are technically called **zero-width assertions** because they correspond to positions, not actual characters in a string; for example, /^*abc*/ will search for *abc* at the beginning of the line, where the ^ represents a position, not an actual character. See Table 17.10 for a list of anchoring metacharacters.

Table 17.10   Anchors (Assertions)

Metacharacter	What It Matches
^	Matches to beginning of line or beginning of a string.
$	Matches to end of line or end of a string.
\b	Matches a word boundary (when not inside *[ ]*).
\B	Matches a nonword boundary.

EXAMPLE 17.26

```
<html>
  <head><title></title></head>
  <body>
```

EXAMPLE 17.26 (CONTINUED)

```
       <script type="text/javascript">
1          var reg_expression = /^Will/;  // Beginning of line anchor
2          var textString=prompt("Type a string of text","");
3          var result=reg_expression.test(textString);  // Returns true
                                                         // or false
           document.write(result+"<br />");
           if (result){
             document.write("<b>The regular expression /^Will/ matched
                             the string\""+ textString +"\".<br />");
           }
           else{
             alert("No Match!");
           }
       </script>
     </body>
   </html>
```

EXPLANATION

1 The variable is assigned a regular expression containing the beginning of line anchor metacharacter, the caret, followed by *Will.*

2 The variable *textString* is assigned user input; in this example, *Willie Wonker* was entered.

3 The regular expression *test()* method will return *true* because the string *Willie Wonker* begins with *Will.* See Figure 17.28.

true
The regular expression /^Will/ matched the string"Willie Wonker".

false

Figure 17.28 The user entered *Willie Wonker. Will* is at the beginning of the line, so this tests true (top); if the user enters *I know Willie,* and *Will* is not at the beginning of the line, the input would test *false* (bottom).

EXAMPLE 17.27

```
<html>
  <head><title>Beginning of Line Anchor</title></head>
  <body>
    <script type="text/javascript">
1     var reg_expression = /^[JK]/;
2     var textString=prompt("Type a string of text","");
3     var result=reg_expression.test(textString);  // Returns true
                                                    // or false
      document.write(result+"<br />");
      if (result){
        document.write("<b>The regular expression /^[JK]/ matched
                        the string\""+ textString +"\".<br />");
      }
      else{
        alert("No Match!");
      }
    </script>
  </body>
</html>
```

EXPLANATION

1   A regular expression contains a beginning of line anchor, the caret. The regular expression reads: Find either an uppercase *J* or uppercase *K* at the beginning of the line or string.

2   The variable *textString* is assigned user input; in this example, *Jack and Jill*.

3   The regular expression *test()* method will return *true* because the string *Jack* matches an uppercase letter *J* and is found at the beginning of the string. See Figure 17.29.

---

true
The regular expression /^[JK]/ matched the string"Jack and Jill".

---

true
The regular expression /^[JK]/ matched the string"Karen Evich".

Figure 17.29   The string must begin with either a *J* or *K*. The user entered *Jack and Jill* (top) and this returns *true*; the user entered *Karen Evich* (bottom) and this also returns *true*.

EXAMPLE 17.28

```
      <html>
        <head><title>End of Line Anchor</title></head>
        <body>
          <script type="text/javascript">
1           var reg_expression = /50$/;
2           var textString=prompt("Type a string of text","");
3           var result=reg_expression.test(textString); // Returns true
                                                         // or false
            document.write(result+"<br />");
            if (result){
              document.write("<b>The regular expression /50$/ matched
                              the string\""+ textString +"\".<br />");
            }
            else{
              alert("No Match!");
            }
          </script>
        </body>
      </html>
```

EXPLANATION

1   The regular expression */50$/* is assigned to the variable. The pattern contains the dollar sign ($) metacharacter, representing the end of line anchor only when the $ is the last character in the pattern. The expression reads: Find a *5* and a *0* followed by a newline.

2   The user is prompted for a string of text.

3   If the string ends in 50, the regex test method returns *true*; otherwise *false*.

EXAMPLE 17.29

```
      <html>
        <head><title>Anchors</title></head>
        <body>
          <script type="text/javascript">
1           var reg_expression = /^[A-Z][a-z]+\s\d$/;
                // At the beginning of the string, find one uppercase
                // letter, followed by one or more lowercase letters,
                // a space, and one digit.
2           var string=prompt("Enter a name and a number","");
3           if ( reg_expression.test(string)){
              alert("It Matched!!");
            }
```

Continues

EXAMPLE 17.29 (CONTINUED)

```
        else{
           alert("No Match!");
        }
     </script>
  </body>
</html>
```

EXPLANATION

1   The regular expression reads: Look at the beginning of the line, ^, find an upper-case letter, *[A-Z]*, followed by one or more lowercase letters, *[a-z]+*, a single whitespace, *\s*, and a digit at the end of the line, *\d$*.

2   The user is prompted for input.

3   The regular expression *test()* method tests to see if there was a match and returns *true* if so, and *false* if not. See Figures 17.30 and 17.31.

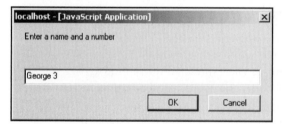

Figure 17.30   The string begins with a capital letter, followed by one or more lowercase letters, a space, and ends with one digit (left); the input sequence matched, so this message is displayed (right).

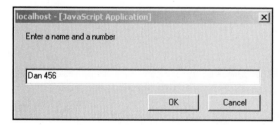

Figure 17.31   The regular expression does not match because the string ends in more than one digit (left); the input sequence did not match, so this message is displayed (right).

EXAMPLE   17.30

```
<html>
   <head><title>The Word Boundary</title></head>
   <body>
      <script type="text/javascript">
         // Anchoring a word with \b
1        var reg_expression = /\blove\b/;
         var textString=prompt("Type a string of text","");
2        var result=reg_expression.test(textString);   // Returns true
                                                        // or false
         document.write(result+"<br />");
         if (result){
            document.write("<b>The regular expression /\\blove\\b/
                 matched the string \""+ textString +"\".<br />");
         }
         else{
            alert("No Match!");
         }
      </script>
   </body>
</html>
```

EXPLANATION

1   The regular expression contains the \b metacharacter, representing a word boundary, not a specific character. The expression reads: Find a word beginning and ending with *love*. This means that *gloves, lover, clover*, and so on, will not be found.

2   The regular expression *test()* method will return *true* because the string *love* is within word boundary anchors \b. See Figure 17.32.

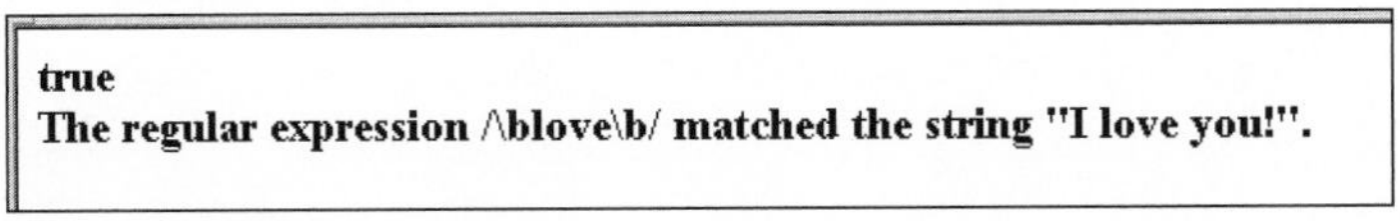

---

true
The regular expression /\blove\b/ matched the string "I love you!".

Figure 17.32   The user entered *I love you!*. The word *love* is between word boundaries (\ *b*). The match was successful.

17.4.6   Alternation

Alternation allows the regular expression to contain alternative patterns to be matched; for example, the regular expression */John|Karen|Steve/* will match a line containing *John* or *Karen* or *Steve*. If *Karen, John*, or *Steve* are all on different lines, all lines are matched. Each of the alternative expressions is separated by a vertical bar (the pipe symbol, |) and the expressions can consist of any number of characters, unlike the character class that only matches for one character; thus, */a|b|c/* is the same as *[abc]*, whereas */ab|de/* cannot be represented as *[abde]*. The pattern */ab|de/* is either *ab* or *de*, whereas the class *[abcd]* represents only **one** character in the set *a*, *b*, *c*, or *d*.

EXAMPLE 17.31

```
<html>
  <head><title>Alternation</title></head>
  <body>
    <script type="text/javascript">
      // Alternation: this or that or whatever...
1     var reg_expression = /Steve|Dan|Tom/;
      var textString=prompt("Type a string of text","");
2     var result=reg_expression.test(textString);  // Returns true
                                                    // or false
      document.write(result+"<br />");
      if (result){
        document.write("<b>The regular expression /Steve|Dan|Tom/
                matched the string\""+ textString +"\".<br />");
      }
      else{
        alert("No Match!");
      }
    </script>
  </body>
</html>
```

EXPLANATION

1   The pipe symbol, |, is used in the regular expression to match on a set of alternative patterns. If any of the patterns, *Steve*, *Dan*, or *Tom*, are found, the match is successful.

2   The *test()* method will return *true* if the user enters either *Steve*, *Dan*, or *Tom*. See Figure 17.33.

---

true
The regular expression /Steve|Dan|Tom/ matched the string"Do you know Tommy?".

---

true
The regular expression /Steve|Dan|Tom/ matched the string"Dan is my son.".

---

true
The regular expression /Steve|Dan|Tom/ matched the string"Steve Dobbins is Christian's daddy.".

Figure 17.33 The user entered *Do you know Tommy?*. Pattern *Tom* was matched in the string.

Grouping or Clustering.   Grouping occurs when a set of characters are enclosed in parentheses, such as /(ma)/ or /(John|Joe) Brown. If the regular expression pattern is enclosed in parentheses, a group or subpattern is created. Then instead of the greedy metacharacters matching on zero, one, or more of the previous single characters, they can match on the previous subpattern. For example, /(ma)+/ means search for "ma" or "mama" or "mamama," and so forth; one or more occurrences of the pattern "ma". If the parentheses are removed and the regular expression is /ma+/, we would be searching for an "m" followed by one or more occurrences of an "a," such a "ma," "maaaaa." Alternation can also be controlled if the patterns are enclosed in parentheses. In the example, /(John|Joe) Brown/, the regular expression reads: search for "John Brown" or "Joe Brown". The grouping creates a subpattern of either "John" or "Joe" followed by the pattern "Brown". Without grouping (i.e., /John|John Brown/), the regular expression reads: search for "John" or "Joe Brown". This process of grouping characters together is also called **clustering**.

```
<html>
    <head><title>Grouping or Clustering</title></head>
    <body>
        <script type="text/javascript">
            // Grouping with parentheses
1           var reg_expression = /^(Sam|Dan|Tom) Robbins/;
2           var textString=prompt("Type a string of text","");
3           var result=reg_expression.test(textString);  // Returns true
                                                          // or false
            document.write(result+"<br />");
            if (result){
                document.write("<b>The regular expression /^(Sam|Dan|Tom)
                Robbins/ matched the string\""+ textString +"\".<br />");
            }
            else{
                alert("No Match!");
            }
        </script>
    </body>
</html>
```

1   By enclosing *Sam*, *Dan*, and *Tom* in parentheses, the alternative now becomes either *Sam Robbins*, *Dan Robbins*, or *Tom Robbins*. Without the parentheses, the regular expression matches *Sam*, or *Dan*, or *Tom Robbins*. The caret metacharacter ^ anchors all of the patterns to the beginning of the line.

2   The user input is assigned to the variable called *textString*.

3   The *test()* method checks to see if the string contains one of the alternatives: *Sam Robbins* or *Dan Robbins* or *Tom Robbins*. If it does, *true* is returned; otherwise, *false* is returned. See Figure 17.34.

---

true
The regular expression /^(Sam|Dan|Tom) Robbins/ matched the string"Dan Robbins is my
brother.".

Figure 17.34 The user entered *Dan Robbins* as one of the alternatives. *Sam Robbins* or *Tom Robbins* would also be okay.

Remembering or Capturing.   Besides grouping, when the regular expression pattern is enclosed in parentheses, the subpattern created is being captured, meaning the subpattern is saved in special numbered class properties, starting with $1, then $2, and so on. For example, in the grouping example where we created a regular expression: /(ma)/, capturing will assign "ma" to $1 if "ma" if matched. We can say that "ma" is remembered in $1. If we have the expression /(John) (Doe)/, "John" will be captured in $1 and "Doe" in $2 if the pattern "John Doe" is matched. For each subpattern in the expression, the number of the property will be incremented by one: $1, $2, $3, and so on. The dollar sign properties can be applied to the *RegExp* object, not an instance of the object. and then used later in the program as shown in Example 17.33.They will persist until another successful pattern match occurs, at which time they will all be cleared. Even if the intention was to control the greedy metacharacter or the behavior of alternation as shown in the previous grouping examples, the subpatterns are automatically captured and saved as a side effect.[2] For more information on this go to *http://developer.netscape.com/docs/manuals/communicator/ jsguide/reobjud.hmt#1007373.*

EXAMPLE 17.33

```
    <html>
       <head><title>Capturing</title></head>
       <body>
         <h3>
         <script type="text/javascript">
1           textString = "Everyone likes William Rogers and his friends."
2           var reg_expression = /(William)\s(Rogers)/;
3           myArray=textString.match(reg_expression);
4           document.write(myArray);  // Three element array
5           document.write("<br>"+RegExp.$1 + " "+RegExp.$2 +"<br>");
            /* alert(myArray[1] + " "+ myArray[2]);
            match and exec create an array consisting of the string, and
            the captured patterns. myArray[0] is "William Rogers"
            myArray[1] is "William"  myArray[2] is "Rogers".*/
         </script>
```

---

2. It is possible to prevent a subpattern from being saved.

EXAMPLE   17.33 (CONTINUED)

```
            </h3>
        </body>
    </html>
```

EXPLANATION

1   The string called *textString* is created.

2   The regular expression contains two subpatterns, *William* and *Rogers*, both enclosed in parentheses.

3   When either the *String* object's *match()* method or the *RegExp* object's *exec()* method are applied to the regular expression containing subpatterns, an array is returned, where the first element of the array is the regular expression string, and the next elements are the values of the subpatterns.

4   The array elements are displayed, separated by commas.

5   The subpatterns are class properties of the *RegExp* object. *$1* represents the first captured subpattern, *William*, and *$2* represents the second captured subpattern, *Rogers*. See Figure 17.35.

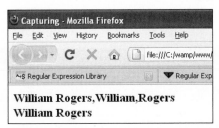

Figure 17.35   Capturing portions of a regular expression using the *RegExp* object.

EXAMPLE   17.34

```
    <html>
        <head><title>Capture and Replace</title></head>
        <body>
          <big>
          <script type = "text/javascript">
1             var string="Tommy Savage:203-123-4444:12 Main St."
2             var newString=string.replace(/(Tommy) (Savage)/, "$2, $1");
3             document.write(newString +"<br />");
          </script>
          </big>
        </body>
    </html>
```

1   A string is assigned to the variable, called *string*.

2   The *replace()* method will search for the pattern *Tommy Savage*. Because the search side of the *replace()* method contains the pattern *Tommy* enclosed in parentheses and the pattern *Savage* enclosed in parentheses, each of these subpatterns will be stored in *$1* and *$2*, respectively. A third pattern would be stored in *$3* and a fourth pattern in *$4*, and so on. On the replacement side of the *replace()* method, *$2* and *$1* are replaced in the string, so that *Savage* is first, then a comma, and then *Tommy*. The first and last names have been reversed.

3   The new string is displayed. See Figure 17.36.

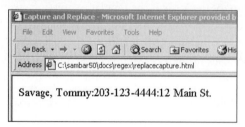

Figure 17.36   Output from Example 17.34.

EXAMPLE   17.35

```
<html>
  <head><title>Capture and Replace</title></head>
  <body>
    <big>
      <script type = "text/javascript">
1       var string="Tommy Savage:203-123-4444:12 Main St."
2       var newString=string.replace(/(\w+)\s(\w+)/, "$2, $1");
3       document.write(newString +"<br />");
      </script>
    </big>
  </body>
</html>
```

EXPLANATION

1   A string is created to be used by the *replace()* method in line 2.

2   The *replace()* method searches for one or more alphanumeric word characters, followed by a single space, and another set of alphanumeric word characters. The word characters are enclosed in parentheses, and thus captured. *$1* will contain *Tommy*, and *$2* will contain *Savage*. On the replacement side, *$1* and *$2* are reversed. After the replacement is made, a new string is created.

3   The value of *newString* shows that the capturing and the substitution occurred successfully, leaving the remainder of the string as it was. See Figure 17.37.

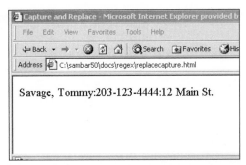

Figure 17.37 Subpatterns are used in string replacement.

17.5 Form Validation with Regular Expressions

When you fill out a form on the Web, you are typically asked for your name, phone number, address (a popup menu of all the states is usually provided), and then all sorts of credit card information. Sometimes it takes four or five tries to get it right because you didn't complete the form exactly the way you were asked. A message will appear and you won't be allowed to submit the form until you get it right. Behind the scenes a JavaScript program is validating the form.

17.5.1 Checking for Empty Fields

There's a form waiting to be filled out. Some of the fields are optional, and some are mandatory. The question is this: Did the user fill in the mandatory fields? If he or she didn't, the form can't be processed properly. Checking for empty or null fields is one of the first things you might want to do.

EXAMPLE 17.36

```
    <html>
       <head><title>Checking for Empty Fields</title>
          <script type="text/javascript">
1             function validate_text(form1) {
2                if ( form1.user_name.value == "" ||
                         form1.user_name.value == null){
                   alert("You must enter your name.");
                   return false;
                }
3                if ( form1.user_phone.value == "" ||
                         form1.user_phone.value == null){
                   alert("You must enter your phone.");
                   return false;
                }
```

Continues

EXAMPLE   17.36 (CONTINUED)

```
                else {
4                    return true;
                }
            }
        </script>
    </head>
    <body>
        <hr />
        <h2> Checking for Empty fields </h2>
5       <form name="formtest" action="/cgi-bin/form1.cgi" method="get"
            onSubmit="return validate_text(formtest)">
        Please enter your name: <br />
6       <input type="text" size=50 name="user_name" />
        <p>
            Please enter your phone number: <br />
7           <input type="text" size=30 name="user_phone" />
        </p><p>
            <input type=submit value="Send">
            <input type=reset value="Clear">
        </p>
    </form>
    </body>
</html>
```

EXPLANATION

1   A user-defined function called *validate_text()* is defined. It takes one parameter, a reference to a form.

2   If the value in the first text field is an empty string (represents a string with no text) or null (represents no value), the user is sent an alert asking him or her to fill in his or her name. If a *false* value is returned, the form is not submitted.

3   If the value in the second text field is an empty string or null, the user is sent an alert asking him or her to fill in a phone number. If a *false* value is returned, the form is not submitted.

4   If both text boxes were filled out, a *true* value is returned, and the form will be submitted to the server's CGI program whose URL is listed in the *action* attribute of the form.

5   The *onSubmit* event is triggered when the user clicks the submit button. The handler function, *validate_text()*, will be called with a reference to this form.

6   The input type for this form is a text box that will get the name of the user.

7   Another text box is created to hold the phone number of the user. See Figure 17.38.

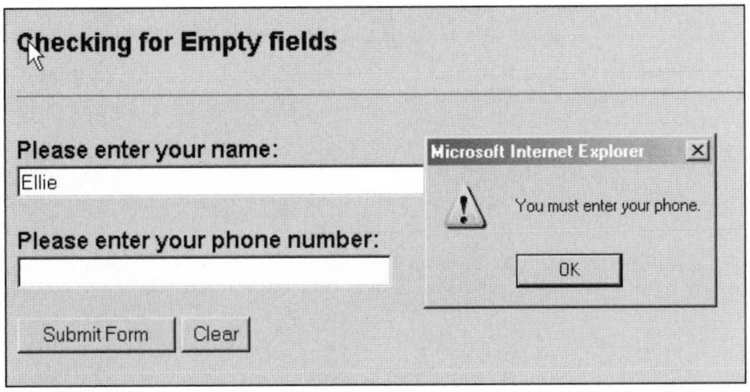

Figure 17.38 The user left the phone number field empty, so the form was not submitted.

17.5.2 Checking for Numeric Zip Codes

If you ask the user for a five-digit zip code, it is easy to check using a regular expression by matching for exactly five digits:

```
/^\d{5}$/
```

Here is another way to say the same thing:

```
/^[0-9][0-9][0-9][0-9][0-9]$/
```

Some longer zip codes contain a dash followed by four numbers. This long zip code format could be represented as:

```
/^\d{5}-?\d{4}$/
```

The beginning and end of line anchors prevent the matched string from containing any extraneous characters at either end of the string. See Example 17.37.

EXAMPLE 17.37

```
    <html>
      <head><title>Testing for a Valid Zip Code</title>
        <script type="text/javascript">
1         function ok_Zip(zip){
2           var regex=/^\d{5}$/;   // Match for 5 numbers
3           if ( regex.test(zip.value) == false) {
              alert("Zip code must contain exactly five numbers!");
              zip.focus();
              return false;
            }
```

Continues

EXAMPLE 17.37 (CONTINUED)

```
4               if ( zip.value == ""){
                    alert("You must enter a zip code");
                    zip.focus();
                    return false;
                }
                return true;
            }
        </script>
    </head>
    <body>
        <big>
            <form name="ZipTest" action="/error" >
                Enter your zip code:
                <input type="text"
                        name="zipcode"
                        size=5 />
                <input type="button"
                        value="Check zip"
5                       onClick="if( ok_Zip(ZipTest.zipcode)) {
                        alert('Zip is valid.')}" />
                <br /><input type="reset">
            </form>
        </big>
    </body>
</html>
```

EXPLANATION

1   The function, called *ok_Zip()*, is defined to validate the zip code entered by the user.

2   The regular expression reads: Look for exactly five digits. The beginning of line and end of line anchors ensure that there will not be any extraneous characters before or after the five digits.

3   The regular expression *test()* method checks that the value entered by the user is a valid zip code. If not, an alert dialog box will tell the user, focus will be returned to the text box, and *false* will be returned.

4   If the user doesn't enter anything, an alert dialog box will appear, focus will be returned to the text box, and *false* will be returned.

5   The *onClick* event is triggered when the user clicks the Check zip button. A Java-Script statement to call the *ok_Zip()* function is assigned to the event. If the user entered a valid zip code, the alert dialog box will pop up and say so. See Figure 17.39.

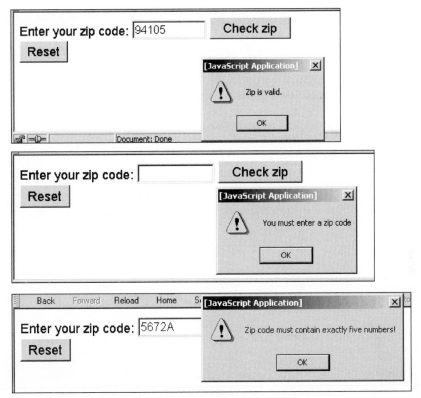

Figure 17.39 The user enters a five-digit zip code (top); the user enters nothing (middle); the user enters four digits and one letter (bottom).

17.5.3 Checking for Alphabetic Data

To test for entries that must consist strictly of alphabetic input, such as a name, state, or country field, the regular expression character set can be used; for example, /[a-zA-z]+/ is a regular expression that matches a string containing one or more uppercase or low-ercase letters, and /^[a-zA-Z]+$/ matches a string containing only one or more upper-case or lowercase letters, because the character set is enclosed within the beginning and ending anchor metacharacters. To represent one or more alphanumeric word characters, [A-Za-z0-9_], you can use the \w metasymbol; for example, /\w+/ represents one or more alphanumeric word characters.

EXAMPLE 17.38

```
        <html>
          <head><title>Testing for Alphabetic Characters</title>
            <script type="text/javascript">
1             function okAlpha(form){
2             var regex=/^[a-zA-Z]+$/;
                //Match for upper- or lowercase letters
                if ( regex.test(form.fname.value) == false) {
                  alert("First name must contain alphabetic characters!");
                  form.fname.focus();
                  return false;
                }
3               if ( form.fname.value == ""){
                  alert("You must enter your first name.");
                  form.fname.focus();
                  return false;
                }
4               return true;
              }
            </script>
          </head>
          <body>
            <big>
5             <form name="alphaTest"
                    method="post"
                    action="/cgi-bin/testing.pl"
6                   onSubmit="return okAlpha(this)" />
                Enter your first name:
                <input type="text"
7                     name="fname"
                      size=20 />
                <p>
8               <input type="submit" value="Submit" />
                <input type="reset" />
            </form>
          </big>
        </body>
      </html>
```

EXPLANATION

1   A function called *okAlpha()* is defined. It takes one parameter, a reference to a form. Its purpose is to make sure the user entered only alphabetic characters in the form.

2   A regular expression is created. It reads: Starting at the beginning of the line, find one or more uppercase or lowercase letters in the character class *[A-Za-z]* followed by the end of line anchor ($). The regular expression is tested against the input that came in from a text box named *text*. If it doesn't match, the alert box will notify the user, and *false* is returned to the *onSubmit* handler on line 6. The form will not be submitted.

EXPLANATION(continued)

3   If the user didn't enter anything at all and the field is empty, another alert will be sent to the user, and *false* will be returned. The form will not be submitted.

4   If the user entered only alphabetic characters in his or her name, *true* will be returned, and the form will be submitted.

5   This is where the HTML form starts.

6   The *onSubmit* handler will be triggered when the user clicks the Submit button, and the *okAlpha()* function will be called, passing a reference to the form called *alphaTest*.

7   The user enters his or her name in the text field called *fname*.

8   After filling out the form, the user will click the Submit button, thereby triggering the *onSubmit* handler on line 6. See Figure 17.40.

Figure 17.40   The user has a digit in her name. She can only enter alphabetic characters, or she will see the warning.

17.5.4   Removing Extraneous Characters

Removing Spaces and Dashes.   To remove any unwanted spaces or dashes from user input, the *String* object's *replace()* method can be used to find the characters and replace them with nothing, as shown in Example 17.39.

EXAMPLE   17.39

```
<html>
  <head><title>Removing Spaces and Dashes</title></head>
  <body bgcolor="magenta">
    <big>
    <h2>Removing Spaces and Hyphens</h2>
    <script type= "text/javascript">
1       var string="444- 33 - 12 34"
2       var regex = /[ -]+/g;
3       var newString=string.replace(regex, "");
        document.write("The original string: "+string);
```

Continues

EXAMPLE 17.39 (CONTINUED)

```
        document.write("<br>The new string: "+ newString +"<br>");
      </script>
      </big>
    </body>
  </html>
```

EXPLANATION

1   The string contains numbers, spaces, and dashes.

2   The variable called *regex* is assigned a regular expression, which means: Search for one or more spaces or dashes, globally (multiple occurrences within the string).

3   The *replace()* method searches in the string for spaces and dashes, and if it finds any, replaces them with the empty string, "", returning the resulting string to *newString*. To change the original string, the return value of the *replace()* method can be returned back to the original string: *var string=string.replace(regex, "")*. See Figure 17.41.

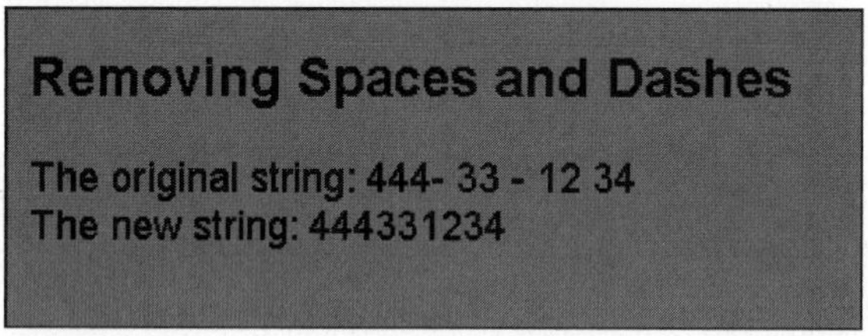

Removing Spaces and Dashes

The original string: 444- 33 - 12 34
The new string: 444331234

Figure 17.41   The *replace()* method is used to remove any spaces or dashes.

Removing Unwanted Parentheses.   You might also want to remove parentheses surrounding area codes or telephone numbers. This is a relatively simple regular expression used in the *replace()* method, as shown in the last example.

EXAMPLE 17.40

```
    <html>
      <head><title>Removing Parens</title></head>
      <body bgcolor="magenta">
        <big>
        <font face="arial">
        <h2>Removing Unwanted Parentheses, Spaces, and Dashes</h2>
        <script type= "text/javascript">
1         var string="(408)-332-1234"
2         var regex = /[() -]+/g;
3         var newString=string.replace(regex, "");
```

EXAMPLE   17.40 (CONTINUED)

```
            document.write("The original string: "+string);
            document.write("<br>The new string: "+ newString +"<br>");
         </script>
         </big>
      </body>
   </html>
```

EXPLANATION

1   The string contains numbers, parentheses, spaces, and dashes.

2   The variable called *regex* is assigned a regular expression, which means: Search for one or more parentheses (open or closed), spaces or dashes, globally (multiple occurrences within the string).

3   The *replace()* method searches in the string for parentheses, spaces, and dashes, and if it finds any, replaces them with the empty string, *""*, returning the resulting string to *newString*. To change the original string, the return value of the *replace()* method can be returned back to the original string: *var string=string.replace(regex, "")*. See Figure 17.42.

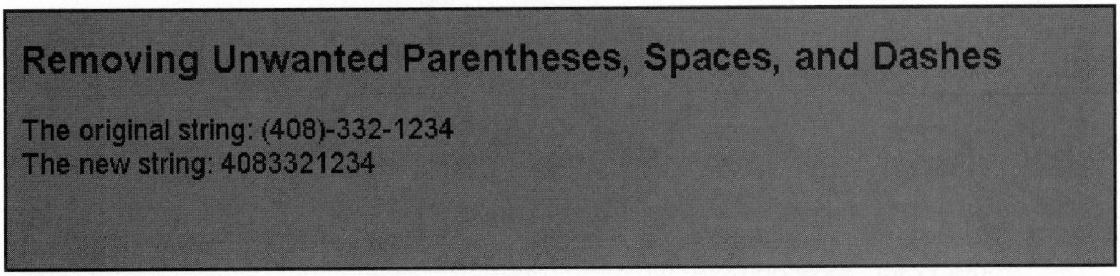

Removing Unwanted Parentheses, Spaces, and Dashes

The original string: (408)-332-1234
The new string: 4083321234

Figure 17.42   Parentheses, as well as spaces and dashes, are removed. Numbers or letters will remain.

Removing any Nondigits.   A character that is not a digit can be represented as *[^0-9]* or as *\D* in a regular expression. You might want to remove any characters that are not digits in the user's input such as zip codes or phone numbers. This can also be done simply with a regular expression and the *replace()* method, as shown in Example 17.41.

EXAMPLE   17.41

```
   <html>
      <head><title>Removing all Nondigits</title></head>
      <body bgcolor="magenta">
         <big>
```

Continues

EXAMPLE 17.41 (CONTINUED)

```
      <h3>If it's not a number, remove it!</h3>
      <script type = "text/javascript">
1       var string="phone is (408)-//[332]-1234@#!!!"
2       var newString=string.replace(/\D/g, "");
        document.write("The orginal string: "+string);
3       document.write("<br>The new string: "+ newString +"<br>");
      </script>
      </big>
    </body>
  </html>
```

EXPLANATION

1   The string contains all kinds of characters, many of which are not numbers.

2   The *replace()* method searches in the string for all nondigit characters, */\D/g*, and if it finds any, replaces them with the empty string, "", returning the resulting string to *newString*. To change the original string, the return value of the *replace()* method can be returned back to the original string: *var string=string.replace(regex, "")*;

3   The new string is displayed after all the nondigit characters were replaced with nothing (i.e., they were removed). See Figure 17.43.

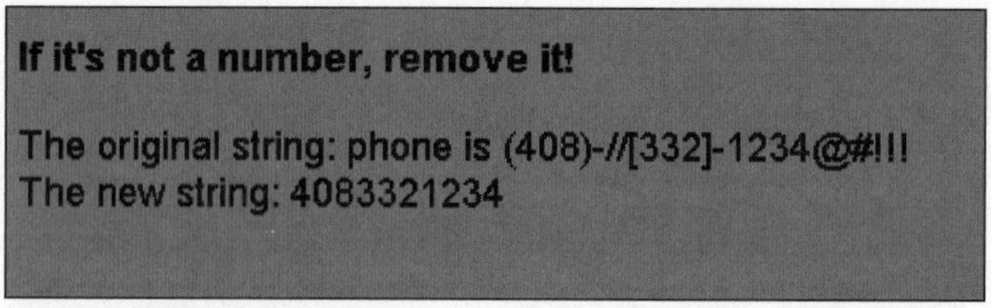

If it's not a number, remove it!

The original string: phone is (408)-//[332]-1234@#!!!
The new string: 4083321234

Figure 17.43   Only numbers will remain in the string. All other characters are removed.

Removing any Nonalphanumeric Characters.   A nonalphanumeric word character *[^0-9a-zA-Z_]*, any character that is not a letter, number, or the underscore, can be represented as \W. Again we can use the *replace()* method to remove those characters from a string.

EXAMPLE 17.42

```
  <html>
    <head><title>Removing Nonalphanumeric Characters</title></head>
    <body bgcolor="magenta">
      <big>
      <h3>If it's not a number or a letter, remove it!</h3>
```

EXAMPLE   17.42 (CONTINUED)

```
            <script type= "text/javascript">
1              var string="(408)-//[332]-1234@#!!!"
2              var newString=string.replace(/\W/g, "");
3              document.write("The original string: "+string);
               document.write("<br>The new string: "+ newString +"<br>");
            </script>
            </big>
          </body>
        </html>
```

EXPLANATION

1   The string contains all kinds of characters, many of which are not letters or
    numbers.

2   The regular expression, /\W/g, means: Search globally for any nonalphanumeric
    characters (\W). The *replace()* method searches for nonalphanumeric characters
    and replaces them with the empty string, *""*, returning the resulting string to *new-
    String*. To change the original string, the return value of the *replace()* method can
    be returned back to the original string: *var string=string.replace(regex, "");*

3   The new string is displayed after all nonalphanumeric characters are removed. See
    Figure 17.44.

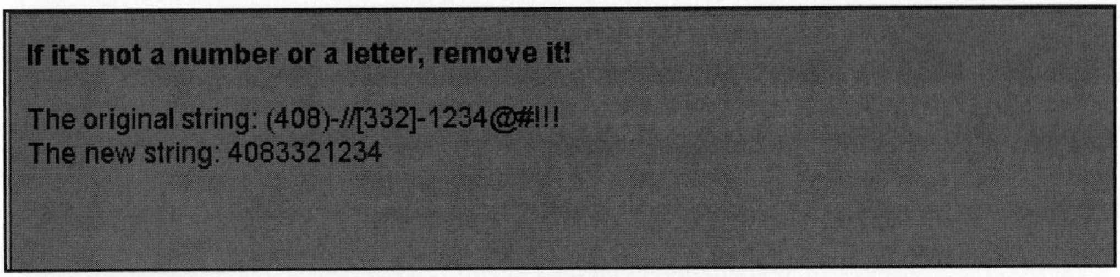

If it's not a number or a letter, remove it!

The original string: (408)-//[332]-1234@#!!!
The new string: 4083321234

Figure 17.44   Any nonalphanumeric characters are removed.

17.5.5   Checking for Valid Social Security Numbers

A Social Security number contains exactly nine numbers. There might be dashes to separate the first three numbers and the last four numbers. The dashes should be optional.
Example 17.43 demonstrates a regular expression that tests for three digits, followed by
an optional dash, followed by two more digits, an optional dash, and finally four digits.
The beginning and end of line anchors ensure that the user does not enter extraneous
characters on either end of his or her Social Security number, such as *abd444-44-
4444xyz*.

EXAMPLE 17.43

```html
     <html>
       <head><title>Testing for a Social Security Number</title>
         <script type="text/javascript">
1          function okSocial(sform){
2             var regex=/^\d{3}-?\d\d-?\d{4}$/;
3             if ( regex.test(sform.ssn.value) == false) {
                 alert("Social Security number invalid!");
                 sform.ssn.focus();
                 return false;
              }
4             if ( sform.ssn.value == ""){
                 alert("Please enter your Social Security number.");
                 sform.ssn.focus();
                 return false;
              }
              return true;
           }
         </script>
       </head>
       <body>
         <big>
           <div align="center">
             <form name="snnTest"
                 method=post
                 action="/cgi-bin/testing"
5                onSubmit="return okSocial(this)" />
               Enter your Social Security number: xxx-xx-xxxx
               <p>
6              <input type="text"
                       name="ssn"
                       size=11 />
               <p>
7              <input type="submit" value="Submit" />
               <input type="reset" />
             </form>
           </big>
         </div>
       </body>
     </html>
```

EXPLANATION

1   The function *okSocial()* is defined. Its purpose is to validate a Social Security number.

2   The regular expression reads: Start at the beginning of the line, look for three digits, one dash (or not one), two more digits, another possible dash, and ending in four digits.

EXPLANATION(CONTINUED)

3   The regular expression *test()* method will return *true* if a valid Social Security number was entered and *false* if not.

4   If nothing was entered in the text box, the user will be alerted, focus will go to the text field, and the form will not be submitted.

5   The *onSubmit* event handler will be triggered when the user clicks the submit button of line 7.

6   The input type is a text field that will hold up to 11 characters.

7   When the user clicks the submit button, the *onSubmit* event handler will be triggered. It will call the *okSocial()* function to validate the Social Security number. See Figure 17.45.

Figure 17.45   The user enters a valid Social Security number.

17.5.6   Checking for Valid Phone Numbers

A valid U.S. phone number has ten digits: an area code of three digits, followed by the subscriber number of seven digits. There might be parentheses surrounding the area code, and dashes or spaces separating the numbers in the subscriber number. With regular expressions you can test for any or all of these conditions and then, if necessary, remove the extraneous characters, leaving just numbers. Example 17.44 demonstrates how to validate a simple U.S. phone number.

EXAMPLE   17.44

```
   <html>
     <head><title>Validating Phone Numbers</title>
       <script type="text/javascript">
         function ok_Phone(phform){
1            var regex = /^\(?\d{3}\)?-?\s*\d{3}\s*-?\d{4}$/;
2            if(regex.test(phform.user_phone.value)){
               return true;
             }
```

Continues

EXAMPLE   17.44 (CONTINUED)

```
              else{
                  alert("Enter a valid phone number");
                  return false;
              }
          }
      </script>
  </head>
  <body>
      <hr />
      <h2>Checking for a Valid Phone Number </h2>
3     <form name="formtest"
              action="http://localhost/cgi-bin/environ.pl"
              method="post"
4             onSubmit="return ok_Phone(this);">
      <p>
      Please enter your phone: <br />
5     <input type="text" size=40 name="user_phone" />
      </p>
      <input type=submit value="Submit" />
      <input type=reset value="Clear" />
      </form>
  </body>
</html>
```

EXPLANATION

1   The regular expression reads: Start at the beginning of the string, look for an option-al literal opening parenthesis, followed by exactly three digits, and an optional clos-ing parenthesis (the area code), followed by an optional dash, zero or more spaces, exactly three digits, zero or more spaces, an optional dash, and ending in exactly four digits, such as (222)-111-2345 or 222-111-2345 or 2221112345.

2   The regular expression is matched, *phform.user_phone.value*, the *test()* method will return *true*, and the form will be submitted; otherwise, the user will be alerted to enter a valid phone number.

3   The HTML form starts here and is named *formtest*.

4   The *onSubmit* event handler is assigned as an attribute of the *<form>* tag. It will be activated when the user clicks the submit button. The handler, *ok_Phone*, passes the form as an argument. The *this* keyword refers to the form named *formtest* and returns a *true* or *false* value. If *true*, the form will be submitted.

5   The user will enter his or her phone number in a text field. See Figure 17.46.

Checking for a Valid Phone Number

Please enter your phone:

```
(456)  444-4444
```

Submit   Clear

Checking for a Valid Phone Number

Please enter your phone:

```
(456)  444-44433
```

Submit   Clear

[JavaScript Application]   ✕

⚠ Enter a valid phone number

OK

Figure 17.46   The user enters a valid phone number (top). Parentheses and the dash are optional; the user enters a number with too many digits, and an alert box appears (bottom).

Go to *http://www.wtng.info*, the World Wide Telephone Guide, to get a listing of phone formats for the world, country by country (see Figure 17.47).

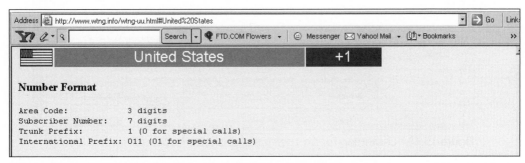

| Address | 🖹 | http://www.wtng.info/wtng-uu.html#United%20States | ▾ | 🔁 Go | Link |

| Y? ✎ ▾ 🔍 | | Search ▾ | 🌸 FTD.COM Flowers ▾ | ☺ Messenger | ✉ Yahoo! Mail ▾ | 📁▾ Bookmarks | ≫ |

🇺🇸 | United States | **+1** |

Number Format

```
Area Code:             3 digits
Subscriber Number:     7 digits
Trunk Prefix:          1 (0 for special calls)
International Prefix:   011 (01 for special calls)
```

Figure 17.47   Go to *http://www.wtng.info/* to look up phone formats around the world.

For international phone numbers, the following formats are accepted (see Figure 17.48):

- +1 (123) 456 7888
- +1123456 7888
- +44 (123) 456 7888
- +44(123) 456 7888 ext 123
- +44 20 7893 2567
- 02345 444 5555 66

Figure 17.48   Searching for an international phone Regex at *regexlib.com*.

17.5.7   Checking for Valid E-Mail Addresses

When validating an e-mail address, you are looking for the typical format found in such addresses. There might be some domain names that are more than three characters, but it isn't typical. Also, just because the user types what looks like a valid e-mail address, that does not mean that it is; for example, the e-mail address *santa@northpole.org* uses a valid syntax, but that fact does not prove that *santa* is a real user.

E-mail addresses usually have the following format:

- An @ sign between the username and address (*lequig@aol.com*).
- At least one dot between the address and domain name (*.com, .mil, .edu, .se*).
- At least six characters (*a@b.se*).[3]

Examples of valid e-mail addresses:

- username@mailserver.com
- *username@mailserver.info*
- *username@mailserver.org.se*
- *username.moretext@mailserver.mil*
- *username@mailserver.co.uk*
- user-name.moretext.sometext@mailserver.se

To break down a simple e-mail regular expression

```
/^(([\-\w]+)\.?)+@(([\-\w]+)\.?)+\.[a-zA-Z]{2,4}$/;
```

use the following steps:

Step 1:	^	Go to the beginning of the line.
Step 2:	([\-\w]+)\.?	The username consists of one or more dashes or word characters grouped by parentheses, followed by one (or not one) literal period. Because the dot is outside the parentheses, there will be either one or zero dots for the list of word characters, not two or three dots in a row.
Step 3:	(([\-\w]+)\.?)+	The username can consist of more than one set of word characters separated by a single dots, as in *Joe.Shmoe.somebody*.
Step 4:	@	A literal @ symbol is required in the e-mail address.
Step 5:	([\-\w]+)\.?)+	The mail server's name is like the user's name, a group of word characters separated by a dot.

3. As of this writing, domain names have at least two characters.

Step 6:   *[a-zA-Z]{2,4}*   The domain name follows the mail server's name. A single dot separates the server from the domain. The domain name consists of between two and four alphabetic characters; for example, *savageman@imefdm.usmc.mil* or *patricia.person@sweden.sun.com*.

Step 7:   *$*   The end of the line anchor assures that no extra characters can be added onto the end of the e-mail address.

Example 17.45 uses a regular expression to check for a valid e-mail address.

EXAMPLE 17.45

```
    <html>
       <head><title>Validating E-Mail Addresses</title>
         <script type="text/javascript">
1          function ok_Email(eform){
2           var regex = /^(([a-zA-Z0-9_\-\.]+)@([a-zA-Z0-9_\-
\.]+)\.([a-zA-Z]{2,5}){1,25})+([;.](([a-zA-Z0-9_\-\.]+)@([a-zA-Z0-9_\-
\.]+)\.([a-zA-Z]{2,5}){1,25})+)*$/;
             // this got the highest rating at regexlib.com!!
3            if(regex.test(eform.user_email.value)){
4              return true;
             }
             else{
5              alert("Enter a valid email address");
               return false;
             }
          }
       </script>
    </head>
    <body>
      <hr />
      <h2> Checking for Valid Email Address </h2>
6     <form name="formtest"
7          action="http://localhost/cgi-bin/environ.pl"
           method="post"
8          onSubmit="return ok_Email(this);">
        <p>
          Please enter your email address: <br />
          <input type="text" size=40 name="user_email" />
        </p><p>
          <input type=submit value="Send" />
        </p>
      </form>
    </body>
  </html>
```

EXPLANATION

1   A function called *ok_Email* is defined. It takes one parameter, a reference to the form started on line 6.

2   This got the highest score at *http://www.regexlib.com*. When you are looking for a regular expression that covers all possibilities, you might spend a week and still not have caught everything. This is where the libraries come in handy. Somebody has already done the hard work.

3   The regular expression *test()* method takes the value of the user input, *user_email.value*, and returns *true* if the pattern in the regular expression matched the user's input.

4   The e-mail address entered is tested to be valid. A *true* value is returned and the form will be submitted to the server. A valid e-mail address does not mean that if mail is sent to that address it will necessarily be delivered; for example, *santa@northpole.org* is syntactically valid, but there is no guarantee that *santa* is a real user (unless you still believe!).

5   If an invalid e-mail address was entered, the alert box will appear with this message. The *ok_Email()* function will return *false*, and the form will not be submitted.

6   The form named *formtest* starts here.

7   This is the URL of the CGI script that will be called on the server side when the form is submitted.

8   The *onSubmit* event handler is triggered when the user clicks the submit button. The value assigned to the event is a function called *ok_Email* that will return *true* if the e-mail address is valid and *false*, if not. The form will be sent to the server only if the return value is *true*. See Figure 17.49.

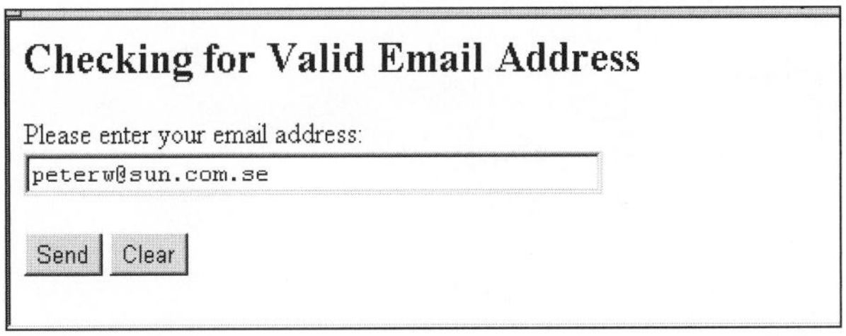

Figure 17.49   The user enters a valid e-mail address.

17.5.8   Credit Card Validation

When validating a credit card number, you can do some preliminary checking but real card validation is done on the server side through a software product designed specifically for that purpose.[4] Before issuing a card, there are certain rules that must be followed when creating card numbers, such as how many numbers there are, what prefix is used by a particular card type, whether the entire number fits a certain formula, and valid expiration dates. For preliminary checking, you can test, for example, to see if a person enters valid digits for a Visa card and that the expiration date is later than the current date, but you can't really tell if the user's card has gone over the limit, was cancelled or stolen, or that he or she even owns it. Checking whether the card is active and has a sufficient balance to cover a sale is performed by the banking system backing the card.

The Expiration Date of the Card.   A valid expiration date is a month and year that haven't gone by. The month and year are represented as two digits: 01 for January, 11 for November, and 03 for the year 2003. The following example defines a function to test for a valid expiration date based on a one- to two-digit month and a two-digit or four-digit year.

EXAMPLE 17.46

```
    <html>
      <head><title>Testing Expiration Dates</title>
        <script type="text/javascript">
1           function validExpire(form) {
2               var now = new Date();
3               var thismonth = (now.getMonth() + 1);
4               var thisyear = now.getFullYear() ;
5               var expireYear = parseInt(form.expireYear.value);
                var yearLength = form.expireYear.value.length;
                var expireMonth = parseInt(form.expireMonth.value);
                if( yearLength == 2 ){
                    expireYear += 2000;
                }
6               if ((expireMonth < thismonth && expireYear == thisyear)
                    || expireMonth > 12){
                    alert("Invalid month");
                    return false;
                }
7               else if ( expireYear < thisyear) {
                    alert("Invalid year");
                    return false;
                }
                else {
                    return true;
                }
            }
        </script>
      </head>
```

---

4. For a guide to credit card validation software, go to *http://www.winsite.com/business/cc/*.

EXAMPLE 17.46 (CONTINUED)

```
        <body>
8         <form name="myForm"
              action="http://127.0.0.1/cgi-bin/env.cgi"
9             onSubmit="return validExpire(this)">
          <p>
            Enter the month (02 or 2):
            <input name="expireMonth" type="text" size=5 />
          </p><p>
            Enter the year (2003 or 03):
            <input name="expireYear" type="text" size=5 />
            <input type="submit" value="submit" />
            <input type="reset" value="clear" />
          </p>
          </form>
        </body>
      </html>
```

EXPLANATION

1   A function called *validExpire()* is defined. It takes one parameter, a reference to a form. Its purpose is to validate the expiration date of a credit card.

2   A new *Date* object is created and assigned to the variable called *now*.

3   Using the *getMonth()* method, we get this month (months start at zero) and add 1.

4   Using the *getFullYear()* method, we get the current year, as *2003*.

5   The *parseInt()* function converts the expiration year, as typed in by the user, to an integer. Then we get the length of the year, and convert the month into an integer. If the number of characters in the year, *yearLength*, is 2, then 2000 is added to the *expireYear* value. If the user typed 02, then the new value is 2002.

6   If the value of *expireMonth* is less than the value of *thisMonth* and the value of *expireYear* is equal to the value of *thisyear*, or the value of *expireMonth* is greater than 12, the number entered is invalid. So a card is invalid if it has a month prior to this month and the card expires this year, or the month is over 12, because there are only 12 months in a year.

7   If the expiration year is prior to this year, it is also invalid.

8   The form starts here.

9   The *onSubmit* event handler is triggered after the user fills out the form and clicks the submit button. When he or she does, the function called *validExpire()* is called. It will return *true* if the expiration date is valid, and the form will be sent to the URL assigned to the *action* attribute of the form. See Figure 17.50.

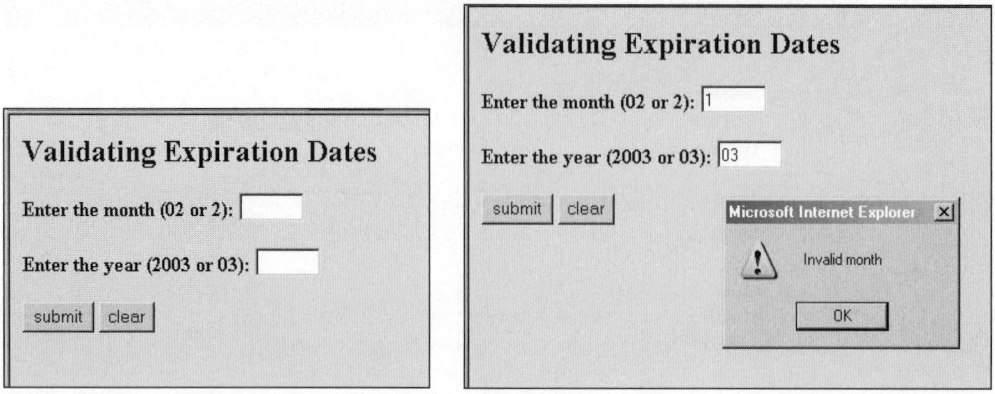

Figure 17.50   The form before the user enters anything (left); the user enters a month and year, but the month has already gone by (right).

Checking for Valid Type, Prefix, and Length.   In Figure 17.51 the major credit cards are listed along with the identifying characteristics of account numbers for each. All the characters must be numbers. Each type of card has a prefix value; for example, MasterCard's prefix is a number between 51 and 56, and Visa's is the number 4. Validation routines to check for a prefix and the correct number of characters are shown in Example 17.47.

These are steps for credit card validation:

1. Remove any spaces or dashes, then test that the result is a numeric value.
2. Check to see if the user has selected a valid credit card type such as MasterCard or Visa, the correct prefix for the card, and a valid length for the number of characters in the card.
3. Apply the Lunh formula for further validation.

EXAMPLE   17.47

```
        <html>
          <head><title>Checking for Valid CC Type and Length</title>
            <script type="text/javascript">
1               function checkCC(myForm){
                  var cc_type;
                  var cc_length;
2                 if (myForm.select1.selectedIndex==0){
                     cc_type="Visa";
                  }
                  else if( myForm.select1.selectedIndex==1){
                     cc_type="MasterCard";
                  }
```

EXAMPLE 17.47 (CONTINUED)

```
                    else if( myForm.select1.selectedIndex==2){
                      cc_type="Discover";
                    }
                    else {
                      alert("You didn't select a card type.");
                    }
3                   cc_length=myForm.text.value.length;
4                   switch(cc_type){
5                     case "Visa" :
6                       if ( cc_length == 13 || cc_length == 16){
                          return true;
                        }
                        else{
                          alert("Invalid length");
                          return false;
                        }
                        break;
7                     case "MasterCard":
                        if ( cc_length == 16){
                          return true;
                        }
                        else{
                          alert("Invalid length");
                          return false;
                        }
                        break;
8                     case "Discover":
                        if ( cc_length == 16){
                          return true;
                        }
                        else{
                          alert("Invalid length");
                          return false;
                        }
                        break;
                      default:
                        alert("Invalid type");
                        return false;
                        break;
                    }
                  }
              </script>
          </head>
          <body bgcolor="lightblue">
            <big>
```

Continues

EXAMPLE 17.47 (CONTINUED)

```
9        <form name="form1" onSubmit="return checkCC(this);">
         Please select a credit card from the menu:
         <p>
10       <select name="select1" size="3">
            <option value="Visa">Visa</option>
            <option value="MC">MasterCard</option>
            <option value="Dis">Discover</option>
         </select>
         <p>
         Please enter your card number:
         </p><p>
11          <input type=textbox name="text" size=30 />
         </p>
12          <input type=submit value="Check card">
            <input type=reset>
       </form>
       </big>
     </body>
   </html>
```

EXPLANATION

1   A function called *checkCC()* is defined. It takes one parameter, a reference to a form.

2   If the value of *selectedIndex is 0*, the first option in the *select* list was chosen, a Visa card. The rest of the statements in this *if* block check to see which card was selected if it wasn't this one.

3   The variable *cc_length* is assigned the number of characters that were typed into the text box; that is, the number of characters in the credit card number.

4   The *switch* statement will be used to check for valid card number lengths for whichever card the user selected from the select menu. The variable *cc_type* contains the card type: Visa, MasterCard, or Discover.

5   If the card is a Visa card, the *case* statements will be used to check for a valid length.

6   The valid length for the Visa credit card number is between 13 and 16 characters (as shown in Figure 17.51). If the card number length is between these numbers, *true* is returned.

7   MasterCard is checked here. Its number must consist of 16 characters.

8   Discover is checked here. Its number must consist of 16 characters.

9   The form starts here. The *onSubmit* handler will be triggered when the user clicks the submit button. At that time the credit card will be checked for a valid number of characters in the number provided by the user. This is not a complete check. You can combine the other functions from this section to provide a more thorough check; we haven't checked here to see if the value entered is numeric, has strange characters, or empty fields.

10 The select menu starts here with three options, each a credit card type.

11 This is the text box where the user enters the card number.

12 When the user clicks the submit button, the *onSubmit* handler is invoked, and if the credit card number passes the validity test, off goes the form! See Figure 17.52.

CARD TYPE	Prefix	Length	Check digit algorithm
MASTERCARD	51-55	16	mod 10
VISA	4	13, 16	mod 10
AMEX	34 37	15	mod 10
Diners Club/ Carte Blanche	300-305 36 38	14	mod 10
Discover	6011	16	mod 10
enRoute	2014 2149	15	any
JCB	3	16	mod 10
JCB	2131 1800	15	mod 10

Figure 17.51 Some valid credit cards, their prefix, length, and whether they pass the Lunh test based on modulus 10, shown later. Source: *http://www.beachnet.com/~hstiles/cardtype.html*.

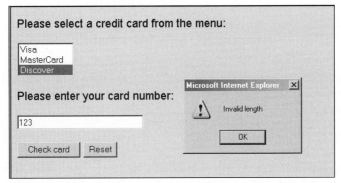

Figure 17.52 The number of characters in the credit card number should be 16 for Discover Card.

The Lunh Formula.   The credit card number can be subjected to an additional mathematical test, called the Lunh formula, which it must pass to be valid. The following steps are required to validate the primary account number:

Step 1: Double the value of every other digit starting with the next-to-rightmost digit.

Step 2: If any of the resulting values has more than two digits, then its digits must be added together to produce a single digit.

Step 3: Add the sum of all the digits **not** doubled in Step 1 to the sum of the digits transformed from Steps 1 and 2.

Step 4: If the result is exactly divisible by 10 (i.e., if the result ends in a zero, 30, 40, 50, etc.), then the number is valid—providing of course that it's of the correct length and bears a correct prefix for that type of card.

For example, to validate the primary account number *49927398716:*

Step 1: Starting from the next to the right-most digit, multiply every other number by 2 (the number in bold text).

```
4   9   9   2   7   3   9   8   7   1   6
    9x2     2x2     3x2     8x2     1x2
    18      4       6       16      2
```

Step 2: If any numbers resulting from Step 1 have more than one digit, add those numbers together.

```
(1+8)   (1+6)
―――――――――――――
  9       7
```

Step 3: Add up the top row of numbers that were not doubled (not in bold) to the bottom row of numbers after Step 2 was finished. Bottom numbers are in parentheses.

```
4 + (9) + 9 + (4) + 7 + (6) + 9 +( 7) + 7 + (2) + 6
```

Step 4: If the result of Step 3 is divisible exactly by 10 (i.e., leaves no remainder), the card is valid. The result of Step 3 is 70. The card number is valid if the card type is valid, as long as the length of numbers entered is valid, and it has the correct prefix for that type of card.

17.5.9   Putting It All Together

After writing the functions that validate each field of the form, they will be put together in a single script to check all form entries. Example 17.48 combines just two of the functions, to keep the example from being too large. One function, *ok_Form()*, calls the functions that check individual entries; for example, *ok_Email()* checks for valid e-mail and returns either *true* or *false*, and *ok_Phone()* checks for a valid phone number. After all of the entries have been checked, the *ok_Form()* function returns either *true* or *false* to the *onSubmit* event handler. If *ok_Form()* returns *true*, the form will be submitted to the server; if not, it is stopped. If we add in all the credit card validation functions, this program will get really large. Why don't you try it?

EXAMPLE 17.48

```
<html>
  <head><title>Validating a Form</title>
    <script type="text/javascript">
1       function ok_Email(myform){
2           var regex=
                /^(([\-\w]+)\.?)+@(([\-\w]+)\.?)+\.[a-zA-Z]{2,4}$/;
3           if(regex.test(myform.user_email.value)){
                return true;
            }
            else{
                alert("Enter a valid email address");
                return false;
            }
        }
4       function ok_Phone(phform){
5           var regex = /^\(?\d{3}\)?-?\s*\d{3}\s*-?\d{4}$/;
6           if(regex.test(phform.value)){
                return true;
            }
            else{
                return false;
            }
        }
7       function ok_Form(myform){
8           if (ok_Email(myform.user_email)== false){
9               alert( "Invalid email address");
10              myform.user_email.focus();
11              myform.user_email.select();
12              return false;
            }
```

Continues

EXAMPLE 17.48 (CONTINUED)

```
13              if (ok_Phone(myform.user_phone) == false){
                    alert( "Invalid phone number");
                    myform.user_phone.focus();
                    myform.user_phone.select();
                    return false;
                }
14              return true;
            }
        </script>
    </head>
    <body bgcolor="lightgreen"> <font face="arial" size="+1">
        <hr />
        <h2> Checking Form Input</h2>
        <form name="myform"
                action="http://localhost/cgi-bin/environ.pl"
                method="post"
15              onSubmit="return ok_Form(this);">
            <p>
            Please enter your email address: <br />
            <input type="text" size=40 name="user_email" />
            </p><p>
            Please enter your phone number: <br />
            <input type="text" size=12 name="user_phone" />
            </p>
            <input type=submit value="Send" />
        </form>
        </font>
    </body>
</html>
```

EXPLANATION

1   The function to validate an e-mail address is defined. It is called by the *ok_Form()* function on line 7.

2   The local variable called *regex* is assigned a regular expression, explained in Example 17.45.

3   The e-mail address entered by the user, *eform.user_email.value*, is tested against the regular expression for validity. The regular expression *test()* method returns *true* or *false* to the *ok_Form* function, line 7.

4   The function to validate a phone number is defined. It is called by the *ok_Phone()* function on line 13.

5   The local variable called *regex* is assigned regular expression.

6   The phone number entered by the user, *eform.user_phform.value*, is tested against the regular expression for validity. The regular expression *test()* method returns *true* or *false* to the *ok_Phone* function, line 13.

EXPLANATION

7   This is the big function that returns the final verdict. Did the user provide a valid e-mail address and phone number? If so, the function returns *true*, line 14.

8   The *ok_Email()* function is called with the user's e-mail input. If the *ok_Email()* function returns *false*, the user entered an invalid address, and will be alerted.

9   The alert dialog box sends this message if the e-mail address is not valid.

10   The *focus()* method puts the cursor in the text box, so that the user can start typing there.

11   The *select()* method highlights the text in a field.

12   If *false* is returned to the *onSubmit* handler on line 15, the form will not be submitted.

13   If an invalid phone number was entered, *false* will be returned to the *onSubmit* handler on line 15.

14   If both the e-mail address and the phone number are valid, the *ok_Form()* function returns *true* to the event handler on line 15, and the form will be submitted to the server's URL assigned to the form's *action* attribute.

15   The *onSubmit* event is triggered when the user clicks the submit button. The handler is a function called *ok_Form()*. It is the main validation function for this form. If *true* is returned, the form will be submitted; otherwise, not. See Figures 17.53, 17.54 and 17.55.

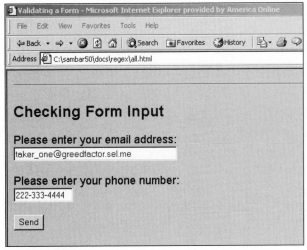

Figure 17.53   The user enters a valid e-mail address.

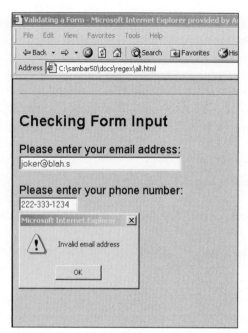

Figure 17.54   The user entered an invalid e-mail address because there is only one letter in the domain name.

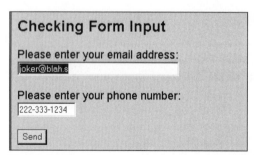

Figure 17.55   The *focus()* and *select()* methods focus on and highlight the invalid entry.

17.6 **What You Should Know**

Regular expressions are huge and they seem to be everywhere. Programming languages are all jumping on the bandwagon to support them. They are particularly useful in Java-Script for validating input data and with regular expression metacharacters give you endless ways to match patterns. After learning how to use regular expressions and pattern matching you should be able to:

1. Define a literal regular expression with JavaScript.
2. Define a regular expression object and use its properties.
3. Use the *test()* and *exec()* methods.
4. Use the regular expression metacharacters to control searches.
5. Perform search and replacements with regular expressions.
6. Validate an e-mail address, phone number, and credit card.
7. Use the *match()* and *search()* methods.
8. Remove extraneous characters from a string.
9. Split up a string by a regular expression delimiter.
10. Use a regular expression library.

Exercises

1. Write a regular expression that will:
   a. Return *true* if a string begins with letters between *a* and *f*, either upper- or lowercase.
   b. Return *true* if a string contains a number.
   c. In the string *My friend is Betsy Ann Savage*, capture the first and last name and display them in reverse, as *Savage, Betsy*.
   d. Replace *Betsy* with *Elizabeth* in the previous string.
   e. In the string *123abcdefg584*, replace all the letters with *XXX*.
   f. Prompt the user for a string of text, then print *true* if the string ends in three or more numbers.
   g. Prompt the user for a string of text, then display the first three characters in the string.
   h. Prompt the user for a string of text that includes letters and numbers, then print *true* if the string does **not** contain the number 4 or the letter *a*, or print *false* if not.
   i. Prompt the user for his or her first and last name. Display *true* if the name starts with an uppercase letter followed by lowercase letters. The last name would be similar to the following: *Jones*, *Smith*, *McFadden*, *O'Reilly*, and *Jones-Smith*.

2. Validate an international phone number that is represented as follows:

   011 49 762 899 20

3. Start with a one- or two-character code for a United Kingdom postal district, such as B for Birmingham or RH for Red Hill, followed by a one- or two-digit number to represent a sector within that district. For example, RH1 is Red Hill district, sector 1; CM23 is the Chelmsford district, sector 23; and B1 is Birmingham district, sector 1. Following the district and sector is a space, followed by a digit and two characters, such as 4GJ.

   For example: *CM23 2QP*   where:
                                               CM = Chelmsford district
                                               23 = sector 23
                                               2QP = a particular road.

   Create a regular expression to validate a UK postal code as just described.

4. Validate a credit card number using the Lunh formula.

chapter

18

An Introduction to
Ajax (with JSON)

18.1 Why Ajax?

JavaScript has gone through kind of a Renaissance of its own since this book was first published in 2002 largely due to the hype and promises it offers. Traditionally Web applications have been somewhat clumsy and slow, and the level of interactivity and usability inferior to their counterpart desktop applications, yet the number of Web applications available continues to grow at an amazing rate. Part of that growth has been spurred on by AJAX, "Asynchronous JavaScript and XML,"[1] not a new programming language, but a methodology for creating fast, rich, user-friendly, and interactive Web applications by allowing a Web page to request small fragments of information from the server instead of an entire page. In this approach, asynchronous means that when a request is initiated by the occurrence of a client event, JavaScript functions using Ajax allow the browser to interact in the background directly with the server, and rather than waiting for the server to respond, continue processing the page. The server will then send its response to Ajax containing only the data that needs changing. Ajax in turn will update that portion of the Web page. For example, if you are filling out a form, instead of waiting until all the fields have been filled and the page submitted, now with Ajax, the fields can be validated as they are filled and the user does not have to sit by waiting for the page to reload before continuing what he or she was doing. This process is shown in Figure 18.1.

As discussed in Chapter 1, "Introduction to JavaScript," Google offers great examples of Ajax with Google Maps and Google Suggests, an application shared now by all major browsers. (In fact, Ajax was made popular in 2005 with Google Suggest.) When the you start searching in the Google search box, each time you press a key, Google lists items that fit that sequence of letters. In a drop-down list, as if by magic, words appear that contain those letters, and after each subsequent key press, the list changes,

---

1. The term Ajax was coined in 2005. Jesse James Garrett thought of the term while in the shower. See *http://en.wikipedia.org/wiki/Ajax_(programming)*.

797

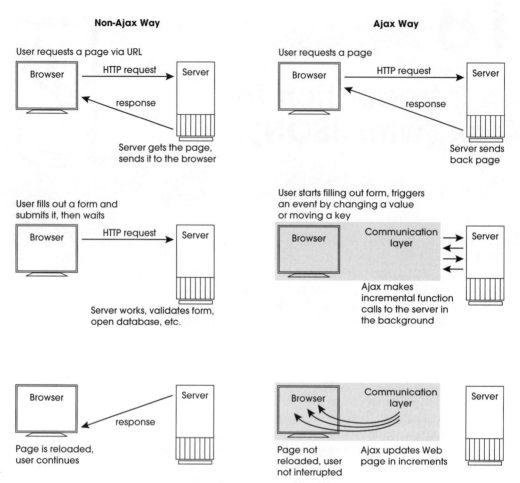

Figure 18.1   The request/response loop with and without Ajax.

reflecting a more refined search. This dynamic and immediate update of the list is an example of Ajax in action. In Figure 18.2, the letters j, a, and v have been typed in the search box. A list of words appears starting with those letters. The user can select any of the suggested items and search for that item without typing any more if he or she sees a word that matches his or her search criteria. There is no delay, no waiting with an Ajax application.

18.2 Why Is Ajax Covered Last?

Why is Ajax the last chapter in this book? If you browse around the Internet for books or tutorials on Ajax, you will soon realize that Ajax requires that you have some basic understanding of everything we have talked about in the preceding chapters because

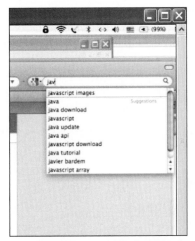

Figure 18.2   Google Suggests. © 2010 Google.

Ajax is based on already existing standards. If you have a strong foundation in the following topics, there is very little new to learn:

- JavaScript
- XML
- HTML
- CSS
- DOM

We have not covered XML in this book, but it has been a standard format since 1998 for sharing structured text-based information between computers. XML is not a requirement for writing Ajax applications, but we will examine an XML document and how Ajax processes its data.

18.3 The Steps for Creating Ajax Communication

We will now go through the steps to create and send requests to the server. We examine each of these steps and then put all of them together in several examples.

1. First and foremost we must create an *XMLHttpRequest* object, a JavaScript object with properties and methods used to handle communication between the browser and server.
2. After we create the request object, we use the object's *open()* method to initialize the object; that is, tell it how the data will be sent, GET or POST (see Chapter 11, "Working with Forms and Input Devices"), and the URL of the file data that is being requested. The URL could be a text file, XML data, or a server-side program such as PHP, ASP.NET, CGI, Java Servlet, and so on.

3. The request is sent to the server with the *send()* method.

4. After the request is sent to the server, the object's *readyState* property keeps track of the state of the request object; for example, if a request has been made, the state changes. With an event handler, a callback function can be executed based on the state of the object. If, for example, the request has been answered and all the information has been sent by the server, the state of the object can be checked and a function called to retrieve and handle the data.

Now we will take a closer look at each of the steps to create Ajax communication between the browser and the server.

18.3.1   Step 1: Create the *XMLHttpRequest* Object

With the HTTP request/response cycle we discussed at the beginning of the book, when the user clicks a link, submits a form, or types an address in the URL, an HTTP connection is made between the browser and the server. The server's response is to send back a new or updated page while the user waits. With applications that make asynchronous calls to the server, there has to be a way to do this without refreshing the page for each HTTP request. This is done with the *XMLHttpRequest* object. This object allows Java-Script to set up a communication channel with the server, exchange data, and update the page without reloading it. Meanwhile the user continues scrolling, typing, and pushing buttons just as he or she would on a desktop application, while Ajax is working with the server in the background.

The *XMLHttpRequest* object is supported by all major browsers (Firefox, Chrome, Opera, and Safari) and is fundamental to all Ajax applications. Internet Explorer 7 comes with the *XMLHttpRequest*, but other versions of Internet Explorer support the ActiveX object, which is not cross-browser compliant. Therefore, when creating a new *XMLHttpRequest* object, most JavaScript programs use *catch* and *try* statements to make sure the object they get back is compatible with their browser. (See Chapter 7, "Functions," for a review of *catch* and *try*.) Example 18.1 demonstrates how to create the *XMLHttpRequest* object for most major browsers. See *https://developer.mozilla.org/en/AJAX/Getting_Started*.

EXAMPLE 18.1

```
      /* Check browser type and create ajaxRequest object
         Put this function in an external .js file and use it for your
         Ajax programs  */
1     function CreateRequestObject(){
2       var ajaxRequest;  // The variable that makes Ajax possible!
3       try{
          // Opera 8.0+, Firefox, Safari
4         ajaxRequest = new XMLHttpRequest();  // Create the object
        }
```

EXAMPLE 18.1 (CONTINUED)

```
            catch (e) {
                // Internet Explorer Browsers
                try{
5                   ajaxRequest = new ActiveXObject("Msxml2.XMLHTTP");
                }
                catch (e) {
                    try{
                        ajaxRequest = new ActiveXObject("Microsoft.XMLHTTP");
                    }
                    catch (e){
                        return false;
                    }
                }
            }
6           return ajaxRequest;
    } //End function
```

EXPLANATION

1   The *CreateRequestObject* function creates the *XMLHttpRequest* object for Ajax to set up communication between JavaScript and the server.

2   This variable will be used to hold a reference to a new Ajax *XMLHttpRequest* object created in this function.

3   If the *try* block has no errors, its statements will be executed; otherwise, the *catch* block will be executed.

4   For most modern browsers, this *try* will succeed. Here the *XMLHttpRequest()* method will create a new object called *ajaxRequest*. (The object name is named any valid variable name.)

5   The *catch* blocks are executed if the browser is Microsoft Internet Explorer. Internet Explorer uses the *ActiveXObject()* method to create the Ajax object rather than the *XMLHttpRequest()* method.

6   If successful, an Ajax request object will be returned from this function.

Properties and Methods.   The *XMLHttpRequest* object has several important properties and methods that will give you information about the status of the request response, the data that was returned from the server, when the state of the server changes, and so on. There are methods to initialize the *XMLHttpRequest* object, send a request, inform you about what is in the response headers, how to cancel a request, and so on. You will see the properties and methods in Tables 18.1 and 18.2 used in the Ajax examples that follow.

Table 18.1   XMLHttpRequest Properties and Event Handlers

XMLHttpRequest Property	Value
status	The HTTP status code of the request response; for example, 200 or 404.
statusText	Returns the HTTP status code from server response as a string us as OK or Not Found.
readyState	A number representing the current state of the object (see Table 18.3).
responseText	Returns a string value of unparsed text as a response from the server.
responseXML	Returns response parsed into a DOM if Content-type is text/xml. Used to get multiple values.
onreadystatechange	The event handler that is called when the *readyState* changes.
onerror	Mozilla event handler that is called when an error happens during a request.
onprogress	Mozilla event handler called as content is loaded.
onload	Mozilla event handler called when the document is finished loading.

Table 18.2   *XMLHttpRequest* Methods

XMLHttpRequest Method	What It Does
abort()	Cancels the request.
getAllResponseHeaders()	Returns a string of all the HTTP headers separated by a newline.
getResponseHeader("server")	Returns the value of a specific HTTP header; for example, "Server" or "Last-Modified".
open()	Initializes the *XMLHttpRequest* object with GET or POST, URL, and so on.
send()	Sends the request.
setRequestHeader()	Adds a key/value pair to add to the header that will be sent to the server.

18.3.2   Step 2: Initializing the Object

Whether retrieving a simple text file, XML file, sending form data, or retrieving information from a database, a request will ask for a resource from the server. To get this information the request object needs to know how the request will be submitted (i.e., GET or POST; use capital letters) and the URL defining the location of the file or server-side script. (When creating HTML forms, this information was normally stored in the ACTION and METHOD attributes of the *<form>* tag.) Once the object has this information, the request can be made.

The *open()* Method.   The *open()* method prepares or initializes the object for communication with the server, whereas the *send()* method actually makes the request. The *open()* method takes three arguments:

1. The request type; that is, how the data is submitted, either GET or POST.[2]
2. The URL of the file or server-side program and parameters representing the data being sent as key/value pairs.
3. An optional third parameter of Boolean true (asynchronous) or false (synchronous). When set to *true*, the default, the processing will continue without waiting for the server to respond, whereas with a *false* setting, the processing will stop until the server responds.

Except for simple file retrieval or searches, the POST method is used, but this requires an additional request header method, and the data represented as name/value pairs is sent to the server as an argument to the *send()* method.

It is important to note that for security reasons, **the URL must be within the same domain as the request object**; for example, JavaScript is not permitted to open an *XMLHttpRequest* to any server other than the same Web server currently being visited by the user.

EXAMPLE (SAMPLE CODE)

```
objectRequest.open("GET", "myfile.txt", true);

objectRequest.open("POST", "http://localhost/hello.php");
```

GET or POST.   The way data is sent to a server with the HTTP protocol depends on whether the method being used is GET or POST. (To review these two methods, go to Chapter 11, section "About HTML Forms" on page 334.) In either case, the data being sent is in a URL-encoded query string consisting of name/value pairs. With the GET method, the browser sends data in the URL (see Figure 18.3), whereas with the POST method it sends additional data to the server specified in headers, a blank line, and finally the data (see Figure 18.4). Ajax handles GET and POST differently as well.

---

2. You can also use the HEAD request method.

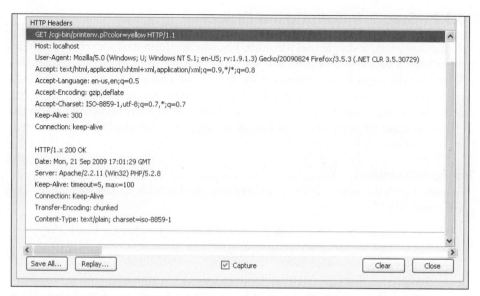

Figure 18.3   Firefox Live Headers shows how the GET method sends data in a query string appended to a the URL and a question mark (shown in highlighted bar).

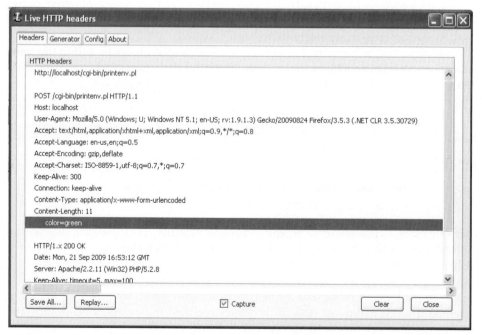

Figure 18.4   Firefox Live Headers add-on shows POST data sent as part of the HTTP header.

When the first parameter to the Ajax *open()* method is GET, the second argument is the URL of the page that is being requested. If the URL is a server-side script, such as PHP or ASP.NET, any input data (name/value pairs), is sent as a URL-encoded query string. A question mark, followed by the query string, is appended to the URL. As you might remember in traditional form processing, if the GET method is used, the data will be attached to the URL in the location box of the browser, visible to all. With Ajax the URL is an argument to the *open()* method and is not visible in the browser window because it is being sent directly from Ajax to the server. For the GET method:

EXAMPLE (SAMPLE CODE)

```
ajaxRequestObject.open("GET","http://localhost/ajaxform.php?username="+
        namevalue+"&userphone="+phonevalue, true);
ajaxRequestObject.send(null);
```

With the POST method, additional data is sent to the server. The first argument to the *open()* method will be POST, the second argument, the URL of the server script, and the third *true* for asynchronous. Instead of attaching the query string to the URL it will be sent as an argument to the *send()* method.

The *setRequestHeader()* method is added to specify the Content-type, set to "application/x-www-form-urlencoded". This is needed for any POST request made via Ajax.

Finally, the *send()* method is called, passing in the parameters that will be sent to the server-side program (without the "?" prefix). This data is formatted as a query string (e.g., "name=value&foo=bar"), and not visible in the browser.

EXAMPLE (SAMPLE CODE)

```
ajaxRequestObject.open("POST", "http://localhost/ajaxform.php", true);
ajaxRequestObject.setRequestHeader("Content-type",
        "application/x-www-form-urlencoded");
ajaxRequestObject.send(username="+namevalue+"&userphone="+phonevalue,
        true);
```

18.3.3 Sending the Request to the Server

Once the object has been initialized, the browser can send a request to the server with the *send()* method. This method takes one argument of "null" if you use the GET method for sending the data. As discussed in the previous section, with the POST method, an additional step is required. The *setRequestHeader()* method tells the server the "Content-type", and the *send()* method sends the query string as name/value pairs to the server.

EXAMPLE (Sample Code)

```
objectRequest.open("GET", "http://localhost/test.php?name=George", true);
  objectRequest.send(null);
```

EXAMPLE (Sample Code)

```
objectRequest.open("POST", "http://localhost/hello.php");
objectRequest.setRequestHeader("Content-Type",
                 "application/x-www-form-urlencoded");
objectRequest.send("first=Joe&last=Blow");
```

18.3.4   Step 3: Monitoring the State of the Server Response

Monitoring the State of the Server.   After sending a request to the server, we need to know when the request has completed and what to do with the information when it comes back. The *onreadystatechange* event handler of the *XMLHttpRequest* object is assigned a function that will be called automatically when the *onreadystatechange* event handler is triggered; that is, when the state of the server changes.

EXAMPLE (Sample Code)

```
ajaxRequest.onreadystatechange = function(){
     // The function will defined later
}
```

What does *readyState* mean? The *XMLHttpRequest* object keeps track of the status of the server's response in another property called *readyState*. This property has one of the values shown in Table 18.3.

Table 18.3   The *readyState* property of the *XMLHttpRequest* Object

Status	Value
0	Object, has been created, not initialized
1	Loading, send method not yet called
2	Loaded, send method called, headers not available
3	Interactive, some data has been received, status and response headers not available
4	Complete, all data has been received and is available

Each time the *readyState* value changes, then the *onreadystatechange* handler is triggered and the function assigned to it called.

When Is the Request Complete?   When the server's response is complete, the *readyState* value will be 4. The next step is to check this value, and if it is 4, retrieve the data from the server's response.

To watch the server response change state, the following code can be added to your program once the Ajax request object has been created. Assuming that the object is named ajaxRequest, the following example tests the *readyState* values and sends an alert stating what each value represents.

EXAMPLE   (SAMPLE CODE)

```
if(ajaxRequest.readyState == 0){
   alert("There is no connection");
}
if(ajaxRequest.readyState == 1){
   alert("The connection is loading");
}
if(ajaxRequest.readyState == 2){
   alert("The data was loaded")
}
if(ajaxRequest.readyState == 3){
   alert("Some data has been retrieved.
         The connection is interactive");
}
if(ajaxRequest.readyState == 4){
   alert("Complete! All of the data has been received");
}
```

Checking the HTTP Status.   We might also want to check the HTTP status returned by the server to the client to determine the outcome of a request. A status returned by the HTTP server of 200 means that the response was successful. (In some of the following examples using a PHP script, Firefox seems to return a status of 0.) An HTTP status of 404 means that the URL cannot be found. There are a number of HTTP status values that can be checked. Some common HTTP status codes are given in Table 18.4.

Table 18.4 Some HTTP Status Codes

HTTP Status Code	
200 OK	OK. The server successfully returned the page.
400 Bad Request	Server didn't understand the request due to malformed syntax.

Continues

Table 18.4 Some HTTP Status Codes (continued)

HTTP Status Code	
401 Unauthorized	The request requires user authentication.
404 Not found	The server found nothing matching the URI given.
500 Internal Server Error	The server encountered an unexpected error and couldn't fulfill the request.
503 Service Unavailable	The server is currently unable to handle the request due to temporary overloading or maintenance.

For a descriptive table of all the HTTP status codes, go to
http://www.google.com/support/webmasters/bin/answer.py?hl=en&answer=40132
and for complete technical definitions of these codes, go to
http://www.w3.org/Protocols/rfc2616/rfc2616-sec10.html.

EXAMPLE (SAMPLE CODE)

```
ajaxRequest.onreadystatechange = function() {
  if (objectRequest.status == 200) {
    // OK
  }
  else if(ajaxRequest.status == 404){
    // Resource not found
  }
  else{
    alert("Error:" + ajaxRequest.statusText);
  }
}
```

18.3.5 Handling the Response with a Callback Function

The function that will check for the status of a request and handle the information returned from the server is called a callback function or an inline function. The object's *onreadystatechange* event handler is assigned a reference to the callback function.

The data sent back from a server can be retrieved with two other properties of the *XMLHttpRequest* object called the *responseText* property and the *responseXML* property.

The *responseText* Property.   For simple Ajax applications, such as getting text from a file, you can retrieve the server's response in a string with the *responseText* property.

EXAMPLE   (SAMPLE CODE)

```
//Callback function
ajaxRequest.onreadystatechange = function() {
  var textObj;
  textObj=document.getElementById("message");
  if(ajaxRequest.readyState == 4){
    //alert(ajaxRequest.status);
    if(ajaxRequest.status==200){
      textObj.innerHTML=ajaxRequest.responseText; /* Get text
          in a string returned by the server. */
    }
  }
  else if(ajaxRequest.status == 404){ //Bad URL
    textObj.innerHTML="Resource unavailable";
  }
  else{
    alert("Error:" +
      ajaxRequest.statusText);
  }
}
```

The responseXML property.   The 'x' in Ajax stands for XML, and although you don't have to use XML to create Ajax applications, data from more complex and structured XML documents can be returned by an HTTP request and assigned to the object's *responseXML* property. This property contains an XML document object, which can be examined and parsed using the DOM, in the same way we used the DOM in Chapter 15, "The W3C DOM and JavaScript." The following example demonstrates how to create a simple XML file and how to use Ajax to retrieve the file data and use the DOM to access the information (see Figure 18.5).

EXAMPLE   (SAMPLE CODE)

```
var xml = ajaxRequest.responseXML;  //Get an XML object
alert(xml);
```

Figure 18.5   The Ajax *responseXML* property contains an XML document object.

Checking HTTP Response Headers. HTTP response headers define various characteristics of the data that has been requested, providing information such as the server type, the last date when the page was modified, the Content-type, and so forth. JavaScript can retrieve this HTTP header information with two methods, the *getAllResponseHeaders()* method and the *getResponseHeader()* method. The *getAllResponseHeaders()* method returns a complete list of all the response headers as name/value pairs, each separated by a newline (see Figure 18.5). The *getResponseHeader()* method returns a string containing a specific response header of the *XMLHttpRequest* object.

The following piece of code highlights how to get all the HTTP response headers, whereas if you want only one header value you could use the *getResponseHeader()* method as:

```
alert(ajaxRequest.getResponseHeader("Content-type");

ajaxRequest.onreadystatechange = function() {
  if (ajaxRequest.readyState == 4) {
    if (ajaxRequest.status == 200) {
      headers=ajaxRequest.getAllResponseHeaders();
      alert(headers);
    }
  }
}
```

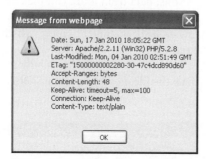

Figure 18.6 HTTP response headers.

18.3.6   The Browser Cache Issue

Normally the browser caches banners, advertising, graphs, photos, and entire Web pages in a folder so that you can hit the back button or click a link to a page you just visited, and the image or page will be pulled from the cache. If you request a page with the same URL as used before, the response is already in the cache and that response will be used instead of requesting it again. Because the browser doesn't have to make an HTTP request for a cached page, the speed of the page load is greatly improved. When using Ajax, on the other hand, which is all based on making HTTP requests to a server, this can be a problem. For example, if you are using Ajax to update a table containing stock data, and the table is to be refreshed every 4 or 5 minutes in real time, the Ajax request will grab the cached page from the previous request, not what is wanted. The page will not reflect the changes because the browser will load from the cache rather than by making another request to the same URL.

The HTTP specification states that the response to a GET request is cacheable but any responses to the POST method are not cacheable, unless the response includes appropriate Cache-Control or Expires header fields, meaning that a query using the POST method will normally be resubmitted and reprocessed for every request. If using the GET method, there are a number of techniques to ensure that a new HTTP request is made every time a request is made. The simplest solution is to change the URL in the Ajax *open()* method to trick the browser into reloading the document for what appears to be a new page. By adding a parameter that is constantly changing in the URL, each request will be unique and therefore, not cached. This can be accomplished by adding a timestamp or a random number value as a parameter to the URL. The value should be different each time, and although it will have no effect on the requested page, it makes the browser see this as a URL that has never been visited before.

EXAMPLE   (SAMPLE CODE)

```
var url = "http://mydomain?myParams="+"&pseudoParam= "+
    new Date().getTime();

var url = "http://mydomain?myParams=" + "&pseudoParam=" +
    Math.random();
```

By adding a new value to the URL, the browser will refresh the page each time there is a request for that page.

You can also add headers to the request object with the *setRequestHeader()* method. Setting the "If-Modified-Since" value to a date earlier than now causes the browser to check to see if the data has changed since that date and send a new request. As long as the date is a past date, it doesn't matter what date you use. If these headers fail on a particular browser, use the random number or date options shown above.

EXAMPLE   (SAMPLE CODE)

```
ajaxRequest.setRequestHeader('If-Modified-Since', 'Sat, 03 Jan
                             2010 00:00:00GMT');
ajaxRequest.setRequestHeader("Cache-Control", "no-cache");
```

18.4 Putting It All Together

The steps we have covered are summarized in the following Ajax examples to demonstrate how to communicate with the server. The first example demonstrates how to use Ajax to get the server's time and respond to key events, the next two examples work with a text file and an XML file, and demonstrate how to retrieve display the content of both types of files, and the last example uses Ajax with forms using both the GET and POST methods. All of the programs go through the following steps:

1. The user clicks a button or presses a key to initiate a function that will start the process of Ajax communicating with the server.
2. Most important, JavaScript uses the *XMLHttpRequest* constructor method to create a new object that will serve as the Ajax communication layer between the browser and the server. (If not this, IFrames or cookies can be used, but will not be covered in this text.)
3. Once the *XMLHttpRequest* object is created, it is initialized with the object's *open()* method to set up the type of HTTP request (GET or POST), the URL (where the request is going), and whether the request will be asynchronous (true and the default), or synchronous (false).
4. The request is then sent to the server with the object's *send()* method.
5. The server processes the request and sends a response to the browser in either XML or text format. It contains the data only of the page elements that need to be changed. In most cases this data will include just a fraction of the total page markup.
6. JavaScript processes the server response, updates the relevant page content, or performs another operation with the new data received from the server.

Connecting to a Server Program.   If you are ready to start using PHP and Apache to test these examples, go to *http://sourceforge.net/projects/xampp/XAMPP* and download XAMPP. It is a very easy to install Apache Distribution for Linux, Solaris, Windows and Mac OS X. The package includes the Apache Web server, MySQL, PHP, Perl, an FTP server, and phpMyAdmin. Once you have installed XAMPP, you will be able to start up the services with the XAMPP control panel by clicking on the XAMPP icon (see Figure 18.7) or going to the Start menu (Windows) or Application menu (MacOS). When you get to the XAMPP control panel (see Figure 18.8), just click to start Apache to get your Apache HTTP server running. PHP scripts will be stored in the same place as HTML files, under the server's root, and should be given a *.php* extension. There are many tutorials and books on PHP. Of course we recommend *PHP and MySQL by Example* by Ellie Quigley and Marko Gargenta (Prentice Hall, ISBN 0-13-187508-6).

Figure 18.7   XAMPP icon to open the control panel.

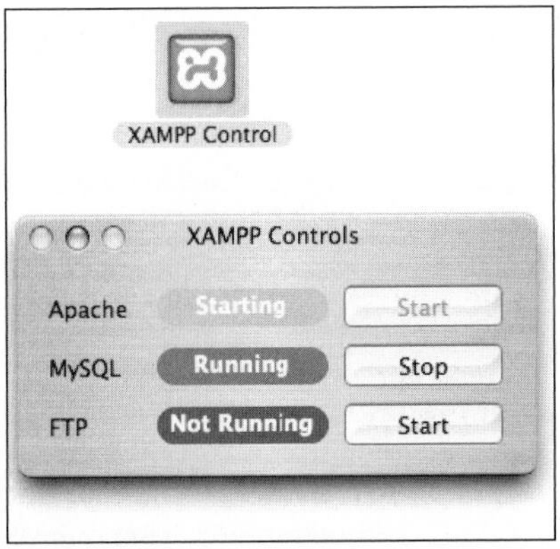

Figure 18.8   Starting the Apache server with XAMPP.

An Ajax Example with PHP.   Example 18.2 demonstrates an asynchronous interaction between the browser and server using Ajax. The PHP server-side script, executing in the background, will be called every time the user types in a letter and releases the key. When a key is released, a request is sent to the server, the PHP script is executed, and the response is returned back from the server as text that can be inserted in an HTML *div* container along with the current time as hour/minute/second. If the delete key is pressed and released the letter will be removed in the text box as well as in the *div* container. You can see how, with some more extensive programming on the PHP side, you could make your "search suggest" application, by creating an array of search strings. If the user typed a letter or letters in a search box on the browser, Ajax would send each letter to the server. The server script would then match each letter against the strings in its array, and if there was a match, return the response in a string to the browser. Because this text cannot assume you are already savvy in PHP, it won't be attempted here, but there are many tutorials on the Web to demonstrate how this is done. For some good examples, see: *http://www.dynamicajax.com/fr/AJAX_Suggest_Tutorial-271_290_312.html* or *http://www.w3schools.com/php/php_ajax_suggest.asp*.

Example 18.2 contains the Ajax code where communication between browser and server takes place. The CSS style sheet for Example 18.2 is located in an external file (Example 18.3). Another file called *ajaxCreateRequest.js* (Example 18.4) contains the code for cross-browser checking and most important creating a new a *XMLHttpRequest* object.

The Client Side script—"ajaxGetText.html"

EXAMPLE   18.2

```
    <html>
      <head><title>First Ajax Script</title>
1         <link rel="stylesheet" type="text/css" href="ajaxStyle.css" />
2         <script type="text/javascript"
                  src="ajaxCreateRequest.js"></script>
```

Continues

EXAMPLE   18.2 (CONTINUED)

```
            <script type="text/javascript">
3              function goAjax(){
4                 var ajaxRequest=createRequest();   /* Cross-browser check;
                                        Get a new XMLHttpRequest object */
                  if( ajaxRequest != false){   /* If we got back a request
                      object create callback function to check state of the
                      request*/
5                 ajaxRequest.onreadystatechange = function(){
6                    if(ajaxRequest.readyState == 4){
7                       if(ajaxRequest.status==200){
8                          document.getElementById("message").innerHTML=
                                            ajaxRequest.responseText;
                        }
                     }
                  } // End callback function
9                 yourname=document.getElementById("username").value;
10                ajaxRequest.open("GET",
                     "http://localhost/serverTime.php?name=" + yourname +
                                      "&random=" + Math.random()
                  );
11                ajaxRequest.send(null);
               } //End if
               else{ alert("Browser problem was encountered!");}
            } // End ajaxFunction()
         </script>
      </head>
      <body>
         <form name="myForm">
12          Your name: <input type="text" onKeyUp="goAjax();"
                            name="username" id="username" /> <br />
            <p>
13             <div id="message" class="divStyle">
               <!-- This is where the Ajax output will be displayed -->
               </div>
            </p>
         </form>
      </body>
   </html
```

1   The CSS style sheet is loaded from a file called "ajaxintro.css". It defines the background color as aliceblue and the style of the <div> contents that will be displayed in the browser, a dark green container with white letters. See Example 18.3.

2   A .js file is loaded here. It contains a JavaScript function that performs a cross-browser check and creates and returns the *XMLHttpRequest* object. If the object cannot be created, the function will return *false*. Example 18.4 contains the function found in an external file called "ajaxCreateRequest.js".

EXPLANATION (CONTINUED)

3   This function is where the Ajax communication between the browser and server will happen. It is called when the *onKeyUp* event handler is triggered; that is, when the user presses a key and releases it (line 12).

4   This function will be called every time the user releases a key. It is responsible for all the Ajax activity, once an *XMLHttpRequest* object has been created.

5   The callback function (also called inline function) monitors the state of the server. When the *onreadystate* event handler sees that the server has changed state, the callback function is executed.

6   If the *readyState* property is 4, the HTTP request has completed.

7   If the HTTP server status is 200 OK, then the server was successful and we are ready to view the response.

8   The *getElementById()* method will return a reference to the *div* container name message (line 13). The *ajaxRequest.responseText* property contains the ASCII text that was returned. The value of the *innerHTML* property contains that returned text that will be displayed in the *<div>* container.

9   The *getElementById()* method will get the name that the user typed in the text field and assign it to a variable called *yourname*.

10   The request object's *open()* method initializes the *XMLHttpRequest* object. The request will be sent as an HTTP GET request to start a server-side PHP program on the localhost (see Example 18.5). The parameters are two URL encoded key/value pairs: The first is the name of the user (name=yourname) and the second is a random number value.

11   The *send()* method is responsible for sending the request to the server. When using the GET method, the argument is set to *null*.

12   The HTML form has one input device, a textbox. After the user types a character in the box and releases the key, the *onKeyUp* event handler will be triggered and call the *goAjax()* function.

13   When the server responds, it will send back text that will be displayed in this *div* container. The *div* container will be styled by the class *divStyle* defined in the external .css file shown next.

The CSS File—"ajaxStyle.css"

EXAMPLE 18.3

```
body{background-color:aliceblue;}
.divStyle { /* class for the <div> container
          background-color:aliceblue;
          margin-left:20%;
          margin-right:20%;
          border-style:solid;
          color:white;
          font-size:150%
}
```

Creating the Request Object—"ajaxCreateRequest.js"

EXAMPLE 18.4

```
/* Check browser type and create ajax request object
   Put this function in an external .js file and use it for your
   Ajax programs  */
function CreateRequest(){
   var ajaxRequest;  // The variable that makes Ajax possible!
   try{
      // Opera 8.0+, Firefox, Safari
      ajaxRequest = new XMLHttpRequest();  // Create the object
   }
   catch (e){
      // Internet Explorer Browsers
      try{
         ajaxRequest = new ActiveXObject("Msxml2.XMLHTTP");
      }
      catch (e) {
         try{
            ajaxRequest = new ActiveXObject("Microsoft.XMLHTTP");
         }
         catch (e){
            return false;
         }
      }
   }
   return ajaxRequest;
} //End function
```

The Server-Side PHP Script—"serverTime.php"

EXAMPLE 18.5

```
1  <?php
      //Server side script to handle request
2     extract($_REQUEST);
3     echo "Welcome, $name!";
4     echo "<br />Time now is ", date("h:i:s A "),".";
   ?>
```

EXPLANATION

1   The PHP server-side file, called serverTime.php is located in the server's root directory (e.g., *htdocs*, *www*, etc.) and will be executed by the server. Its output will be sent back to the browser and displayed in the *div* container defined in the HTML document. To run this script, you must have an HTTP server and PHP installed. See XAMPP at *http://sourceforge.net/projects/xampp/XAMPP* for installing the Apache and PHP.

EXPLANATION (CONTINUED)

2   This PHP function extracts the data from a global associative array called *$_REQUEST*. It contains any name/value pairs of the HTML form sent with either GET or POST requests; in this example, the array contains two elements: *name* and *"Ellie"*. PHP's *extract()* function creates a variable, *$name*, for the *name* and assigns it the value *"Ellie"*. (This information was sent in the request object's *open()* method as "http://localhost/serverTime.php?**name="+yourname+"&random=**" + Math.random()).

3   The PHP *echo* statement returns the value of *$name* to the server where it is then sent back to the Ajax program in the Ajax request object's *responseText* property.

4   The PHP *date()* function returns the hour, minute, and second, AM or PM. This data is updated in the Ajax program every time the server sends a response. Results of this process are shown in Figures 18.9 through 18.13.

Figure 18.9   The page as it is initially displayed.

Figure 18.10   Once the user starts typing, the *div* box appears with the letters and time.

Figure 18.11   Each time a letter is typed, it is added to the name in the *div* box while time is changing.

Figure 18.12   User types more letters, *div* box and server time are updated.

Figure 18.13   If the delete key is pressed the letters start disappearing in the *div* box and time is updated.

18.4.1   Using Ajax to Retrieve Text From a File

In Example 18.6, we use Ajax to request and return ASCII text from a file and display the response results in a *div* container. For a more sophisticated example of an Ajax program using a text file, see *http://www.dynamicdrive.com/dynamicindex2/ajaxticker.htm*. This Ajax ticker program adds the ability to periodically refetch the contents of an external file. All source code is provided.

At *http://www.JavaScriptkit.com/dhtmltutors/ajaxticker/index.shtml* you can find another excellent tutorial on how to combine RSS, Ajax, and JavaScript to create a live RSS ticker.

Example 18.6 provides an Ajax program to get text from a file. The CSS file (Example 18.9) and the JavaScript file (Example 18.8) to create the request object are external file. The text file is shown in Example 18.7.

The Ajax Program—"ajaxGetText.htm"

EXAMPLE   18.6

```
      <html>
        <head><title>Reading From a Text File with Ajax</title>
          <link rel="stylesheet" type="text/css" href="ajaxTextFile.css" />
          <script type="text/javascript" src="ajaxCreateRequest.js">
          </script>
          <script type="text/javascript">
            function getText(url){
1             var ajaxRequest=createRequest();   /* Cross-browser check;
                                    Get a new XMLHttpRequest object */
              if( ajaxRequest != false){ /* If we got back a request
                  object create callback function to check state of
                  the request*/
2               ajaxRequest.onreadystatechange = function() {
3                 if (ajaxRequest.readyState == 4) {
                    if (ajaxRequest.status == 200 ||
                                        ajaxRequest.status==0){
4                     document.getElementById('data').innerHTML=
                                        ajaxRequest.responseText;
                    }
                    else {
                      alert('There was a problem with the request.');
                    }
                  }
                } // End callback function
              }
5             ajaxRequest.open('GET', url, true); // Initialize the
                                                  // object
              ajaxRequest.setRequestHeader('If-Modified-Since',
                              'Sat, 03 Jan 2010 00:00:00GMT');
                              // Deal with the cache
6             ajaxRequest.send(null); // Send the request
```

Continues

EXAMPLE   18.6 (CONTINUED)

```
            } //End getText() function
        </script>
    </head>
    <body>
        <span style="cursor: pointer; text-decoration: underline"
7               onclick="getText('ajaxtext.txt')">
        Fetch text from a file
        </span>
        <p>
8           <div id="data" class="divStyle">
            </div>
        </p>
    </body>
</html>
```

EXPLANATION

1   A new *XMLHttpRequest* object, called *ajaxRequest*, is created (code is in "ajaxRequest.js", Example 18.8).

2   The callback function is defined and assigned to the *onreadystatechange* event handler used to monitor the state of the server.

3   When the *readyState* of the server is 4, the request is complete. If the HTTP status is OK (200), the program proceeds.

4   The *getElementById()* method will return a reference to the *div* container named "data" on line 8. The *ajaxRequest.responseText* property contains the ASCII text that was returned. The *innerHTML* property will put that text in the *<div>* container.

5   The *XMLHttpRequest* object's *open()* method initializes the object. The request will be sent as an HTTP GET request to get data from a file called "ajaxtext.txt". (When using Internet Explorer the URL was *http://localhost/ajaxtext.txt* with Firefox just the name of the file was given.)

6   The request is sent to the server.

7   When the user clicks the underlined text defined by the *span* tag, the *getText()* function will be launched. Its argument is the name of the text file that will be processed, shown in Example 18.7.

8   This is the *<div>* container where the results of the HTTP request will be displayed. See Figure 18.14.

The Text File—"ajaxText.txt"

EXAMPLE   18.7

Once upon a time there were
three little bears.

The Ajax Request File—"AjaxRequest.js"

EXAMPLE   18.8

```
      /* Check browser type and create ajax request object
         Put this function in an external .js file and use it for your
         Ajax programs. Fully explained in Example 18.1. */
1     function CreateRequest(){
2       var ajaxRequest;  // The variable that makes Ajax possible!
3       try{
           // Opera 8.0+, Firefox, Safari
4         ajaxRequest = new XMLHttpRequest();   // Create the object
         }
         catch (e){
           // Internet Explorer Browsers
           try{
5            ajaxRequest = new ActiveXObject("Msxml2.XMLHTTP");
           }
           catch (e) {
           try{
6            ajaxRequest = new ActiveXObject("Microsoft.XMLHTTP");
           }
           catch (e){
7              return false;
             }
           }
         }
8       return ajaxRequest;
      } //End function
```

The CSS File—"ajaxTextFile.css"

EXAMPLE   18.9

```
      body{background-color:aliceblue;}
      .divStyle {
              margin-left:5px;
              margin-right:200px;
              border-style:solid;
              border-color:blue;
              font-size:150%;

      }
```

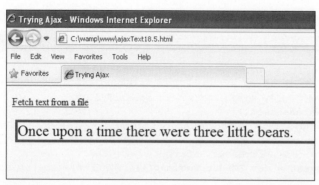

Figure 18.14 A text file is retrieved and it contents displayed in a *div* container.

18.4.2   Using Ajax to Retrieve XML from a File

XML is the Extensible Markup Language. Although similar in structure to HTML, XML was designed to transport and store data, whereas HTML was designed to describe the layout and looks of the data. With XML you create markup that defines the structure of a document, but instead of having predefined tags as with HTML, you make your own. The XML tree looks similar to the HTML upside-down document tree, starting with a root element at the top and branching down to parents, attributes, children, and so on. XML has rules, very XML-specific syntax rules on how to create a "well-formed" document. It is not hard to learn, but if you are unfamiliar with XML, go to the W3C schools Web site where you will find an excellent tutorial at *http://www.w3schools.com/xml/xml_tree.asp*.

XML data is often stored in external files as plain text. The data in the XML files can be easily exchanged between different programs, applications, and computers. In this chapter we are using Ajax to exchange data between a client and server. In the previous example the server returned a string of text from a simple text file. In this example we will use Ajax to get data from an XML file as an object and use the XML DOM to parse and display the data. And finally, at the end of this chapter, we will use an easier technology, called JSON, to make exchanging and parsing data a little simpler. In fact JSON is said to be rapidly replacing XML because of its easy lightweight data-interchange format.

The XML file for the following example, called "bookstore.xml", is found in Example 18.10.[3] If you are not familiar with XML, this file is a good example of how the markup is structured. The Ajax program (Example 18.11) makes a request to the server to get the XML file. The server returns an XML object, and the rest of the program uses DOM methods and properties to parse out the data from the XML object and to create the elements and text nodes that will be placed in an HTML *div* container.

---

3. This example uses an XML file slightly modified from one found in the W3Schools XML tutorial.

The XML File (bookstore.xml)

EXAMPLE 18.10

```xml
<bookstore>
  <book category="COOKING">
    <title>The Art of Simple Food</title>
    <author>Alice Waters</author>
    <published>2007</published>
    <price>35.00</price>
  </book>
  <book category="AUTOBIOGRAPHY">
    <title>Moments of Being</title>
    <author>Virginia Woolf</author>
    <published>1985</published>
    <price>14.00</price>
  </book>
  <book category="FICTION">
    <title>Plain Truth</title>
    <author>Judy Picoult</author>
    <published>2000</published>
    <price>15.00</price>
  </book>
</bookstore>
```

Ajax Program

EXAMPLE 18.11

```html
<html>
  <head><title>Reading from an XML file</title>
    <script type="text/javascript" src="ajaxCreateRequest.js">
    </script>
    <script type="text/javascript">
1       function makeRequest(url){
        var httpRequest=createRequest();   /* Cross-browser check;
                                    Get a new XMLHttpRequest object */
        if( httpRequest != false){      // If we got back a request
                                        // object
          httpRequest.open('GET', url, true);
          httpRequest.setRequestHeader('If-Modified-Since',
                             'Sat, 03 Jan 2010 00:00:00GMT');
          httpRequest.send(null);
          httpRequest.onreadystatechange = function() {
2           getXMLContents(httpRequest); };
        }
        else{ alert("There was a problem with your request.");}
      } // End createRequest function
```

Continues

EXAMPLE　**18.11** (CONTINUED)

```
3   function getXMLContents(httpRequest) {
        if (httpRequest.readyState == 4) {
            if (httpRequest.status == 200) {
4               var xml = httpRequest.responseXML;
5               var booklist = xml.getElementsByTagName("book");
6               for( j=0; j < booklist.length; j++){
                    var book=booklist[j];
7                   var category=book.getAttribute("category");
                    for(i=0;i<book.childNodes.length; i++){
8                       switch(book.childNodes[i].nodeName){
                            case "title":
                                title=book.childNodes[i].firstChild.nodeValue;
                            case "author":
                                author=book.childNodes[i].firstChild.nodeValue;
                            case "price":
                                price=book.childNodes[i].firstChild.nodeValue;
                            case "published":
                                published=book.childNodes[i].firstChild.nodeValue;
                        }
                    } //End inner for loop
9                   var para=document.createElement("p");
                    var brtag1=document.createElement("br");
                    var brtag2=document.createElement("br")
                    var brtag3=document.createElement("br")
10                  var categoryTxt=document.createTextNode("Category:
                                                            "+category);
                    var titleTxt=document.createTextNode("Title: " + title);
                    var authorTxt=document.createTextNode("Author: "+author);
                    var priceTxt=document.createTextNode("Price: "+ price);

11                  para.appendChild(categoryTxt);
                    para.appendChild(brtag1);
                    para.appendChild(titleTxt);
                    para.appendChild(brtag2);
                    para.appendChild(authorTxt);
                    para.appendChild(brtag3);
                    para.appendChild(priceTxt);

12                  document.getElementById('data').appendChild(para);
                }
            }else { alert('There was a problem with the request.');}
        }
    }
        </script>
    </head>
```

EXAMPLE 18.11 (CONTINUED)

```
        <body>
          <span style="cursor: pointer; text-decoration: underline"
13              onclick="makeRequest('http://localhost/bookstore.xml')">
          Get book details
          </span>
14        <div id=data>
          </div>
        </body>
      </html>
```

EXPLANATION

1   This function creates the *XMLHttpRequest* object, initializes it with the GET method and the XML file, called "bookstore.xml", sends the request to the server, and calls the *getXMLContents()* function when the state of the server changes to 4 (complete).

2   This function takes the *XMLHttpRequest* object as its argument. It is called when the *onreadystatechange* event handler is notified that the server's *readyState* has changed.

3   This function checks when the server has completed the request and fetches the contents of the XML file.

4   The *httpRequest.responseXML* **property contains the data returned from the XML file as an XML document object.**

5   The *getElementsByTagName()* method gets a reference to all the *<book>* tags stored as an array in the XML object. Look at "bookstore.xml" to see the structure.

6   The outer for loop will iterate through each book in the array of books, called *booklist*.

7   The XML DOM *getAttribute()* method returns the value of an attribute by its name, which is "category".

8   For the name of each book, *childNodes[i].nodeName*, the *switch* statement will use the *nodeValue* property to get the text for the title, author, and so on.

9   Using the DOM, elements are created that will be inserted in the *div* container on line 14. A paragraph (*p*) and break (*br*) elements are created to hold the book values.

10 Next, the *textNodes* are created that will be appended to the paragraph.

11 Once all the text nodes are created, they are appended to the paragraph with break tags after each line of text.

12 Now, the new paragraph, built entirely with DOM methods, is inserted into the *div* container defined on line 14.

13 When the user clicks the underlined text, defined by the *<span>* tag, the Ajax program is launched.

14 This is the *<div>* container that will display the output from the XML file returned from the server. See Figure 18.15.

Figure 18.15 XML file has been read and processed by Ajax and the DOM.

18.4.3   Ajax and Forms

There are several reasons why you might choose to use Ajax for forms in your Web page.

1. Faster validation.
2. Auto-completing the form fields.
3. Spell checking in real time.
4. Updating content (weather updates, auctions, stock tickers).
5. Dynamically updating a list based on user input.

When creating non-Ajax HTML forms, the *<form>* tag takes an ACTION attribute and a METHOD attribute. The ACTION attribute is used to specify the URL of a server-side program that will deal with form input after the submit button is clicked, and the METHOD attribute determines how the input will be sent, either with the HTTP GET or POST methods. In the traditional HTML form, the form will have a submit button that, when clicked, causes the browser to bundle up the input data into a URI encoded query string consisting of name/value pairs. This encoded data will be sent to the server-side program named in the ACTION attribute of the form. If the method is GET, the query string will be appended to the URL prepended with a question mark, visible in the location box of the browser. If the method is POST, the encoded data will be sent as a message body in an HTTP header to the server. This POST data will not be visible in the location box and is not limited in size so this method is normally used to send data from a form. The server-side program (e.g., PHP, ASP.NET, CGI), will then process the data and send back its response in a brand new page while the user waits. Example 18.12 is a traditional HTML form.

A Traditional HTML Form

EXAMPLE 18.12

```
        <html>
          <head><title>An HTML Form</title></head>
          <body>
1           <form ACTION="http://localhost/guestbook.php" METHOD="post"><p>
              <p>
              Your name:
2             <input type="text" name="username" size="50" /><br />
              Your phone:
              <input type="text" name="userphone" size=50/><br />
              <p>
3             <input type="submit" value="Submit" />
            </form>
          </body>
        </html>
```

When creating HTML forms with AJAX, the *<form>* tag will not be given an ACTION or a METHOD attribute and the submit button will not be used to submit the form data. Instead, an event handler will trigger off the chain of events that deal with the communication between the browser and server. Whether using GET or POST, because Ajax is making server requests, the user will not have to wait for an entire page to be returned before continuing to work on the page. The next examples will demonstrate how to create and process forms with Ajax.

The GET Method.   Example 18.13 demonstrates how to create an Ajax form using the GET method. The example can be divided into four parts. First the program checks for the type of browser being used and creates the Ajax request object. The second part creates the Ajax functions that will send a request to the server, check for the state of the server, and when the server completes a request, will handle the data that comes back. In the next part, the HTML form is created with a *div* container to hold the data that will come back from the server. Finally the server-side PHP program on the server side receives the form data from the server, handles it, and sends it back to the server. The PHP program might be responsible for validating logins, sending database queries, reading or writing to files, starting sessions, cookies, and so on.

The Ajax Program

EXAMPLE 18.13

```
      <html>
        <head><title>Get method Ajax form</title>
          <link rel="stylesheet" type="text/css" href="ajaxGETstyle.css" />
          <script type="text/javascript" src="ajaxCreateRequest.js">
          </script>
          <script type="text/javascript">
1           function goAjax(){
              var ajaxRequest=createRequest();
              if(ajaxRequest != false){
2               ajaxRequest.onreadystatechange = function(){
3                 var textObj=document.getElementById("message");
                  if(ajaxRequest.readyState == 4){
                    //alert(ajaxRequest.status);
                    if(ajaxRequest.status==200){
4                     textObj.innerHTML=ajaxRequest.responseText;
                    }
                  }
                  else if(ajaxRequest.status == 404){
                    textObj.innerHTML="Resource unavailable";
                  }
                  else{
                    textObj.innerHTML="Error!!";
                  }
                }
    var namevalue=
5       encodeURIComponent(document.getElementById("username").value)
    var phonevalue=
        encodeURIComponent(document.getElementById("userphone").value)
6 ajaxRequest.open("GET","http://localhost/ajaxform.php?username="+
        namevalue+"&userphone="+phonevalue, true);
    ajaxRequest.setRequestHeader('If-Modified-Since',
        'Sat, 03 Jan 2010 00:00:00GMT');
7 ajaxRequest.send(null);
            }
          else{alert("Browser encountered a problem!");}
        } // End goAjax()function
      </script>
    </head>
    <body>
8     <form action="">
        Your name: <input type="text" size=50 id=username
                          name='username' /> <br />
          <p>
        Your phone: <input type="text" size=50 id=userphone
                          name="userphone" /><br />
```

EXAMPLE   18.13 (CONTINUED)

```
         <p>
9        <input type="button" value="submit" onClick="goAjax()"; />
      </form>
10    <div id="message" class="divStyle">
      </div>
   </body>
</html>
```

EXPLANATION

1   The *goAjax()* function is returned an *XMLHttpRequest* object from the *createRequest()* function found in the external .js file called "ajaxCreateRequest.js" shown in Example 18.14. The CSS style sheet is in Example 18.15.

2   The *onreadystate* event handler will start the callback function when the state of the server request changes.

3   The *getElementById()* method will return a reference to the *div* container using its *id* called "message".

4   When the server has completed successfully, its response will be returned as text. The *innerHTML* property contains the response text that is assigned to the *div* container on line 10 and will be displayed in the browser.

5   To avoid unexpected requests to the server, the *encodeURIComponent* encodes any user-entered parameters that will be passed as part of a *URI*. The value typed by the user into the form for the username will be assigned to the variable *namevalue*.

6   The *XMLHttpRequest* object is initialized. It will use the GET method. The URL is a server-side PHP program (Example 18.16) that will be passed parameters, appended to a ?, consisting of the user's name and phone number.

7   An *XMLHttpRequest* is sent to the server.

8   The HTML form starts here. Notice the ACTION and METHOD attributes are NOT specified as they are in non-Ajax forms.

9   Even though this button looks like a "submit" button, it is really an ordinary button with an *onClick* event handler that when clicked, will start the *goAjax()* function. In non-Ajax form submission, the submit button normally causes the contents of the form to be sent to the URL assigned to the form's ACTION attribute.

10   The *div* container will display the results that were returned to the server from the PHP program listed as a parameter in the *open()* method on line 6.

The File to Create an Ajax Request Object

EXAMPLE 18.14

```
/* Check browser type and create ajax request object */

function createRequest(){
  var ajaxRequest;  // The variable that makes Ajax possible!
  try{
    // Opera 8.0+, Firefox, Safari
    ajaxRequest = new XMLHttpRequest();
  }
  catch (e){
    // Internet Explorer Browsers
    try{
      ajaxRequest = new ActiveXObject("Msxml2.XMLHTTP");
    }
    catch (e) {
      try{
        ajaxRequest = new ActiveXObject("Microsoft.XMLHTTP");
      }
      catch (e){
        return false;
      }
    }
  }
  return ajaxRequest;
}
```

The CSS Style Sheet File

EXAMPLE 18.15

```
body{background-color:blue;color:white;font-size:120%}
.divStyle {
          background-color:lightblue;
          margin-left:50px;
          margin-right:100px;
          border-style:solid;
          color:darkblue;
          font-size:120%
}
```

The Server-Side PHP Script

EXAMPLE   18.16

```php
   <?php
1    extract($_REQUEST);
2    if( empty($username)){
3        echo "<span style='color:red'>Please enter your name.
         </span><br />";
4        exit;
     }
5    if (empty($userphone)){
         echo "<span style='color:red'>Please enter your phone number.
         </span><br />";
         exit;
     }
6    echo "Welcome <b>$username</b>. Your phone number is
     <b>$userphone</b>.";
   ?>
```

EXPLANATION

1   This PHP function extracts the data from a global associative array called
    $_REQUEST. It contains any name/value pairs submitted from the HTML form
    and sent with either GET or POST requests; in this example, the array contains
    two sets of name/value pairs:
        username => "Ebenezer Scrooge"
        userphone => "0207 626 4388"

    PHP's *extract* function creates a variable, *$username*, for the name and assigns it
    the value "Ebenezer Scrooge" and another variable called *$userphone* with a value
    of "0207 626 4388". (This information was sent in the server request in a param-
    eter: ?username="namevalue+"&userphone="+phonevalue. Figure 18.16 shows a
    completed form.

2   If the variable is empty (i.e., null), tell the user.

3   If the user didn't enter anything in the textfield, he or she will be sent this message
    in red letters defined by the *<span>* tag (see Figure 18.17).

4   The PHP program exits here.

5   If the user doesn't type anything in the phone field, he will get a message in red
    telling him or her to enter his or her phone number (see Figure 18.18).

6   The PHP program echo's a string of text to the server. The server will respond by
    sending the text to the Ajax program where it will be received (line 3 in the Ajax
    program) and displayed (line 4 in the Ajax program).

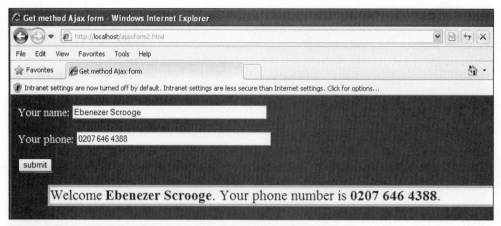

Figure 18.16 Ajax and form submission with the GET method.

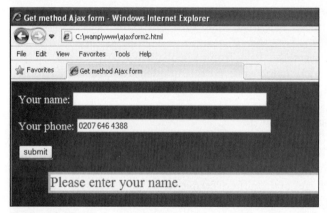

Figure 18.17 The user didn't enter his name. PHP responded with the message in red text.

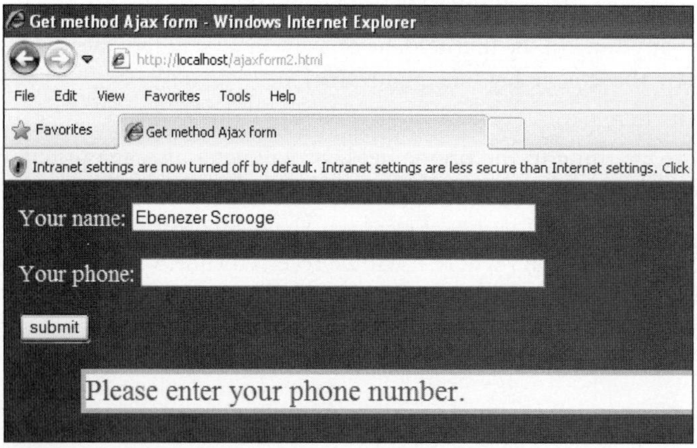

Figure 18.18 The user didn't enter his phone number. PHP sent back the message in red text.

The POST Method. In Example 18.17, rather than repeating the previous example in its entirety, only the code where changes are made for the POST method is highlighted. The *setRequestHeader* for the *Content-type* has been added and the *send()* method contains the query string data that will be sent to the server. The line controlling caching has been removed, because with the POST method caching is not an issue. The output is identical to what is shown in Figures 18.16, 18.17, and 18.18.

```
EXAMPLE   18.17

/* Section of the Ajax Program highlighting changes to make a POST
   request */

ajaxRequest.onreadystatechange = function(){
  var textObj;
  textObj=document.getElementById("message");
  if(ajaxRequest.readyState == 4){
    if(ajaxRequest.status==200){
      textObj.innerHTML=ajaxRequest.responseText;
    }
  }
  else if(ajaxRequest.status == 404){
    textObj.innerHTML="Resource unavailable";
  }
  else{
    textObj.innerHTML="Error!! Firefox request aborted.
        Status: "+ajaxRequest.status;
  }
}
      var namevalue=
        encodeURIComponent(document.getElementById("username").value)
      var phonevalue=
        encodeURIComponent(document.getElementById("userphone").value)
            /* This is where the code changes for the POST method */
1           ajaxRequest.open("POST", "http://localhost/ajaxform.php")
2           ajaxRequest.setRequestHeader("Content-type",
                          "application/x-www-form-urlencoded");
3           ajaxRequest.send("username="+namevalue+
                          "&userphone="+phonevalue);
         }
       </script>
     </head>
     <body>
4      <form>
         Your name: <input type="text" size=50 id=username
                        name='username' /> <br />
         <p>
           Your phone: <input type="text" size=50 id=userphone
                          name="userphone" /><br />
```

Continues

EXAMPLE   18.17 (CONTINUED)

```
    <p>
       <input type="button" value="submit"
              onClick="ajaxFunction()"; />
    </form>
    <div id="message" class="divStyle">
    </div>
    </p>

  </body>
</html>
```

EXPLANATION

1   When the *XMLHttpRequest* object is initialized, the *open()* method takes two pa-
    rameters in this example: the HTTP method is POST, and the URL is the name of
    the server-side PHP script that will process form input sent by the server. The de-
    fault is asynchronous, *true*, specified as a third parameter.

2   With the POST method another header is sent to the server specifying the "Con-
    tent-type".

3   Instead of sending the query string as a set of parameters to the *open()* method,
    they are sent to the server by the *send()* method.

4   This is where the HTML form starts. There are no attributes.

18.5 Ajax and JSON

What is JSON? JSON, **JavaScript O**bject Notation, like Ajax, is not a programming language, but a subset of JavaScript. It is a text-based format that provides an easy way to
exchange and parse data over a network. Although JSON was originally tied to Java-
Script, it is language independent and is now used by Ruby, PHP, C++, Python, Java, Perl,
and so on. The JSON format is often used for serialization and transmitting structured
data with Ajax.

   If you recall, in Example 18.11 when using Ajax and XML, there was a lot involved.
First, you had to understand how XML structures its data, and next how to create the
XML DOM object when the server returns the contents of the XML file, and finally how
to use the DOM to parse the data. JSON offers a nice alternative to using XML. Instead
JSON represents data as an array or associative array (JavaScript object) and any lan-
guage that supports this representation of data can use it.

   Most modern browsers are providing an implementation of native JSON so that you
can use parse and string methods provided by the browser to handle JSON data. For
example, Firefox 3.5, Internet Explorer 8, Google Chrome, and Apple Safari have introduced support for native JSON, and the ECMAScript Fifth Edition (ES5) Draft Specification is being finalized to support it. Using native JSON is much faster and convenient
than importing libraries. There are a number of Ajax frameworks including Yahoo! UI

Library, jQuery, Dojo, and mootools that support JSON. The JSON Web site provides a short and succinct discussion on the JSON technology (see Figure 18.19).

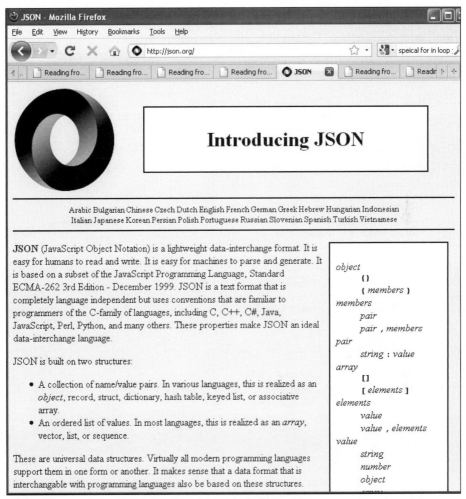

Figure 18.19 The JSON Web site.

18.5.1   JSON Data Structures

JSON is based on two data structures we discussed in Chapters 8 and 9: arrays and objects. As you might recall, the array is indexed by numbers or strings, and the object consists of properties and their corresponding values. It is possible to nest these data structures, so you might have an array of objects, an array of arrays, an object with nested properties and values, and so on. For both of these structures, we use the literal notation.

> ## EXAMPLE (SAMPLE CODE)
>
> Example: (JavaScript array)
>
> ```
> var friends = [ "John", "Jane", "Niveeta", "Su" ];
> ```
>
> Example: (JavaScript object literal)
>
> ```
> var soldier = {
>                 name: undefined,
>                 rank: "captain",
>                 picture: "keeweeboy.jpg",
>                 salary: 50000,
>                 enlisted: true
> }
> ```

Table 18.5   JSON's Basic Types

Data Type	Example
Number	5, 5.435
String	"John Doe", 'red'
Boolean	true or false
Array	[1,2,3,4.5] ["Bob","Jim","Joe"]

Object	{ "Name": "John",
	  "Age" : 35,
	  "Status": true,
	}

null	null

18.5.2   Steps to Use JSON

Create a .json File.   To use JSON, the object literal or array will be placed in a file named with a *.json* extension (see Chapter 8 to review object literals). The object or array will not be named in the file. It would look like this:

```
{   "namev: undefined,
    "rank": "captain",
    "picturev: "keeweeboy.jpg",
    "salary": 50000,
    "enlisted": true
}
```

Create the Ajax Program.   The Ajax program will make a request to the server to get text in the *.json* file. The server will return the text in the *requestResponseText* property of the Ajax request object. Next Ajax must convert the JSON text into a JavaScript object (or array). To accomplish this, we can use the JavaScript built-in *eval()* function, as long as security is not an issue. For our demo it is not, because Ajax communication is permitted within this domain where the page originated, and therefore, trusted. (Later we will download the JSON library, *json2*, to accomplish the same task.)

The *eval()* function evaluates the text and creates a JavaScript data structure, consisting of key/value pairs, either an array or object.

```
var myObject = eval('(' + myJSONtext + ')');
```

Now with the dot notation, we can get the values associated with the keys; for example,

```
name = myObject.name  // object notation
color = myObject[0]   // array notation
```

After the data has been parsed and stored in variable, it is ready to be displayed in the browser.

Steps for Using Ajax and a JSON Array

EXAMPLE 18.18

```
1. The JSON text file, "colors.json" contains the following array:

     [ "red", "blue", "green", "yellow" ]


------------------------------------------------------------
2. The Ajax program requests the file and evals the response.

// Segment from the Ajax program
function getXMLContents(httpRequest) {
  if (httpRequest.readyState == 4) {
    if (httpRequest.status == 200) {
      var colors = eval('('+httpRequest.responseText +')') ;
      alert(colors);
      // alert("I like "+ colors[3])   Prints "yellow"
    }
    else {
      alert('There was a problem with the request.');
    }
  }
}
```

Continues

EXAMPLE 18.18 (CONTINUED)

3. After the *eval()* evaluates the string returned from the server, it is converted into an array and displayed below:

Steps for Using Ajax and a JSON Object

EXAMPLE 18.19

1. The JSON text file, "**person.json**" contains an object literal:

```
{ "Name": "Joe Shmoe",
  "Salary": 100000.50,
  "Age": 35,
  "Married": true
}
```

----

2. The Ajax program requests the file and evals the response:

```
// Segment from the Ajax program
function getXMLContents(httpRequest) {
  if (httpRequest.readyState == 4) {
    if (httpRequest.status == 200) {
      var person = eval('('+httpRequest.responseText +')') ;
      var name=person.Name;
      var salary=person.Salary;
      var age=person.Age;
      var married=person.Married;
      alert("Name: "+name +
               "\nSalary: " + salary +
               "\nAge: " + age +
               "\nMarried: "+ married
           );
    }
    else {
      alert('There was a problem with the request.');
    }
  }
}
```

EXAMPLE 18.19 (CONTINUED)

3. Output after the eval().

Message from webpage

Name: Joe Shmoe
Salary: 100000.5
Age: 35
Married: true

OK

18.5.3 Putting It All Together with JSON

In the next set of examples, we will create a JSON text file, with the structure of a Java-Script object (in fact, any program employing hashes or associative arrays could read this file), use an Ajax program to request the file and, after getting a response from the server, read and parse the JSON data with JavaScript's *eval()* function, then place the parsed data in a *div* container and display it (shown in Figure 18.20).

The JSON File (ajaxCar.json)

EXAMPLE 18.20

```
1 { "make":"Honda Civic",
   "year":2006,
   "price":18000,
2  "owner":{
           "name":"Henry Lee",
           "cellphone": "222-222-2222",
3          "address":{"street": "10 Main",
                      "city": "San Francisco",
                      "state": "CA"
               }
   },
   "dealer": "SF Honda"
4 }
```

EXPLANATION

1 This is a JSON object consisting of properties and their values (key/value pairs).

2 The *owner* property has nested properties. If the object is named "car", then to get the cell phone number for the *owner*, the dot notation is used to separate the properties; for example, *car.owner.cellphone* will get the value "222-222-2222".

Continues

EXPLANATION(CONTINUED)

3   The address property also has nested property/value pairs. To get the value of the
    state, you would say *car.owner.address.state.*

4   JSON structure must be syntactically correct or the JavaScript *eval()* will not be
    able to evaluate properly, all strings quoted, curly braces lined up. It appears that
    if you want to create an array of hashes, the syntax requires an object notation
    rather than array notation; that is, use curly braces on the outside of the whole
    structure, not [ ].

Ajax Program with JSON and *eval()*

EXAMPLE   18.21

```
<html>
<head><title>Reading from an JSON file</title>
  <script type="text/javascript">
    function makeRequest() {
      var httpRequest;
      if (window.XMLHttpRequest) { // Mozilla, Safari, ...
        httpRequest = new XMLHttpRequest();
        if (httpRequest.overrideMimeType) {
          httpRequest.overrideMimeType('text/xml');
        }
      }
      else if (window.ActiveXObject) { // IE
        try {
          httpRequest = new ActiveXObject("Msxml2.XMLHTTP");
        }
        catch (e) {
          try {
            httpRequest = new ActiveXObject("Microsoft.XMLHTTP");
          }
          catch (e) {}
        }
      }
      if (!httpRequest) {
        alert('Giving up :( Cannot create an XMLHTTP instance');
        return false;
      }
      httpRequest.onreadystatechange = function() {
        getXMLContents(httpRequest); };
      httpRequest.open('GET', "file:///C:/wamp/www/ajaxCar.json",
                      true);
      /* Check that you use the correct URL for your browser. IE
         wanted "http://localhost/ajaxCar.json". Firefox complained
         about the a not well-formed .json file */
```

EXAMPLE   18.21 (CONTINUED)

```
              httpRequest.setRequestHeader('If-Modified-Since',
                                   'Sat, 03 Jan 2010 00:00:00GMT');
              httpRequest.setRequestHeader("Content-type",
                                      "application/json");
              httpRequest.send('');

              function getXMLContents(httpRequest) {
                 var httpRequest;
                 if (httpRequest.readyState == 4) {
                    if (httpRequest.status == 200) {
                       textObj=document.getElementById("data");
1                      var carObject = eval('('+ httpRequest.responseText
                                               +')') ;
                       // alert(carObject.make); Using the object's property
2                      var details="";
3                      for(var property in carObject){
                          if (property == "owner"){ // Nested associative
                                                    // array
                             details += "owner name = " +
                                 carObject[property].name + "<br />";
                             details += "owner cell phone =
                                 " carObject[property].cellphone + "<br />";
                          }
                          else{
4                            details += property + " = " +
                                            carObject[property] + "<br />";
                          }
                       }
5                      textObj.innerHTML=details; // Put data in document
                    }                              // Figure 18.20
                    else {
                       alert('There was a problem with the request.');
                    }
                 }
              }
           }
        </script>
     </head>
     <body>
        <span style="cursor: pointer; text-decoration: underline"
6              onclick="makeRequest()">
           Get car details
        </span>
7       <div id=data>
        </div>
     </body>
  </html>
```

EXPLANATION

1   The JavaScript *eval()* function evaluates and/or executes a string of JavaScript code. First, *eval()* determines if the argument is a valid string, i.e., the JSON string that was returned from the server. Then *eval()* parses the string. The string returned from the *eval()* is a JavaScript object.

2   The variable details will hold the properties and values of the JavaScript object.

3   JavaScript's special *for/in* loop provides a mechanism for stepping through all the properties of an object. It iterates through the *carObject*, retrieving both properties and values to be placed in the *div* container on line 8.

If the property is "owner", it has a nested set of key/value pairs as shown here:

```
{ "make":"Honda Civic",
  "year":2006,
  "price":18000,
  "owner":{
        "name":"Henry Lee",
        "cellphone": "222-222-2222",
        "address":{"street": "10 Main",
                   "city": "San Francisco",
                   "state": "CA"
        }
  },
  "dealer": "SF Honda"
}
```

The special *for/in* loop iterates through the object's properties. To get the value of a property, the property is placed between square brackets (associative array) preceded by the name of the object. In a nested object, the dot syntax is used to get to the nested property as: *carObject["owner"].name* or *carObject["owner"].address.street*.

4   Each time through the loop, a property and its value will be added to the *details* variable until all properties/values have been collected. In this example, the address was not included, only to keep the program size smaller.

5   The DOM's *innerHTML* property will be assigned all of the details collected for the *carObject* and placed in the *div* container on line 8, Figure 18.20.

6   When the user clicks this button, the *makeRequest()* function will be called to create an Ajax request object and handle the JSON data (see page 840).

7   This is the *div* container where the display data will be placed. The results is shown in Figure 18.20.

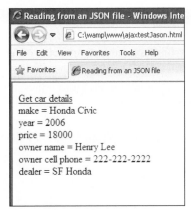

Figure 18.20 After reading and parsing data from a JSON file.

18.5.4 Solving the *eval()* Security Problem

Using the JavaScript *eval()* function to parse Ajax data is not recommended as a secure approach for handling data coming from an Ajax request as it makes the program vulnerable to cross-site scripting (XSS). There are a number of sites that deal specifically with this issue[4] (see *http://www.blackhat.com/presentations*). If your browser supports native JSON, you can use the JSON *parse()* method to take the place of *eval()*. If the browser doesn't support native JSON, there are public domain libraries available that are easy to download and use with no fuss.

Example 18.22 is a simple test to see if your browser supports JSON. This script was executed using Firefox 3.5.7 and Internet Explorer 8.0. Firefox ran the script without a problem (see Figure 18.21), whereas Internet Explorer produced an error that it didn't recognize "JSON" (see Figure 18.22). The problem was easy to solve by downloading the *json2* library and including it in the script, see Example 18.23 .

EXAMPLE 18.22

```
    <script type="text/javascript">
        // Testing native JSON support  Firefox
1       var jsonString = '{"name":"Joe Shmoe", "phone":"415-111-1111"}';
2       var employee=JSON.parse(jsonString);
3       alert("Name: " + employee.name +"\nPhone: "+ employee.phone);
    </script>
```

---

4. "The eval technique is subject to security vulnerabilities if the data and the entire JavaScript environment is not within the control of a single trusted source. If the data is itself not trusted, for example, it may be subject to malicious JavaScript code injection attacks; unless some additional means is used to validate the data first."—*http://en.wikipedia.org/wiki/JSON.*

EXPLANATION

1   The string called jsonString consists of what will represent a JavaScript object with properties and values. The data in a .json file would not have the outer single quotes.

2   The *JSON.parse()* method evaluates the string and converts it to a JavaScript object, the same way the JavaScript *eval()* function works when evaluating an expression (discussed in "The eval() Function" on page 118).

3   Using the JavaScript object, we can get the name and phone values for the object with the dot syntax.

Figure 18.21   JSON support with Firefox.

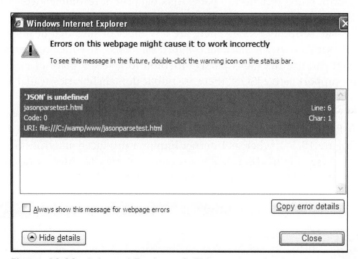

Figure 18.22   Internet Explorer 8: This version does not recognize the JSON *parse()* method.

EXAMPLE 18.23

```
1  <script type="text/javascript" src="json2.js">
   </script>
   <script type="text/javascript">
2    var jsonString = '{"name":"Joe Shmoe", "phone":"415-111-1111"}';
3    var employee=JSON.parse(jsonString);
     alert("Name: " + employee.name + "\nPhone: "+ employee.phone);
   </script>
```

EXPLANATION

1   The JavaScript program will use the *json2.js* library.

2   A string is created containing the text that will be parsed by the library's *JSON.parse()* method.

3   The *JSON.parse()* method converts the string, called jsonString, into a JavaScript object (see Figure 18.23).

Figure 18.23   After adding the json2.js library, Internet Explorer works fine.

Douglas Crockford at JSON.org has provided a set of routines that will convert any JavaScript data type into a JSON string. Go to *http://www.JSON.org/JSON.js* for a free download of the most current library for parsing and stringifying JSON objects, *json2.js*. With this library you can read JSON strings and write them to the server. Example 18.24 demonstrates how to use the *json2.js* library to create a JavaScript object from the text coming from the JSON file.

The steps are:

1. Make sure the *.json* file is in the correct object format. (The MIME type is "application/json" and may have to be set in your server so that Firefox does not read the JSON file as an XML file resulting in a "not well-formed" error.)

2. At the top of your Ajax program add the *<script>* tag *src* attribute to the name of the JSON library, in this case "json2.js":

   ```
   <script type="text/javascript" src="json2.js">
   ```

3. In the Ajax program, read the object in as text from the *XMLHttpRequest* object's *responseText* property into a string variable.

4. Use the *JSON.parse()* method to turn the string into a JavaScript object.

5. Use the properties and values of the object to get the information from the object such as *myObject.name*, *myObject.phone*, and so on.

Jason and Ajax Using JSON Library

EXAMPLE 18.24

```
1  <script type="text/javascript" src="json2.js">
   /* Add the src attribute to your Ajax program to include the
      json2.js libaray
      Code for creating the XMLHttpRequest object is not included
      here. You can find it in Example 18.1.
   */
2  function getXMLContents(httpRequest) {
      if (httpRequest.readyState == 4) {
        if (httpRequest.status == 200) {
          textObj=document.getElementById("data");
3         var jasonString = httpRequest.responseText;
          alert(jasonString);        // see Figure 18.24.
4         var carObject=JSON.parse(jasonString);
          var details="";
5         for(var property in carObject){
              if (property == "owner"){
                  details += "owner name = " +
                             carObject[property].name + "<br />";
                  details += "owner cell phone = " +
                             carObject[property].cellphone + "<br />";
              }
              else{
                  details += property + " = " +
                  carObject[property] + "<br />";
              }
          }
          textObj.innerHTML=details;          // see Figure 18.25.
        }
        else {
          alert('There was a problem with the request.');
        }
      }
   }
   </script>
   </head>
   <body>
     <span style="cursor: pointer; text-decoration: underline"
6         onclick="makeRequest('ajaxCar.json')">
        Get car details
     </span>
7  <div id="data">
     </div>
   </body>
   </html>
```

EXPLANATION

1   The *json2* library provides methods to encode JavaScript objects to JSON, and decode the resulting text back to JavaScript objects. The original json2 library documentation can be found at json.org/js.html.

2   This function is where the server's response is handled and parsed. The *XMLHttpRequest* object, called *httpRequest* in this example, was returned from the functions not listed but found in Example 18.1.

3   The *XMLHttpRequest* object's *responseText* property contains the response from the server request, a string of text from the "ajaxCar.json" file (see Figure 18.24).

4   The *JSON.parse* method from the *json2* library takes a string and turns it into a JavaScript object.

5   The special *for* loop is going through all the properties in the *carObject*, retrieving both properties and values to be placed in the *div* container on line 7.

6   The JSON file will be requested from the server. It has a .json extension. The URL might be *http://localhost/ajaxCar.json*, depending on your browser.

7   The *<div>* tag is given an *id* called "data". See Figure 18.25.

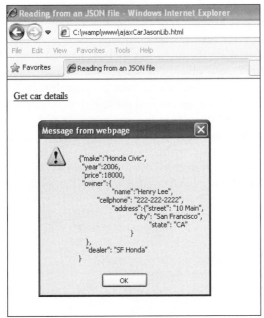

Figure 18.24 The JSON string.

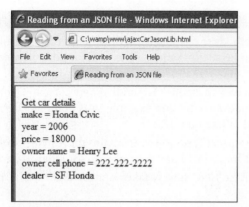

Figure 18.25 After parsing the JSON string.

18.6 Debugging Ajax with Firebug

Firebug (see Figure 18.26) is a Firefox extension that lets you debug and profile your Ajax, HTML, CSS, JavaScript, and DOM applications by using tabbed browsing and a console for errors and log messages. Firebug appears either as a separate window or as a small panel at the bottom of your browser. The FireBug console can log all Ajax requests live, and allows you to inspect the responses that are normally invisible. You can see the value of the *XMLHttpRequest* object, the server's status, the *readyState*, and so on. and with the Script debugger step through the your program line by line or stop at specified breakpoints watching the changes in real time. Firebug's inspectors allow you to see the CSS rules and watch DOM nodes as they are being created, modified, and removed by JavaScript in real time. Firebug's Script tab contains a powerful debugger that lets you pause JavaScript execution on any line. You can then step forward line-by-line to analyze how the state of the program changes in real time. Firebug also lets you specify the circumstances under which a breakpoint is triggered and lets you browse code as well as edit it.

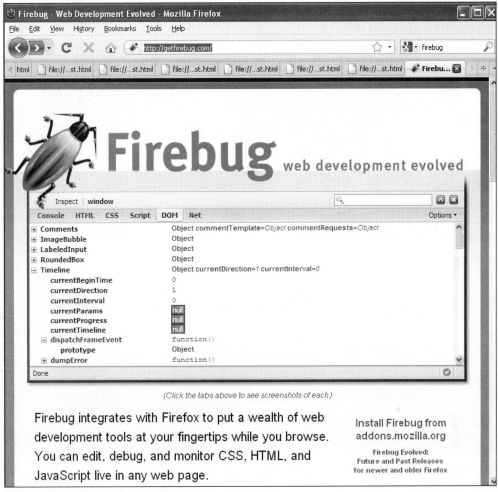

Figure 18.26   The Firebug Web site.

If you want to test your pages in Internet Explorer, Opera, and Safari, the solution is Firebug Lite, a JavaScript file you can insert into your pages to simulate some Firebug features in browsers that are not named Firefox. Firebug Lite creates the variable "firebug" and doesn't affect or interfere with HTML elements that aren't created by itself. Go to *http://getfirebug.com/* for more information.

Figure 18.27 shows Firebug in its own window with breakpoints. The yellow arrow on the left is the line that is currently executing. The problem: Firefox returns an HTTP status of 0 instead of 200. By placing the cursor on the status variable, Firebug will show that the value is 0. The pane at the bottom of the Firebug window monitors the value of variables, breakpoints and the state of the program's stack. The little blue arrow to the left of the Console tab lets you step through the program one line at a time. The red dots to the left of the program are breakpoints obtained simply by clicking on a line number. Firebug comes with full documentation and there are a number of tutorials on the Web to help you understand how to use it most effectively. For an excellent video demonstration on using this debugger with Ajax, see "Introduction to Debugging AJAX Application with Firebug" on YouTube at *http://www.youtube.com/watch?v=W4jXAaEMp2M* (see Figure 18.28).

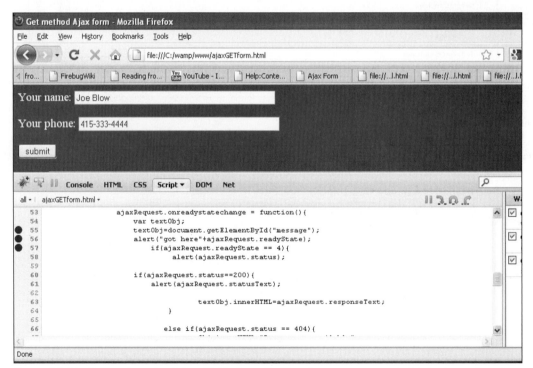

Figure 18.27   Setting breakpoints with Firebug. Putting the cursor on a variable shows its value.

Figure 18.28 A video to teach you how to use Firebug.

18.6.1 Basic Instructions for Using Firefox

Step 1. From the Firefox browser window where your program output is displayed, Go to the Tools menu in your browser menu bar. Under Add-ons, click on Firebug and a new window will pop up. Click Open Firebug.

Step 2. The Firebug screen will be split in two parts: the upper half will be the web page you are displaying and the lower half will be Firebug displaying the code behind the Web page you are watching. By selecting the feature of the program you want to check (i.e., HTML, JavaScript, the DOM, and the NET) you can scroll through the program code looking for that.

Step 3. Click on the different sections of the site (always on the bottom half of the screen) and on top notice how the area you clicked is highlighted. That will help you identify the bugs.

Step 4. You can set breakpoints by clicking on any line in your code and then moving your cursor over one of the lines to see what's going on. You can view CSS, the

DOM tree, and check to see what is happening on the network. There are more features than can be covered in this text, but the Firebug documentation and online help are excellent if you want to use this tool to help you identify the bugs in your program.

18.6.2   What You Should Know

This chapter focused on Ajax, making asynchronous server requests using JavaScript. The main idea was that the browser fetched small pieces of content from the server bypassing the normal request/response cycle. Rather, Ajax represents a communications layer allowing a page to be updated without interrupting the user's interaction with the page. After studying this chapter, you should understand:

1. What Ajax stands for.
2. Why use Ajax.
3. What asynchronous means.
4. How to create an *XMLHttpRequest* object.
5. How to handle browser differences.
6. How to initialize the *XMLHttpRequest* object.
7. How to send a request to the server.
8. How to check the state of the server request.
9. How to get the response from the server.
10. How to get and display the contents of a text file.
11. How to get and parse the contents of an XML file.
12. How to handle GET and POST requests.
13. How to use the DOM and an XML object.
14. The advantages of using JSON.
15. How to get and parse JSON data.
16. How to get and install the *json2* library.
17. What Firebug is used for.

Exercises

1. Create an Ajax program that reads text from a simple text file and displays the output in an alert box.

2. Using the Ajax program you just completed, add some checks to monitor the state of the server by displaying the *readyState* values as they change.

3. Create a form text box and two radio buttons. Ask the user for his or her name and to check one of the radio buttons, either "male" or "female". Use the POST method and send the form data to a server-side script such as PHP or ASP.NET. Return the information and display it in a yellow *div* container.

4. Convert the "bookstore.xml" file into a JSON file. Use an Ajax program to read from the JSON file and parse its data. Download the json2 library and use it.

5. Install Firebug or Firebug Lite and use it to examine one of the Ajax programs you have just completed.

Index